HISTORY

OF THE

CHURCH OF JESUS CHRIST

OF

LATTER-DAY SAINTS.

PERIOD I.

History of Joseph Smith, the Prophet

BY HIMSELF.

VOLUME VI.

AN INTRODUCTION AND NOTES

BY

B. H ROBERTS

PUBLISHED BY THE CHURCH.

DESERET BOOK COMPANY
44 EAST SOUTH TEMPLE
SALT LAKE CITY, UTAH

1980

Lithographed by

DESERET PRESS

in the United States of America

TABLE OF CONTENTS.

VOLUME VI.

INTRODUCTION.

CHAPTER I.

AN ESTIMATE OF THE PROPHET JOSEPH AS A RELIGIOUS LEADER—ANTI-
MORMON MEETING AT CARTHAGE—HISTORICAL SKETCH—IMPORT-
ANT CONFERENCE OF THE TWELVE HELD IN BOSTON.

CHAPTER II.

MOVEMENTS OF APOSTLES IN THE EAST—THE NAUVOO MANSION—ROCK-
WELL ACQUITTED—SPECIAL CONFERENCE AT NAUVOO—DISCOURSE
OF THE PROPHET ON THE DEMISE OF JAMES ADAMS.

CHAPTER III.

ANCIENT RUINS IN AMERICA, BOOK OF MORMON EVIDENCES—THE PROPHET ON THE U. S. CONSTITUTION AND THE BIBLE—MISREPRESENTATIONS CORRECTED—LETTER TO THE U. S. PRESIDENTIAL CANDIDATES—THE PROPHET'S ADDRESS TO THE SAINTS.

CHAPTER IV.

CORRESPONDENCE BETWEEN JAMES ARLINGTON BENNETT AND PRESIDENT JOSEPH SMITH—RENEWAL OF PETITIONS TO CONGRESS FOR REDRESS OF MISSOURI GRIEVANCES—PRESIDENT JOSEPH SMITH'S APPEAL TO THE GREEN MOUNTAIN BOYS, VERMONT—STATUS OF THE NAUVOO LEGION IN ILLINOIS MILITIA.

CHAPTER V.

THE AVERY KIDNAPPING—DEFENSIVE PREPARATIONS AGAINST MISSOURI
MOBS—APPEALS TO THE GENERAL GOVERNMENT FOR PROTEC-
TION—NAUVOO LEGION OFFERED AS UNITED STATES TROOPS.

CHAPTER VI.

MEMORIAL OF CITY COUNCIL TO CONGRESS ANENT MISSOURI AFFAIRS
—ROCKWELL RETURNS TO NAUVOO—RECITAL OF HIS ADVEN-
TURES—AVERY'S ACQUITTAL BY MISSOURI'S COURTS—NAU-
VOO'S POLICE FORCE INCREASED PUBLICATION
ON MORMONISM, PRO ET CON—1843.

CHAPTER VII.

PRESIDENT SMITH'S CORRESPONDENCE WITH JOHN C. CALHOUN—CART-
WRIGHT DROWNING CASE, ENGLAND—CITY GUARDS INCREASED—
FEARS OF LAW AND MARKS—INVESTIGATION BY THE CITY COUN-
CIL—RESISTANCE OF OFFICERS AT CARTHAGE—ANTI-MOR-
MON OBJECTIONS TO CITY ORDINANCES—THE PROPH-
ET'S DIFFICULTIES WITH FRANCIS M. HIGBEE—
REGULATIONS FOR THE SALE OF SPIRITUOUS
LIQUORS.

CHAPTER VIII.

PRESENTATION OF THE BOOK OF MORMON TO QUEEN VICTORIA—THE SEALING POWERS OF THE PRIESTHOOD—GOVERNOR FORD'S WARNING TO THE PEOPLE OF HANCOCK COUNTY—APOSTROPHE TO MISSOURI—JOSEPH SMITH NOMINATED FOR PRESIDENT OF THE UNITED STATES—HIS VIEWS ON THE POWERS AND POLICY OF THE GOVERNMENT OF THE UNITED STATES.

CHAPTER IX

CHAPTER X.

CHAPTER XI.

ORSON PRATT SENT TO WASHINGTON AS AGENT OF NAUVOO—AMOS
FIELDING TO ENGLAND, DITTO—COMMENT ON THE CANDIDACY OF
JOSEPH SMITH FOR PRESIDENT OF THE U. S.—CONSPIRACY OF THE
LAWS, HIGBEES, FOSTERS ET AL AGAINST JOSEPH SMITH—
THE PROPHET'S MEMORIAL TO CONGRESS—OCCUPA-
TION OF THE WEST CONTEMPLATED.

CHAPTER XII.

THE AUTHORITIES OF NAUVOO VS. THE HIGBEES ET AL.—DEDICATION
OF THE MASONIC HALL—THE CHURCH CONFERENCE IN APRIL,
1844—ADDRESS OF PRESIDENT SIDNEY RIGDON.

CHAPTER XIII.

CONFERENCE OF THE CHURCH, APRIL, 1844, CONTINUED—ADDRESS OF
PATRIARCH HYRUM SMITH—THE BUILDING OF THE TEMPLE.

CHAPTER XIV.

CONFERENCE OF THE CHURCH, APRIL, 1844 (CONTINUED)—THE KING
FOLLETT SERMON—THE CHARACTER OF GOD— RELIGIOUS FREEDOM—GOD
AN EXALTED MAN—ETERNAL LIFE TO KNOW GOD AND JESUS CHRIST—
EVERLASTING BURNINGS—MEANING OF THE HEBREW SCRIPTURES—
A COUNCIL OF THE GODS—MEANING OF THE WORD CREATE—THE
IMMORTAL INTELLIGENCE—THE RELATION OF MAN TO GOD—
OUR GREATEST RESPONSIBILITY—THE UNPARDONABLE SIN
—THE FORGIVENESS OF SIN—THE SECOND DEATH.

CHAPTER XV.

GENERAL CONFERENCE FOR APRIL, 1844, (CONCLUDED)—THE ANNOUNCE-
MENT THAT THE WHOLE LAND OF AMERICA IS ZION—
INSTRUCTIONS TO ELDERS SET APART FOR MISSIONS—
A GENERAL CONFERENCE IN ENGLAND.

CHAPTER XVI.

DIFFICULTIES WITH THE HIGBEES AND FOSTERS, CONFERENCES APPOINTED
BY THE TWELVE THROUGHOUT THE UNITED STATES—INSTRUCTIONS
TO REUBEN HEDLOCK, PRESIDENT OF THE BRITISH MISSION—
PREPARATIONS FOR ENLARGEMENT OF THE WORK—
FRANCIS M. HIGBEE'S SUIT AGAINST PRESIDENT
SMITH—THE PROPHET RELEASED.

CHAPTER XVII.

ADDRESS OF THE PROPHET—HIS PROPHETIC CALLING AND THE RESUR-
RECTION—STATUS OF AFFAIRS AT NAUVOO—HYDE'S REPORT
FROM WASHINGTON OF THE WESTERN MOVEMENT—OREGON.

CHAPTER XVIII.

THE STATE PRESIDENTIAL CONVENTION AT NAUVOO—THE STATES REPRE-
SENTED—SPEECH OF JOHN S. REID, ESQ.—EARLY DAYS
WITH THE PROPHET.

CHAPTER XIX.

CHARGES AGAINST PRESIDENT SMITH BEFORE THE CIRCUIT COURT—HIS
VOLUNTARY APPEARANCE AT COURT—TREAT-
MENT—RETURN TO NAUVOO.

CHAPTER XX.

CASE OF JEREMIAH SMITH BEFORE MUNICIPAL COURT AT NAUVOO—AFFI-
DAVITS OF CRIMES OF CHAUNCEY L. HIGBEE—
APPEARANCE OF THE "EXPOSITOR."

CHAPTER XXI.

THE DESTRUCTION OF THE "NAUVOO EXPOSITOR"—PROCEEDINGS OF
THE NAUVOO CITY COUNCIL AND MAYOR.

CHAPTER XXII.

PRESIDENT SMITH ARRESTED FOR RIOT IN RELATION TO "EXPOSITOR"
AFFAIR—HABEAS CORPUS PROCEEDINGS BEFORE MUNICIPAL
COURT—A CALL FROM ARKANSAS—THE PROPHET'S
DREAMS — MASS MEETING AT WARSAW — LETTERS
TO GOVERNOR FORD ON "EXPOSITOR" AFFAIR.

CHAPTER XXIII.

DISCOURSE OF THE PROPHET—THE GODHEAD—THE MOB UPRISING—
ARREST OF PRESIDENT SMITH ET AL. OVER THE "EXPOSI-
TOR" AFFAIR BEFORE ESQUIRE WELLS.

CHAPTER XXIV.

RUMORS OF INVASION FROM MISSOURI—THE LEGION ORDERED TO ASSIST
THE CITY MARSHAL—NAUVOO PLACED UNDER MARTIAL
LAW—THE MAYOR'S ADDRESS TO THE LEGION.

CHAPTER XXV.

ATTEMPTS TO DRAFT SAINTS INTO MOB SERVICE AGAINST NAUVOO—
THREATENED INVASION FROM MISSOURI—JAMES A.
BENNETT URGED TO COME TO NAUVOO.

CHAPTER XXVI.

THE TWELVE CALLED FROM EASTERN MISSION—GOVERNOR FORD AT CAR-
THAGE—NAUVOO DELEGATION TO GOVERNOR—THREATS AND CON-
SPIRACY AGAINST THE PROPHET'S LIFE — GOVERNOR FORD
INVITED TO NAUVOO TO INVESTIGATE CONDITIONS.

CHAPTER XXVII.

PREPARATIONS TO DEFEND NAUVOO—MOB MOVEMENTS ON CARTHAGE ROAD —
GOVERNOR FORD'S REVIEW OF HANCOCK COUNTY DIFFICULTIES—
JOSEPH SMITH'S ACCOUNT OF THE SAME DIFFICULTIES—
DEFENSE OF HIS OWN AND ASSOCIATES' COURSE.

CHAPTER XXVIII.

GOVERNOR FORD'S WRONG VIEWPOINT—ELDER TAYLOR'S ACCOUNT OF THE
INTERVIEW WITH THE GOVERNOR AT CARTHAGE—CLOSE OF THE
PROPHET'S JOURNAL NARRATIVE OF HIS LIFE.

CHAPTER XXIX

THE PROPHET STARTS FOR THE ROCKY MOUNTAINS—THE COUNSEL OF FALSE
BRETHREN—THE RETURN TO NAUVOO—THE SURRENDER
AND ARRIVAL AT CARTHAGE.

CHAPTER XXX.

ARREST OF JOSEPH AND HYRUM SMITH ON A CHARGE OF TREASON—FALSE

IMPRISONMENT—ELDER TAYLOR'S PROTEST—FALSE IMPRISONMENT.

CHAPTER XXXI.

INTERVIEW IN CARTHAGE PRISON BETWEEN GOVERNOR FORD AND THE PROPHET
—TAYLOR'S REPORT OF THE INTERVIEW—TESTIMONY TO THE EXISTENCE OF
A CARTHAGE CONSPIRACY AGAINST THE PROPHET'S LIFE.

CHAPTER XXXII.

THE PROPHET IN CARTHAGE PRISON—THE UNION OF JUDICIAL, EXECUTIVE, AND MILITARY AUTHORITY IN DEALING WITH THE PRISONERS—THE LAST NIGHT IN PRISON.

CHAPTER XXXIII.

THE DAY OF THE MARTYRDOM—THREATS—REPEATED WARNINGS OF THE PRISON- ERS' DANGER GIVEN TO GOVERNOR FORD—THE CARTHAGE GREYS AS GUARDS.

CHAPTER XXXIV

DEPARTURE OF GOVERNOR FORD FOR NAUVOO—THE AFTERNOON IN CARTHAGE PRISON—THE ASSAULT ON THE PRISON—THE MARTYRDOM OF JOSEPH AND HYRUM SMITH.

CHAPTER XXXV.

GOVERNOR FORD IN NAUVOO—NEWS OF THE MARTYRDOM MESSAGE TO NAUVOO —ARRIVAL OF THE BODIES—SORROWFUL SCENES—THE BURIAL.

INTRODUCTION.

I. The Time Period.

The time-period covered in this sixth volume of the HISTORY OF THE CHURCH is less than one year. Nine months and twenty-eight days, to be exact; or from the 1st of September, 1843, to the 29th of June, 1844. Events within this period are therefore given in elaborate detail. The general reader and the student of our history will find in this volume a larger collection of documents, official and otherwise, covering this period, than will be found elsewhere.

This volume also closes the first Period of our Church History, the period marked off by two events: (1) the birth of the Prophet Joseph Smith; and (2) his martyrdom and that of his brother Hyrum, at Carthage, Illinois.

The Journal History of the Prophet, that great source of historical knowledge concerning the development of the New Dispensation, closes with his entry of the 22nd of June, 1844. After that, for our knowledge of the remaining events of the Prophet's life, we are dependent upon collections of *data* by the Church historians from public and private sources, of which collections there are two: the first extends from the 22nd of June to the 29th of that month, and forms the concluding chapters of this volume; the second begins also with the 22nd of June, and extends to the 8th of August, 1844; at which time the Twelve Apostles were sustained for the time being as the presiding council of the Church. This second collection of *data* by the Church historians will open Volume VII of this HISTORY.

In the present volume we see the Prophet's brave struggle against the overwhelming odds of his foes—foes within the Church, false brethren; and foes without the Church—the combination of political and sectarian enemies fixed in their determination to kill him, destroy Nauvoo, and expel the Saints from Illinois: for all these things were included in the program of the anti-Mormons of Illinois, even before the death of the Prophet was encompassed. Three score and seven years now give perspective to the stirring events in which the really great drama was enacted; and from that vantage ground of perspective said events may be reviewed to the enlightenment of those who seek to know the truth, and the injustice of the things enacted in Illinois during the closing months of the Prophet Joseph's earthly career.

II. *Why the Latter-day Saints were Welcomed to Illinois.*

On the one hand, in the above mentioned struggle, was a people who but a few years before had been welcomed into Illinois as exiles from a neighboring state, the victims of a cruel and ignorant intolerance. They were welcomed, in part, because of the injustice to which they had been subjected in a neighboring state, and because their physical sufferings, arising from want of shelter and food in an inclement season of the year to which they were exposed, was such as to move adamantine hearts to pity. Also they were welcomed because, as pointed out in the Introduction to Volume IV of this HISTORY, the state of Illinois needed augmentation of her population by just such a people as the Latter-day Saints were—industrious, frugal, skilled mechanics, successful farmers, experienced men of affairs, men capable of trade and commerce, enterprising and with a larger proportion of educated men and women among them than was to be found among the people of western Illinois in those days. I do not here employ the language of adulation on the one hand, nor seek to make invidious distinctions upon the other. Either would be vain, since the well-known and accepted facts of history would disprove the declarations made if not founded in truth. The fact is, however, that all that is claimed above for the Missouri exiled Latter-day Saints is true and well-attested by their achievements in settling Nauvoo, which in four years rose from a ware-house or two and a few half tumble-down shacks on the banks of the river, and called "Commerce," to the dignity of being the first city in Illinois in population and commercial enterprise, and also gave promise of developing into a manufacturing center of great importance. This last item was evidenced in the fact that the founder of Nauvoo, President Joseph Smith, and the Nauvoo city council appreciated the possibilities in the water power of the Lower Des Moines Rapids in the Mississippi, at the head of which the city was located. Reference to his journal entry for the 23rd of September (this volume, p. 80) will witness that he suggested that a petition be sent to the national Congress for the construction of a canal around the rapids to overcome the obstruction for the free passage of river craft, which the rapids prevented during the low water period of each year, and thus enhance the value of the great stream to the inland commerce of the west.* Reference again to President Smith's journal

---

* That the general government of the United States has since constructed such a canal from Keokuk to Montrose, directly opposite Nauvoo on the west, and at a cost of more than four and a half million dollars, completing it in 1877, is noted in this volume, p. 80 and foot note.

entry for the 8th of December, 1843 (this volume, p. 103) will disclose the fact that he gave instruction in the forenoon to his clerk to draw a plan for a dam in the Mississippi; and that in the afternoon of the same day the city council met and passed an ordinance authorizing Joseph Smith to "erect a dam of suitable height to propel mills and machinery from any point within the limits of said city, and below the Nauvoo House;" also in connection with this dam to construct a "harbor or basin for steamboats and other craft;" and to construct docks, wharfs and landings," the wharfage fees to be "regulated by ordinance of said city (this volume p. 106).

III. Nauvoo as a Possible Manufacturing Center.

What further contributed to the promise that Nauvoo would be a great manufacturing center as well as the center of an immense agricultural region with a splendid commercial outlet, was the fact that artisans and tradesmen of the very first order in skill, were rapidly gathering into the city, not only from the New England and other Eastern states of our own country, but also from the British Isles. It was inevitable if let alone that Nauvoo would become the greatest manufacturing center of Illinois, and among the first of such cities in the United States. The Prophet did not live to see even a commencement made upon these large enterprises he had conceived, but subsequently his zealous followers organized a company to carry them to a successful conclusion under the title of "The Nauvoo Water Power Company,"* which began the construction of the dam on the 29th of April, 1845; but which had to be abandoned because of the hostilities that soon after increased and continued until they culminated in the expulsion of the Latter-day Saints from Illinois.†

* See *Nauvoo Neighbor* for March 5th and March 12th. John E. Page was president of the company; and in a communication to the *Neighbor* (March 12, 1845) urging a vigorous prosecution of the enterprise, he said:

"We have commenced active operations for the building of a dam in the river, as noticed in the *Neighbor* of last week.   *   *   *

"Here is the proud and gallant Mississippi, with her rapid current, tumbling to the broad Atlantic, seeming to say (as she quickens her pace over the rugged rocks of the lower rapids just opposite to our beautiful Nauvoo) only improve my shores and banks, ye Saints, as ye improve my neighboring soil; and I will propel your mills, cotton and woollen manufactories, by which your laborers can find employ, and your poor can be clothed and fed."

† As the suggestion of Joseph Smith for building the canal around the Des Moines Rapids by the general government of the United States was carried out; so also is the water power of the Des Moines Rapids being utilized for manufacturing and other purposes, first suggested by the Prophet, but now, of course, in a way and on a larger scale than it was possible even for men to dream of when the

In addition to these measures, manufacturing and agricultural associations were incorporated; also the "Nauvoo House Associations" for the erection of a hotel, ambitious to be known as the finest hostelry in the Upper Mississippi country. One of the agricultural associations, known as the "Big Field Corporation," held six sections, or three thousand eight hundred and forty acres of land east of Nauvoo; and the year following the Prophet's death the company harvested about thirty thousand bushels of corn, nearly the same amount of wheat, besides an "abundance of oats, barley, buckwheat. potatoes and other vegetables.*

IV. Educational Measures at Nauvoo.

And not only in material things was the superior character of Nauvoo's founders and builders proclaimed; but equally broad and comprehensive were their preparations for an educational system. By their city charter they were empowered to establish an institution of learning within the limits of the city for the teaching of the arts and sciences and learned professions, to be called the "University of the City of Nauvoo;" also a common school system for the city, all of which was in course of development even in the early years of Nauvoo's existence. And in addition to these direct educational institutions of common schools and projected university, literary and dramatic associations were organized, as also choral and band organizations for the cultivation of musical talents and to promote the pleasure and refinement of society; while the religious zeal of the community expressed itself in the rapidly rising walls of the splendid temple—soon to be the most solid and pretentious building in the state; and in the tireless missionary enterprise of the dominant Church.

city council of Nauvoo, in 1843, authorized the construction of a dam to harness this power in the Mississippi for the service of man. This, however, is now nearly an accomplished fact through the enterprise of the Keokuk and Hamilton Water Power Company, which, between Hamilton on the Illinois side, and Keokuk on the Iowa side of the Mississippi (eight or nine miles below Nauvoo), has in course of construction a dam which, including abutments, will be 4,700 feet in length, will stand 32 feet above the river bed, and be 42 feet wide at its base, built of solid concrete. In connection with the dam, and incident to it will be wharfage and a large drydock for the construction and repair of floating craft. There will be developed and for sale as the result of this enterprise, 200,000 horsepower for the service of St. Louis and other towns of Missouri, Illinois and Iowa. The dam and power house will be built at a cost of $22,000,000.

* See "History of the Mormon Church," *Americana* magazine, number for January, 1911, Ch. LIX; also Elder John Taylor's Journal entry for 5th of September, 1844.

V. Jealousy of Nauvoo's Promising Greatness.

Nothing was lacking, then, in the promises of constant and rapid growth, of prosperity and future greatness of Nauvoo. Small wonder if the narrow bigotry and jealousy of small-souled men of the time and vicinity—especially those who were inhabitants of rival towns, particularly those of Warsaw and Carthage—were envious of Nauvoo's prosperity and promise of future greatness. Hitherto this element of jealousy of Nauvoo's prosperity and promise of future greatness has not been accorded the importance due to it as a contributing cause to the warfare made upon that city and the Saints. Little doubt, however, can be entertained, now attention has been called to it, but what as a contributing cause jealousy of Nauvoo stood next to religious prejudice and political distrust and hatred.

A correspondent from Fair Haven, Connecticut, to a gentleman in Nauvoo, set forth this matter most convincingly. An excerpt of the letter was published in the *Nauvoo Neighbor* of August 7th, 1844. It is proper to say that the writer was not a member of the Mormon Church; "but," as the editor of the *Neighbor* describes him, "a citizen of Connecticut, loving law and liberty and life;" and now the paragraph dealing with the point under discussion:

"It is now known here that the lazy speculators of Warsaw, and the still lazier office drones at Carthage, cared nothing for Joseph Smith personally, or for his tenets either; but the prosperity of Nauvoo increasing as it did, beyond any former parallel, even in the western world, excited in their bosoms envy, hatred and all ungodliness. This is the true secret of all their barbarous movements against Mormonism—and they supposed by destroying the Smiths they should extinguish their religion, disperse the Mormons—depopulating and desolating Nauvoo."

Also a correspondent to the *State Register* published at Springfield, Illinois, speaking of Thomas C. Sharp, editor of the *Warsaw Signal* and the anti-Mormon disturbances in Hancock county said:

"He [Sharp] is also described as having made himself the 'organ of a gang of town lot speculators at Warsaw,' who are afraid that Nauvoo is about to kill off their town and render speculation abortive.'"*

Mr. Backenstos in January, 1845, when the repeal of the Nauvoo Charter was under discussion in the Illinois legislature, referred to this same subject in a speech on the floor of the house of representatives, in the course of which he said;

"Town rivalry had also something to do with this opposition to Nauvoo. While Warsaw was on the decline, Nauvoo was rapidly in-

*The *Register* article is copied into the the *Nauvoo Neighbor* for November 13th, 1844.

creasing in wealth and population; a plan to bring about a re-action was soon concocted by the leading men of Warsaw, who made one pilgrimage after another to Nauvoo, imploring the Mormon Prophet to aid them in building up a city adjoining the town of Warsaw, by settling a portion of the Mormon population in and about Warsaw, and commence the building of a new city. The bubble soon exploded, and the speculation failed. This gave rise to dissatisfaction with some who had heretofore been exceedingly polite to '*Lieutenant General Joseph Smith!*' "*

Thus in every way, to refer back to the point of starting the discussion of this subdivision, the Latter-day Saints are proven by their achievements and the foundations they laid for the future greatness of their city, to be a superior people, and hence a desirable addition to the population of the then-young commonwealth of Illinois.

VI. The Character of the People of Western Illinois.

On the other hand there was a population in western Illinois, and perhaps more especially in Hancock county, which had more than its full share of lawless and desperate men; who, as by a law of social gravitation, seek the frontiers of civilization. Moreover it is notorious that the whole upper Mississippi was a rendezvous for gamblers, counterfeiters, horse thieves, murderers and other criminals that infested the great river, which gave easy ingress and egress to a frontier wilderness on the one hand, and to such centers of population and activity, on the other, as New Orleans, St. Louis, and many minor places, besides. "I must give some account of the anti-Mormons," says Governor Ford in his History of Illinois, when referring to the inhabitants of Hancock county. "I had a good opportunity to know the settlers of Hancock county," he continues. "I had attended the circuit courts there as state's attorney, from 1830, when the county was first organized, up to 1834; and to my certain knowledge the early settlers, with some honorable exceptions, were in popular language, hard cases" (page 406). Then for a period of several years to the advent of the "Mormons" he had no means of knowing the character of the people who drifted into the country: "But," he adds, "having passed my whole life on the frontier, on the outer edge of the settlements, I have frequently seen that a few first settlers would fix the character of a settlement for good or for bad, for many years after its commencement. If bad men began the settlement, bad men would be attracted to them, upon the well known principle that birds of a feather will flock together. Rogues will find each other out, and so will honest men. From all which it appears extremely probable, that the later

*Nauvoo Neighbor, March 12th, 1845.

immigrants were many of them attracted to Hancock by a secret sympathy between them and the early settlers."

Indeed the governor suggests that it may have been "the promptings of a secret instinct," which led the "Mormons" to "discern their fellows" and induced them to settle in Hancock in preference to other localities open to them. All which may be regarded as an ingenious thrust at the Latter-day Saints, but which fails of reaching its mark from the fact that it was the criminal element chiefly in Hancock county's population which arrayed itself in antagonism against the Saints, and against whom they were arrayed in all their conflicts in that county. Whereas, under the governor's theory, this criminal element among the "old citizens" and the Saints should have been as hand in glove in their co-operation of encompassing evil things. But to the contrary; from the time the "Mormons" appeared on the scenes at Commerce, in 1839, until they were expelled, they steadfastly and emphatically set their faces against the evils that cursed that community, and denounced all manner of evil both as manifested in a few of their own delinquent members, apostates and camp followers who trailed after the main body of the Church from Missouri, as well as in others: such as dram-drinking, swearing, Sabbath-breaking, contracting debts under pretense of poverty and distress without any prospects or intention of paying,* and especially did they denounce stealing, under any and all pretexts what soever.†

And as it was largely the criminal element among the "old citizens" that was arrayed against the Saints (with unprincipled politicians and a few bigoted and jealous religious leaders added), so was it the conservative and law-abiding portion of the community among whom they had many friends; and nearly all of whom were at least so far friendly with the Saints that they could not be induced to oppose them, much less join in acts of mob violence to the injury of their persons or property; for which reason this portion of the non-Mormon population were called by the contemptuous name of "Jack-Mormons," which epithet was invented by the editor of the Warsaw *Signal*, Thomas C. Sharp, who also originated the term "Jack-Mason" when editing an anti-Masonic paper in western New York. In all probability it was this second name which suggested the first.

*See John Taylor's communication to the Quincy *Argus*, May 1st, 1839. HISTORY OF THE CHURCH, Vol. III, Chapter XXIII.

†See Denunciation of Thieves, 1844, by Hyrum Smith; by President Smith and the formal action of the Apostles quorum, this HISTORY Vol. IV, Chapter XVII. Also the minutes of the conference held at Nauvoo April, 1843, this HISTORY, Vol V, Chapter XVII.

VII. *Educational Status of the People of Western Illinois.*

Education among the masses of Hancock's non-Mormon population was of the meagrest kind. Even Mr. Gregg, the historian of the county, who always gives the best report possible of conditions, remarks, when treating of the county's educational status, that "a new country and among pioneers, is not the place where prosperous colleges and seminaries, or even high schools, are actually found. Hence common schools and, in many instances, very 'common' ones at that, were the best means of education in Hancock county in early days," But this is said of the schools of Hancock county; the greater number of the adult population, 1839-1846, which represent the years when the Saints lived in the county, had migrated from states where educational opportunities were even fewer and less advanced than in western Illinois. Even some of the men prominent in political life in the state were men of extremely limited education. Joseph Duncan, elected governor of Illinois in 1834, and who had served four terms in Congress previous to his election as governor, had but a limited education," says Gregg.* And of Thomas Carlin, who was the governor of Illinois when the exiled Saints moved into the state—he had previously held many minor offices —the same authority says: "He had but a meager education."†

But while the above represents the educational conditions both among the masses of Hancock county and western Illinois in general, and of some of the men in public life, it is also true that there were here and there men in Hancock and surrounding counties of good education and enlightened culture, such as Stephen A. Douglas, O. H. Browning, Major Warren, John J. Hardin, General Minor R. Deming, Samuel Marshal, Judge Jesse B. Thomas, Josiah Lamborn, Governor Ford and others.

VIII. *The Political Phase.*

It has already been observed in these volumes (Vol. IV, Introduction) that in addition to the Latter-day Saints being welcomed into Illinois on account of their economic value in a newly and sparsely settled country, as wealth creators through their industry, frugality and skill in mechanics and husbandry, political parties of Illinois both Whigs and Democrats vied with each other in heartiness of welcome, each hoping to profit by the influx of the new population in both state

*History of Hancock County, p. 158.
†Ibid.

and national elections. Hence it was possible to obtain for Nauvoo the exceptiona powers that constituted her, under the letter of her charter, an autonomy within the limits of her boundaries more akin to a sovereign state than to a municipality within a state and a county. And such were the powers claimed for her by her founders.*
Hence also that catering to the misconception and wrong interpretations of the chartered powers of Nauvoo by lawyers and politicians seeking professional and political favors of the people, which encouraged the belief that the city government was the omnipotent political power within the city limits; and that her municipal court was not only equal to, but even superior to the state courts—"for all other courts were restricted," it was contended,while the municipal court of Nauvoo was not restricted! Similar claims of absolutism were made respecting the city council as a law-making power; and thus were the people of Nauvoo misled by their legal and political advisers, who gave false counsel instead of true, and who encouraged the people in their prejudices and flattered their vanity rather than corrected their errors by an appeal to sound judgment and to the law.

IX. *Mischief Arising from False Legal and Political Counsel.*

Much mischief arose from this source. It was because of these misconceptions in respect of the character of their city government that led to the enactment of those ill advised and unwarranted city ordinances—

That made gold and silver alone legal tender within the city;

That declared Joseph Smith exempt from arrest on requisitions from Missouri founded upon the old difficulties in that state, and providing that persons making an attempt to arrest him might be taken with or without process, imprisoned for life, and might not be pardoned by the governor without consent of the mayor;†

That authorized the city council, marshal, constables and city watch to require all strangers entering the city or already tarrying there to give their names, former residence and for what intent they were tarrying in the city, and answer such other questions as the officers respectively deemed proper to ask; refusal to give the desired information, or giving false names or information subjected them to the same penalties as "vagrants and disorderly persons;"

That further authorized and required the above named officers to

* See this HISTORY Vol. V, Ch. xxiv and Vol. IV. Introduction pp, xxii *et seq.*
† This ordinance about a month after its enactment was repealed at the suggestion of President Smith. See this volume pp. 55-6.

"hail and take all persons found strolling about the city at night after nine o'clock and before sunrise, and to confine them in ward for trial under the ordinances concerning vagrants and disorderly persons, unless they could give a good account of themselves for being out "after nine o'clock;"

That further authorized and required the aforesaid officers to enter all hotels or houses of public entertainment, and such other habitations as they may judge proper, and require the inmates to give immediate information of all persons residing in said hotel or habitation, and their business, occupation or movements, under penalty of forfeiture of license, if a public house, and they and the transient persons subject to the penalties visited upon vagrants for failure to give the information required, or giving false information; while the officer who should "refuse or neglect to perform the above duties should be fined $100, and be broke of his office;"

That forbade the search and seizure of person or property by foreign process [*i. e.* other process than that issuing from the city's authority] within the city of Nauvoo, leading to the widespread belief that the design of said ordinance was "to hinder the execution of the statutes of Illinois" within said city;*

That asked the general government to ratify the Nauvoo Charter, and in addition constitute the city a territorial government, by granting "all rights, powers, privileges and immunities belonging to territories and not repugnant to the constitution of the United States," with power granted to the mayor to call to his aid a sufficient number of the United States troops, in connection with the Nauvoo Legion, to repel the invasion of mobs, keep the public peace, protect the innocent from lawless banditti; the United States officers to obey the requisition of this ordinance; and the Nauvoo Legion, when in service quelling mobs and preserving the public peace, to be under the same regulations, rules and laws of pay as the troops of the United States; the territorial privileges to continue until the "state of Missouri restores to those exiled citizens [the Latter-day Saints] the lands, rights, privileges, property, and damages for all losses" they had sustained by being banished from that commonwealth;†

And, finally, that asserted the right of the municipal court to arrest

---

* This alleged "design" of the ordinance President Smith specifically denied in the open session of the city council, and to a committee of lawyers from Carthage, who waited upon the city council to protest against this ordinance; and the ordinance was amended by a third section disclaiming such alleged intention, but still retaining the feature that forced state process to be served through the agency of Nauvoo's city officers. See this vol. pp. 173-4.

† This volume pp. 130-132.

process issued by the state's circuit courts, and even by the United States courts, by *habeas corpus* proceedings; and insisted, not only upon the right to pass judgment upon the sufficiency of writs under which arrests were made, but upon the right also to go behind the writs and try the cases upon their merits.

X. *Subserviency of Politicians and Lawyers.*

Blame for this political subserviency and misleading political and legal advice, may not be charged on one party more than another. If Cyrus Walker, a Whig candidate for congress, assented to the doctrine as understood by Nauvoo's leading men, that the municipal court of Nauvoo held the power under *habeas corpus* procedure to arrest execution of process of the state courts, as he did,* so, too, did Joseph P. Hoge, Democratic nominee; and even Governor Ford, when requested to call out the militia to rearrest Joseph Smith after he had been liberated from the custody of Sheriff Reynolds, agent of Missouri, under *habeas corpus* proceedings, took refuge behind the *habeas corpus* proceedings of the Municipal Court at Nauvoo. In that case the court not only inquired into the sufficiency of the writ of requisition from Missouri, and granted by Governor Ford himself, but also went back of the writ and tried the case *exparte* on its merits, and finally discharged the prisoner, both "for want of substance in the warrant, * * * as well as upon the merits of the case."† When answering the request of Missouri to rearrest Joseph Smith, Governor Ford, I say, at least took refuge behind the aforesaid proceedings of the Municipal Court to the extent of saying, in the face of that procedure, that "no process, officer or authority of Illinois had been resisted or interfered with,"‡ and therefore refused to call out the militia to rearrest President Smith.

It is but fair to Governor Ford, however, to say that in his inaugural speech of December 8th, 1842, he pointed out what he regarded as objectionable features in the Nauvoo charter, and recommended its modification.§ and later censured the lawyers for misleading the Nauvoo city authorities in this matter, in the following passage from a letter to the Mayor and City Council of Nauvoo, under date of June 22nd, 1844.

You have also assumed to yourselves more power than you are entitled to in relation to *habeas corpus* under your charter. I know that you have been told by lawyers, for the purpose of gaining your favor,

---

* This HISTORY Vol. V, pp. 467-8, 472.

† This HISTORY, Vov. V. pp. 473-4.

‡ See Ford's letter to Thomas Reynolds, Governor of Missouri, under date of August 14, 1843. This HISTORY, Vol. V, pp. 553-6.

§ Ibid p. 200.

that you have this power to any extent. In this they have deceived you for their own base purposes. Your charter supposes that you may pass ordinances, a breach of which will result in the imprisonment of the offender.

For the purpose of giving more speedy relief to such persons authority was given to the Municipal Court to issue writs of *habeas corpus* in all cases arising under the ordinances of the city.

It was never supposed by the Legislature, nor can the language of your charter be tortured to mean that a jurisdiction was intended to be conferred which would apply to all cases of imprisonment under the general laws of the state or of the United States, as well as the city ordinances.

To which President Smith replied:

Whatever power we have exercised in the *habeas corpus* has been done in accordance with the letter of the Charter and Constitution as we confidently understood them; and that, too, with the ablest counsel; but if it be so that we have erred in this thing, let the Supreme Court correct the evil. We have never gone contrary to constitutional law, so far as we have been able to learn it. If lawyers have belied their profession to abuse us the evil be on their heads.*

XI   The Fate of a Balance of Power Factor in Politics.

Being misled by false legal and political advice was not the only misfortune of the kind perpetrated upon the Saints, first by the subserviency of, and then the betrayal by, politicians and lawyers. The hope of both parties to secure political advantage by the influx of the new Latter-day Saint population into the state has been already referred to; as also the efforts of both parties to gain their favor by granting exceptional favors to them in founding Nauvoo. When, however, the time for voting came, and the Saints voted according to their convictions of duty, or as their inclinations prompted, the defeated party or candidates blamed them for the defeat, and straightway favored the adoption of an anti-Mormon policy, which found support not only in the defeated party, but also among those who felt a grievance against the Saints on other accounts; some because Nauvoo's prosperity and constantly increasing importance as a center of population and trade and commerce was rapidly eclipsing all other towns of the state; and others, over-anxious to retard, if not destroy, a rival system on account of religious prejudice. When an anti-Mormon party took the field, pledged itself to repeal the Nauvoo charter, and to drive the Mormons from the state—as was the pledge of Joseph Duncan, Whig candidate for Governor of Illinois in 1841,† there was really no other course for the Saints to pursue but to combine solidly for the defeat of the candidate and

* This HISTORY, Vol. VI. Ch. XXVI, where both letters will be found at length.
† See Ford's *History of Illinois*, p. 269; also this HISTORY, Vol IV, pp. 479-481 and footnotes; Vol. V, p. 490.

party making such pledges; the instinct of self-preservation impelled such a course, rather than the prompting of inclination.

For a time, as in all such cases, the party receiving the support of this practically solid Mormon vote could be relied upon to protect and defend those who had made success possible for them; but at the first indication that the hold of the favored party upon such vote is precarious, that there is a possibility that it might go to the other side,* naturally the ardor of their friendship, seldom or never sincere, cools; and they are ready to combine for the destruction of their former allies as others have been. And when in addition to precariousness of hold upon those who possess the balance of power there stands up in the back ground of things the possibility that the balance of power party may become strong enough in the political subdivision in which they are located to run affairs on their own account, the likelihood of all parties combining against them becomes all the more assured. In Illinois the Latter-day Saints ran the entire political gamut of experience as a "balance of power" factor in the politics of western Illinois. The final phase of that experience had been reached when at a mass meeting held at Carthage on the sixth of September, 1843, it was—

Resolved, That as it has been too common for several years past for politicians of both political parties, not only of this county, but likewise of the state, to go to Nauvoo and truckle to the heads of the Mormon clan for their influence, we pledge ourselves that we will not support any man of either party in the future who shall thus debase himself.†

Politicians still sought Mormon aid to encompass their own political ends, but, as Governor Ford later remarked, "'they were willing and anxious for Mormon voters at elections, but they were unwilling to risk their popularity with the people, by taking part in their favor even when law and justice, and the Constitution, were all on their side;"† and

---

*Such appeared to be the very great probability in the election of 1843. As will be remembered by the readers of Vol. IV of this History, Cyrus Walker, Esq., Whig candidate for Congress, rendered valuable service in delivering the Prophet from the hands of those bent upon running him into Missouri for trial on the old complaint against him in that state. That service could only be obtained in that crisis by Joseph Smith pledging himself to vote for Walker, which was interpreted to meam, of course, the Mormon vote; and it was generally conceded that the Whigs receiving the Mormon vote would be successful. Before the day of election, however, there had arisen strong reasons for believing that the arrest of the Prophet and the effort to take him to Missouri, as also Walker's appearance upon the scene to effect his liberation, was itself a political trick to secure the Mormon vote for the Whig party, which was thwarted by the Mormons voting, at the last moment, the Democratic ticket. (See Vol. V, Chapter XXVI).

†Ford's History of Illinois, p. 364.

so finally all parties turned against them, and they were at the last, as we shall see in a future volume of this history, expelled without mercy from the state.

XII. Joseph Smith's Candidacy for the Presidency.

The mischief that threatened during the Prophet's life time, and which finally befell the Saints, was clearly foreseen by the Church leaders; and the desire to escape from the threatening portents of it prompted the nomination of Joseph Smith for the office of President of the United States, in the general election of 1844. Of course there could be no hope seriously entertained that he would be elected; but, as explained by an editorial in the *Times and Seasons*,* if the Saints could not succeed in electing their candidate, they would have the satisfaction of knowing that they had acted conscientiously; they had used their best judgment, under the circumstances, and if they had to throw away their votes, it was better to do so upon a worthy than upon an unworthy individual who might use the weapon they put into his hand to destroy them. The Prophet himself evidently regarded his nomination humorously rather than seriously, except that it might result in withdrawing the Saints from the position of shuttle-cock between the battle doors of the two old political parties. "I care but little about the presidential chair," he said on one occasion. "I would not give half as much for the office of President of the United States as I would for the one I now hold as Lieutenant General of the Nauvoo Legion." Again he said: "When I get hold of eastern papers, and see how popular I am; I am afraid myself that I shall be elected; but if I should be, I would not say [*i. e.* to the Latter-day Saints] your cause is just but I can do nothing for you."

As a further evidence that Joseph Smith did not regard his candidacy as likely to be successful, he was, at the time of his nomination and afterwards, pushing vigorously his project of a western movement for the Church. He had drawn up a memorial and ordinance to the national congress asking to be authorized by the general government to raise one hundred thousand armed volunteers to police the inter-mountain and Pacific coast west from Oregon to Texas, for the purpose of assuring Texas her independence, and maintaining the claims of the United States to Oregon, and affording the whole western population of our country protection from Indian depredations; and thus contribute to the rapid settlement and development of that noble extent of country lying between the Mississippi and the Pacific Ocean. His agents, Orson Hyde and Orson Pratt, presented the matter to sen-

*See this volume, pp. 214-217, where the editorial is given *in extenso*.

ators and representatives at Washington, and a number favored the project of the removal of the Mormons to the west, but generally urged that Joseph Smith go without seeking special authorization from the government. Reference to Orson Hyde's report of the procedure among congressmen and their views upon the subject will be found in his two important communications to the Prophet from Washington, in chapter XVI of this volume. Mr. John Wentworth, representative to Congress from northern Illinois, introduced President Smith's Memorial and Ordinance into the House on the 25th of May, to be read for the information of the House; but before the reading was concluded, objection was made, and as it required unanimous consent to have it read, further reading was prevented. A vote to suspend the rules in order that Mr. Wentworth might secure the reading of the memorial stood 79 yeas, and 86 nays, which vote gives evidence at least of a widespread desire to have the matter presented to the House.*

XIII. Missouri as a Factor in the Affairs of Nauvoo.

In addition to all the Illinois factors that entered into the complex situation confronting the Saints at Nauvoo, at the time of the Prophet's death, and some time previous to his arrest, was the attitude and course pursued by Missouri with reference to Nauvoo and the Saints, Disgraced as a state by her own conduct towards the Latter-day Saints, when they were inhabitants within her borders, her people were all too willing to co-operate with any party or agency that would continue to make war upon them. If the state of Illinois which with open arms had received the people that Missouri exiled from her borders, under such circumstances of cruelty, could also be brought to drive them from that state, it would be regarded, in a way, as a vindication of Missouri and the course she had taken in her treatment of the Saints, since in effect it would say, that the people of Illinois, no less than the people of Missouri, found it impossible to tolerate the "Mormons;" and therefore there must be something fundamentally wrong with them, rather than with the people of these states. Hence the anti-Mormons of Hancock and adjoining counties in Illinois, always found support in whatever of violence or wrong they planned against the Saints. Hence the constant threats of invasion of mobs from Missouri, emphasized by occasional kidnapping expeditions into Hancock county, together with frequent requisitions upon the Illinois authorities for the arrest and extradition of Joseph Smith on the old charges against him in Missouri. And these

*See Chapter XI, this volume, where the memorial itself, Hyde's two letters and the action in the House of Representatives will he found in full.

Missouri threats and outrages were not among the least of the annoy-
ances and anxieties of the Saints; and they make clear the necessity
that was felt for an efficient militia force at Nauvoo. Hence the
Nauvoo Legion and the lively interest manifested in its frequent
musters and drills, and its thorough equipment; all of which, but for
the constant danger of invasion from Missouri mobs, and the co-operation with them of like forces in Illinois, would have been inconsistent
with the deportment of a religious community whose mission was one of
peace and good will towards men; and who had been especially commanded to "renounce war and proclaim peace" (Doc and Cov. Sec. 98,
16); and commanded also to "sue for peace," both to those who had
"smitten" them—the revelation was given after the expulsion from
Jackson county, Missouri—and "to all people;" and "lift up an ensign
of peace, and make a proclamation of peace unto the ends of the earth"
(Doc. and Cov. sec 105: 38-40). But invasions from Missouri constantly menacing them, and the danger of mob violence breaking out in
Illinois, justified the organization of the Legion, and the maintenance
of its efficiency by full equipment of arms and frequent drills and musters; for the right of self-preservation is not abrogated by any divine
law given to the Saints; and duty to protect home and family against
the assaults of the evil-disposed, presses as firmly upon the Saints, as
upon those who have not definitely pledged themselves to a program of
righteousness.

XIV. Apostate Conspirators at Nauvoo.

One other factor only remains to be mentioned of those that enter
into that combination of forces that resulted in the death of the Prophet
and the Patriarch. That is the conspiracy of apostates within Nauvoo
itself.

The apostates and their sympathizers were headed by a coterie of
prominent young men: The two Law brothers, William and Wilson;
Robert D. and Charles A. Foster, brothers; Francis M. and Chauncey
L. Higbee, brothers, and unworthy sons of that most faithful man and
the Prophet's devoted friend, Judge Elias Higbee (See Vol. IV pp. 81-
100 passim); Sylvester Emmons and Joseph H. Jackson. Of these,
William Law was counselor in the First Presidency, and Wilson Law
was a major general, and commander of one of the cohorts of the
Nauvoo Legion, and all were or had been more or less prominent in the
public life of Nauvoo.

The cause of their apostasy seems to have been the baneful influence
of John C. Bennett's immoralities; for these men were quite generally
associates of his before his flight from Nauvoo. They evidently lost

the spirit of the gospel, wandered through sin into spiritual darkness, and seemingly were obsessed by a murderous spirit against the Prophet who boldly revealed their wickedness and publicly denounced their conduct; and in retaliation this coterie of apostates entered into conspiracies to encompass President Smith's death, and that of his brother Hyrum. They were in communication with the Prophet's enemies in Missouri, and sought to betray him into their hands. They were among the chief actors in all schemes of opposition and conspiracies against him in the closing year of his life, including those plots which eventuated in the martyrdom of both Prophet and Patriarch at Carthage.

XV.   The "Expositor" Affair.

Such are the chief factors that enter into the combination of events detailed in this volume of HISTORY and which have a direct relationship to the martyrdom of the Smith brothers. They existed as combustible matarials awaiting only the spark that would set them aflame to work death and destruction.

The spark came. It came in the destruction of the *Nauvoo Expositor*, published by the above mentioned coterie of apostates. It was the intention of the *Expositor*, as its name would indicate, to make an *expose* of alleged conditions in Nauvoo, in the moral, social, religious and political phase of them. Also to agitate for the *"unconditional repeal of the Nauvoo Charter."* This was a challenge to mortal combat, the issue being the life of the city of Nauvoo; and after that the question of the existence of the Church in Illinois, or even within the confines of the United States; for undoubtedly the city charter once repealed, carrying with it the disorganization of the Legion, protection for the Saints, as matters stood in 1844, both civil and military, would be gone. It was a life and death struggle then that the advent of the *Expositor* inaugurated. The Saints stood at such disadvantage in the proposed contest that if the *Expositor* was allowed to run its course it would inevitably have won its case against the city; and against the Church, so far as the latter continuing in Illinois, and perhaps as far as its continuance in the United States was concerned.

The new marriage system, involving the practice, within certain limitations and under very special conditions, of a plurality of wives, constituted a ground of appeal to popular prejudices and passions that would have been absolutely resistless if the paper had been allowed to proceed. The charter would have been repealed; the city government destroyed, or at the least modified and placed in the hands of an apostate or anti-Mormon minority whose administration would have been intolerable to the large majority of Nauvoo's citizens; and finally the scenes of Missouri would have been re-enacted in an Illinois setting.

In the presence of such difficulties, what was to be done? In addition to declaring the existence of the practice of plural marriage, not yet announced or publicly taught as a doctrine of the Church, and agitating for the unqualified repeal of the Nauvoo charter, gross immoralities were charged against leading citizens which doubtless rendered the paper grossly libelous. In other cities such an avowed enemy as the *Expositor* was, would have been destroyed by a mob. For the people of Nauvoo to have so proceeded would have been a departure from their principles of upholding law and order, and would have brought upon them the people of the surrounding counties, and from Missouri in overwhelming numbers. Mob violence could not be thought of; and yet the safety of the community imperatively demanded the suppression of the *Expositor* at any cost.

Under these circumstances the city council met and took under consideration the *Expositor* and the necessity of destroying it. As their charter conferred upon the city the right to remove nuisances, the city council declared the *Expositor* press a nuisance and directed the Mayor to have it destroyed, which he did by giving an order to that effect, and it was destroyed without riot or tumult.

The legality of the action of the Mayor and City Council was, of course, questionable, though some sought to defend it on legal grounds; but it must be conceded that neither proof nor argument for legality are convincing. On the grounds of expediency or necessity the action is more defensible. The existence of the city, the preservation of the Latter-day Saints until provision could be made for a retreat from Illinois—which retreat was even then being provided for by the Prophet in the projected movement of the Church to the west—demanded the cessation of the publication of the *Expositor*. By proceeding at least under the forms of law, the city council, though they might be conscious of the illegality of their action, avoided the necessity of the people resorting to mob action for self-preservation, and made it possible for the legality of their course to be determined in the courts, and the parties injured to recover compensation for the press and damages by civil process. Meantime the libelous press with its mission of destruction of the Saints at Nauvoo was silenced; and had events taken the course which the action of the city council provided, a respite would have been gained from impending violence, during which arrangements for the retreat of the Saints from Illinois could have been completed and a goal of safety won for them. Under a plea, then, of absolute necessity to self-preservation of a community, and to achieve the retreat here alluded to, and with the certainty that those injured in property by the *Expositor's* destruction would be fully compensated in civil action before the courts—the action of the mayor and city council of Nauvoo is defensible, even if not on the ground of the legality of their procedure.*

XVI. The Appeal to the Mob Spirit.

Events did not take the course planned for them. The uproar that followed the destruction of the *Expositor* press, put all reason at defiance. At Warsaw a mass meeting was held which issued a statement, in connection with the resolutions it passed, that "A mob at Nauvoo, under a city ordinance, has violated the highest privilege in government: and to seek redress in the ordinary way would be utterly ineffectual * * * *Resolved*, that we hold ourselves at all times in readiness to co-operate with our fellow citizens in this state, Missouri, and Iowa, to exterminate, *utterly exterminate* the wicked and abominable Mormon leaders, the authors of our troubles. * * * The time, in our opinion, has arrived when the adherents of Smith as a body should be driven from the surrounding settlements into Nauvoo. That the Prophet and his miscreant adherents should then be demanded at their hands; and, if not surrendered, a war of extermination should be waged to the entire destruction, if necessary for our protection, of his adherents. And we hereby recommend this resolution to the consideration of the several townships, to the mass convention to be held at Carthage."

The Carthage meeting held a few days later embodied the above in their resolutions, as did other mass meetings held at various places. The *Warsaw Signal* in its impression of June 12th, passionately said:†

"We have only to state that this [i. e. The destruction of the *Expositor* press] is sufficient! War and extermination is inevitable! CITIZENS ARISE, ONE and ALL!!! Can you stand by, and suffer such INFERNAL DEVILS! to ROB men of their property rights, without avenging them? We have no time to comment: every man will make his own. LET IT BE MADE WITH POWDER and BALL!!!"

All the combustible material to which attention is called in this Introduction was instantly aflame at the destruction of the *Expositor* press. Every passion was appealed to, jealousy, envy, cupidity, hatred. All the lawless elements of the community were practically invited to

---

*See Chapter XXX, *passim* this volume for a discussion of the *Expositor*; also Taylor-Colfax Discussion on the "Mormon" Question, p. 20. Also an editorial from the Nauvoo *Neighbor*, see p. 496, this volume.

†I follow the typing and punctuation from the *Signal* as given by the late John Hay, secretary of state, *Atlantic Monthly* of December, 1869.

assemble and run riot in lawless violence, and excess of carnage and destruction of property and life.   Nothing but the wholesome fear of the strength and effectiveness of the Nauvoo Legion at that time held this lawless element in check.

It was all in vain that hearings were had before the municipal court of Nauvoo, on the *Expositor* matter; in vain that a subsequent hearing was had before Esquire Wells, then not a Mormon and living outside of Nauvoo limits; in vain that the *Nauvoo Neighbor* sought to conciliate the awakening wrath that was aroused in the community, by pleading that if the city council had "exceeded the law of the land, a higher court could regulate the proceedings;" in vain that President Smith urged Governor Ford to come to Nauvoo to make personal investigation of conditions and take the necessary steps to prevent riot and war—all was in vain; preparations were in the making on all sides for an uprising angainst Nauvoo and the Saints, and there was nothing left but to defend the city by placing it under martial law and calling upon the Legion to resist the threatened assault, which act was made the basis for the subsequent charge of "treason."

Then followed in quick succession the demand of the governor for the Mayor and members of the City Council to come to Carthage and submit to trial under circumstances that inevitably meant death; the inspiration of the Prophet to go to the West and all would be well; the crossing of the Mississippi by the Prophet and a few trusted friends to make preparations for that journey; the accusation by false friends of cowardice on the Prophet's part, the flight as of a false shepherd leaving the flock to be devoured by wolves; the lightning-like retort of the Prophet—"*If my life is of no value to my friends, it is of none to myself;*" the return to Nauvoo; the subsequent going to Carthage to submit to the demands of the governor of Illinois in every particular, and the well-known story of Carthage jail—the martyrdom.

XVII. *The Prophet's Nobility in the hour of Trial.*

The bearing of the Prophet throughout the closing months with which this volume deals is admirable.   There is no faltering or evidence of weakness at any point of his conduct.   If criticised at all it would be for over-daring, for over self-confidence, that approached sublimity. Strong men through wickedness fell away from their discipleship, and conspired against him; the Prophet reproved them in the gate, and proclaimed their iniquities in public when hope of reforming them was gone.   He saw mobs forming for the destruction of himself and Nauvoo and his people; he calmly prepared to meet force with force, and drilled and prepared his legion for the conflict, entrenched some of the approaches to the city, and picketed them with guards; as mayor of the city he placed the city under martial law; and as lieutenant-general he took personal command of the Nauvoo Legion and stood ready to defend the rights of himself and his people, for which his revolutionary ancestry had fought in the war for American independence. He believed gloriously in the right of self-defense, and resistance to oppression by physical force if necessary. To his uncle John Smith at Ramus who had asked for counsel in the disturbed state of things, he wrote ten days before his death:

"I write these few lines to inform you that we feel determined in this place not to be dismayed if hell boils over all at once. We feel to hope for the best, and determined to prepare for the worst, and we want this to be your motto in common with us: *We will never ground our arms until we give them up by death.*"

And from Carthage prison, on the morning of the day of his martyrdom, he wrote to his wife for transmission to his people:

"There is one principle which is eternal: It is the duty of all men to protect their lives and the lives of their household, whenever necessity requires, and no power has a right to forbid it, should the last extreme arrive; but I anticipate no such extreme; *but caution is the parent of safety.*"

When the jail in Carthage was assailed, and the mob was pouring murderous volleys into the room occupied by himself and friends, the Prophet turned from the prostrate form of his murdered brother to face death-dealing guns and bravely returned the fire of his assailants, "bringing his man down every time," and compelling even John Hay, who but reluctantly accords the Prophet any quality of virtue, to confess that he "made a handsome fight" in the jail.*

XVIII. *Always the Prophet-Teacher.*

But what was more wonderful than the manifestation of moral and physical courage and good generalship during these turbulent months of his career, was the pursuance of his duties as a teacher of religious truth—his calling as a Prophet of God. Notwithstanding he was troubled on every side, he could compose his mind to instruct the

*This is the late Secretary of State John Hay, in the *Atlantic Monthly* for December, 1869; "Joe Smith died bravely, he stood by the jam of the door and fired four shots, bringing his man down every time. He shot an Irishman named Wills, who was in the affair from his congenital love of a brawl, in the arm; Gallagher, a Southerner from the Mississippi bottom, in the face; Voorhees, a half-grown hobbledehoy from Bear Creek, in the shoulder; and another gentleman, whose name I will not mention, as he is prepared to prove an *alibi*, and besides stands six feet two in his moccasins." In a later paragraph he refers to "the handsome fight in the jail."

Church on such doctrines as the complete salvation of their dead; how to proceed with the administration of all ordinances given for and in behalf of the dead; the doctrine of the resurrection and the reality of spiritual existences; the plurality of Divine Intelligences, or Gods; the nature of man's spirit; the doctrine of eternal progress for intelligences who keep the estates through which they are appointed to pass; the nature and character of the Godhead, and the relationship of man to God.   All these themes and many more he dwelt upon in public discourse and private interview and written communications.   He lived his life, as I have said elsewhere, *in cresendo*, it grew in intensity and volume as he approached its close.   Higher and still higher the inspiration of God directed his thoughts; bolder were his conceptions, and clearer his expositions of them.   So far was he from being a "fallen prophet" in the closing months of his career, as apostates charged, that he grew stronger with each passing day; more impressive in weight of personal character, and charm of manner; for he preserved amid all the conflicts and trials through which he passed—until the shadows of impending death began to fall upon him in Carthage prison—the natural sweetness of his nature, and the intellectual playfulness characteristic of him from boyhood—*so do not fallen prophets.*

*   *   *   *   *   *   *

Side by side on the banks of the majestic river that half encircles Nauvoo, the "beautiful," carrying with it also the idea of "rest," peacefully sleep the brothers, Joseph and Hyrum Smith, the Prophet and the Patriarch of the Church in the New Dispensation of the Gospel. Their lives were interlaced by almost daily associations from childhood to the last awful scene of martyrdom. It was therefore most fitting that they should be buried beside each other, on the banks of the "Father of Waters" in the city they had founded, where they had toiled and suffered and achieved; where their joys rose to greater heights and their sorrows sounded greater depths than falls to the lot of but few men in this world. Undisturbed may their death slumber be until it shall be ended by the trump of God, calling them forth to a glorious resurrection.

*   *   *   *   *   *   *

Prophet and Patriarch

In the Temple square at Salt Lake City, where tens of thousands, made up of people of nearly every nation in the world view them, stand two bronze statues, life size, on granite bases. They are the statues of the Brothers Smith, the Prophet and the Patriarch of the New Dispensation of the Gospel. On the granite basements, respectively, are bronze tablets on which is engraved the Life Record of these men, and what is character-istic of each.

The text of the bronze plate of Hyrum Smith's statue is as follows:

HYRUM SMITH.

The Patriarch and a witness of the Book of Mormon.

An elder brother, and the steadfast friend and counselor of Jeseph Smith, the Prophet.

Born at Tunbridge, Vermont, February 9th, 1800; suffered martyr-dom with the Prophet at Carthage, Illinois, on the 27th of June, 1844.

The friendship of the brothers Hyrum and Joseph Smith is foremost among the few great friendships of the world's history. Their names will be classed among the martyrs for religion.

The Book of Mormon—the plates of which Hyrum Smith both saw and handled; the revelations in the Book of Doctrine and Covenants; the Church of Jesus Christ of Latter-day Saints—these, to bring them forth for the salvation of the world, cost the best blood of the 19th century.

"I could pray in my heart that all men were like my brother Hyrum, who possesses the mildness of a lamb and the integrity of Job, and, in short, the meekness and humility of Christ. I love him with that love that is stronger than death."—*Joseph Smith.*

"If ever there was an exemplary, honest and virtuous man, the embodiment of all that is noble in the human form, Hyrum Smith was the representative."—*President John Taylor.*

As he shared in the labors, so does he share in the honor and glory of the New Dispensation with his Prophet Brother.

In life they were not divided; in death they were not separated; in glory they are one.

The text on the west side of the base of Joseph Smith's tablet is:

JOSEPH SMITH.

The Prophet of the New Dispensation of the Gospel of Jesus Christ our Lord. He was born at Sharon, Vermont, on the 23rd of December, 1805; and suffered Martyrdom for the word of God and the testimony of Jesus at Carthage, Illinois, on the 27th of June, 1844.

HIS VISION OF GOD.

I saw two Personages whose glory and brightness defy all descrip-tion. One of them spake unto me and said:

"*This is my Beloved Son: hear Him.*"

I asked which of all the sects was right, and which I should join. I was answered I must join none of them; they were all wrong; they teach for doctrine the commandments of men; I received a promise that the fulness of the Gospel would at some future time be made known to me.

THE BOOK OF MORMON.

This book was revealed to him, and he translated it by the gift and power of God. It is an inspired history of ancient America, and contains the fullness of the Gospel. It is the American Testament of our Lord and Savior Jesus Christ.

THE ORGANIZATION OF THE CHURCH.

Joseph Smith received divine authority through the ministration of angels to teach the Gospel and administer the ordinances thereof. He established again in the earth the Church of Jesus Christ, organizing it by the will and commandment of God on the 6th day of April, 1830.

He also received commission to gather Israel and establish Zion on this land of America; to erect temples and perform all ordinances therein both for the living and the dead; and prepare the way for the glorious coming of the Lord Jesus Christ to reign on earth.

The contents of the tablet on the east side of the base of the Prophet's statue are these gems from his teachings:

TRUTH GEMS.

The glory of God is intelligence.

It is impossible for a man to be saved in ignorance.

Whatever principles of intelligence we attain unto in this life will rise with us in the resurrection.

There is a law irrevocably decreed in heaven before the foundations of this world upon which all blessings are predicated; and when we obtain any blessing from God it is by obedience to that law on which it is predicated.

This is the work and glory of God: to bring to pass the immortality and eternal life of man.

Adam fell that man might be; and men are that they might have joy.

The intelligence of spirits had no beginning, neither will it have an end. Jesus was in the beginning with the Father: man was also in the beginning with God. Intelligence, or the light of truth, was not created or made, neither indeed can be.

The spirit and body is the soul of man; and the resurrection from the dead is the redemption of the soul.

It is the first principle of the Gospel to know for a certainty the character of God; and to know that man, (as Moses) may converse with Him as one man converses with another.

This message of the Prophet, and these doctrines of the east bronze tablet, together with other doctrines taught by him in this PERIOD I of our CHURCH HISTORY, and to be found scattered through the six volumes now published of that history, await only the mind of some God-inspired Spencer to cast them into synthetical form—to be adequately presented and witnessed—to constitute Mormonism both the Religion and the Philosophy of modern times—to bring to pass and to glorify the Golden Age of the long-promised Millennium of Christian hope.

HISTORY

OF THE

CHURCH OF JESUS CHRIST OF LATTER-DAY SAINTS

VOL. VI

HISTORY

OF THE

CHURCH OF JESUS CHRIST

OF

LATTER-DAY SAINTS.

PERIOD I.

HISTORY OF JOSEPH SMITH, THE PROPHET.

CHAPTER I.

AN ESTIMATE OF THE PROPHET JOSEPH AS A RELIGIOUS
LEADER—ANTI-MORMON MEETING AT CARTHAGE—HISTOR-
ICAL SKETCH—IMPORTANT CONFERENCE OF THE TWELVE
HELD IN BOSTON.

Friday, September 1, 1843. — A conference was held
in Buffalo, New York, Elder John P. Greene presiding;
Wm. H. Folsom,* clerk: 13 branches, 1 High Priest, 58

---

* William H. Folsom named above afterward became prominent as an architect
in Utah. He was born in Portsmouth, New Hampshire, in March, 1815, and died
in Salt Lake City, 1901, at the advanced age of 86 years. When a boy he moved to
Buffalo N.Y. with his parents. When in his twenty fifth year he heard a Mormon
Elder preach and was converted to the gospel and joined the Church. As a consequence of this act he was ostracised by his people. He took his family and moved
to Nauvoo and established himself as an architect and builder, and assisted in the
construction of the Nauvoo Temple.

Brother Folsom was expelled from Nauvoo at the time of the general exodus of
the Saints and settled for a time at Keokuk. He subsequently moved to Council
Bluffs, and in 1860 went on to Salt Lake valley. His ability as an architect and
builder was soon required by President Brigham Young. President Young
conceived the general plan of the now celebrated "Mormon Tabernacle" at Salt Lake
City, but William Folsom took President Young's suggestions and worked out the
plans. While others scouted the idea of the structure, Folsom had faith in it, and
as a consequence he has associated his name inseparably with the building, that

Elders, 2 Teachers, 1 Deacon, and 247 members were represented.

I attended the meeting of the High Council as a witness
in the case of Cowles* vs. George J. Adams. Charges not
sustained.

Saturday, 2. — I was not well, and therefore adjourned
Mayor's Court.

Sunday, 3. — I attended council with my brother
Hyrum, Newel K. Whitney, Willard Richards, William
Law and William Marks, and gave instructions to the
brethren in relation to things in futurity.

A tremendous storm at Chester, Penn. The creek rose
twenty-three feet in two hours, and swept away all the
bridges, many factories and houses, and upwards of
twenty persons drowned.

A conference was held at Hayward's Hotel, Manchester,
England.

Minutes of the Manchester Conference, held 3rd of September, 1843.

Charles Miller, President; William Walker, Clerk. Present: 1
Patriarch, 1 High Priest, 25 Elders, 40 Priests, 21 Teachers, and 4
Deacons.

Total number of members represented was as follows: 1,549
members, including 44 Elders, 99 Priests, 56 Teachers, 22 Deacons.
Baptized since last general conference, 80; cut off, 29; emigrated, 18;
removed, 26; died, 4.

Monday, 4. — Attended mayor's court and tried three
cases—viz.,

City *versus* A. Dodge, S. Dodge, and Luther Purtelow.
The two first I fined five dollars, and the last one
dollar and costs. One, p. m., called and gave licence for

stands as one of the world's centers of interest and curiosity. He was the architect and superintendent of construction of the Manti Temple, and was an able
assistant in the construction of all the Temples in Utah. He was the designer of
the Salt Lake Theater, and of many other buildings that are this day admired for
their architectural grace and durability.

* This was Austin Cowles, for some time counselor in the Nauvoo stake of Zion
(HISTORY OF THE CHURCH, Vol. IV, p. 323) and subsequently a member of the High
Council. The nature of the charges made against George J. Adams at this time is
not known.

a circus performance, which I attended with my family until five, p. m.

I copy from the *New York Sun* as follows: —

"JOE SMITH, THE MORMON PROPHET."[*]

This Joe Smith must be set down as an extraordinary character, a prophet-hero, as Carlyle might call him. He is one of the great men of this age, and in future history will rank with those who, in one way or another, have stamped their impress strongly on society.

Nothing can be more plebeian, in seeming, than this Joe Smith. Little of dignity is there in his cognomen; but few in this age have done such deeds, and performed such apparent miracles. It is no small thing, in the blaze of this nineteenth century, to give to men a new revelation, found a new religion, establish new forms of worship, to build a city, with new laws, institutions, and orders of architecture, — to establish ecclesiastic, civil and military jurisdiction, found colleges, send out missionaries, and make proselytes in two hemispheres: yet all this has been done by Joe Smith, and that against every sort of opposition, ridicule and persecution. This sect has its martyrs also; and the spirit in which they were imprisoned and murdered in Missouri, does not appear to have differed much from that which has attended religious persecutions in all ages of the world.

That Joe Smith, the founder of the Mormons, is a man of great talent, a deep thinker, and eloquent speaker, an able writer, and a man of great mental power, no one can doubt who has watched his career. That his followers are deceived, we all believe; but, should the inherent corruptions of Mormonism fail to develop themselves sufficiently to convince its followers of their error, where will the thing end? A great military despotism is growing up in the fertile West, increasing faster in proportion, than the surrounding population, spreading its influence around, and marshalling multitudes under its banners, causing serious alarm to every patriot.

What is the reason that men are so blind that they cannot or will not see the hand of the Lord in His work of the last days!

Tuesday, 5. — Went to the office at nine, a. m., with Mr. Hamilton, of Carthage, who had obtained a deed from

---

[*] This article is much of the complexion of one published many years later — 1882 — by Josiah Quincy of Boston, who visited the Prophet about eight or nine months later, and published an account of his visit, and his impression of the Prophet in his "Figures of the Past," under the title "Joseph Smith at Nauvoo."

the sheriff of the county for lot 2, block 103, in the city of Nauvoo, for taxes, although I had previously paid them; which is another specimen of the oppression, injustice, and rascality of Mr. Collector Bagby, who by such foul means robs me and other Saints, and abuses all who come unfortunately in his power.

I requested my clerk to make out a bill of fare for the "Mansion."

The ship *Metoka* sailed from Liverpool with a company of Saints on board.

Wednesday, 6. — I went to the recorder's about half past six, a. m., and found him in bed.

Held mayor's court in the case, "City *versus* Joseph Owen."

*Anti-Mormon Meeting at Carthage, Seat of Hancock, County Illinois.**

Meeting convened pursuant to adjournment. The former chairman† not being present.

EdsonWhitney, Esq., was called to the chair, and the meeting being organized, the following preamble and resolutions were submitted by the committee, and unanimously adopted: —

PREAMBLE AND RESOLUTIONS.

This meeting having convened for the purpose of taking under advisement a subject of vital importance not only to this county, but to all the surrounding counties, regret that we are necessarily and irresistibly forced to the conclusion that a certain class of people have obtruded themselves upon us, calling themselves Mormons, or Latter-day Saints, and under the sacred garb of Christianity, assumed, as we honestly believe, that they may the more easily, under such a cloak, perpetrate the most lawless and diabolical deeds that have ever, in any age of the world, disgraced the human species.

In evidence of the above charge, we find them yielding implicit obedience to the ostensible head and founder of this sect, who is a pretended prophet of the Lord, and under this Heaven-daring assump-

---

* This was an adjourned meeting from one of the same character which had met at the same place on the 19th of August previous, which after hearing Anti-Mormon addresses and appointing committees to draft resolutions against the Mormons, adjourned to meet again on the above date, 6th of September. (See HISTORY OF THE CHURCH, Vol. IV pp. 537—8).

† The former chairman was Major Reuben Groves. (See minutes of the 19th of August, above note.)

tion claiming to set aside, by his vile and blasphemous lies, all those moral and religious institutions which have been established by the Bible, and which have in all ages been cherished by men as the only means of maintaining those social blessings which are so indispensably necessary for our happiness.

We believe that such an individual, regardless as he must be of his obligations to God, and at the same time entertaining the most absolute contempt for the laws of man, cannot fail to become a most dangerous character, especially when he shall have been able to place himself at the head of a numerous horde, either equally reckless and unprincipled as himself, or else made his pliant tools by the most absurd credulity that has astonished the world since its foundation.

In the opinion of this meeting, a crisis has arrived, when many of the evils to be expected from a state of things so threatening have transpired. We feel convinced that circumstances have even now occurred which prove to us most conclusively that Joseph Smith, the false Prophet before alluded to, has evinced, in many instances, a most shameless disregard for all the forms and restraints of law, by boldly and presumptuously calling in question the acts of certain officers, who had fearlessly discharged the duties absolutely imposed upon them by the laws, particulary when they have come in contact with his own sordid and selfish interests.

He has been heard to threaten—nay, he *has* committed violence upon the person of an officer, because that officer dared honestly to do his duties according to law.

He has caused his city council to pass laws contrary to the laws of the state, and subversive of the rights of citizens of this state.

Citizens have been arrested, tried and punished for breaches of those mock laws, from time to time, in such manner, that they have been compelled to the humiliating necessity of seeking an asylum elsewhere, in order to escape the tyranny and oppression of this modern Caligula.

He has caused the writ of *habeas corpus* to be issued by the municipal court of the city of Nauvoo, in a case not provided for in the charter of this city, and indeed contrary to the letter of that instrument; and, himself a prisoner, arrested under grave charges made by a neighboring state, brought before said court, tried, and acquitted; thereby securing his own rescue from the custody of the law.

Citizens from the adjoining counties have been denied the right to regain property stolen and taken to Nauvoo, even after they have discovered both the thief and the property; and themselves, under the most frivolus pretenses, arrested, fined, and other property rifled from them, to satisfy the mock judgments and costs of his cormorant officers.

Persons upon whom stolen property has been found in the city of Nauvoo, have been brought before this religio-political chief; and he, in the capacity of mayor of the city, has refused to convict, where the cases have been most clear and palpable.

We have had men of the most vicious and abominable habits imposed upon us to fill our most important county offices, by his dictum, in order, as we verily believe, that he may the more certainly control our destinies, and render himself, through the instrumentality of these base creatures of his ill-directed power, as absolutely a despot over the citizens of this county as he now is over the serfs of his own servile clan.

And, to crown all, he claims to merge all religion, all law, and both moral and political justice, in the knavish pretension that he receives fresh from heaven divine instructions in all matters pertaining to these things; thereby making his own depraved will the rule by which he would have all men governed.

He has caused large bodies of his ragamuffin soldiery to arm themselves, and turn out in pursuit of officers legally authorized to arrest himself; he being charged with high crimes and misdemeanors committed in the state of Missouri, and those officers arrested by the vilest hypocrisy, and placed in duress, that he might enable himself to march triumphantly into Nauvoo, and bid defiance to the laws of the land.

In view of the above grievances, this meeting feel that it is their bounden duty to resist, by every laudable means, all such unwarrantable attacks upon their liberties. Therefore—

Resolved, 1st. That inasmuch as we honestly believe that the combination of people calling themselves Mormons, or Latter-day Saints, have given strong indications, in their recent movements, that they are unwilling to submit to the ordinary restraints of law, we are therefore forced to the conclusion that the time is not far distant when the citizens of this country will be compelled to assert their rights in some way.

Resolved, 2nd. That while we would deprecate anything like lawless violence, without justifiable cause, yet we pledge ourselves in the most solemn manner to resist all the wrongs which may be hereafter attempted to be imposed on this community by the Mormons, to the utmost of our ability,—peaceably, if we can, but forcibly, if we must.

Resolved, 3rd. That in the event of our being forced into a collision with that people, we pledge ourselves that we will stand by and support each other in every emergency up to the death.

Resolved, 4th. That we believe that it is also the interest of our friends in the neighboring counties and also neighboring states to begin to take a firm and decided stand against the high pretensions and base designs of this latter-day would-be Mahomet.

Resolved, 5th. That provided we must necessarily, for the well-being of this community, the protection of our dearest rights, and the preservation of our excellent institutions, adopt measures to humble the pride and arrogance of that audacius despot; we therefore call upon all good and honest men, without distinction of party or place, to come to the rescue.

Resolved, 6th. That we pledge ourselves in the most determined manner that if the authorities of the State of Missouri shall make another demand for the body of Joseph Smith, and our Governor shall issue another warrant to stand ready at all times to serve the officer into whose hands such warrant may come, as a *posse*, in order that it may not be said of us, in future, that the most outrageous culprits have been suffered "to go unwhipped of justice."

Resolved, 7th. That a corresponding committee be appointed to communicate with the different parts of this county, and also with other counties; and we would also recommend to all surrounding counties to appoint like committees for the purpose of a mutual interchange of views in regard to the subjects embraced in these proceedings.

Resolved, 8th. That as it has been too common for several years past for politicians of both political parties, not only of this county, but likewise of the state, to go to Nauvoo and truckle to the heads of the Mormon clan for their influence, we pledge ourselves that we will not support any man of either party in future who shall thus debase himself.

Resolved, 9th. That if the Mormons carry out the threats they have made in regards to the lives of several of our citizens, we will, if failing to obtain speedy redress from the laws of the land, take summary and signal vengeance upon them as a people.

Resolved, 10th. That when the Government ceases to afford protection, the citizens of course fall back upon their original inherent right of self-defense.

In pursuance of the 7th resolution, the following gentlemen were appointed to act as a central corresponding committee at Carthage— namely, Captain Robert F. Smith, Major T. J. Bartlet, Harmon T. Wilson, Frank A. Worrel, and Walter Bagby.

On motion of Henry Stevens, it was ordered that committees, consisting of two persons, be appointed in each election precinct of this county, for the purpose of communicating with the central committee at Carthage; and that those two may add to their number at discretion.

On motion of Daniel Beaver, it was made the duty of the person whose name stands first on the list of each committee to act as chairman; and that all communications from the other committees, or from any other source, shall be added.

The following gentlemen were then appointed by the chair as committees in the several precincts, to wit: —

Green Plains—Edson Whitney and Levi Williams.

Bear Creek—William White and Andrew Moore.

Chili—Stephen Owen and Arthur Morgan.

Augusta—William D. Abernethy and Alexander Oliver.

Saint Mary's—William Darnell and Daniel Beaver.

Fountain Green—Thomas Geddis and S. H. Tyler.

La Harpe—Jesse Gilmer and Charles Comstock.

Camp Creek—James Graham and Thomas Harris.

Appanooce—John McCanley and John R. Atherton.

Montebello—Samuel Steel and Benjamin B. Gates.

Warsaw—Thomas C. Sharp and Mark Aldrich.

On motion of Levi Williams, Colonel Root, of McDonough county, was added to the central corresponding committee of Carthage.

On motion of Henry Newton, Esq.,

Resolved, That the central committee of correspondence act as a general committee of supervision; and, in case of a contingency occurring requiring aid, that they immediately call on the precinct committees and upon all others favorable to our cause to furnish such aid as the exigency of the case may require.

On the motion of Charles C. Stevens, the following supplementary resolutions were unanimously adopted: —

Resolved, That the president of this meeting be requested to communicate with the Governor of Missouri, and respectfully request him to make another demand upon the authorities of this state for the body of Joseph Smith, commonly called the Mormon Prophet; and in the event of a requisition and an order for his arrest and delivery to the proper officers of the state of Missouri, we offer our services to enforce said order, and pledge ourselves to sustain the supremacy of the laws at all hazards and under all circumstances.

Resolved, That a copy of the proceedings of this meeting be forwarded to the publisher of the *Warsaw Message, Quincy Whig*, and *Quincy Herald*, for publication, with a request to them to add a note, soliciting all editors friendly to our cause in this state, Missouri, and Iowa Territory, to copy.

It was then moved and seconded, That this meeting adjourn, subject to the call of the central corresponding committee.

EDSON WHITNEY, Chairman.

W. D. ABERNETHY, Secretary.

Editors throughout Illinois, Missouri, Iowa Territory, friendly to the Anti-Mormon cause, are requested to publish the proceedings, in to-day's paper, of a meeting held at Carthage on the 6th instant.

Thursday, 7.— I took home the letter written to Harrisburg* for the Church History, a small fragment of which only has been preserved, and is as follows:—

Historical Sketch of the Church of Jesus Christ of Latter-day Saints.

Messrs. Editors,—The Church of Jesus Christ of Latter-day Saints was founded upon direct revelation, as the true Church of God has ever been, according to the Scriptures (Amos iii: 7, and Acts i: 2); and through the will and blessings of God, I have been an instrument in His hands, thus far, to move forward the cause of Zion: therefore, in order to fulfill the solicitations of your letter of July last, I shall commence with my life.

[Then follows a brief historical sketch of the Church from the birth of the Prophet to the settlement of the Saints at Nauvoo, much in the strain of the *"Wentworth Letter"* already published in this HISTORY, (Vol. IV, Ch. xxxi); and for the reason that all the historical data in this I. Daniel Rupp sketch is contained in the *Wentworth Letter*, it is thought unnecessary to reproduce it here, excepting the closing paragraphs which deal with conditions and prospects at Nauvoo, on the date at which we have arrived in our HISTORY, viz. September, 1843.—Editor.]

Nauvoo, upon every point connected with increase and prosperity has exceeded the most sanguine expectations of thousands. It now contains near 3,500 houses, and more than 15,000 inhabitants. The charter contains, among its important powers, privileges or immunities, a grant for "The University of Nauvoo," with the same liberal powers of the city, where all the arts and sciences will grow with the growth and strengthen the strength of this beloved city of the Saints of the last days.

Another very commendatory provision of the charter is that that portion of the citizens subject to military duty are organized into a body of independent military men, styled the "Nauvoo Legion," whose highest officer holds the rank and is commissioned lieutenant-general. This Legion, like other independent bodies of troops in this Republican Government, is at the disposal of the Governor of the state, and President of the United States. There is also an act of incorporation for an Agricultural and Manufacturing Association, as well as the Nauvoo House Association.

Since the organization of this Church, its progress has been rapid, and its gain in numbers regular. Besides these United States, where

* This was a Brief Historical Account of the Rise and Progress of the Church prepared for one I. Daniel Rupp, of Harrisburg, Penn. It was published in 1844, in a "History of Religious Denominations," p. 409.

nearly every place of notoriety has heard the glad tidings of the Gospel of the Son of God, England, Ireland and Scotland have shared largely in the fullness of the everlasting Gospel, and thousands have already gathered with their kindred Saints to this the corner stone of Zion. Missionaries of this Church have gone to the East Indies, to Australia, Germany, Constantinople, Egypt, Palestine, the islands of the Pacific, and are now preparing to open the door in the extensive dominions of Russia.

There is no correct data by which the exact number of members composing this now extensive and still extending Church of Jesus Christ of Latter-day Saints can be known. Should it be supposed at 150,000,* it might still be short of the truth.

Believing the Bible to say what it means and mean what it says, and guided by revelation, according to the ancient order of the fathers, to whom came what little light we enjoy, and circumscribed only by the eternal limits of truth, this Church must continue the even tenor of its way.

Called at the office, and administered the laying on of hands to Sister Partington and her two children.

Dreadful conflagration at Stuhlweissenburg, in Hungary. About six hundred houses destroyed.

Friday, 8.—My wife being sick, I was at home all day.

Stephen Markham started for Dixon with the court papers in relation to the writ of habeas corpus, and as a witness.

I directed William Clayton to go to Augusta, Iowa, to get a deed signed by Mr. Moffit for the steamer *Maid of Iowa.*

Muster day of the first cohort.

The Twelve held a meeting in Boylston Hall, Boston. Present—Elders Heber C. Kimball, Orson Pratt, George A. Smith, Wilford Woodruff, John E. Page.

Saturday, 9.— My wife a little more comfortable. William Clayton went to Augusta, got the deed signed by Mr. Moffit and his wife, and returned in the evening.

General training of the Nauvoo Legion.

The quorum of the Twelve met the church in Boston, at Boylston Hall, in conference. Sixteen branches were represented, containing 878 members. A great deal of valuable instruction was given by the Twelve, and the hall, a very large one, was crowded. A number were baptized during conference, which lasted three days. The minutes of conference I here insert:—

Important Conference of the Twelve, Held at Boylston Hall, Boston, September 9, 1843.

Present of the Quorum of the Twelve—Elders Brigham Young, Heber C. Kimball, Parley P. Pratt, Orson Pratt, Orson Hyde, John E. Page. Wilford Woodruff, George A. Smith.

[*Reported by Wilford Woodruff.*]

Conference opened with prayer by Elder George A. Smith.

After the various branches in the New England States were represented, Elder P. P. Pratt made a few remarks, of which the following is a synopsis:

Some Elders tell us that they have taught the gathering according to the Scriptures. But it is not sufficient to teach the principle from the Scriptures alone; for if there was no other guide, the people would be left in doubt as to whether they should gather to Jerusalem, Africa, America, or elsewhere. It is right to teach the gathering according to the Scriptures, although some predictions of the Prophets are obscure; but we are not left to them alone. We know and all the Saints ought to know that God has appointed a place and time of gathering and has raised up a Prophet to bring it about, of which we are witnesses. Our message is that we are witnesses of the fulfillment of the predictions of the Prophets.

We have not to lay down a long, round-about [system] of arguments and calculations. The specific time and place are pointed out, the stakes are driven, the foundations of the city and temple are laid, and a people already gathered. We therefore know where to go; and to reject the revelations of God, which have pointed out these things to us, only brings condemnation. If this is not the case, then our faith is vain, and our works and hopes are vain also.

We worship a God who can inspire His servants to tell the people what to do. We have already got the opinions of men enough concerning the coming of Jesus Christ; but we need the voice of a Prophet in such a case and we have it. I am willing to risk my all upon it: and if the Elders understand the principle of gathering, and teach it correctly, the people will have the correct spirit of the gathering.

It is time we come out and declared boldly and definitely what God had for the people. We want more than opinions—we want your works. He has said he would send a Prophet to prepare the way. And

let me ask these profound sectarians, why He has not done it? If the
angels found a God in heaven able to give instructions, shield them
from sword and famine, &c., why have we not found Him? Let the
teachers bear the message they are entrusted with; and if the people
wish then for Scripture, tell them that their message is in fulfillment of
prophecy; but let them have the whole message.

Elder E. P. Maginn said he for one had taught the gathering according to the Scriptures; but he considered all modern revelations
Scripture as well as those given anciently.

Elder Brigham Young addressed the meeting on the subject of our
faith. We hear the Elders represent the feeling of the brethren concerning the gathering. This is right. The Spirit of the Lord Jesus
Christ is a gathering spirit. Its tendency is to gather the virtuous and
good, the honest and meek of the earth, and, in fine, the Saints of God.
The time has come when the Lord is determined to fulfill his purposes.
The people are apt to say that if they had lived in the days of Jesus
Christ they would have received His work. But judge ye if the people
are better now than then. They are not. When the full, set time was
come, the Lord came in the flesh to do His work, whether the people
were prepared or not; and He would not have come at all, if He had
waited till the people were prepared to receive Him. It was decreed
from all eternity that He should come, and He came. The people were
not prepared then, nor are they any more prepared now. And now the
full set time has come for the Lord God Almighty to set His hand to
redeem Israel. We are not bound to make the people believe, but we
are bound to preach the Gospel; and having done this, our garments
are clear.

The Lord does not require every soul to leave his home as soon as
He believes. Some may be wanted to go to the isles of the sea, and
some to go north,and some south. But He *does* require them to hearken
to counsel, and follow that course which He points out, whether to
gather or stay to do some other work.

The Spirit of the Lord and His work are on the alert, and those who
keep up with the work must be on the alert also. The Spirit of the
Lord will leave them who sit down and refuse to obey. When the
Lord says, "Gather yourselves together," why do you ask Him what
for? Had you not rather enjoy the society of Saints than sinners whom
you cannot love? Is it not the principle of the Saints to mingle together and promote the great cause in which they are engaged?

Perhaps some of you are ready to ask, "Cannot the Lord save us as
well where we are as to gather together?" Yes, if the Lord says so.
But if He commands us to come out and gather together, He will not
save us by staying at home. Have you not received the Gospel? Yes.

Then do you believe what we say? Have you not received the Holy Ghost, by receiving the Gospel which we have brought unto you? Yes. thousands have; and it stands as a testimony that God has got a Prophet on the earth. You might have been baptized seventy times seven in any way except the way God had ordained and pointed out, and you would not have received the Holy Ghost. This also is a testimony to you.

Are you engaged with us in this great work? "Yes, certainly," you answer, "heart and hand." "Can we do any good?" Yes, you can. The sectarian world send the Bible to the nations of the earth. The poor among them put sixpence, fifty cents or a dollar into the box to carry out that object; and can the Latter-day Saints do nothing? Let them do what God requires. He has required that we should build a house unto His name, that the ordinances and blessings of His kingdom may be revealed, and that the Elders may be endowed, go forth and gather together the blood of Ephraim—the people of God, from the ends of the earth.

Can you get an endowment in Boston or anywhere, except where God appoints? No, only in that place which God has pointed out. Now, query—Could Moses have obtained the law if he had stayed in the midst of the children of Israel, instead of going up on to the mountain? The Lord said, "Go and do so and so; stand before Pharaoh; pull off they shoes, for the place is holy." Moses obeyed, and obtained blessings which he would not have received if he had been disobedient.

Has the Lord spoken in these last days, and required us to build Him a house? Then why query about it? If He has spoken, it is enough. I do not care whether the people gather or not, if they don't want to do so. I do not wish to save the people against their will. I want them to choose whether they will gather and be saved with the righteous, or remain with the wicked and be damned. I would like to have all people bow down to the Lord Jesus Christ; but it is one of the decrees of the Lord that all persons shall act upon their agency, which was the case even with the angels who fell from heaven.

Now, will you help us to build the Nauvoo House and Temple? If so, you will be blessed: if not, we will build it without you. And if you don't hearken, you will not have the Spirit of the Lord; for the Spirit of the Lord is on the move.

The Apostles tried to gather the people together in their day. Christ said He would gather the Jews oft as a hen gathereth her chickens under her wings, but they would not. Neither God nor angels care whether men hear or forbear: they will carry on their work; for the full, set time is come for God to set up His kingdom, and we go about it. We must build a house, and get an endowment, preach the gospel, warn the people, gather the Saints, build up Zion, finish our work, and be prepared for the coming of Christ.

Now, we want to send four missionaries to the Pacific Islands, and we want a little clothing, and beds, and money to pay their passage. Can you do something for them? This is not all. We want you to give all you have to spare towards building the Temple. We shall be able to build it, if we have to work with a sword in one hand. But perhaps you are afraid you will not have enough for yourself, when you get there; yet how easy it is for the Lord to take it away from you by fire or otherwise!

Elder Maginn had an ivory cane. I asked him for it, but he declined making me a present of it. Not long after, he had it stolen from him in a crowd, and it now does neither of us any good. Perhaps your purse may slip through your pocket, or you may lose your property; for the Lord can give and take away. Jacob, with his faith, obtained all the best cattle his father-in-law had.

If I had a wife and ten children, I would give all my money to build the Temple and Nauvoo House, and I would trust in God for their support. Yet I will be richer for it; for God would prosper me in business. Men are apt to serve God on Sunday, and neglect Him all the week. Who blesses you and all the people? God. But do the people acknowledge the hand of God in all these things? No; they turn away from Him, and do not acknowledge Him, or realize from whom their blessings flow. They know not who blesses them. It never comes into their hearts. So with the farmer. The blessings are constantly flowing to him, and he considers not whence they come.

Let me tell you a secret. When the Lord shakes the earth, and every valley shall be exalted, and every mountain and hill shall be made low, He will bring gold for brass, silver for iron, brass for wood, and iron for stones. Then you will have no use for gold, for money and gods as you now have. You will not care so much about it; but the Lord will think as much of it then as now.

But now we want some of the gods of the Gentiles—some of the gold and silver to build the Temple and Nauvoo House for the accommodation of the kings, princes and nobles of the earth, when they come to inquire after the wisdom of Zion, that they may have a place for their entertainment, and for the weary traveler to be refreshed. Let us have your gold to take to Nauvoo for this purpose.

Is there wisdom in Zion? We think so, and the world begins to think so. Let the world come forward and translate the plates that have of late come forth,* if they have wisdom to do it. The Lord

---

* Having reference to certain plates known as the "Kinderhook Plates," found at Kinderhook, Illinois, April, 1843. See this HISTORY, Vol. V., pp. 372-378.

intends to take away the gods of the Gentiles: He pulleth down and He buildeth up at His own pleasure.

Sacrifice your gods for the building up of Zion. Administer of your substance. Send our missionaries to the islands of the seas. Don't be afraid of a dollar, or a hundred dollars, or even a thousand dollars. I would not. I have made a sacrifice of all I possessed a good many times. I am richer the more I give; for the Lord has promised and does reward me a hundredfold; and if I sacrifice all for the cause of God, no good thing will be withheld from me. I have taken this course to get rich. I have given all I had, and God has given many blessings in consequence. If I am too bold in asking, be too bold in giving. I ask, expecting to receive. Put your shoulders to the wheel with all your might. Give your all, and become rich by receiving a hundredfold.

Adjourned until half-past two o'clock. when the meeting was opened by singing.

Prayer by Elder Parley P. Pratt. Singing.

Elder Parley P. Pratt said: I have a few remarks to make concerning the subject spoken of in the forenoon by Elder Brigham Young, who said we wanted all your gold, silver, and precious things. We not only want your all as pertaining to gold, silver, &c., but we want you, your wives and children, and all you have to be engaged in the work of the Lord.

I don't know that I can give you a better pattern of what we want than the case of Joseph in Egypt. Israelites will get all they can. They are very great to go ahead. The Egyptians believed in dreams; and by the peculiar gift of interpretation of dreams, Joseph entered into a great scheme of speculation. He used the gift of interpretation to become great in the eyes of the Egyptians. He obtained great political influence, came out with gold ornaments, and rode in the king's chariot in great splendor. He laid up corn in great abundance during the seven years of plenty; and when the famine came, he got all their gold, silver, cattle, land, property, and, finally their persons. * * *

God is the origin of power—the Sovereign. He made the people and the earth, and He has the right to reign. There will be good times and good government, when the world will acknowledge the God of heaven as the Lawgiver, and not till then; and if I could live under His government, I should be thankful, although I am a real Republican in principle, and would rather live under the voice of the people than the voice of one man. But it will be for the good and happiness of man when that government is established, which we pray for when we say, "Thy kingdom come, Thy will be done on earth as it is in heaven;" and until that time arrives we must pray for it.

This Joseph in Egypt—the speculator—what a great and good man he was! I love him, I admire his course, and I believe a little of his blood is in my veins. But had Joseph been like the religious world at the present day—had he said he had got religion and done with the world, he would not have rode the king's horse, worn his robe, or had to do with gold and silver; and he would have done no good, built no storehouses, and saved no corn, for fear of speculation.

But he acted differently. And there is an ancient prediction respecting our modern prophet, Joseph—namely, that a prophet and seer should be raised up, and those who seek to destroy him shall be confounded. This has proved true. Upwards of thirty law suits have been brought against the Lord's anointed, and his persecutors have as often been confounded. He has been raised and supported according to the prophecy, to do a work on the earth, and the Lord has been with him. Every weapon formed against him has been broken. He has overcome all the lawsuits which have been brought against him, and no accusation has been sustained against him; yet he will lay a plan to speculate as large as ancient Joseph did; he will have power to buy up all the rest of the world.

What Elder Young said is good. We want all he spoke of, and a great deal more, We do not want it for ourselves, but for you. We want you to use it; and we have a Prophet who tells how, when and where to use it. Take your means and unite your exertions in this work. We want you to take that course which will save you. Build up a city and temples, and enjoy them, and do as the Lord tells you, and hearken to counsel.

We have prophets to tell us what to do, and we should get as much wisdom as the world. If they want a railroad built, all they have to do is to open books. The people subscribe stock, a railroad is soon built, and an income is realized. The Saints ought to be as well united as the world, and do the things that God has required, that a great nation may be saved from all nations.

The old gentleman [Satan] that rules the nations has ruled long enough; and if I were an infidel, I would like to have the Lord raise up a Joseph, or a Daniel, or a Mordecai, or an Esther, to obtain political, temporal, and spiritual power, and cause a change for the good of the world. Thank heaven, he has begun to raise them up. He has raised up another Joseph to do the great work of God, and it will continue on until the saying goes forth that the Lord has built up Zion.

The kingdom of God must be established, and it will be. I read that gold, silver, power, thrones, and dominions will be connected with the great work of God in the last days. Then let us wake up to see what God says shall come to pass, and let us enlarge our hearts and prepare for the great and glorious work.

Do the Saints here in Boston know that they are identified with the laying of the foundation, and establishing of a great and mighty kingdom, which is to include all the great and glorious work to be fulfilled in the last dispensation and fullness of times? And I prophesy, in the name of the Lord, that whether the Saints of Boston or any other place, stand for it or rise against it, numberless millions will celebrate that day when the foundation of this work was laid.

Elder George A. Smith said: I am pleased with the many remarks which have been made this day. You can easily see a similarity between the two Josephs, and the revelations that are given for the salvation of the present generation. Joseph in Egypt, a savior of his father's house and the Egyptians: Joseph [Smith] at this day holds the keys of salvation not only to the Gentiles, but also to the house of Israel.

I do not know but some may have reflections different from my own. I will, however, show how the Lord deals with mankind. Some may say, "Who can believe that God who dwells in heaven will condescend to speak to the people about building Him a house in this day of religion and science?

This may be considered simple in the eyes of many; but the day was when the salvation or damnation of the whole world hung upon as small a circumstance. "Noah, by faith, being warned of God of things not seen as yet, moved with fear, prepared an ark to the saving of his house, by which he condemned the world, and became heir of the righteous which is by faith."

Had the editors of this day lived then, I think they would have said and written more against it than they have against Joseph Smith and the revelations he has received and published.

We find God was in the habit of telling men to do many simple things, even to the giving of a law concerning the protection of birds' nests. You talk about God condescending to speak of small things in the last days, but it is only as it was in the days of Moses; for we read in the Bible how God commanded the children of Israel, when they found a bird's nest, (Deut. xxii: 7) not to take the dam with the young: "But thou shalt in any wise let the dam go, and take the young to thee." Why? "That it may be well with thee, and that thou mayst prolong thy days."

We see from this, that however small and simple the commandments of God appear to be, they are great in their results. Connecting this with the law of God to Israel concerning the eating of locusts, beetles and grasshoppers (Leviticus xi: 22). "Even these of them ye may eat; the locust after his kind, and the bald locust after his kind, and the beetle after his kind, and the grasshopper after his kind."

Is this as small business for the Lord to talk about as it is for Him to command the Saints to build a tavern or boarding house for visitors who constantly go to Nauvoo, which, when done, will do much good for the spreading of the work to all nations. What good could arise from a law of God permitting the eating of beetles and grasshoppers, I cannot say.

All the prophecies have aimed at the gathering of the people, and saving them in the last days. But it is better never to have known the Master's will than to know it and not perform it; and my advice is, If you cannot take hold of the work and go through the whole course, stop and go no further. If you have not courage to go on at the expense of all things, it is better to turn back.

We do not want to deceive you. Our traditions have taught us to be very religious, to wear long faces, never to tell an amusing story, nor to laugh, &c. This was the case with the long-faced Christians in Missouri, and they were the first to strike a dagger to our hearts. It is better for a man to act out what he is than to be a hypocrite. "Pure religion and undefiled before God and the Father, is this," says James, "to visit the fatherless and widows in their affliction, and to keep himself unspotted from the world."

I do not like that religion which lies in a man's long face, or his coat or his hat. If I wear a strange hat, it is not because of my religion: for where the religion of a man is in the shape of a hat or coat, it is not very extensive anywhere else.

Some of the Elders want to appear very big, and to be called great preachers; but whenever I have seen them trying to preach something large and mysterious, to get a name, I have concluded they have yet much to learn. I have been eleven years a member of this Church, and was a believer two years before I entered it; and during that time I have seen many Elders who like to preach large and mysterious sermons.

As many are desirous of hearing mysteries, I will rehearse a short sermon of mysteries for their edification. Elder Kimball has had a long standing in the Church. He has preached much, done much good, brought many souls into the kingdom, had great influence, and is considered the most successful minister among us.

Elder Amasa Lyman and myself went into Pike county, Illinois, to preach where the Elders had preached all the mysteries about beasts, heads and horns. They wanted us to preach mysteries. We told them we were not qualified to preach mysteries; but if they would send for Elder Kimball he would preach them. So they sent about forty miles for Elder Kimball, and brought him down, they were so anxious to hear mysteries.

When he came, he had a large congregation assembled. He arose and remarked that he understood they had sent for him to come and preach the mysteries to them. "I am well qualified, and fully competent to do it, and am happy to have the privilege. I want the attention of all." When every mind was stretched and eager to learn these great mysteries he said, "The first mystery I shall present before you is this, "Look at Elder Amasa Lyman; he needs a pair of pantaloons and a new hat. But it appears you do not see it; consequently I want to open your eyes and reveal to you a great mystery; for an Elder in the Church has need of a hat and a pair of breeches as well as yourselves, and *especially* when the Saints *know* he is so much in need of them!" He preached a few more mysteries of the same nature, and the result of this sermon was that Elder Lyman got a pair of pants and a new hat, and Elder Kimball and myself each a barrel of flour for our families.

Elder Brigham Young arose and said: I will make an apology for my remarks in the former part of the day. Some may think I spoke very plainly; but the object I had in view was to teach you your duty, as I am aware the people are not made to feel it; and the apology I have to make is this: I will turn Thomsonian doctor, and give the composition without cream and sugar,—it matters not whether I get friends or foes. If this work does not live, I do not want to live; for it is my life, my joy, my all; and if it sinks, God knows I do not want to swim.

I wish you to understand this—that he that gathereth not with us scattereth, and they have not the Spirit of God. We live in anticipation of the day when mobs cannot harm us, and they who have tasted the bitter cup feel to realize this hope. Wake up, ye Elders of Israel who have sought to build yourselves up, and not the kingdom of God, and put on your sword. Wake up, ye that have daubed with untempered mortar! Hearken and hear me; for I say unto you, in the name of Jesus Christ, that if you do not help us to build the Temple and the Nauvoo House, you shall not inherit the land of Zion.

If you do not help to build up Zion and the cause of God, and help me and my brethren on our way when we want to go on the Lord's business, you shall not partake of the blessings which are laid up in store for the Saints. Many Elders seek to build themselves up, and not the work of the Lord. They will say "Put gold rings on my fingers; give me what I want;" and they care nothing about the Temple. This they should not do. I will not allow myself to do so; and when any one does this, no matter who he may be, even though he was one

of the Twelve, he will not prosper. Those of the Twelve and others of
the Elders who have apostatized, I have known their hearts and their
breathings. I have known their movements although they thought I did
not know much. But I knew all about them; and when I see men
preaching to build themselves up, and not Zion, I know what it will
end in. But you may say you are young. I don't care if you are.
Are you old enough to know what you are about? If so, preach and
labor for the building up of the city of Zion; concentrate your means
and influence there, and not scatter abroad. Instead of which, some of
the Elders appear to be dumb and lazy, and care for nothing but
themselves.

Now, ye Elders, will you be faithful? If not, you will not be
chosen, for the day of choosing is at the door. Why be afraid of a
sacrifice? I have given my all many times, and am willing to do it
again. I would be glad to hear the Lord say through His servant
Joseph, "Let my servant Brigham give again all that he has," I would
obey it in a moment, if it took the last coat off my back.

A hymn was sung.

Elder Kimball arose and said: I get up of necessity to say a few
words. I am unwell, but I feel the importance of this work. I have
been a member of this Church twelve years. I came out of the Baptist church and joined this with all my heart, as I was seeking after
truth. I have passed through everything but death; in fact I have been
brought into situations even worse than death. It has been my lot and
privilege to sacrifice all I possessed from time to time; and we have
come here to call for help to build the Temple and Nauvoo House. I
have spent thirty dollars to get here, and have collected fifteen and
that with much difficulty.

We were commanded of the Lord to come: but it seems as though
but few felt interested in it. Here I see four brethren going as missionaries to the Sandwich Islands, and destitute of means to help themselves. I could weep for them. I feel interested in this great work·
We are seeking to bring about a work that could never before be performed.

When the time is brought about that we are to receive our inheritances, the more faithful we are, the larger will be our reward. We
have come out to reap, but do we have time to reap new grain? No;
for it takes all our time to try to save that which is already reaped.

We have reapers in the field, and we are trying to save the wheat·
We want to get it on the barn floor, so that we may thrash it. We
have come after it to warn you. You think Elder Young put the flail
on rather heavy; but it is nothing to be compared with the thrashing
you will get in Zion, and those who have the hardest heads will, of

course, have to be thrashed the hardest. But don't be troubled about the chaff when it comes to the barn, for God will prepare a great winnowing mill which will blow all the chaff away, and the wheat will be found before the mill: then it has to go through the smut machine, then ground, then put through the bolting machine, and many will bolt in going through. I speak in parables. I compare the Saints to a good cow. When you milk her clean, she will always have an abundance of milk to give; but if you only milk her a little, and don't strip her, she will soon dry up. So with the Saints: if they do but little in building up Zion, they soon have but little to do with. This was the case in Cincinnati.

The night before arriving at Cincinnati, I had a dream while on the steamboat. I dreamt that I had a wagon with a rack on it, and an individual with me. We were going to a field of wheat of mine that had been cut, bound and shocked up, in order to haul into the barn. When we came to the field, I jumped off the wagon, and got over the fence to examine it, pulled off the cap sheaf, and behold it was oats. Pulling the bundles apart, I found there were clusters of rats. On further examination I found clusters of mice, and the oats were all eaten up.

In my dream I was going to haul in wheat, but to my astonishment it was oats, and they were all eaten up by the rats and mice.

I thought these rats and mice were the Elders and official members who had been in and lain on the Church at Cincinnati—lived on the wheat—eaten it up instead of building up new branches; so that when the Twelve came along, they could not get anything for the Temple or Nauvoo House, or hardly a place to stay. The rats had eaten up the wheat, so we had to go to the world for a home to stay while we were there.

We do not profess to be polished stones like Elders Almon W. Babbitt, George J. Adams, James Blakeslee, and Eli P. Maginn, &c., &c.; but we are rough stones out of the mountain; and when we roll through the forest, and knock the bark from the trees, it does not hurt us, even if we should get a corner knocked off occasionally; for the more we roll about, and knock the corners off, the better we are; but if we were polished and smooth when we get the corners knocked off, it would deface us.

Joseph Smith never professed to be a dressed, smooth, polished stone, but to have come rough out of the mountain; and he has been rolling among the rocks and trees, yet it has not hurt him at all: but he will be as smooth and polished in the end as any other stone, while many who were so very polished and smooth in the beginning get badly defaced and spoiled while they are rolling about.

Elder Parley P. Pratt said—Some are going to Zion, and the rest want to know what they shall do. The Lord, through Jeremiah (iii, 14,15) says, "I will take you one of a city, and two of a family, and I will bring you to Zion: and I will give you pastors according to mine heart, which shall feed you with knowledge and understanding." Inasmuch as you hearken to counsel, you will know what the will of the Lord is concerning you in all things. Meet often together to worship God and to speak to each other of the things of God. Gather as soon as you can. Come up to the mountain of the Lord's house, and there learn of these things, that the Scriptures may be fulfilled.

Elder Orson Pratt said—I do not know that I can say anything to impress the subjects which have been spoken upon more fully upon your minds than has been done. There are some things, however, I wish to mention. We have learned from what we have heard this day that great blessings will be given to the faithful when the Temple is finished. I will speak of some of the consequences that will follow, if we do not obey.

When the Temple is reared, God will manifest Himself in a peculiar manner. If we are obedient, He has told us He will make manifest to us things we are ignorant of. He has said He will reveal things which pertain to this dispensation that have been hidden and kept secret from the foundation of the world.

No former age or generation of the world have had the same things revealed: all other dispensations will be swallowed up in this. He declares, in His revelations, the consequences of not building the house unto His name within such a time. The Lord says, If you build the house in that time, you shall be blessed; but if not, you shall be rejected as a church with your dead, saith the Lord. So, if that house is not built, then in vain are all our cares; our faith and works, our meetings and hopes are vain also; our performances and acts will be void.

The servants of God who are faithful and do their duty will get the blessing; and we are determined to do our duty, and lay these principles before the Saints, so that they may have the privilege of contributing. We will turn this responsibility upon the heads of the Saints; then our garments will be clear, and the Lord is able and will be willing to endow all the faithful in some other place.

This Church, in its infancy, was directed to do a certain work, and the consequences pointed out. The Lord gave a revelation several years since to the Church to appoint our wise men, and send up our moneys by them to buy land: if not, we should not have an inheritance, but our enemies should be upon us. We went through and told the Saints these things; but did the churches do as God commanded? No, they did not. But the revelation was fulfilled, and the enemies of the Saints came upon them, and drove them from their houses and homes, and finally from the State of Missouri. This was in consequence of their disobeying the commandments of God through His servant Joseph.

Many suppose they must get direct revelation from God for themselves. Not so. He has a prophet, and he says the Church shall give heed to the words of the Prophet, as he is to hold the keys of the kingdom of God in this life and in the world to come. Then it is of much consequence that you give heed to his word.

Says one, Suppose we are not satisfied that this is the work of God? You can ask God if the work is true, and He will give you a testimony. You can put every confidence in the Book of Mormon and in Joseph, the Prophet; and if you are not satisfied, go to God. I doubt in my own mind if men can stand what they will have to pass through, unless they do get a witnes for themselves; and I pray you to give heed to the words which the Twelve have taught you, and ask God to help you.

The conference was adjourned until ten o'clock tomorrow morning.

Sunday, 10th. Conference met according to adjournment.

Meeting was opened by singing, and prayer by Elder Maginn; after which Elder Wilford Woodruff addressed the assembly from Amos iii: 7— "Surely the Lord God will do nothing, but he revealeth his secret unto his servants the prophets?" According to the testimony of the Scriptures in all ages of the world, whenever God was about to bring a judgment upon the world or accomplish any great work, the first thing he did was to raise up a Prophet, and reveal unto him the secret, and send him to warn the people, so that they may be left without excuse. This was the case in the days of Noah and Lot. God was about to bring judgments upon the people, and he raised up those Prophets who warned the people of it: yet they gave no heed to them, but rejected their testimony; and the judgments came upon the people, so that they were destroyed, while the Prophets were saved by pursuing the course marked out by the Lord.

Jesus Christ testified to the Jews of the things that awaited them as a nation, the fall of Jerusalem, and their dispersion among the Gentile world; but they did not believe it. Yet the secret of all these things was revealed to the Prophets and Apostles. They believed it, and looked for its fulfillment; and it came to pass as it was predicted, though contrary to the expectation of the Jewish nation.

In like manner do we look for the certain fulfillment of those tremendous events upon the heads of the Gentile world which have been spoken of and pointed out by all the holy Prophets and Apostles since the world began, they having spoken as they were moved upon by the power of God and the gift of the Holy Ghost, events which more deeply concern the Gentile world than the overthrow of Jerusalem and the dispersion of the Jews did the Jewish nation; for while they stumbled at the stone they were broken; but when it falls upon the heads of the Gentile world, it will grind them to powder.

The full set time is come for the Lord to set His hand to accomplish these mighty events; and as He has done in other ages, so has He done now—He has raised up a Prophet, and is revealing unto him His secrets. Through that Prophet He has brought to light the fullness of the everlasting Gospel to the present generation, and is again once more for the last time establishing His Church upon the foundation of the ancient Apostles and Prophets, which is revelation, Jesus Christ being the chief corner stone.

In the Church is now found judges as at the first, and counselors as at the beginning; also Apostles, Prophets, Evangelists, Pastors, and Teachers, with gifts and graces, for the perfecting of the Saints, the work of the ministry, and the edifying of the body of Christ.

The Lord has raised up His servants, and sent them into the vineyard to prune it once more for the last time, to preach the Gospel of Jesus Christ, and to warn the nations, that they may be left without excuse in the day of their visitation; also to gather the honest in heart and the meek of the earth, that Zion may be built up, and the sayings of the Prophets fulfilled.

One of the secrets that God has revealed unto his Prophet in these days is the Book of Mormon; and it was a secret to the whole world until it was revealed unto Joseph Smith, whom God has raised up as a Prophet, Seer, and Revelator unto His people. This record contains an account of the ancient inhabitants of this continent and of the cities with which they overspread this land from sea to sea, the ruins of which still remain as standing monuments of the arts, science, power, and greatness of their founders. It also points out the establishing of this our own nation, with the conditions for its progress, and those predictions contained in the Book of Mormon—the stick of Joseph in the hand of Ephraim, will as truly be fulfilled as those contained in the Bible—the stick and record of Judah; and both these sticks or records contain prophecies of great import concerning the Gentile nations, and especially this land and nation, which are not yet fulfilled, but must shortly come to pass: yea, their fulfillment is nigh, even at the doors.

Though the secrets which God is revealing through His servant the Prophet in these last days may be unpopular and unbelieved in by the world, yet their unbelief will not make the truth of God of none effect, any more than it did in the days of Lot and Noah, or at the fall of Jerusalem.

When Jesus Christ said there should not be left one stone upon another in the temple that should not be thrown down, the Jewish nation did not believe it, neither would they receive such testimony; but they looked at outward circumstances, and were ready to say, "Who can prevail against us? What nation like unto our nation? We have held the giving of the law, the oracles, and the Urim and Thummim; the lawgiver has never departed from between our feet; we have held the power of government from generation to generation; and what nation hath power now to prevail against us?"

Through this order of reasoning they were blinded, and knew not the day of their visitation: they understood not the things that belonged to their peace; they rejected their Lord and King, contended against the word and testimony, and finally put Him to death on the cross, with many who followed Him. But this did not hinder the fulfillment of His predictions concerning that nation. The words of the Lord had gone forth out of His mouth, and could not return unto Him void. The things that belonged to their peace were hid from their eyes, and they were counted unworthy as a nation. The kingdom was to be rent out of their hands and given to another; the die was cast, and judgment must come.

Jerusalem was soon surrounded by the Roman army, led on by the inspired Titus; and a scene of calamity, judgment, and woe immediately overspread the inhabitants of that city, which was devoted to destruction,—such a calamity as never before rested upon the nation of Israel. Blood flowed through their streets; tens of thousands fell by the edge of the sword, and thousands by famine. Women were evil towards the children of their own bosoms in the straitness of the siege, the spectacle of which shocked the Roman soldiers as they entered the city. The Jews were crucified in such numbers by their enemies that they could find no more wood for crosses, or room for their bodies; and while despair was in every face, and every heart sinking while suffering under the chastening hand of God, their enemies rushed upon them in the city to strike the last fatal blow; and, as their last resort, they rushed for safety into the temple, which was soon on fire, and they sank in the midst of the flames with the cry of their sufferings ascending up on high, accompanied by the smoke of the crackling spires and towers.

The remaining population were sold as slaves, and driven like the dumb ass under his burthen, and scattered, as corn is sifted in a sieve, throughout the Gentile world. Jerusalem was razed from its foundations, the ruins of the temple thrown down, and the foundation thereof ploughed up, that not one stone was left upon another. Christ said that Jerusalem should be trodden down of the Gentiles until the times of the Gentiles be fulfilled, which has been the case to the very letter until the present generation.

Will not God in like manner as truly and faithfully bring to pass those great, important and tremendous events upon the heads of the Gentile world which have been proclaimed by the Prophets Isaiah, Jeremiah, Ezekiel, Daniel, and many other holy Prophets: also by Christ and the Apostles on the continent of Asia, as well as by Lehi, Nephi, Alma, Moroni, and others on this continent—all of whom have proclaimed these things as they were moved upon by the Spirit of inspiration, the power of God, and the gift of the Holy Ghost?

The Apostle says that "No prophecy of the Scripture is of any private interpretation, for the prophecy came not of old time by the will of man: but holy men of God spake as they were moved by the Holy Ghost."

Isaiah's soul seemed to be on fire, and his mind wrapt in the visions of the Almighty, while he declared, in the name of the Lord, that it should come to pass in the last days that God should set His hand again the second time to recover the remnant of His people, assemble the outcasts of Israel, gather together the dispersed of Judah, destroy the tongue of the Egyptian sea and make men go over dry-shod, gather them to Jerusalem on horses, mules, swift beasts, and in chariots, and rebuild Jerusalem upon her own heaps; while, at the same time, the destroyer of the Gentiles will be on his way; and while God was turning the captivity of Israel, he would put all their curses and afflictions upon the heads of the Gentiles, their enemies, who had not sought to recover, but to destroy them, and had trodden them under foot from generation to generation.

At the same time the standard should be lifted up, that the honest in heart, the meek of the earth among the Gentiles, should seek unto it; and that Zion should be redeemed and be built up a holy city, that the glory and power of God should rest upon her, and be seen upon her; that the watchman upon Mount Ephraim might cry—"Arise ye, and let us go up unto Zion, the city of the Lord our God;" that the Gentiles might come to her light, and kings to the brightness of her rising; that the Saints of God may have a place to flee to and stand in holy places while judgment works in the earth; that when the sword of God that is bathed in heaven falls upon Idumea, or the world,—when the Lord pleads with all flesh by sword and by fire, and the slain of the Lord are many, the Saints may escape these calamities by fleeing to the places of refuge, like Lot and Noah.

Isaiah, in his 24th chapter, gives something of an account of the calamities and judgments which shall come upon the heads of the Gentile nations, and this because they have transgressed the laws, changed the ordinance, and broken the everlasting covenant. The Apostle Paul says to his Roman brethren, that if the Gentiles do not continue in the goodnes of God, they, like the house of Israel, should be cut off. Though Babylon says, "I sit as a queen, and am no widow, and shall see no sorrow," the Revelator says, "Therefore shall her plagues come in one day, death and mourning and famine; and she shall be utterly burned with fire, for strong is the Lord God who judgeth her."

Jesus communicated the parable of the fig-tree, which in putting forth its leaves betokens the approach of summer; and so likewise, when we see the signs in the sun, moon, and stars, and in the heavens and the earth of which He spoke, we might know that His coming is near—that the generation in which those signs appeared should not pass away till all should be fulfilled.

These things are about to come to pass upon the heads of the present generation, notwithstanding they are not looking for it, neither do they believe it. Yet their unbelief will not make the truth of God of none effect. The signs are appearing in the heavens and on the earth, and all things indicate the fulfillment of the Prophets. The fig-tree is leafing, summer is nigh, and the Lord has sent his angels to lay the foundation of this great and important work.

Then why should not God reveal His secrets unto His servants the Prophets, that the Saints might be led in paths of safety, and escape those evils which are about to engulf a whole generation in ruin?

Monday, 11. Conference met at Boylston Hall at nine o'clock, a. m. Present of the quorum of the Twelve, Elders Brigham Young, Parley P. Pratt, Orson Pratt, John E. Page, Wilford Woodruff, George A. Smith, Heber C. Kimball, and Orson Hyde.

Opened with prayer by Elder Page.

Elder Brigham Young stated the object of the meeting. The first item of business is the spread of the Gospel of salvation. I want to state what devolves upon the Twelve. Nine years ago a revelation was given which was fulfilled in 1835; and when fulfilled, the Prophet lifted up his head and rejoiced before the Lord. Previously, the responsibility of spreading the Gospel rested on him; now it is on the Twelve. This is the relation we hold between the living and the dead— to direct how you may escape.

Last winter we were directed to send men to the nations of the earth. Elder Addison Pratt had been to the Sandwich Islands, and proffered his services. We have power to ordain them, and call upon the Church to assist in sending them. Here are four men willing to go, and we do not wish them to cease trying, unless it be to die trying. One of them is ill. If he stays, he will die. I would go, or die trying.

We call on the churches to fit out these men with necessaries. Elder Eli P. Maginn and Elder Philip B. Lewis we call on to fit them out. If

Elder Lewis does not, Maginn will do it himself. This takes the responsibility from us.

If the Saints will not help, the curse of God will rest upon them. If the Temple at Nauvoo is not built, we will receive our endowments, if we have to go into the wilderness and build an altar of stone. If a man gives his all, it is all God requires. Brother Kimball has received one dollar since he came to Boston, and seventeen dollars and a half before, towards building the Temple. A book is kept of all sums given. This book will also be opened. All is recorded. I have received twenty-three dollars, and I have spent about forty-five or fifty dollars. I am rich, and expect to be so throughout all eternity, with the help of God and my brethren. I can get home, if I can sell land. Some of the Twelve are more destitute; but they are the best set of boys you ever saw.

During the persecution in Missouri, when the mob came against Far West, Elder Kimball stood near me in one of the companies; and every time they formed, he rammed down another ball into his old musket, until he got five balls in. We are a good-feeling set of men, because of the Spirit which is in us. What produces it? The impulse of the heart. We should feel the same on the desert of Arabia, or on the islands of the sea; we feel happy wherever we are. When we ask for victuals, and get turned away, as we often have been, we feel just as well.

The Spirit which is in me prompts me to look forward to something better. We have a prospect of selling shares of the Nauvoo House, and of obtaining subscriptions for the Temple, and we feel better.

Here are twelwe men, and I defy all creation to bring a charge of dishonesty against them. We had to give security for the faithful performance of our duty as agents for the Nauvoo House and Temple. This has been heretofore unheard of in the Church. I glory in it. The financial affairs of the Church rest on our shoulders, and God is going to whip us into it. When men are in future called to do like Brigham, I will be one to bind them: this is a precedent. We are the only legally authorized agents of the Church to manage affairs, give counsel to emigrants how to dispose of goods, &c.

Some men come into this Church through designing purposes. Mr. Cowen, who lives about 30 miles above Nauvoo, wanted Brother Joseph to make a settlement at Shoquokon. Several of the brethren went there and preached, and some families moved up with the intention of settling. Mr. Cowen was all love—a charming fellow, and calculated to magnetize. He is now in the Eastern country, and going amongst the brethren. He gives one a kiss, and says he, "I am not a Mormon, but expect to be: Brother Joseph and myself are confidential friends. Can't you lend me five hundred dollars? I have got land, and I will give you a mortgage." At the same time, he knew quite well that his land was in a perfect swamp, and that the place was not fit for a settlement. Even the captains of steamers could with difficulty be persuaded upon to call there, either on account of goods or passengers. His name is John F. Cowen, and he stands five feet six inches high. There are others.

I would ask the Latter-day Saints, Do you know your benefactors? Do you know the source from whence you derive your knowledge? Take in the publications and periodicals of the Church. They give you intelligence of all matters pertaining to this dispensation with revelations for the guidance of the Church.

I know that men who go through the world with the truth have not much influence; but let them come with silk velvet lips and sophistry, and they will have an influence. It is your privilege to be discerners of spirits. If you don't know me or the Twelve, walk with us fifty years, and perhaps you will know us then; and if such a man as Cowen comes along, will you trust him or me? No power can hide the heart from the discerning eye. If we are ignorant, what knowledge have the rest of the people? I sit down with all my ignorance, and read people's hearts as I see their faces, and they can't help themselves.

No one has ever stepped aside but I have known it. I know the result of their actions, and they cannot help themselves. If you find out my heart, you are welcome to it. If any of the Twelve take a wrong path, or a course by themselves, I know the path, and know the end of it. They are soon in the ditch, crying for help. I sit down and let others run. I strike with a crooked stick to hit the whole.

Now, the Twelve must be helped home, and there must be something for the Temple and the Nauvoo House. We have got a plot of the city of Nauvoo for lithographing. If any wish to advance the money to lithograph, and have a few thousands struck off, they shall be paid till they are satisfied. There was not wealth enough in New York and the regions round about. [He here exhibited the map of Nauvoo.] He concluded with a few remarks relative to the circumstances of Elder Hyde, who had just returned from his mission to Jerusalem.

Elder Parley P. Pratt spoke as follows:—In the middle of last April I arrived at Nauvoo houseless and with a large family. Brother Joseph said to me, "Brother Parley, stay at home and build a house." I was behindhand in instructions and information, while others had been at home learning the great things of God. I have now come East principally on business, though I always have a mission, wherever I am. I speak for my brethren: they have an absolute claim; it belongs to them, and they want it. It is justly theirs. I ask for nothing for myself.

Elder Heber C. Kimball said, I suppose you all understand what

Elder Young has said, and I consider his counsel good. He is my superior and my head in the council of the Twelve. If I go astray, it will be through ignorance. We must be subject to the powers that be; and there are no powers but what are ordained of God; and if we reject their counsel, we shall be damned. Some of our finest-looking and smartest men have fallen.

I consider those trees in the forest which have the largest and highest tops are in the greatest danger: they are blown down; and there is no way of restoring them but to cut them off. Let the stump go back, and new sprouts come out. Those who have most responsibility are in most danger. We must be careful how we treat God's officers.

No man ever fell, unless it was through rejecting counsel. I as well as my brethren see this. My superior knows more than I, because he is nearer the fountain. To get knowledge, begin at the foot of the stream, and drink all up till you get to the fountain, and then you get all the knowledge.

It is necessary for the people here to obey counsel. God has sent me forth, through his servants, to take my part in this great work, and the work is true. I know there are but few in this Church who will be able to walk in this narrow path. We must keep the celestial law in the flesh. The more simple we teach, the better for us.

It is a wrong idea of Elders whipping sects. Try and win the people; salt both sheep and shepherd too; get them up so that they will lick the salt out of your hands. [An infidel here handed money to Brother Kimball, who prophesied that he would be a Saint and an Elder, and all his family should be Saints.] Give them good salt, gain the affections of the shepherd, and the whole flock will come. Now, we get sheep up to lick; and when the old shepherd of the sheep comes up to lick salt, the Elders will hit him over the head with a cane. Their religion is as dear to them as ours to us. Don't feed too much salt at once, but give a little at a time, or they are cloyed.

Elders of Israel, be wise! Give short discourses, as long ones cloy your hearers, who will say, "A good discourse, but I got tired."

Never infringe on the right of other people, and never tear down other people's houses until you have built a better. We are sent to preach repentance, and let people alone. How do you like to go into other Churches and hear them abuse us? Do as you would be done by. Persuade men, and not compel them, unless the time spoken of by the Savior comes, when the Lord shall say unto His servants "Go out into the highways and hedges, and compel them to come in, that my house may be filled." (Luke 14 ch., 23 v.) Let men be humble, kind and affectionate.

CHAPTER II.

MOVEMENTS OF APOSTLES IN THE EAST—THE NAUVOO MAN-
SION—ROCKWELL ACQUITTED—SPECIAL CONFERENCE AT
NAUVOO—DISCOURSE OF THE PROPHET ON THE DEMISE
OF JAMES ADAMS.

Sunday, September 10, 1843.—Cold, and considerable rain.
Kindled a fire in the office for the first time this   The Drought
fall. This is the first rain of any consequence   of 1843.
since the first of June. There have been occasional—say
three or four slight showers, but not enough to wet the
potatoe hills, and the vegetables in the gardens have generally stopped growing, on account of the drougth. Even
corn is seriously injured,—much of it by a worm in the
ear. Early potatoes are scarcely worth digging.

Monday, 11.—Early in the morning a petition was presented to me, as Lieut.-General, to devise means to get
the public arms of the State for the Legion; whereupon I
appointed William W. Phelps, Henry Miller, and Hosea
Stout a committee to wait on Governor Ford on the
subject.

Election for probate justice; weather cold; people cold.
Greenleaf received most of the votes in Nauvoo—say
seven hundred votes.

Six, p. m., I met with my Brother Hyrum, William
Law, Newel K. Whitney, and Willard Richards in my
private room, where we had a season of prayer for Brother
Law's little daughter, who was sick, and Emma, who was
somewhat better.

Tuesday, 12.—Rainy day.

Elder Woodruff left Boston for Portland by railroad and
Woodruff in a while passing through Chester woods, the en-
Train Wreck. gine was thrown off the tracks, and with the
baggage cars smashed to pieces. Several of the passenger cars mounted the ruins, but none of the passengers
were injured, except two very slightly. The engineer,
however, was killed instantaneously. Elder Woodruff,
with most of the passengers, remained all night in the
woods, and found it very cold.

Wednesday, 13.—I attended a lecture at the Grove, by
Mr. John Finch, a Socialist, from England, and said a
few words in reply.

The following article appears [this day] in the *Neighbor*, copied from *The New Haven*, Conn., *Herald:*—

NAUVOO AND JOSEPH SMITH.

A gentleman of this town, (New Haven, Conn.) of undoubted
veracity, who has lately spent several weeks at Nauvoo and among the
Mormons, informs us that the general impression abroad in regard to
that place and people is very erroneous. During his residence there
he became quite familiar with their manners, principles, and habits,
and says there is not a more industrious, moral, and well-ordered town
in the country. Society is as much diversified there as it is here, the
Mormons constituting about two-thirds of the population,while all religious sects are as freely tolerated as in any other part of the State. He was
at the late trial and acquittal of Joseph Smith,and says that the charges
against him were of the most frivolous and unsubstantial nature. He
[Joseph Smith] is an agreeable man in conversation,is respected by those
who know him, and is 'as much sinned against as sinning.' He only
claims the privilege of exercising and enjoying his own religion,—a
privilege which he and his followers cheerfully award to others. They
invite immigrants to come among them, and receive those who design
to enter into the Mormon community with great attention and kindness.
Houses are prepared for their reception, to which they are conducted
on their arrival by a committee appointed for that purpose, whose next
business is to attend to their immediate wants and see them comfortably
situated. Education is by no means neglected, proper schools and
teachers being provided, and temperance reigns throughout. It has
now about 15,000 to 18,000 inhabitants, and promises to become a place
of extensive business, four or five steamboats stopping there every day.

The gentleman remarked to us that he wished he could speak as well of his own native town as he could of Nauvoo. This is news to us, as no doubt it will be to many; but no one who knows him can doubt the integrity of our informant.

Thursday, 14.—I attended a second lecture on Socialism, by Mr. Finch; and after he got through, I made a few remarks, alluding to Sidney Rigdon and Alexander Campbell getting up a community at Kirtland, and of the big fish there eating up all the little fish. *I said I did not believe the doctrine.*

The Prophet on Socialism.

Mr. Finch replied in a few minutes, and said—"I am the voice of one crying in the wilderness. I am the spiritual Prophet—Mr. Smith the temporal."

Elder John Taylor replied to the lecture at some length.

Friday, 15.—I put up a sign.

"NAUVOO MANSION."

In consequence of my house being constantly crowded with strangers and other persons wishing to see me, or who had business in the city, I found myself unable to support so much company free of charge, which I have done from the foundation of the Church. My house has been a home and resting-place for thousands, and my family many times obliged to do without food, after having fed all they had to visitors; and I could have continued the same liberal course, had it not been for the cruel and untiring persecution of my relentless enemies. I have been reduced to the necessity of opening "The Mansion" as a hotel. I have provided the best table accommodations in the city; and the Mansion, being large and convenient, renders travelers more comfortable than any other place on the Upper Mississippi. I have erected a large and commodious brick stable, and it is capable of accommodating seventy-five horses at one time, and storing the requisite amount of forage, and is unsurpassed by any similar establishment in the State.

"Nauvoo Mansion" Made a Hotel.

There was an officers' drill in Nauvoo.

Rhoda Ann, daughter of Willard and Jenetta Richards, was born at fifteen minutes to three, p. m., in Nauvoo.

Saturday, 16.—General parade of the Nauvoo Legion

Legion Parade and Inspection.

near my farm. Went in company with my staff to the muster, was met by an escort, and arrived before the Legion about noon. I was received and saluted with military honors. The Legion was dismissed at about one, p. m., for two hours, and I rode home to dinner. I returned about twenty minutes after three, attended the review, and with my staff inspected the Legion; after which, I took my post and gave orders.

After the inspection, I made a speech to the Legion on their increasing prosperity, and requested the officers to increase the Legion in numbers.

I was highly gratified with the officers and soldiers, and I felt extremely well myself.

About sundown the Legion was dismissed. I rode home with my staff, highly delighted with the day's performance, and well paid for my services.

Sunday, 17.—I was at meeting; and while Elder Almon W. Babbitt was preaching, I took my post as Mayor outside the assembly to keep order and set an example to the other officers.

After preaching, I gave some instructions about order in the congregation, men among women, and women among men, horses in the assembly, and men and boys on the stand who do not belong there, &c.

In the evening Mr. Blodgett, a Unitarian minister, preached. I was gratified with his sermon in general, but differed in opinion on some points, on which I freely expressed myself to his great satisfaction,—*viz.*, on persecution making the work spread, like rooting up a flower-garden or kicking back the sun!

Monday, 18.— I received a letter from Governor Ford as follows:—

Letter of Governor Ford to the Prophet.

SPRINGFIELD, September 13, 1843.

DEAR SIR,—In answer to your letter, I have the honor to reply, that I will consider it my duty to prevent the invasion of this State, if in my power, by any persons elsewhere for any hostile purposes whatever.

From information in my possession, I am of opinion that there is but little danger of any such invasion. It is altogether more likely that some other mode of annoyance will be adopted. My enemies here, I think, are endeavoring to put something of the kind on foot.

I am, most respectfully,

Your obedient servant,

THOMAS FORD.

I attended a council at my old house.

A conference was held at Preston, Halifax County, Nova Scotia. 1 Elder, 1 Teacher, 1 Deacon, and 14 members were represented. Robert Dixon, president; J. Jermen, clerk. — Conference in Nova Scotia.

David Greenleaf was elected probate judge for the county of Hancock, by a majority of 598 votes.

Tuesday, 19.—I directed Brother Phelps to answer the letter recently received from the Governor, and to enclose a copy of the resolutions passed at the meeting of the mobocracy at Carthage; which he did.

Wrote a letter to J. B. Backenstos.

A portion of the Twelve were present at a general muster of the independent companies of Boston. Saw a sham battle, in which thirty-five brass cannon were discharged seven times. One party was commanded by the Governor of Mass., and the other by the officer next in rank.

Wednesday, 20.—Visited my farm, accompanied by my Brother Hyrum.

The *Neighbor* has the following:—

PORTER ROCKWELL.

A few short months ago, it was heralded through this State that Porter Rockwell was the individual who attempted to murder ex-Governor Boggs, of Missouri. It was confidently stated that Joseph Smith was accessory before the fact. The thing was swallowed as a precious morsel by the enemies of Mormonism. It was iterated and reiterated by the public journals, and the general expression of a certain class was that Mr. Smith ought to be hung; there was no doubt of his guilt; he was one of the most inhuman, diabolical, dangerous, and malignant persons in the universe; and when a requisition was made for him by the Governor of Missouri, it was considered worse than "arson" or "treason" that he should be acquitted by the legal authorities of this State, under *habeas corpus;* and afterwards, when Porter Rockwell was taken, it was exultingly stated that they had got the scoundrel, and that he would now receive the due demerit of his crime. How stands the matter when it is investigated—investigated by a Missouri court? The following will show:—

The last *Independence Expositor* says:— "Orin Porter Rockwell, the Mormon confined in our county jail, some time since, for the attempted assassination of ex-Governor Boggs, was indicted by our last grand jury for escaping from our county jail some time since, and sent to Clay county for trial. Owing, however, to some informality in the proceedings, he was remanded to this county again for trial. There was not sufficient proof adduced against him to predicate an indictment for shooting ex-Govornor Boggs, and the grand jury therefore did not indict him for that offense."—[*St. Louis New Era.*]

It appears, then, after all the bluster, the hue-and-cry about Mormon outrages, Mormon intrigue, "blood," "arson," and "murder," that "there was not sufficient proof adduced against him to predicate an indictment for shooting ex-Governor Boggs, and the grand jury therefore did not indict him for that offense." This speaks for itself: it needs no comment. We are glad, for the sake of suffering innocence, that Mr. Rockwell stands clear in the eyes of the law. Thus it seeme that after exerting all their malice and hellish rage to implicate the innocent, they can find no proof against him. But yet he must be again incarcerated, without proof, for another hearing. This is Missouri justice. If he was guilty of breaking jail, why not try and punish him for that before that court? Where is the necessity of remanding him to another county for another hearing? It is evident that they wish to immolate him, and, by offering him as a sacrifice, glut their thirst for innocent blood.

I answered Governor Ford's letter received on the 18th. Elder Brigham Young instructed Elder Addison Pratt

Pacific Island Mission.

to go and engage a passage for himself and Elders Noah Rogers, Knowlton F. Hanks, and B. F. Grouard, as missionaries to the Pacific Islands, although they had not one-tenth of the means on hand to pay their passage.

In the evening, Elders Brigham Young, Heber C. Kimball, Orson Pratt, Wilford Woodruff, George A. Smith, and John E. Page visited Mr. O. S. Fowler, the phrenologist, who examined their heads and gave their phrenological charts.

Thursday, 21.—Made affidavit with Willard Richards and William Clayton to Auditor of State *v.* Walter Bagby.

About eleven, a. m., called with my Brother Samuel H. to see about getting a copy of his blessing, and wished Doctor Richards much joy in his new daughter.

About noon, went on board the *Maid of Iowa*, with William Clayton, clerk of the boat.

One, p. m., the thermometer stood at 100 deg. in the shade.

Friday, 22.—The Twelve visited the Navy Yard and Harbor of Boston, the *Mississippi* steamship, the ropewalk, the Bunker-hill monument, the State-house, and the State's prison. In the evening they addressed the Saints in Boylston Hall.

Elder Addison Pratt, accompanied by Elder Philip B. Lewis engaged a passage to the Society Islands at $100 each for himself, Noah Rogers, Knowlton F. Hanks, and B. F. Grouard.

Saturday. 23.—Elder Stephen Markham returned from Dixon, the trial of Reynolds and Wilson being postponed till May next.

Bishop George Miller returned from the Pinery. He reports the water in Black River so low that they could not get their raft into the Mississippi. Report from the Pinery.

I had an interview with Elder Orson Spencer, from whom I borrowed $75 for the Temple.

Sunday, 24.—I preached on the stand about one hour on the 2nd chapter of Acts, designing to show the folly of common stock. In Nauvoo every Stewardship vs. Common Stock.

one is steward over his own. After preaching, I called upon the brethren to draw stone for the Temple, and gave notice for a special conference for the 6th of October next. Adjourned the meeting about one, p. m., on account of the prospect of rain. Judge McBride and a lawyer from Missouri were present at the meeting.

Monday, 25.—Wet day. At home. Held a conversation with the Missouri lawyer.

Tuesday, 26 —Held Mayor's Court, and tried the case of "Dana *v.* Leeches." No cause of action. Called at the store about six, p. m., and directed the clerk to issue papers in the case of "Medagh *v.* Hovey."

Wednesday, 27.—The *Neighbor* of this date has the following editorial:—

CONCERNING HORSE THIEVES.

We find that the *Quincy Whig* has some very righteous remarks to make concerning the Mormons, emanating from the purest principles of patriotism. (?) The editor has had some "*private* conversation" with some individual or individuals about certain charges brought against the Mormons, particulary that of screening horse thieves.

We think that the *Whig* has not done itself much credit in advocating the principles contained in those resolutions. We leave that, however, for a discerning public to judge.

Concerning the horse thieves, however, the informant of the *Whig* would have shown himself a better friend to society to have given information to the proper authorities, and had these pests of society brought to condign punishment. And the editor of that paper would have proved himself more patriotic by telling us who these people are that are screened in our midst, than dealing thus in generals and stabbing in the dark.

Come, Mr. *Whig*, out with it, and let us know who it is that is found transgressing. Who knows but that, far fallen as we are, there yet may be virtue enough left to prosecute a horse thief! We have tried this more than once, and prosecuted them as far as Carthage; but no sooner do they arrive in the jail there than we lose all track of them. The lock of the door is so slippery, that it lets them all out. We presume, however, that it is on account of the honesty of the people. (?) We are pleased to find that the *Whig* is in the secret!

Mr. Ivins, of this city, had a horse stolen last week, and we frequently have occurrences of the kind. Will the editor of that paper be so kind as to ask his informant who the thieves are, and where they live, and give us the desired information? and we shall esteem it a peculiar favor.

I was at home all day, and gave Brother Phelps the privilege of occupying the small house near the store.

Thursday, 28.—At half-past eleven, a. m., a council convened over the store, consisting of myself, my brother Hyrum, Uncle John Smith, Newel K. Whitney, George Miller, Willard Richards, John Taylor, Amasa Lyman, John M. Bernhisel, and Lucien Woodworth; and at seven in the evening we met in the front upper room of the Mansion, with William Law and William Marks. By the common consent and unanimous voice of the council, I was chosen president of the special council.

Meeting of a Special Council.

The president led in prayer that his days might be prolonged until his mission on the earth is accomplished, have dominion over his enemies, all their households be blessed, and all the Church and the world.

Friday, 29.—Elder Brigham Young started from Boston for Nauvoo. The Twelve were now scattered among the branches in the Eastern States.

Saturday, 30.—Rainy, and strong west wind.

Elders Young and Woodruff stayed at Elder Forster's, in New York.

Sunday, October 1, 1843.—I copy the following from the *Times and Seasons* of this date:—

WHO SHALL BE OUR NEXT PRESIDENT?

This question we frequently hear asked, and it is a question of no small importance to the Latter-day Saints.

We, as a people, have labored and are still laboring under great injustice from the hands of a neighboring state. The Latter-day Saints have had their property destroyed, and their houses made desolate by the hands of the Missourians; murders have been committed with impunity, and many, in consequence of oppression, barbarism, and cruelty, have slept the sleep of death. They [the Saints] have been obliged to flee from their possessions into a distant land, in the chilling frosts of winter, robbed, spoiled, desolate, houseless, and homeless, without any just pretext or shadow of law, without having violated the laws of that state, or the United States; and have had to wander as exiles in a strange land, without as yet being able to obtain any redress for their grievances.

We have hitherto adopted every legal measure. First, we petitioned the State of Missouri, but in vain. We have memorialized Congress, but they have turned a deaf ear to our supplication, and referred us again to the State and *justice* of Missouri. Doubtless many of the members of that honorable body were not sufficiently informed of the enormity and extent of the crimes of our persecutors, nor of the indelible stain which our national escutcheon has received through their inhuman daring. They have been allowed to revel in blood and luxuriate in the miseries of the oppressed, and no man has laid it to heart.

The fact is that gentlemen of respectability and refinement, who live in a civilized society, find it difficult to believe that such enormities could be practiced in a Republican government. But our wrong cannot slumber. Such tyranny and oppression must not be passed over in silence. Our injuries, though past, are not forgotten by us; they still rankle in our bosoms, and the blood of the innocent yet cries for justice; and as American citizens we have appealed and shall still continue to appeal to the legally-constituted authorities of the land for redress, in the hopes that justice, which has long slumbered, may be aroused in our defense; that the spirit which burned in the bosoms of the patriots of '76 may fire the souls of their descendants; and though slow, that their indignation may yet be aroused at the injustice of the oppressor; and that they may yet mete out justice to our adversaries, and step forward in the defense of the innocent.

We shall ask no one to commit themselves on our account. We want no steps taken but what are legal, constitutional and honorable. But we are *American citizens*; and as American citizens we have rights in common with all that live under the folds of the "star-spangled banner." Our rights have been trampled upon by lawless miscreants. We have been robbed of our liberties by mobocratic influence, and all those honorable ties that ought to govern and characterize Columbia's sons have been trampled in the dust. Still we are *American Citizens*; and as American citizens we claim the privilege of being heard in the councils of our nation. We have been wronged, abused, robbed, and banished; and we seek redress. Such crimes can not slumber in Republican America. The cause of common humanity would revolt at it, and Republicanism would hide its head in disgust.

We make these remarks for the purpose of drawing the attention of our brethren to this subject, both at home and abroad, that we may fix upon the man who will be the most likely to render us assistance in obtaining redress for our grievances; and not only give our own votes, but use our influence to obtain others; and if the voice of suffering innocence will not sufficiently arouse the rulers of our nation to investigate our case, perhaps a vote of from fifty to one hundred thousand may rouse them from their lethargy.

We shall fix upon the man of our choice, and notify our friends duly.

I published the following in the same number of the *Times and Seasons*:—

THE APPOINTMENT OF A MISSION TO RUSSIA.

To all the Saints and honourable men of the earth to whom the Lord has given liberally of this world's goods, *greeting*:

Our worthy Brother, Elder George J. Adams, has been appointed by the First Presidency of the Church of Jesus Christ of Latter-day Saints at Nauvoo to present to them the importance, as well as the things connected with his mission to Russia, to introduce the fullness of the Gospel to the people of that vast empire, and also to which is attached some of the most important things concerning the advancement and building up of the kingdom of God in the last days, which cannot be explained at this time. But as the mission is attended with much expense, all those who feel disposed to bestow according as God has blessed them shall receive the blessings of Israel's God, and tenfold shall be added unto them, as well as the prayers of the Saints of God.

With sentiments of high esteem, we subscribe ourselves your friends and brethren in the now and everlasting covenant,

JOSEPH SMITH,
HYRUM SMITH.
Presidents of the Church of Jesus Christ of Latter-day Saints.*

I attended meeting this morning, and adjourned it in consequence of the cold and rain. The afternoon being more pleasant, the people assembled, and were addressed by Elders Marks, Charles C. Rich and Bishop Jacob Foutz.

Council met in the evening same as on Thursday previous.

Monday, 2.—At home.

Tuesday, 3.—Elders Brigham Young, Heber C. Kimball, Orson Hyde, George A. Smith, Wilford Woodruff, and Jedediah M. Grant spent the day in visiting the Saints in Philadelphia. In the evening they partook of an oyster supper, on the invitation of Mr. Jeffreys.

Movements of Apostles in the East.

* The fact that Sidney Rigdon and Wm. Law did not sign this document as in the First Presidency, should be noted.

The brethren assembled with their wives, to the number of about one hundred couple, and dined at the Mansion as an opening to the house. A very pleasant day, and all things passed off well.

The following is extracted from the *Neighbor* of this date.

PLEASURE PARTY AND DINNER AT THE NAUVOO MANSION.

General Joseph Smith, the proprietor of said house, provided a luxurious feast for a pleasure party; and all having partaken of the luxuries of a well-spread board, the cloth was removed, and a committee appointed to draft resolutions suitable to the occasion. They adjourned for a few moments and returned, when Robert D. Foster was appointed chairman.

The object of the meeting was then briefly stated by the chairman; after which a hymn was sung, and prayer by Elder Taylor. The chairman then arose and made some appropriate remarks for the occasion, touching upon the rise and progress of the city, the varied scenes through which the Saints had to pass, the persecutions and abuses the Prophets had to undergo, &c., &c. After which he read the following resolutions and toast, which were unanimously adopted:—

Resolved, 1st. That a vote of thanks be presented to General Joseph Smith and lady, through the medium of the *Nauvoo Neighbor*, for the very bountiful feast by them provided, for the accommodation of this party of more than one hundred couple at their Mansion.

Resolved, 2nd. General Joseph Smith, whether we view him as a Prophet at the head of the Church, a General at the head of the Legion, a Mayor at the head of the City Council, or as a landlord at the head of his table, if he has equals, he has no superiors.

Resolved, 3rd. Nauvoo, the great emporium of the West, the center of all centers, a city of three years' growth, a population of 15,000 souls congregated from the four quarters of the globe, embracing the intelligence of all nations, with industry, frugality, economy, virtue, and brotherly love, unsurpassed by any age in the world,—a suitable home for the Saints.

Resolved, 4th. Nauvoo Legion, a well disciplined and faithful band of invincibles, ready at all times to defend their country with this motto, "Vive la Republique."

Resolved, 5th. Nauvoo Charter, like the laws of the Medes and Persians, an unalterable decree by a patriotic band of wise legislators for the protection of the innocent.

Resolved, 6th. Thomas Ford, Governor of Illinois, fearless and faithful in the discharge of all official duties,—long may he live, and blessings attend his administration.

Colonel Francis M. Higbee was then called to the stand, who addressed the audience in a very spirited and appropriate manner for the day.

Professor Orson Spencer was then called, who arose, and in his usual easy and eloquent manner highly entertained the company for nearly half-an-hour.

The next called was Elder John Taylor, who alone was capable of putting on the top stone of the entertainment. His address was highly interesting, combining, like a Lacoon, a volume in every gesture.

General Smith then arose, and, in a very touching and suitable manner, tendered his thanks to the company for the encomiums and honors conferred on him. He recited the many woes through which he had passed, the persecutions which he had suffered, and the love he had for the brethren and citizens of Nauvoo. He tendered his gratitude for the pleasing prospects that surrounded him to the great Giver of all good. He said he thought that his case was similar to that of old Job's —that after he had suffered and drank the very dregs of affliction, the Lord had remembered him in mercy, and was about to bless him abundantly.

After he had done, Mrs. Emma Smith presented her thanks, through the chair, to the company present; after which, a motion was made and carried, to adjourn, whereupon the company were called to their feet. Benediction by Elder Taylor, and the party retired with the most perfect satisfaction and good humor as was ever witnessed on such occasions.

ROBERT D. FOSTER, Chairman.

In the evening Mr. William Backenstos and Clara M. Wasson were married at the Mansion. I solemnized the marriage in presence of a select party.

Wednesday, 4.—I extract the following from the *Neighbor* of this date:—

ANTI-MORMONISM.

With respect to the Carthage meeting, I take upon myself to deny the charges *in toto*, and challenge them to the proof. If we harbor horse-thieves among us, as is basely asserted, let the man that has lost his horse publish his name and the name of the villain, or how he knows him to be a Mormon, and where he is harbored, that we may have something more than vague assertions. They well know that no such proof can be produced, but that the charges had their birth in the minds of one or two heartless scoundrels thirsting for revenge for their late disappointments. The whole of the charges are a tissue of falsehoods got up with the idea of intimidating a peaceable body of citizens. But, sir, we set such designing knaves at defiance and laugh at their threats, treating them with utter contempt, but ever ready to abide by the truth.

JOHN GREENHOW.

Elder Reuben Hedlock wrote the following letter:—

Elder Reuben Hedlock to the First Presidency.

LIVERPOOL, October 4, 1843.

To the First Presidency and Quorum of the Twelve Apostles, greeting:—

DEAR AND MUCH ESTEEMED BRETHREN,—I hasten to inform you of my arrival in Liverpool on the 30th day of September, in company with Elders John Cairns, James Sloan and wife, James Houston, and William G. Jermon. We left six of the Twelve in the city of New York, the 2nd day of September, and came on board of the ship *Columbus.* Our passage money was five dollars. We had a very hard passage. We were very much crowded in the steerage. There were 236 persons— Dutch, Irish, English and Scotch, and as dirty as any I ever saw. We were not much sick; the weather was cold. Had it been otherwise, we should have suffered more. A steamer leaves for New York to-day, and I thought I would announce to you my arrival by this opportunity, and such information as I was in possession of up to this date. There is a ship to sail on the 14th instant, by which I shall write you again.

I found Elders Hyrum Clark, Thomas Ward, and Amos Fielding in Liverpool, and they were well; and as far as I was informed by them, the Church is in a good state and on the increase; it numbers somewhere between eight and nine thousand members. There is a great want of laborers in the vineyard. Many of the first Elders have left this for Nauvoo, leaving their places vacant. I presented to the Presidency here your decision relative to the printing. Elders Ward and Fielding received it, and manifested a desire to abide by it. Elder Fielding wept when I showed him your decision concerning him and his coming to Nauvoo by the first ship to see you face to face. The brethren say here that he has been too hasty in some things, and has given some an offense; but I do not as yet know anything derogatory to his character that I could say aught against him. I shall write you all the particulars as fast as I come in possession of them. As regards the printing in this land, we shall stop it after the next number is published. In it we wish to publish the news from Nauvoo for the benefit of the Saints, and to announce our arrival in this country.

Permit me here to give you my opinion as regards the printing in this land, and I will cheerfully abide your advice notwithstanding. After we stop the *Star*, we shall have during the shipping season to advertise and give general information in the emigration business to the Saints scattered abroad. I think it would be best to republish the *Times and Seasons* for the benefit of the Church. The duties on books are £2-10s. per hundredweight; and there are now 1,600 *Stars* circulated here at the present, and the demands of our publications are on the increase. The duties would almost reprint the *Times and Seasons,* and then we could do our advertising on the last page, if thought advisable. We could afford it as cheap as the present *Star,* and pay you something for the privilege of publishing, as well as to pay it to the crown. I have not yet learned the amount of funds remaining here subject to your order. I have not had much time as yet to inquire into those matters, in consequence of the multitude of business in unloading our freight from shipboard.

The brethren that came with me wish to say to those whom it may concern, that they are well, and will in a few days leave for their fields of labor.

I shall write to you once a month, no preventing Providence, and should be glad to have you write to me as often, and give me your advice and counsel relating to those things you,in your wisdom,may think beneficial to the Saints and emigration in this land.

I wish Elder Taylor would forward to me the amount of the number that will make the volume of the *Times and Seasons* complete by the first opportunity. By so doing I can sell the 200 volumes to advantage. I will try to forward to him what I can obtain for the *Times and Seasons* already here. If it should be thought wisdom to reprint the *Times and Seasons* here, I wish Brother Taylor would be particular to send, so that we could obtain them, if possible. I am informed by Elder Ward that they have not received any intelligence from you since last February.

I wish you would write me your mind concerning the printing immediately on the receipt of this sheet, so that our communication with the Saints in England may not be stopped long.

I am, as ever, your humble servant in the bonds of the new and everlasting covenant,

REUBEN HEDLOCK.

I was at the mansion preparing some legal papers.— Justin Butterfield, Esq., U. S. Attorney for Illinois, arrived this afternoon; and I spent the rest of the day in riding and chatting with him.

The Prophet's visit with Justin Butterfield.

Council of the quorum [special council, see p. 39] met and adjourned to Sunday evening; my Brother Hyrum's child being sick.

The quorum of the Twelve started from Philadelphia for Pittsburgh.

Thursday, 5.—This morning I rode out with Esquire Butterfield to the farm.

In the afternoon, rode to the prairie to show some of the brethren some land. Evening, at home, and walked up and down the streets with my scribe. Gave instructions to try those persons who were preaching, teaching, or practicing the doctrine of plurality of wives; for, according to the law, I hold the keys of this power in the last days; for there is never but one on earth at a time on whom the power and its keys are conferred; *and I have constantly said no man shall have but one wife at a time, unless the Lord directs otherwise.*

Instructions Respecting Plurality of Wives.

Friday, 6.—I attended special conference; but as few people were out, in consequence of the weather proving unfavorable, the organization of the conference was adjourned until to morrow, or the first pleasant day.

After giving notice that President Rigdon's case would be considered, &c., I walked towards home, and gave instructions to my scribe to cause all the papers relating to my land-claims in the Half Breed Tract in Iowa, to be placed in the hands of Esquire Butterfield.

The Prophet's Dissatisfaction with Sidney Rigdon.

Saturday, 7.—I attended conference.

Sunday, 8.—Slight frost last night. Conference convened in the morning; but, as it rained, adjourned till Monday at ten, a. m.

Prayer-meeting at my house in the evening. Quorum present; also, in addition, Sisters Adams, Elizabeth Ann Whitney, my aunt Clarissa Smith, and my mother.

My brother Hyrum and his wife were blessed, ordained and anointed.

The Twelve arrived at Pittsburgh at ten, a. m., and again left by the steamer *Raritan*, at eleven, a. m., *en route* for Nauvoo.

Monday, 9.—Attended conference, and preached a funeral sermon on the death of General James Adams; a brief synopsis of which, as reported by Dr. Willard Richards, will be found in the minutes below.

I here insert the conference minutes.

MINUTES OF A SPECIAL CONFERENCE.

The Church of Jesus Christ of Latter-day Saints, in Special Conference, held in the City of Nauvoo, commencing on the 6th of October, 1843.

Friday, October 6, ten o'clock, a. m.

The weather proving unfavorable, the organization of the Conference was postponed until the next day at ten o'clock, a. m.

Saturday, ten o'clock, a. m.

Conference assembled and proceeded to business.

President Joseph Smith was called to the chair, and Gustavus Hills was chosen clerk.

Singing by the choir, and prayer by Elder Almon W. Babbitt.

The president stated the items of business to be brought before the conference to be—

1st. The case and standing of Elder Sidney Rigdon, Counselor in the First Presidency.

2nd. The further progress of the Temple; after which, any miscellaneous business.

Elder Sidney Rigdon addressed the conference on the subject of his situation and circumstances among the Saints.

President Joseph Smith addressed the conference, inviting an expression of any charges or complaints which the conference had to make. He stated his dissatisfaction with Elder Sidney Rigdon as a Counselor, not having received any material benefit from his labors or counsels since their escape from Missouri. Several complaints were then brought forward in reference to his management in the post office; a supposed corespondence and connection with John C. Bennett, with Ex-Governor Carlin, and with the Missourians, of a treacherous character; also his leaguing with dishonest persons in endeavoring to defraud the innocent.

President Joseph Smith related to the conference the detention of a document from Justin Butterfield, Esq., which was designed for the benefit of himself, (President Smith,) but was not handed over for some three or four weeks, greatly to his disadvantage; also, an indirect testimony from Missouri, through the mother of Orrin P. Rockwell, that said Rigdon and others had given information, by letter, of President Smith's visit to Dixon, advising them to proceed to that place and arrest him there. He stated that, in consequence of these and other circumstances, and Elder Rigdon's unprofitableness to him as a Counselor, he did not wish to retain him in that station, unless those difficulties could be removed; but desired his salvation, and expressed his willingness that he should retain a place among the Saints.

Elder Almon W. Babbitt suggested the propriety of limiting the complaints and proofs to circumstances that had transpired since the last conference.

President Joseph Smith replied, and showed the legality and propriety of a thorough investigation, without such limitation.

Elder Sidney Rigdon pleaded, concerning the document from Justin Butterfield, Esq., that he received it in answer to some inquiries which he [Rigdon] had transmitted to him [Butterfield]; that he [Rigdon] received it at a time when he was sick, and unable to examine it; did not know that it was designed for the perusal and benefit of President Joseph Smith; that he had, consequently, ordered it to be laid aside, where it remained until inquired for by Joseph Smith. He had never written to Missouri concerning the visit of Joseph Smith to Dixon, and knew of no other person having done so. That, concerning certain rumors of belligerent operations under Governor Carlin's administration, he had related them, not to alarm or disturb any one; but that he had the rumors from good authorities, and supposed them well founded. That he had never received but one communication from John C. Bennett, and that of a business character, except one addressed to him conjointly with Elder Orson Pratt, which he handed over to President Smith. That he had never written any letters to John C. Bennett.

The weather becoming inclement, conference adjourned until Sunday, ten o'clock, a. m.

Sunday, 8th, ten o'clock, a. m.

Conference assembled agreeably to adjournment.

Singing by the choir, and prayer by Elder William W. Phelps.

Elder Sidney Rigdon resumed his plea of defense. He related the circumstances of his reception in the city of Quincy, after his escape from Missouri,—the cause of his delay in not going to the city of Washington, on an express to which he had been appointed: and closed with a moving appeal to President Joseph Smith, concerning their former friendship, associations, and sufferings; and expressed his willingness to resign his place, though with sorrowful and indescribable feelings. During this address, the sympathies of the congregation were highly excited.

Elder Almon W. Babbitt related a conversation he had had with Esquire Johnson, in which he exonerated Elder Sidney Rigdon from the charge or suspicion of having had a treacherous correspondence with ex-Governor Carlin.

President Joseph Smith arose and explained to the congregation the supposed treacherous correspondence with ex-Governor Carlin, and expressed entire lack of confidence in his integrity and steadfastness, judging from their past intercourse.

Patriarch Hyrum Smith followed with appropriate and impressive remarks on the attributes of mercy in God, as that by which He influences, controls and conquers; and the propriety and importance of the Saints exercising the same attribute towards their fellows, and especially towards their aged companion and fellow-servant in the cause of truth and righteousness.

Elder Almon W. Babbitt and President William Law followed with remarks in defense of Elder Sidney Rigdon.

On motion by President William Marks, and seconded by Patriarch Hyrum Smith, conference voted that Elder Sidney Rigdon be permitted to retain his station as Counselor in the First Presidency.

*President Joseph Smith arose and said, "I have thrown him off my shoulders, and you have again put him on me. You may carry him, but I will not."** *

Singing. Prayer by Elder William Law.

Conference adjourned for one hour.

Three, p. m.

Conference assembled; but in consequence of the inclemency of the weather, business was postponed until Monday, ten o'clock, a. m.

Monday, ten o'clock, a. m.

Conference assembled, and resumed business.

Singing by the choir. Prayer by Elder Alpheus Cutler.

The business pertaining to the Temple was then announced by the President as next in order.

Elder Alpheus Cutler, on the part of the Temple Committee, represented the work of the Temple to be retarded for want of team work and provisions—also of iron, steel, blasting powder, and clothing,—giving as his opinion that the walls could easily be completed next season, if these embarrassments were removed, and the brethren would come forward to sustain them in the work with the means that were in their hands.

Elder Reynolds Cahoon followed, seconding the remarks of Elder Cutler, and setting forth the importance of the Saints using their utmost exertions to fulfill the revelation concerning the Temple, earnestly exhorting the Saints here and abroad to roll in the necessary means into the hands of the Trustee, that the work may advance with rapidity.

* This paragraph in Italics appears as footnote in the Ms. History.

President Hyrum Smith followed with pertinent remarks on the importance of the work—the ease with which it might be advanced to its completion,—that it had already become a monument for the people abroad to gaze on with astonishment. He concluded with some advice to parents to restrain their children from vice and folly, and employ them in some business of profit to themselves, to the Temple, or elsewhere.

On motion by Elder William Law, and seconded by President Hyrum Smith, conference voted that we, as a conference and individuals, will use all the means, exertions, and influence in our power to sustain the Temple Committee in advancing the work of the Temple.

Conference adjourned for one hour.

Two o'clock, p. m.

Conference re-assembled, and listened with profound attention to an impressive discourse from President Joseph Smith, commemorative of the decease of James Adams, Esq., late of this city, and an honorable, worthy, useful and esteemed member of the Church of Jesus Christ of Latter-day Saints.

THE PROPHET'S REMARKS ON THE DEMISE OF JAMES ADAMS.

All men know that they must die. And it is important that we should understand the reasons and causes of our exposure to the vicissitudes of life and of death, and the designs and purposes of God in our coming into the world, our sufferings here, and our departure hence. What is the object of our coming into existence, then dying and falling away, to be here no more? It is but reasonable to suppose that God would reveal something in reference to the matter, and it is a subject we ought to study more than any other. We ought to study it day and night, for the world is ignorant in reference to their true condition and relation. If we have any claim on our Heavenly Father for anything, it is for knowledge on this important subject. Could we read and comprehend all that has been written from the days of Adam, on the relation of man to God and angels in a future state, we should know very little about it. Reading the experience of others, or the revelation given to *them*, can never give *us* a comprehensive view of our condition and true relation to God. Knowledge of these things can only be obtained by experience through the ordinances of God set forth for that purpose. Could you gaze into heaven five minutes, you would know more than you would by reading all that ever was written on the subject.

We are only capable of comprehending that certain things exist, which we may acquire by certain fixed principles. If men would acquire salvation, they have got to be subject, before they leave this

world, to certain rules and principles, which were fixed by an unalterable decree before the world was.

The disappointment of hopes and expectations at the resurrection
would be indescribably dreadful.

The organization of the spiritual and heavenly worlds, and of spiritual and heavenly beings, was agreeable to the most perfect order and
harmony: their limits and bounds were fixed irrevocably, and voluntarily subscribed to in their heavenly estate by themselves, and were by
our first parents subscribed to upon the earth. Hence the importance
of embracing and subscribing to principles of eternal truth by all men
upon the earth that expect eternal life.

I assure the Saints that truth, in reference to these matters, can and
may be known through the revelations of God in the way of His ordinances, and in answer to prayer. The Hebrew Church "came unto the
spirits of just men made perfect, and unto an innumerable company of
angels, unto God the Father of all, and to Jesus Christ, the Mediator
of the new covenant." What did they learn by coming of the spirits of
just men made perfect? Is it written? No. What they learned has
not been and could not have been written. What object was gained by
this communication with the spirits of the just? It was the established
order of the kingdom of God: the keys of power and knowledge were
with them to communicate to the Saints. Hence the importance of
understanding the distinction between the spirits of the just and
angels.

Spirits can only be revealed in flaming fire or glory. Angels have
advanced further, their light and glory being tabernacled; and hence
they appear in bodily shape. The spirits of just men are made ministering servants to those who are sealed unto life eternal, and it is through
them that the sealing power comes down.

Patriarch Adams is now one of the spirits of the just men made
perfect; and, if revealed now, must be revealed in fire; and the glory
could not be endured. Jesus showed Himself to His disciples, and they
thought it was His spirit, and they were afraid to approach His spirit.
Angels have advanced higher in knowledge and power than spirits.

Concerning Brother James Adams, it should appear strange that so
good and so great a man was hated. The deceased ought never to have
had an enemy. But so it was. Wherever light shone, it stirred up
darkness. Truth and error, good and evil cannot be reconciled. Judge
Adams had some enemies, but such a man ought not to have had one.
I saw him first at Springfield, when on my way from Missouri to Washington. He sought me out when a stranger, took me to his home, encouraged and cheered me, and gave me money. He has been a most
intimate friend. I anointed him to the patriarchal power—to receive

the keys of knowledge and power, by revelation to himself. He has had revelations concerning his departure, and has gone to a more important work. When men are prepared, they are better off to go hence. Brother Adams has gone to open up a more effectual door for the dead. The spirits of the just are exalted to a greater and more glorious work; hence they are blessed in their departure to the world of spirits. Enveloped in flaming fire, they are not far from us, and know and understand our thoughts, feelings, and motions, and are often pained therewith.

Flesh and blood cannot go there; but flesh and bones, quickened by the Spirit of God, can.

If we would be sober and watch in fasting and prayer, God would turn away sickness from our midst.

Hasten the work in the Temple, renew your exertions to forward all the work of the last days, and walk before the Lord in soberness and righteousness. Let the Elders and Saints do away with light-mindedness, and be sober.

Such is a faint outline of the discourse of President Joseph Smith, which was delivered with his usual feeling and pathos, and was listened to with the most profound and eager attention by the multitude, who hung upon his instructions, anxious to learn and pursue the path of eternal life.

After singing by the choir, and prayer by the President, Conference adjourned *sine die*, with the benediction of the President.

JOSEPH SMITH, President.

GUSTAVUS HILLS, Clerk.

The missionaries to the Society Islands went on board the ship *Timoleon*, Captain Plasket, at New Bedford, and got under way. Elder Philip B. Lewis donated $300 towards their passage and fitout. Elder Knowlton F. Hanks' health was very poor.

Pacific Islands Mission Embarks.

CHAPTER III.

ANCIENT RUINS IN AMERICA, BOOK OF MORMON EVIDENCE—
THE PROPHET ON THE U. S. CONSTITUTION AND THE
BIBLE—MISREPRESENTATIONS CORRECTED—LETTER TO
THE U. S. PRESIDENTIAL CANDIDATES—THE PROPHET'S
ADDRESS TO THE SAINTS.

Tuesday, October 10, 1843.—My brother Hyrum was
appointed, by the voice of the Spirit, one of the Temple
Committee, in place of Judge Elias Higbee, deceased.

I spent the day in council with J. and O. C. Skinner
and the Rhodes' about the sale of land, and appointed
William Clayton to buy the property.

Wednesday, 11.—I was at home this morning. In the
afternoon I went with my brother Hyrum, William Law,
and our wives, to Brother John Benbow's.

The following is from the *Times and Seasons:*—

ANCIENT RUINS—INTRODUCTORY.

Every day adds fresh testimony to the already accumulated evidence
on the authenticity of the Book of Mormon. At the time that book
was translated, there was very little known about ruined cities and
dilapidated buildings. The general presumption was that no people
possessing more intelligence than our present race of Indians had ever
inhabited this continent; and the accounts given in the Book of Mormon
concerning large cities and civilized people having inhabited this land
were generally disbelieved and pronounced a humbug. Priest, since
then, has thrown some light on this interesting subject. Stephens, in
his "Incidents of Travels in Central America," has thrown in a flood of
testimony, and from the following statements it is evident that the Book
of Mormon does not give a more extensive account of large and popul-
ous cities than those discoveries demonstrate to be even now in
existence.—Ed.]

(Article from the Texas Telegraph, October 11.)

We have been informed by a gentleman who has traversed a large
portion of the Indian country of Northern Texas, and the country

lying between Santa Fe and the Pacific, that there are vestiges of ancient cities and ruined castles or temples on the Rio Puerco, and on the Colorado of the West.

He says that on one of the branches of the Rio Puerco, a few days' travel from Santa Fe, there is an immense pile of ruins that appear to belong to an ancient temple. Portions of the walls are still standing, consisting of huge blocks of limestone regularly hewn and laid in cement. The building occupies an extent of more than an acre. It is two or three stories high, has no roof, but contains many rooms, generally of a square form, without windows; and the lower rooms are so dark and gloomy that they resemble caverns rather than the apartments of an edifice built for a human habitation.

Our informant did not give the style of architecture, but he believes it could not be erected by Spaniards or Europeans, as the stones are much worn by the rains, and indicate that the building has stood many hundred years. From his description, we are induced to believe that it resembles the ruins of Palenque or Otulum.

He says there are many similar ruins on the Colorado of the West, which empties in the Californian sea. In one of the valleys of the Cordilleras traversed by this river, and about four hundred miles from its mouth, there is a large temple still standing, its walls and spires presenting scarcely any traces of dilapidation; and were it not for the want of a roof, it might still be rendered habitable. Near it, scattered along the declivity of a mountain, are the ruins of what must have been once a large city.

The traces of a large aqueduct, part of which is, however, in the solid rock, are still visible. Neither the Indians residing in the vicinity nor the oldest Spanish settlers of the nearest settlements can give any account of the origin of these buildings. They merely know that they have stood there from the earliest periods to which their traditions extend.

The antiquarian who is desirous to trace the Aztec or the Toltec races in their migrations from the northern regions of America may find in their ancient edifices many subjects of curious speculation.

Thursday, 12.—Prayer-meeting in my room. We prayed for William Marks, who was sick.

I sent William Clayton to Lathrop, to borrow $50, that I might be able to redeem $5000 worth of property, which was published to be sold to-day at Rhodes'; but Lathrop refused. He also went to Eli Chase's, but was refused by him. I was grieved that the brethren felt so penurious in their spirit, although they professed to be guided by the revelations which the Lord gives through me. On my afterwards giving a pledge that I would repay the $50 in forty-eight hours, Lathrop lent the money and enabled me to redeem the land.

I received the following from H. R. Hotchkiss:

Letter—H. R. Hotchkiss to Joseph Smith.

NEW YORK, 27th September, 1843.

Rev. Joseph Smith.

DEAR SIR,—I see by the newspapers that there has been a meeting of citizens at Carthage relative to the Mormons, and that several severe resolutions have been passed condemning the conduct of the Mormons. Knowing how little I can rely upon public rumor upon such subjects, I have taken the liberty of applying directly to you for correct information, and solicit as a particular favor that you will communicate at your earliest convenience the facts in the case.

Of course I feel an interest in the prosperity of Nauvoo, and an interest also in the success of the Mormon enterprise, and a deep interest in the welfare of your people; and the more so, certainly, as their pecuniary interest is identified with my own. I make this frank acknowledgment, because it is always best for men of sense to talk as they mean. I should, however, be solicitous for a successful termination of your great enterprise, had I not one dollar invested in Nauvoo, because the complete triumph of energetic exertions is always gratifying to all business men.

Your obedient servant,

HORACE R. HOTCHKISS.

I wrote this reply:—

Letter—Joseph Smith to H. R. Hotchkiss.

NAUVOO, Ill., Oct. 12, 1843,

DEAR SIR,—Your letter of the 27th ult. is at hand, soliciting information concerning the "Carthage resolutions." In answer to your very candid inquiry and interest relative to our welfare, brevity will suffice. Unprincipled men and disappointed demagogues, with here and there an "untamed sucker," composed that disgraceful and disgracing as well as mobocratic assemblage; and I feel proud to say that patriots and honest men generally frown upon such audacious proceedings as beneath the dignity of freemen. It is to be hoped that public opinion will continue to spurn at such doings, and leave the actors to fester in their own shame.

With the smiling prospects around us at present, success seems certain; and, with the blessings of Jehovah, we shall reap the reward of virtue and goodness. I go for the good of the world; and if all honest men would do so, mean men would be scarce. You are at liberty to use this to counteract falsehoods as you may deem proper.

Respectfully, I am your obedient servant,

JOSEPH SMITH.

Friday, 13.—First severe frost at Nauvoo this season. Ice on the water.

At home; made arrangements to prepare provisions for the workmen in the pinery. From ten, a. m. to three, p. m., presided in municipal court, on *habeas corpus* in favor of Charles Drown, to be delivered from the custody of Samuel Waterman. The prisoner being sick, adjourned the case to the 16th.

In the afternoon, trying a span of grey horses in the carriage.

Dr. Turner, a phrenologist, came in. I gratified his curiosity for about an hour by allowing him to examine my head.

I was engaged settling accounts with D. S. Hollister.

Saturday, 14.—In the morning, at home, having a long

Location of the mind.

conversation with a physiologist and mesmeriser. I asked them to prove that the mind of man was seated in one part of the brain more than another.

Sat in City Council till one, p. m., which passed "An Ordinance concerning the inspection of flour," and appointed William E. Horner inspector of flour for the city of Nauvoo.

Sunday, 15.—Cool, calm, and cloudy. At eleven, a. m., I preached at the stand east of the Temple. The following synopsis was reported by Dr. Willard Richards:—

The Prophet on the Constitution of the United States and the Bible—Temporal Economies.

It is one of the first principles of my life, and one that I have cultivated from my childhood, having been taught it by my father, to allow every one the liberty of conscience. I am the greatest advocate of the

Constitution of the United States there is on the earth. In my feelings I am always ready to die for the protection of the weak and oppressed in their just rights. The only fault I find with the Constitution is, it is not broad enough to cover the whole ground.

Although it provides that all men shall enjoy religious freedom, yet it does not provide the manner by which that freedom can be preserved, nor for the punishment of Government officers who refuse to protect the people in their religious rights, or punish those mobs, states, or communities who interfere with the rights of the people on account of their religion. Its sentiments are good, but it provides no means of enforcing them. It has but this one fault. Under its provision, a man or a people who are able to protect themselves can get along well enough; but those who have the misfortune to be weak or unpopular are left to the merciless rage of popular fury.

The Constitution should contain a provision that every officer of the Government who should neglect or refuse to extend the protection guaranteed in the Constitution should be subject to capital punishment; and then the president of the United States would not say, "*Your cause is just, but I can do nothing for you,*" a governor issue exterminating orders, or judges say, "The men ought to have the protection of law, but it won't please the mob; the men must die, anyhow, to satisfy the clamor of the rabble; they must be hung, or Missouri be damned to all eternity." Executive writs could be issued when they ought to be, and not be made instruments of cruelty to oppress the innocent, and persecute men whose religion is unpopular.

I cannot believe in any of the creeds of the different denominations, because they all have some things in them I cannot subscribe to, though all of them have some truth. I want to come up into the presence of God, and learn all things; but the creeds set up stakes, and say, "Hitherto shalt thou come, and no further;" which I cannot subscribe to.

I believe the Bible as it read when it came from the pen of the original writers. Ignorant translators, careless transcribers, or designing and corrupt priests have committed many errors. As it read, Gen. vi. 6, "It repented the Lord that he had made man on the earth;" also, Num. xxiii. 19, "God is not a man, that he should lie; neither the Son of man, that he should repent;" which I do not believe. But it ought to read, "It repented *Noah* that God made man." This I believe, and then the other quotation stands fair. If any man will prove to me, by one passage of Holy Writ, one item I believe to be false, I will renounce and disclaim it as far as I promulged it.

The first principles of the Gospel, as I believe, are, faith, repentance, baptism for the remission of sins, with the promise of the Holy Ghost.

Look at Heb. vi. 1 for contradictions—"Therefore leaving the principles of the doctrine of Christ, let us go on unto perfection." If a man
leaves the principles of the doctrine of Christ, how can he be saved in
the principles? This is a contradiction. I don't believe it. I will
render it as it should be—"Therefore *not* leaving the principles of the
doctrine of Christ, let us go on unto perfection, not laying again the
foundation of repentance from dead works, and of faith toward God,
of the doctrine of baptisms, and of laying on of hands, and of resurrection of the dead, and of eternal judgment."

It is one thing to see the kingdom of God, and another thing to enter
into it. We must have a change of heart to see the kingdom of God,
and subscribe the articles of adoption to enter therein.

No man can receive the Holy Ghost without receiving revelations.
The Holy Ghost is a revelator.

I prophesy, in the name of the Lord God of Israel, anguish and wrath
and tribulation and the withdrawing of the Spirit of God from the earth
await this generation, until they are visited with utter desolation. This
generation is as corrupt as the generation of the Jews that crucified
Christ; and if He were here to-day, and should preach the same doctrine
He did then, they would put Him to death. I defy all the world to
destroy the work of God; and I prophesy they never will have power to
kill me till my work is accomplished, and I am ready to die.

I will now speak a little on the economy of this city. I think there
are too many merchants among you. I would like to see more wool
and raw materials instead of manufactured goods, and the money be
brought here to pay the poor for manufacturing goods. Set our women
to work, and stop their spinning street yarns and talking about spiritual
wives.

Instead of going abroad to buy goods, lay your money out in the
country, and buy grain, cattle, flax, wool, and work it up yourselves.

I proclaim, in the name of the Lord God Almighty, that I will fellowship nothing in the Church but virtue, integrity, and uprightness.

We cannot build up a city on merchandise. I would not run after the
merchants. I would sow a little flax, if I had but a garden spot, and
make clothing of it.

The temporal economy of this people should be to establish and encourage manufactures, and not to take usury for their money. I do not
want to bind the poor here to starve. Go out into the country and into
the neighbouring cities, and get food, and gird up your loins, and be
sober. When you get food, return, if you have a mind to.

Some say it is better to give to the poor than build the Temple. The
building of the Temple has sustained the poor who were driven from
Missouri, and kept them from starving; and it has been the best means
for this object which could be devised.

Oh, all ye rich men of the Latter-day Saints from abroad, I would invite you to bring up some of your money—your gold, your silver, and your precious things, and give to the Temple. We want iron, steel, spades, and quarrying and mechanical tools.

It would be a good plan to get up a forge to manufacture iron, and bring in raw materials of every variety, and erect manufacturing establishments of all kinds, and surround the rapids with mills and machinery.

I never stole the value of a pin's head, or a picayune in my life; and when you are hungry don't steal. Come to me, and I will feed you.

The secret of masonry is to keep a secret. It is good economy to entertain strangers—to entertain sectarians. Come up to Nauvoo, ye sectarian priests of the everlasting Gospel, as they call it, and you shall have my pulpit all day.

Woe to ye rich men, who refuse to give to the poor, and then come and ask me for bread. Away with all your meanness, and be liberal. We need purging, purifying and cleansing. You that have little faith in your Elders when you are sick, get some little simple remedy in the first stages. If you send for a doctor at all, send in the first stages.

All ye doctors who are fools, not well read, and do not understand the human constitution, stop your practice. And all ye lawyers who have no business, only as you hatch it up, would to God you would go to work or run away!"

Monday, 16.—At home nearly all day, attending to family concerns.

Went to municipal court, and adjourned hearing of the case* to the 17th.

Tuesday, 17.—Went to municipal court. The prosecutor not appearing, court ordered that the prisoner be discharged.

Wednesday, 18.—Pleasant and comfortable day.

Fifteen deaths have occured during the past week in the city.

Thursday, 19.—Warm and pleasant day. The water has risen about two feet in the Mississippi, and is still rising.

The Prophet's Visit to Macedonia.

About noon, started for Macedonia, in company with Brother William Clayton. Arrived there about

---

* This was the case of Chas. Drown on *habeas corpus* referred to under date of 13th of October.

sundown, and I stayed at Brother Benjamin F. Johnson's for the night.

Friday, 20.—In the evening I gave instructions to Benjamin F. Johnson and others in relation to the blessings of the everlasting covenant and the sealings of the Priesthood.

Elder John P. Greene returned from a Mission to the State of New York, with about 100 emigrants, some of them from Pennsylvania, who joined his company on the way.

Warm, smoky day, with strong wind, very dark evening.

Saturday, 21.—We left Macedonia, and arrived home about two p. m.   Pleasant cool day.

Sunday, 22.—Meeting at the stand.   Elder Rigdon preached half-an hour on "Poor Rich Folks."

I remained at home all day, and held a prayer-meeting at my house at two, p. m.; tweuty-four persons present.

Elders Young, Kimball, and George A. Smith returned from their mission to the Eastern States, having, in connection with Elders Orson Pratt and Wilford Woodruff, visited the branches in Kentucky, Ohio, Pennsylvania, New Yersey, New York, Connecticut, Massachusetts, Rhode Island, New Hampshire, and Maine; held conferences, set in order the churches, collected tithings for the Temple and subscriptions for the Nauvoo House, baptized many, and stirred up a general system of gathering among the Saints in the Eastern countries.   They have been absent nearly four months, and have accomplished a good work.   I was very glad to see them, and blessed them in the name of the Lord.   Elders Daniel Spencer and Bradford Elliot also returned from their missions, and quite a respectable number of Saints came in their company.

Labors of the Apostles in the East.

Pleasant, cool day.

Monday, 23.—Those of the Twelve who returned from the East yesterday visited me through the day, and paid over the means they had received for the Temple and the

Nauvoo House. I immediately gave directions to send to St. Louis for groceries and different articles necessary for the Temple and the workmen thereon.

This morning President Hyrum Smith entered upon the duties of his office, having previously been appointed by the voice of the Spirit to supply the place of the late Elias Higbee, deceased, as one of the Temple Committee. On his arrival Hyrum Smith Appointed on Temple Committee. at the Temple he was greeted by a hearty welcome from those engaged on the works, and the universal feeling is that great good will result from this appointment.

The day cloudy, with strong east wind.

Tuesday, 24.—William W. Phelps and Colonel Dunham started for Springfield to see the Governor, and endeavor to obtain from him the quota of State arms which belong to the Legion.

Morning warm and pleasant; afternoon wind west by north. At four, a little rain, accompanied by snow, for the first time this fall.

Wednesday, 25.—Ice one-third of an inch thick on small bodies of water. Cloudy and cold day.

In the evening settled the taxes for the Temple and Nauvoo House.

Eleven deaths in the city reported this week.

Friday, 27.—I was at home and received a visit from Bishop George Miller and Elder Peter Haws, who have just returned from their trip to Mississippi and Alabama.

Many emigrants have arrived in Nauvoo the last few weeks.

Prayer-meeting at my house in the evening.

Saturday, 28.—Cold east wind. At home all day.

Sunday, 29.—Meeting at the stand, south side of the Temple, from eleven, a. m. to two, p. m. Elders Brigham Young and John Taylor preached. Dr. Willard Richards called for a collection of $8, to buy a new book in which to record history, which sum was made up.

At nine, a. m., Elders Richards, Miller and Haws

ordained William C. Steffey (who was going to Texas on business,) an Elder.

Two, p. m., prayer-meeting in my house; twenty-five present. I gave instructions on the priesthood.

Monday, 30.—At nine, a. m., went to mayor's court, and adjourned it for one week.

Twelve, noon, attended a court in the office, when the parties agreed to leave their difficulty to be settled by the arbitration of Brother Flagg.

I received $300 from Brother Spencer, and immediately paid it to Dr. Robert D. Foster.

On account of the cold weather, most of the masons have discontinued the work on the Temple.

Tuesday, 31.—At nine, a. m., Mr. Moore was brought before me for a breach of city ordinance, which was proved, and I fined him $5.

I rode out with Hyrum in the carriage to the prairie, returning about three, p. m. Snow on the ground this morning; cold east wind, and rain all day.

Wednesday, November 1, 1843.—In the evening there was a prayer-meeting in the mansion; twenty-nine present.

Thursday, 2 —Sitting in council with Hyrum, Brigham Young, Heber C. Kimball, Willard Richards, John Taylor, William Law, and William Clayton, at ten, a. m., on the subject of the following letter from Joseph L. Heywood:—

Letter: Joseph L. Heywood to Joseph Smith.

QUINCY, October 23, 1843.

Gen. Joseph Smith.

DEAR SIR,—In a conversation with Colonel Frierson. of this place, a short time since, he expressed, in very warm terms, feelings of sympathy for the wrongs yourself and brethren suffered in Missouri, as well as his sense of the vindictive feelings the authorities of that State still manifest towards you personally.

Mr. F. has not yet had the pleasure of a personal acquaintance with yourself, although he says he had the pleasure of meeting your lady at her sister's residence on Rock River. Mr. F. has been written by the Hon. B. Rhett, of S. Carolina, upon the subject of the *Persecution*: and

Mr. F. thinks, of all men, he would be the best qualified to present a petition in our behalf; and says, should such an arrangement meet your approbation, he will use his influence in favor of a petition; and says he knows of some honorable men in Missouri who, he has no doubt, are anxious to wipe off the stain that rests upon them, by [making] some just reparation.

I submit, by permission of Mr. F., a copy of a letter he has written to a distinguished citizen of South Carolina, together with a circular put out confidentially by the friends of Mr. Calhoun, of S. C., whom with my present feelings I should cheerfully support for our next President, and who, I have no doubt would be preferred, by the brethren to Mr. Van Buren.

If the plan suggested of memorializing Congress should meet your approbation, please inform me. Colonel Frierson promises his aid in such an event, and says he would go to Nauvoo and assist in arranging papers relative to such a step. Please accept my assurances of love and esteem for yourself and family, and a prayer that wisdom from on high may direct you in your deliberations.

I remain your brother in Christ,

JOS. L. HEYWOOD.

We agreed to write a letter to the five candidates for the Presidency of the United States, to inquire what their feelings were towards us as a people, and what their course of action would be in relation to the cruelty and oppression that we have suffered from the State of Missouri, if they were elected. *Letters to Candidates for Presidency of the U. S. Decided upon*

The Twelve Apostles published the following in the *Times and Seasons*: —

An Epistle of the Twelve, to the Elders and Churches Abroad.

On our late mission to the Eastern States, we discovered that the publications at Nauvoo were very little patronised by the Saints and branches in the various sections of the country where we passed, while the common newspapers of the day received a liberal support by those who pretend to "hunger and thirst after righteousness." We feel justified, therefore, in reprobating such a course as detrimental to the general good of the whole Church, that shows a lack of charity in the Elders.

"Do men gather grapes of thorns, or figs of thistles?"

Nauvoo at present is the seat of the First Presidency, the place of the

gathering for all Saints, and the great center of the world for pure
religion, revelation, truth, virtue, knowledge, and everything else preparatory to the coming of the Son of Man. The best news, the best
people, and the best plan of salvation must be there. Wherefore,

Resolved unanimously that the traveling Elders are hereby instructed
to use due diligence in obtaining subscribers for the *Times and Seasons*
and *Nauvoo Neighbor*, and forward the pay by safe hands to the
publishers at Nauvoo, that the Saints and the world may receive "line
upon line and precept upon precept, here a little and there a little,"
together with such extracts of translations and revelations as the Presidency of the Church may direct, for the edification of the whole body
of the Church in righteousness.

Done in council at Nauvoo, Nov. 2nd, 1843.

BRIGHAM YOUNG,
President of the Twelve.

WILLARD RICHARDS, Clerk.

Friday, 3rd.—I continued in council all day.

Died at sea, Elder Knowlton F. Hanks. The following
extract is from a letter of Addison Pratt, one of the
Pacific Islands missionaries:—

[Under this date there is inserted in the Prophet's History a long
letter from Elder Addison Pratt of the Pacific Island mission, describing
in great detail the last illness, death and burial at sea of Elder Knowl-
lton F. Hanks. Elder Hanks died of consumption; and of the death the
Prophet remarks: "Elder Hanks is the first Elder who has died at sea
while on a foreign mission. He was a faithful Elder, cut off by consumption in the flower of his days."]

Saturday, 4.—Elders Richards and Taylor were with
me at the Mansion, assisting writing letters.

Wrote to John C. Calhoun as follows:—

*President Smith's Letter to John C. Calhoun, and other Presidential
Candidates.*

Hon. John C. Calhoun.

DEAR SIR,—As we understand you are a candidate for the Presidency
at the next election; and as the Latter-day Saints (sometimes called
"Mormons," who now constitute a numerous class in the school politic of
this vast republic,) have been robbed of an immense amount of property, and endured nameless sufferings by the State of Missouri, and
from her borders have been driven by force of arms, contrary to our
national covenants; and as in vain we have sought redress by all constitutional, legal, and honorable means, in her courts, her executive

councils, and her legislative halls; and as we have petitioned Congress to take cognizance of our sufferings without effect, we have judged it wisdom to address you this communication, and solicit an immediate, specific, and candid reply to "*What will be your rule of action relative to us as a people*," should fortune favor your ascension to the chief magistracy?

Most respectfully, sir, your friend,

and the friend of peace, good order,

and constitutional rights,

JOSEPH SMITH.

In behalf of the Church of Jesus Christ of Latter-day Saints.

Similar letters were written to Gen. Lewis Cass, Hon. Richard M. Johnson, Hon. Henry Clay, and President Martin Van Buren. To Mr. Van Buren's letter I added the following:—

Post Script to Van Buren.

Also whether your views or feelings have changed since the subject matter of this communication was presented you in your then official capacity at Washington, in the year 1841, and by you treated with a coldness, indifference, and neglect, bordering on contempt.

Elder Wilford Woodruff arrived at Nauvoo with paper for the use of the printing office.

Sunday, 5.—Rode out with mother and others for her health.

At dinner I was taken suddenly sick; went to the door and vomited all my dinner, dislocated my jaw, and raised fresh blood, and had many symptoms of being poisoned. The Prophet poisoned.

In the evening a prayer-meeting in the hall over the store.

Mr. Cole having kept a school in the hall for some time, the noise proved a nuisance for the clerks in the history office, and I gave Dr. W. Richards orders to tell Mr. Cole he must find some other room in which to teach school, as the room is needed for councils.

Meeting at the stand. Elder Rigdon preached.

Received a letter from Reuben Hedlock, dated Liverpool, October 16. He informs me there is a great call for

preaching, and many Elders are wanted throughout the
British Isles. Much opposition. The Saints
are anxious to have the *Star* continue its
publication, as 1,600 copies are circulated.

Also received a letter from Hyrum Clark, giving a
partial account of the business affairs of the emigration
and publishing offices.

Monday, 6.—Domestic affairs kept me busy in the
morning, and in the afternoon listened to William W.
Phelps giving a relation of his visit to the governor, which
amused me.

It has been very cool for some days past.

Elder Erastus Snow arrived with a company from Massachusetts.

Tuesday, 7.—Mr. Cole moved the tables back into the
hall, when Richards and Phelps called to
report that the noise in the school disturbed
them in the progress of writing the History.

I gave orders that Cole must look out for another place, as the history must continue and not be
disturbed, as there are but few subjects that I have felt a
greater anxiety about than my history, which has been a
very difficult task, on account of the death of my best
clerks and the apostasy of others, and the stealing of
records by John Whitmer, Cyrus Smalling and others.

The quorum of the Twelve—viz., President Brigham
Young, Parly P. Pratt, Orson Pratt, Wilford Woodruff,
John Taylor, George A. Smith, and Willard Richards,
assembled in the mayor's office, and voted to raise $500 to
get paper, &c., to print the *Doctrine and Covenants*.
Also voted that Parley P. Pratt, Wilford
Woodruff, and John Taylor be a committee to
borrow or get the money, and that President
Young go along with them.

Wednesday, 8.—From nine to eleven, a. m., had an
interview with Richards and Phelps, read and heard read
part of my history, then attended to settling some accounts

with several individuals. In the afternoon, I examined a sample of fringe designed for the pulpits of the Temple; and from two to three, conversed with Phelps, Lewis, John Butler and others.

The *Neighbor* has the following:—

Misrepresentations Corrected.

We know that statements made by the Carthage mob in their resolutions, as published in the late *Warsaw Message*, were false. We also felt convinced that the parties themselves were apprized of that fact, and that it was a thing generally understood by the public; and therefore we did not trouble ourselves about it. But having the following testimonies and affidavits sent us for publication, we insert them for the information of those who may not have had opportunities of informing themselves relative to this subject.

STATE OF ILLINOIS, ⎰
　LEE COUNTY. ⎰ ss.

We the undersigned citizens of the town of Dixon, county of Lee, State of Illinois, being duly sworn according to law, depose and say that we have seen the article entitled "Statement of facts connected with the arrest of Joseph Smith and his discharge therefrom," published in the *Warsaw Message* of the date of 15th of July, A.D. 1843; and have also seen an editorial article in the same number of said paper, in which it is stated that said statement of facts was furnished by E. Southwick, one of Mr. Smith's attorneys in said case; and that we know the fact stated in that statement—to wit, that Reynolds, for a considerable length of time immediately after his arrival at Dixon, did peremptorily refuse to allow Smith a private interview with his counsel; and that said Reynolds did expressly state that no conversation could be had with Smith by his attorneys, unless he, Reynolds, was present at such conversation.

The length of time which such refusal to allow said private conversation continued, was, in the belief of these deponents, at least one hour; and that such private conversation was not permitted by Reynolds, until after being informed by at least two of these deponents (Messrs. Dixon and Sanger) that such private interview must be allowed Mr. Smith, as that was a right he had guaranteed to him by law.

JOHN DIXON,　　　　J. D. McCOMSAY,
ISAAC ROBINSON,　　J. ALBERT HELFENSTEIN,
L. P. SANGER.　　　　S. G. PATRICK,
　　　　E. SOUTHWICK.

Sworn and subscribed to before me at Dixon, this 29th day of July, 1843.

FREDERICK R. DUTCHER,
Justice of the Peace for Lee County, Ill.

We, the undersigned, state under oath that we traveled in company with Joseph H. Reynolds, the agent of the State of Missouri, from Dixon to Nauvoo, at the time he had Joseph Smith in custody with the intention of taking him to Missouri, between the 26th of June last and the 1st instant; and that the Mormons, friends of Mr. Smith, who met us on said journey, before we arrived at Nauvoo, conducted themselves, so far as we could perceive and were able to judge, with the strictest propriety; and to our knowledge made use of no means of intimidation towards either H. T. Wilson or said Reynolds; but, on the contrary, several of them, and said Smith among that number, pledged themselves that said Wilson and Reynolds should be personally safe; and that said Mormons, none of them as we could perceive, were armed, so far as was discernible; and further, that the statement made in the *Old School Democrat* of the 12th instant, over the signature of T. H. Reynolds, that he and said Wilson were disarmed soon after they were arrested on the trespass suit commenced against them by said Smith, and that their arms were not returned to them until after the said Smith's discharge at Nauvoo, was incorrect. And in relation to this, these deponents say that said Wilson and Raynolds were arrested on said action of trespass at Dixon, on Saturday morning, the 24th of June last. That they were not disarmed by the sheriff of Lee county, who had them in custody, nor by any other person, until the following day, at Paw-paw Grove, thirty-two miles distant from Dixon; and that the arms of said Wilson and Reynolds were restored to them by the said sheriff of Lee county, who had them in custody for default of bail, at their (Wilson and Reynolds') own request, while on the journey from Dixon to Nauvoo, before the company had arrived within at least eigthy miles of Nauvoo.

J. D. McCOMSAY,
L. P. SANGER,
E. SOUTHWICK,
S. G. PATRICK.

Sworn and subscribed to before my, at Dixon, this 29th day of July, A.D. 1843.

FREDERICK R. DUTCHER,
Justice of the Peace.

To the Editor of the Warsaw Message:

GENTLEMEN:—It appears from an article in your paper of the 15th of July under the editorial head, that there is a question of veracity therein

raised, between Mr. H. T. Wilson and myself, relative to the proceed
ings had after the late arrest by him of Joseph Smith. Now, in order
that the public may no longer be deceived in the premises, be pleased
to publish, together with this note, the above affidavits, that the charge
of falsehood may attach where it properly belongs.

Very respectfully yours,
E. SOUTHWICK.

DIXON, July 29, 1843.

I wrote to the *Times and Seasons:*—

Communication of President Joseph Smith to the Saints.

Messrs. Taylor and Woodruff:

It has been so long since I addressed the Saints through the medium
of the *Times and Seasons*, that I feel confident that a few words from
my pen, by way of advice, will be well received, as well as a "way-
mark" to guide the "faithful" in future. I was sorry to learn, by your
remarks upon the resolutions of the "Twelve" concerning your papers,
which appeared not long since, that many of the Saints abroad were
more apt to patronize the common newspapers of the day than yours,
for the important reason that the Church of Jesus Christ of Latter-day
Saints has the words of eternal life, and your paper, as it has hitherto
done, must continue to publish such portions of them for the benefit of
the Saints and the salvation of mankind as wisdom shall from time to
time direct.

Freedom is a sweet blessing. Men have a right to take and read
what papers they please; "but do men gather grapes of thorns, or figs
of thistles?" It certainly is no more than just to suppose that *charity
begins at home*; and if so, what must such as profess to be Saints think,
when they patronize the splendor of Babylon and leave the virtue of
Zion to linger for want of bread?

Beside which, if virtue is justified rather than vanity, the best of
everything calculated to happify man and dignify society will—yea,
must be in Nauvoo. And as the new commandment given anciently
was *to love one another*, even so the works of the Saints at home and
abroad will bear its own testimony whether *they love the brethren.*

In all the world the *Times and Seasons* is the only paper that virtually
sustains, according to the forms of Scripture and prophecy, "Apostles,
Prophets, Evangelists," and revelations. And what shall be said of
him that, like the "Levite," passes on the other side of the way, when
we behold men who "have borne the heat and the burden of the day"
struggling against the popular opinions of a vain world, the burlesque
of a giddy throng, the vulgarity of a self-wise multitude, and the falsehoods of what may justly be termed the "civilized meanness of the

age," and not lending a helping hand? The 25th chapter of Matthew contains the simple answer.

Now, let me say once for all, like the Psalmist of old, "How good and how pleasant it is for brethren to dwell together in unity." "As the precious ointment upon the head that ran down upon Aaron's beard, that went down to the skirts of his garments, as the dew of Hermon that descended upon the mountains of Zion," is such unity; for there the Lord commanded the blessing, even life for evermore!" Unity is power; and when the brethren as one man sustain the *Times and Seasons*, they sustain me, by giving a spread to the revelations, faith, works, history and progress of the Church. The brethren who conduct the paper have been appointed to that important station, because they are worthy and well qualified; and what a blessed sign of a faithful friend to God and man is it to see the charity of a brother support his brethren, as an evidence that he means to pass from death into life?

Many of the articles which appear in the *Times and Seasons* are extracts of revelations, translations, or are the united voice of conferences, which, like "apples of gold in pictures of silver," are treasures more than meat for the called, chosen and faithful among the Saints, and should be more than *drink* to those that hunger and thirst after righteousness. As Nauvoo is rising in glory and greatness, so shall I expect to see the *Times and Seasons* increase in circulation by the vigilance of the Elders and Saints, so as to be a herald of truth and a standard of pure and undefiled religion. Finally, men and brethren, when you support my friends, you support me. In the bonds of the new and everlasting covenant,

I am your humble servant,

JOSEPH SMITH.

CHAPTER IV.

CORRESPONDENCE BETWEEN JAMES ARLINGTON BENNETT AND
PRESIDENT JOSEPH SMITH—RENEWAL OF PETITIONS TO
CONGRESS FOR REDRESS OF MISSOURI GRIEVANCES—PRES-
IDENT JOSEPH SMITH'S APPEAL TO THE "GREEN MOUNTAIN
BOYS"—VERMONT—STATUS OF THE NAUVOO LEGION IN
ILLINOIS MILITIA.

Thursday, November, 9, 1843.—At the office, dictating
letters and signing deeds.

The missionaries to the Pacific Islands touched at Cape
de Verde Islands, and laid in a supply of fruits of various
kinds.

Saturday, 11.—A company of Saints arrived from England. The work is still prospering in that
country, poverty and distress are making
rapid strides, and the situation of the laboring
classes is getting every day more deplorable. **Prosperity of the Work in England.**

City Council met. Hyrum Smith, president *pro tem.*
Albert P. Rockwood assessor and collector for 1st ward;
Daniel Hendricks for 2nd ward; Jonathan H. Hale, 3rd
ward; and Henry G. Sherwood for 4th ward.

Sunday, 12.—Prayer-meeting in the evening, in the
south-east room of my old house.

Clear, cold.

Monday 13.—Having received a letter from James
Arlington Bennett, Esq., I copy it:—

Letter: James Arlington Bennett to President Joseph Smith.

ARLINGTON HOUSE, Oct. 24, 1843.

DEAR GENERAL:—I am happy to know that you have taken possession
of your new establishment, and presume you will be eminently successful and happy in it, together with your good lady and family.

You are no doubt already aware that I have had a most interesting
visit from your most excellent and worthy friend, President B. Young,
with whom I have had a glorious frolic in the clear blue ocean; for

most assuredly a frolic it was, without a moment's reflection or consideration.

Nothing of this kind would in the least attach me to your person or cause. I am capable of being a most *undeviating friend*, without being governed by the smallest religious influence.

As you have proved yourself to be a philosophical divine, you will excuse me when I say that we must leave their influence to the mass. The boldness of your plans and measures, together with their unparalleled success so far, are calculated to throw a charm over your whole being, and to point you out as the most extraordinary man of the present age.

But my mind is of so mathematical and philosophical a cast, that the divinity of Moses makes no impression on me, and you will not be offended when I say that I rate you higher as a legislator than I do Moses, because we have you present with us for examination, whereas Moses derives his chief authority from prescription and the lapse of time.

I cannot, however, say but you are both right, it being out of the power of man to prove you wrong. It is no mathematical problem, and can therefore get no mathematical solution. I say, therefore, Go a-head: you have my good wishes. You know Mahomet had his *"right hand man."*

The celebrated Thomas Brown, at New York, is now engaged in cutting your head on a beautiful cornelian stone, as your *private seal*, which will be set in gold to your order, and sent to you. It will be a gem, and just what you want. His sister is a member of your Church. The expense of this seal, set in gold, will be about $40; and Mr. Brown assures me that if he were not so poor a man, he would present it to you free.

You can, however, accept it or not, as he can apply to it another use. I am myself short for cash; for although I had sometime since $2,000 paid me by the Harpers, publishers, as the first instalment on the purchase of my copyright, yet I had got so much behind during the hard times, that it all went to clear up old scores. I expect $38,000 more, however, in semi-annual payments, from those gentlemen, within the limits of ten years; a large portion of which I intend to use in the State of Illinois, in the purchase and conduct of a large tract of land; and therefore should I be compelled to announce in this quarter that I have no connection with the Nauvoo Legion, you will of course remain silent, as I shall do it in such a way as will make all things right.

I may yet run for a high office in your state, when you would be sure of my best services in your behalf; therefore, a known connection with you would be against our mutual interest. It can be shown that a commission in the Legion was a *Herald* hoax, coined for the fun of it by me, as it is not believed even now by the public. In short, I expect to be yet, through your influence, governor of the State of Illinois.

My respects to Brothers Young, Richards, Mrs. Emma, and all friends.

Yours most respectfully,

JAMES ARLINTON BENNETT.

P.S.—As the office of inspector-general confers no command on me, being a mere honorary title,—if, therefore, there is any gentleman in Nauvoo who would like to fill it in a practical way, I shall with great pleasure and good-will resign it to him, by receiving advice from you to that effect. It is an office that should be filled by some scientific officer.

J. A. B.

I insert my reply:—

Letter: President Joseph Smith to James Arlington Bennett.

NAUVOO, ILLINOIS, Nov. 13, 1843.

DEAR SIR:—Your letter of the 24th ult. has been regularly received, its contents duly appreciated, and its whole tenor candidly considered; and, according to my manner of judging all things in righteousness, I proceed to answer you, and shall leave you to meditate whether "mathematical problems," founded upon the truth of revelation, or religion as promulgated by me, or by Moses, can be solved by rules and principles existing in the systems of common knowledge.

How far you are capable of being "a most undeviating friend, without being governed by the smallest religious influence," will best be decided by your survivors, as all past experience most assuredly proves. Without controversy, that friendship which intelligent beings would accept as sincere must arise from love, and that love grow out of virtue, which is as much a part of religion as light is a part of Jehovah. Hence the saying of Jesus, "Greater love hath no man than this, that a man lay down his life for his friends."

You observed, "as I have proven myself to be a philosophical divine" I must excuse you when you say that we must leave these *influences* to the mass. The meaning of "philosophical divine" may be taken in various ways. If, as the learned world apply the term, you infer that I have achieved a victory, and been strengthened by a scientific religion, as practiced by the popular sects of the age, through the aid of colleges, seminaries, Bible societies, missionary boards, financial organizations, and gospel money schemes, then you are wrong. Such a combination of men and means shows a form of godliness without the power; for is it not written, "I will destroy the wisdom of the wise." "Beware lest any man spoil you through philosophy and vain deceit, after the rudiments of the world, and not after the doctrines of Christ." But if the inference is that by more love, more light, more virtue, and more truth from the Lord, I have succeeded as a man of God, then you reason truly, though the weight of the sentiment is lost, when the *"influence is left to the mass."* "Do men gather grapes of thorns, or figs of thistles?"

Of course you follow out the figure, and say, the boldness of my plans and measures, together with their unparalleled success, so far, are calculated to throw a charm over my whole being, and to point me out as the most extraordinary man of the present age! The *boldness of my plans and measures* can readily be tested by the touchstone of all schemes, systems, projects, and adventures—*truth;* for truth is a matter of fact; and the fact is, that by the power of God I translated the Book of Mormon from hieroglyphics, the knowledge of which was lost to the world, in which wonderful event I stood alone. an unlearned youth, to combat the worldly wisdom and multiplied ignorance of eigtheen centuries, with a new revelation, which (if they would receive the everlasting Gospel,) would open the eyes of more than eight hundred millions of people, and make "plain the old paths," wherein if a man walk in all the ordinances of God blameless, he shall inherit eternal life; and Jesus Christ, who was, and is, and is to come, has borne me safely over every snare and plan laid in secret or openly, through priestly hypocrisy, sectarian prejudice, popular philosophy, executive power, or law-defying mobocracy, to destroy me.

If, then, the hand of God in all these things that I have accomplished towards the salvation of a priest-ridden generation, in the short space of twelve years, through the boldness of the plan of preaching the Gospel, and the boldness of the means of declaring repentance and baptism for the remission of sins, and a reception of the Holy Ghost by laying on of the hands, agreeably to the authority of the Priesthood, and the still more bold measures of receiving direct revelation from God, through the Comforter, as promised, and by which means all holy men from ancient times till now have spoken and revealed the will of God to men, with the consequent "success" of the gathering of the Saints, throws any "charm" around my being, and "points me out as the most extraordinary man of the age," it demonstrates the fact that truth is mighty and must prevail, and that one man empowered from Jehovah has more influence with the children of the kingdom than eight hundred millions led by the precepts of men. God exalts the humble, and debases the haughty.

But let me assure you in the name of Jesus, "who spake as never man spake," that the "boldness of the plans and measures," as you term them, but which should be denominated the righteousness of the cause, the truth of the system, and power of God, which "so far" has borne me and the Church, (in which I glory in having the privilege of being a member,) successfully through the storm of reproach, folly, ignorance, malice, persecution, falsehood, sacerdotal wrath, newspaper satire, pamphlet libels, and the combined influence of the powers of earth and hell,—I say these powers of righteousness and truth are not the decrees or rules of an ambitious and aspiring Nimrod, Pharaoh, Nebuchadnezzar, Alexander, Mahomet, Bonaparte, or other great sounding heroes that dazzled forth with a trail of pomp and circumstances for a little season, like a comet, and then disappeared, leaving a wide waste where such an existence once was, with only a name; nor where the glorious results of what you term "boldness of plans and measures," with the attendant "success," matured by the self-aggrandizing wisdom of the priests of Baal, the scribes and Pharisees of the Jews, popes and bishops of Christendom, or pagans of Juggernaut: nor were they extended by the divisions and subdivisions of a Luther or Calvin, a Wesley, or even a Campbell, supported by a galaxy of clergymen and churchmen, of whatever name or nature, bound apart by cast-iron creeds, and fastened to set stakes by chain-cable opinions, without revelation. Nor are they the lions of the land, or the leviathans of the sea, moving among the elements, as distant chimeras to fatten the fancy of the infidel; but they are as the stone cut out of the mountain without hands, and will become a great mountain, and fill the whole earth.*   *   *   *   *   *

It seems that your mind is of such "a mathematical and philosophical cast," that the divinity of Moses makes no impression upon you, and that I will not be offended when you say that you rate me higher as a legislator than you do Moses, because you have me present with you for examination; that "Moses derives his chief authority from prescription and the lapse of time." You cannot, however, say but we are both right, it being out of the power of man to prove us wrong. "It is no mathematical problem, and can therefore get no mathematical solution."

* The omitted part of the letter is a paragraph in which are quoted a number of foreign phrases from Egyptian, Hebrew, Greek, German, Portuguese and other tongues; which are in no way germane to the subject discussed, but are a mere pedantic display, doubtless admitted, in this instance, in a spirit of humor by President Smith, as an offset to Bennett's assumption of so lofty an intellect—a mind of "so mathematical and philosophical a cast—that the divinity of Moses," etc., made no "impression" on him. The display of foreign phrases was doubtless the work of W. W. Phelps, who had some smattering knowledge of languages, which he was ever fond of displaying. Unfortunately similar displays were injected into President Smith's appeal to his native state—Vermont; and his paper, "Views of the Powers and Policy of the Government of the United States." These injections were also doubtless the work of Elder Phelps, who was one of the Prophet's clerks and amenuenses when the documents named above were prepared. Because these displays of pedantry mar these documents, and are in no way germane to the subjects of which they treat, and are not really the work of President Smith, they are omitted from the papers referred to as published in this HISTORY, the omission being indicated by elipses signs.

Now, sir, to cut the matter short, and not dally with your learned ideas, for fashion's sake you have here given your opinion, without reserve, that revelation, the knowledge of God, prophetic vision, the truth of eternity, cannot be solved as a mathematical problem. The first question then is, What is a mathematical problem? and the natural answer is, A statement, proposition or question that can be solved, ascertained, unfolded or demonstrated by knowledge, facts or figures; for "mathematical" is an adjective derived from *mathesis* (Gr.), meaning, in English, learning or knowledge. "Problem" is derived from *probleme* (French), or *problema* (Italian, or Spanish), and in each language means a question or proposition, whether true or false. "Solve" is derived from the Latin verb "*solvo*," to explain or answer.

One thing more in order to prove the work as we proceed. It is necessary to have witnesses, two or three of whose testimonies, according to the laws or rules of God and man, are sufficient to establish any one point.

Now for the question. How much are one and one? Two. How much is one from two? One. Very well; one question or problem is solved by figures. Now, let me ask one for facts: Was there ever such a place on the earth as Egypt? Geography says yes; ancient history says yes; and the Bible says yes: so three witnesses have solved that question. Again: Lived there ever such a man as Moses in Egypt? The same witnesses reply, *Certainly.* And was he a Prophet? The same witnesses, or a part, have left on record that Moses predicted in Leviticus that if Israel broke the covenant they had made, the Lord would scatter them among the nations, till the land enjoyed her Sabbaths: and, subsequently, these witnesses have testified of their captivity in Babylon and other places, in fulfillment. But to make assurance doubly sure, Moses prays that the ground might open and swallow up Korah and his company for transgression, and it was so: and he endorses the prophecy of Balaam, which said, Out of Jacob shall come he that shall have dominion, and shall destroy him that remaineth of the city: and Jesus Christ, as Him that "had dominion," about fifteen hundred years after, in accordance with this and the prediction of Moses, David, Isaiah, and many others, came, saying, Moses wrote of me, declaring the dispersion of the Jews, and the utter destruction of the city; and the Apostles were his witnesses, unimpeached, especially Jude, who not only endorses the facts of Moses "divinity," but also the events of Balaam and Korah, with many others, *as true.*

Besides these tangible facts, so easily proven and demonstrated by simple rules and testimony unimpeached, the art (now lost,) of embalming human bodies, and preserving them in the catacombs of Egypt, whereby men, women and children, as *mummies*, after a lapse of near three thousand five hundred years, come forth among the living; and although *dead,* the papyrus which has lived in their bosoms, unharmed, speaks for them in language like the sound of an earthquake. *Ecce veritas! Ecce cadaveros!* Behold the truth! Behold the mummies!

Oh, my dear sir, the sunken Tyre and Sidon, the melancholy dust where the city of Jerusalem once was, and the mourning of the Jews among the nations, together with such a cloud of witnesses, if you had been as well acquainted with your God and Bible as with your purse and pence table, the divinity of Moses would have dispelled the fog of five thousand years and filled you with light; for facts, like diamonds, not only cut glass, but they are the most precious jewels on earth. The spirit of prophecy is the testimony of Jesus.

The world at large is ever ready to credit the writings of Homer. Hesiod, Plutarch, Socrates, Pythagoras, Virgil, Josephus, Mahomet, and an hundred others; but where, tell me, where, have they left a line—a simple method of solving the truth of the plan of eternal life? Says the Savior, "If any man will do his [the Father's] will, he shall know of the doctrine, whether it be of God, or whether I speak of myself." Here, then, is a method of solving the divinity of men by the divinity within yourself, that as far exceeds the calculations of numbers as the sun exceeds a candle. Would to God that all men understood it and were willing to be governed by it, that when one had filled the measure of his days, he could exclaim like Jesus, *Veni mori, et reviviscere!'*

Your good wishes to go ahead, coupled with Mahomet and a right hand man, are rather more vain than virtuous. Why, sir, Cæsar had his right hand Brutus, who was his left hand assassin,—not, however, applying the allusion to you.

As to the private seal you mention, if sent to me, I shall receive it with the gratitude of a servant of God, and pray that the donor may receive a reward in the resurrection of the just.

The summit of your future fame seems to be hid in the political policy of a "mathematical problem" for the chief magistracy of this state, which I suppose might be solved by "double position," where the *errors* of the *supposition* are used to produce a true answer.

But, sir, when I leave the dignity and honor I received from heaven, to boost a man into power, through the aid of my friends, where the evil and designing, after the object has been accomplished, can lock up the clemency intended as a reciprocation for such favors, and where the wicked and unprincipled, as a matter of course, would seize the opportunity to flintify the hearts of the nation against me for dabbling at a sly game in politics,—verily I say, when I leave the dignity and honor of heaven, to gratify the ambition and vanity of man or men,

may my power cease, like the strength of Samson, when he was shorn
of his locks, while asleep in the lap of Delilah. Truly said the Savior,
"Cast not your pearls before swine, lest they trample them under their
feet, and turn again and rend you."

Shall I, who have witnessed the visions of eternity, and beheld the
glorious mansions of bliss, and the regions and the misery of the
damned,—shall I turn to be a Judas? Shall I, who have heard the
voice of God, and communed with angels, and spake as moved by the
Holy Ghost for the renewal of the everlasting covenant, and for the
gathering of Israel in the last days,—shall I worm myself into a political hypocrite? Shall I, who hold the keys of the last kingdom, in which
is the dispensation of the fullness of all things spoken by the mouths
of all the holy Prophets since the world began, under the sealing power
of the Melchisedec Priesthood,—shall I stoop from the sublime authority
of Almighty God, to be handled as a monkey's cat-paw, and pettify
myself into a clown to act the farce of political demagoguery? No—
verily no! The whole earth shall bear me witness that I, like the
towering rock in the midst of the ocean, which has withstood the
mighty surges of the warring waves for centuries, *am impregnable*, and
am a faithful friend to virtue, and a fearless foe to vice,—no odds
whether the former was sold as a pearl in Asia or hid as a gem in
America, and the latter dazzles in palaces or glimmers among the tombs.

I combat the errors of ages; I meet the violence of mobs; I cope
with illegal proceedings from executive authority; I cut the gordian
knot of powers, and I solve mathematical problems of universities,
*with truth—diamond truth; and God is my "right hand man."**

And to close, let me say in the name of Jesus Christ to you, and to
presidents, emperors, kings, queens, governors, rulers, nobles, and
men in authority everywhere, Do the works of righteousness, execute
justice and judgment in the earth, that God may bless you and her
inhabitants; and

> The laurel that grows on the top of the mountain
>   Shall green for your fame while the sun sheds a ray;
> And the lily that blows by the side of the fountain
>   Will bloom for your virtue till earth melts away.

With due consideration and respect, I have the honor to be

Your most obedient servant,   JOSEPH SMITH.

P.S. The court-martial will attend to your case in the Nauvoo
Legion.   J. S.

* Not in the blasphemous sense attributed to him by some anti-Mormon writers;
namely, that God was subordinate to him—his right hand man (See Riley's "Founder of Mormonism" ch. x); but in the sense of the passage near the close of his address to "The Green Mountain Boys" (this chapter)—"And Jesus Christ, the Son
of God, is my Great Counselor"—reverently said.

Tuesday, 14.—In the evening called at the office with Mr. Southwick, of Dixon, and had my letter to James Arlington Bennett read.

Wednesday, 15.—Mayor's court in the office. "Erskine *versus* Pullen." Nonsuit.

P. M. At the office. Suggested the idea of preparing a grammar of the Egyptian language.

Prayer-meeting at the old house. I spoke of a petition to Congress, my letter to Bennett, and intention to write a proclamation to the kings of the earth.

Grammar for the Egyptian Language Suggested.

Thursday, 16.—Held a court — "Averett *versus* Bostwick."

At home the remainder of the day. Chilly east wind and foggy.

Friday, 17.—Deeded lot 4, block 135, to Sally Phelps, wife of W. W. Phelps.

About ten, a.m., called in the office with Esquire Southwick, of Dixon.

Thunder, lightning and rain last night. Warm and foggy morning.

Saturday, 18.—Rode out on horseback to the prairie, accompanied by Mr. Southwick.

Conference of the church held at Halifax, Nova Scotia. Robert Dixon, president; Edward Cook, secretary. Two branches were represented, containing 2 Elders, 1 Teacher, 2 Deacons, and 34 members.

Sunday, 19.—Eleven a.m. to two p.m., prayer-meeting at the old house, and fasting.

In the evening, prayer-meeting and breaking of bread, &c.

Monday, 20.—Two gentlemen from Vermont put up at the Mansion. I rode round with them in the afternoon to show them the improvements in the city. In the evening, several of the Twelve and others called to visit me. My family sang hymns,

Meeting at the Prophet's Home.

and Elder John Taylor prayed and gave an address, to which they paid great attention, and seemed very much interested.

Tuesday, 21.—Council of the Twelve and others at my old house all day. Dictated to my clerk an appeal to the Green Mountain boys of Vermont, my native State.

Also instructed Elders Richards, Hyde, Taylor and Phelps to write a "Proclamation to the Kings of the Earth."

Wednesday, 22.—Rode out to the prairie with W. Clayton and Lorenzo D. Wasson, and found Arthur Smith cutting timber on my land without my consent, which I objected to.

Prayer-meeting in the evening at the old house.

Five deaths in the city during the past week.

Thursday, 23.—Met in council in the old house; then walked down to the river to look at the stream,
Canal Around
the Rapids. rocks, &c., about half-past eleven, a.m. Suggested the idea of petitioning Congress for a grant to make a canal over the falls, or a dam to turn the water to the city, so that we might erect mills and other machinery.*

Issued a writ of habeas corpus, on application of John M. Finch.

Friday, 24.—Attended Municipal Court "on habeas corpus, John M. Finch at suit of Amos Davis." Finch discharged, Davis to pay costs, it being a vexatious and malicious suit.

The young men have established a debating society in Nauvoo, to discuss topics of various descriptions.

---

* The General Government finally constructed a canal around the rapids at a cost of $4,582,000, completing the work in 1877. The canal is seven and a half miles in length and has in it three locks, overcoming the obstruction in river navigation which the Des Moines rapids in early days presented. It is called the Des Moines Rapids Canal.

Saturday, 25.—Colonel Frierson, United States Surveyor from Quincy, arrived in Nauvoo. In the evening the High Council sat on the case of Harrison Sagers, charged with seduction, and having stated that I had taught it was right. Charge not sustained. I was present with several of the Twelve, and gave an address tending to do away with every evil, and exhorting them to practice virtue and holiness before the Lord; told them that the Church had not received any permission from me to commit fornication, adultery, or any corrupt action; but my every word and action has been to the contrary. If a man commit adultery, he cannot receive the celestial kingdom of God. Even if he is saved in any kingdom, it cannot be the celestial kingdom. I did think that the many examples that have been made manifest, such as John C. Bennett's and others, were sufficient to show the fallacy of such a course of conduct.

The Prophet's Stand on Chastity and General Morality.

I condemned such actions *in toto*, and warned the people present against committing such evils; for it will surely bring a curse upon any person who commits such deeds.

After adjournment, held a council, and agreed to meet Mr. Frierson* at the Mansion to morrow morning.

I received a letter signed by George B. Wallace and six other Elders, requesting permission for Elder John E. Page to remain in Boston the ensuing winter. Also a letter from John E. Page, giving his assent to the petition, to which the Twelve Apostles wrote the following reply:—

Letter: Brigham Young in Behalf of the Twelve to Elder John E. Page, Appointing him to go to Washington.

Elder John E. Page:

BELOVED BROTHER:—Your letter dated at Boston, in connection with

---

* This Col. Frierson resided at Quincy, was a political representative of John C. Calhoun, then an active aspirant for the presidency of the United States. See letter of Joseph L. Heywood, pp. 62, 63.

some one hundred and fifty of the brethren, is received, and we proceed
to reply. Your letter is not before us this moment; consequently you
must excuse a reference to dates and names which have escaped our
recollection. But the subject is fresh, and the letter was read in a
council of Presidents Joseph, Hyrum, and the Twelve, when the word
of the Lord came through Joseph the Seer thus:—"Let my servant
John E. Page take his departure *speedily* from the city of Boston, and
go directly to the city of Washington, and there labor diligently in
proclaiming my Gospel to the inhabitants thereof: and if he is humble
and faithful, lo! I will be with him, and will give him the hearts of the
people, that he may do them good and build up a church unto my
name in that city."

Now, Brother Page, if you wish to follow counsel and do the will of
the Lord, as we believe you desire to do, call the church at Boston
together, *without delay*, and read this letter to them, calling upon
them to assist you on your mission, and go thy way speedily unto the
place which is appointed unto you by the voice of the Lord, and build
up a church in the city of Washington; for it is expedient and absolutely necessary that we have a foothold in that popular city. Let
your words be soft unto the people, but full of the spirit and power of
the Holy Ghost. *Do not challenge the sects for debate*, but treat them as
brethren and friends; and the God of heaven will bless you, and we will
bless you in the name of the Lord Jesus, and the people will rise up
and bless you, and call you a sweet messenger of peace. You will
pardon us for giving you such counsel, for we feel to do it in the name
of the Lord.

When you have built a church at Washington so as to warrant the
expense. It will be wisdom for you to send or take your wife to Washington; so says President Joseph.

All things go on smoothly here. As to the reports circulated while
we were in Boston, there is nothing of them. Brother Joseph has commenced living in his new house, and enjoys himself well. He has raised
a sign, entitled "Nauvoo Mansion," and has all the best company in the
city. Many strangers from abroad call on him, feeling perfect liberty
so to do, since he has made his house public; and it is exerting a blessed influence on the public mind.

The Temple has been progressing rapidly until the recent frosts.
The walls are now above the windows of the first story, and some of
the circular windows are partly laid. The brethren of the Twelve have
all arrived home, are tolerably well, and their families, except Sister
Hyde, who has been very sick, and is yet, though at last report rather
better. No prospect of any of the Twelve leaving home this winter

that we know of. Elder Snow has arrived with his company from Boston, generally in good spirits.

The devil howls some: may be you will hear him as far as Boston, for there cannot a blackleg be guilty of any crime in Nauvoo, but somebody will lay it to the servants of God. We shall give the substance of this communication to your wife same mail.

We remain your brother in the new and everlasting covenant, in behalf of the quorum,

BRIGHAM YOUNG, President.

W. RICHARDS, Clerk.

Sunday, 26.—I met with Hyrum, the Twelve and others, in council with Colonel Frierson, at the Mansion, concerning petitioning Congress for redress of grievances. Read to him the affi- davits of Hyrum Smith, Brigham Young, Parley P. Pratt, Lyman Wight, George W. Pitkin and Sidney Rigdon, taken before the municipal court on *habeas corpus*, and conversed with him thereon.

Renewal of Petitions to Congress.

At eleven, a.m., Elder Orson Pratt preached in the Assembly Room.

In the evening, Elder Parley P. Pratt lectured in the Mansion. Rainy, muddy day.

Monday, 27.—Wet day. Being quite unwell, I stayed at home.

Tuesday, 28.—At home. Colonel Frierson wrote a Memorial to Congress.*

Wednesday, 29.—At home. Clear and cold. Colonel Frierson left for home, taking with him a copy of the Memorial, to get signers in Quincy. I here insert a copy of the—

* The reason Col. John Frierson interested himself in this matter was that Hon. R. B. Rhett a representative in the National Congress from South Carolina, and a political friend of John C. Calhoun, had expressed a willingness to present to Congress a memorial for a redress of grievances suffered by the Saints in Missouri; and of course all this in the interest of Calhoun as candidate for President. See pp. 62,63; also *Nauvoo Neighbor* for the 5th June, 1844.

MEMORIAL.

To the Honorable the Senate and House of Representatives of the United States, in Congress Assembled.

The memorial of the undersigned inhabitants of Hancock county, in the State of Illinois, respectfully showeth—

That they belong to the society of Latter-day Saints, commonly called "Mormons;" that a portion of our people commenced settling in Jackson county, Missouri, in the summer of 1831, where they purchased lands and settled upon them with the intention and expectation of becoming permanent citizens in common with others.

From a very early period after the settlement began, a very unfriendly feeling was manifested by the neighboring people; and as the society increased, this unfriendly spirit also increased, until it degenerated into a cruel and unrelenting persecution, and the society was at last compelled to leave the county. An account of these unprovoked persecutions has been published to the world; yet we deem it not improper to embody a few of the most prominent items in the memorial, and lay them before your honorable body.

On the 20th July, 1833, a mob collected at Independence, a deputation or committee from which called upon a few members of our Church there, and stated to them that the store, printing office, and all mechanic shops belonging to our people must be closed forthwith, and the society leave the county immediately.

These conditions were so unexpected and so hard, that a short time was asked for to consider on the subject before an answer could be given, which was refused; and when some of our men answered that they could not consent to comply with such propositions, the work of destruction commenced.

The printing office—a valuable two-story brick building, was destroyed by the mob, and with it much valuable property. They next went to the store for the same purpose; but one of the owners thereof agreeing to close it, they abandoned their design.

A series of outrages was then commenced by the mob upon individual members of our society. Bishop Partridge was dragged from his house and family, where he was first partially stripped of his clothes, and then tarred and feathered from head to foot. Mr. Charles Allen was also tarred at the same time.

Three days afterwards the mob assembled in great numbers, bearing a red flag, and proclaiming that unless the society would leave *en masse*, every man of them should be killed. Being in a defenseless situation, to avoid a general massacre, a treaty was entered into and ratified, by which it was agreed that one-half of the society should leave the county by the 1st of January, and the remainder by the 1st of April following.

In October, while our people were gathering their crops and otherwise preparing to fulfil their part of the treaty, the mob again collected without any provocation, shot at some of our people, whipped others, threw down their houses, and committed many other depredations. The members of the society were for some time harassed both day and night, their houses assailed and broken open, and their women and children insulted and abused.

The store-house of A. S. Gilbert and Company was broken open, ransacked, and some of the goods strewed in the streets. These repeated assaults so aroused the indignant feelings of our people, that a small party thereof, on one occasion, when wantonly abused, resisted the mob. A conflict ensued, in which one of our people and some two or three of their assailants were killed.

This unfortunate event raised the whole county in arms, and we were required forthwith to surrender our arms and leave the county. Fifty-one guns were given up, which have never been returned or paid for to this day.

Parties of the mob, from thirty to seventy in number, then scoured the county in every direction, threatening and abusing women and children, until they were forced first to take shelter in the woods and prairies at a very inclement season of the year, and finally to make their escape to Clay county, where the people permitted them to take refuge for a time.

After the society had left Jackson county, their buildings, amounting to about two hundred, were either burned or otherwise destroyed, with a great portion of their crops, as well as furniture, stock, &c.; for which they have not as yet received any remuneration.

The society remained in Clay county nearly three years, when, in compliance with the demands of the citizens there, it was determined to remove to that section of country known afterwards as Caldwell county.

In order to secure our people from molestation, the members of the society bought out most of the former inhabitants of what is now Caldwell county, and also entered much of the wild land then belonging to the United States in that section of country, fondly hoping that as we were American citizens, obeying the laws and assisting to support the government, we would be protected in the use of homes which we had honestly purchased from the General Government and fully paid for.

Here we were permitted to enjoy peace for a season; but as our society increased in numbers and settlements were made in Daviess and Carrol counties, unfounded jealousies sprang up among our neighbors, and the spirit of the mob was soon manifested again. The people of our Church who had located themselves at De Witt were compelled by the mob to leave the place, notwithstanding the militia were called out for their protection.

From De Witt the mob went to Daviess county, and, while on their way, took some of our people prisoners, and greatly abused and mistreated them. Our people had been driven by force from Jackson county; they had been compelled to leave Clay county, and sell their lands there, for which they have never been paid: they had finally settled in Caldwell county, where they had purchased and paid for nearly all the Government land within its limits, in order to secure homes where they could live and worship in peace; but even here they were soon followed by the mob.

The society remained in Caldwell from 1836 until the fall of 1838, and during that time had acquired by purchase from the Government, the settlers, and preemptioners, almost all the lands in the county of Caldwell, and a portion of those in Daviess and Carrol counties.

Those counties, when our people first commenced their settlements, were for the most part wild and uncultivated, and they had converted them into large and well improved farms, well stocked. Lands had risen in value, from 10 to 25 dollars per acre, and those counties were rapidly advancing in cultivation and wealth.

In August, 1838, a riot commenced, growing out of the attempt of a member of the society to vote, which resulted in creating great excitement and many scenes of lawless outrage. A large mob, under the conduct of Cornelius Gilliam, came into the vicinity of Far West, drove off our stock, and abused our people. Another party came into Caldwell county, took away our horses and cattle, burnt our houses, and ordered the inhabitents to leave their homes immediately.

By order of Brigadier-General Doniphan and Colonel Hinkle, a company of about sixty men, under the command of David W. Patten, went to disperse this mob. A conflict ensued, in which Captain Patten and two of his men were killed, and others wounded.* A mob party, from two to three hundred in number, many of whom are supposed to have come from Chariton county, fell on our people, and, notwithstanding they begged for quarters, shot down and killed eighteen, as they would so many wild beasts.

They were finally compelled to flee from those counties; and on the 11th October, 1838, they sought safety by that means, with their families,

* This is an error. Col. Frierson has confounded two incidents—the "Battle" at Crooked River, and a movement in Daviess county. General Doniphan gave no orders in respect of the skirmish in which David Patten lost his life, usually called the "Battle of Crooked River;" but he and also General Park gave some orders to Col. Wight and Col. Hinkle in relation to movements of militia in Daviess county against Millport and Gallatin. (See Vol. iii, ch. xii.)

leaving many of their effects behind. That they had previously applied to the constituted authorities of Missouri for protection, but in vain.

The society were pursued by the mob, conflicts ensued, deaths occurred on each side, and finally a force was organized under the authority of the Governor of the state of Missouri, with orders to drive us from the State, *or exterminate us.*

Abandoned and attacked by those to whom we had looked for *protection*, we determined to make no further resistance, but submit to the authorities of the State and yield to our fate, however hard it might be. Several members of the society were arrested and imprisoned on a charge of treason against the State: and the rest, amounting to above 14,000 souls, fled into the other States, principally into Illinois, where they now reside.

Your memorialists would further state that they have heretofore petitioned your honorable body, praying redress for the injuries set forth in this memorial; but the committee to whom our petition was referred reported, in substance, that the General Government had no power in the case, and that we must look for relief to the courts and the legislature of Missouri.

In reply, your memorialists would beg leave to state that they have repeatedly appealed to the authorities of Missouri in vain; that though they are American citizens, at all times ready to obey the laws and support the institutions of the country, none of us would dare enter Missouri for any such purpose, or for any purposes whatever.

Our property was seized by the mob or lawlessly confiscated by the State; and we were forced, at the point of the bayonet, to sign deeds of trust relinquishing our property. But the exterminating order of the Governor of Missouri is still in force, and we dare not return to claim our just rights. The widows and orphans of those slain, who could legally sign no deeds of trust, dare not return to claim the inheritance left them by their murdered parents.

It is true the Constitution of the United States gives to us, in common with all other native or adopted citizens, the right to enter and settle in Missouri; but an executive order has been issued to exterminate us if we enter the State, and a part of the Constitution becomes a nullity, so far as we are concerned.

Had any foreign state or power committed a similar outrage upon us, we cannot for a moment doubt that the strong arm of the General Government would have been stretched out to redress our wrongs; and we flatter ourselver that the same power will either redress our grievances or shield us from harm in our efforts to regain our lost property, which we fairly purchased from the General Government.

Finally, your memorialists pray your honorable body to take their wrongs into consideration, receive testimony in the case, and grant such relief as by the Constitution and laws you may have power to give.

And your memorialists will ever pray.

Eleven copies were also made for circulation and signatures by Thomas Bullock, one of my clerks.

Activities in Renewal of Appeals to Congress.

Four, p.m. A meeting of the citizens in the assmbly room, [over President Smith's store] when Brigham Young was chosen chairman of the meeting, and Willard Richards, clerk.

The object of the meeting was briefly explained by the clerk, followed by Judge Phelps, which was to petition Congress for redress of grievances in relation to the Missouri persecutions.

Voted that the chairman appoint a committee to get the names of memorialists in this city.

The chairman appointed the assessors and collectors in their several wards.

Voted that the same committee collect means to purchase paper. President Sidney Rigdon to go to La Harpe, and Elder Heber C. Kimball to Ramus, to procure signers.

The charmain appointed committees to visit other places.

Joseph Smith, the Mayor, made some remarks, and his Appeal to the Green Mountain Boys was read by William W. Phelps, as follows:—

President Smith's Appeal to his Native State—Vermont.

I was born in Sharon, Vermont, in 1805, where the first quarter of my life grew with the growth and strengthened with the strength of that "first-born" State of the "United Thirteen." From the old "French War" to the final consummation of American Independence, my fathers, heart to heart, and shoulder to shoulder, with the noble fathers of our liberty, fought and bled; and with the most of that venerable band of patriots, they have gone to rest, bequeathing a glorious country, with all her inherent rights, to millions of posterity. Like other honest citizens, I not only (when manhood came,) sought my own peace, prosperity, and happiness, but also the peace, prosperity, and happiness of my friends; and, with all the rights and realm before me, and the revelations of Jesus Christ to guide me into all truth, I had good reasons to enter into the blessings and privileges of an American citizen, the rights of a Green Mountain Boy, unmolested, and enjoy life and religion according to the most virtuous and enlightened customs, rules, and etiquette of the nineteenth century. But, to the disgrace of the United States, it is not so. These rights and privileges, together with a large amount of property, have been wrested from me, and thousands of my friends, by lawless mobs in Missouri, supported by executive authority; and the crime of plundering our property, and the unconstitutional and barbarous act of our expulsion, and even the inhumanity of murdering men, women, and children, have received the *pass-word of "justifiable"* by legislative enactments; and the horrid deeds, doleful and disgraceful as they are, have been paid for by Government.

In vain have we sought for redress of grievances and a restoration to our rights in the courts and legislature of Missouri. In vain have we sought for our rights and the remuneration for our property in the halls of Congress and at the hands of the President. The only consolation yet experienced from these highest tribunals and *mercy-seats* of our bleeding country *is that our cause is just, but the Government has no power to redress us.*

Our arms were forcibly taken from us by those Missouri marauders; and, in spite of every effort to have them returned, the State of Missouri still retains them: and the United States militia law, with this fact before the Government, still compels us to military duty; and, for a lack of said arms, the law *forces us to pay fines.* As Shakespeare would say *"thereby hangs a tale."*

Several hundred thousand dollars' worth of land in Missouri was purchased at the United States Land Offices in that district of country and the money, without doubt, has been appropriated to strengthen the army and navy, or increase the power and glory of the nation in some other way. And notwithstanding Missouri has robbed and mobbed me and twelve or fifteen thousand innocent inhabitants, murdered hundreds, and expelled the residue, at the point of the bayonet, without law, contrary to the express language of the Constitution of the United States and every State in the Union, and contrary to the custom and usage of civilized nations, and especially one holding up the motto, *"The asylum of the oppressed,"* yet the comfort we receive to raise our wounded bodies and invigorate our troubled spirits, on account of such immense sacrifices of life, property, patience, and right, and as an equivalent for the enormous taxes we are compelled to pay to support these functionaries in a dignified manner, after we have petitioned and pleaded with tears, and been showed like a caravan of foreign animals, for the peculiar gratification of connoiseurs in humanity, that flare along in public life like lamps upon lamp-posts, because they are better calculated for the schemes of the night than for the scenes of the day, is, as President Van Buren said, *Your cause is just, but Government has no power to redress you!*

No wonder, after the Pharisee's prayer, the publican smote his breast and said, "*Lord be merciful to me a sinner!*" What must the manacled nations think of freemen's rights in the land of liberty? *   *   *   *

Now, therefore, having failed in every attempt to obtain satisfaction at the tribunals, where all men seek for it, according to the rules of right, I am compelled to appeal to the honor and patriotism of my native State—to the clemency and valor of "Green Mountain Boys;" for throughout the various periods of the world, whenever a nation, kingdom, state, family, or individual has received an insult or an injury from a superior force, (unless satisaction was made,) it has been the custom to call in the aid of friends to assist in obtaining redress. For proof we have only to refer to the recovery of Lot and his effects by Abraham in the days of Sodom and Gomorrah, or to turn to the relief afforded by France and Holland for the achievement of the Independence of these United States, without bringing up the great bulk of historical facts, rules, laws, decrees, and treaties, and Bible records, by which nations have been governed, to show that mutual alliance for the general benefit of mankind to retaliate and repel foreign aggressions. To punish and prevent home wrongs, when the conservators of justice and the laws have failed to afford a remedy, are not only common and in the highest sense justifiable and wise, but they are also proper expedients to promote the enjoyment of equal rights, the pursuit of happiness, the preservation of life, and the benefit of posterity.

With all these facts before me, and a pure desire to ameliorate the condition of the poor and unfortunate among men, and, if possible, to entice all men from evil to good, and with firm reliance that God will reward the just, I have been stimulated to call upon my native State for a "union of all honest men," and to appeal to the valor of the "Green Mountain Boys" by all honorable methods and means to assist me in obtaining justice from Missouri, not only for the property she has stolen and confiscated, the murders she has commited among my friends, and for our expulsion from the State, but also to humble and chastise or abase her for the disgrace she has brought upon constitutional liberty until she atones for her sins.

I appeal also to the fraternity of brethren who are bound by kindred ties to assist a brother in distress in all cases where it can be done ac-

---

* The omission here indicated is the paragraph of foreign phrases not germane to the matter as explained in the footnote at page 75.

cording to the rules of order, to extend the boon of benevolence and protection in avenging the Lord of His enemies, as if a Solomon, a Hiram, a St. John, or a Washington raised his hands before a wondering world, and exclaimed, "My life for his!" Light, liberty, and virtue forever!

I bring this appeal before my native State, for the solemn reason that an injury has been done, and crimes have been committed, which a sovereign State, of the Federal compact, one of the great family of "*E pluribus unum*," refuses to compensate, by consent of parties, rules of law, customs of nations, or in any other way. I bring it also because the National Government has fallen short of affording the necessary relief, as before stated, *for want of power*, leaving a large body of her own free citizens, whose wealth went freely into her treasury for lands, and whose gold and silver for taxes still fills the pockets of her dignitaries "in ermine and lace," defrauded, robbed, plundered, ravished, driven, exiled, and banished from the "Independent Republic of Missouri!"

And in the appeal let me say, Raise your towers, pile your monuments to the skies, build your steam frigates, spread yourselves far and wide, and open the iron eyes of your bulwarks by sea and land; and let the towering church steeples marshal the country like the dreadful splendor of an army with bayonets. But remember the flood of Noah; remember the fate of Sodom and Gomorrah; remember the dispersion and confusion at the tower of Babel; remember the destruction of Pharaoh and his hosts; remember the handwriting upon the wall, "*Mene, mene, tekel upharsin;*" remember the angel's visit to Sennacherib, and the one hundred and eighty-five thousand Assyrians; remember the end of the Jews and Jerusalem, and remember the Lord Almighty will avenge the blood of His Saints that now crimsons the skirts of Missouri! Shall wisdom cry aloud, and her speech not be heard?

Has the majesty of American liberty sunk into such vile servitude and oppression, that justice has fled? Have the glory and influence of a Washington, an Adams, a Jefferson, a Lafayette, and a host of others, forever departed; and the wrath of a Cain, a Judas, and a Nero whirled forth in the heraldry of hell, to sprinkle our garments with blood, and lighten the darkness of midnight with the blaze of our dwellings? Where is the patriotism of '76? Where is the virtue of our forefathers? and where is the sacred honor of freemen!

Must we, because we believe in the fulness of the Gospel of Jesus Christ, the administration of angels, and the communion of the Holy Ghost, like the Prophets and Apostles of old,—must we be mobbed with impunity, be exiled from our habitations and property without remedy, murdered without mercy, and Government find the weapons and pay the vagabonds for doing the jobs, and give them the plunder into the bargain? Must we, because we believe in enjoying the constitutional privilege and right of worshiping Almighty God according to the dictates of our own consciences, and because we believe in repentance, and baptism for the remission of sins, the gift of the Holy Ghost by the laying on of hands, the resurrection of the dead, the millennium, the day of judgment, and the Book of Mormon as the history of the aborigines of this continent,—must we be expelled from the institutions of our country, the rights of citizenship and the graves of our friends and brethren, and the Government lock the gate of humanity and shut the door of redress against us? If so, farewell freedom! adieu to personal safety! and let the red hot wrath of an offended God purify the nation of such sinks of corruption; for that realm is hurrying to ruin where vice has the power to expel virtue.

My father, who stood several times in the battles of the American Revolution, till his companions in arms had been shot dead at his feet, was forced from his home in Far West, Missouri, by those civilized—or satanized—savages, in the dreary season of winter, to seek a shelter in another State; and the vicissitudes and sufferings consequent to his flight brought his honored grey head to the grave a few months after. And my youngest brother also, in the vigor and bloom of youth, from his great exposure and fatigue in endeavoring to assist his parents on their journey, (I and my brother Hyrum being in chains, in dungeons, in Missouri, *where they tried to feed us with—human flesh*) was likewise so debilated that he found a premature grave shortly after my father; and my mother, too, though she yet lingers among us, from her extreme exposure in that dreadful tragedy, was filled with rheumatic affections and other diseases, which leave her no enjoyment of health. She is sinking in grief and pain, broken-hearted, from Missouri persecution.

O death! wilt thou not give to every honest man a heated dart to sting those wretches while they pollute the land? And O Grave! wilt thou not *open the trap door* to the pit of ungodly men, that they may stumble in?

I appeal to the "Green Mountain Boys" of my native State to rise in the majesty of virtuous freemen, and by all honorable means help to bring Missouri to the bar of justice. If there is one whisper from the spirit of an Ethen Allen, or a gleam from the shade of a General Stark, let it mingle with our sense of honor and fire our bosoms for the cause of suffering innocence, for the reputation of our disgraced country, and for the glory of God; and may all the earth bear me witness, if Missouri—blood-stained Missouri, escapes the due merit of her crimes—the vengeance she so justly deserves—that Vermont is a hypocrite, a *coward*, and this nation the hotbed of political demagogues!

I make this appeal to the sons of liberty of my native State for help to frustrate the wicked designs of sinful men. I make it to hush the violence of mobs. I make it to cope with the unhallowed influence of wicked men in high places. I make it to resent the insult and injury made to an innocent, unoffending people, by a lawless ruffian State. I make it to obtain justice where law is put at defiance. I make it to wipe off the stain of blood from our nation's escutcheon. I make it to show presidents, governors, and rulers prudence. I make it to fill honorable men with discretion. I make it to teach senators wisdom. I I make it to teach judges justice. I make it to point clergymen to the path of virtue. And I make it to turn the hearts of this nation to the truth and realities of pure and undefiled religion, that they may escape the perdition of ungodly men; and Jesus Christ, the Son of God, is my Great Counselor.

Wherefore let the rich and the learned, the wise and the noble, the poor and the needy, the bond and the free, both black and white, take heed to their ways, and a leave to the knowledge of God, and execute justice and judgment upon the earth in righteousness, and prepare to meet the judge of the quick and the dead, for the hour of His coming is nigh.

> And I must go on as the herald of grace,
> Till the wide-spreading conflict is over.
> And burst through the curtains of tyrannic night;
> Yes, I must go on to gather our race,
> Till the high blazing flame of Jehovah
> Illumines the globe as a triumph of right.

As a friend of equal rights to all men, and a messenger of the everlasting Gospel of Jesus Christ, I have the honor to be,

Your devoted servant,
JOSEPH SMITH.

Sidney Rigdon spoke.

Parley P. Pratt confessed he was wrong in one thing in Missouri; that is, he left alive, and left them alive; and asked forgiveness, and promised never to do so again.

Parley P. Pratt offered to deliver the President's "Appeal to the Green Mountain Boys" to all the large towns in New York, if he could have a copy.

The President offered a copy and it was voted that

Elder Pratt shall have this mission granted him, and voted in addition that he go to all the towns in Vermont.

The Chairman [Brigham Young] spoke.

The Mayor [President Smith] spoke. Said he rose to make a confession, that he used all his influence to prevent the brethren from fighting when mobbed in Missouri. If I did wrong, I will not do so any more. It was a suggestion of the head. He would never do so again; but when the mobs come upon you, kill them. I never will restrain you again, but will go and help you.

The Chairman [Brigham Young] spoke again; acknowledged his wrong; said he would never put his hand on Brother Hosea Stout's shoulder again to hold him back when he was abused.

John Taylor spoke of Missouri; said he would never submit to such treatment again.

Mayor [President Smith] spoke again. If I do not stand with those who will stand by me in the hour of trouble and danger, without faltering, I give you leave to shoot me.*

Mayor read a letter in reply to one he wrote to Henry Clay.

Parley P. Pratt stated that the history of the persecution was put into the hand of Henry Clay.

* Relative to the spirit of this meeting in Nauvoo on the 29th of November, 1843; and also of many of the articles published as Editorials, and letters that were written about this time to public men, the reader should be reminded that these leading brethren of the Church were speaking and writing under a great stress of feeling—under a sense of outraged justice. Their minds had been refreshed and their feelings again wrought up by the detailed recital of the acts of injustice endured in Missouri by the Memorial to congress drawn up by Colonel Frierson; and under such circumstances it is scarcely to be expected that strong men will not give expression to the vehemence they feel. Edmund Burke once said in defense of the rashness expressed in both speech and action of some of the patriots of the American Revolution, that *"It is not fair to judge the temper or the disposition of any man or set of men when they are composed and at rest from their conduct or there expressions in a state of disturbance and irritation."* The justice of Burke's assertion has never been questioned, and without any wresting whatsoever it may be applied to the prominent Church leaders on the occasion of this meeting at Nauvoo; and, moreover, they saw again forming those mobocratic tendencies in Illinois from which they had suffered in Missouri.

Moved by Joseph Smith, That every man in the meeting who could wield a pen write an address to his mother country. Carried.

Mayor read the Memorial to Congress. The State rights doctrines are what feed mobs. They are a dead carcass —a stink, and they shall ascend up as a stink offering in the nose of the Almighty.

They shall be oppressed as they have oppressed us, not by "Mormons," but by others in power. They shall drink a drink offering, the bitterest dregs, not from the "Mormons," but from a meaner source than themselves. God shall curse them.

Adjourned till next Monday evening, early candle-light.

At ten, a.m., rode out with Mr. Jackson At home most all day.

The "Appeal to the Green Mountain Boys" sent to press.

Severe frost, so that the ice is on the water in the house.

W. L. D. Ewing writes to Major John Bills—

Letter: W. L. D. Ewing, State Auditor, Illinois, to Major John Bills—Legion Affairs.

The foregoing opinions constitute my reason for refusing to issue the warrants in your favor. I am not satisfied myself entirely of the correctness of the opinions of the Attorney-General. If you should be dissatisfied with the decision, I would advise you to raise the question before the Supreme Court, which will be in session on the 2nd Monday of December. I am the more anxious that this should be done because I wish to be satisfied whether I was correct or not in issuing warrants to you in the spring. Be pleased to advise me on the subject.

Respectfully,

W. L. D. EWING, Auditor.

Enclosing the opinion of the Attorney-General, Josiah Lamborn, as follows:—

Letter: J. Lamborn, Attorney General of Illinois—Legal Opinion of Above.

SPRINGFIELD, ILLINOIS, Nov. 30, 1843.

I have examined the claim of J. C. Bennett as brigade-inspector of the Nauvoo Legion, and it is my opinion that the claim should be disallowed.

The Legislature, in giving authority for the organization of a body of "independent military men" at Nauvoo, intended, no doubt, that all expenses, &c., except "their proportion of public arms," should be defrayed by the city and its privileged Legion.

They occupy a novel position, disconnected from the military communities of the whole State, and in no way subject to the regular military officers, possessing an exemption even from subjection to the general military laws, with a law-making power invested in their own Legion. It is not reasonable to suppose that the Legislature would confer so many exclusive favors, and yet pay those who profit by this condition of things as much as is paid to regular militia officers.

In the absence of any express provision by law to authorize the payment of the claim, 1 can see nothing from which an authority of the kind could be derived, and therefore advise accordingly.

J. LAMBORN, Attorney-General.

And copy of letter from J. N. McDougall to General W. L. D. Ewing:—

Letter: J. N. McDougall to State Auditor.

SPRINGFIELD, ILLINOIS, Nov. 30, 1843.

General W. L. D. Ewing, Auditor, &c.—

I have examined the claim of John Bills, brigade-major of the Nauvoo Legion, for services under the 53rd section of the militia law, and have arrived at the conclusion that the Nauvoo Legion are not to be considered as a part of the regular militia of this State, and that the general law has no further application to them than is expressly provided for in the law authorizing their organization. The law providing for the organization of the Legion making no provision for the payment of its officers by the State, it is my opinion that the above claim ought not to be audited.

The Legion was organized by the City Council, is subject to their control for the purpose of enforcing their ordinances. It is entirely independent of the general military law, may have a different organization, make laws for its own government, and seems evidently designed to sustain the municipal authorities of Nauvoo. If there are expenses to be paid, the municipality of which they form a very important element, must meet them. I am, with great respect,

Your obedient servant,

J. N. McDOUGALL.

Mr. Ewing reported to Major Bills that the returns made

out [for Mr. Bills], and sent to the State Department, were the best reports by any brigade-major in the State, and did him great credit: the refusal to pay him for his services is a mere pretext, as the Nauvoo Charter requires that the Nauvoo Legion shall perform the same amount of duty as is now or may hereafter be required of the regular militia of the State, and shall be at the disposal of the Governor for the public defense and the execution of the laws of the State, and be entitled to their proportion of the State arms; and were it not for the prejudice against us on account of our religion, his claim would have been paid without a word of complaint.

CHAPTER V.

THE AVERY KIDNAPPING—DEFENSIVE PREPARATIONS AGAINST
MISSOURI MOBS—APPEALS TO THE GENERAL GOVERNMENT
FOR PROTECTION—NAUVOO LEGION OFFERED AS UNITED
STATES TROOPS.

Friday, December 1, 1843.—At home. In the evening,
walking out and administering to the sick.

At noon, Dr. Willard Richards called on me to get a
petition to Congress for an appropriation to improve the
Rapids.

Progress of
the Work.
I continue to receive letters from Elders
in the different States, giving news of the progress of the work.

Clear and cold day. Some ice floating in the river.

Saturday 2.—Prayer-meeting from one to six p. m.,
in the assembly room over the store. Orson Hyde, Parley P. Pratt, Wilford Woodruff, George A. Smith, and
Orson Spencer received their endowments and further instructions in the Priesthood. About thirty-five persons
present.

A conference was held at Alexander in Genesee county, New York. Ten branches, containing 44 Elders and
206 members, were represented. Two High Priests, one
Seventy, 21 Elders and one Deacon present.

Sunday, 3.—I arrived at the assembly room* about
noon: found all present, except Hyrum
and his wife. He had slipped and turned
his knee-joint backward, and sprained the
large muscle of his leg, and I had been ministering unto
him. Emma had been unwell during the night. After the meeting was organized, William W. Phelps

Hyrum Smith
Meets with an
Accident

* This was the upper room of President Smith's brick store.

December 1843]   HISTORY OF THE CHURCH.   **99**

read my "Appeal to the Green Mountain Boys," which was dedicated by prayer after all had spoken upon it. We also prayed for Nathan Pratt, who was very sick, Hyrum, and others. I afterwards instructed them in the things of the Priesthood.

Monday, 4.—At six in the evening, I attended the adjourned meeting of citizens in the assembly room, which was crowded with a select congregation. Many could not get admission. There were two Missourians present. I made some observations at the opening of the meeting, requested them to be calm and cool, but let the spirit of '76 burn in their bosoms, and when occasion requires, say little, but act; and when the mob comes, mow a hole through them.

My "Appeal to the Green Mountain Boys" was read by W. W. Phelps.

Elder Parley P. Pratt read his "Appeal to the State of New York."

My clerk, Willard Richards, read the memorial to Congress, when the assembly unanimously voted their approbation of the memorial, when I spoke two-and-a-half hours, relating many circumstances which transpired in Missouri, not mentioned in the memorial. I have already had thirty-eight vexatious lawsuits, and have paid Missouri $150,000 for land. I borrowed $500 of Judge Young in Washington, to pay the expenses of the party that accompanied me, and had to borrow of others. Number of the Prophet's Vexatious Lawsuits

Daniel Avery and his son were kidnapped from the neighborhood of Warsaw by a company of Missourians, assisted by some anti-Mormons of this county, and carried into Missouri.*

Tuesday, 5.—Six p. m., met the Twelve, also Phelps, Clayton, and Turley, in council, in the office, on important business.

* This occurred on the 2nd of December. See Avery's Affidavit, Chapter VI, this volume.

Advised the Twelve to raise money to send to Elder Hyde, who is east, for him to get paper to print the Doctrine and Covenants, and get new type and metal for sterotyping the same.

Wednesday, 6.—At home and took the following affidavit:—

Chapman's Affidavit in the Avery Case.

STATE OF ILLINOIS, }
CITY OF NAUVOO. } ss.

On the sixth day of December, in the year of our Lord one thousand eight hundred and forty-three, came Delmore Chapman before me, Joseph Smith, mayor of said city; and after being duly sworn, deposeth and saith that on the nineteenth day of November, 1843, a man named Richardson came to one of his neighbors living in Bear Creek precinct, in the county of Hancock, named Philander Avery, and enticed him to the Mississippi at Warsaw, by false pretenses; and from thence by a company he was forced over the river and taken to Monticello jail; and that on the second day of December, some of the same party and others came to the aforesaid Bear Creek and kidnapped Daniel Avery, the father of the aforesaid Philander Avery, and by force of arms hurried him across the said Mississippi river into the State of Missouri, to aforesaid jail at Monticello, Lewis county, where your said affiant verily believes they are both now incarcerated illegally and inhumanly in prison; and further report says that some of them are to come to Nauvoo next, to kidnap Nelson Turner; and further your affiant saith not.

DELMORE CHAPMAN.

Subscribed and sworn to before me, this sixth day of December, 1843.   JOSEPH SMITH, Mayor.

Upon which I wrote to his Excellency Thomas Ford:—

LETTER—PRESIDENT JOSEPH SMITH TO GOVERNOR FORD.

NAUVOO, December 6, 1843.

SIR:—The enclosed affidavit is forwarded to your Excellency for instructions to know what shall be done in the premises. I shall act according to the best of my judgment, constitutionally, till I receive your instructions, and in the meantime shall forward, as soon as they can be had, all the facts relative to the case as a suitable person will go immediately to the place and get the necessary affidavits. Send your instructions by the bearer.

Respectfully, I have the honor to be,

Your obedient servant,

JOSEPH SMITH,

Lieutenant-General of N. L.

P. S. Shall any portion of the Legion be called out?

N. B. An express has just reached me that Governor Reynolds will make another demand for me. I rely on the honor of Illinois, for no writ can legally issue against me. I have suffered from their insatiable thirst for my blood long enough, and want the peace of my family to remain undisturbed.

Wednesday, 6.—Esquire Goodwin and others, not members of the Church, petitioned the Governor not to help Missouri to persecute the Saints.

Thursday, 7.—At eleven a. m. a meeting of the citizens of Nauvoo was held. The minutes of which I extract from the *Neighbor* as follows:—

PUBLIC MEETING AT NAUVOO.

At a meeting of the citizens of Nauvoo, held near the Temple, on the 7th day of December, 1843, Alpheus Cutler was called to the chair, and Willard Richards appointed secretary; whereupon, after the object of the meeting was stated, a committee of three—namely, W. W. Phelps, Reynolds Cahoon, and Hosea Stout, were appointed to draft a preamble and resolutions expressive of the sentiments of the people of the city of Nauvoo relative to the repeated unlawful demands by the State of Missouri for the body of General Joseph Smith, as well as the common, cruel practice of kidnapping citizens of Illinois, and forcing them across the Mississippi river, and then incarcerating them in the dungeons or prisons of Missouri. And after a few minutes' absence they returned with the following:—

RESOLUTIONS.

Whereas, the State of Missouri, with the Governor at the head, continues to make demands upon the executive of Illinois for the body of General Joseph Smith, as we verily believe, to keep up a system of persecution against the Church of Latter-day Saints, for the purpose of justifying the said State of Missouri in her diabolical, unheard of, cruel and unconstitutional warfare against said Church of Latter-day Saints, and which she has practiced during the last twelve years, whereby many have been murdered, mobbed and ravished, and the whole community expelled from the State:

And also to heave dust in the eyes of the nation and the world, while she, as a State, with the Government to back her, continues to slip over the river to steal the property of the Latter-day Saints, and kidnap the members of said Church to glut her vengeance, malice, revenge, and avarice, and to make slaves of the said captives or murder them: Therefore,

Resolved unanimously: As we do know that Joseph Smith is not guilty of any charge made against him by the said State of Missouri, but is a good, industrious, well-meaning, and worthy citizen of Illinois, and an officer that does faithfully and impartially administer the laws of the State, that we as citizens of Illinois, crave the protection of the Constitution and laws of the oountry as an *ægis* to shield him, the said General Joseph Smith, from such cruel persecutions, beseeching the Governor of Illinois not to issue any more writs against the said General Joseph Smith, or other Latter-day Saints (unless they are guilty), but to let the Latter-day Saints "breathe awhile like other men," and enjoy the liberty guaranted to every honest citizen by the Magna Charta of our common country.

Resolved, That as citizens of the State of Illinois, we solicit the attention of the Governor and officers generally of the State to take some lawful means and measures to regain the citizens that have been kidnapped by the Missourians, and to prevent the said Missourians and government from committing further violence upon the citizens of Illinois.

Resolved, as the sense of this meeting, That, according to the true meaning of the law, those citizens of any section of country who do not rise up as virtuous freemen (when any portion of inhabitants congregate or combine to injure, slander, or deprive another portion of their rights,) and magnify the law, to clear themselves from such unhallowed attempts to subvert order and law, that they by their silence make themselves accessories of the crime of such unlawful assemblage or outrageous individuals.

Resolved, unimously, That we solicit the Governor by all honorable means to grant us peace, for we will have it.

                                        ALPHEUS CUTLER, Chairman.
WILLARD RICHARDS, Secretary.

In the afternoon, Lucien Woodworth started with the papers to the Governor, and the petition from Goodwin and others, and Delmore Chapman's affidavit.

The German brethren met at the assembly room at six p. m., and choose Bishop Daniel Garn as their Presiding Elder, and organized to have preaching in their native language.

Provision for German Meetings.

Directed copies of my Appeal to the various authorities of Vermont and the United States.

Friday, 8.—At eleven a. m. I went to my office and gave instructions to my clerk for the drawing of a draft of a dam on the Mississippi river, and directed that the city council be called at four this afternoon to make preparations for any invasion from Missouri.

Precautionary Steps against Missouri Invasion

Willard Richards and Philip B. Lewis made an affidavit, which I insert:—

Richards' and Lewis' Affidavit.

STATE OF ILLINOIS, ⎱ ss.
CITY OF NAUVOO. ⎰

On the 8th day of December, 1843, came Willard Richards and Philip B. Lewis before me, Joseph Smith, Mayor of said city, and after being duly sworn, depose and say that they have been informed that two men have been kidnapped recently by the Missourians, in connection with some of the lawless inhabitants of the county of Hancock, and that rumors are now afloat that it is the intention of said lawless persons, in connection with the aforesaid Missourians, to kidnap some of the citizens of this city; and further your affiants would state that they are of opinion, to prevent difficulties of such a vexatious nature, that something should be done to secure the peace of this city from being disturbed. And further your affiants say not.

WILLARD RICHARDS,
PHILIP B. LEWIS.

Subscribed and sworn to before me, this 8th day of December, 1843.

W. W. PHELPS, Clerk.

Whereupon I issued the following notification:—

An Order to the City Marshal.

STATE OF ILLINOIS, ⎱ ss.
CITY OF NAUVOO. ⎰

To the Marshal of said City, Greeting:—

Whereas complaint has been made to me upon oath, that some persons have been kidnapped by the Missourians, in connection with

some of the lawless inhabitants of Hancock county, and that threats
have been made that some of the citizens of Nauvoo will be kidnapped
or arrested, and forcibly carried away from said city without being allowed the benefit of the writ of *habeas corpus*, according to the ordinance in such case made and provided, you will therefore take the
necessary measures to have the rights of the citizens of this city held
sacred, and the ordinances of said city duly carried into full force and
effect. To which end, should you judge that the peace and safety of
the city require it, you are further notified to call for a suitable portion of the Nauvoo Legion to be in complete readiness to compel obedience to the ordinances of the said city.

Given under my hand and seal this 8th day of December, 1843.

JOSEPH SMITH, Mayor,

W. W. PHELPS, Clerk, M. C.

In consequence thereof, I received from the City Marshal:—

The City Marshal's Reply.

CITY OF NAUVOO, December 8, 1843.

SIR:—Your order to have the ordinances of this city fully
carried into effect will be duly attended to; but in order so to do, it will
be necessary for you as Mayor of the city, to issue orders to Major
General Wilson Law for a suitable portion of the Nauvoo Legion to be
in readiness to *compel obedience* to said ordinances, if necessary.

Respectfully, &c.,

HENRY G. SHERWOOD, City Marshal.

To Joseph Smith, Mayor.

And I issued:—

Mayor's Order to the Commander of the Nauvoo Legion.

"HEADQUARTERS NAUVOO LEGION,
CITY OF NAUVOO, Dec. 8, 1843.

The Marshal of this city having made a demand of me for a suitable
portion of the Nauvoo Legion to protect the rights of the citizens and
carry the ordinances of said city into full effect, you are hereby directed
and required to hold in readiness such portions of the said Nauvoo Legion, which you have the honor to command, as may be necessary to
compel obedience to the ordinances of said city and secure the peace of
the citizens, and call them out, if occasion require, without further notice.

With due regard, I have the honor to be

Your obedient servant

JOSEPH SMITH,

Lieutenant-General. N. L.

Major-General Wilson Law,
Commanding Nauvoo Legion.

Four p. m., attended City Council, which passed "An extra ordinance for the extra case of Joseph Smith and others."

Special Ordinance in the Prophet's Case, vs. Missouri.

Whereas, Joseph Smith has been three times arrested and three times acquitted upon writs founded upon supposed crimes or charges preferred by the State of Missouri, which acquittals were made from investigations upon writs of *habeas corpus*—namely one in the United States Court for the district of Illinois, one in the Circuit Court of the State of Illinois, and one in the Municipal Court of Nauvoo:

And whereas, a *nolle prosequi* has once been entered in the courts of Missouri upon all the cases of Missouri against Joseph Smith and others:

And whereas, there appears to be a determined resolution by the State of Missouri to continue these unjust, illegal, and murderous demands for the body of General Joseph Smith:

And whereas, it has become intolerable to be thus continually harassed and robbed of our money to defray the expenses of these prosecutions:

And whereas, according to the Constitution of Illinois, "all men are born equally free and independent, and have certain inherent and indefeasible rights, among which are those of enjoying and defending life and liberty, and of acquiring, possessing, and protecting property and reputation, and pursuing their own happiness:"

And whereas, it is our bounden duty, by all common means, if possible, to put a stop to such vexatious lawsuits and save expense: Therefore—

Section 1. Be it ordained by the City Council of the City of Nauvoo, according to the intent and meaning of the Charter for the "benefit and convenience" of Nauvoo, that hereafter, if any person or persons shall come with process, demand, or requisition, founded upon the aforesaid Missouri difficulties, to arrest said Joseph Smith, he or they so offending shall be subject to be arrested by any officer of the city, with or without process, and tried by the Municipal Court, upon testimony, and, if found guilty, sentenced to imprisonment in the city prison for life; which convict or convicts can only be pardoned by the Governor, with the consent of the Mayor of said city.

Section 2. And be it further ordained that the preceding section shall apply to the case of every and all persons that may be arrested, demanded, or required upon any charge founded in the aforesaid Missouri difficulties.

Section 3. And be it further ordained that the jury that makes the presentment, in any case above specified, shall not, nor either of them, act as jurors on the final trial; but the trial shall be conducted according to the fifth and sixth articles of the amendment to the Constitution of the United States.

Passed December 8, 1843.

JOSEPH SMITH, Mayor.

WILLARD RICHARDS, Recorder.*

The City Council also passed "An ordinance to erect a dam in the Mississippi river, and for other purposes."

Ordinance Providing for the Erection of a Dam in the Mississippi.

Section 1. Be it ordained by the City Council of the City of Nauvoo, that Joseph Smith and his successors for the term of perpetual succession are hereby authorized and empowered to erect a dam, of suitable height to propel mills and machinery, from any point within the limits of said city and below the Nauvoo House, and in a proper direction to reach the island this side of Montrose; but not to interfere with the main channel of the Mississippi river.

Section 2. And be it further ordained that the said Joseph Smith and his successors are further authorized to erect north of the aforesaid island, a dam, pier, or breakwater to intersect the sandbar above.

Section 3. Be it further ordained that said Joseph Smith and his successors are also authorized and have full liberty to use the said dam and water for the purpose of propelling mills and machinery, and shall be governed in their rates of toll and rules of manufactory by ordinance of said city.

Section 4. And be it further ordained that the said Joseph Smith and his successors are further authorized and empowered to use the space within the limits of the said dam as a harbor or basin for steamboats and other water craft; and for which purpose they may construct docks, wharfs, and landings, and receive such fees for wharfage as may be regulated by ordinance of said city.

Section 5. And be it further ordained that said Joseph Smith and his successors are further authorized to build an embankment on the east side of the aforesaid island, to connect the said dam with the pier on the north, and to use the top of said dam for a public road or highway, receiving for compensation from those who cross upon it such rates as may be allowed by ordinance of said city.

Passed December 8, 1843.

JOSEPH SMITH, Mayor.

WILLARD RICHARDS, Recorder.

*The Ordinance was about a month later repealed at the suggestion of President Smith.

I suggested to the Council the idea of petitioning Congress to receive the City of Nauvoo under the protection of the United States Government, to acknowledge the Nauvoo Legion as U. S. troops, and to assist in fortifications and other purposes, and that a messenger be sent to Congress for this purpose at the expense of the city.

Petition for Nauvoo to Be Placed under the General Government

Messrs. John Taylor, Orson Spencer, and Orson Pratt were appointed a committee to draft a memorial according to my suggestions.

Saturday, 9.—At home.

Prayer-meeting in the assembly room.

I copy from the *Neighbor*.

PUBLIC MEETING AT NAUVOO MAKING AN APPEAL TO THE GENERAL GOVERNMENT ON SUNDRY LOCAL AFFAIRS.

At a very large meeting of the citizens of Nauvoo, held at the corner of Main and Water streets, Mr. Heber C. Kimball was elected chairman, and John M. Bernhisel appointed secretary. Mr. George A. Smith having made a few observations, Mr. John Taylor read the preamble and resolutions of a meeting held at the temple, on the 7th instant; also an ordinance entitled "An extra ordinance for the extra case of Joseph Smith and others," recently passed by the City Council of the City of Nauvoo; likewise the fifth and sixth articles of the amendments of the Constitution of the United States, and the opinion of the Attorney-General of the State of Illinois on the subject of the organization of the Nauvoo Legion, he being of the opinion that said Legion was disconnected from the military communities of the whole State, and in no way subject to the regular military officers, possessing an exemption even from subjection to the general military laws, with a law-making power vested in their own Legion.

After some pertinent remarks by Mr. Taylor, General Joseph Smith briefly addressed the meeting. He dissented entirely from the opinion of the Attorney-General, and observed that it was stated in the Charter that the Legion was a part of the Militia of Illinois, and that his commission declared that he (General Smith) was the Lieutenant-General of the Nauvoo Legion and of the Militia of the State of Illinois; and as such, it was not only his duty to enforce the city ordinance, but the laws of the State, when called on by the Governor. He also stated that he had been informed that the Chief Magistrate of Missouri had it in contemplation to make another requisition on the Governor of Illinois for him (Joseph Smith).

The meeting then adjourned *sine die*.

H. C. KIMBALL, Chairman.

J. M. BERNHISEL, Secretary.

Received the following:—

Letter of Wilson Law to Joseph Smith Anent the Legion.

NAUVOO LEGION, NAUVOO CITY,
December 9, 1843.

Lieutenant-General Joseph Smith.

In consequence of the orders I received from you ' to hold in readiness a sufficient portion of the legion, &c.,—to make said forces efficient," it will be necessary to supply them with munitions of war, which of course must be done at the expense of the city. You will therefore please to give orders to the commandants of cohorts on their application to you on the city treasury for whatever amount you may think proper on the present occasion.

Most respectfully your obedient servant,
WILSON LAW,
Major-General, N. L.

Sunday, 10.—Rainy day. I stayed at home.

A prayer-meeting held this evening in the assembly room. I was not present. Brigham Young presided. Several sick persons were prayed for.

By letter from J. White, deputy sheriff of Clark county, Missouri, I learn that Mr. Daniel Avery is in Marion county prison, without trial. The sheriff requests several men to go there as witnesses. It is evidently a trap to get some more of our people into their power. When I was in prison in Missouri, my witnesses were arrested before they got into court to testify, except one, who was kicked out of the court by an officer, Lieutenant Cook, who damned him, and ordered some of his company to shoot him. After which, the State's attorney, Birch, turned to me tauntingly, saying, "Why the hell don't you bring on your witnesses?" and Judge King laughed at my discomfiture. The Saints have had enough of Missouri mob justice.

Avery Case—a Reminiscence of Missouri Days.

Monday, 11. The following affidavit will show that some of the citizens of Illinois are so far fallen and so much governed by mobocratic influence as to assist the Missouri wretches in their hellish designs:—

Affidavit of Sission Chase—The Avery Case.

STATE OF ILLINOIS, } ss.
HANCOCK COUNTY.

On the 11th day of December, 1843, came Sission A. Chase before me Aaron Johnson, a Justice of the Peace of said county; and, after being duly sworn, deposeth and saith that the crime of kidnapping has been committed in Hancock County; and on the 2nd day of this present December, 1843, at the house of Schrench Freeman, about four miles and a half south of Warsaw, in said county, your said affiant heard a man by the name of John Elliot say that he was going a shooting turkeys. When asked what he was going to shoot them with, he showed a brace of pistols and a large hickory cane. Your affiant observed that he thought he could not kill turkeys with such weapons; and the said Elliot said that there was a certain cock he meant to take before night, and they would do for that. He, the said Elliot, went off, and your affiant did not see him till Sunday evening the 3rd, when your affiant asked the said Elliot if he had caught his turkey; and he replied, yes, the one he was after—a Mormon Elder. Your affiant then asked him who he was; and he said, Daniel Avery. Your affiant then asked the said Elliot what had been done with said Avery; and he said we put him on to a horse, tied his legs, and guarded him to the river, from whence, about ten o'clock at night, we took him into Clark county, Missouri, for stealing a horse four years ago, where they would try him; and if found guilty, they would then take him into another county, where there was a jail, as there was none in Clark county. On the 4th day of December, I asked him if they had writs or authority to take Mr. Avery. He replied, we all had writs. On the 5th, said Elliot said he expected to get into difficulty on account of this scrape; but if any Mormon makes any business with me, I will shoot him. And further your affiant says not.

SISSION A. CHASE.

Subscribed and sworn to this 11th day of December, 1843, before me
AARON JOHNSON, J. P.

Which I sent to the Governor, with this letter:—

Letter—Joseph Smith to Governor Ford.

NAUVOO, December 11, 1843.

SIR:—I herewith forward your Excellency another affidavit on the subject of the late kidnapping, and shall continue [to do] the same as they come to hand, expecting your cordial co-operation in the premises that the laws may be magnified and made honorable, and our lives held precious, our friends saved from jeopardy, and the captives freed.

Respectfully, I have the honor to be

Your obedient servant,

JOSEPH SMITH.

Meetings were held and resolutions passed in all the wards of the city, requesting the city coun-

Nauvoo's Police Force Enlarged. cil to raise a company of forty men to act as police.

Last night, two ruffians, whose names are unknown, went to the house of Brother Richard Badham—a farmer living on the prairie, robbed the house of $4.50, threatened his life, stabbed him in the abdomen, when part of his caul gushed out. Dr. John M. Bernhisel dressed his wounds today, and he thinks there is a prospect of his recovering.

Tuesday, 12.--In office at nine a. m., and wrote a letter to my uncle:—

Letter—Joseph Smith to John Smith—The Latter Appointed a Patriarch.

President John Smith:—The petition of a special conference at Macedonia of last November for your appointment as Patriarch in the Church has been received, duly considered, and is granted. You have my best wishes in your behalf, as well as my prayers, that you may fill so honorable and exalted a station with the dignity, sobriety, and grace which has hitherto characterized your conduct and communion with men, as a man of God.

Respectfully yours,

JOSEPH SMITH.

At ten, a. m., attended City Council, which passed an ordinance exempting all church property from city tax.

In accordance with the petitions from the several wards, the council passed the following:—"An ordinance for selecting forty policemen and for other purposes.

Ordinance Enlarging Police Force.

"Section 1. Be it ordained by the City Council of the City of Nauvoo that the Mayor of said city be, and is hereby authorized to select and have in readiness for every emergency forty policemen, to be at his disposal in maintaining the peace and dignity of the citizens, and enforcing the ordinances of the said city, for ferreting out thieves and bringing them to justice, and to act as daily and nightly watchmen, and be under the pay of said city.

Passed December 12, 1843.

JOSEPH SMITH, Mayor.

W. RICHARDS, Recorder.

The Council also passed "An ordinance for the health and convenience of travelers and other persons."

Ordinance on the Personal Sale of Liquors.

Section 1. Be it ordained by the City Council of Nauvoo, that the Mayor of the city be and is hereby authorized to sell or give spirits of any quantity as he in his wisdom shall judge to be for the health and comfort, or convenience of such travelers or other persons as shall visit his house from time to time.

Passed December 12, 1843.

JOSEPH SMITH, Mayor.

WILLARD RICHARDS, Recorder.

Wednesday, 13.—At home.

I insert an editorial from the *Neighbor*:—

PUBLIC MEETING AT NAUVOO—THE AGGRESSIONS OF MISSOURI.

It will be seen in another column that a public meeting was held in this place for the purpose of providing some remedy for the repeated aggressions of the State of Missouri; since which time an ordinance has been passed by the City Council to carry into effect that object, and to prevent the citizens of this place from being any longer imposed upon by the continued illegal proceedings of the state and citizens of Missouri.

We think that it is high time that something should be done to screen ourselves from the continued aggressions of the meddling, troublesome, bloodthirsty herd; and we know of no means that will be more efficient and lawful than the one adopted.

We have done good for evil long enough, in all conscience. We think that we have fulfilled the Scriptures every whit. They have smitten us on the one cheek, and we have turned the other, and they have smitten that also.

We have also fulfilled the law, and more than fulfilled it. And for sake of peace, when we knew that we had violated no law, nor in anywise subjected ourselves to persecutions, we have endured the wrong patiently, without offering violence or in anywise injuring the heartless wretches who could be trusted with such a dishonorable document.

Those vagabonds have been suffered to prowl at large, and boast of their inglorious deeds in our midst; and no man has injured them, or said, Why do you so?

The time, however, is now gone by for this mode of proceeding, and those vagabonds must keep within their own borders and let peaceable citizens alone, or receive the due merit of their crimes. We think that this ordinance passed by the City Council is wise, judicious, and well-timed,and is well calculated to protect peaceable citizens in their rights, and to prevent those lawless vagabonds from interfering with the rights of peaceable citizens.

To those unaquainted with our relationship to Missouri, and the accumulated wrongs and repeated aggressions that we have received from the hands of that State, our language may appear harsh and illtimed; but those who are in possession of those facts know better. Their merciless, unrelenting, inhuman prosecutions and persecutions, from the time of our first settlement in that state until the present, have been wholly and entirely unprovoked and without the shadow of law.

Joseph Smith has been suffered to be taken time and again by them; we say suffered, because he could not be legally and constitutionally taken, Joseph Smith never committed the crimes of which he is charged. He is an innocent man.

But allowing their false, diabolical accusations to be true, what then? Does it follow that he is continually to be followed for the same offense? Verily no. The Constitution of the United States expressly says—"Nor shall any person be subject for the same offense to be *twice* put in jeopardy of life or limb." And yet we find that the State of Missouri has put Joseph Smith in jeopardy no less than four or five times. He was tried once by a military tribunal in Missouri, and sentenced to be shot. He was afterwards tried by a pretended civil (mobocratic) court; and since then he has been several times apprehended, tried, and acquitted for the same offense, in this State, by Missouri requisitions.

Is he still illegally and unconstitutionally to be held in abeyance by these miscreants? or shall we as freeborn American citizens, assert our rights, put the law in force upon those lawless, prowling vagabonds and say that he shall be free?

Shall we suffer our pockets to be picked through the influence of these scoundrels eternally, by defending ourselves against vexatious lawsuits? or shall we take a more summary way, and by a legal course punish the aggressors, proclaim our freedom, and shield ourselves under the broad folds of the Constitution? The latter is the course for us to pursue.

The ordinance passed by the City Council will secure this object;

and we are glad to find that the opinion of J. Lamborn, attorney general, and J. N. McDougall, correspond so much with our own—"That the Nauvoo Legion is an independent military organization, and is by law expressly required to sustain the municipal laws of Nauvoo.

What are we to say about these kidnappers who infest our borders and carry away our citizens—those infernals in human shape?

The whole European world has been engaged in a warfare against those who traffic in human blood. Negotiations have been made, treaties entered into, and fleets have been sent out, through the combined efforts of the nations, to put a stop to this inhuman traffic. But what would those nations think, if they were told the fact that in America—Republican America, the boasted cradle of liberty and land of freedom,—that those dealers in human flesh and blood, negro dealers and drivers, are allowed with impunity to steal white men, and those sons of liberty can obtain no redress.

Great God! has it come to this, that freeborn American citizens must be kidnapped by negro drivers? What are our authorities doing! Why are not these wretches brought to justice? We have heard that one or two of the citizens of Illinois have been engaged in assisting these wretches. We shall try to find out who they are and their whereabouts and make them known; and then, if they are not brought to condign punishment, we shall say that justice has fled from Illinois."

Thursday, 14.—At home.

Philander Avery arrived in Nauvoo, having made his escape from his kidnappers in Missouri.

I received the following milk-and-water letter from Governor Ford:—

Letter—Governor Ford to President Smith.

SPRINGFIELD, December 12, 1843.

General Joseph Smith.

SIR:—I have received your favor of the 6th instant, together with the proceedings of a public meeting of the citizens of Nauvoo, on the subject of the late kidnapping, by the people of Missouri and others, of two citizens of this State.

You request to know if any portion of the Legion shall be called out. My answer is, No. The Militia cannot be called out, except in the cases specified by me in my letter to Governor Reynolds, dated in the month of August last, in which I took the ground that the Militia can only be called out to repel an invasion, suppress an insurrection, or on some extreme emergency; and not to suppress, prevent, or punish individual crimes. I still am of the opinion that the ground assumed by me on that occasion is the true one. The prevention and punishment of individual offenses has been confided by the constitution and laws of this State to the judicial power, and not to the executive.

If a citizen of the State has been kidnapped, or if property has been stolen from this State, and carried to the State of Missouri, those who have done either are guilty of an indictable offense. But the constitution and the laws have provided no means whereby either the person or property taken away can be returned, except by an appeal to the laws of Missouri. The Governor has no legal right to demand the return of either. The only power I would have would be simply this: If any of the guilty persons should be charged with larceny or kidnapping, by indictment or affidavit, duly certified, and with having fled to Missouri, then I would have the power, and it would become my duty to make a demand upon the Governor of Missouri for the surrender of the fugitives, to be tried by the courts of this State. I am fully satisfied that in ordinary cases this is all the power I would possess. It would be simply a power to be exercised in aid of the judicial power. Any other powers to be exercised by the Governor would be to make him a dictator and a despot. It is true that an extraordinary case might arise, in which the inhabitants of one State might arise in warlike and hostile array against those of another; in which case a state of war would exist, and then only could I interfere.

I would advise your citizens to be strictly peaceable towards the people of Missouri. You ought to be aware that in every country individuals are liable to be visited with wrong, which the law is slow to redress, and *some of which are never redressed in this world.* This fact, however, has never been held to be a justification for violence, not warranted by law.

If any of the people of Nauvoo should invade Missouri for the purpose of rescuing persons there in jail, the consequence would be that indictments would be presented against them, and demands made upon me for their arrest and surrender; which demands I would be compelled to obey, and thus they would be harassed by interminable demands and prosecutions; and very likely it would lead to a species of border warfare, which would be exceedingly annoying to a peaceable city, and, if you could be placed in the wrong, might lead to exceedingly unpleasant consequences with reference both to law and public opinion.

You inform me that you are informed that Governor Reynolds is about to make a new demand for you; and you implore my protection from what you term this renewed persecution. In the month of August last, I was furnished by your friends with a very large amount of affidavits and evidence, said to be intended to show cause why no further writs should be issued against you. As they are very voluminous, I have not yet read them, and probably never will, unless a new demand should be made; in which case they will receive a careful perusal; and you may rest assured that no steps will be taken by me but such as the constitution and laws may require.

I am, very respectfully, &c.,

THOMAS FORD.

It appears from this letter, that Governor Ford has never taken pains to examine the evidences placed in his hands, "and probably never will," in relation to the Missouri writs; and evidently as little pains to examine the Constitution of the United States or even reflect upon the ordinary principles of human rights, to suppose that a State, after having, by a union of executive, judicial and military powers, exterminated 15,000 of its innocent inhabitants, who were not even charged with any crime, robbing them of all they possessed on earth, murdering scores of men, women and children, and expelling all the others from the State, among strangers, in mid-winter, destitute of everything upon the face of the earth that could possibly have a tendency to make life desirable, should be constitutionally entitled to demand back from banishment persons who have thus suffered its absolute decrees of exile, to satiate a yet unsatiated thirst for human blood and torture. O reason, where art thou fled! O humanity, where hast thou hidden thyself? Patriots of '76, has your blood been spilt in vain, that in 1843 the Executive of a great Republican State can coolly say, "I have not yet read them, and probably never will?" Is liberty only a name? Is protection of person and property fled from free America? *Let those answer who can.*

Friday, 15.—I awoke this morning in good health, but was soon suddenly seized with a great dryness of the mouth and throat, sickness of the stomach, and vomited freely. My wife waited on me, assisted by my scribe, Dr. Willard Richards, and his brother Levi, who administered to me herbs and mild drinks. I was never prostrated so low, in so short a time, before; but by evening was considerably revived.

Very warm for the season.

Saturday, 16.—This morning I felt considerably better; arose at 10, and sat all day in the City Council, which was held in my house for my accommodation.

The Mayor, Aldermen, and Councilors signed officially the Memorial to Congress for redress of losses and griev-

Comment on
Appeal to the
General Gov-
ernment for
Protection.

ances in Missouri. While discussing the petition to Congress, I prophesied, by virtue of the holy Priesthood vested in me, and in the name of the Lord Jesus Christ, that, if Congress will not hear our petition and grant us protection, they shall be broken up as a government.*   *   *   *

I informed the Council that it was my wish they should ask the privilege of calling on Government for the United States troops to protect us in our privileges, which is not unconstitutional, but lies in the breast of Congress.

Heber C. Kimball was duly elected city auctioneer, in place of Charles Warner, removed.

The Council passed ''An ordinance regulating merchants and grocers;'' also ''An ordinance concerning the landing of steamers;'' and Jonathan Dunham was appointed wharf-master for one year.

* This prediction doubtless has reference to the party in power; to the "government" considered as the administration; not to the "government" considered as the country; but the administration party, the Democratic Party, which had controlled the destiny of the country for forty years.   It is matter of history that a few years later the party then in power lost control of the national government, followed by the terrible conflict of the Civil War.   The Party against which the above prediction was made so far lost its influence that it did not again return to power for a quarter of a century; and when it did return to power it was with such modified views as to many great questions of government, that it could scarcly be regarded as the same party except in name.

Lest it should be urged that the Whig party was in control of the government in 1843, I call attention to the fact that while General Harrison, a Whig, was elected in 1840, he was President only one month, as he died on the 4th of April, 1841. His whole cabinet, excepting Mr. Webster, Secretary of State, resigned, and the Vice President became President.   Though elected by the Whigs Mr. Tyler was a Democrat "and the Whig administration had but a month's actual existence.' (See History of the United States, Morris, pp 311, 312).

Heber C. Kimball and George A. Smith were appointed a committee to wait on Mr. Davidson Hibbard, and solicit from him a block of land, whereon to erect a city prison.

After Council, conversed with some of the Twelve, brother Turley and others, till 8 p. m. Prayer meeting in the evening.

Warm, foggy, and muddy day.

Sunday, 17.—At home till 4 p. m.; attended prayer meeting at the assembly room. Samuel Harrison Smith admitted. Returned home at 7.

River clear of ice as far up as the Stone Tavern.

Mr. King Follet, one of the constables of Hancock County, started with ten men this afternoon to arrest John Elliott for kidnapping Daniel Avery, upon a warrant granted by Aaron Johnson, Esq., J. P.

Monday, 18.—After dinner, Constable Follet returned with John Elliott, a schoolmaster, when an examination was had before Esq. Johnson, in the assembly room. Elliott was found guilty of kidnapping Avery, and bound over in the sum of $3,000 to the Circuit court of Carthage for trial. I endeavored to have the court reduce those bonds, as Mr. Elliott was comparatively a stranger in Nauvoo; but did not succeed.

During the investigation, testimony appeared to show that Elliott had threatened my life; and for this I made affidavit and brought him to trial before Robert D. Foster, J. P., immediately after he had been bound over by Esq. Johnson. I extract from the proceedings, in part, from the *Neighbor:*—

THE TRIAL OF JOHN ELLIOTT.

The prisoner was brought forward, and the court said it was his privilege to plead for a change of venue, by paying the costs; but as the costs were not forthcoming, the court proceeded.

Mr. Styles then read the "Act to regulate the apprehension of offenders and for other purposes," p 219, r. s. The act sets forth that the use of threatening language is sufficient to criminate individuals. This we are prepared to prove.

Sisson Chase sworn.

The testimony was similar to that before deliverd, [in Chase affidavit see p. 109] with the following additional items:—

I did ask him if he had authority. In the morning he said that he would not care about shooting some of the Mormons. In conversation with him, he carried the idea that a conspiracy was formed against Joseph Smith and others, and that some of them would be shot. These conversations were had at different times. He thought Mr. Smith was a bad character. He thought they ought to be taken. Question: Who? Joseph Smith and some others.

I told him he had been taken, but had been acquitted. He did not thank the Governor for that. He carried the idea that there was a conspiracy against his life, and said we have a plan in operation that will pop him over.

Mr. Elliott sworn.

By the Court: Is your residence, Mr. Elliott, in this county? Yes.

Messrs. Marr and Styles, attorneys, resident in Nauvoo, made some thrilling remarks pertaining to the outrageous proceedings of Missouri. The diabolical conduct of those wretches who could be engaged in destroying and kidnapping their fellowmen was portrayed in glowing colors.

Judge Phelps and General Smith then followed on the same subject: their language was thrillingly eloquent and powerful. If ever inhumanity and deeds of blood were depicted in their true colors, it was on that occasion: their thoughts flashed as fire, and they spake in "words that burned." We never saw the character of General Smith so clearly developed; for while he abhorred and depicted the fiendish crime that the culprit stood charged with in its true colors, he pitied the poor wretch that then stood before him, and with feelings of commiseration, benevolence, and philanthrophy, withdrew his charge—wished, if it was within the power of the court, that the culprit might be forgiven,—promised to pay all the charges, and invited him and those of his friends who came along with him, to come to his house, and they should be taken care of. It would be superfluous for us to attempt to give even a faint outline of the remarks made by the above-named gentlemen. We hope to have at least a synopsis of their speeches for publication, which we are sure would be highly interesting to our readers. Upon the whole, although a painful, yet it was an interesting occasion and will long be remembered; and unless Mr. Elliott's heart and those of his friends were made of adamant, it must have made an indelible impression on their minds, and almost made them hate themselves.

I received from Aaron Johnson, Esq., the following demand:—

Legion Aid Applied For.

CITY OF NAUVOO, December 18, 1843.

SIR:—I have been informed that a writ issued by me for the body of Levi Williams, for kidnapping Daniel Avery, will be resisted by an armed force: Therefore, according to the provision of the Charter, I wish you to order me a detachment of the Nauvoo Legion—say 100 men, to enforce the law of the State, and bring the said Williams to justice.

AARON JOHNSON, J. P.

Which demand I complied with by writing to Major-General Wilson Law.

Detachment of the Legion Ordered into Service.

CITY OF NAUVOO, Dec. 18, 1843.

SIR:—You will detach 100 men, under the direction of Aaron Johnson, a Justice of the Peace, for the purpose of assisting the constable in executing the law of the State in taking Levi Williams, who is charged with kidnapping Daniel Avery.

Yours,

JOSEPH SMITH, Lieut-Gen., N. L.

To MAJOR-GEN. WILSON LAW,
Commanding Nauvoo Legion.

Gen. Wilson detached Colonel Stephen Markham with 100 men for that purpose.

About 10 p. m., two young men arrived as express, stating that a mob was collecting at Warsaw, also at Colonel Levi Williams' house; and messengers had gone to the mob in Missouri to reinforce their number there.

<small>Rumors of Mob Risings.</small>

Dr. Richards made the following affidavit:—

Affidavit of Willard Richards that Nauvoo was in Danger.

STATE OF ILLINOIS, CITY OF NAUVOO,
December 18, 1843.

Personally appeared Willard Richards before me, Joseph Smith, Mayor of said city, and upon his oath deposeth and saith that from information he has received, he verily believes that the peace of said city is in danger from a mobocratic assemblage at Warsaw, and a force collected under the command of Colonel Levi Williams in the lower part of the county, and runners having been sent to Missouri to excite the Missourians to join the mobbers in this county, for the purpose of making a descent on said city, or disturbing its peaceable inhabitants; and further your deponent saith not.

WILLARD RICHARDS.

Subscribed and sworn to before me this 18th December, 1843.

W. W. PHELPS,
Clerk of the Mayor's Court.

Whereupon I wrote to Major-General Wilson Law:—

Legion Ordered into Service.

CITY OF NAUVOO, Dec. 18, 1843.

SIR:—I am credibly informed that a warlike force is collecting at or near Warsaw, for the purpose of some violent move towards this city or some of the inhabitants thereof. You will therefore order out such a portion of the Nauvoo Legion as may be necessary to repel any such mobocratic or hostile design of the same unlawful force, and also as may be sufficient to secure the peace of the citizens, according to law.

Yours,

JOSEPH SMITH, Lieut-Gen. N. L.

MAJOR-GEN. WILSON LAW,
Commanding Nauvoo Legion.

I returned home to rest about one o'clock in the morning of the 19th.

Tuesday, 19.—At home. About 9 a. m., a part of the company who went with Hosea Stout returned, and stated

Moves and Counter Moves of Forces.

that they went within two miles of Colonel Williams', when they were informed that a body of men, armed with rifles, &c., were collected at his house, and he judged it prudent to return for weapons and help; also that Brother Chester Loveland told them that he had seen thirty armed men following Constable King Follett some miles on his way, when he had Elliott in custody.

Esq. Johnson immediately wrote to Loveland to have him come to Nauvoo and make affidavit of the warlike movements of the mob, that he might send to the Governor.

I directed my clerks to make copies of the affidavits respecting the kidnapping of the Averys to send to Governor Ford, that he might be left without excuse, although he may probably not read them.

Elder William Martindale writes from Washington, Wayne county, Iowa:—

STRANGE CELESTIAL PHENOMENON—1860.

A singular phenomenon was seen in this neighborhood. Jesse Fox, William and Lorenzo Fox, David Bale, James Wilson, and William Cole, with some others, retired to the house of Solomon Mendenhall, at which place they stayed a short time. While there they discovered a ball rising from the east in an oblique line; and as it ascended it moved towards the west with great rapidity until it was high in the heavens, leaving a streak of light behind it, which to the natural eye, had the appearance of being thirty or forty feet in length. This light remained stationary for about one minute. Both ends then coming round, formed a figure 8, which figure also retained its position for the same space of time. It then was transformed into a figure 6, which also remained for about a minute. It then was formed into a cypher or 0, which remained for about three minutes. The figures put together made 1860 in large figures in the heavens. The phenomenon was indeed singular, and has been a matter of great speculation with us.

At one p. m. I was present when the Legion paraded near the Temple, were inspected by the officers, and instructed to prepare themselves with arms and ammunition and to hold themselves in readiness, for a moment's notice. Brother Henry Boley was shot severely under the arm by the accidental discharge of his gun.

Legion Parade

Amos S. Chase made the following affidavit:—

Affidavit of Amos Chase.

STATE OF ILLINOIS, }
CITY OF NAUVOO. } ss.

On the 19th day of December, 1843, came Amos S. Chase before me Joseph Smith, Mayor of said city; and after being duly sworn, deposeth and saith that on the 18th day of December, 1843, he was about four miles below Warsaw, in Hancock County, shortly after the constable arrested John Elliott for being concerned in kidnapping Daniel Avery, not long since, and saw the men of the neighborhood gathering with arms to retake the said John Elliott; and when asked what they would do, if the Governor did not sanction such an unlawful course, several of them replied, "Damn the Governor! If he opens his head, we will punch a hole through him! He dare not open his head! We will serve him the same sauce we will the Mormons." The said mob then went to Warsaw, where your affiant saw them with their arms; and further your affiant saith not.

AMOS S. CHASE,

Subscribed and sworn to before me this 19th day of December, 1843.

W. W. PHELPS, Clerk, M. C.

Wednesday, 20.—At home, in good health and spirits, counseling and attending to business in general.

The Clerk of the Municipal Court took the following affidavits:—

AFFIDAVITS OF PHILANDER AVERY—MISSOURI KIDNAPPING.

STATE OF ILLINOIS,) ss.
CITY OF NAUVOO.)

On the 20th day of December, 1843, personally appeared before me, Willard Richards, clerk of the Municipal Court of said city Philander Avery, of Bear Creek precinct, in said county, and after being duly sworn, deposeth and saith that on the 19th day of November, 1843, at his house, in the precinct aforesaid, Ebenezer Richardson, of Lee county, Territory of Iowa, by false pretenses, persuaded your affiant to accompany said Richardson to the Missisippi river at Warsaw, where your affiant was seized by one Joseph C. McCoy, of Clark county, Missouri, in connection with the said Richardson, and about one dozen of other individuals, whose names are unknown to your affiant, and by them forced across said Mississippi River, where they bound your affiant; and Mark Childs swore that your affiant had stolen said McCoy's horse and colt, and that his father Daniel Avery had secreted said horse and colt, and said Richardson threatened your affiant with death or seven years' imprisonment, in order to persuade him to make false statements, and testify that his father, Daniel Avery, had stolen said McCoy's horse and colt, which statements your affiant made, and swore to the same, while in duress, with a bowie-knife presented to intimidate. And your affiant further saith that the testimony he gave concerning his father's guilt, was extorted from him through fear, while in duress, and said testimony was absolutely false, and your affiant fully believes that his father is innocent of the crime of stealing said McCoy's horse and colt; and further your deponent saith not.

PHILANDER AVERY.

Subscribed and sworn to before me; in testimony whereof

[L. S.]   I have set my hand and affixed the seal of said court at Nauvoo aforesaid, this 20th day of December, A. D. 1843.

WILLARD RICHARDS,

Clerk of the Municipal Court of the City of Nauvoo,

Affidavit of the Hamiltons.

STATE OF ILLINOIS, } ss.
COUNTY OF HANCOCK,

On the 20th day of December, 1843, personally appeared before me Aaron Johnson, a Justice of the Peace in and for said county, Andrew H. Hamilton, and James B. Hamilton, of Bear Creek precinct, in said county, and, after being duly sworn, depose and say that on the evening of the 2nd day of December, 1843, at Vernon Doty's mill, in said precinct, Colonel Levi Williams, of said Hancock county, as principal, and his son, John Williams, with William Middleton, of the county of Clark and State of Missouri, Captain McCoy, of the said county of Clark and State of Missouri, John Fox of Green Plains precinct, and about a dozen other men, armed with pistols, dirks and bowie knives came forcibly upon Daniel Avery at said Doty's mill, and seized and bound him. The said Avery told them to stand off. They said they had a writ. He observed, he would not resist legal authority. They said they would take said Avery to Warsaw, and there to try him. The said Avery replied, "I understand you: you will take me to Warsaw, and there pass me over the river to Missouri." Some of said gang then shouted, "Lay hold of him; G—d d—n him, lay hold of him: there's no use of parleying;" at which Colonel Levi Williams, with a large bowie-knife in his hand, and others, then forced the said Daniel Avery to submit, telling him (without a writ,) that his life would be taken if he did not submit. They then tied him with silk handkerchiefs. Colonel Levi Williams and another person then led the said Daniel Avery away: and as they passed your affiants within the distance of about four rods, the said Daniel Avery cried out to one of your said affiants, "tell my friends where I am gone." Colonel Williams told said Avery to hold his peace, for it was of no use. William Middleton then got a horse; and after tying him upon said horse, as sworn to before by another witness, they then conveyed him to Missouri without a writ or trial, as your affiants verily believe; and further they say not.

ANDREW M. HAMILTON.
JAMES B. HAMILTON.

Subscribed and sworn to this 20th day of December, 1843, before me.

AARON JOHNSON, J. P.

CHAPTER VI.

MEMORIAL OF CITY COUNCIL TO CONGRESS ANENT MISSOURI
AFFAIRS—ROCKWELL'S RETURN TO NAUVOO—RECITAL OF
HIS ADVENTURES—AVERY'S ACQUITTAL BY MISSOURI'S
COURTS—NAUVOO'S POLICE FORCE INCREASED—PUBLICA-
TIONS ON MORMONISM, PRO ET CON—1843.

Thursday, December 21, 1843.—About one o'clock in the
morning I was alarmed by the firing of a gun, got up, and
went down to the river bank to see the guard, and inquire the cause of it. To my surprise, they had not
heard it, although I felt sure it was fired in Montrose.
The morning proved it to be correct, some rowdies in
Montrose had been firing in the night.

At noon met with the City Council which voted that
Councilor Orson Pratt present the Memorial and Ordinance to Congress.

Passed "An ordinance to prevent unlawful search or
seizure of person or property by foreign [i.e. outside]
process in the city of Nauvoo."

Heber C. Kimball resigned his office as city auctioneer
and Charles Warner was re-elected.

John P. Greene was duly elected city marshal, in the
room of Henry G. Sherwood, who expects to leave soon.

I gave instructions to the marshal and policemen to
see that all carrion is removed out of the city,
The Prophet for a Clean, Orderly City. and all houses kept in order,—to stop the
boys when fighting in the streets, and prevent
children from floating off on the ice, and correct anything
out of order, like fathers; and I offered to build the city
jail, if it was left to my dictation, which the Council
authorized me to do.

I insert the Memorial from the City Council to the Congress of the United States for redress of grievances and protection from further persecution, which was signed by them:—

MEMORIAL OF THE CITY COUNCIL TO CONGRESS.

"To the Honorable Senators and Representatives of the United States of America in Congress assembled,

We, the undersigned members of the City Council of the City of Nauvoo, citizens of Hancock County, Illinois, and exiles from the State of Missouri, being in council assembled, unanimously and respectfully, for ourselves, and in behalf of many thousands of other exiles, memorialize the honorable Senators and Representatives of our nation upon the subject of the unparalleled persecutions and cruelties inflicted upon us and upon our constituents by the constituted authorities of the State of Missouri, and likewise upon the subject of the present unfortunate circumstances in which we are placed in the land of our exile. As a history of the Missouri outrages has been extensively published, both in this country and in Europe, it is deemed unnecessary to particularize all of the wrongs and grievances inflicted upon us in this memorial. As there is an abundance of well-attested documents to which your honorable body can at any time refer, hence we only embody the following important items for your consideration.

First:—Your memorialists, as freeborn citizens of this great republic, relying with the utmost confidence upon the sacred "articles of the Constitution," by which the several States are bound together, and considering ourselves entitled to all the privileges and immunities of free citizens in what State soever we desired to locate ourselves, commenced a settlement in the county of Jackson, on the western frontiers of the State of Missouri, in the summer of 1831.

There we purchased lands from the Government, erected several hundred houses, made extensive improvements, and shortly the wild and lonely prairies and stately forests were converted into well cultivated and fruitful fields. There we expected to spend our days in the enjoyment of all the rights and liberties bequeathed to us by the sufferings and blood of our noble ancestors. But alas! our expectations were vain.

Two years had scarcely elapsed before we were unlawfully and unconstitutionally assaulted by an organized mob, consisting of the highest officers in the county, both civil and military, who openly and boldly avowed their determination in a written circular to drive us from said county.

As a specimen of their treasonable and cruel designs, your honorable body are referred to said circular, of which the following is but a short extract,—namely: "We the undersigned citizens of Jackson county, believing that an important crisis is at hand, as regards our civil society, in consequence of a pretended religious sect of people that have settled and are still settling in our county, styling themselves Mormons, and intending as we do to rid our society, 'peaceably if we can, forcibly if we must;' and believing as we do that the arm of the civil law does not afford us a guarantee, or at least a sufficient one, against the evils which are now inflicted upon us, and seem to be increasing by the said religious sect, deem it expedient and of the highest importance to form ourselves into a company for the better and easier accomplishment of our purpose."

This document was closed in the following words:—"We therefore agree that, after timely warning, and receiving an adequate compensation for what little property they cannot take with them, they refuse to leave us in peace, as they found us, we agree to use such means as may be sufficient to remove them; and to that end we each pledge to each other our bodily powers, our lives, fortunes, and sacred honors."

To this unconstitutional document were attached the names of nearly every officer in the county, together with the names of hundreds of others.

It was by this band of murderers that your memorialists, in the year 1833, were plundered of their property and robbed of their peaceable homes. It was by them that their fields were laid waste, their houses burned, and their men, women, and children, to the number of about twelve hundred persons, banished as exiles from the county, while others were cruelly murdered by their hands.

Second: After our expulsion from Jackson county, we settled in Clay county, on the opposite side of the Missouri river, where we purchased lands both from the old settlers and from the [U. S.] Land Office: but soon we were again violently threatened by mobs, and obliged to leave our homes, and seek out a new location.

Third: Our next settlement was in Caldwell county, where we purchased the most of the land in said county, beside a part of the lands in Daviess and Carroll counties. These counties were almost entirely in a wild and uncultivated state; but, by the persevering industry of our citizens, large and extensive farms were opened in every direction, well stocked with numerous flocks and herds. We also commenced settlements in several other counties of the state, and once more confidently hoped to enjoy the hard-earned fruits of our labor unmolested.

But our hopes were soon blasted. The cruel and murderous spirit which first began to manifest itself in the constituted authorities and inhabitants of Jackson county, and afterwards in Clay and the surrounding counties, receiving no check either from the civil or military power of the state, had in the meantime taken courage, and boldly and fearlessly spread its contaminating and treasonable influence into every department of the government of said state. Lieutenant-Governor Boggs, a resident of Jackson county, who acted a conspicuous part in our expulsion from said county, instead of being tried for treason and rebellion against the Constitution, and suffering the just penalty of his crimes, was actually elected governor; and placed in the executive chair.

Thus the inhabitants of the State were greatly encouraged to renew with redoubled fury, their unlawful attacks upon our defenseless settlements. Men, women, and children were driven away in every direction before their merciless persecutors, robbed of their possessions, their property, their provisions, and their all, cast forth upon the bleak, snowy prairies, houseless and unprotected. Many sank down and expired under their accumulated sufferings, while others, after enduring hunger and the severities of the season, suffering all but death, arrived in Caldwell county, to which place they were driven from all the surrounding counties, only to witness a still more heart-rending scene.

In vain had we appealed to the constituted authorities of Missouri for protection and redress of our former grievances. In vain we now stretched out our hands and appealed as the citizens of this great republic to the sympathies, to the justice, and magnanimity of those in power. In vain we implored again and again at the feet of Governor Boggs, our former persecutor, for aid and protection against the ravages and murders now inflicted upon our defenseless and unoffending citizens. The cry of American citizens, already twice driven and deprived of liberty, could not penetrate their adamantine hearts.

The Governor, instead of sending us aid, issued a proclamation for our extermination and banishment, ordered out the forces of the State, placed them under the command of General Clark, who, to execute these exterminating orders, marched several thousand troops into our settlements in Caldwell county, where, unrestrained by fear of law or justice, and urged on by the highest authority of the state, they laid waste our fields of corn, shot down our cattle and hogs for sport, burned our dwellings, inhumanly butchered some eighteen or twenty defenseless citizens, dragged from their hiding-places little children, and placing the muzzles of their guns to their heads, shot them [such acts being accompanied] with the most horrid oaths and imprecations·

An aged hero and patriot of the Revolution, who served under General Washington, while in the act of pleading for quarter, was cruelly murdered and hewed in pieces with an old corn cutter; and in addition to all these savage acts of barbarity, they forcibly dragged virtuous and inoffensive females from their dwellings, bound them upon benches used for public worship, where they in great numbers ravished them in the most brutal manner.

Some fifty or sixty of the citizens were thrust into prisons and dungeons, where, bound in chains, they were fed on human flesh, while their families and some fifteen thousand others were at the point of the bayonet, forcibly expelled from the State.

In the meantime, to pay the expenses of these horrid outrages, they confiscated our property, and robbed us of all our possessions.

Before our final expulsion, with a faint and lingering hope we petitioned the State legislature then in session, unwilling to believe that the virtue and patriotism of the venerable fathers of the Revolution had fled from the bosoms of their illustrious descendants—unwilling to believe that American citizens could appeal in vain for a restoration of liberty cruelly wrested from them by cruel tyrants. But in the language of our noble ancestors, "our repeated petitions were only answered by repeated injuries."

The legislature, instead of hearing the cries of 15,000 suffering, bleeding, unoffending citizens, sanctioned and sealed the unconstitutional acts of the governor and his troops, by appropriating 200,000 dollars to defray the expenses of exterminating us from the State. No friendly arm was stretched out to protect us. The last ray of hope for redress in that State was now entirely extinguished. We saw no other alternative but to bow down our necks and wear the cruel yoke of oppression, and quietly and submissively suffer ourselves to be banished as exiles from our possessions, our property, and our sacred homes, or otherwise see our wives and children coldly butchered and murdered by tyrants in power.

Fourth. Our next permanent settlement was in the land of our exile, the State of Illinois, in the spring of 1839; but even here we are not secure from our relentless persecutor, the State of Missouri. Not satisfied in having drenched her soil in the blood of innocence, and expelling us from her borders, she pursues her unfortunate victims into banishment, seizing upon and kidnapping them in their defenseless moments, dragging them across the Mississippi river, upon their inhospitable shores, there they are tortured, whipped, immured in dungeons, and finally hung [as a means of torture, but not unto death] by the neck without any legal process what ever.

We have memorialized the former Executive of this State, Governor Carlin, upon these lawless outrages committed upon our citizens; but he renderd us no protection. Missouri, receiving no check in her murderous career, continues her depredations, again and again kidnapping our citizens and robbing us of our property; while others, who fortunately survived the execution of her bloody edicts, are again and again demanded by the Executive of that State, on pretense of some crime said to have been committed by them during the exterminating expedition against our people.

As an instance, General Joseph Smith, one of your memorialists, has been three times demanded, tried, and acquitted by the courts of this State, upon investigation under writs of *habeas corpus,* once by the United States Court for the District of Illinois, again by the Circuit Court of the State of Illinois, and lastly by the Municipal Court of the City of Nauvoo, when at the same time a *nolle prosequi* had been entered by the courts of Missouri upon all the cases of that State against Joseph Smith and others.

Thus the said Joseph Smith has been several times tried for the same alleged offense, put in jeopardy of life and limb, contrary to the fifth article of the amendments to the Constitution of the United States; and thus we have been continually harassed and robbed of our money to defray the expenses of these vexatious prosecutions. And what at the present time seems to be still more alarming, is the hostility manifested by some of the authorities and citizens of this State [Illinois.] Conventions have been called, inflammatory speeches made, and many unlawful and unconstitutional resolutions adopted to deprive us of our rights, our liberties, and the peaceable enjoyment of our possessions.

From the present hostile aspect, and from bitter experience in the State of Missouri, it is greatly feared lest the barbarous scenes acted in that State will be re-acted in this. If Missouri goes unpunished, others will be greatly encouraged to follow her murderous examples.

The afflictions of your memorialists have already been overwhelming—too much for humanity, too much for American citizens to endure without complaint. We have groaned under the iron hand of tyranny and oppression these many years. We have been robbed of our property to the amount of two millions of dollars. We have been hunted as wild beasts of the forest. We have seen our aged fathers who fought in the Revolution and our innocent children alike slaughtered by our persecutors; we have seen the fair daughters of American citizens insulted and abused in the most inhuman manner; and finally we have seen fifteen thousand souls—men, women and children, driven by force of arms during the severities of the winter from their sacred homes and firesides, penniless and unprotected, to a land of strangers.

Under all these afflicting circumstances, we imploringly stretch forth

our hands towards the highest councils of our nation, and humbly
appeal to the illustrious Senators and Representatives of a great and
free people for redress and protection.

Hear, O hear the petitioning voice of many thousands of American
citizens, who now groan in exile on Columbia's free soil! Hear, O hear
the weeping and bitter lamentations of widows and orphans, whose
husbands and fathers have been cruelly martyred in the land where
the proud eagle exulting soars! Let it not be recorded in the archives
of the nations that Columbia's exiles sought protection and redress at
your hands, but sought it in vain. It is in your power to save us, our
wives, and our children from a repetition of the bloodthirsty scenes of
Missouri, and greatly relieve the fears of a persecuted and injured
people, by ordaining for their protection the following ordinance,
namely—

AN ORDINANCE

*For the protection of the people styled the Church of Jesus Christ
of Latter-day Saints, residing on the western borders of the
State of Illinois.*

PREAMBLE.

Whereas the State of Missouri at sundry times has unconstitutionally
deprived a certain portion of her citizens (called "Mormons,") of their
rights, property, lands, and even of their lives:

And whereas, in the years 1838 and 1839 the said State of Missouri
with impunity did illegally and inhumanly exile and banish for ever
from her limits and jurisdiction all the said citizens (called "Mormons,")
that remained alive.

And whereas, after being hospitably received by the citizens of
Illinois, the said State of Illinois did grant, enact, and charter for
the benefit and convenience of the said exiled "Mormons" as follows:—

[Here in the original document is inserted the city charter of
Nauvoo already published, Vol. IV, pp 239-249.]

And whereas, by the 10th article of the Constitution of the United
States as amended—"Art. 10. The powers not delegated to the United
States by the Constitution, nor prohibited by it to the States, are reserved to the States respectively, or to the people;" and whereas, according to the fourth article and section second, "The citizens of each
state shall be entitled to all privileges and immunities of citizens in the
several States:" and whereas, according to the second paragraph of the

third section of said Constitution, "The Congress shall have power to dispose of and make the needful rules and regulations respecting territory;" and whereas the said Congress has the power to protect each state against invasion and insurrection: and whereas most of the inhabitants of the city of Nauvoo are exiles from the State of Missouri: and whereas most of the lands owned in the State of Missouri were purchased from the United States, and patented by the United States to the amount of more than $200,000 worth: and whereas the United States are bound to clear the title and protect it: and whereas the said exiles or expelled "Mormons" have lost in property and damages about two millions of dollars: and whereas the said State of Missouri continues her ravages, persecutions, and plunderings, by kidnapping said exiles from Illinois, and by other depredations:

Now, therefore, to show the fatherly care of the United States, to ratify the said charter, to protect the said exiles from mob violence, and shield them in their rights: —

Section 1. Be it ordained by the Senate and House of Representatives of the United States of America in Congress assembled, that all the rights, powers, privileges, and immunities belonging to Territories, and not repugnant to the Constitution of the United States, are hereby granted and secured to the inhabitants of the city of Nauvoo, in addition to the spirit, letter, meaning, and provisions of the afore-mentioned charter, or act of incorporation from the State of Illinois, until the State of Missouri restores to those exiled citizens the lands, rights, privileges, property, and damage for all losses.

Section 2. And be it further ordained, in order to effect the object and further intention of this ordinance, and for the peace, security, happiness, convenience, benefit, and prosperity of the said city of Nauvoo, and for the common weal and honor of our country, that the mayor of Nauvoo be, and he is hereby empowered by this consent of the President of the United States; whenever the actual necessity of the case and the public safety shall require it, to call to his aid a sufficient number of United States forces, in connection with the Nauvoo Legion, to repel the invasion of mobs, keep the public peace, and protect the innocent from the unhallowed ravages of lawless banditti that escape justice on the western frontier; and also to preserve the power and dignity of the Union.

Section 3. And be it further ordained that the officers of the United States army are hereby required to obey the requisitions of this ordinance.

Section 4. And be it further ordained that, for all services rendered in quelling mobs and preserving the public peace the said Nauvoo

Legion shall be under the same regulations, rules, and laws of pay as the troops of the United States.

City of Nauvoo, Illinois, December 21st, 1843.

HYRUM SMITH,   BENJAMIN WARRINGTON,
JOHN TAYLOR,   DANIEL SPENCER,
ORSON PRATT,   BRIGHAM YOUNG,
W. W. PHELPS,   ORSON HYDE,
HEBER C. KIMBALL,
                                        Councilors;

ORSON SPENCER,
DANIEL H. WELLS,
SAMUEL BENNETT,
GEO. A. SMITH,
GEO. W. HARRIS,
                                        Aldermen;

JOSEPH SMITH, Mayor;
WILLARD RICHARDS, Recorder;
JOHN P. GREENE, Marshal. *

Two letters came into the post-office from the sheriff of Clark County, Missouri. From them it appears that that State wishes to continue the old game of seizing witnesses and making prisoners of them, to cover up her mobocracy and kidnapping under a legal form. The following answer was written:—

Letter: W. W. Phelps to J. White, Esq., Anent Avery Affair.

CITY OF NAUVOO, ILL., Dec. 21, 1843.

SIR,—Two letters were put into my hands this morning relative to the witnesses of Mr. Avery's innocence as to being accessory to horse stealing some four years since. In the first place, Mr. Avery was abducted from this State without process, contrary to law. In the second place, the principal for felony by the law of Missouri should be indicted within three years, &c. Again, the revised statutes of Missouri have a wise provision in such cases as Mr. Avery's. If Mr. Avery, therefore, will sue out a commission according to the law con

---

*There was also a Memorial prepared by the Prophet from the inhabitants of Hancock county generally to the same effect as the above, but it was never extensively signed or presented to Congress.

cerning depositions, (R. S., page 219 to 222,) directed to Alderman Geo. W. Harris, an acting justice of the peace for the city of Nauvoo, and county of Hancock, the necessary testimony to establish Mr. Avery's innocence will be taken according to law, and forwarded to the proper officer in due time.

Respectfully, &c..

W. W. PHELPS.

J. WHITE, ESQ., Dep. Sheriff,
    Clark Co., Waterloo, Mo.

P.S. You will have the politeness to show this to Mr. Avery.

In the evening I was visited by several strangers, and had considerable conversation with them.

Friday, 22.—At home at nine o'clock, a. m., reading a magazine to my children.

A little after twelve went into the store-room occupied by Butler and Lewis, and commenced a conversation with Dr. John F. Charles, to convince him that mobocracy is not justifiable, and that I did not deal in politics.

Attitude of Prophet on Mobocracy and Politics.

David Holman, living about two miles from Ramus, went out in the evening with his family visiting. About ten o'clock he discovered his house on fire. The neigbors had inquired how long he would be gone. A man rode to Carthage. A company went up, secured the provisions to themselves, and fired the house.

Warm and pleasant weather.

Saturday, 23.—At home, counseling the brethren who called on me, and attending to my domestic duties, making preparations for a Christmas dinner party.

Prayer meeting in the Assembly Room.

Sunday, 24.—At home. Received a visit from Mr. Richardson, one of the men who assisted in kidnapping Avery. He manifested some repentance and sorrow for his part in that transaction, and promised to use what influence he had with the Missourians to have Avery set at liberty.

Monday, 25.—This morning, about one o'clock, I was
aroused by an English sister, Lettice Rushton,
A Christmas Serenade. widow of Richard Rushton, Senior, (who, ten
years ago, lost her sight,) accompanied by
three of her sons, with their wives, and her two daughters,
with their husbands, and several of her neighbors, singing,
"Mortals, awake! with angels join," &c., which caused a
thrill of pleasure to run through my soul. All of my
family and boarders arose to hear the serenade, and I felt
to thank my Heavenly Father for their visit, and blessed
them in the name of the Lord. They also visited my
brother Hyrum, who was awakened from his sleep. He
arose and went out of doors. He shook hands with and
blessed each one of them in the name of the Lord, and
said that he thought at first that a cohort of angels
had come to visit him, it was such heavenly music to
him.

At home all day. About noon, gave counsel to some
brethren who called on me from Morley Settlement, and
told them to keep law on their side, and they would come
out well enough.

At two o'clock, about fifty couples sat down at my table
to dine. While I was eating, my scribe called, requesting
me to solemnize the marriage of his brother, Dr. Levi
Richards, and Sara Griffiths; but as I could not leave, I
referred him to President Brigham Young, who married
them.

A large party supped at my house, and spent the
evening in music, dancing, &c., in a most
Rockwell's Return to Nauvoo. cheerful and friendly manner. During the
festivities, a man with his hair long and falling
over his shoulders, and apparently drunk, came in and
acted like a Missourian. I requested the captain of the
police to put him out of doors. A scuffle ensued, and I
had an opportunity to look him full in the face, when, to
my great surprise and joy untold, I discovered it was my
long-tried, warm, but cruelly persecuted friend, Orrin

Porter Rockwell, just arrived from nearly a year's imprisonment, without conviction, in Missouri.

The following is his statement of his experience and sufferings by that people:—

ROCKWELL'S EXPERIENCE IN MISSOURI.

I, Orrin Porter Rockwell, was on my way from New Jersey to Nauvoo; and while at St. Louis, on the 4th March, 1843, was arrested by a Mr. Fox, on oath of Elias Parker, who swore I was the O. P. Rockwell advertised in the papers as having attempted to assassinate Lilburn W. Boggs, and was taken before a magistrate in St. Louis.

I was then put into the St. Louis county jail, and kept two days with a pair of iron hobbles on my ankles. About midnight, was taken into the stage coach in charge of Fox, and started for Jefferson City. There were nine passengers, two of them women. I sat on the middle seat. One of the men behind me commenced gouging me in the back. I spoke to him, and told him that it was dark, and I could not see him, but that he was no gentleman. One of the ladies whispered to him, and he ceased the operation.

The next night, the driver, being drunk, ran against a tree, and broke the king bolt; and not knowing what to do, ironed as I was, I crawled into the boot, and found an extra bolt, and in the dark fixed the coach, got it off the tree, and we started on. Soon after, ran against a bank, and could not move. I was asleep at the time, but the bustle awoke me, when I told them, if they would take off my irons, I would get off and drive, as the driver was too drunk to manage the horses. They refused. I, however, got hold of the lines, and, by the help of other passengers lifting at the wheels, got it righted, and I drove to the next stand, near the Osage river. The roads were very bad, and the load heavy; so we got along slowly.

There was an officer of the U. S. army in the coach. We were two days and two nights from St. Louis in reaching Jefferson City, where I was lodged in the jail two days and two nights. The U. S. officer went on.

Started on for Independence, still in charge of Fox. At Boonville, overtook the U. S. officer. We three were all that were in the coach all the way from Boonville to Independence. Sheriff Reynolds told me afterwards that when he looked into the stage he took me for the guard, and the officer for the prisoner, for he looked like the guilty one.

Was about four days going to Independence: arrived there just at night. A large crowd gathered around, making many remarks. Some were for hanging me at once. I was then placed in the jail. In two or three days, underwent a sham trial before a justice of the peace. The courthouse was crowded, and the men were armed with hickory clubs. They set on boys from ten to twelve years of age to kick and punch me, which they did repeatedly. While in court, Fox was the main witness introduced, and he swore falsely.

Fox swore that I had stated to him that I had not been in the county for five years. I informed the court that Fox swore falsely, in proof thereof that the people of Independence knew that I had traveled through Independence several times during that time, for the people were all well aware of my having visited this place, which fact alone should satisfy them that Fox was swearing for money, which I afterwards learned that he obtained and divided with Parker.

The magistrate committed me to prison for my safe preservation, as he was afraid the people would kill me; but he could find no crime against me. This I was told by the officer who conveyed me to prison.

I was re-committed to jail, still wearing the iron hobbles, and was kept in the upper part in the day-time, and in the dungeon at night, with a little dirty straw for a bed, without any bedding, no fire, and very cold weather. For eighteen days I was not free from shaking with cold. I then got permission to buy 1½ bushels of charcoal, which I put into an old kettle, and kept a little fire. When that was gone, I could not obtain any more.

After I was arrested at St. Louis, I was visited by Joseph Wood, an apostate "Mormon," who professed to be a lawyer. He was accompanied by Mr. Blanerhasset, who told me that everything I had would be taken from me, and proposed to take charge, keep, and return to me any property I might have with me. I let him have a pair of pistols, a bowie knife, and watch, which he never returned to me.

After the weather got a little warmer, they furnished me with a few old newspapers to read. A family lived at the corner of the jail. The women once in a while used to send out a little negro girl with a small basket of victuals. She handed up to the grate a big Missouri whip-stock, with a piece of twine, which I tied to the pole and drew up the basket, and let it down again.

I made a pin-hook and tied to the twine, and baited with a chunk of corn-dodger hard enough to knock a negro down with, and stuck it out of the grated window and fished for pukes. When passers-by came along, they would stop and gawk at me awhile, and pass on.

A preacher who had a family of girls lived on the opposite side of the street. The girls would watch and laugh at them, and call out and ask me if I got any bites. I replied, No, but some glorious nibbles.

Numbers were put into the jail with me at different times, and taken out again. One of them, who was charged with a fraudulent issue of U. S. Treasury notes, was allowed to have his saddle-bags with him. They contained some fire-steels, gun-flints, and articles of Indian trade. I sawed the irons nearly off with one of the fire-steels. He got the negro girl to get him a knife, and I finished cutting the fetters with it. He would frequently call for a good supper and pay for it, which was allowed him, but not allowed me. He was very anxious to escape, and urged me to undertake it with him. He ordered a good supper, and he ate very heartily. I would not eat, telling him that he could not run if he ate so much. Nearly dusk, as the jailer came in to get the dishes, we sprang to the door, and I locked him in, and threw the key into the garden. In coming down stairs, we met the jailer's wife. I told her that her husband was unharmed; I had only locked him up. We had a board fence to climb over, which was about twelve feet high. I climbed it, and ran about twenty rods, when he called me to come and help him over, which I did. If I had not, I should have escaped. The pure air had so great an effect upon me, that I gave out and slacked my pace, The populace of the place came up, and I told them to run; they would soon catch him; and that I had given out and could not run. They soon returned with him. I fell into the crowd and walked back to the jail yard.

Sheriff J. H. Reynolds laid his hand upon my shoulder, he being the first to approach me. Asked where the key was. I told him, In the garden.

Smallwood Nowlin was the first who proposed to hang me on the spot, when Reynolds gave me a push towards the crowd, and said, "There he is, G— d —n him! Do what you damn please with him." Nowlin's son in-law (by marrying one of his mulatto wenches), a Mexican, stepped up to me to lay hold of me, when I told him to stand off, or I would mash his face. He stepped back.

I then walked up stairs into the jail. Was followed by Reynolds and others, until the room and stairs were full. Reynolds asked me what I had cut my irons off with. I went to the saddle-bags and handed him the knife and fire-steel. While feeling for them, I got hold of a piece of buckskin that had some three or four pounds of bullets tied up in it, which I intended to use in mashing in the head of any one that should attempt to put a rope on my neck. A rope was passed along over the heads of the people into the room to a bald-headed man. About this time pistols could be heard cocking in every part of the room, and bowie-knives were produced as if for fight. In a few minutes the room was clear of all but three or four persons.

I was then put into the dungeon, my feet ironed together, my right hand to my left foot, so close that I could not half straighten myself. The irons, when put on my wrists, were so small that they would hardly go on, and swelled them; but in eighteen days I could slip them up and turn them around my arm at the elbow. I was fed on cold corndodger and meat of the poorest description; and if I did not eat it all up, it was returned the next time.

About a month after the court sat, my irons were taken off, and I was so weak that I had to be led to the court-room by the officer. I was notified that a bill was found against me for breaking jail, and that the grand jury had failed to find a bill against me on the charge of shooting Boggs, as charged in the advertisement offering a reward for my apprehension.

I was taken into court, and was asked by the judge if I had any counsel. I told him I had not. He asked if I had any means to employ a counsel. I answered that I had none with me that I could control. He then said, Here are a number of counselors: if I was acquainted with any of them, I could take my choice. I told him I would make choice of Mr. Doniphan, who arose and made a speech, saying he was crowded with business, but that here are plenty of young lawyers who could plead for me as well as he could. The judge heard his plea, and then told me he did not consider that a sufficient excuse, and I could consider Mr. Doniphan my counsel.

I was then ordered back to jail, and ironed again in the same way. Mr. Doniphan asked for and obtained a change of venue to Clay County, which is in another district.

When the officers came to Independence jail for me, they requested me to get ready in a hurry, as they feared the mob would kill me. I told them I wanted to put on a clean shirt, if it cost me my life, as I had not been permitted to enjoy the luxury of a change of linen since I had boarded at the expense of Jackson County. While I was changing my shirt, the officers several times told me to hurry, or the mob would be on me and kill me.

When I got ready to start, the officers furnished me a very hard-trotting horse, with a miserable poor saddle, tied my feet under the horse with ropes, and my hands behind my back, and started off at a good round trot, in charge of two officers. In a short time a strange gentleman fell into our company, who was also on horseback. It was six miles to the ferry, where we could cross the Missouri river. When we got there, we saw the boat land on the opposite side, when several men got off the boat, and took a course to the woods, through which the road ran. The boat returned. This stranger asked—"Where are those men going?" and was answered—"They are going to the woods to hew timber."

We then crossed, and took our way for Liberty. When we left the boat, we saw no signs of people, nor heard any sound of axes. After traveling some two or three miles, the woods became dense and brushy: we heard the crackling of brush, and the noise of men traveling through it. The officers and stranger appeared frightened, and urged speed, keeping close watch. We came to an opening in the woods, when the noise of crackling of brush ceased. We traveled safely to Liberty, where this stranger told his friends that he overheard several men in Independence planning to waylay me in the thick timber on the Missouri bottom, at the place where we heard the noises; but his being in company counteracted their plot. I was then lodged in Liberty jail. In a few days afterwards I learned that the men who went into the brush told it, that they went into the woods according to agreement to waylay me; but when they saw this stranger, it frustrated their plans.

In about ten days, on pretext of informality in the papers, I was remanded back to Independence jail. It was rumored that I was again going to be waylaid, when the two officers from Clay county took me by a different road, and so I escaped the second time.

When I was put in Independence jail, l was again ironed hand and foot, and put in the dungeon, in which condition I remained about two months. During this time, Joseph H. Reynolds, the sheriff, told me he was going to arrest Joseph Smith, and they had received letters from Nauvoo which satisfied them that Joseph Smith had unlimited confidence in me, that I was capable of toting him in a carriage or on horseback anywhere that I pleased; and if I would only tote him out by riding or any other way, so that they could apprehend him, I might please myself whether I stayed in Illinois or came back to Missouri; they would protect me, and any pile that I would name the citizens of Jackson county would donate, club together, and raise, and that I should never suffer for want afterwards: "you only deliver Joe Smith into our hands, and name your pile." I replied—"I will see you all damned first, and then I won't."

About the time that Joseph was arrested by Reynolds at Dixon, I knew that they were after him, and [yet had] no means under heaven of giving him any information. My anxiety became so intense upon the subject, knowing their determination to kill him, that my flesh twitched on my bones. I could not help it; twitch it would. While undergoing this sensation, I heard a dove alight on the window in the upper room of the jail, and commence cooing, and then went off. In a short time, he came back to the window, where a pane was broken: he crept through between the bars of iron, which were about two and-a-half inches apart.

I saw it fly round the trap-door several times: it did not alight, but continued cooing until it crept through the bars again, and flew out through the broken window.

I relate this, as it was the only occurrence of the kind that happened during my long and weary imprisonment; but it proved a comfort to me: the twitching of my flesh ceased, and I was fully satisfied from that moment that they would not get Joseph into Missouri, and that I should regain my freedom. From the best estimates that can be made, this incident occurred about the time when Joseph was in the custody of Reynolds.

In a few days afterwards, Sheriff Reynolds came into the jail and told me that he had made a failure in the arrest of Joseph.

After the lawyers had been about two months making out fresh papers, I was again conveyed to Liberty jail on a miserable horse, with feet and hands tied as before, but [by] a different road.

In a few days afterwards, my mother found where I was, and she came to see me and brought me $100, whereby I was enabled to fee Mr. Doniphan for his services as counsel.

The time of trial being continually delayed, I began to be uneasy. I was handcuffed in the dungeon, which is the basement story of the prison, and is about nine feet high. I took down the stove-pipe, pushed my clothes up through the stove-pipe hole, and then crawled through the hole in the floor, which was made of logs about fourteen inches thick, into the upper room. The hole was so small that it scratched my flesh, and made me bleed from many wounds. I then examined the inside door, and with the bail of the water pail I unbolted it; but finding I could not get through the outside door, I returned to my dungeon through the same narrow pass.

The following night I made another attempt through the same way; but, failing to get through the outside door, I lay down on the upper floor, where the boys who were bringing my food next morning found me. They made an alarm, when five or six men came and again conveyed me down into the dungeon. It caused quite an excitement.

My mother, learning that Mr. Doniphan had returned home, went to him, and prevailed on him to come and speak to me at the dungeon grate. While he was talking to me, a little boy, the son of a poor widow, about five or six years old, who had previously been to see me, finding I had no fire, had run home and brought some fire and chips to the grate. Mr. Doniphan said—"You little devil you, what are you doing here with this fire?" He replied, "I am going to give it to Mr. Rockwell, so that he can warm him." Doniphan then said—"You little devil you, take this fire and leave;" when the little urchin replied (looking him in the face)—"Mr. Doniphan, you go to hell: I am going to give Mr. Rockwell this fire, so that he can warm him;" and he pushed it through the grate, gave me the chips, and continued to supply my daily wants of chips and fire while I continued in the dungeon.

From Mr. Doniphan I learned that a special term of court was called, and my trial would come on in about fifteen days. The night following this visit, some men came to the grates of my dungeon, and asked if I wanted to get out. I told them, No, as I had been informed that day that I should have a trial in a fortnight. They replied—"Honor bright: if you wish to get out, we'll let you out in a few minutes." I replied that I would rather remain, as my trial would come on so soon. Next morning one of the men came, put some money in the cleft of a stick, and put it through the hole to me. He refused to tell his name; but I knew by his voice that he was one of the men who came to me in the night.

The trial came on according to my last notification. I was tried for breaking Independence jail; and although the law of Missouri reads that, in order to break jail, a man must break a lock, a door, or a wall, still Judge King ruled that it was breaking jail to walk out when the door is open; and under this ruling the jury brought in a verdict of "five minutes' imprisonment in the county jail;" but I was kept there four or five hours, during which time several attempts were made to get up some other charge against me.

About 8 p.m. on December 13th, General Doniphan took me out and told me I must take across the country on foot, and not walk on any traveled road, unless it was during the night, as they would be apt to follow and again take me, as they did not care on what grounds, so they could make me trouble.

I accordingly started, accompanied by my mother, and went to the house of a widow, where I obtained my first supper in freedom for more than nine months. We then traveled two miles and obtained $4.

I then took through the woods to the road, where I heard two men riding on horseback. I hid behind a shady tree, and overheard one of them say, "He has not been gone many minutes: we shall soon overtake him."

I went round the houses and traveled in the fields by the side of the road. The moon was in its first quarter, and I traveled during the night about twenty-five miles. I carried a little food with me, and next day traveled on the road, and walked past Crooked River to a Mr. Taylor's, with all the skin off my feet.

A neighbor offered to take me in for the night, if I would go back two miles. I did so, found his wife very cross with her husband, who said, "Stranger, you see my wife is very cross. I have got some whisky; let's drink: my wife will soon have something to eat." When supper was eaten, she became good tempered. I stayed in peace through the night. Next morning I ate breakfast with them, and gave them fifty cents, when the man brought out a horse, and sent a little boy with me fourteen miles, which was a very great relief to my weary feet.

The next night I stopped near where the Haun's Mill massacre took place.

The third day I walked till noon, and then hired a man to carry me the remainder of the day for seventy-five cents. Stayed at a house where I was well acquainted; but the people did not recognize me, and I did not make myself known. Paid fifty cents for supper, lodging, breakfast, and being sent twelve miles on horseback the next morning.

I then continued my journey about thirty miles, where I rested three days to recruit my feet. I was then carried twenty-five miles on horseback, and walked the same day twenty-five miles. The day following I walked forty miles, and then waited another day and engaged a man to carry me to Montrose, to which place I was three days in going. I immediately crossed the river to Nauvoo in a small boat, and came straight to the Mansion.

Daniel Avery was liberated from his imprisonment in
Release of Missouri by *habeas corpus*. This was, no
Daniel Avery. doubt, on account of our vigilance in communicating with the Governor, and endeavoring to prosecute the kidnappers, and continually making public the conduct of Missouri.

Warm day; rain in the evening.

A PLAN FOR WOMEN'S SUBSCRIPTIONS TO THE TEMPLE.
(From the Millenial Star.)

We have much pleasure in publishing and recommending the following plan to be adopted amongst the sisters of the Church of Jesus Christ of Latter-day Saints in England. We believe that the completion of the Temple is as near the hearts of the sisters as to the hearts of the brethren, and that the following proposed [plan] will be responded to on the part of the English sisters in a manner that shall reflect honor upon themselves, and be materially instrumental in forwarding the great work.

NAUVOO, Dec. 25, 1843.

To the Sisters of the Church of Jesus Christ in England, Greeting:—

DEAR SISTERS:—This is to inform you that we have here entered into a small weekly subscription for the benefit of the Temple funds. One thousand have already joined it, while many more are expected, by which we trust to help forward the great work very much. The amount is only one cent or a halfpenny per week.

As Brother Amos Fielding is waiting for this, I cannot enlarge more than to say that myself and Sister Thompson are engaged in collecting the same.

　　　　　We remain,

　　　　　　　　　Your affectionate sisters in Christ,

　　　　　　　　　　　MARY SMITH,

　　　　　　　　　　　M. R. THOMPSON.

NAUVOO, Dec. 25, 1843.

The ladies' subscription for the Temple, of one cent per week, is fully sanctioned by the First Presidency.

　　　　　　　　　　　HYRUM SMITH.

We feel much to encourage this plan, and trust that the sisters in England will manifest that they will not be behind the sisters in Nauvoo in this laudable work. One thing in connection with this work we would mention, and request that it be attended to with the strictest accuracy; that is, that the name of each individual be recorded, and the amount which they subscribe, in order that such names may be transmitted to Nauvoo, where they will have to be entered in the books of the Lord's House. The sisters or others who may collect the subscriptions will please to be very particular on this point.

Tuesday, 26.—At home. I rejoiced that Rockwell had returned from the clutches of Missouri, and that God had delivered him out of their hands. Brother Daniel Avery also arrived about dusk this evening; and the Missourians have no longer the pleasure of exulting over any Mormon victims for the present; but their blood-thirstiness will not long be satisfied unless they seek out another victim on whom to glut their malice and vengeance.

Prophet's Joy at the Return of Rockwell and Avery.

Wednesday, 27.—Cold: a little ice in the river, which has been clear for some time past.

I received letters from General Lewis Cass, of Michigan, and Hon. John C. Calhoun, of South Carolina, in answer to mine of Nov. 4.

Mr. Keith gave a lecture and concert of music in the assembly room this evening.

MR. ROCKWELL.

(*Editorial From the Neighbor.*)

The name of this individual is, no doubt, familiar to most of our readers. He has obtained some celebrity in the world also, not for his reputed virtue, but for his supposed crimes.

It will be recollected that he is the person who was basely and falsely implicated, along with Joseph Smith, as the reputed [would be] murderer of ex-Governor Boggs, while Mr. Smith was charged with being accessory before the fact. A vexatious lawsuit was instituted against Joseph Smith, wherein he was charged with the above-named crime; and finally, after many attempts of the governor of Missouri to get him into his power, was acquitted by the United States Court for the district of Illinois,

Stories of murder and blood were circulated from Maine to Missouri; they were iterated and reiterated by the newspapers of the whole Union, and painted in the most glowing colors that human ingenuity could invent. Mr. Rockwell was branded as a murderer, and Joseph Smith as accessory before the fact, without any other evidence than a story fabricated by some of our generous politicians, engendered in falsehood by hearts as dark as Erebus for religious and political effect.

This demagoguery and political corruption has caused an innocent man to be immolated in a Missouri dungeon for upwards of eight months, without the slightest evidence of his guilt, or even the most remote evidence of crime leading to his committal. He was taken without process, and committed to jail upon mere supposition, and finally acquitted without any shadow of proof having been adduced from beginning to end. This is the way that Missouri treats free-born American citizens, and they can obtain no redress.

Mr. Rockwell arrived here on Monday night, and has given us some of the details of his history since he was first taken in Missouri to the present time; and we can assure our readers that it will "a tale unfold" relative to that state, which even many of those who have been driven therefrom will find it difficult to believe that there did exist such monsters in human shape.

Thursday, 28.—At home. Elder Orson Hyde returned

frcm Adams county, having obtained quite a number of signatures to the Memorial to Congress, and made an affidavit of what he learned in Warsaw concerning the mob.

Affidavit of Orson Hyde—Disclosing Plan To Drive the Saints.

STATE OF ILLINOIS, ⎫ ss.
CITY OF NAUVOO.   ⎭

On the 28th day of December, 1843, came Orson Hyde before me, Joseph Smith, mayor of said city; and after being duly sworn, deposeth and saith that on the 26th instant, as he was passing from Lima to Nauvoo, through that part of Hancock county where Colonel Levi Williams resides, he was credibly informed that on Saturday previous the anti-Mormons held a meeting, drew up an article, and passed several resolutions, among which were these:—"We will revere and hold sacred and inviolate the Constitution of the United States, and also the Constitution of this State. We will visit the Mormons residing in our vicinity and require them to give up their guns; and such as do it shall dwell here in peace; but those who will not do it may have thirteen days to leave in; and if they are not off in that time, we will drive them." The above is the substance, but perhaps not the very words. They also swear that the Mormons shall never raise another crop in that region, &c.; &c., and further this deponent saith not.

ORSON HYDE.

Subscribed and sworn to before me this 28th of December, 1843,

W. W. PHELPS, Clerk, M. C.

Daniel Avery having made affidavit of the cruel treatment he had recently received at the hands of Missourians, I here insert it:—

Affidavit of Daniel Avery—His Treatment in Missouri.

STATE OF ILLINOIS, ⎫ ss.
CITY OF NAUVOO.   ⎭

On the 28th day of December, 1843, came Daniel Avery before me, Joseph Smith, mayor of the city aforesaid, and after being duly sworn, deposeth and saith that on the second day of December, 1843, he was unlawfully arrested by force and arms, and kidnapped at Doty's Mill in Bear Creek precinct, Hancock county, and State aforesaid, by Colonel Levi Williams, his son John Williams, of Hancock county; John Elliott, a schoolmaster, from four-and-a-half miles below Warsaw; William Middleton and Joseph McCoy, of Clark county, Missouri, and four others. Colonel Williams held his bowie-knife to his breast. Six of the others stood with their pistols cocked and their fingers upon the triggers, muzzles presented at his body, ready to fire; and two stood with clubs, and amidst the most horrid oaths and imprecations, took and bound with silk handkerchiefs your said affiant, and led him away between two men, one holding a savage bowie-knife on one side, and the other a cocked pistol on the other side, (having taken away your said affiant's weapons while binding him in the mill,) and led your affiant about a mile. Your affiant refused to walk any further, and they put him upon a horse, and tied his legs under the horse; and John Elliott, the aforesaid schoolmaster, led the horse as fast as he could make his way, through a thicket and by-way to the house of the aforesaid Colonel Williams. Here the kidnappers ate and drank; and after they had unbound me, (for they had bound me so tight that I was in great pain,) I was also suffered to partake.

They then put me upon the horse again, and bound me, and started for the river, the said schoolmaster Elliott leading the horse. When we came near a schoolhouse where there was a meeting, they came to a halt, sent messengers to the meeting, and in the course of half an hour they returned with an armed mob, with rifles and other weapons, sufficient to make the whole company number about twenty. Being all on horseback, they formed a circle, with your affiant in the center, (who up to that time had acquainted every man he saw that *they were kidnapping him*, and marched in that order to a house on a point below Warsaw; and as I was very cold from being bound, they took me into the house to warm. I now called for a trial, as I had told them all the way that I never resisted legal authority. They said they were hunting a magistrate. Said I, "I understand you; you mean to force me into Missouri." McCoy returned, and said, "We are ready." It was about midnight. We went about three hundred yards up the river to a skiff. I refused to cross as they had promised me a trial. They forced me into a skiff and bound me, and five men put me across. Their names, so far as I could ascertain, are William Middleton, William Clark, Joseph McCoy, John Elliott, and Charles Coolidge. They landed at the tavern on the south side of the Des Moines, and took me into a back room, threw down a buffalo robe for my bed; but as my arms were bound so tight that I could not rest, I complained; told Middleton that was not the way he was used at my house. They felt at my arms and exclaimed, "By God, they are not too tight!" I begged to have one arm liberated, and finally they untied both, and I slept (under guard) on the buffalo robe before the fire.

About noon they got ready and started with me, guarded upon a horse, for McCoy's in Clark county, Missouri, about twelve miles distant. It being night when we arrived, and I unwell through fatigue and confinement and the abuses before received, I went to bed. They had sent runners ahead; and after I had been in bed awhile, the sheriff came up from Waterloo, the county seat, a distance of about two miles, to arrest me and take me before a magistrate that night; but Middleton and McCoy objected, as I was sick. The sheriff, however, executed his writ, and left me in their care till morning. It being late before we breakfasted, he came in the morning and made the second scope of his authority and took me. He quizzed me the night before, to draw something out for testimony; but as innocence cannot be affected by truth, he was as wise at one end of the story as the other.

At Waterloo I was examined by a magistrate, who committed me upon the substance of an affidavit made by my son in duress with a bowie-knife at his breast, and upon a promise that he should be liberated from Monticello jail, where he was confined after being kidnapped some three or four weeks previous. My bonds were fixed at $1000; and as I had no bail in such a strange place, I was started for Palmyra jail, in Marion county. The deputy sheriff took me to Musgrove, the sheriff, a distance of ten miles. Here I sued out a writ of habeas corpus, but the judge remanded me to prison.

At Monticello my chains were taken off, and I was at liberty in the midst of a strong guard to view the town. Here a lawyer agreed to take me and my son through court (as the Missourians say,) for a horse. Saw my son in the prison; said he was forced at the point of a bowie-knife to make an affidavit against me; but he knew I was innocent.

I tried to be left with him in jail; but no, I was compelled to go to Palmyra, where I arrived the next evening. The sheriff thrust me into the dungeon without waiting to eat, warm, or anything else. The next morning the blacksmith came into the jail and ironed me to the middle of a great chain that was fast to the floor, where I remained in the horrid gloom of a Missouri prison two weeks.

From thence the deputy sheriff started, with me chained upon the horse in this wise. He then chained my right leg, and then passed the chain up to my left hand. In this way I traveled nine miles, when we stopped, and he changed the chain from my hand to the horse's neck. We arrived at Monticello, and I was chained all night.

The next day I was conveyed to Waterloo, and delivered into the custody of the sheriff of Clark county. I was kept under a strong guard by day, and at night chained to one of the guards or to the bed-post.

I was informed that Middleton and McCoy procured an indictment against me, by giving bonds to the amount of some two or three hundred dollars, that they would hunt up testimony to the point for next court, there being nothing against me but the affidavit of my son before alluded to; and so the grand jury found a bill.

Ellison, my lawyer, deceived me, and put over my case for six months, because, as I suppose, I, being kidnapped, had no fees for him. I objected to having my trial put off for six months. I did not fancy the dungeon of Palmyra prison. The court concluded to let me to bail under bonds of $1000, but this I could not obtain. Subsequently it was reduced to $500, but all in vain, for I was unaquainted with the people.

This was on Saturday, and I was thus left to meditate on the mischief that may be made out of a little matter by meddlesome men.

On Monday I sued out a writ of habeas corpus; and after a fair hearing of the matter, I received the following order:—

STATE OF MISSOURI, } ss.
COUNTY OF CLARK. }

December, 25, 1843.

Ordered by the Clark County Court that Samuel Musgrove, sheriff of Clark county, discharge Daniel Avery from imprisonment, on an indictment found against him for the alleged crime of stealing a mare of Joseph McCoy.

By order of Court.

[L.S.]   Witness—Willis Curd, Clerk of said court, and seal of office this 25th of December, 1843.

Done at office in Waterloo, date above.

WILLIS CURD, Clerk.

HONS. JOHN W. DEWELLIN, } Judges.
    HENRY SNIVELY, }

Very early on Tuesday morning your affiant started for Nauvoo and arrived the same evening about sundown, a distance of nearly twenty miles so crippled from the iron bondage and hard usage of Missouri, that he is hardly able to walk. To those who assisted your said affiant to obtain his release from bondage, he tenders his grateful acknowledgements; and further your affiant saith not.

Subscribed and sworn to before me, this 28th day of December, 1843.

DANIEL AVERY.

W. W. PHELPS, Clerk, M. C.

Friday, 29.—At home. In the forenoon, W. W. Phelps called and gave us a lesson on eloquence, and read my Appeal to the Green Mountain Boys, and also a New Year's hymn without rhyme. Three p. m., I related to Dr. Bernhisel and Joseph H. Jackson* my commencement in receiving revelations. Mr. Jackson said he was almost persuaded to be one with me. I replied, I would that he were not only almost, but altogether.

Joseph H. Jackson—Prophet's Interview with.

At four p. m., I met with the city council.

Having selected forty men to act as city policemen, they met with the Council, and were sworn into office to support the Constitution of the United States and the State of Illinois, and obey the ordinances of this city and the instructions of the Mayor, according to the best of their ability.

Police Force of Nauvoo Increased.

Names of police called by Captain Jonathan Dunham:

Jonathan Dunham, High Policeman,	Charles C. Rich, 1st Lieutenant,
Hosea Stout, 2nd Lieutenant,	Shadrack, Roundy, 3rd Lieut.,
John Pack, Ensign,	Jesse P. Harmon, Orderly Sergt.
John D. Lee, 2nd Sergeant,	Daniel Carn, 3rd Sergeant,
Josiah Arnold, 4th Sergeant,	James Emmett, 1st Corporal,
Alexander Mills, 2nd Corporal,	Steven H. Goddard, 3rd Corporal
William Pace, 4th Corporal,	Abraham C. Hodge, Pioneer,
Levi W. Hancock, Fifer,	Daniel M. Repsher, Fifer.
Richard D. Sprague, Drummer,	Samuel Billings, Drummer,

*This man afterwards was discovered to be an adventurer and a most desperate character. Gregg in his Prophet of Palmyra, chapter XXX, speaks of him as "an adventurer of fine appearance and gentlemanly manners, who appeared in the county (Hancock) during the troubles; went to Nauvoo, and became intimate with Smith and the leaders; afterwards turned against them—went to Warsaw and issued a pamphlet—claiming to be an expose of Mormonism and the evil purposes and practices of the Prophet * * * He was an entire stranger to the county and its people; no one knew whence he came or what became of him afterwards, when the excitement was all over. Hence it is just to say, that the equivocal position in which he stood very justly tended to lessen confidence of the public in his statements, and his little book made slight impression. The Mormons charged that he was an adventurer of the worst class—himself a counterfeiter, etc., and that he quarreled with the Prophet and the authorities because he was detected and exposed." Gregg also says that this "Expose was much of the same character as that of General Bennett's." (Ibid.)

Abraham O. Smoot,
John Lytle,
Andrew Lytle.
Howard Egan,
Benjamin Boyce,
Lorenzo Clark,
Davies McOlney,
Abram Palmer,
Isaac C. Haight,
John L. Butler,
Elbridge Tufts,
Truman R. Barlow,

Dwight Harding,
Simeon A. Dunn,
Appleton M. Harmon,
James Pace,
Francis M. Edwards.
William H. Edwards,
Moses M. Sanders,
Warren A. Smith,
George W. Clyde,
Vernon H. Bruce,
Armsted Moffet,
Azra Adams.

The Mayor said—

Address of the Mayor to the Nauvoo Police.

It is expected that a part will be on duty while others rest. It might be expected that thieves had crept into the Church for the purpose of concealing their wickedness under the garb of sanctity.

It is an abominable thing to set a thief to catch a thief; and I would look with the utmost contempt upon men who do this as guilty of a mean or cowardly act.

Some city councils have taken thieves out of their prisons, and employed them as policemen, under the old and foolish adage—"Set a rogue to catch a rogue," which is decidedly wrong, and is corrupt in policy.

You will act under the direction of Jonathan Dunham—we will call him High Policeman. In reality he is the captain of the police: but as men are apt to be frightened at a military title, we will use a civil title, as these policemen are all civil officers of the city.

Captain Dunham is the man to send after a thief. He will not come back, after following him a mile, to ask if he may shoot him, if he resists. Some men have strange ears and changeable hearts: they become transformed from their original purity and integrity, and become altogether different from what they were.

If the bloodthirsty hell-hounds of Missouri continue their persecution, we will be forbearing, until we are compelled to strike; then do it decently and in good order, and break the yoke effectually, so that it cannot be mended. The mob have been so repulsed in their last attempt at kidnapping, they may stand in fear, at least for a short time.

We will be in peace with all men, so long as they will mind their own business and let us alone. Even "Peace with Missouri" shall be the motto of the Church of Jesus Christ of Latter-day Saints, from this time forth, if they will stop their persecution and oppressive warfare against us. Let them alone, for they stink in the nostrils of the Almighty: let them alone. Porter Rockwell has come home clear. A Missouri grand jury could not find a bill against him even in Jackson county; and that proves me clear of the charge of being accessory of shooting Lilburn W. Boggs. Many of our difficulties from the State of Missouri are hurled upon us through the influence of some of our near neighbors.

Governor Ford has boasted of being a law-abiding man. A governor certainly should be law-abiding. It is therefore our best policy to acquaint the Executive, by affidavits, of every violation of our rights, so that when the onset comes, he will be obliged by law to send the militia to our support. Let us keep cool as a cucumber on a frosty morning. Do not be excited. Say nothing about Missouri's oppresion. "A soft answer turns away wrath but grievous words stir up anger," therefore we "poor pussy" this generation.

Keep a strict account of the time you serve as policemen. Have the ordinances of the city always in your possession, and study them, and ferret out all grogshops, gambling-houses, brothels, and disorderly conduct; and if a transgressor resists, cuff his ears. If anyone lifts a weapon or presents a pistol at you, take his life, if need be, to preserve your own; but enforce the ordinances, and preserve the peace of the city, and take care of your own lives. Let no horses be taken away out of the city, or anything else stolen, if you can help it.

Let Missouri alone. Keep out of her territory. Don't go over there on any business whatever. Any of this people would be subject to cruel abuse, if found in that State, in the same manner that Porter Rockwell has been. He was seized in St. Louis while attending to his lawful business, picked up and ironed, and thrown in jail without any form of law, conveyed to Independence in the custody of a ruffian who swore falsely in the hope of getting a reward, kept in irons all the way, lodged in Independence jail without even the form of an inquiry, chained double in a filthy, damp. unventilated dungeon,—chained hand and foot, so that he could not straighten for months, till his body was reduced to a mere skeleton, and he unable to walk when the irons were taken off, and he had to be led,—half fed on the refuse of what dogs would not eat: his case presented to a Jackson county grand jury, and not evidence enough to warrant them in even finding an indictment. After which, the Missouri court, in the plenitude of their justice, transmitted the innocent and unindicted man back to the dungeon, without fire, provisions, or any other comfort,—hoping by this torture, no doubt, to produce death, or force him to accede to an infamous proposition, "that whether Jo Smith was guilty or innocent, only come out against him, you shall have your liberty, and receive a liberal reward." After months have passed away, without any shadow of law, the door is opened, and he is told to "slip off privately, or the people will hang you." Keep out of Missouri, if you don't want such treatment as this; for the Averys, Rockwell, and many others have been thankful to get away with their lives.

If any man attempts to bribe you in any way whatever, or persuade you to neglect your duty, tell the same to me. Let us have a reformation.

There are speculators in this State who are wanting to sell revolving pistols to us, in order to fight the Missourians, and at the same time inciting the Missourians to fight us. Don't buy: it would be better to buy ploughshares and raise corn with them.

My life is more in danger from some little dough-head of a fool in this city than from all my numerous and inveterate enemies abroad. I am exposed to far greater danger from traitors among ourselves than from enemies without, although my life has been sought for many years by the civil and military authorities, priests, and people of Missouri; and if I can escape from the ungrateful treachery of assassins, I can live as Cæsar might have lived, were it not for a right-hand Brutus. I have had pretended friends betray me. All the enemies upon the face of the earth may roar and exert all their power to bring about my death, but they can accomplish nothing, unless some who are among us and enjoy our society, have been with us in our councils, participated in our confidence, taken us by the hand, called us brother, saluted us with a kiss, join with our enemies, turn our virtues into faults, and, by falsehood and deceit, stir up their wrath and indignation against us, and bring their united vengeance upon our heads. All the hue-and-cry of the chief priests and elders against the Savior, could not bring down the wrath of the Jewish nation upon His head, and thereby cause the crucifixion of the Son of God, until Judas said unto them, "Whomsoever I shall kiss, he is the man; hold him fast." Judas was one of the Twelve Apostles, even their treasurer, and dipt with their Master in the dish, and through his treachery, the crucifixion was brought about; and *we have a Judas in our midst.*

The Mayor blesses the Police.

It shall be said in time to come, Where are our old policemen? Let us have one of the old policemen, to stand at our window, guard our interest, and protect our families, and we shall be safe.

If you will magnify your office, the full confidence of Israel shall be the blessing that shall be conferred on you in time to come.

Counselor Hyrum Smith spoke of the importance of the police office.

The Mayor said that if any one offered a bribe to a policeman, the city will pay that policeman twice the amount effered for the information, when reported to the Mayor.

Friday, 29.—My clerk made copies of five affidavits made yesterday by Elder Orson Hyde, Mr. Daniel Avery, and others, and sent the same to the Governor, with the following letter:—

Letter to Governor Ford—Accompanying Affidavits.

NAUVOO, December 30, 1843.

SIR:—I forward to your Excellency a number of affidavits relative to the late kidnapping of the Averys, and upon other matters. When the mob made efforts to resist the laws, Joseph Smith, as Mayor, gave notice to Major-General Law to hold a portion of the Nauvoo Legion in readiness; and Aaron Johnson, Esq., called for some troops to maintain the laws: but I am happy to say, none were ordered to march, as it was deemed most advisable to let Colonel Levi Williams and his mob flourish until indictments could be made at the Circuit Court of Hancock county.

We shall continue to keep your Excellency informed upon all matters of moment touching the premises.

Saturday, 30.—At nine, a.m., held Mayor's court. Two boys, Roswell and Evander White, were brought up for stealing six hens and a rooster. They were sentenced to pay for the fowls, and to ten days' hard labor each on the streets.

In the afternoon, met in the assembly room with the quorum. William Law and wife were not present. Warm and rainy.

Sunday, 31st.—At home.

In the afternoon, called with Elder Parley P. Pratt to see his wife.

At early candle-light, went to prayer-meeting; administered the sacrament; after which I retired. At midnight, about fifty musicians and singers sang Phelps' New Year's Hymn under my window.

Warm and rainy.   No ice to be seen.

The subjoined list shows a few of the publications for and against the Saints during the year.

Pro et con Mormonism, publications for the year 1843.

The *Alton Telegraph* published several very severe articles against the Church.

Edward Brotherton published a scurrilous pamphlet at Manchester, England. entitled "Mormonism—its Rise and Progress, and the Prophet Joseph Smith."

The *Richmond Palladium* published an amusing and fovorable article on "Mormonism."

The *Boston Bee* published a series of articles favorable to the Saints, which had a beneficial effect in putting down prejudice and misrepresentation.

A favorable account of a visit to Nauvoo was published by Samuel A. Prior, Methodist minister.

The *Morning Star,* a Freewill Baptist paper, published a long and bitter article against the Latter-day Saints, entitled "Mormon Perversion."

A favorable article, entitled "Nauvoo and Mormonism," was published by a Traveler.

The *Quincy Whig* published several bitter articles against me.

The *Warsaw Message,* and subsequently the *Warsaw Signal*, published a continual tirade of abuse, misrepresentation, and lies against the Saints.

The *New Haven* (Con.) *Herald* published a favorable account of the "Mormons" in Nauvoo.

CHAPTER VII.

PRESIDENT SMITH'S CORRESPONDENCE WITH JOHN C. CAL-
HOUN—CARTWRIGHT DROWNING CASE, ENGLAND—CITY
GUARDS INCREASED—FEARS OF LAW AND MARKS—INVES-
TIGATION BY THE CITY COUNCIL—RESISTANCE OF OFFI-
CERS AT CARTHAGE—ANTI-MORMON OBJECTIONS TO CITY
ORDINANCES—THE PROPHET'S DIFFICULTIES WITH FRAN-
CIS M. HIGBEE—REGULATIONS FOR THE SALE OF SPIR-
ITUOUS LIQUORS.

Monday, January 1, 1844.—A cold, blustering rain-storm ushered in the new year.

At sunrise, Thomas Miller, James Leach, James Bridges, and John Frodsham were brought before me by the police, charged with disorderly conduct. Fined Miller $5: the others were discharged.

A large party took a new year's supper at my house, and had music and dancing till morning. I was in my private room with my family, Elder John Taylor and other friends. New Year's at the Mansion.

Tuesday 2.—Two p. m., Hyrum Dayton was brought before Mayor's court for disorderly conduct in resisting and abusing the police: fined $25 and costs. His son, Lysander Dayton, for the same offense, was sentenced to ten days' hard labor, on the public streets; and subsequently, for contempt of court, ten days more.

Snow one inch deep.

I here insert Mr. Calhoun's answer to my letter of inquiry, dated November 4, 1843:—

Letter: John C. Calhoun to Joseph Smith—Defining What Former's Policy would be Towards the Saints if Elected President.

FORT HILL, December 2, 1843.

Sir:—You ask me what would be my rule of action relative the Mormons or Latter-day Saints, should I be elected President; to which I answer, that if I should be elected, I would strive to administer the government according to the Constitution and the laws of the union; and that as they make no distinction between citizens of different religious creeds I should make none. As far as it depends on the Executive department, all should have the full benefit of both, and none should be exempt from their operation

But as you refer to the case of Missouri, candor compels me to repeat what I said to you at Washington, that, according to my views, the case does not come within the jurisdiction of the Federal Government, which is one of limited and specific powers.

With respect, I am, &c,, &c.,
J. C. CALHOUN.

MR. JOSEPH SMITH.

To which I wrote the following reply:—

Letter: Joseph Smith to John C. Calhoun—The Latter's Policy Towards the Latter-day Saints, if Elected President of the U. S. Considered.

NAUVOO, ILLINOIS, January 2, 1844.

Sir:—Your reply to my letter of last November, concerning your rule of action towards the Latter-day Saints, if elected President, is at hand; and that you and your friends of the same opinion relative to the matter in question may not be disappointed as to me or my mind upon so grave a subject, permit me, as a law-abiding man, as a well-wisher to the perpetuity of constitutional rights and liberty, and as a friend to the free worship of Almighty God by all, according to the dictates of every person's own conscience, to say that *I am surprised* that a man or men in the highest stations of public life should have made up such a fragile "view" of a case, than which there is not one on the face of the globe fraught with so much consequence to the happiness of men in this world or the world to come.

To be sure, the first paragraph of your letter appears very complacent and fair on a white sheet of paper. And who, that is ambitious for greatness and power, would not have said the same thing? Your oath binds you to support the Constitution and laws; and as all creeds and religions are alike tolerated, they must, of course, all be justified or condemned according to merit or demerit. But why—tell me why are all the principal men held up for public stations *so cautiously careful* not to publish to the world that they will *judge a righteous judgment, law or no law?* for laws and opinions, like the vanes of steeples, change with the wind.

One Congress passes a law, another repeals it; and one statesman says that the Constitution means this, and another that; and who does not know that all may be wrong? the opinion and pledge, therefore, in the first paragraph of your reply to my question, like the forced steam from the engine of a steam-boat, makes the show of a bright cloud at first; but when it comes in contact with a purer atmosphere, dissolves to common air again.

Your second pargraph leaves you naked before yourself, like a likeness in a mirror, when you say, that according to your *view*, the Federal Government is "one of limited and specific powers," and has no jurisdiction in the case of the "Mormons." So then a State can at any time expel any portion of her citizens with impunity: and, in the language of Mr. Van Buren, frosted over with your gracious *"views of the case,"* though the cause is ever so just, Goverment can do nothing for them, because it has no power.

Go on, then, Missouri, after another set of inhabitants (as the Latter-day Saints did,) have entered some two or three hundred thousand dollars' worth of land, and made extensive improvements thereon; go on, then, I say; banish the occupants or owners, or kill them, as the mobbers did many of the Latter-day Saints, and take their land and property as spoil; and let the Legislature, as in the case of the "Mormons," appropriate a couple of hundred thousand dollars to pay the mob for doing that job; for the renowned Senator from South Carolina, Mr. J. C. Calhoun, says the powers of the Federal Government are so *specific and limited that it has no jurisdiction of the case!* O ye people who groan under the oppression of tyrants!—ye exiled Poles, who have felt the iron hand of Russian grasp!—ye poor and unfortunate among all nations! come to the asylum of the oppressed; buy ye lands of the General Government; pay in your money to the treasury to strenghten the army and the navy; worship God according to the dictates of your own consciences; pay in your taxes to support the great heads of a glorious nation: but remember a *"sovereign State"* is so much more powerful than the United States, the parent Government, that it can exile you at pleasure, mob you with impunity, confiscate your lands and property, have the Legislature sanction it,—yea, even murder you as an edict of an emperor, *and it does no wrong;* for the noble Senator of South Carolina says the power of the federal Government is *so limited and specific, that it has no jurisdiction of the case!* What think ye of *imperium in imperio?*

Ye spirits of the blessed of all ages, hark! Ye shades of departed statesmen, listen! Abraham, Moses, Homer, Socrates, Solon, Solomon, and all that ever thought of right and wrong, look down from your exaltations. if you have any; for it is said, "In the midst of counselors there *is safety;"* and when you have learned that fifteen thousand innocent citizens, after having purchased their lands of the United States and paid for them, were expelled from a "sovereign State," by order of the Governor, at the point of the bayonet, their arms taken from them by the same authority, and their right of migration into said State denied, under pain of imprisonment, whipping, robbing, mobbing, and even death, and no justice or recompense allowed; and, from the Legislature with the Governor at the head, down to the Justice of the Peace, with a bottle of whisky in one hand and a bowie-knife in the other, hear them all declare that there is no justice for a "Mormon" in that State; and judge ye a righteous judgment, and tell me when the virtue of the States was stolen, where the honor of the General Government lies hid, and what clothes a senator with wisdom. O nullifying Carolina! O little tempestuous Rhode Island! Would it not be well for the great men of the nation to read the fable of the *partial judge*; and when part of the free citizens of a State had been expelled contrary to the Constitution, mobbed, robbed, plundered, and many murdered, instead of searching into the course taken with Joanna Southcott, Ann Lee, the French Prophets, the Quakers of New England, and rebellious negroes in the slave States, to hear both sides and then judge, rather than have the mortification to say, "Oh, it is *my* bull that has killed *your* ox! That alters the case! I must inquire into it; *and if, and if—*!

If the General Government has no power to reinstate expelled citizens to their rights, there is a monstrous hypocrite fed and fostered from the hard earnings of the people! A real "bull beggar" upheld by sycophants. And although you may wink to the priests to stigmatize, wheedle the drunkards to swear, and raise the hue-and-cry of—"Impostor! false prophet! G— d—n old Joe Smith!" yet remember, if the Latter-day Saints are not restored to all their rights and paid for all their losses, according to the known rules of justice and judgment, reciprocation and common honesty among men, that God will come out of His hiding place, and vex this nation with a sore vexation: yea, the consuming wrath of an offended God shall smoke through the nation with as much distress and woe as independence has blazed through with pleasure and delight. Where is the strength of Government? Where is the patriotism of a Washington, a Warren, and Adams? And where is a spark from the watch-fire of '76, by which one candle might be lit that would glimmer upon the confines of Democracy? Well may it be said that one man is not a state, nor one state the nation.

In the days of General Jackson, when France refused the first instalment for spoliations, there was power, force, and honor enough to resent injustice and insult, and the money came: and shall Missouri, filled with negro-drivers and white men stealers, go "unwhipped of justice" for tenfold greater sins than France? No! verily, no! While

I have powers of body and mind—while water runs and grass grows—while virtue is lovely and vice hateful; and while a stone points out a sacred spot where a fragment of American liberty once was, I or my posterity will plead the cause of injured innocence, until Missouri makes atonement for all her sins, or sinks disgraced, degraded, and damned to hell, "where the worm dieth not, and the fire is not quenched."

Why, sir, the powers not delegated to the United States and the States belong to the people, and Congress sent to do the people's business have all power; and shall fifteen thousand citizens groan in exile? O vain men! will ye not, if ye do not restore them to their rights and $2,000,000 worth of property, relinquish to them, (the Latter-day Saints,) as a body, their portion of power that belongs to them according to the Constitution? Power has its convenience as well as inconvenience. "The world was not made for Cæsar alone, but for Cassius too."

I will give you a parable. A certain lord had a vineyard in a goodly land, which men labored in at their pleasure. A few meek men also went and purchased with money from some of these chief men that labored at pleasure a portion of land in the vineyard, at a very remote part of it, and began to improve it, and to eat and drink the fruit thereof,—when some vile persons, who regarded not man, neither feared the lord of the vineyard, rose up suddenly and robbed these meek men, and drove them from their possessions, killing many.

This barbarous act made no small stir among the men in the vineyard; and all that portion who were attached to that part of the vineyard where the men were robbed rose up in grand council, with their chief man, who had firstly ordered the deed to be done, and made a covenant not to pay for the cruel deed, but to keep the spoil, and never let those meek men set their feet on that soil again, neither recompense them for it.

Now, these meek men, in their distress, wisely sought redress of those wicked men in every possible manner, and got none. They then supplicated the chief men, who held the vineyard at pleasure, and who had the power to sell and defend it, for redress and redemption; and those men, loving the fame and favor of the multitude more than the glory of the lord of the vineyard, answered—"Your cause is just, but we can do nothing for you, because we have no power."

Now, when the lord of the vineyard saw that virtue and innocence were not regarded, and his vineyard occupied by wicked men, he sent men and took the possession of it to himself, and destroyed those unfaithful servants, and appointed them their portion among hypocrites.

And let me say that all men who say that Congress has no power to restore and defend the rights of her citizens have not the love of the truth abiding in them. Congress has power to protect the nation against foreign invasion and internal broil; and whenever that body passes an act to maintain right with any power, or to restore right to any portion of her citizens, it is the *supreme law of the land*; and should a State re fuse submission, that State is guilty of *insurrection or rebellion*, and the President has as much power to repel it as Washington had to march against the "whisky boys at Pittsburg," or General Jackson had to send an armed force to suppress the rebellion of South Carolina.

To close, I would admonish you, before you let your "*candor compel*" you again to write upon a subject great as the salvation of man, consequential as the life of the Savior, broad as the principles of eternal truth, and valuable as the jewels of eternity, to read in the 8th section and 1st article of the Costitution of the United States, the *first*, *fourteenth* and *seventeenth* "specific" and not very "limited powers" of the Federal Government, what can be done to protect the lives, property, and rights of a virtuous people, when the administrators of the law and law-makers are unbought by bribes, uncorrupted by patronage, untempted by gold, unawed by fear, and uncontaminated tangling alliances—even like Cæsar's wife, not only *unspotted*, *but unsuspected!* And God, who cooled the heat of a Nebuchadnezzar's furnace or shut the mouths of lions for the honor of a Daniel, will raise your mind above the narrow notion that the General Government has no power, to the sublime idea that Congress, with the President as Executor, is as almighty in its sphere as Jehovah is in his.

With great respect, I have the honour to be

Your obedient servant,

JOSEPH SMITH.

HON. ("MR") J. C. CALHOUN,
    Fort Hill, S. C.

Jonathan Pugmire, Senior, and Thomas Cartwright discharged by Judge Whitehead, at Chester, England. The judge would not allow the costs of prosecution or witnesses to be paid by the Crown. It was very evident that the Church of England ministers were at the bottom of the machinations, and were sorely discomfited at the result. I insert the statement of the unfortunate occurrence given by Jonathan Pugmire, Junior:—

Release of Pugmire and Cartwright from Prison, England.

Cartwright Drowning—Accident at a Baptism in England.

Thomas Cartwright was baptized November 6, 1843, unknown to his wife, by Elder Jonathan Pugmire, Senior; but she had mistrusted he had gone to the water, and went to Pugmire's house the same evening, and inquired where Tom was, (meaning her husband). Mrs. Pugmire answered she did not know.

After this, Mrs. Cartwright went out and met them returning from the waters of baptism, and shouted—"Damn you, I'll dip ye!" and expressing her determination to have revenge on Pugmire's family, she used a great deal of very bad language.

Some of the neighbors (not belonging to the Church) advised her not to speak too much against the Latter-day Saints, as she might yet become convinced of the truth of their doctrines and be baptized herself. She replied, "I hope to God, if ever I am such a fool, that I'll be drowned in the attempt!"

A short time afterwards, in consequence of her husband talking to her about the truths of the Gospel, she consented to go to Pugmire's house and hear for herself.

After attending a few times, she told her husband she had a dream, in which she saw it was a fearful thing to fall in the hands of the living God, and requested to be baptized.

Mrs. Pugmire talked with her, reminding her of her harsh expression. She confessed all, and said, "I am very sorry; and as my conduct is known to all this neighborhood, I do not wish to have my baptism public, but to have it done privately; and I wish no female to accompany me to the water but you."

On the night of her baptism (November 23, 1843), she was conducted to the water by her husband and Elder Pugmire, witnessed by Mrs. Pugmire and James Moore. Previous to this time, Elder Pugmire had baptized eight or ten persons in the same place.

On arriving at the water, they found the creek had overflowed its banks, in consequence of a heavy rain which had fallen that day. Elder Pugmire examined its banks, and concluded he could attend to the ordinance without going into the regular bed of the creek.

This was done; but on raising Mrs. Cartwright, and as they were walking out, they both went under the water.

It was afterwards discovered that the water had undermined the bank, and it gave way under their feet. Meantime, Thomas Cartwright leaped into the creek and seized hold of his wife's petticoat; but the water carried her off, and left the garment in his hand.

James Moore got hold of Elder Pugmire by the hair of his head, Mrs. Pugmire holding Moore's hand, and thus they dragged him out.

Moore then ran to the village to give the alarm. On his return, he found Cartwright about one hundred yards from where he leaped in, with his head above water, holding on to the stump of a tree. He said he could not have remained in that situation one minute longer.

George Knowlen swam the stream and got him out; but his wife was not found until the day following, when she was found about two hundred yards from where the accident occurred, standing upon her feet, with her head above water, the stream having fallen about two feet.

On Pugmire reaching home, a Church of England minister had him arrested and dragged from his family the same evening, and kept in custody of a constable until a coroner's inquest was held on the body of the deceased.

After she was buried, Cartwright was arrested, and both were sent to Chester jail, to wait their trial befor the judge of assize. They were in confinement six weeks and three days before their trial came on.

The judge (Whitehead) remarked to the jury that baptism was an ordinance of our religion, and that it was a mere accident which had occurred. He advised the jurymen to be very careful how they examined the case before them—that it was an ordinance instituted by God (at that moment the Lord spoke by the voice of thunder, which shook the court house,) and advised the prisoners to be very careful in the future to select a proper place for the performance of that rite. They were then set free.

During their imprisonment, Pugmire had a vision, in which he was informed that they would be liberated; and he told Cartwright to be of good cheer, for they certainly would be acquitted.

Wednesday 3.—At home.

At noon, met with the City Council. The following is a copy of the minutes:—

Difficulty of Wm. Law et al. With the Police.

SPECIAL CITY COUNCIL, Jan. 3, 1844, 12 o'clock.

Names of members called. All present.

The mayor directed the marshal to notify William Law and John Snyder that the council was in session, and informed the council that William Law had said to his brother Hyrum that the police had been sworn by him (the Prophet) secretly to put Law out of the way. [The Prophet said] "I have had no private conversation with any of the police but the high policeman, Jonathan Dunham, and that was to request him to have especial care of my personal safety, as I apprehended attempts to kidnap me by the Missourians." He called on the policemen to say if they had received any private oath from him, when they all said, "No."

Councilor Hyrum Smith said that William Law told him the police had sworn him (Law) to keep the secret, which was that he was to be put out of the way in three months.

The mayor said he wished policemen to understand forever that all he wanted was that they should execute the ordinances of the city and his orders according to law.

Several of the police called for the individual to be named who made the statement to William Law.

The mayor said he thought proper that William Law should come and make his statement to the council on oath.

The mayor then said to the police, "If you see a man stealing, and you have told him three times to stand, and warned him that he is a dead man if he does not stand, and he runs shoot off his legs. The design of the office of the police is to stop thieving; but an enemy should not be harmed until he draws weapons upon you."

William Law came in, and was sworn to tell the whole truth touching the case before the council.

William Law said he had been informed that some of the policemen had had another oath administered besides the one administered to them publicly: that one of them said there was a Judas in General Smith's cabinet,—one who stood next to him; and he must be taken care of, and that he must not be allowed to go into the world, but must be taken care of; and he was not only a dough-head and a traitor like Judas, but an assassin like Brutus: that the idea had been advanced that the scriptures support such a doctrine.

Alderman Harris.   Who is the person? and who told you?

Law.   l am under obligations *not* to tell.

Alderman Harris.   That is immaterial.   You are bound to disclose the whole truth here by virtue of your oath.

Law.   I am afraid to tell.   One oath is as good as another.

The Mayor said he would protect him.   He was bound to tell.

Law.   Eli Norton told me.

Alderman Harris.   Was Eli Norton of the police?

Law.   No; but he got his information from Daniel Carn, who is a policeman.

The marshal was sent to bring Eli Norton.

The mayor said to the police—"On conditions I have had no private conversation with any of you, rise up and change the breech of your gun upwards," when all arose and changed the positions of their guns as indicated.

Counselor Hyrum Smith considered the matter very alarming when he heard it.   He referred to Dr. Sampson Avard's and John Carl's treachery and false swearing in Missouri, and rehearsed what was said by the mayor to the police in the former council.

The mayor said, "The reason why I made the remarks I did was on account of the reports brought from Missouri jail by O. P. Rockwell, that my enemies were determined to get me into their power and take my life, and thereby thought they would accomplish the overthrow of 'Mormonism.' And to enable them to effect this, they had secured the services of some of my most confidential friends, whom I did not suspect, and who were living in Nauvoo, to deliver me into their hands so that their religious organizations upon their own principles might stand; for they feared that 'Mormonism' would destroy their present religious creeds, organizations, and orthodox systems. They did not design to try me, but hang me, or take my life anyhow: that they had a man in our midst who would fix me out, if they could not get me into their power without." He then referred to his remarks at the previous council.

Minutes of last council being called for, were then read.

Eli Norton sworn.

Question by the Mayor Did Carn say I had administered a private oath?

Norton. No. Did not say much about Law. Did not say you had ever administered any private oath. Carn never intimated to me that Law must be put out of the way. Did not call William Law's name, nor any other name. Did not say the policemen had received a private oath. Understood Carn to say they had received private instructions; and if a man could not keep a secret, he was not worthy of a place in the Church. Did not say the mayor had given him a private charge. Did not tell where the danger was expected to come from. Told me there were dough-heads about. Did not say the dough-heads were in danger, but the mayor was in danger from the dough-heads.

Question by William Law: Did you not understand from Brother Carn that he was suspicious of some person near Joseph being a dough-head, and that that person was myself?

Answer: He mentioned a dough-head as being very near Joseph, and he guessed you was the man; and I thought it might be that Daniteism was not done with.

Mayor: Tell what you know that made you so alarmed about Brother Law.

Answer: There was no chain to the conversation; but I drew the inference that Brother Law was the dough-head from Carn's conversation; but Carn did not name Law.

Daniel Carn was sworn: Said, "I told Brother Norton that certain men had been counseled by the Prophet to invest their means in publishing the new translation of the Bible; and they instead of obeying that counsel, had used their property for the purpose of building a steam-mill and raising a hundred acres of hemp; and the Lord had not blessed them in the business, but sunk their hemp in the Mississippi river. I told him it was my opinion that Brother Law was the dough-head referred to.

I have had no secret conversation whatever with the mayor, and never received any charge except the one, with the rest of the police, before the city council.

The mayor suggested the propriety, since Rockwell and others are clear, and we have the promise of protection from the governor; and as the police are now well organized, that they put up their guns and that the council pass such an order. The Danite system alluded to by Norton never had any existence. It was a term made use of by some of the brethren in Far West, and grew out of an expression I made use of when the brethren were preparing to defend themselves from the Missouri mob, in reference to the stealing of Macaiah's images (Judges chapter 18)—If the enemy comes, the Danites will be after them, meaning the brethren in self-defense.

The mayor instructed the police to lay up their arms till further orders.

At half past four p. m. council adjourned.

The council spent nearly the whole day in investigating the subject and examining these two witnesses. The police were all sworn and cross-examined by William Law and the aldermen, and the result showed nothing but imagination, having grown out of the surmises of Daniel Carn; upon which Law became satisfied, shook hands with me, declaring he did not believe a word of the story, and said he would stand by me to the death, and called the whole council and the police to witness his declaration. *Reconciliation of the Prophet and Wm. Law.*

Thursday 4.—At home.

I took dinner in the north room, and was remarking to Brother Phelps what a kind, provident wife I had,—that when I wanted a little bread and milk, she would load the table with so many good things, it would destroy my appetite. At this moment Emma came in, while Phelps, in continuation of the conversation said, "You must do as Bonaparte did—have a little table, just large enough for the victuals you want your- *Repartee of Joseph and Emma Smith* self.'' Mrs. Smith replied, ''Mr. Smith is a bigger man than Bonaparte: he can never eat without his friends.'' I remarked, ''That is the wisest thing I ever heard you say.''

Friday 5.—At home.

Last night I dreamed I saw two serpents swallowing each other tail foremost.

Another tempest in a tea-pot, or big fuss about nothing at all. In consequence of the night being severely cold, Alarm of William Marks. some persons built a fire on the bank of the river, nearly opposit William Marks' house. He then became afraid, and concluded he must either be the Brutus or the dough-head, and lay awake all night, thinking the police had built the fire to kill him by! In the morning he called on me, reported the circumstances and expressed his fears, when another session of inquiry was held by the city council at his request, and the police sworn and questioned. The following is a synopsis of the minutes:—

Special Session o the City Council—Fears of Wm. Law and Marks.

Friday, January 5, 1844, 11 a. m.

Names of members called.

Prayer by O. Spencer.

Minutes of the last two councils read and approved.

Object of the council stated by the mayor, similar to the last council as William Law and William Marks had considered themselves in danger. When he heard the report he was unwilling to believe anything about it, from the course the thing took in the last council; but, for the sake of others, he had called this council.

As Leonard Soby was going home night before last, he was hailed by a supposed policeman with a gun, which frightened him. Soby says that a policeman had told him that Marks and Law must not cross his tracks; that Warren Smith said at another time that William Marks and William Law were enemies to Joseph.

I have never thought even to dream of doing anything against the peace of the inhabitants of this city. Did not know I had any enemies in this city: have stayed at home and heard but little: did not know that there was so much evil surmising among the people. My long forbearance to my enemies ought to be sufficient testimony of my peaceful disposition toward all men. It occurred to my mind that it was not fear, but got up for effect; but I do not know it. I want the council to investigate this matter.

William Marks sworn. Testified that on Monday evening Brother Soby came up and said, "Are you aware of the danger you are in?" Marks replied, "No."

Soby: "Your life is threatened; a policeman stopped me in the dark last night as I was going home; I was alarmed. I supposed the threats were from that policeman, but I was mistaken. Another policeman, Warren Smith, said last Sunday that Joseph had enemies—that Law and myself were Joseph's enemies, and if they came in his way they might be popped over. A fire was kindled in the street near my house, and I thought I was watched. Francis Higbee told me, and a man in the east part of the town told me; and a man came from the other side of the river and told the story to that man, as he said. Yesterday morning, Hyrum Smith, Wilson Law, and William Law met in the street, and I told the story as before related.

Mayor. Did ever anybody tell you I directed you to be watched?

William Marks. No.

Marshal went for Francis M. Higbee and George W. Crouse.

Leonard Soby sworn. On Sunday, 31st December last, I met Warren Smith in Crouse's store; asked him if he knew who the Brutus was. Warren Smith said he believed William Law was one, and Marks another; they had better not come in his way. Did not say he would shoot them, or endanger their life in any way. Did not know whether there were any private instructions, or not. Believed Brother Marks was in danger. Did not think Marks in any danger from Joseph. Thought Warren Smith was under a wrong impression with regard to Marks. Warren Smith said, "He, Marks, had better not cross my path when I am on duty." I gathered the idea there was something wrong with Brother Warren Smith. Do not recollect any person present.

Mayor. Did Warren Smith or any other policeman give you to understand that I had authorized him to believe there was any difficulty between me and Brother Law or Marks?

Soby. No. He did not think Warren Smith would transcend his official duties towards Law or Marks. Felt at the time Marks and Law were in danger. Did not think they were in danger, if they did not rise up against the authorities.

Did not say he had any instruction. Said to Mr. Marks, "You have enemies." My impression was that somebody had been to Joseph to make a bad impression on his mind. Warren Smith did mention brother Marks' name, I think.

Thirty policemen, all who were present, sworn. Testified that General Smith had never given them any private instruction concerning the case before the council.

Warren Smith said Soby asked his opinion who was the Judas. I said, from rumor, I would suspect William Law. Does not believe he mentioned Marks' name. My opinion was founded on rumor. Brother Isaac Hill said Brother Law was in a bad situation—was kicking, and if he did not mind, he would go over the board. If he had his property in available means and was away, he would feel better. Have heard it talked of that Brother Law was not going to stand. Hil did not tell what he was kicking at. I understand a Brutus to mean a treacherous man.

George W. Crouse sworn. Does not recollect any conversation between Warren Smith and Leonard Soby, at his store, relative to the case in question. Had a discussion about the duties of policemen.

Councilor John Taylor said it was customary in all cities for policemen to go armed in time of danger.

Councilor Orson Hyde confirmed Councilor Taylor's observation.

Councilor Hyrum Smith spoke. Told a story of the old Dutchman and the ox. Soby makes me think of an old Dutchman that had an ox—the first animal he ever owned in his life, and he broke him to ride; then he filled a sack with rocks and laid it on the ox's back, and got on himself, and told his son to hide by the roadside, and when he came along, to jump out and hollo boo, as he wanted to know how well his ox was broke. The son did accordingly. The ox was frightened, and threw the old man off. "Father," said the son, "I did as you told me." "Yes," said the old man; "but you made too big a boo."

Francis M. Higbee sworn. Have received the impression from rumor that Mr. Law, Mr. Marks and probably one or two others, could not subscribe to all things in the Church, and there were some private matters that might make trouble. Don't know of anyone being in danger. No one told me the police had received any private instruction. Could not tell who he had received these rumors from.

William Law spoke. Said he had no personal feeling against Warren Smith. Some two or three years since, he sued Brother Warren, and stayed the suit, &c. Was suspicious Warren Smith's feelings might have risen from that source.

Councilor Hyrum Smith, Daniel Carn, Warren Smith, Leonard Soby, and William Marks addressed the council.

The mayor spoke. Said no one had come to him with tales about William Marks, to prejudice his mind against him. Was totally ignorant of it. I said to Brother Dunham,—If any man approach my house with arms, or attempted to disturb my house, I wanted the police to take care of that individual, whoever he might be. I repeat the instruction, and am perfectly astonished that Brother Law, Marks, or any other man should entertain such an idea [that they were in danger.] I live above suspicion on this subject from any source whatever. I never could bring my feelings to take revenge on my enemies. The City Council did not concoct the idea of having a police. The several wards petitioned for a police to protect them against invasion—wanted citizens to pass the streets at any time of night without molestation; but if the police see a man breaking in to my house or barn, or anybody's house or barn, tell him to stand, and inquire his business. I think it possible that some person has been practicing fraud on Brother Soby and the police and upon individuals, as the police, according to their instructions, had laid away their guns.

Don't guard Brother Marks' house any more. Men must not pervert the power entrusted to them like ex-Governor Boggs, whose executive oath required him to protect the Saints in Missouri, but perverted his power to enforce their extermination from the State.

Brother Soby does not know that it was a policeman who stopped him. Brother Marks does not know that the police kindled the fire before his house. Let the police have canes. Let the citizens pass and repass at all times of night.

Councilor Taylor spoke. Thought the conclusion drawn up by Brother Soby, that Joseph or somebody was going to get revenged by setting the guard to kill Marks, was the most contemptible that could be imagined; and if Brother Soby had had the respect for Brother Joseph he ought to have had, he could not have formed such a conclusion.

Mayor referred to Francis Higbee's testimony. Thought Francis Higbee had better stay at home and hold his tongue, lest rumor turn upon him and disclose some private matters which he would prefer kept hid. Did not believe there was any rumor of the kind afloat, or he could have told some of the names of his informants. Thought the young men of the city had better withdraw from his society, and let him stand on his own merits. I by no means consider him the standard of the city.

There has been a system of corruption and debauchery, which these rumors have grown out of; and the individuals who are the authors of them are those who do not want a police: they want to prowl in the streets at pleasure without interruption.

Alderman Orson Spencer spoke, approving the conduct of the police. General Wilson Law said. "I am Joseph's friend: he has no better friend in the world: I am ready to lay down my life for him;" and upon that the mayor and General Wilson Law shook hands.

The ordinance concerning the forty policemen read twice.

The mayor objected to assuming the entire disposal of the police beyond the definition of the ordinance.

Alderman George A. Smith said he could sleep with a fire near his house, if there were some of the police warming themselves by it; and he believed any honest man could do the same.

The police received the thanks of the council.

The cross-examination and speeches are generally omitted.

Council adjourned at dusk for the want of candles.

Reflections of the Prophet as to Traitors in High Places

What can be the matter with these men? Is it that the wicked flee when no man pursueth, that hit pigeons always flutter, that drowning men catch at straws, or that Presidents Law and Marks are absolutely traitors to the Church, that my remarks should produce such an excitement in their minds. Can it be possible that the traitor whom Porter Rockwell reports to me as being in correspondence with my Missouri enemies, is one of my quorum? The people in the town were astonished, almost every man saying to his neighbor, "Is it possible that Brother Law or Brother Marks is a traitor, and would deliver Brother Joseph into the hands of his enemies in Missouri?" If not, what can be the meaning of all this? "The righteous are as bold as a lion."

A number of gentlemen boarding at my house conversed with me on national affairs. I sent for Brother Phelps, who came and read my letter to John C. Calhoun, with which they were highly edified.

Elder Brigham Young went to La Harpe for the purpose of instructing the Saints.

Commenced snowing a little before sunset, and continued all night.

Saturday, 6.—Snow about four inches deep. I rode out with Emma in a sleigh.

The Bishops and lesser Priesthood met at Henry W. Miller's hall.

Sunday, 7.—At home in the morning. In the afternoon, rode out to my farm, and preached in Brother Cornelius P. Lott's house.

The Twelve Apostles attended meetings and preached in different parts of the city.

At six p. m. attended prayer-meeting with the quorum in the assembly room. Law and Marks absent.

Monday, 8.—At home in the morning.

At eleven went to my office to investigate a difficulty between John D. Parker and his wife. After laboring with them about two hours, brought about a reconciliation.

I also had an interview with William Law in the streets.

My uncle, John Smith, from Macedonia, visited me.

Amos Fielding arrived from Liverpool.

Tuesday, 9.—At home.

I insert the following from the *Neighbor,* as a specimen of the respect which the Carthage mob has for law or justice:

DISGRACEFUL AFFAIR AT CARTHAGE—OFFICERS RESISTED.

On Tuesday last Horace S. Eldredge, one of our county officers, went to Carthage for the purpose of arresting Milton Cook, on the charge of bastardy, and bringing him before R. D. Foster, justice of the peace of this county, before whom affidavit had been made to that effect. He found the accused in Bartlett's grocery, (Carthage,) and arrested him.

Cook had a gun that he said he had loaded for the purpose, and would make a hole through the constable if he molested him, and swore he would not be taken.

Harmon T. Wilson and others then stepped forward to his assistance, and said that they had sworn to stand by him, and that he should not go. He [Eldredge] then returned with his process to the justice of the peace, and told him what had occurred.

Mr. R. D. Foster then summoned eleven men to go along with the constable and assist him in bringing the delinquent. They went out and drove to the grocery, where they expected to find him; but he was not there. They then went out for a short time, without making known their business, when they saw an armed force gathering.

They shortly afterwards returned to the grocery, and saw him there where he swore he would not be taken. There was also an armed force standing in the door, who also swore he should not be taken.

The officer having the process, Mr. Markham and Mr. Eagle stepped forward and wished to reason the case with them, the officer at the same time demanding their assistance. They were met with an armed force of about twenty, four of whom stood in the doorway, two with guns and bayonets, and two with pistols.

The two having the bayonets charged directly at Mr. Markham, and swore they would run him through, and rushed upon him with their bayonets. He, however, warded off their blows with his arm, and the bayonet glanced and struck Mr. John Eagle in the abdomen. The bayonet went through his clothes, scratched his body, and glanced off without doing any further injury, other than giving him a slight cut in the hand.

Those having the pistols then attempted to shoot, when Mr.Markham seized the hand of one of them that held the pistol, and prevented him from firing. The other put his pistol to Mr. Eagle's breast, and swore he would shoot him.

The company at that time used all their force, and crowded the officers and their assistants some distance back, and carried off and secreted the prisoner. The officer and his company then went to the tavern to stay all night.

The next morning, about eight o'clock, the constable and Mr. Markham went to the grocery and searched, and Bartlett said that he was gone—that he had taken his horse and gone out of town.

They then saw a company of men gathered at Harmon T. Wilson's store, armed with guns, bayonets, pistols, clubs, and other missiles. Mr. Markham went to the store, where he found the constable and the prisoner. There were fifty in and about the store, all armed.

Mr. Eldredge then told the company present who he was, and demanded all in the house to assist in taking the prisoner, and then seized him. As soon as he laid hold of the prisoner, about six or eight men laid hold of the constable. Mr. Markham assisted the constable. When Mr. Markham had nearly succeeded in liberating the constable, a man who was called Dr. Morrison, drew his pistol and shot at Markham. The ball missed Markham, but came so near Mr. Coltrin's head, who was one of the assistants, as to graze his forehead.

As there were only four of the assistants in the store, they were overpowered by superior numbers, and the prisoner was taken away from them.

They saw that it would be impossible to take him without bloodshed, and consequently returned home. The parties engaged in this affray swore that, regardless of all law, they would defend the prisoner, and he should not be taken.

We have received the above particulars from Mr. Markham, and can consequently rely upon the correctness of the statement, as he is one of the parties mentioned. The woman who was *enciente*, who made the affidavit, is not in the Church, neither is Mr. Eagle—the person who was struck with the bayonet. Mr. Eagle has gone to the governor to make complaint.

We think that it is high time that prompt measures be taken to put a stop to such abominable outrages. If officers can be insulted in this manner and the law violated with impunity, we think that we shall speedily slide back into the barbarous ages.

Some of our mobocratic friends who assembled at a mobocratic meeting some time ago in Carthage, were considerably chagrined at our terming them mobocrats. We wonder whether they now believe that they are, or not? If such proceedings as those are cherished, fare well to our Republican institutions! farewell to law, equity, and justice! and farewell to all those sacred ties that bind men to their fellowmen!

We would here ask where the sheriff was. Why was he not applied to? We merely ask for information. We don't know that he was present or applied to. If he was, it certainly was his duty to see the law magnified.

Wednesday 10.—At home.

Ordained Uncle John Smith a patriarch. Enjoyed myself well in an interview with the brethren, and concluded to take a ride part way with my uncle on his return to Macedonia.

John Smith, Uncle of the Prophet, Ordained a Patriarch.

In consequence of a visit from some gentlemen from Carthage, I called the City Council together at seven p. m. I copy the minutes:—

Special Session of City Council; Complaints of Carthage Citizens Considered.

January 10, 1844, 7. p. m.

Names of members called.

The mayor said:—"Messrs. Backman, Hamilton, and Sherman, lawyers from Carthage, have called on me and told me that the occasion of the excitement at Carthage and the resistance to the law, in the case of the arrest of Cook, was the late ordinance of this council to prevent unlawful search or seizure of person or property by foreign process in the city of Nauvoo; that they considered said ordinance was designed to hinder the execution of the statutes of Illinois within this city; consequently, they, the old citizens, felt disposed to stop the execution of processes issuing from the city precincts. They also raised objections against the process by Justice Foster for the apprehension of Cook. because it was made returnable to him alone, whereas they said the statute required it to be made returnable before himself or some other justice.

I explained to them the nature and reason of the ordinance—that was to prevent kidnapping under the pretense of law or process, and to facilitate the apprehension of thieves, &c., in this city, by throwing all foreign processes into the hands of the marshal, who would be most likely to know the hiding-places of fugitives from justice, who might secrete themselves in our city; and said that if any wrong impression had gone abroad with regard to the motives of the council in passing said ordinance, I would call the council immediately, that they might have the opportunity of giving any explanation necessary, so that the public might understand the ordinance in its true light. I have therefore called the council accordingly. I also referred the lawyers from Carthage to the statute which requires all processes issued in cases of bastardy to be returnable alone to the justice issuing the same, which they doubted until I showed them the law, when they looked a little crest-fallen and foolish."

After deliberation, an additional section relative to the foregoing ordinance was read three times, and passed, by way of amendment:—

"Secttion 3. Be it ordained by the city council of the city of Nauvoo, that nothing in the foreging ordinance shall be so construed as to prevent, hinder, or thwart the designs of justice, or to retard the civil officers of the state or county in the discharge of their official duties, but to aid and assist them within the limits of this city.

"Passed January 10, 1844.

"JOSEPH SMITH, Mayor.
"WILLARD RICHARDS, Recorder."
Council adjourned.

Wrote a letter to Esquire Backman to inform him what the City Council had done.

I received a long equivocating letter from Francis M. Higbee, charging me with having slandered his character and demanding a public trial before the Church. It contains no denial of the charges which he accuses me of having spoken against him, but is full of bombast.

Complaints of F. M. Higbee against the Prophet.

Thursday 11.—At home.

Rode out, ten a. m., and returned at half-past one p. m.

This morning William Jones, who had stayed all night at Wilson's Tavern in Carthage, was arrested without process by Colonel Levi Williams and his company, who kept him in custody until noon without rations.

The Twelve Apostles gave an invitation to the Saints in Nauvoo to cut and draw for me seventy-five or one hundred cords of wood on the 15th and 16th instant.

Friday 12.—Thaw: snow nearly gone.

A conference was held in Brownstown, Main county, Michigan. Elder Mephibosheth Sirrine, president; and Gehiel Savage, clerk. Nine branches were Conference in represented, containing 6 elders, 9 priests, Michigan 7 teachers,1 deacon, 136 members,and 45 scattered members; one hundred members having removed from that state to Nauvoo since the conference in July last.

Saturday 13.—At home in the morning.

At ten o'clock, attended City Council, where a bill for an ordinance concerning the recording of deeds in this city was taken under consideration, and read twice. It elicited much discussion.

The ten policemen who were not present at the meeting of the City Council on the 5th instant were sworn in the matter of William Law and William Marks, and testified they had received no private instructions whatever from me.

A discussion took place on the subject of granting licenses for the sale of spirits.

I signed resolutions passed at a court martial held this morning.

Stephen M. Farnsworth was chosen president of the priests' quorum, and William Carmichael and William Box his counselors.

Sunday 14.—At home all day.

A prayer-meeting was held at the assembly room. I did not attend.

Warm and rainy towards evening.

The Twelve Apostles preached at private houses in various parts of the city.

A branch of the Church was organized in New Orleans, with 34 members. T. B. Jackaway, president, and E. L. Brown, clerk.

Monday 15.—At home. Wrote to Sister Maria L. Campbell, Elmira, N. Y.

At nine, a. m., teams began to arrive with wood, according to the appointment of the Twelve Apostles, there

A Wood Bee.

being about 200 of the brethren chopping in the woods, and from thirty to forty teams engaged in drawing the wood to my house. About 100 loads were drawn, and as many more chopped, and left to be drawn another day.

At ten, a. m., Dr. Richards called, and told me it was reported that Francis M. Higbee was going to put me un-

Threats of Francis M. Higbee.

der $10,000 bonds for speaking against him. At the same time, Constable Eldredge summoned me to attend a court as witness before Esquire Johnson; and I went accordingly, to give my testimony.

The Twelve Apostles wrote the following letter:—

L:*tter: The Twelve Apostles to the Saints at Morley Settlement— Material Help Asked for.*

NAUVOO, January 15, 1844.

To President Isaac Morley and the Saints at Morley Settlement, the Twelve send greeting:—

BELOVED BRETHREN—While the work of the Lord is great and sought out by all them that have pleasure therein, the Lord of the vineyard has laid special charges upon some of His servants to execute; and while we are striving by all means to raise funds to hasten the Temple the approaching spring, we are not unmindful of the "History of the Church," the "Great Proclamation to the Kings of the Earth," and the "Memorials to Congress," &c., all of which are now before the Church, though their progress is retarded for the want of the necessaries of life, in the families of those who are employed in this business.

Two or three clerks are necessarily employed, and that continually, by our Prophet, who cheerfully devote their time—not a *tenth*, but the *whole*, to roll on these desirable objects; but their hands are palsied and their pens stayed, more or less. Therefore, with the approbation of our President, we again call on you, as those who have ever been ready to listen to the wants of the Church, that you would raise such collections of provisions as you may have at your disposal, and forward the same *without delay* to us, for the special benefit of the clerks of President Smith or the Church. Asking no more, it is right they should not go hungry or naked.

Do you ask what is wanting? We answer, Look to your own households, and say what it requires to make them comfortable, and you will know just what is wanting by these men. *Eatables of every kind*, and even soap to keep their hands clean, is scarce at Nauvoo, and it takes many lights to keep the pen in motion these long evenings.

The President has plenty to do without supporting a number of clerks, whose business as deeply concerns every other individual in the Church as himself, although he has done it to a great extent and with great inconvenience; and we are confident that when you are made acquainted with the facts, you will be unwilling that *Joseph* should *do all, and get all the blessing*. And as you shall continue your liberality in temporal things, God shall pour out upon your heads blessings spiritual and temporal; and *now* is the time for *action*.

All is peace at Nauvoo, and the last report from the Carthagenians was, they were beginning to think it was time to throw down their arms and attempt a compromise. But the "Mormons" can truly say they have had no quarrel with them. It has all been between the citizens and the law, their own officers being the executors thereof; and we feel disposed to let them fight it out among themselves, while we live in peace and laugh at their folly.

With our prayers and blessings, we subscribe ourselves

Your brethren in Christ Jesus.

In behalf of the quorum,

B. YOUNG, President.

W. RICHARDS, Clerk.

The Municipal Court issued a warrant for the arrest of Francis M. Higbee, on affidavit of Orson Pratt.

East wind in forenoon, and some rain. Brisk wind from N.W. in afternoon.

Benjamin Andrews published in the *Times and Seasons*
"An Appeal to the people of the State of
Maine," setting forth the persecutions, murders, and robberies committed upon the Saints
by the people of the State of Missouri, and soliciting the
assistance of his native State in procuring redress.

Andrews'
Appeal to the
State of Maine

Tuesday, 16.—Cold and windy.

At ten, a.m., Francis M. Higbee was brought up before
the Municipal Court, on complaint of Orson
Pratt, for absenting himself from City Council
without leave, when summoned as a witness,
and for slanderous and abusive language towards one of the members of the Council.

Francis M.
Higbee on
Trial—Recon-
ciliation with
Prophet.

The court adjourned, and the City Council commenced
their session, continuing till two o'clock, during which
time a reconciliation took place with Francis M. Higbee,
who had written a slanderous letter concerning me, and
said many hard things, which he acknowledged; and I
forgave him. I went before the Council and stated that
all difficulties between me and F. M. Higbee were eternally buried, and I was to be his friend for ever. To which
F. M. Higbee replied, "I will be his friend for ever, and
his right-hand man."

A number of the brethren assembled and chopped up
the firewood which had been hauled to my house yesterday, and piled it up ready for use.

The following "Ordinance concerning the sale of Spirituous Liquors" was passed by the City Council:

An Ordinance concerning the Sale of Spirituous Liquors.

Whereas, the use and sale of distilled and fermented liquors for all
purposes of beverage and drink by persons in health are viewed by this
City Council with unqualified disapprobation:

Whereas, nevertheless the aforesaid liquors are considered highly
beneficial for medical and mechanical purposes, and may be safely
employed for such uses, under the counsel of discreet persons:
Therefore,

Sect. 1. Be it ordained by the City Council of the city of Nauvoo, that the Mayor of this city is hereby authorized to sell said liquors in such quantities as he may deem expedient.

Sect. 2. Be it further ordained, that other persons not exceeding one to each ward of the city, may also sell said liquors in like quantities for medical and mechanical purposes by obtaining a license of the Mayor of the city. The above ordinance to be in full force and effect immediately after its passage,—all ordinances to the contrary notwithstanding.

Passed January 16, 1844.

JOSEPH SMITH, Mayor.

W. RICHARDS, Recorder.

An ordinance was also passed, authorizing Henry G. Sherwood to make out a city directory, and to establish an intelligence office in the city. Also the following ordinance:—

An Ordinance concerning Witnesses and Jurors' Fees,

Be it ordained by the City Council of the city of Nauvoo, that hereafter all persons subpœnaed and attending upon courts of trial as witnesses, or as jurors in civil cases, shall not be compelled to testify or be held in attendance either as witness or juror, unless they shall first be tendered the sum of fifty cents per day for each witness and each juror subpœnaed.

Passed January 16, 1844.

JOSEPH SMITH, Mayor.

W. RICHARDS, Recorder.

Wednesday, 17.—At home settling accounts with various individuals. Gave deed of a lot to John Lytle.

The steamer *Shepherdess* sank near St. Louis, drowning forty passengers.

Thursday, 18.—At home, and wrote letters to Reuben McBride and Joseph Coe, Kirtland; Clark Leal, of Fountain Green; and to Justin J. Butterfield, Esq., Chicago.

This afternoon a man called on Brother Nelson Judd, and said he wanted to sell him some wood below Davidson Hibbard's. He went to see the wood, the man saying he would meet him at the place. When below, Hibbard's two

men came up on horseback, and told him they had a
warrant for him, for taking away Avery's

Assault Upon
Nelson Judd. things from Bear Creek. One shot at him
twice and the other snapped at him twice
with their pistols. Judd then coolly said, "Now, 'tis
my turn," putting his hand into his pocket, although he
knew he had no pistols: yet the men fled.

There was a cotillion party at the Mansion this evening.

Friday, 19.—Rode out in the course of the day. In the
evening, gave a lecture on the Constitution of the United
States, and on the candidates for the Presidency.

Mild weather. Cloudy in the afternoon.

A meeting was held in the assembly room to devise
means for the founding of another library institution in
Nauvoo.

CHAPTER VIII.

PRESENTATION OF THE BOOK OF MORMON TO QUEEN VICTO-
RIA—THE SEALING POWERS OF THE PRIESTHOOD—GOV-
ERNOR FORD'S WARNING TO THE PEOPLE OF HANCOCK
COUNTY—APOSTROPHE TO MISSOURI—JOSEPH SMITH NOM-
INATED FOR PRESIDENT OF THE UNITED STATES—HIS
VIEWS ON THE POWERS AND POLICY OF THE GOVERNMENT
OF THE UNITED STATES.

Saturday, January 20th, 1844.—Held Mayor's Court on
the case—"City of Nauvoo *versus* Stephen Wilkinson,"
for breach of ordinance. I discharged the defendant, he
paying costs.

At six, p. m., prayer-meeting in the assembly room.
I was at home.

The High Council met, but, having no business, adjourned.

"STANZAS"

On the Presentation of the Book of Mormon to Queen Victoria.

BY MISS E. R. SNOW.

Before leaving London, Elder Lorenzo Snow presented to her Majesty Queen Victoria, and his Royal Highness Prince Albert, through
the politeness of Sir Henry Wheatly, two neatly bound copies of the
Book of Mormon, which had been donated by President Brigham
Young, and left in the care of Elder Snow for that purpose; which circumstance suggested the following lines:—

> Of all the monarchs of the earth
>   That wear the robes of royalty,
> She has inherited by birth
>   The broadest wreath of majesty.

From her wide territorial wing
    The sun does not withdraw its light,
While earth's diurnal motions bring
    To other nations day and night.

All earthly thrones are tottering things,
    Where lights and shadows intervene;
And regal honor often brings
    The scaffold or the guillotine.

But still her sceptre is appproved;
    All nations deck the wreath she wears:
Yet, like the youth whom Jesus loved,
    One thing is lacking even there.

But lo! a prize possessing more
    Of worth than gems with honor rife—
A herald of salvation bore
    To her the words of endless life.

That GIFT, however fools deride,
    Is worthy of her royal care:
She'd better lay her crown aside
    Than spurn the light reflected there.

Oh would she now her influence bend—
    The influence of royalty,
Messiah's kingdom to extend,
    And Zion's "nursing mother" be.

Thus with the glory of her name
    Inscribed on Zion's lofty spire,
She'd win a wreath of endless fame,
    To last when other wreaths expire.

Though over millions called to reign—
    Herself a powerful nation's boast,
'Twould be her everlasting gain
    To serve the King, the Lord of Hosts.

For there are crowns and thrones on high,
    And kingdoms there to be conferred;
There honors wait that never die;
    There fame's immortal trump is heard.

Truth echoes—'tis Jehovah's word;
   Let kings and queens and princes hear;
In distant isles the sound is heard;
   Ye heavens rejoice!   O earth, give ear!

The time, the time is now at hand
   To give a glorious period birth:
The son of God will take command
   And rule the nations of the earth.

Nauvoo, Jan. 20, 1844.

Sunday 21.—Preached at the southeast corner of the temple to several thousand people, although the weather was somewhat unpleasant. My subject was the sealing of the hearts of the fathers to the children, and the hearts of the children to the fathers.

[The following synopsis was reported by Elder Wilford Woodruff:]—

Discourse: The Sealing Power in the Priesthood.

When I consider the surrounding circumstances in which I am placed this day, standing in the open air with weak lungs, and somewhat out of health, I feel that I must have the prayers and faith of my brethren that God may strengthen me and pour out His special blessing upon me, if you get very much from me this day.

There are many people assembled here to-day, and throughout the city, and from various parts of the world, who say that they have received to a certainty a portion of the knowledge from God, by revelation, in the way that He has ordained and pointed out.

I shall take the broad ground, then, that we have received a portion of knowledge from God by immediate revelation, and from the same source we can receive all knowledge.

What shall I talk about to-day? I know what Brother Cahoon wants me to speak about. He wants me to speak about the coming of Elijah in the last days. I can see it in his eye. I will speak upon that subject then.

The Bible says, "I will send you Elijah the Prophet before the coming of the great and dreadful day of the Lord; and he shall turn the hearts of the fathers to the children, and the hearts of the children to the fathers, lest I come and smite the earth with a curse."

Now, the word *turn* here should be translated *bind*, or seal. But what is the object of this important mission? or how is it to be fulfilled? The keys are to be delivered, the spirit of Elijah is to come, the Gospel to be established, the Saints of God gathered, Zion built up, and the Saints to come up as saviors on Mount Zion.

But how are they to become saviors on Mount Zion? By building their temples, erecting their baptismal fonts, and going forth and receiving all the ordinances, baptisms, confirmations, washings, anointings, ordinations and sealing powers upon their heads, in behalf of all their progenitors who are dead, and redeem them that they may come forth in the first resurrection and be exalted to thrones of glory with them; and herein is the chain that binds the hearts of the fathers to the children, and the children to the fathers, which fulfills the mission of Elijah. And I would to God that this temple was now done, that we might go into it, and go to work and improve our time, and make use of the seals while they are on earth.

The Saints have not too much time to save and redeem their dead, and gather together their living relatives, that they may be saved also, before the earth will be smitten, and the consumption decreed falls upon the world.

I would advise all the Saints to go to with their might and gather together all their living relatives to this place, that they may be sealed and saved, that they may be prepared against the day that the destroying angel goes forth; and if the whole Church should go to with all their might to save their dead, seal their posterity, and gather their living friends, and spend none of their time in behalf of the world, they would hardly get through before night would come, when no man can work; and my only trouble at the present time is concerning ourselves, that the Saints *will be divided, broken up, and scattered*, before we get our salvation secure; for there are so many fools in the world for the devil to operate upon, it gives him the advantage oftentimes.

The question is frequently asked "Can we not be saved without going through with all those ordinances, &c.?" I would answer, No, not the fullness of salvation. Jesus said, "There are many mansions in my Father's house, and I will go and prepare a place for you." *House* here named should have been translated kingdom; and any person who is exalted to the highest mansion has to abide a celestial law, and the whole law too.

But there has been a great difficulty in getting anything into the heads of this generation. It has been like splitting hemlock knots with a corn-dodger for a wedge, and a pumpkin for a beetle. Even the Saints are slow to understand.

I have tried for a number of years to get the minds of the Saints prepared to receive the things of God; but we frequently see some of them, after suffering all they have for the work of God, will fly to pieces like glass as soon as anything comes that is contrary to their traditions: they cannot stand the fire at all. How many will be able to abide a celestial law, and go through and receive their exaltation, I am unable to say, as many are called, but few are chosen.

Prayer-meeting in the Assembly Room.

Monday, 22.—Rainy; wind easterly; mud very deep.

Rented the Nauvoo Mansion and stables to Ebenezer Robinson for one thousand dollars per annum and board for myself and family and horses, reserving to myself three rooms in the house. <small>Nauvoo Mansion Leased.</small>

Prayer-meeting at President Young's; ten present.

Tuesday. 23.—Ebenezer Robinson took possession of the Nauvoo Mansion, to continue it as a public-house. W. W. Phelps, Newel K. Whitney and Willard Richards valued the printing office and lot at $1,500; printing apparatus, $950; bindery, $112; foundry, $270; total, $2,832. I having sold the concern to John Taylor, who in consideration was to assume the responsibility of the Lawrence estate. <small>Sale of the Printing Establishment to John Taylor</small>

There was a cotillion party in the evening at the Nauvoo Mansion. The night was clear and cold.

The ship *Fanny*, Captain Patterson, sailed from Liverpool with 210 Saints on board.

Wednesday, 24.—Called at my office about one o'clock. I think the appraised valuation of the printing office rather too low.

Weather very cold.

The mob party at Carthage, Warsaw, and Green Plains continued their agitation.

Thursday, 25.—At home.

Prayer-meeting at Brother Brigham's: eight of the Twelve Apostles present. Weather extremely cold.

I approved of the doings of a generel court-martial held January 13th.

Friday, 26.—I dictated to my clerk an article on the situation of the nation, referring to the President's Message, &c.

Prayer-meeting at Brother Young's: eight of the Twelve Apostles present. Elder Orson Hyde went to Carthage to preach. Weather clear and cool.

Saturday, 27.—Weather extremely cold and clear.

Prayer-meeting in the assembly room. High Council met, but, having no business, adjourned.

Sunday, 28.—I had some company in the evening from Warsaw. I conversed with them on politics, religion, &c. Prayer-meeting in the assembly room. Weather very cold.

I insert the following from the *Millennial Star:*—

Importance of Elders Keeping Journals, Case of Healing Recorded.

MR. EDITOR:—The idea has frequently crossed my mind, that were the Elders of the Church of Jesus Christ in this age to keep a journal of their travels and ministry, and record all the healings and miracles they had witnessed from time to time,—that should their separate journals be afterwards collected together and published in a volume, I am inclined to believe that a far greater number of manifest displays of the power of God would be therein recorded than is found in the journals of the Elders of the Church of Jesus Christ in the early ages, at least so far as they are faithfully handed down to us in the New Testament Scriptures.

And although, as in days of old, we are frequently branded with the epithets of "fools, fanatics, religious enthusiasts, dupes, and vile impostors," yet "what we have felt and seen, with confidence we tell."

We have frequently heard from individuals on whose testimony we can rely with the greatest confidence, of extraordinary displays of the power of God in the gift of healing; such, for instance, as the blind receiving their sight, the deaf having their hearing restored, the lame man being made to "leap as an hart," the dumb spirit being cast out, and one instance of the dead being restored to life.

Another instance of the kind last mentioned, with a heart overflowing with gratitude, I desire to record. On the afternoon of yesterday, a child of mine, a girl aged eight years, was sliding on the rails of the staircase, when on a sudden she turned over, and fell from top to bottom with a most tremendous crash, falling on her head, and being completely double when picked up by her mother,—so much so indeed, that her brother, who heard the noise, looked out of the kitchen, and seeing something lying in the passage motionless, concluded that his sister had thrown some dirty linen over the rails, and took no further notice. Her mother, on hearing the noise occasioned by her fall, hastened out of the parlor to the fatal spot, and immediately discovered it was poor Mary Jane, who lay motionless, speechless, senseless, yea, lifeless. She instantly took her up in her arms, and when she beheld her appearance, in an agony she cried out, "My child is dead! she has fallen and killed herself."

By this time I had hastened to the horrid scene, where I beheld my lovely girl stretched on the lap of her disconsolate mother, without the slightest appearance of life. I immediately examined her, and found that she breathed not, and that her pulsation had ceased. Her eyes also were wide open, and quite fixed as in death, and there appeared to be gathering over them the film of dissolution. In fact, if it be true that Eutychus (the young man mentioned in the 20th chapter of the Acts of the Apostles, who fell from an upper story,) was taken up dead, it is equally true that my daugther was taken up dead, for there was not the slightest vestige of life apparent.

At this moment, with heart uplifted to my Heavenly Father, I, in mighty faith, placed my hands upon her and ejaculated, "Lord, heal my child!" when in one moment she shewed signs of life, and attempted to speak.

I immediately gave her to drink a little cold water, and bathed her head with the same. She then sat up and vomited considerably, and she is now so far recovered as this morning to sing a verse of a hymn and walk about as usual.

During my presidency over the Liverpool Conference, which is nearly eighteen months, I have witnessed many cases of healing, but never any so very striking as the one I have just related.

If you deem the narrative worthy of a place in your pages of the *Millennial Star*, you are quite at liberty to insert it.

I remain, dear brother,

Yours sincerely in the Gospel of Jesus,

GEORGE MITCHELSON.

Monday, 29.—At ten, a.m., the Twelve Apostles, together with Brother Hyrum and John P. Greene, met at the mayor's office, to take into consideration the proper course for this people to pursue in relation to the coming Presidential election.

The Presidential Election Considered.

The candidates for the office of President of the United States at present before the people are Martin Van Buren and Henry Clay. It is morally impossible for this people, in justice to themselves, to vote for the re-election of President Van Buren—a man who criminally neglected his duties as chief magistrate in the cold and unblushing manner which he did, when appealed to for aid in the Missouri difficulties. His heartless reply burns like a firebrand in the breast of every true friend of liberty—*"Your cause is just, but I can do nothing for you."*

As to Mr. Clay, his sentiments and cool contempt of the people's rights are manifested in his reply—*"You had better go to Oregon for redress,"* which would prohibit any true lover of our constitutional privileges from supporting him at the ballot-box.

It was therefore moved by Willard Richards, and voted unanimously—

That we will have an independent electoral ticket, and that Joseph Smith be a candidate for the next Presidency; and that we use all honorable means in our power to secure his election.

I said—

The Prophet on the Campaign.

If you attempt to accomplish this, you must send every man in the city who is able to speak in public throughout the land to electioneer and make stump speches, advocate the "Mormon" religion, purity of elections, and call upon the people to stand by the law and put down mobocracy. David Yearsly must go,—Parley P. Pratt to New York, Erastus Snow to Vermont, and Sidney Rigdon to Pennsylvania.

After the April Conference we will have General Conferences all over the nation, and I will attend as many as convenient. Tell the people we have had Whig and Democratic Presidents long enough: we want a President of the United States. If I ever get into the presidential chair. I will protect the people in their rights and liberties. I will not electioneer for myself. Hyrum, Brigham, Parley and Taylor must go. Clayton must go, or he will apostatize. The Whigs are striving for a king under the garb of Democracy. There is oratory enough in the Church to carry me into the presidential chair the first slide.

Captain White, of Quincy, was at the Mansion last night,

and this morning drank a toast. * * * "May Nauvoo become the empire seat of government!"

I dictated to Brother Phelps the heads of my pamphlet, entitled, "Views on the Powers and Policy of the Government of the United States."

A Millerite lecturer came into the office with Brother Clayton, about five, p.m. I had some conversation with him about the definition of the Greek word Hades, and the Hebrew word Sheol, &c He lectured in the evening in the hall.

Commencement of the Prophet's Views on Powers and Policy of U.S.

Prayer-meeting at Elder Brigham Young's.

Governor Ford wrote the following expostulatory epistle to the citizens of Hancock County, through the *Warsaw Signal:—*

Governor Ford's Warning to the People of Hancock County.

SPRINGFIELD, January 29, 1844.

DEAR SIR:—I have received the copy of the proceeding and reso-lutions of a meeting of the citizens of Hancock County, which you did me the honor to send me.

I have observed with regret that occasions have been presented for disturbing the peace of your county; and if I knew what I could legally do to apply a corrective, I would be very ready to do it. But if you are a lawyer, or at all conversant with the law, you will know that I, as a Governor, have no right to interfere in your difficulties.

As yet, I believe that there has been nothing like war among you: and I hope that all of you will have the good sense to see the necessity of preserving peace. If there is anything wrong in the Nauvoo char-ters, or in the mode of administering them, you will see that nothing short of legislative or judicial power is capable of enforcing a remedy.

I myself had the honor of calling the attention of the Legislature to this subject at the last session; but a large majority of both political parties in that body either did not see the evil which you complain of, or, if they did, they repeatedly refused to correct it. And yet a call is made upon me to do that which all parties refused to do at the last session.

I have also been called upon to take away the arms from the *Mormons*, to raise the militia to arrest a supposed fugitive, and in fact t o repeal some of the ordinances of the City of Nauvoo.

Hancock County is justly famed for its intelligence; and I cannot believe that any of its citizens are so ignorant as not to know that I have no power to do these things.

The absurd and preposterous nature of these requests give some color to the charge that they are made for political effect only. I hope that this charge is untrue; for, in all candor, it would be more creditable to those concerned to have their errors attributed to ignorance than to a disposition to embroil the country in the horrors of war for the advancement of party ends.

But if there should be any truth in the charge, (which God forbid.) I affectionately entreat all the good citizens engaged in it to lay aside their designs and yield up their ears to the voice of justice, reason, and humanity. All that I can do at present is to admonish both parties to beware of carrying matters to extremity.

Let it come to this—let a state of war ensue, and I will be compelled to interfere with executive power. In that case also, I wish, in a friendly, affectionate, and candid manner, to tell the citizens o Hancock County, *Mormons* and all, that my interference will be against those who shall be the first transgressors.

I am bound by the laws and Constitution to regard you all as citizens of the State, possessed of equal rights and privileges, and to cherish the rights of one as dearly as the rights of another. I can know no distinction among you except that of assailant and assailed.

I hope, dear sir, you will do me the favor to publish this letter in the papers of your county, for the satisfaction of all persons concerned.

I am, with the highest respect,

Your obedient servant,

THOMAS FORD.

Tuesday 30.—At eleven, a.m., I went into the office with Colonel Jackson.

One, p.m., held mayor's court at my office, on the case "City *versus* Thomas Coates." Fined the defendant $25 and costs for beating John Ellison.

A Millerite preached again in the assembly room, and Elder Rigdon replied to him. There was a full house.

Prayer-meeting at Elder Brigham Young's.

Wednesday, 31.—Eleven, a. m., I called at the office, and told Benjamin Winchester to go to Warsaw and preach the first principles of the Gospel, get some lexicons, and return home.

Winchester's Mission to Warsaw.

Prayer-meeting at Elder Brigham Young's in the evening. There seems to be quite a revival throughout Nauvoo, and an inquiry after the things of God, by all the quorums and the Church in general.

Sidney Rigdon published a lengthy appeal to the Legislature of the State of Pennsylvania, setting forth in pathetic style the grievances he had Rigdon's suffered through the persecution against the Appeal to Pennsylvania. Church by the State of Missouri, which concludes as follows:—

Peroration of Rigdon's Appeal to Pennsylvania.

In confidence of the purity and patriotism of the representatives of the people of his native state, your memorialist comes to your honorable body, through this his winged messenger, to tell you that the altar which was erected by the blood of your ancestors to civil and religious liberty, from whence ascended up the holy incense of pure patriotism and universal good will to man, into the presence of Jehovah, a savior of life, is thrown down, and the worshipers thereat have been driven away, or else they are lying slain at the place of the altar. He comes to tell your honorable body that the temple your fathers erected to freedom, whither their sons assembled to hear herprecepts and cherish her doctrines in their hearts, has been desecrated—its portals closed, so that those who go up thither are forbidden to enter.

He comes to tell your honorable body that the blood of the heroes and patriots of the revolution, who have been slain by wicked hands for enjoying their religious rights, the boon of Heaven to man, has cried and is crying in the ears of the Lord of Sabaoth, saying, "Redress, redress our wrongs, O Lord God of the whole earth."

He comes to tell your honorable body that the dying groans of infant innocence and the shrieks of insulted and abused females, and many of them widows of revolutionary patriots, have ascended up into the ears of Omnipotence, and are registered in the archives of eternity, to be had in the day of retribution as a testimony against the whole nation, unless their cries and groans are heard by the representatives of the people, and ample redress made, as far as the nation can make it, or else the wrath of the almighty will come down in fury against the whole nation.

Under all these circumstances, your memorialist prays to be heard by your honorable body touching all the matters of his memorial. And as a memorial will be presented to Congress this session for redress of our grievances, he prays your honorable body will instruct the whole delegation of Pennsylvania, in both houses, to use all their influence in the national councils to have redress granted.

And, as in duty bound, your memorialist will ever pray.

SIDNEY RIGDON.

Miss E. R. Snow published the following apostrophe to—

"MISSOURI."

What aileth thee, O Missouri! that thy face should gather blackness? and why are thy features so terribly distorted?

Rottenness has seized upon thy vitals, corruption is preying upon thy inward parts, and the breath of thy lips is full of destructive contagion.

What meaneth thy shaking? and why art thou terrified? Thou hast become like Belshazzar. *"Mene, mene, tekel, upharsin!"* is indeed written against thee; but it is the work of thine own hand; the characters upon thy wall are of thine own inscription; and wherefore dost thou tremble?

Wouldst thou know the interpretation thereof? Hast thou sought for a Daniel to declare it unto thee? Verily one greater than a Daniel was in thy midst; but thou hast butchered the Saints, and hast hunted the Prophets like Ahab of old.

Thou has extinguished the light of thy own glory; thou hast plucked from thy head the crown of honor; thou hast divested thyself of the robe of respectability; thou hast thrust from thine own bosom the veins that flowed with virtue and integrity.

Thou hast violated the laws of our sacred constitution; thou hast unsheathed the sword against thy dearest national rights, by rising up against thine own citizens, and moistening thy soil with the blood of those that legally inherited it.

When thou hadst torn from helpless innocence its rightful protectors thou didst pollute the holy sanctuary of female virtue, and barbarously trampled upon the most sacred gems of domestic felicity.

Therefore the daughters of Columbia count thee a reproach, and blush with indignation at the mention of thy name.

Thou hast become an ignominious stain on the escutcheon of a noble, free and independent republic; thou hast become a stink in the nostrils of the Goddess of Liberty.

Thou art fallen—thou art fallen beneath the weight of thine own unhallowed deeds, and thine iniquities are pressing as a heavy load upon thee.

But although thy glory has departed—though thou hast gone down like a star that is set forever, thy memory will not be erased; thou wilt be had in remembrance even until the Saints of God shall forget that the way to the celestial kingdom is "through great tribulation."

Though thou shouldst be severed from the body of the Union, like a mortified member—though the lion from the thicket should devour thee, thy doings will be perpetuated; mention will be made of them by the generations to come.

Thou art already associated with Herod, Nero, and the bloody Inquisition; thy name has become synonymous with oppression, cruelty, treachery, and murder.

Thou wilt rank high with the haters of righteousness and the shedders of innocent blood: the hosts of tyrants are waiting beneath to meet thee at thy coming.

O ye wise legislators! ye executives of the nation! ye distributors of justice! ye advocates of equal rights! arise and redress the wrongs of an innocent people, and redeem the cause of insulted liberty.

Let not the contagious spirit of corruption wither the sacred wreath that encircles you, and spread a cloud of darkness over the glory of your star-spangled banner;

Lest the monarchs of the earth should have you in derision; lest you should be weighed in the balance with the heathen nations, and should be found wanting; lest the arm of the Lord should be revealed in judgment against you; lest an arrow of vengeance from the almighty should pierce the rotten fabric of a once sheltering constitution, and your boasted confidence become like an oak dismembered of its branches, whose shattered trunk is torn piecemeal by the uprising of the tempest!

For the cries of the widow and fatherless, the groans of the oppressed and the prayers of the suffering exile have come up before the God of Hosts, who brought our pilgrim fathers across the boisterous ocean, and raised up a Washington to break the yoke of foreign oppression.

Morley Settlement, January, 1844.

Thursday, February 1.—At home: weather cold.

Phinehas Richards published a thrilling appeal to the inhabitants of his native state of Massachusetts, to consider the wrongs sustained in the loss of lives and property, and other damages

An Appeal to Massachusetts —Phinehas Richards.

done to the Church of Jesus Christ of Latter-day Saints, of which he is a member.

Elder Reuben Hedlock wrote to President Brigham Young, giving the names of those who had emigrated at the expense of the office, amounting to $2,378; which is due from the emigrants.

Friday, 2.—Dr. Willard Richards called and read Phinehas Richards' appeal to the inhabitants of Massachusetts, for redress of Missouri grievances.

Prayer-meeting at Elder Brigham Young's. Weather cold.

I went into the assembly room, where I found Elders Wilford Woodruff, Willard Richards, and W. W. Phelps, to whom I related the following dream, which Elder Wilford Woodruff reported:

The Prophet's Dream—Troubled Waters Overcome.

I was standing on a peninsula, in the midst of a vast body of water where there appeared to be a large harbor or pier built out for boats to come to. I was surrounded by my friends, and while looking at this harbor I saw a steamboat approaching the harbor. There were bridges on the pier for persons to cross, and there came up a wind and drove the steamboat under one of the bridges and upset it.

I ran up to the boat, expecting the persons would all drown; and wishing to do something to assist them, I put my hand against the side of the boat, and with one surge I shoved it under the bridge and righted it up, and then told them to take care of themselves. But it was not long before I saw them starting out into the channel or main body of the water again.

The storms were raging and the waters rough. I said to my friends that if they did not understand the signs of the times and the spirit of prophecy, they would be apt to be lost.

It was but a few moments after when we saw the waves break over the boat, and she soon foundered and went down with all on board.

The storm and waters were still very rough; yet I told my friends around me that I believed I could stem those waves and that storm, and swim in the waters better than the steamboat did; at any rate I was determined to try it. But my friends laughed at me, and told me I could not stand at all, but would be drowned.

The waters looked clear and beautiful, though exceedingly rough; and I said I believed I could swim, and I would try it anyhow. They said I would drown. I said I would have a frolic in the water first, if I did; and I drove off in the raging waves.

I had swam but a short distance when a towering wave overwhelmed me for a time; but I soon found myself on the top of it, and soon I met the second wave in the same way; and for a while I struggled hard to live in the midst of the storm and waves, and soon found I gained upon every wave, and skimmed the torrent better; and I soon had power to swim with my head out of water: so the waves did not break over me at all, and I found that I had swam a great distance; and in looking about, I saw my brother Samuel by my side.

I asked him how he liked it. He said, "First rate," and I thought so too. I was soon enabled to swim with my head and shoulders out of water, and I could swim as fast as any steamboat.

In a little time it became calm, and I could rush through the water, and only go in to my loins, and soon I only went in to my knees, and finally could tread on the top of the water, and went almost with the speed of an arrow.

I said to Samuel, See how swift I can go! I thought it was great sport and pleasure to travel with such speed, and I awoke.

Saturday 3.—Prayer-meeting in the assembly room. The High Council met. Did but little business.

A rather favorable article appears in Niles' *National Register* of this date, noticing the correspondence between myself and John C. Calhoun, a copy of which is contained in the political department of the same number.

It also notices the correspondence between myself and James Arlington Bennett, publishing the same, with some of our city ordinances. The editor also quotes the following from the *Hawk Eye*:—

Mormon Improvements.

Atthough much complaint has been made about the Mormons, we saw on our late trip evidences of improvement on our prairies which we consider highly creditable to the Mormons who made them, without whom we doubt whether they would have been made for many years to come. All those who have traveled over the large prairie between Fort Madison, Warsaw and Carthage, remember how dreary it was a few years since. Now it is studded with houses and good farms. The English, who understand hedging and ditching far better than our people, have gone upon that prairie and have enclosed extensive fields in this manner. Along the old Rock Island tract, which we traveled seven years ago, and which was then a dreary waste, we saw a field enclosed with a good sod fence, six miles long and one wide. We think such enterprise is worthy to be mentioned. As long as the Mormons are harmless, and do not interfere with the rights of our people we think they should be treated well. We shall never convince them that they are a deluded people, as far as their religious notions are concerned, in any other way.

Sunday 4.—I attended prayer-meeting with the quorum in the assembly room, and made some remarks respecting the hundred and forty-four thousand mentioned by John the Revelator, showing that the selection of persons to form that number had already commenced.

The 144,000 Selection Begun.

President Brigham Young held a meeting at Brother Chamberlain's, in the neighborhood north of the city; and Elder Wilford Woodruff, at Thomas Kingston's, six miles east of the city.

Monday 5.—The regular session of the Municipal Court was opened in the Mayor's office. Present, George W. Harris, George A. Smith, and N. K. Whitney. Adjourned to the Nauvoo Mansion, on account of the severity of the weather. I presided as Chief Justice. The assessors of the different wards in the city presented their tax-lists, which occupied nearly all day. The court remitted the taxes of the widows and of the poor who were unable to pay.

City Council.

In the afternoon, Elder William Weeks (whom I had employed as architect of the Temple,) came in for instruction. I instructed him in relation to the circular windows designed to light the offices in the dead work of the arch between stories. He said that round windows in the broad side of a building were a violation of all the known rules of architecture, and contended that they should be semicircular—that the

Architecture of the Nauvoo Temple.

building was too low for round windows. I told him I would have the circles, if he had to make the Temple ten feet higher than it was originally calculated; that one light at the centre of each circular window would be sufficient to light the whole room; that when the whole building was thus illuminated, the effect would be remarkably grand. "I wish you to carry out *my* designs. I have seen in vision the splendid appearance of that building illuminated, and will have it built according to the pattern shown me."

Called at my office in the evening, and revised my "Views of the Powers and Policy of the Government of the United States." I was the first one who publicly proposed a national bank on the principles set forth in that pamphlet. Originality of
Bank Views.

Tuesday, 6.—Very cold day.

I spent the evening with my brother Hyrum, Sidney Rigdon, and the Twelve Apostles and their wives, at Elder John Taylor's; took supper, and had a very pleasant time.

Wednesday, 7.—An exceedingly cold day. In the evening I met with my brother Hyrum and the Twelve Apostles in my office, at their request, to devise means to promote the interests of the General Government. I completed and signed my "Views of the Powers and Policy of the Government of the United States," which I here insert:

Views of the Powers and Policy of the Government of the United States.—Joseph Smith.

Born in a land of liberty, and breathing an air uncorrupted with the sirocco of barbarous climes, I ever feel a double anxiety for the happiness of all men, both in time and in eternity.

My cogitations, like Daniel's, have for a long time troubled me, when I viewed the condition of men throughout the world, and more especially in this boasted realm, where the Declaration of Independence "holds these thruths to be self-evident, that all men are created equal; that they are endowed by their Creator with certain unalienable rights; that among these are life, liberty, and the pursuit of happiness;" but at the same time some two or three millions of people are held as slaves for life, because the spirit in them is covered with a darker skin than ours; and hundreds of our own kindred for an infraction, or supposed infraction, of some over-wise statute, have to be incarcerated in dungeon gloom, or penitentiaries, while the duellist, the debauchee, and the defaulter for millions, and other criminals, take the uppermost rooms at feasts, or, like the bird of passage, find a more congenial clime by flight.

The wisdom which ought to characterize the freest, wisest, and most noble nation of the nineteenth century, should, like the sun in his meridian splendor, warm every object beneath its rays; and the main efforts of her officers, who are nothing more nor less than the servants of the people, ought to be directed to ameliorate the condition of all, black or white, bond or free; for the best of books says, "God hath made of one blood all nations of men for to dwell on all the face of the earth."

Our common country presents to all men the same advantages, the facilities, the same prospects, the same honors, and the same rewards; and without hypocrisy, the Constitution, when it says, "We, the people of the United States, in order to form a more perfect union, establish justice, ensure domestic tranquility, provide for the common defense, promote the general welfare, and secure the blessings of liberty to ourselves and our posterity, do ordain and establish this Constitution for the United States of America," meant just what it said without reference to color or condition, *ad infinitum*.

The aspirations and expectations of a virtuous people, environed with so wise, so liberal, so deep, so broad, and so high a charter of *equal rights* as appears in said Constitution, ought to be treated by those to whom the administration of the laws is entrusted with as much sanctity as the prayers of the Saints are treated in heaven, that love, confidence, and union, like the sun, moon, and stars, should bear witness,

> "For ever singing as they shine,
> The hand that made us is divine!"

Unity is power; and when I reflect on the importance of it to the stability of all governments, I am astounded at the silly moves of persons and parties to foment discord in order to ride into power on the current of popular excitement; nor am I less surprised at the stretches of power or restrictions of right which too often appear as acts of legislators to pave the way to some favorite political scheme as destitute of intrinsic merit as a wolf's heart is of the milk of human kindness. A Frenchman would say, "*Presque tout aimer richesses et pouvoir.*" (Almost all men like wealth and power.)

I must dwell on this subject longer than others; for nearly one hundred years ago that golden patriot, Benjamin Franklin, drew up a plan of union for the then colonies of Great Britain, that *now* are such an independent nation, which, among many wise provisions for obedient children under their father's more rugged hand, had this:—"They have power to make laws, and lay and levy such general duties, imports, or taxes as to them shall appear most equal and just, (considering the ability and other circumstances of the inhabitants in the several colonies,) and such as may be collected with the least inconvenience to the people, rather discouraging luxury than loading industry with unnecessary burthens." Great Britain surely lacked the laudable humanity and fostering clemency to grant such a just plan of union; but the sentiment remains, like the land that honored its birth, as a pattern for wise men *to study the convenience of the people more than the comfort of the cabinet.*

And one of the most noble fathers of our freedom and country's glory, great in war, great in peace, great in the estimation of the world, and great in the hearts of his countrymen, (the illustrious Washington,) said in his first inaugural address to Congress—"I behold the surest pledges that as, on one side, no local prejudices or attachments, no separate views or party animosities will misdirect the comprehensive and equal eye which ought to watch over this great assemblage of communities and interests, so, on another, that the foundations of our national policy will be laid in the pure and immutable principles of private morality, and the pre-eminence of free government be exemplified by all the attributes which can win the affections of its citizens and command the respect of the world."

Verily, here shine the virtue and wisdom of a statesman in such lucid rays, that had every succeeding Congress followed the rich instruction in all their deliberations and enactments, for the benefit and convenience of the whole community and the communities of which it is composed, no sound of a rebellion in South Carolina, no rupture in Rhode Island, no mob in Missouri expelling her citizens by Executive authority, corruption in the ballot-boxes, a border warfare between Ohio and Michigan, hard times and distress, outbreak upon outbreak in the principal cities, murder, robbery, and defalcation, scarcity of money, and a thousand other difficulties, would have torn asunder the bonds of the Union, destroyed the confidence of man with man, and left the great body of the people to mourn over misfortunes in poverty brought on by corrupt legislation in an hour of proud vanity for self-aggrandizement.

The great Washington, soon after the foregoing faithful admonition for the common welfare of his nation, further advised Congress that "among the many interesting objects which will engage your attention, that of providing for the common defense will merit particular regard. To be prepared for war is one of the most effectual means of preserving peace." As the Italian would say—"*Buono aviso.*"

The elder Adams, in his inaugural address, gives national pride such a grand turn of justification, that every honest citizen must look back upon the infancy of the United States with an approving smile, and rejoice that patriotism in their rulers, virtue in the people, and prosperity in the Union once crowded the expectations of hope, unveiled the sophistry of the hypocrite, and silenced the folly of foes. Mr. Adams said, "If national pride is ever justifiable or excusable, it is when it springs not from *power* or riches, grandeur or glory, but from conviction of national innocence, information, and benevolence."

There is no doubt such was actually the case with our young realm at the close of the last century. Peace, prosperity, and union filled the country with religious toleration, temporal enjoyment, and virtuous enterprise; and grandly,too,when the deadly winter of the"StampAct," the "Tea Act," and other close communion acts of Royalty had choked the growth of freedom of speech, liberty of the press, and liberty of conscience—did light, liberty, and loyalty flourish like the cedars of God.

The respected and venerable Thomas Jefferson, in his inaugural address, made more than forty years ago, shows what a beautiful prospect an innocent, virtuous nation presents to the sage's eye,where there is space for enterprise, hands for industry, heads for heroes, and hearts for moral greatness. He said, "A rising nation spread over a wide and fruitful land, traversing all the seas with the rich productions of their industry, engaged in commerce with nations who feel power and forget right, advancing rapidly to destinies beyond the reach of mortal eye,— when I contemplate these transcendent objects, and see the honor, the happiness, and the hopes of this beloved country committed to the issue and the auspices of this day, I shrink from the contemplation, and humble myself before the magnitude of the undertaking."

Such a prospect was truly soul-stirring to a good man. But "since the fathers have fallen asleep," wicked and designing men have unrobed the Government of its glory; and the people, if not in dust and ashes, or in sackcloth, have to lament in poverty her departed greatness, while demagogues build fires in the north and south, east and west, to keep up their spirits *till it is better times.* But year after year has left the people to *hope*, till the very name of *Congress* or *State Legislature* is as horrible to the sensitive friend of his country as the house of "Bluebard" is to children, or "Crockford's" Hell of London to meek men.*

When the people are secure and their rights properly respected, then the four main pillars of prosperity—viz., agriculture, manufactures,

* Reference is had to Crockford's famous gaming club house at No. 50 on the west side of St. James St., London.

navigation, and commerce, need the fostering care of Government; and in so goodly a country as ours, where the soil, the climate, the rivers, the lakes, and the sea coast, the productions, the timber, the minerals, and the inhabitants are so diversified, that a pleasing variety accommodates all tastes, trades, and calculations, it certainly is the highest point of supervision to protect the whole northern and southern, eastern and western, centre and circumference of the realm, by a judicious tariff. It is an old saying and a true one, "If you wish to be *respected*, respect yourselves."

I will adopt in part the language of Mr. Madison's inaugural address, —"To cherish peace and friendly intercourse with all nations, having correspondent dispositions; to maintain sincere neutrality towards belligerent nations; to prefer in all cases amicable discussion and reasonable accommodation of differences to a decision of them by an appeal to arms; to exclude foreign intrigues and foreign partialities, so degrading to all countries, and so baneful to free ones; to foster a spirit of independence too just to invade the rights of others, too proud to surrender our own, too liberal to indulge unworthy prejudices ourselves, and too elevated not to look down upon them in others; to hold the union of the States as the basis of their peace and happiness; to support the Constitution, which is the cement of the Union, as well in its limitations as in its authorities; to respect the rights and authorities reserved to the States and to the people as equally incorporated with and essential to the success of the general system; to avoid the slightest interference with the rights of conscience or the functions of religion, so wisely exempted from civil jurisdiction; to preserve in their full energy the other salutary provisions in behalf of private and personal rights, and of the freedom of the press,—so far as intention aids in the fulfillment of duty, are consummations too big with benefits not to captivate the energies of all honest men to achieve them, when they can be brought to pass by reciprocation, friendly alliances, wise legislation, and honorable treaties."

The Government has once flourished under the guidance of trusty servants; and the Hon. Mr. Monroe, in his day, while speaking of the Constitution, says, "Our commerce has been wisely regulated with foreign nations and between the States. New States have been admitted into our Union. Our Territory has been enlarged by fair and honorable treaty, and with great advantage to the original States; the States respectively protected by the national Government, under a mild paternal system against foreign dangers, and enjoying within their separate spheres, by a wise partition of power, a just proportion of the sovereignty, have improved their police, extended their settlements, and attained a strength and maturity which are the best proofs of

wholesome laws well administered.   And if we look to the condition of
individuals, what a proud spectacle does it exhibit! On whom has oppression fallen in any quarter of our Union? Who has been deprived of
any right of person or property?—who restrained from offering his
vows in the mode which he prefers to the Divine Author of his being?
It is well known that all these blessings have been enjoyed in their full-
est extent; and I add, with peculiar satisfaction, that there has been
no example of a capital punishment being inflicted on any one for the
crime of high treason." What a delightful picture of power, policy,
and prosperity! Truly the wise man's proverb is just—Righteousness
exalteth a nation, but sin is a reproach to any people.

But this is not all. The same honorable statesman, after having had
about forty years' experience in the Government, under the full tide of
successful experiment, gives the following commendatory assurance of
the efficiency of the *Magna Charta* to answer its great end and aim—
to protect the people in their rights. "Such, then, is the happy Government under which we live; a Government adequate to every purpose
for which the social compact is formed; a Government elective in all its
branches, under which every citizen may by his merit obtain the highest
trust recognized by the Constitution, which contains within it no cause
of discord, none to put at variance one portion of the community with
another; a Government which protects every citizen in the full enjoyment of his rights, and is able to protect the nation against injustice
from foreign powers."

Again, the younger Adams, in the silver age of our country's advancement to fame, in his inaugural address (1825), thus candidly declares the majesty of the youthful republic in its increasing greatness:
—"The year of jubilee, since the first formation of our union, has just
elapsed: that of the Declaration of Independence is at hand. The consummation of both was effected by this Constitution. Since that period,
a population of four millions has multiplied to twelve. A Territory,
bounded by the Mississippi, has been extended from sea to sea. New
States have been admitted to the Union, in numbers nearly equal to
those of the first confederation. Treaties of peace, amity, and commerce have been concluded with the principal dominions of the earth.
The people of other nations, the inhabitants of regions acquired, not by
conquest, but by compact, have been united with us in the participa-
tion of our rights and duties, of our burdens and blessings. The forest
has fallen by the ax of our woodsman. The soil has been made to teem
by the tillage of our farmers. Our commerce has whitened every ocean.
The dominion of man over physical nature has been extended by the
invention of our artists.   Liberty and law have marched hand in hand.
All the purposes of human association have been accomplished as effec-

tively as under any other Government on the globe, and at a cost little exceeding, in a whole generation, the expenditures of other nations in a single year."

In continuation of such noble sentiments, General Jackson, upon his ascension to the great chair of the chief magistracy, said, "As long as our Government is administered for the good of the people, and is regulated by their will, as long as it secures to us the rights of person and property, liberty of conscience, and of the press, it will be worth defending; and so long as it is worth defending, a patriotic militia will cover it with an impenetrable *ægis*."

General Jackson's administration may be denominated the *acme* of American glory, liberty, and prosperity; for the national debt, which in 1815, on account of the late war, was $125,000,000, and being lessened gradually, was paid up in his golden day, and preparations were made to destribute the surplus revenue among the several States; and that august patriot, to use his own words in his farewell address, retired. leaving "a great people prosperous and happy, in the full enjoyment of liberty and peace, honored and respected by every nation of the world."

At the age, then, of sixty years, our blooming Republic began to decline under the withering touch of Martin Van Buren! Disappointed ambition, thirst for power, pride, corruption, party spirit, faction, patronage, perquisites, fame, tangling alliances, priestcraft, and spiritual wickedness in *high places*, struck hands and revelled in midnight splendor.

Trouble, vexation, perplexity, and contention, mingled with hope, fear, and murmuring, rumbled through the Union and agitated the whole nation, as would an earthquake at the centre of the earth, the world heaving the sea beyond its bounds and shaking the everlasting hills; so, in hopes of better times, while jealousy, hypocritical pretensions, and pompous ambition were luxuriating on the ill-gotten spoils of the people, they rose in their majesty like a tornado, and swept through the land, till General Harrison appeared as a star among the storm-clouds for better weather.

The calm came, and the language of that venerable patriot, in his inaugural address, while descanting upon the merits of the Constitution and its framers, thus expressed himself:—"There were in it features which appeared not to be in harmony with their ideas of a simple representative Democracy or Republic. And knowing the tendency of power to increase itself, particularly when executed by a single individual, predictions were made that, at no very remote period, the Government would terminate in virtual monarchy.

"It would not become me to say that the fears of these patriots have been already realized. But as I sincerely believe that the tendency of measures and of men's opinions for some years past has been in that direction, it is, I conceive, strictly proper that I should take this occasion to repeat the assurances I have heretofore given of my determination to arrest the progress of that tendency, if it really exists, and restore the Government to its pristine health and vigor."

This good man died before he had the opportunity of applying one balm to ease the pain of our groaning country, and I am willing the nation should be the judge, whether General Harrison, in his exalted station, upon the eve of his entrance into the world of spirits, told the truth, or not, with acting President Tyler's three years of perplexity, and pseudo-Whig-Democrat reign to heal the breaches or show the wounds, *secundum artem.*

Subsequent events, all things considered, Van Buren's downfall, Harrison's exit, and Tyler's self-sufficient turn to the whole, go to show*— * * * * *certainly there is a God in heaven to reveal secrets.*

No honest man can doubt for a moment but the glory of American liberty is on the wane, and that calamity and confusion will sooner or later destroy the peace of the people. Speculators will urge a national bank as a savior of credit and comfort. A hireling pseudo-priesthood will plausibly push abolition doctrines and doings and "human rights" into Congress, and into every other place where conquest smells of fame, or opposition swells to popularity. Democracy, Whiggery, and cliquery will attract their elements and foment divisions among the people, to accomplish fancied schemes and accumulate power, while poverty, driven to despair, like hunger forcing its way through a wall, will break through the statutes of men to save life, and mend the breach in prison glooms.

A still higher grade of what the "nobility of nations" call "great men" will dally with all rights, in order to smuggle a fortune at "one fell swoop," mortgage Texas, possess Oregon, and claim all the unsettled regions of the world for hunting and trapping; and should an humble, honest man, red, black, or white, exhibit a better title, these gentry have only to clothe the judge with richer ermine, and spangle the lawyer's finger with finer rings, to have the judgment of his peers and the honor of his lords as a pattern of honesty, virtue, and humanity, while the motto hangs on his nation's escutcheon—*"Every man has his price!"*

Now, O people! people! turn unto the Lord and live, and reform this nation. Frustrate the designs of wicked men. Reduce Congress at

* For Explanation of Elipses see footnote p. 75 this volume.

least two-thirds. Two Senators from a State and two members to a million of population will do more business than the army that now occupy the halls of the national Legislature. Pay them two dollars and their board per diem (except Sundays.) That is more than the farmer gets, and he lives honestly. Curtail the officers of Government in pay, number, and power; for the Philistine lords have shorn our nation of its goodly locks in the lap of Delilah.

Petition your State Legislatures to pardon every convict in their several penitentiaries, blessing them as they go, and saying to them, in the name of the Lord, *Go thy way, and sin no more.*

Advise your legislators, when they make laws for larceny, burglary, or any felony, to make the penalty applicable to work upon roads. public works, or any place where the culprit can be taught more wisdom and more virtue, and become more enlightened. Rigor and seclusion will never do as much to reform the propensities of men as reason and friendship. Murder only can claim confinement or death. Let the penitentiaries be turned into seminaries of learning, where intelligence, like the angels of heaven, would banish such fragments of barbarism. Imprisonment for debt is a meaner practice than the savage tolerates, with all his ferocity. *"Amor vincit omnia."*

Petition, also, ye goodly inhabitants of the slave States, your legislators to abolish slavery by the year 1850, or now, and save the abolitionist from reproach and ruin, infamy and shame.

Pray Congress to pay every man a reasonable price for his slaves out of the surplus revenue arising from the sale of public lands, and from the deduction of pay from the members of Congress.

Break off the shackles from the poor black man, and hire him to labor like other human beings; for "an hour of virtuous liberty on earth is worth a whole etermity of bondage." Abolish the practice in the army and navy of trying men by court-martial for desertion. If a soldier or marine runs away, send him his wages, with this instruction, that his country will never trust him again; he has forfeited his honor.

Make honor the standard with all men. Be sure that good is rendered for evil in all cases; and the whole nation, like a kingdom of kings and priests, will rise up in righteousness, and be respected as wise and worthy on earth, and as just and holy for heaven, by Jehovah, the Author of perfection.

More economy in the national and state governments would make less taxes among the people; more equality through the cities, towns, and country, would make less distinction among the people; and more honesty and familiarity in societies would make less hypocrisy and flattery in all branches of the community; and open, frank, candid decorum to all men. in this boasted land of liberty, would beget esteem, confidence, union, and love; and the neighbor from any state or from any country, of whatever color, clime or tongue, could rejoice when he put his foot on the sacred soil of freedom, and exclaim, The very name of "*American*" is fraught with "*friendship!*" Oh, then, create confidence, restore freedom, break down slavery, banish imprisonment for debt, and be in love, fellowship and peace with all the world! Remember that honesty is not subject to law. The law was made for transgressors. Wherefore a * * * * good name is better than riches.

For the accommodation of the people in every state and territory, let Congress show their wisdom by granting a national bank, with branches in each State and Territory, where the capital stock shall be held by the nation for the Central bank, and by the states and territories for the branches; and whose officers and directors shall be elected yearly by the people, with wages at the rate of two dollars per day for services; which several banks shall never issue any more bills than the amount of capital stock in her vaults and the interest.

The net gain of the Central bank shall be applied to the national revenue, and that of the branches to the states and territories' revenues. And the bills shall be par throughout the nation, which will mercifully cure that fatal disorder known in cities as *brokerage*, and leave the people's money in their own pockets.

Give every man his constitutional freedom and the president full power to send an army to suppress mobs, and the States authority to repeal and impugn that relic of folly which makes it necessary for the governor of a state to make the demand of the President for troops, in case of invasion or rebellion.

The governor himself may be a mobber; and instead of being punished, as he should be, for murder or treason, he may destroy the very lives, rights, and property he should protect. Like the good Samaritan, send every lawyer as soon as he repents and obeys the ordinances of heaven, to preach the Gospel to the destitute, without purse or scrip, pouring in the oil and the wine. A learned Priesthood is certainly more honorable than "*an hireling clergy.*"

As to the contiguous territories to the United States, wisdom would direct no tangling alliance. Oregon belongs to this government honorably; and when we have the red man's consent, let the Union spread from the east to the west sea; and if Texas petitions Congress to be adopted among the sons of liberty, give her the right hand of fellowship, and refuse not the same friendly grip to Canada and Mexico. And when the right arm of freemen is stretched out in the character of a navy for the protection of rights, commerce, and honor, let the iron eyes of power watch from Maine to Mexico, and from California to Columbia. Thus may union be strengthened, and foreign speculation prevented from opposing broadside to broadside.

Seventy years have done much for this goodly land. They have burst the chains of oppression and monarchy, and multiplied its inhabitants from two to twenty millions, with a proportionate share of knowledge keen enough to circumnavigate the globe, draw the lightning from the clouds, and cope with all the crowned heads of the world.

Then why—oh, why will a once flourishing people not arise, phœnix-like over the cinders of Martin Van Buren's power, and over the sinking fragments and smoking ruins of other catamount politicians, and over the windfalls of Benton, Calhoun, Clay, Wright, and a caravan of other equally unfortunate law doctors, and cheerfully help to spread a plaster and bind up the *burnt, bleeding wounds,* of a sore but blessed country?

The Southern people are hospitable and noble. They will help to rid so *free* a country of every vestige of slavery, whenever they are assured of an equivalent for their property. The country will be full of money and confidence when a National Bank of twenty millions, and a State Bank in every state, with a million or more, gives a tone to monetary matters, and make a circulating medium as valuable in the purses of a whole community as in the coffers of a speculating banker or broker.

The people may have faults, but they should never be trifled with. I think Mr. Pitt's quotation in the British Parliament of Mr. Prior's couplet for the husband and wife, to apply to the course which the King and ministry of England should pursue to the then colonies of the *now* United States, might be a genuine rule of action for some of the *breath-made* men in high places to use towards the posterity of this noble, daring people:—

> "Be to her faults a little blind;
> Be to her virtues very kind."

We have had Democratic Presidents, Whig Presidents, a pseudo-Democratic-Whig President, and now it is time to have a *President of the United States*; and let the people of the whole Union, like the inflexible Romans, whenever they find a *promise* made by a candidate that is not *practiced* as an officer, hurl the miserable sycophant from his exaltation, as God did Nebuchadnezzar, to crop the grass of the field with a beast's heart among the cattle.

Mr. Van Buren said, in his inaugural address, that he went in the Presidential chair the inflexible and uncompromising opponent of every attempt, on the part of Congress, to abolish slavery in the District of Columbia, against the wishes of the slave-holding States, and also with a determination equally decided to resist the slightest interference with it in the States where it exists.

Poor little Matty made this rhapsodical sweep with the fact before his eyes, that the State of New York, his native State, had abol-

ished slavery without a struggle or a groan. Great God, how independent! From henceforth slavery is tolerated where it exists, constitution or no constitution, people or no people, right or wrong: *Vox Matti!*
Vox Diaboli! And peradventure, his great "sub-treasury" scheme
was a piece of the same mind. But the man and his measures have such
a striking resemblance to the anecdote of the Welshman and his cart-
tongue, that when the Constitution was so long that it allowed slavery at
the capitol of a free people, it could not be cut off; but when it was so
short that it needed a *sub-treasury* to save the funds of the nation, it
could be spliced! Oh, granny, granny, what a long tail our puss has
got.* * * * But his mighty whisk through the great national
fire, for the presidential chestnuts, *burnt the locks of his glory with the
blaze of his folly!*

In the United States the people are the government, and their united
voice is the only sovereign that should rule, the only power that should
be obeyed, and the only gentlemen that should be honored at home and
abroad, on the land and on the sea. Wherefore, were I the president
of the United States, by the voice of a virtuous people, I would honor
the old paths of the venerated fathers of freedom; I would walk in the
tracks of the illustrious patriots who carried the ark of the Government upon their shoulders with an eye single to the glory of the people,
and when that people petitioned to abolish slavery in the slave states,
I would use all honorable means to have their prayers granted, and,
give liberty to the captive by paying the Southern gentlemen a reasonable equivalent for his property, that the whole nation might be free
indeed!

When the people petitioned for a National Bank, I would use my best
endeavors to have their prayers answered, and establish one on national principles to save taxes, and make them the controllers of its
ways and means. And when the people petitioned to possess the territory of Oregon, or any other contiguous territory, I would lend the influence of a Chief Magistrate to grant so reasonable a request, that
they might extend the mighty efforts and enterprise of a free people
from the east to the west sea, and make the wilderness blossom as the
rose. And when a neighboring realm petitioned to join the union of
liberty's sons, my voice would be, *Come*—yea, come, Texas; come Mexico,
come Canada; and come, all the world: let us be brethren, let us be one
great family, and let there be a universal peace. Abolish the cruel
custom of prisons (except certain cases), penitentiaries, court-martials
for desertion; and let reason and friendship reign over the ruins of ignorance and barbarity; yea, I would, as the universal friend of man, open
the prisons, open the eyes, open the ears, and open the hearts of all

* For explanation of Elipses see footnote p. 75 this volume.

people, to behold and enjoy freedom—unadulterated freedom; and God who once cleansed the violence of the earth with a flood, whose Son laid down His life for the salvation of all His Father gave him out of the world, and who has promised that He will come and purify the world again with fire in the last days, should be supplicated by me for the good of all people.   With the highest esteem, I am a friend of virtue and of the people,

JOSEPH SMITH,

NAUVOO, ILLINOIS, February 7, 1844.

CHAPTER IX.

Wednesday, February 7, 1844.—A piece of doggerel appears in the *Warsaw Message* of this date, entitled "Buckeye's Lamentations for the Want of More Wives," evidently the production of Wilson Law, and breathing a very foul and malicious spirit.

Thursday, 8.—Held Mayor's court, and tried two negroes for attempting to marry white women: fined one $25, and the other $5. In the evening there was a political meeting in the assembly room, when Brother Phelps publicly read for the first time my "Views of the Powers and Policy of the General Government." I addressed the meeting as follows:—

Views of the Prophet on His Candidacy for President of United States.

I would not have suffered my name to have been used by my friends on anywise as President of the United States, or candidate for that office, if I and my friends could have had the privilege of enjoying our religious and civil rights as American citizens, even those rights which the Constitution guarantees unto all her citizens alike. But this as a people we have been denied from the beginning. Persecution has rolled upon our heads from time to time, from portions of the United States, like peals of thunder, because of our religion; and no portion of the Government as yet has stepped forward for our relief. And in view of these things, I feel it to be my right and privilege to obtain what influence and power I can, lawfully, in the United States, for the protection of injured innocence; and if I lose my life in a good cause I am willing to be sacrificed on the altar of virtue, righteousness and truth, in maintaining the laws and Constitution of the United States, if need be, for the general good of mankind.

I was followed by Elders Hyde and Taylor, and a unanimous vote was taken to maintain my political views.

Friday, 9.—Held Mayor's court in my dining-room on the case, "Nauvoo *versus* William Withers," for assault. Case withdrawn on my recommendation.

This evening a public meeting was held. I extract from the *Neighbor*:—

PUBLIC MEETING.

On Friday, the 9th instant, a public meeting was held in the assembly room, at which a public address of General Joseph Smith's to the citizens of the United States was read by Judge Phelps. The address is certainly an able document, big with meaning and interest, clearly pointing out the way for the temporal salvation of this Union, showing what would be our best policy, pointing out the rocks and quick-sand where the political bark is in danger of being wrecked, and the way to escape it, and evincing a knowledge and foresight of our political economy worthy of the writer.

Appropriate remarks were made by several gentlemen after the reading of the address.

Saturday, 10.—I instructed the marshal to inform Mr. Cole, who kept a select school in the assembly room, that I must for the future have that room for my own use.

Prayer-meeting in the assembly room. Prayed for Sister Richards and others, who were sick.

A conference was held at Tuscaloosa county, Alabama: Elder John Brown, president; and George W. Stewart, clerk. Three branches were represented, containing nine elders, two priests, three teachers, three deacons, and 123 members.

Sunday, 11.—Snow on the ground. Thaw commenced in the afternoon. I was at home.

Monday, 12.—I sat in the city council, and recommended the repeal of the ordinances entitled "An extra ordinance for the extra case of Joseph Smith," "An ordinance to prevent unlawful search or seizure of persons or property, by foreign* process, in the city of Nauvoo," and "An ordinance regulating the currency;" and they were repealed accordingly. The Memorial to Congress, passed December 21, 1843, was again read, and signed by the councilors, aldermen, mayor, recorder, and marshal.

I instructed Councilor Orson Pratt to call all the Illinois representatives together, and tell them our sufferings have been such that we must have that document passed, and we *will* have it.

"You must go in for it. Go to John Quincy Adams and ask him to call the delegates from Massachusetts separate from the Illinois delegation, and demand the same. Go to Henry Clay and other prominent men. Call public meetings in the city of Washington. Take the saloon, publish the admittance so much per ticket, invite the members of both houses to come and hear you, and roar upon them. You may take all my writings you think anything of and read to them, &c., and you shall prosper, in the name of God. Amen."

The recorder presented the report of the attendance of the city council, from which it appears that I have sat with them eleven sessions, from the 14th of October, 1843, to the 16th of January, 1844, inclusive.

Councilor Orson Pratt nominated George P. Stiles as councilor during his absence, which was confirmed by the council.

I burned $81 of city scrip according to ordinance.

Thawing. Streets very dirty.

Tuesday, 13.—I was at home. Settled with Theodore Turley, and gave him the deed of a lot.

Having received an invitation from Brother Joseph L. Heywood to visit Quincy, I wrote him in reply:—

---

*That is, process outside of the city government.

Letter:—Joseph Smith to Joseph L. Heywood—Anent a visit to Quincy.

NAUVOO, February 13, 1844.

DEAR BROTHER HEYWOOD,—I sit down at this time to acknowledge the receipt of, and reciprocate the friendly feelings manifest in yours of the 7th instant; and, although surrounded by a press of business, shall take pleasure in spending a few moments to reply.

I would take the greatest pleasure imaginable in coming down to Quincy on a visit to see you and all my friends in your city, would business and circumstances permit; but it would be a matter of impossibility almost for me to leave home at the present time, in consequence of a multitude of business which I have daily to attend to. Moreover, wisdom and prudence seem to forbid my coming, on account of the bitter feeling which manifests itself in various places between this and Quincy,—not that I have any apprehensions for my personal safety; for the same kind hand which hath hitherto been my shield and support would save me from the power of my wicked persecutors; but something might grow out of it which would prompt my adversaries to get out another illegal writ, and would eventually, probably, cost me some three or four thousand dollars, as in other cases, and under which I have still to labor to disadvantage. Under these considerations, therefore, I am compelled to decline paying you a visit for the present. At the same time, in connection with Mrs. Smith, I tender my warmest acknowledgement for the invitation.

I am pleased to hear of the prosperity of your branch, and hope it will continue; for, although I never feel to force my doctrine upon any person; I rejoice to see prejudice give way to truth, and the traditions of men dispersed by the pure principles of the Gospel of Jesus Christ.

I should be pleased to have the privilege of forming an acquaintance with your partner, Mr. Kimball, and his lady; and should they ever come up this way, I hope they will call and see me.

As respects things in Nauvoo, I have nothing to say but good. Although the mobocrats of this county breathe out their shame with a continual foam, and threaten extermination, &c..the citizens of Nauvoo are at peace; they fear no danger, for the report of mobs has become so common, that the "Mormons" pay no attention to it whatever. Each man minds his own business, and all are making improvements as fast as they can. In fact, things in general seem prosperous and pleasing; and I never saw a better feeling amongst the Saints than at the present time.

My family have been somewhat sick of late, and continue so, especially my youngest boy.

Accept, dear sir, the warmest respects of myself and Mrs. Smith, and please present the same to your lady. In the meantime I remain your friend and brother,

JOSEPH SMITH.

President Brigham Young returned from Bear creek settlements, where he had been preaching for the last few days.

Wednesday, 14.—At home through the day. In the evening the assembly room was filled by the brethren, when my "Views of the Powers and Policy of the Government of the United States" was again read. I afterwards spoke on the same subject at a considerable length.

Thursday, 15.—At home. A beautiful day.

I insert the following article from the *Times and Seasons:*—

WHO SHALL BE OUR NEXT PRESIDENT?

This is an inquiry which to us as a people is a matter of the most paramount importance, and requires our most serious, calm, and dispassionate reflection. Executive power, when correctly wielded, is a great blessing to the people of this great commonwealth, and forms one of the firmest pillars of our confederation. It watches the interests of the whole community with a fatherly care; it wisely balances the other legislative powers when over-heated by party spirit or sectional feeling; it watches with jealous care our interests and commerce with foreign nations, and gives tone and efficacy to legislative enactments.

The President stands at the head of these United States, and is the mouth-piece of this vast republic. If he be a man of an enlightened mind and a capacious soul,—if he be a virtuous man, a statesman, a patriot, and a man of unflinching integrity,—if he possess the same spirit that fired the souls of our venerable sires, who founded this great commonwealth, and wishes to promote the good of the whole republic, he may indeed be made a blessing to the community.

But if he prostrates his high and honorable calling to base and unworthy purposes,— if he make use of the power which the people have placed in his hands for their interests to gratify his ambition, for the purpose of self-aggrandizement or pecuniary interest,—if he meanly pander with demagogues, loses sight of the interest of the nation, and sacrifice the Union on the altar of sectional interests or party views, he renders himself unworthy of the dignified trust reposed in him, debases the nation in the eyes of the civilized world, and produces misery and confusion at home. "When the wicked rule, the people mourn."

There is perhaps no body of people in the United States who are at the present time more interested about the issue of the presidential contest than are the Latter-day Saints. And our situation in regard to the two great political parties is a most novel one. It is a fact well understood that we have suffered great injustice from the State of Missouri, that we have petitioned to the authorities of that state for redress in vain, that we have also memorialized Congress under the late administration, and have obtained the heartless reply that "Congress has no power to redress your grievances."

After having taken all the legal and constitutional steps that we can, we are still groaning under accumulated wrongs. Is there no power anywhere to redress our grievances? Missouri lacks the disposition and Congress lacks both the disposition and power (?); and thus fifteen thousand inhabitants of these United States can with impunity be dispossessed of their property; have their houses burned, their property confiscated, many of their numbers murdered, and the remainder driven from their homes and left to wander as exiles in this boasted land of freedom and equal rights; and after appealing again and again to the legally-constituted authorities of our land for redress, we are coolly told by our highest tribunals, "We can do nothing for you."

We have paid hundreds of thousands of dollars into the coffers of Congress for their lands, and they stand virtually pledged to defend us in our rights, but they have not done it. If a man steals a dollar from his neighbor, or steals a horse or a hog, he [the neighbor] can obtain redress; but we have been robbed by wholesale, the most daring murders have been committed, and we are coolly told that we can obtain no redress. If a steamboat is set on fire on our coast by foreigners, even when she is engaged in aiding and abetting the enemies of that power, it becomes a matter of national interference and legislation; or if a foreigner, as in the case of McLeod, is taken on our land and tried for supposed crimes committed by him against our citizens, his nation interferes, and it becomes a matter of negotiation and legislation. But our authorities can calmly look on and see the citizens of a county butchered with impunity: they can see two counties dispossessed of their inhabitants, their houses burned, and their property confiscated; and when the cries of fifteen thousand men women and children salute their ears, they deliberately tell us that we can obtain no redress.

Hear it, therefore, ye mobbers! Proclaim it to all the scoundrels in the Union!   Let a standard be erected around which shall rally all the renegadoes of the land: assemble yourselves and rob at pleasure; murder till you are satiated with blood; drive men, women and children from their homes: there is no law to protect them, and Congress has no power to redress their grievances; and the great father of the Union (the President) has not got an ear to listen to their complaints.

What shall we do under this state of things?   In the event of either of the prominent candidates, Van Buren or Clay, obtaining the presidential chair, we should not be placed in any better situation.

In speaking of Mr. Clay, his politics are diametrically opposed to ours.   He inclines strongly to the old school of Federalists, and as a matter of course would not favor our cause, neither could we conscientiously vote for him.   And we have yet stronger objections to Mr. Van Buren on other grounds.   He has sung the old song of Congress— "Congress has no power to redress your grievances."

But did the matter rest here, it would not be so bad.   He was in the presidential chair at the time of our former difficulties.   We appealed to him on that occasion, but we appealed in vain, and his sentiments are yet *unchanged*.

But all these things are tolerable in comparison to what we have yet to state.   We have been informed from a respectable source that there is an understanding between Mr. Benton, of Missouri, and Mr. Van Buren, and a conditional compact entered into, that if Mr. Benton will use his influence to get Mr. Van Buren elected, Van Buren when elected, shall use his executive influence to wipe away the stain from Missouri by a further persecution of the "Mormons," and wreaking out vengeance on their heads, either by extermination or by some other summary process.   We could scarcely credit the statement; and we hope yet, for the sake of humanity, that the suggestion is false: but we have too good reason to believe that we are correctly informed.

If, then, this is the case, can we conscientiously vote for a man of this description, and put the weapons into his hands to cut our throat with?   We cannot.   And however much we might wish to sustain the Democratic nomination, we cannot—we will not vote for Van Buren. Our interests, our property, our lives, and the lives of our families are too dear to us to be sacrificed at the shrine of party spirit and to gratify party feelings.   We have been sold once in the State of Missouri, and our liberties bartered away by political demagogues, through executive intrigue, and we wish not to be betrayed again by Benton and Van Buren.

Under these circumstances, the question again arises, Whom shall we support?   GENERAL JOSEPH SMITH—a man of sterling worth and integrity and of enlarged views—a man who has raised himself from the humblest walks in life to stand at the head of a large, intelligent, respectable, and increasing society, that has spread not only in this land, but in distant nations,—a man whose talents and genius are of an exalted nature, and whose experience has rendered him in every way adequate to the onerous duty. Honorable, fearless, and energetic, he would administer justice with an impartial hand, and magnify and dignify the office of Chief Magistrate of this land; and we feel assured that there is not a man in the United States more competent for the task.

One great reason that we have for pursuing our present course is, that at every election we have been made a political target for the filthy demagogues in the country to shoot their loathsome arrows at. And every story has been put into requisition to blast our fame from the old fabrication of "walk on the water" down to "the murder of ex-Governor Boggs." The journals have teemed with this filthy trash, and even men who ought to have more respect for themselves—men contending for the gubernatorial chair have made use of terms so degrading, so mean, so humiliating, that a Billingsgate fisherwoman would have considered herself disgraced with. We refuse any longer to be thus bedaubed for either party. We tell all such to let their filth flow in its own legitimate channel, for we are sick of the loathsome smell.

Gentlemen, we are not going either to "murder ex-Governor Boggs, nor a Mormon in this state for not giving us his money," nor are we going to "walk on the water," "nor drown a woman," nor "defraud the poor of their property," nor send "destroying angels after General Bennett to kill him," nor "marry spiritual wives," nor commit any other outrageous act this election to help any party with. You must get some other persons to perform these kind offices for you for the future. We withdraw.

Under existing circumstances, we have no other alternative; and if we can accomplish our object, well: if not, we shall have the satisfaction of knowing that we have acted conscientiously, and have used our best judgment. And if we have to throw away our votes, we had better do so upon a worthy rather than upon an unworthy individual, who might make use of the weapon we put in his hand to destroy us with.

Whatever may be the opinions of men in general in regard to Mr. Smith, we know that he needs only to be known to be admired; and that it is the principles of honor, integrity, patriotism, and philanthropy that have elevated him in the minds of his friends; and the same principles, if seen and known, would beget the esteem and confidence of all the patriotic and virtuous throughout the Union.

Whatever, therefore, be the opinions of other men, our course is marked out, and our motto henceforth will be—*General Joseph Smith.*

Friday, 16.—At home. This evening I spent two hours in the office. Settled with Brother Whitney; gave him deed of several town lots, and took his receipt in full.

Saturday, 17.—I wrote the following article:—

PACIFIC INUENDO.

The very candid, pacific, and highly creditable *advice* which Governor Ford has done himself the honor to address to "the citizens of Hancock county, Mormons and all," and which appears in the *Warsaw Signal* of the 14th instant, is like the balm of Gilead, well calculated to ease the pain which has troubled the heads and hearts of the Carthagenians, Warsawvians, and other over-jealous bodies for *weal and woe.*

It certainly must be admitted, on all hands, that Governor Ford has exalted himself as a mediator, patriot, lawyer, governor, peacemaker, and friend of all, not only to magnify the law and make it honorable, but also in pointing out the part of peace.

Such is what the Latter-day Saints have ever sought at the hands of those in authority; and with an approving conscience clear as the crystal spring, and with a laudable intention warm as the summer zephyr, and with a charitable prayer mellow as the morning dew, it is now our highest consolation to hope that all difficulties will cease, and give way to reason, sense, peace, and goodwill.

The Saints, if they will be humble and wise, can now practice what they preach, and soften by good examples, rather than harden by a distant course of conduct, the hearts of the people.

For general information, it may be well to say that there has never been any cause for alarm as to the Latter-day Saints. The legislature of Illinois granted a liberal charter for the City of Nauvoo; and let every honest man in the Union who has any knowledge of her say whether she has not flourished beyond the most sanguine anticipations of all. And while they witness her growing glory, let them solemnly testify whether Nauvoo has willfully injured the country, county, or a single individual one cent.

With the strictest scrutiny publish the facts, whether a particle of law has been evaded or broken: virtue and innocence need no artificial covering. Political views and party distinctions never should disturb the harmony of society; and when the whole truth comes before a virtuous people, we are willing to abide the issue.

We will here refer to the three last dismissals upon writs of *habeas corpus,* of Joseph Smith, when arrested under the requisitions of Missouri.

The first, in June, 1841, was tried at Monmouth, before Judge Douglas, of the fifth judicial circuit: and as no exceptions have been taken to that decision by the state of Missouri—but Missouri previously entered a *nolle prosequi* on all the old indictments against the Mormons in the difficulties of 1838—it is taken and granted that that decision was just!

The second, in December, 1842, was tried at Springfield before Judge Pope in the U. S. District Court; and from that honorable discharge, as no exceptions from any source have been made to those proceedings, it follows as a matter of course that that decision was just!

And the third, in July, 1843, was tried at the city of Nauvoo, before the Municipal Court of said city; and as no exceptions to that discharge have been taken, and as the governor says there is "evidence on the other side to show that the sheriff of Lee county *voluntarily* carried Mr. Reynolds (who had Mr. Smith in custody,) to the city of Nauvoo without any coercion on the part of any one," it must be admitted that that decision was just!

But is any man unconvinced of the justness of these strictures relative to the two last cases, let the astounding fact go forth, that *Orrin Porter Rockwell,* whom Boggs swore was the principal in his [attempted] assassination, and as accessory to which Mr. Smith was arrested, has returned home, "clear of sin." In fact, there was not a witness to get up an indictment against him.

The Messrs. Averys, who were unlawfully transported out of this state, have returned to their families in peace; and there seems to be no ground for contention. no cause for jealousy, and no excuse for a surmise that any man, woman, or child will suffer the least inconvenience from General Smith, the charter of Nauvoo, the city of Nauvoo, or even any of her citizens.

There is nothing for a bone of contention! Even those ordinances which appeared to excite the feeling of some people have recently been repealed; so that if the "intelligent" inhabitants of Hancock county want peace, want to abide by the Governor's advice, want to have a character at home, and really mean to follow the Savior's golden rule, "To do unto others as they would wish others to do unto them," they will be still now, and let their own works praise them in the gates of justice and in the eyes of the surrounding world. Wise men ought to have understanding enough to conquer men with kindness.

"A soft answer turneth away wrath," says the wise man; and it will be greatly to the credit of the Latter-day Saints to show the love of God, by now kindly treating those who may have, in an unconscious moment, done wrong; for truly said Jesus, Pray for thine enemies.

Humanity towards all, reason and refinement to enforce virtue, and good for evil are so eminently designed to cure more disorders of society than an appeal to arms, or even argument untempered with friendship, and the one thing needful that no vision for the future, guide-board for the distant, or expositor for the present, need trouble any one with what he ought to do.

His own good, his family's good, his neighbor's good, his country's good, and all good seem to whisper to every person—The governor has told you what to do. Now do it.

The constitution expects every man to do his duty; and when he fails the law urges him; or should he do too much, the same master rebukes him.

Should reason, liberty, law, light, and philanthropy now guide the destinies of Hancock county with as much sincerity as has been manifested for her notoriety or welfare, there can be no doubt that peace, prosperity, and happiness will prevail, and that future generations as well as the present one will call Governor Ford *a peacemaker*. The Latter-day Saints will, at all events, and profit by the instruction, and call upon honest men to help them cherish all the love, all the friendship, all the courtesy, all the kindly feelings, and all the generosity that ought to characterize clever people in a clever neighborhood, and leave candid men to judge which tree exhibits the best fruit—the one with the most clubs and sticks thrown into its boughs and the grass trodden down under it, or the one with no sticks in it, some dead limbs, and rank grass growing under it; for by their signs ye can know their fruit, and by the fruit ye know the trees.

Our motto, then, is Peace with all! If we have joy in the love of God, let us try to give a reason of that joy, which all the world cannot gainsay or resist. And may be, like as when Paul started with recommendations to Damascus to persecute the Saints, some one who has raised his hand against us with letters to men in high places may see a light at noonday, above the brightness of the sun, and hear the voice of Jesus saying, "It is hard for thee to kick against the pricks."

Intelligence is sometimes the messenger of safety. And, willing to aid the governor in his laudable endeavors to cultivate peace and honor the laws, believing that very few of the citizens of Hancock county will be found in the negative of such a goodly course, and considering his views a kind of manifesto, or olive leaf, which shows that there is rest for the soles of the Saints' feet we give it a place in the *Neighbor*, wishing it God speed, and saying, God bless good men and good measures! And as Nauvoo has been, so it will continue to be, a good city, affording a good market to a good country; and let those who do not mean to try the way of transgressors, say "Amen."

The High Council met and settled several cases of difficulty betwixt brethren.

The Anti-Mormons held a convention at Carthage, the object being to devise ways and means of ex- pelling the Saints from the State. Among other resolutions was one appointing the 9th of March next as the day of fasting and prayer, wherein the pious of all orders are requested to pray to Almighty God that He would speedily bring the false Prophet Joseph Smith to deep repentance, or that He will make a public example of him and his leading accomplices.

Anti-Mormon Convention at Carthage.

The ice broke up in the river.

Sunday, 18.—Beautiful day. Southwest wind.

A very large assembly of the Saints met at the stand, near the Temple, when I preached a lengthy discourse.

Four p. m., went to my office with Hyrum and two gentlemen from St. Louis. Heard Dr. Richards read my correspondence with Senator Calhoun, and Phelps read my "Views of the Power and Policy of the General Government."

At seven, attended prayer-meeting in the assembly room.

Monday, 19.—At nine a. m. went to my office with Dr. Bernhisel, who proposed some alterations in my views of the government. Phelps read the same, and the doctor seemed better pleased with it than before.

To the Editor of the Neighbor:—

SIR,—I wish to say to you, as there seems to be a prospect of peace, that it will be more love-like, more God-like, and man-like, to say nothing about the *Warsaw Signal.*

If the editor breathes out that old sulphurous blast, let him go and besmear his reputation and the reputation of those that uphold him with soot and dirt, but as for us and all honest men, we will act well our part, for there the honor lies.

We will honor the advice of Governor Ford, cultivate peace and friendship with all, mind our own business, and come off with flying colors, respected, because, in respecting others, we respect ourselves.

Respectfully, I am
JOSEPH SMITH.

A conference was held in Halifax, Halifax county,

Nova Scotia, Elder Robert Dickson, president. Two branches were represented, consisting of thirty members, three elders, one priest, one teacher, and two deacons.

The wild geese commenced flying north.

Tuesday, 20.—At ten a. m. went to my office, where the Twelve Apostles and some others met in council with Brothers Mitchell Curtis and Stephen Curtis, who left the pinery on Black river, 1st January. They were sent by Lyman Wight and Bishop Miller to know whether Lyman should preach to the Indians, the Menominees and Chippeways having requested it.

Delegation from Lyman Wight on Indian Affairs

The Chippeways had given Brother Wight some wampum as a token of peace, and the brethren had given them half a barrel of flour and an ox to keep the Indians from starving, and Wight had gone through to Green Bay with them to make a road.

I told them to tell Brother Wight I had no counsel to give him on the subject. He is there on his own ground and must act on his own responsibility, and do what he thinks best in relation to the Indians, understanding the laws and nature of the subject as well as I can here, and he shall never be brought into difficulty about it by us.

I instructed the Twelve Apostles to send out a delegation and investigate the locations of California and Oregon, and hunt out a good location, where we can remove to after the temple is completed, and where we can build a city in a day, and have a government of our own, get up into the mountains, where the devil cannot dig us out, and live in a healthful climate, where we can live as old as we have a mind to.

Western Movement for the Church Contemplated

Warm. The ice floating down the river.

A meeting of the citizens of Hancock county was held at the court-house in Carthage. Passed a resolution that the second Saturday of March be appointed for a general wolf-hunt, being the same day

A Wolf Hunt Called for Hancock Co.

selected by the convention of the 17th instant for a day of fasting and prayer for my destruction.

Wednesday 21.—The Rev. Mr. De Wolfe, Episcopalian, lectured in the assembly room in the evening. I attended and, after the sermon, at his request, spoke to the people, showing them that to get salvation we must not only do some things, but everything which God has commanded. Men may preach and practice everything except those things which God commands us to do, and will be damned at last. We may tithe mint and rue, and all manner of herbs, and still not obey the commandments of God. The object with me is to obey and teach others to obey God in just what He tells us to do. It mattereth not whether the principle is popular or unpopular, I will always maintain a true principle, even if I stand alone in it.

The Prophet on the Necessity of Complete Obedience to God.

My *Pacific Inuendo*, written on the 17th instant, appeared in the *Neighbor* of to-day, in connection with Governor Ford's letter of the 29th of January.

Ice left the west bank of the river, opposite the lower brick house.

Very warm and pleasant.

Council of the Twelve met in my office. I insert the minutes:—

Minutes of a Council Meeting of the Twelve.

At a meeting of the Twelve, at the mayor's office, Nauvoo, February 21, 1844, seven o'clock, p. m., Brigham Young, Parley P. Pratt, Orson Pratt, Wilford Woodruff, John Taylor, George A. Smith, Willard Richards and four others being present, called by previous notice, by instruction of President Joseph Smith on the 20th instant, for the purpose of selecting a company to explore Oregon and California, and select a site for a new city for the Saints.

Jonathan Dunham, Phineas H. Young, David D. Yearsley, and David Fullmer, volunteered to go; and Alphonzo Young, James Emmett, George D. Watt, and Daniel Spencer were requested to go.

Voted the above persons to be notified to meet with the council on Friday evening next, at the assembly room,

WILLARD RICHARDS, Clerk.

Thursday, 22.—At home.

Ice continues to run in the river. Very pleasant, cool nights.

Friday, 23.—W. W. Phelps received a letter from John Whitmer in relation to certain records, and a book containing some of the early history of the Church which had been written by my clerks, and was Church property, and which had been fraudulently detained from my possession by John Whitmer; to which Dr. Richards replied.

Met with the Twelve in the assembly room concerning the Oregon and California Exploring Expedition; Hyrum and Sidney present. I told them I wanted an exploration of all that mountain country.

The Western Exploring Equipment.

Perhaps it would be best to go direct to Santa Fe. "Send twenty-five men: let them preach the Gospel wherever they go. Let that man go that can raise $500, a good horse and mule, a double barrel gun, one-barrel rifle, and the other smooth bore, a saddle and bridle, a pair of revolving pistols, bowie-knife, and a good sabre. Appoint a leader, and let them beat up for volunteers. I want every man that goes to be a king and a priest. When he gets on the mountains he may want to talk with his God; when with the savage nations have power to govern, &c. If we don't get volunteers, wait till after the election."

George D. Watt said, "Gentlemen, I shall go." Samuel Bent, Joseph A. Kelting, David Fullmer, James Emmett, Daniel Spencer, Samuel Rolfe, Daniel Avery, and Samuel W. Richards, volunteered to go.

Saturday, 24.—At home. Had an interview with Brother Phelps at nine o'clock.

Seth Palmer, Amos Fielding, Charles Shumway, and John S. Fullmer volunteered to go to Oregon and California.

Fifteen hundred copies of my "Views" out of press.

Very pleasant the past two weeks; the pleasantest February I ever saw.

President Brigham Young went to Knowlton's settlement on Bear creek, and preached.

Sunday, 25.—I preached at the temple block. Hyrum also preached.

Evening, I attended prayer-meeting in the assembly room. We prayed that "General Joseph Smith's Views of the Powers and Policy of the United States," might be spread far and wide, and be the means of opening the hearts of the people. I gave some important instructions, and prophesied that within five years we should be out of the power of our old enemies, whether they were apostates or of the world; and told the brethren to record it, that when it comes to pass they need not say they had forgotten the saying.

A Prophecy of Deliverance of the Saints

Some rain in the evening; cloudy and foggy.

Monday, 26.—At home. A cold wind from the north. Rainy, dull day.

In the afternoon, held court at the Mansion. City of Nauvoo *versus* Orsimus F. Botswick, on complaint of Hyrum Smith for slanderous language concerning him and certain females of Nauvoo. Bostwick was fined $50 and costs. Francis M. Higbee, his attorney, gave notice he should appeal to the municipal court, and then to the circuit court. I told Higbee what I thought of him for trying to carry such a suit to Carthage—it was to stir up the mob and bring them upon us.

The Case of Botswick Slander of Hyrum Smith.

Prayer-meeting in the assembly room in the afternoon. My uncle John Smith and lady were present, were anointed, and received blessings; and in the evening Father Morley was also blessed.

Ira S. Miles volunteered to join the mountain exploring expedition.

Tuesday, 27.—At home. Cool and clear. River clear of ice.

In the afternoon, visited the printing office.

Mailed my "Views of Powers and Policy," &c., to the

President and cabinet, supreme judges, senators, representatives, principal newspapers in the United States, (all the German), and many postmasters and individuals.

Almon L. Fullmer and Hosea Stout volunteered to go on the Western Exploring Expedition.

Wednesday, 28.—At home. Rainy day.

At four, p. m., steamboat *General Brooke* passed up the river: first boat this season. No ice in sight.

In the evening I sent Brother Coolidge to Brother Phelps, to call the brethren and pray for Brother Coolidge's sick child, as he thought it could not live till morning. Elder John Taylor and others prayed for him.

Dr. Alphonzo Young published an appeal to his native state of Tennessee, giving a history of our Missouri troubles, and asking the influence of that state to obtain redress.

The *Neighbor* of to-day publishes the following:—

FOR PRESIDENT, JOSEPH SMITH.

Having now raised the name of our General and Prophet to the head of our columns, it becomes us, as Latter day Saints, to be prudent and energetic in the cause that we pursue, and not let any secondary influences control our minds or govern our proceedings.

The step that we have taken is a bold one, and requires our united efforts, perseverance, and diligence; but important as it may be, it is no greater than others have taken, and they have conceived that they had a right, without molestation, to pursue that course, and to vote for that man whose election they in their wisdom thought would be most conducive to the public weal.

As American citizens, then we presume that all will concede to us this right; and whatever may be their views respecting the policy of such a step, they will acknowledge that we act legally, justly, and constitutionally in pursuing our present course.

Some have nominated Henry Clay, some Colonel Johnson, others John C. Calhoun, others Daniel Webster, and others Martin Van Buren.

Those several committees, unquestionably thought that they had each of them made the wisest selection in naming the man of their choice. They selected their several candidates because they thought they were the wisest, the greatest statesmen, and the most competent to fill the presidential chair, whilst they severally thought that the other candidates were incompetent.

We have governed by the same principles; and if others think they have made the wisest selection, so do we. If others think they have nominated the greatest statesman, so do we; and while those several committees think that none of the nominations made are so good as their own, we think that the man of our choice is the most able, the most competent, the best qualified, and would fill the Presidential chair with greater dignity to the nation; and that his election would be conducive of more happiness and prosperity at home and abroad than that of any other man in these United States.

This is a thing that we, as Latter-day Saints, know; and it now devolves upon us as an imperative duty to make others acquainted with the same things, and to use all our influence at home and abroad for the accomplishment of this object.

Mr. Smith is not so generally known personally as are several of the above-named candidates; and although he has been much spoken of as a man, he has been a great deal calumniated and misrepresented, and his true character is very little known.

It is for us to take away this false coloring; and by lecturing, by publishing, and circulating his works, his political views, his honor, integrity and virtue, to stop the foul mouth of slander, and present him before the public in his own colors, that he may be known, respected, and supported.

Thomas S. Edwards volunteered to join the exploring expedition to the Rocky Mountains.

Thursday, 29.—Called at my office, and gave Brother Phelps the *Zanesville Gazette* of January 31, containing the speech of Cassius M. Clay, delivered in Scott county, Kentucky, December 30, 1843, on annexing Texas to the United States; and instructed him to reply to the same, and gave him the subject matter, and directed the manner I wished it done; and then rode out with Porter Rockwell.

A Reply Sketched to Cassius M. Clay.

The steamer *Ohio* went up the river.

Moses Smith and Rufus Beach volunteered to join the Oregon exploring expedition.

Friday, March 1.—Very frosty night; showery day, west wind.

Spent the day in counseling.

Letters from the elders show a rapid progress of the work of the Lord in different parts of the Union. Elder John E. Page has gone to Washington for the purpose of proclaiming to the rulers of our nation the principles of eternal truth. By a letter received from him, we learn he has been preaching and baptizing in Boston and vicinity.

The High Council to the Saints in Nauvoo.

The High Council of the Church of Jesus Christ of Latter-day Saints at Nauvoo to the Saints of this [Nauvoo] Stake, greeting.

BELOVED BRETHREN,—Realizing as we do, the importance of the work in which we are engaged, we deem it expedient to lay before you such matters from time to time as in our opinion will be beneficial to the Saints, and the spirit in us may seem to require.

We would remind our brethren, the elders, who have at sundry times been sent forth as flaming heralds, messengers of the everlasting Gospel, who proclaim a message of salvation to their fellow-men, thereby gathering and bringing up to Zion the scattered elect of God, to be taught more perfectly he principles of salvation; that whilst their message is abroad we have had our mission to remain at Nauvoo and to participate with the Saints in the blessing of poverty, if such it may be called; amid sickness and distress, in the vexations and turmoils of the unruly and ungodly, for which no man has paid us, for days, weeks, months, and years; that our time has been spent in endeavoring to settle difficulties, set in order the things needful to salvation; in trying to reconcile and cement the feelings of our brethren to each other in the spirit of the Gospel; whilst at times, circumstances of a more painful nature have been presented.

Individuals have been brought before us charged with high crimes in violation of the laws of heaven, on whom much patient exertion in the labors of love have by us been bestowed, to reclaim them from the error and evil of their doings.

We regret to have it to say that in some instances our efforts have been fruitless; for after we have found in them an obstinate and unyielding spirit to the principles of right, we have (reluctantly) been compelled to sever them from the Church as withered branches.

Such persons not unfrequently manifest their wickedness by their trifling with and bidding defiance to all and every good rule, regulation and law, set forth for the guidance of all Saints.

One single trait of their depravity is frequently manifested by their going to some ignorant elder and getting re-baptized into the Church, not having first made the least satisfaction (as was required) to such as they have injured.

We have to say that baptism in such cases is not valid and cannot profit. We here continue to say; let such expelled person first be reconciled to his injured brother, and bring forth fruit mete for repentance; or, in case of dissatisfaction with our decision, take an appeal and reverse it, if found wrong.

Expelled persons not complying with these rules (which are in accordance with the order of heaven), whom we have been once necessitated to withdraw fellowship from, cannot be restored in any illegal way; and we would say that all such clandestine entering into the Church is climbing up some other way, and that such persons can only be considered as thieves and robbers. We would also remind the elders that it is improper for them to re-baptize any such expelled persons while they remain thus obstinate; and that it will subject them to censure, and bring them to trial before a proper tribunal of the Church.

We therefore hope, for the future, that certain officious, forward-feeling elders will be more prudent in such cases hereafter.

We remain yours in the bonds of the new and everlasting covenant,

WILLIAM MARKS,
CHARLES C. RICH,
Presidents.

SAMUEL BENT,	L. DUNBAR WILSON,
DAVID FULLMER,	THOMAS GROVER,
NEWEL KNIGHT,	LEONARD SOBY,
JAMES ALLRED,	ALPHEUS CUTLER,
GEORGE W. HARRIS,	AARON JOHNSON,
WILLIAM HUNTINGTON, SEN.,	HENRY G. SHERWOOD,

Counselors.

HOSEA STOUT, Clerk.

The *Times and Seasons* of March 1st presents my name to the public as candidate for president of the United States.

Jonathan Dunham filed his bonds with the recorder, and took the oath of office as wharf-master of the city of Nauvoo.

Elder Wilford Woodruff very sick; the 37th anniversary of his birthday.

Saturday, 2.—Ten a. m. held Mayor's court. Reproved Elder S. B. Stoddard for giving appearance of evil in attempting to be bail for Orsimus F. Boswick. Brother Stoddard afterwards explained to my satisfaction.

President Brigham Young visited Macedonia, accompanied by his brother, L. D. Young, and preached there on the Sabbath.

Sunday, 3.—Ground covered with snow. Attended prayer-meeting in the evening.

Monday, 4.—I suggested the name of James Arlington Bennett, of Long Island, as a candidate for Vice-President.

At early candle-light, the First Presidency, Twelve Apostles, temple committee, and others, met in council. I insert the minutes.

Minutes of a Council Meeting—Twelve and Temple Committee.

George Coray came in, and said he was sent by Lyman Wight to get sheep, &c, to carry to the Pine country, to receipt for them, or agree to pay lumber.

President Joseph suggested that it was best to let the Nauvoo House remain as it is until the temple is completed, as we need the temple more than anything else.

Elder Haws said there was some dissatisfaction about being sent from the Pinery without accounts, &c., and could not have credit on tithing, and one month at the Pinery is only called fifteen days here.

President Joseph told them that they should have their number of days in full. "We will let the Nauvoo house stand until the temple is done, and we will put all our forces on the Temple, turn our lumber towards the Temple, and cover it in this fall, and sell the remainder to get blasting powder, fuse, rope, steel, &c.

And when the temple is completed, no man shall pass the threshold till he has paid five dollars; and every stranger shall pay five dollars towards liquidating the cash debts on the Temple, and I will not have the house dirtied.

Let Woodworth go to the pinery, take the things wanted, and bring back the lumber, and his wages go on as usual.

Let a special conference be called on the 6th of April, and all the elders called home who can come. Let the people of this city come together on Thursday, at nine o'clock in 'the morning. After two or three lectures, we will call on the people to fill up the boxes with liberal contributions, to procure cash materials for the temple.

I instructed a letter to be written to James Arlington

Bennett to consult him on the subject of nominating him for Vice-President. I here insert the letter: —

Letter—Willard Richards to James Arlington Bennett—The Matter of Bennett Becoming Candidate for Vice-President of U. S.

NAUVOO, March 4, 1844.

DEAR GENERAL,—Yours of the 1st of February, was duly received, and produced the most pleasing sensations among your friends here, and especially with the Prophet, who said, "Tell General Bennett I am perfectly satisfied with his explanation; and as to *temper,* I had not even thought of it."

You suggest that Brother Joseph's correspondence with Mr. Calhoun would appear in some degree to contradict the noble sentiments expressed in that able document to yourself; but if you will notice that his communication to you was written as an individual, and that to Mr. Calhoun as the voice of the people he represents, I think you will dis-cover no discrepancy; but if so, tell me particulars without delay, and you shall have an explanation.

I have recently mailed to you General Smith's "Views of the Powers and Policy of the Government of the United States," which were drawn forth in consequence of his friends selecting him as a candidate for the next Presidency, which he very reluctantly acquiesced in, and it seems would not, only to support a favorite maxim—*"The people must govern;"* but having once been prevailed upon to suffer his name to go abroad as a candidate, it is desirable to him of course, as to every patriot, that those who have brought him forward should use all honor-able means to sustain him in the canvass; and if I had not felt dis-posed to uphold him before the people, I never would have been the first to urge his nomination; and during the short space since his name has been published, his friends have been astonished at the flood of influence that is rolling through the Western States in his favor, and in many instances where we might have least expected it.

I need not assert what the wisest of the wise admit without argument—that General Smith is the greatest statesman of the 19th century. Then why should not the nation secure to themselves his superior tal-ents, that they may rise higher and higher in the estimation of the crowned heads of the nations, and exalt themselves through his wisdom?

Your friends here consider your letter about the Governorship of Illinois just like every man in your quarter, mere sport, child's sport; for who would stoop to the play of a single State, when the whole nation was on the board?—a cheaper game!

General Smith says, if he must be President, Arlington Bennett must be Vice-President. To this his friends are agreed—agreed in every-thing; and in this consists our power: consequently, your name will appear in our next paper as our candidate for Vice-President of the United States. You will receive our undivided support, and we expect the same in return for General Smith for the Presidency; and we will go it with the rush of a whirlwind, so peaceful, so gentle, that it will not be felt by the nation till the battle is won.

Dear General, if glory, honor, force, and power in righteous principles are desired by you, now is your time. You are safe in following the counsel of that man who holds communion with heaven; and I assure you, if you act well your part, victory's the prize.

Brother Arlington, look well to "General Smith's Views," and his letter to Calhoun, and comprehend him fully. Say to the *New York Herald*, now is the time for your exaltation; raise your standard high, sound your trumpet long and loud, support General Smith and myself at the next election; and when we are exalted, you shall not be forgotten.

Hold forth no false shadows to honest men; yet though there is but one best piece to the fatted calf, yet there are many good slices; therefore you will not forget the "*Advertiser*," "*Niles Register*," "*Globe*," &c., &c.

Get up an electoral ticket—New York, New Jersey, Pennsylvania, and any other state within your reach. Open your mouth wide, and God shall fill it. Cut your quill, and the ink shall flow freely.

Commence at your own mansion and stay not, only for electioneering purposes, till by some popular route you reach Nauvoo; and if you preach Mormonism it will help you. At every stage, tavern, boat and company, expose the wickedness of Martinism in saying, if he is elected President, he will annihilate the Mormons, and proclaim the sycophancy of the candidates generally, and uphold Joseph against every aspersion and you shall triumph gloriously.

We have many things to say to you, which we must keep till we see you face to face.

All is right at Nauvoo. We are now fitting out a noble company to explore Oregon and California, and progressing rapidly with the great Temple, which we expect to roof this season, though there is yet a chance at the *eleventh hour* for you to bring in your thousand, and secure your "penny."

On the 6th of April is our special conference at Nauvoo. I wish you could be here on that occasion, but the time is too short. From that period our Elders will go forth by hundreds or thousands and search the land, preaching religion and politics; and if God goes with them, who can withstand their influence?

My words are the words of your friends here—Come and see us.

Brother Joseph's, Young's, and Bernhisel's respects to you. Mrs.
Richards' kind respects with mine to yourself and love to all yours.

Most respectfully yours,
WILLARD RICHARDS.

The temple committee proposed to establish a powder
manufactory.

CHAPTER X.

URGING THE BUILDING OF THE TEMPLE—TENDERS OF PEACE
TO MISSOURI—PROPHET'S DISCOURSE ON ELIAS, ELIJAH,
MESSIAH—LYMAN WIGHT'S PROPOSAL OF A SOUTHWEST
MOVEMENT FOR THE CHURCH.

Tuesday, March 5, 1844.—I saw Hyrum Kimball at Bryant's store, and gave him a lecture on his resisting the ordinances of the city, by telling the captains of the steamboats they need not pay wharfage, &c.

Rode out with Emma.

At two, p. m., met with the City Council. I copy the minutes:—

Special Session of the City Council.

March 5, 1844, 2 p. m.

Names of members called. Quorum present.

Mayor stated that he had called the council, because that when the wharf-master called on the steamboats for wharfage, the officers of the boats declined paying, assigning as a reason that Hyrum Kimball and —— Morrison had told them that they owned the land, and they need pay no wharfage to the city; and he called the council to know their views on the subject, as he had told Hyrum Kimball that he should see the ordinances executed; and if the boats did not pay, he should blow them up and all those who upheld them in resisting the ordinances. Every measure is taken to palsy the hands of the officers of the city; and I want to know how to remedy the evil, or whether I shall abandon the ordinances, &c.

Alderman Harris said that it was the mayor's duty to enforce the ordinances of the city, and that no man has a right to build a wharf without leave from the city council.

Councilor Phelps suggested the propriety of licensing those who owned wharves to collect a tax for the landing of the boat.

Alderman Wells concurred.

Mayor said the land on the water's edge was a street.

Alderman Wells suggested the propriety of having the street worked as soon as may be.

Councilor Phelps said, if Water street extended round the city, then Kimball had been constructing a nuisance.

Mayor spoke in explanation, and said that Kimball said, if the city would make a wharf, he would give up what he had done.

Councilor Orson Spencer said he wished the mayor to execute the law of the city.

Councilor Brigham Young concurred.

Councilor W. W. Phelps proposed that Water street be worked the whole length.

Councilor Taylor said, "I go in for executing the laws of the city."

Marshal stated that Morrison said he had a bond for a deed to low-water mark, and the city could not take his personal rights, and he objected to the boats paying wharfage.

Councilor Orson Pratt said, if Kimball or Morrison or any one else has built wharves since that street was laid out, they could get no damages.

Councilor Daniel Spencer considered the ordinance passed good, and it ought to be enforced.

Councilor Hyrum Smith, believed it was our duty to stand up to the ordinances.

Moved by Brigham Young that the city council instruct the Mayor to order the supervisor to open Water street from Joseph Smith's store north to the north line of the city.

Councilor Phelps approved of the motion, that the road might be cleared from rafts, and the rafts might also pay license.

Councilor Warrington said the upper stone house was in the street.

Mayor said that was the greatest nuisance there was in the street.

Councilor Orson Spencer was in favor [i.e., of the motion to open Water street.] Motion carried unanimously.

The governor having refused to issue commissions to the aldermen-elect of the city, Councilor Whitney inquired who were aldermen.

The mayor explained that if the governor refuses to grant a commission, it does not disqualify the officer elect from acting in his office; consequently, there is no virtue in the commission, but the virtue of the office consists in the election.

Councilor Young thought they were aldermen all the time or none of the time.

Mayor said he wanted all the aldermen to be added to the city council.

Alderman Wells said he considered the election made the aldermen, and not the commission.

Mayor said if he had been elected alderman and filed his bonds, he would act as councilor and magistrate.

Noah Packard sent a memorial to the governor, senate, and house of representatives of Massachusetts, his native state, setting forth in detail the sufferings of the Saints in Missouri, and their expulsion from that state.

Packard's Memorial to Legislature of Massachusetts

Wednesday, 6 —Went to my office, and thence with Brother Phelps to Mr. Bryant's, to see him about his uniting with Hiram Kimball and others to resist the ordinances of the city.

The *Neighbor* publishes the name of James Arlington Bennett as candidate for Vice-President.

Thursday, 7.—A splendid day; wind from the southwest.

Minutes of a General Meeting in the Interest of the Temple.

[Reported by Elders Willard Richards and Wilford Woodruff.]

A vast assembly of Saints met at the Temple of the Lord at nine o'clock a. m., by a special appointment of President Joseph Smith, for the purpose of advancing the progress of the Temple, &c.

The Patriarch, Hyrum Smith, was present; also of the Twelve Apostles, Brigham Young, Heber C. Kimball, Parley P. Pratt, Orson Pratt, Willard Richards, Wilford Woodruff, John Taylor, and George A. Smith; also the temple committee and about eight thousand Saints.

A hymn was sung by the choir; prayer by Elder Parley P. Pratt, when another hymn was sung.

Patriarch Hyrum Smith took the stand and said, The object of the meeting is to stir up your minds by way of remembrance. It is necessary to have a starting-point, which is to build the Temple.

With the assistance of the sisters, we expect to get the nails and glass; and with the assistance of the brethren, we expect to do the rest. I will proclaim in public and in private thet the sisters bought the glass and nails by penny subscription. Choose ye this day whom ye will serve.

We shall call upon this vast multitude for a donation to buy powder and fuse-ropes to blast the rocks in the quarry. We want the brethren to at least do as much as the sisters.

We do not intend to finish the Nauvoo House this season, but to take all the hands and finish the Temple this summer, or the walls of it, and get the roof on by December, and do off the inside next winter; and about a year from this spring we will dedicate it.

We can do anything we undertake. We have power, and we can do great things. In five years to come the work will progress more than it has done for ten years past.

Isaiah said we should perform a marvelous work and a wonder. I don't wonder he said so, if he saw this vast multitude; and I think this people is abundantly able to build this temple, and much depends upon it for our endowments and sealing powers; and many blessings depend upon it.

President Joseph Smith then arrived, took the stand, arose, and, after requesting Orson Pratt to come to the stand and take his post, said:—

I do not know whether the object of the meeting has been told you or not. I apologize for not coming sooner.

I have had so much on my mind since I saw you, that I hardly know where to begin or what to say; but one of the grand objects I had in view in calling this meeting was to make a few remarks relative to the laws and ordinances of the city and the building of the temple.

The reason I want to speak of the city ordinances is that the officers have difficulty in administering them.

We are republicans, and wish to have the people rule; but they must rule in righteousness. Some would complain with what God Himself would do.

The laws or ordinances are enacted by the city council on petition of the people; and they can all be repealed, if they wish it, and petition accordingly.

At all events, the people ought not to complain of the officers; but if they are not satisfied, they should complain to the lawmakers by petition.

I am instructed by the city council to tell this people that if there is any law passed by us which you dislike. we will repeal it, for we are your servants. Those who complain of our rights and charters are wicked and corrupt, and the devil is in them.

The reason I called up this subject is, we have a gang of simple fellows here who do not know where their elbows or heads are. If you preach virtue to them, they will oppose that; or if you preach a Methodist God to them, they will oppose that; and the same if you preach anything else; and if there is any case tried by the authorities of Nauvoo, they want it appealed to Carthage to the circuit court. Mr. Orsimus F. Bostwick's case had to go to Carthage. Our lawyers will appeal anything to the circuit court.

I want the people to speak out and say whether such men should be tolerated and supported in our midst; and I want to know if the citizens will sustain me when my hands are raised to heaven for and in behalf of the people.

From this time I design to bring such characters who act against the interests of the city before a committee of the whole; and I will have the voice of the people, which is republican, and is likely to be the voice of God; and as long as I have a tongue to speak, I will expose the iniquity of the lawyers and wicked men.

I fear not their boiling over nor the boiling over of hell, their thunders, nor the lightning of their forked tongues.

If these things cannot be put a stop to, I will give such men into the hands of the Missouri mob. The hands of the officers of the city falter and are palsied by their conduct.

There is another person I will speak about. He is a Mormon—a certain man who lived here before we came here; the two first letters of his name are Hiram Kimball. When a man is baptized and becomes a member of the Church, I have a right to talk about him, and reprove him in public or private, whenever it is necessary, or he deserves it.

When the city passed an ordinance to collect wharfage from steamboats, he goes and tells the captains of the steamboats that he owned the landing, and that they need not pay wharfage.

I espise the man who will betray you with a kiss; and I am determined to use up these men, if they will not stop their operations. If this is not true, let him come forward and throw off the imputation.

When they appeal to Carthage, I will appeal to this people, which is the highest court. I despise the lawyers who haggle on lawsuits, and I would rather die a thousand deaths than appeal to Carthage,

Kimball and Morrison say they own the wharves; but the fact is, the city owns them, sixty-four feet from high water mark. From the printing office to the north limits of the city is public ground, as Water street runs along the beach, and the beach belongs to the city and not to individuals.

Another thing: I want to speak about the lawyers of this city. I have good feelings towards them; nevertheless I will reprove the lawyers and doctors anyhow. Jesus did, and every prophet has; and if I am a prophet, I shall do it: at any rate, I shall do it, for I profess to be a prophet.

The maritime laws of the United States have ceded up the right to regulate all tolls, wharfage, &c., to the respective corporations who have jurisdiction, and not to individuals.

Our lawyers have read so little that they are ignorant of this: they have never stuck their noses into a book on maritime law in their lives, and, as Pope says:—

> Shallow draughts intoxicate the brain;
> Drink deep, or taste not the Pierian Spring.

Our city lawyers are fools to undertake to practice law when they know nothing about it.

I want from this time forth every fool to stay at home and let the steamboats and captains alone. No vessel could land anywhere, if subject to individual laws.

The corporation owns the streets of the city, and has as much right to tax the boats to make wharves as to tax citizens to make roads. Let every man in this city stay at home, and let the boat-captains, peace-officers and everybody alone.

How are we to keep peace in the city, defend ourselves against mobs, and keep innocent blood from being shed? By striking a blow at everything that rises up in disorder.

I will wage an eternal warfare with those that oppose me while I am laboring in behalf of the city. I will disgrace every man by publishing him on the house top, who will not be still and mind his own business. Let them entirely alone, and they will use themselves up.

I was visited by an old gentleman this morning, who told me that the spirit of mobocracy was about subsiding. A couple of merchants in this city (I will not tell their names,) have told the country people not to bring butter, eggs, &c., to Nauvoo for sale; at least, so the people abroad say.

Now, if they will not let the people bring their produce, the people will not buy their goods; and the result will be, the merchants will get a spirit of mobocracy.

Another man (I will not call his name,) has been writing to the *New York Tribune*, some of the most disgraceful things possible to name. He says, in that article, that there are a great many donations to the Temple which have been appropriated to other purposes.

His object evidently was to stigmatize the trustee and excite prejudice against us abroad. But I pledge myself that whoever has contributed any old shoes, harness, horses, wagons, or anything else, if he will come forward, will show that every farthing is on the book and has been appropriated for the building of the Temple.

I pledge myself that if he finds the first farthing that we cannot show where it has been appropriated, I will give him my head for a football.

He also states that the Temple cannot be built, it costs so much. Who does not know that we can put the roof on the building this season, if we have a mind to? By turning all the means from the Nauvoo House and doubling our diligence we can do it.

There are men in our midst who are trying to build up themselves at our expense, and others who are watching for iniquity, and will make a man an offender for a word. The best way for such men is to be still. If I did not love men, I would not reprove them, but would work in the darkness as they do.

As to who is the author of the article in the *Tribune*, read it and you will see for yourselves. He is not a lawyer; he is nearer related to a doctor—a small man. (Mr. McNeil inquired if he was the man.) No; I do not know you: you are a stranger. But I will rest myself and give way for others.

President Hyrum Smith arose and made a few remarks. He compared the lawyers to polliwogs, wigglers, and toads. He said they would dry up next fall. "Those characters, I presume, were made in gizzard making time, when it was cheaper to get gizzards than souls; for if a soul cost $5, a gizzard would cost nothing: like tree toads, they change color to suit the object they are upon. They ought to be ferreted out like rats. You could describe them as you would a hedgehog: they are in every hedge, stinking like the skunk."*

Charles Foster asked if Joseph meant him.

Joseph said, "I will reply by asking you a question."

Foster: "That is no way."

Joseph. "Yes, that is the way the Quakers do. But Jesus said, "Whose image and superscription is this? Why did you apply the remarks to yourself? Why did you ask if we meant you?

Foster. "Then I understand you meant me.

Joseph. "You said it."

Foster. "You shall hear from me."

Joseph. "As Mayor, I fine you $10 for that threat, and for disturbing the meeting."

Doctor Foster spoke in palliation of his brother Charles, and asked Joseph to await, &c. He said, "He has not threatened you." Joseph said, "He has." Doctor Foster said: "No one has heard him threaten you," when hundreds cried, "I have!" Doctor Foster continued to speak, when the Mayor called him to order, or, said he, "I will fine you."

William W. Phelps then read General Smith's "Views of the Powers and Policy of the General Government of the United States;" after which, it was voted, unanimously, with one exception, to uphold General Smith for the Presidency of the United States.

* Nauvoo was unfortunate in being overrun with pettifogging lawyers at this time, and it was to these, doubtless, that the disparaging remarks of both the Prophet and Hyrum, rspecting lawyers referred. It is unfortunate that they did not segregate the pettifoggers from the worthy men of the profession; than whom no class of citizens, and no other profession, render more valuable service to the state.

An article was also read by W. W. Phelps, entitled, "A Voice of Innocence from Nauvoo," and all the assembly said "Amen" twice.

At thirty minutes past twelve, the meeting adjourned till two p. m.

When the people assembled according to adjournment, choir sang a hymn. Prayer by Elder Orson Pratt. Singing.

President Brigham Young addressed the congregation. He said: I wish to speak upon the duty of lawyers, as they have been spoken of this morning. They were first among the children of Israel to explain the laws of Moses to the common people.

I class myself as a lawyer in Israel. My business is to make peace among the people; and when any man who calls himself a lawyer takes a course to break peace instead of making it, he is out of the line of his duty. A lawyer's duty is to read the law well himself, then tell the people what it is, and let them act upon it, and keep peace; and let them receive pay like any laboring man.

It is desirable for justices of the peace, when men call for writs, to inquire into the merits of the case, and tell the parties how to settle it, and thus put down lawsuits. To cure lawing, let us pay attention to our business.

When we hear a story, never tell it again, and it will be a perfect cure. If your brother mistreats you, let him alone; if your enemy cheats you, let it go; cease to deal with men who abuse you. If all men had taken the straightforward course that some have, we should not have such disorderly men in our midst.

I have no objection to any man coming here, but I will have nothing to do with men who will abuse me at midnight and at noonday. Our difficulties and persecutions have always arisen from men right in our midst.

It is the lust of individuals to rob us of everything, and to take advantage of divisions that may arise among us to build themselves up. I feel that I want every man should stay and lift up holy hands without dubiety, wrath or doubting.

To the men who own land here I would say: Do not think you can sell your lands here, and then go off and spend it somewhere else in abusing the Mormons. I tell you nay; for know it, ye people, that Israel is here; and they are the head, and not the tail; and the people must learn it. All those who have gone from us have gone from the head to the tail.

The grand object before us is to build the temple this season.

We have heard the effects of slander, and we want a cure and balm; and I carry one with me all the while, and I want all of you to do the same. I will tell you what it is: it is to mind your own business, and let others alone, and suffer wrong rather than do wrong. If any take your property away, let them alone, and have nothing to do with them.

A spirit has been manifested to divide the Saints. It was manifest in the last election. It was said, if they did not look out, the Saints on the flat would beat the Saints on the hill.

Great God! how such a thing looks, that the Saints should be afraid of beating one another in the election, or being beat? I would ask, who built up this city? Would steamboats have landed here, if the Saints had not come? Or could you, even the speculators, have sold your lands for anything here, if the Saints had not come? They might have sold for a few bear and wolf skins, but not for money.

If any of you wish to know how to have your bread fall butter-side up, butter it on both sides, and then it will fall butter-side up. Oppose this work, and it will roll over you.

When did this work ever stop since it began? Never. The only thing the Saints now want to know is—what does the Lord want of us, and we are ready to do it.

Well, then, build the Temple of the Lord. Keep the law of God, ye Saints, and the hypocrite and scoundrel will flee out of your midst and tremble, for the fire of God will be too hot for them.

I expect the Saints are so anxious to work, and so ready to do right, that God has whispered to the Prophet, "Build the Temple, and let the Nauvoo House alone at present." I would not sue a man, if he owed me five hundred or a thousand dollars, should he come to me and say he would not pay me.

Elder John Taylor remarked that it was said by some discontented persons that the municipal officers of the city were acting in an arbitrary manner, which was false. He then went to explain the principles of Democracy, until it was announced that it would be desirable to set a contribution on foot immediately to get fuse rope and blasting powder, as a boat was coming down the river, and the messenger was waiting to go down to St. Louis.

Elder Taylor paused awhile for this purpose, and a collection amounting to about sixty dollars was made. He then continued his speech: "When society was first organized they found themselves without legislature, congress, house of lords, or anything of the kind, every man was lord over his own house.

Difficulties began to arise, and the people began to contend and combine together in governments. By-and-by, some two or three requested that they might return to their original customs, and the government said they might. This was the situation of this city in the main, when we asked for a charter.

Of General Joseph Smith some are afraid, and think it doubtful about his election; and, like the ostrich, stick their heads under a bush, and leave their bodies out, so that we can all see them; and after this it will be a by-word—"That man is an ostrich who hides his head in this cause." He spoke also on going on with the temple.

President Brigham Young said—"Those who have not paid their property tithing we shall call upon, and take dinner; and we had rather be saved that trouble, and have them come up and pay. You will want a blessing in the temple when it is done."

President Joseph Smith remarked:—In relation to those who give in property for the temple. We want them to bring it to the proper source, and to be careful into whose hands it comes, that it may be entered into the Church books, so that those whose names are found in the Church books shall have the first claim to receive their endowments in the temple. I intend to keep the door at the dedication myself, and not a man shall pass who has not paid his bonus.

As to politics, I care but little about the presidential chair. I would not give half as much for the office of President of the United States as I would for the one I now hold as Lieutenant-General of the Nauvoo Legion.

We have as good a right to make a political party to gain power to defend ourselves, as for demagogues to make use of our religion to get power to destroy us. In other words, as the world has used the power of government to oppress and persecute us, it is right for us to use it for the protection of our rights. We will whip the mob by getting up a candidate for President.

When I get hold of the Eastern papers, and see how popular I am, I am afraid myself that I shall be elected; but if I should be, I would not say, "*Your cause is just, but I can do nothing for you.*"

What I have said in my views in relation to the annexation of Texas is with some unpopular; the people are opposed to it. Some of the Anti-Mormons are good fellows. I say it, however, in anticipation that they will repent. They object to Texas on account of slavery. Why, it is the very reason she ought to be received, so that we may watch over them; for, of the two evils, we should reject the greatest.

Governor Houston of Texas, says—"if you refuse to receive us into the United States, we must go to the British Government for protection."

This would certainly be bad policy for this nation; the British are now throughout that whole country, trying to bribe all they can; and the first thing they would do, if they got possession, would be to set the negroes and the Indians to fight, and they would use us up. British officers are now running all over Texas to establish British influence in that country.

It will be more honorable for us to receive Texas and set the negroes free, and use the negroes and Indians against our foes. Don't let Texas go, lest our mothers and the daughters of the land should laugh us in the teeth; and if these things are not so, God never spoke by any Prophet since the world began.

How much better it is for the nation to bear a little expense than to have the Indians and British upon us and destroy us all. We should grasp all the territory we can. I know much that I do not tell. I have had bribes offered me, but I have rejected them.

The government will not receive any advice or counsel from me: they are self-sufficient. But they must go to hell and work out their own salvation with fear and trembling.

The South holds the balance of power. By annexing Texas, I can do away with this evil. As soon as Texas was annexed, I would liberate the slaves in two or three States, indemnifying their owners, and send the negroes to Texas, and from Texas to Mexico, where all colors are alike. And if that was not sufficient, I would call upon Canada, and annex it.

Singing by the choir. Prayer by President B. Young.

The barque *Fanny*, Captain Patterson, arrived at New Orleans with 210 souls, led by Elder William Kay. They express, [the opinion] in a letter to the *Millennial Star*, that no people ever had a more prosperous voyage than the Lord has favored this company with; and such a captain and crew, for kindness, could scarcely be met with, the captain frequently administering from the cabin stores unto the necessities of all who required it.

Arrival of Wm. Kay and Company of English Saints.

Elder John E. Page published an address to the inhabitants of Washington.

Friday, 8.—Very heavy rain all night, accompanied by thunder.

Bishop Miller arrived from the Pinery.

At ten a. m., my scribe, Willard Richards, called to tell me that James Arlington Bennett was a native of Ireland, and therefore was not constitutionally elegible to be the Vice-President. He wanted to know who should be nominated for Vice-President. I told him to counsel with others upon that

Jas. A. Bennett Ineligible for Vice-President of U. S.

point, when he said he would call a council this evening.

At seven p. m., the First Presidency, the Twelve, Bishop Miller, Levi Richards, W. W. Phelps, and Lucian Woodworth assembled in the Mayor's office, when W. W. Phelps read the following pacific communication, which I had previously dictated him to write:—

A Friendly Hint to Missouri.

One of the most pleasing scenes that can occur on earth, when a sin has been committed by one person against another, is, to forgive that sin; and then according to the sublime and perfect pattern of the Savior, pray to our Father in heaven to forgive him also.

Verily, verily, such a friendly rebuke is like the mellow zephyr of summer's eve—it soothes, it cheers and gladdens the heart of the humane and the savage. Well might the wise man exclaim, "A soft answer turneth away wrath;" for men of sense, judgment, and observation, in all the various periods of time, have been witnesses, figuratively speaking, that water, not wood, checks the rage of fire.

Jesus said: "Blessed are the peacemakers, for they shall be called the children of God." Wherefore if the nation, a single State, community, or family ought to be grateful for anything, it is peace.

Peace, lovely child of heaven!—peace like light from the same great parent, gratifies, animates, and happifies the just and the unjust, and is the very essence of happiness below, and bliss above.

He that does not strive with all his powers of body and mind, with all his influence at home and abroad, and to cause others to do so too—to seek peace and maintain it for his own benefit and convenience, and for the honor of his State, nation, and country, has no claim on the clemency of man; nor should he be entitled to the friendship of woman or the protection of government.

He is the canker-worm to gnaw his own vitals; and the vulture to prey upon his own body; and he is, as to his own prospects and prosperity in life, a *felo-de-se* of his own pleasure.

A community of such beings are not far from hell on earth, and should be let alone as unfit for the smiles of the free or praise of the brave.

But the peacemaker, O give ear to him! for the words of his mouth and his doctrine drop like the rain, and distil as the dew. They are like the gentle mist upon the herbs, and as the moderate shower upon the grass.

Animation, virtue, love, contentment, philanthropy, benevolence, compassion, humanity and friendship push life into bliss: and men, a

little below the angels, exercising their powers, privileges, and knowledge according to the order, rules, and regulations of revelation, by
Jesus Christ, dwell together in unity; and the sweet odor that is wafted
by the breath of joy and satisfaction from their righteous communion is
like the rich perfume from the consecrated oil that was poured upon
the head of Aaron, or like the luscious fragrance that rises from the
field of Arabian spices.   Yea, more, the voice of the peacemaker—

> It is like the music of the spheres—
> It charms our souls and calms our fears;
> It turns the world to Paradise,
> And men to pearls of greater price.

So much to preface this friendly hint to the state of Missouri: for,
notwithstanding some of her private citizens and public officers have
committed violence, robbery, and even murder upon the rights and persons of the Church of Jesus Christ of Latter-day Saints, yet compassion,
dignity, and a sense of the principles of religion among all classes, and
honor and benevolence, mingled with charity by high-minded patriots,
lead me to suppose that there are many worthy people in that state who
will use their influence and energies to bring about a settlement of all
those old difficulties, and use all consistent means to urge the State, for
her honor, prosperity, and good name, to restore every person she or
her citizens have expelled from her limits, to their rights, and pay them
all damage, that the great body of high-minded and well-disposed
Southern and Western gentlemen and ladies—the real peace-makers of
a western world, will go forth—good Samaritan-like, and pour in the oil
and the wine, till all that can be healed are made whole; and after
repentance, they shall be forgiven; for verily the Scriptures say, "Joy
shall be in heaven over one sinner that repents, more than over ninety-
and-nine just persons that need no repentance."

Kowing the fallibility of man, considering the awful responsibility of
rejecting the cries of the innocent, confident in the virtue and patriotism of the noble-minded Western men, tenacious of their character and
standing, too high to stoop to disgraceful acts, and too proud to tolerate meanness in others; yea, may, I not say, without boasting that
the best blood of the West, united with the honor of the illustrious fathers of freedom, will move, as the forest is moved by a mighty
wind, to promote peace and friendship in every part of our wide-spread,
lovely country.

Filled with a love almost unspeakable, and moved by a desire pleasant as the dew of heaven, I supplicate not only our Father above, but
also the civil, the enlightened, the intelligent, the social, and the best
inhabitants of Missouri—those that feel bound by principles of honor,
justice, moral greatness, and national pride, to arise in the character of

virtuous freemen from the disgrace and reproach that might inadvertantly blur their good names, for want of self-preservation.

Now is the time to brush off the monster that, incubus-like, seems hanging upon the reputation of the whole State. A little exertion, and the infamy of the evil will blacken the guilty only, for is it not written, "The tree is known by its fruit?"

The voice of reason, the voice of humanity, the voice of the nation, and the voice of Heaven seem to say to the honest and virtuous throughout the State of Missouri, wash yourselves, make you clean, lest your negligence should be taken by the world, from the mass of facts before it, that you are guilty!

Let there be one unison of hearts for justice; and when you reflect around your own firesides, remember that fifteen thousand once among you, now not, but who are just as much entitled to the privileges and blessings you enjoy as yourselves, like the widow before the unjust judge, are fervently praying for their rights.

When you meditate upon the massacre at Haun's mill, forget not that the Constitution of your State holds this broad truth to the world, that none shall be deprived of life, liberty, or property, but by the judgement of his peers or the law of the land.

And when you assemble together in towns, counties, or districts, whether to petition your legislature to pay the damage the Saints have sustained in your State, by reason of oppression and misguided zeal, or to restore them to their rights according to Republican principles and benevolent designs, reflect, and make honorable, or annihilate, such statute law as was in force in your state in 1838,—*viz:* "If twelve or more persons shall combine to levy war against any part of the people of this state, or to remove [them] forcibly out of the state or from their habitations, evidenced by taking arms and assembling to accomplish such purpose, every person so offending shall be punished by imprisonment in the Penitentiary for a period not exceeding five years, or by a fine not exceeding five thousand dollars and imprisonment in the county jail not exceeding six months.

Finally, if honor dignifies an honest people, if virtue exalts a commuity, if wisdom guides great men, if principle governs intelligent beings, if humanity spreads comfort among the needy, and if religion affords consolation by showing that charity is the first, best and sweetest token of perfect love, then, O ye good people of Missouri, like the woman in Scripture who had lost one of her ten pieces of silver, arise, search diligently till you find the lost piece, and then make a feast, and call in your friends for joy.

With due consideration, I am the friend of all good men,

JOSEPH SMITH.

NAUVOO, ILL., March 8, 1844.

Brother George A. Smith brought the information that
St. Louis Comment on the Prophet's Candidacy. Brother Farnham had just returned from St. Louis, and said the people in that place were saying, "Things have come to a strange pass. If Joe Smith is elected President, he will raise the devil with Missouri; and if he is not elected, he will raise the devil anyhow."

It was agreed that Colonel Solomon Copeland, living at
Copeland of Tennessee Considered as Candidate for Vice-President. Paris, Henry county, Tennessee, should be written to on the subject of the Vice-Presidency; and that Elder Wilford Woodruff should write the letter, and invite him to visit us, and see if he would suffer his name to run for that office.

Saturday, 9.—Met in the City Council, and gave my reasons in favor of the repeal of the hog law. [The subject was discussed at some length.]

Council adjourned for one hour. In the afternoon City Council rejected the petition to repeal the hog law.

I proposed to license Hiram Kimball and Mr. Morrison, who own the land opposite to the wharf, to make wharves
Matter of Wharfage. and collect wharfage; then the city can dispense with a wharf-master; that Kimball and Morrison pay a tax for the landing of every boat; and they could tax the boat, or not, as they liked.

The Female Relief Society met twice in the assembly room, and sanctioned "The Voice of Innocence From Nauvoo," and then adjourned for one week to accommodate others who could not get into the room at either of the meetings.

Our worthy brother, King Follett, died this morning,
Death of King Follett. occasioned by the accidental breaking of a rope, and the falling of a bucket of rock upon him while engaged in walling up a well, and the men above were in the act of lowering the rock to him.

Elder Follett was one of those who bore the burden, in common with others of his brethren, in the days when men's faith was put to the test. He was a native of Vermont, and moved many years since into Cuyahoga county, Ohio.

There, for the first time, he heard the Gospel preached, united with the Church of Jesus Christ of Latter-day Saints in the spring of 1831, and has been a sharer in the afflictions through which the Saints have passed from that time until the time of his death.

He shared in the violence of Missouri persecution, was cast into prison, and endured many months' imprisonment; and, after long delay, obtained a trial on the charges preferred against him, and was honorably discharged, being acquitted of all the crimes with which a band of wicked persecutors could charge him

All the persecutions he endured only tended to strengthen his faith and confirm his hope; and he died as he had lived, rejoicing in the hope of future felicity.

Having united with the Church in the forty-first year of his age, he filled up the prime of his life in the service of his God, and went to rest in his fifty-sixth year, being fifty-five years, seven months, and fourteen days old when he slept the sleep of death.

So the righteous pass, and so they sleep, until the mandate of Him for whom they suffer and in whom they trust shall call them forth to glory, honor, immortality and eternal life.

Sunday, 10.—Frost in the night; beautiful day. South wind.

Brother King Follett was buried this day with Masonic honors.

I attended meeting at the stand, and preached on the subject of Elias, Elijah, and Messiah. [A sketch of which was reported by Elder Wilford Woodruff, as follows]:—

Discourse of the Prophet.—Elias, Elijah, Messiah.

There is a difference between the spirit and office of Elias and Elijah. It is the spirit of Elias I wish first to speak of; and in order to come at the subject, I will bring some of the testimony from the Scripture and give my own.

In the first place, suffice it to say, I went into the woods to inquire of the Lord, by prayer, His will concerning me, and I saw an angel, and he laid his hands upon my head, and ordained me to a Priest after the order of Aaron, and to hold the keys of this Priesthood, which office was to preach repentance and baptism for the remission of sins, and also to baptize. But I was informed that this office did not extend to the laying on of hands for the giving of the Holy Ghost; that that office was a greater work, and was to be given afterward; but that my ordination was a preparatory work, or a going before, which was the spirit of Elias; for the spirit of Elias was a going before to prepare the way for the greater, which was the case with John the Baptist. He came crying through the wilderness, "Prepare ye the way of the Lord, make his paths straight." And they were informed, if they could receive it, it was the spirit of Elias; and John was very particular to tell the people, he was not that Light, but was sent to bear witness of that Light.

He told the people that his mission was to preach repentance and baptize with water; but it was He that should come after him that should baptize with fire and the Holy Ghost.

If he had been an imposter, he might have gone to work beyond his bounds, and undertook to have performed ordinances which did not belong to that office and calling, under the spirit of Elias.

The spirit of Elias is to prepare the way for a greater revelation of God, which is the Priesthood of Elias, or the Priesthood that Aaron was ordained unto. And when God sends a man into the world to prepare for a greater work, holding the keys of the power of Elias, it was called the doctrine of Elias, even from the early ages of the world.

John's mission was limited to preaching and baptizing; but what he did was legal; and when Jesus Christ came to any of John's disciples, He baptized them with fire and the Holy Ghost.

We find the apostles endowed with greater power than John: their office was more under the spirit and power of Elijah than Elias.

In the case of Phillip when he went down to Samaria, when he was under the spirit of Elias, he baptized both men and women. When Peter and John heard of it, they went down and laid hands upon them, and they received the Holy Ghost. This shows the distinction between the two powers.

When Paul came to certain disciples, he asked if they had received the Holy Ghost? They said, No. Who baptized you, then? We were baptized unto John's baptism. No, you were not baptized unto John's baptism, or you would have been baptized by John. And so Paul went and baptized them, for he knew what the true doctrine was, and he knew that John had not baptized them. And these principles are strange to me, that men who have read the Scriptures of the New Testament are so far from it.

What I want to impress upon your minds is the difference of power in the different parts of the Priesthood, so that when any man comes among you, saying, "I have the spirit of Elias," you can know whether he be true or false; for any man that comes, having the spirit and power of Elias, he will not transcend his bounds.

John did not transcend his bounds, but faithfully performed that part belonging to his office; and every portion of the great building should be prepared right and assigned to its proper place; and it is necessary to know who holds the keys of power, and who does not, or we may be likely to be deceived.

That person who holds the keys of Elias hath a preparatory work. But if I spend much more time in conversing about the spirit of Elias, I shall not have time to do justice to the spirit and power of Elijah.

This is the Elias spoken of in the last days, and here is the rock upon which many split, thinking the time was past in the days of John and Christ, and no more to be. But the spirit of Elias was revealed to me, and I know it is true; therefore I speak with boldness, for I know verily my doctrine is true.

Now for Elijah. The spirit, power, and calling of Elijah is, that ye have power to hold the key of the revelation, ordinances, oracles, powers and endowments of the fullness of the Melchisedeck Priesthood and of the kingdom of God on the earth; and to receive, obtain, and perform all the ordinances belonging to the kingdom of God, even unto the turning of the hearts of the fathers unto the children, and the hearts of the children unto the fathers, even those who are in heaven.

Malachi says, "I will send you Elijah the prophet before the coming of the great and dreadful day of the Lord: and he shall turn the heart of the fathers to the children, and the heart of the children to their fathers, lest I come and smite the earth with a curse."

Now, what I am after is the knowledge of God, and I take my own course to obtain it. What are we to understand by this in the last days?

In the days of Noah, God destroyed the world by a flood, and He has promised to destroy it by fire in the last days: but before it should take place, Elijah should first come and turn the hearts of the fathers to the children, &c.

Now comes the point. What is this office and work of Elijah? It is one of the greatest and most important subjects that God has revealed. He should send Elijah to seal the children to the fathers, and the fathers to the children.

Now was this merely confined to the living, to settle difficulties with families on earth? By no means. It was a far greater work. Elijah! what would you do if you were here? Would you confine your work to the living alone? No: I would refer you to the Scriptures, where the ubject is manifest: that is, without us, they could not be made perfect, nor we without them; the fathers without the children, nor the children without the fathers.

I wish you to understand this subject, for it is important; and if you will receive it, this is the spirit of Elijah, that we redeem our dead, and connect ourselves with our fathers which are in heaven, and seal up our dead to come forth in the first resurrection;and here we want the power of Elijah to seal those who dwell on earth to those who dwell in heaven. This is the power of Elijah and the keys of the kingdom of Jehovah.

Let us suppose a case. Suppose the great God who dwells in heaven should reveal Himself to Father Cutler here, by the opening heavens, and tell him, "I offer up a decree that whatsoever you seal on earth with your decree, I will seal it in heaven; you have the power then; can it be taken off? No. Then what you seal on earth, by the keys of Elijah, is sealed in heaven; and this is the power of Elijah, and this is the difference between the spirit and power of Elias and Elijah; for while the spirit of Elias is a forerunner, the power of Elijah is sufficient to make our calling and election sure; and the same doctrine, where we are exhorted to go on to perfection, not laying again the foundation of repentance from dead works, and of laying on of hands, ressurection of the dead, &c.

We cannot be perfect without the fathers, &c. We must have revelation from them, and we can see that the doctrine of revelation far transcends the doctrine of no revelation; for one truth revealed from heaven is worth all the sectarian notions in existence.

This spirit of Elijah was manifest in the days of the apostles, in delivering certain ones to the buffetings of Satan, that they might be saved in the day of the Lord Jesus. They were sealed by the spirit of Elijah unto the damnation of hell until the day of the Lord, or revelation of Jesus Christ.

Here is the doctrine of election that the world has quarreled so much about; but they do not know anything about it.

The doctrine that the Presbyterians and Methodists have quarreled so much about—once in grace, always in grace, or falling away from grace, I will say a word about. They are both wrong. Truth takes a road between them both, for while the Presbyterian says "once in grace, you cannot fall;" the Methodist says: "You can have grace today, fall from it to-morrow, next day have grace again; and so follow on, changing continually." But the doctrine of the Scriptures and the spirit of Elijah would show them both false, and take a road between them both; for, according to the Scripture, if men have received the good word of God, and tasted of the powers of the world to come, if they shall fall away, it is impossible to renew them again, seeing they have crucified the Son of God afresh, and put Him to an open shame; so there is a possibility of falling away; you could not be renewed again, and the power of Elijah cannot seal against this sin, for this is a reserve made in the seals and power of the Priesthood.

I will make every doctrine plain that I present, and it shall stand upon a firm basis, and I am at the defiance of the world, for I will take shelter under the broad cover of the wings of the work in which I am engaged. It matters not to me if all hell boils over; I regard it only as I would the crackling of the thorns under a pot.

A murderer, for instance, one that sheds innocent blood, cannot have forgiveness. David sought repentance at the hand of God carefully with tears, for the murder of Uriah; but he could only get it through hell: he got a promise that his soul should not be left in hell.

Although David was a king, he never did obtain the spirit and power of Elijah and the fullness of the Priesthood; and the Priesthood that he received, and the throne and kingdom of David is to be taken from him and given to another by the name of David in the last days, raised up out of his lineage.

Peter referred to the same subject on the day of Pentecost, but the multitude did not get the endowment that Peter had; but several days after, the people asked "What shall we do?" Peter says, "1 would ye had done it ignorantly,'' speaking of crucifying the Lord, &c. He did not say to them, "Repent and be baptized, for the remission of your sins;" but he said, "Repent ye therefore, and be converted, that your sins may be blotted out, when the times of refreshing shall come from the presence of the Lord.'' (Acts iii. 19.)

This is the case with murderers. They could not be baptized for the remission of sins for they had shed innocent blood.

Again: The doctrine or sealing power of Elijah is as follows:—If you have power to seal on earth and in heaven, then we should be wise. The first thing you do, go and seal on earth your sons and daughters unto yourself, and yourself unto your fathers in eternal glory. * * * * * * * * I will walk through the gate of heaven and claim what I seal, and those that follow me and my counsel.

The Lord once told me that what I asked for I should have. I have been afraid to ask God to kill my enemies, lest some of them should, peradventure, repent.

I asked a short time since for the Lord to deliver me out of the hands of the Governor of Missouri, and if it needs must be to accomplish it, to take him away; and the next news that came pouring down from there was, that *Governor Reynolds had shot himself.* And I would now say, "Beware, O earth, how you fight against the Saints of God and shed innocent blood; for in the days of Elijah, his enemies came upon him, and fire was called down from heaven and destroyed them.

The spirit of Elias is first, Elijah second, and Messiah last. Elias is a forerunner to prepare the way, and the spirit and power of Elijah is to come after, holding the keys of power, building the Temple to the capstone, placing the seals of the Melchisedec Priesthood upon the house of Israel, and making all things ready; then Messiah comes to His Temple, which is last of all.

Messiah is above the spirit and power of Elijah, for He made the world, and was that spiritual rock unto Moses in the wilderness. Elijah was to come and prepare the way and build up the kingdom before the coming of the great day of the Lord, although the spirit of Elias might begin it.

I have asked of the Lord concerning His coming; and while asking the Lord, He gave a sign and said, "In the days of Noah I set a bow in the heavens as a sign and token that in any year that the bow should be seen the Lord would not come; but there should be seed time and harvest during that year: but whenever you see the bow withdrawn, it shall be a token that there shall be famine, pestilence, and great distress among the nations, and that the coming of the Messiah is not far distant.

But I will take the responsibility upon myself to prophesy in the name of the Lord, that Christ will not come this year, as Father Miller has prophesied, for we have seen the bow; and I also prophesy, in the name of the Lord, that Christ will not come in forty years; and if God ever spoke by my mouth, He will not come in that length of time. Brethren, when you go home, write this down, that it may be remembered.

Jesus Christ never did reveal to any man the precise time that He would come. Go and read the Scriptures, and you cannot find anything that specifies the exact hour He would come; and all that say so are false teachers.

There are some important things concerning the office of the Messiah in the organization of the world. which I will speak of hereafter, May God Almighty bless you and pour out His Spirit upon you, is the prayer of your unworthy servant. Amen.

At half-past three p. m., I met with the Twelve, Bishop Miller and the Temple Committee, in the Nauvoo Mansion.

The following letter from Lyman Wight and others was read:—

Letter:—Lyman Wight to the First Presidency—Preaching the Gospel to the Indians and Proposing to Migrate to Texas.

BLACK RIVER FALLS, Feb. 15, 1844.

To the First Presidency and the Quorum of the Twelve of the Church of Christ of Latter-day Saints.

DEAR BRETHREN,—Through the goodness and mercy of God, the Eternal Father, and grace of our Lord and Savior Jesus Christ, we are permitted to write and send by a special messenger a concise account of our lumbering operations, together with the apparent prospects of the introduction and spread of the Gospel among the Chippewa and Menomanee Indians, and also the projects of our hearts in regard to future operations in spreading the Gospel south in all the extent of America, and the consequences growing out of the same, all of which we beg leave to submit to your consideration that we may have your concurrence, or such views as shall be in accordance with the mind and will of the Lord, and govern ourselves in accordance therewith.

Since we have been here lumbering, we have had many difficulties to encounter; but the main hindrance to our successful operations was the feeding, clothing, and transporting a great many lazy, idle men, who have not produced anything by their pretended labor, and thus eating up all that the diligent and honest could produce by their unceasing application to labor; and we have not yet got entirely clear of such persons.

But under all these mighty clogs and hindrances, we have been able to accomplish and have in progress, so that we can deliver in Nauvoo about one million feet of lumber by the last of July next, which will be a great deal more than what is necessary to build the Temple and the Nauvoo House. Besides all this, we have made valuable improvements here,—all the result of much labor done under trying circumstances.

We have recently ascertained that the lands from the falls of Black River to its sources are the property of the Menomanee Indians, and the general government having urged them to move off the lands in the vicinity of Green Bay to their own lands. The Indians say they will, provided the Government will remove all strange Indians and trespassing white men off their lands; consequently, the agent and superintendent of Indian Affairs are taking such steps as will stop all further trespassing on the Indian lands, on the Wisconsin, Black and Chippewa rivers, under the penalties of the laws relative to the cases.

We sent Brothers Miller and Daniels, in company with the principal chief of the Menomanee Indians, overland to the Wisconsin river, to ascertain more about the matter. They saw the agent; found him a gruff, austere man, determined to stop all trespassing on Indian lands.

The Indians are willing to sell privileges to individuals for lumbering and cutting timber, as they have hitherto done; but the agent is opposed to it. Thus a difficulty arises between themselves.

Now, as regards the introduction of the Gospel of Christ among the Indians here, it will require more exertion, to all appearances, to check the enthusiastic ardor of these our red brethren, until the full principles of faith in our Lord and Savior Jesus Christ shall be reasoned into their minds, than to urge them on to receive it. They have great confidence in us.

The country belonging to these northern Indians is a dreary, cold region, and to a great extent, cranberry marshes, pine barrens, and swamps, with a small amount of good lands, scarce of game, and only valuable in mill privileges and facilities for lumbering purposes.

As to mineral resources, they have not been fully developed. There is no doubt as to the abundance of iron ore, but uncertain as to quality.

Now, under all these circumstances, a few of us here have arrived at this conclusion in our minds (such as can undergo all things,)—that as the Gospel has not been fully opened in all the South and Southwestern States, as also Texas, Mexico, Brazil, &c., together with the West Indian Islands, having produced lumber enough to build the Temple and Nauvoo House,—also having an influence over the Indians, so as to induce them to sell their lands to the United States, and go to a climate southwest, (all according to the policy of the U. S. Government),—and having also become convinced that the Church at Nauvoo or in the Eastern States will not build the Nauvoo House according to the commandment, neither the Temple in a reasonable time, and that we have, so far as we have made trials, got means in the south,—we have in our minds to go to the table-lands of Texas, to a point we may find to be the most eligible, there locate, and let it be a place of gathering for all the South (they being incumbered with that unfortunate race of beings, the negroes); and for us to employ our time and talents in gathering together means to build according to the commandments of our God, and spread the Gospel to the nations according to the will of our Heavenly Father. We, therefore, our beloved brethren, send our worthy Brother Young, with a few of our thoughts, on paper, that you may take the subject-matter under consideration, and return us such instructions as may be according to the mind and will of the Lord our God.

We have thought it best to sell the mills here, if you think it expedient. We feel greatly encouraged to spend and be spent in the cause of Christ, according to the will of our Heavenly Father.

You will, therefore, after due deliberation, send us, by the hands of Brother Young, such instructions as may be the result of your deliberations.

Holding ourselves ready under all circumstances in life to try to do all things whatsoever commanded or instructed to do by those ordained to direct the officers of the Church of Jesus Christ; subscribing ourselves yours truly, while life shall endure,

LYMAN WIGHT,
GEORGE MILLER,
PHINEAS R. BIRD
PIERCE HAWLEY,
JOHN YOUNG.

Select Committee to write expressly the views of the branch of the Church at Black River Falls.

JOSEPH SMITH, P. C.
BRIGHAM YOUNG, P. T.
WILLARD RICHARDS, Clerk.

Also a letter to myself from Lyman Wight and others—

Letter:—Lyman Wight to President Joseph Smith—Suggesting a Southwest Movement for the Church.

BLACK RIVER FALLS, WISCONSIN TERRITORY,
February 15th, 1844.

To Joseph Smith, President of the Church of Jesus Christ of Latter-day Saints, and to the Twelve Apostles, greeting:—

Believing a concert of action in all things in this Church to be highly important, we deem it necessary, under existing circumstances, to make you acquainted with our views, feelings, and temporal and spiritual prospects, as they now exist.

We wrote you last fall a full and complete description of this country as high as the falls on Black River, without exaggeration, giving a slight description of the Pinery.

With the exception of several renegadoes and false brethren, things passed smoothly until some time in the month of January, when we were visited by three different tribes of Lamanites upon the most friendly terms, receiving us as their counselors, both temporal and spiritual.

The names of those tribes are Menomanees, Chippewa, and Winnebagoes. They informed us that all the land above the falls belongs to the Menomanee tribe, and that the agents and the governor, the general agent in the northwest of all the Indian affairs, had agreed with them to remove all the lumbermen from Black River, Chippewa, and Lemanware rivers, by their request; but after a lengthy conversation with them, they felt to treat us as their friends, and not their enemies.

We dispatched two messengers—namely, George Miller and Cyrus Daniels, to go immediately to Wisconsin, where they met with the agent, who gave them to understand we could get the timber, which is already cut, at a reasonable rate, and for any future prospect we will be under the necessity of entering into a contract.

We calculate the present prospect for lumber betwixt this and the last of July next will be from eight to twelve hundred thousand feet, which we deem will be all sufficient to finish the two houses, which will accomplish the mission on which we started to this country.

We, therefore, as a brahch and a member of the body of the Church of Jesus Christ of Latter-day Saints chose the following committee—namely, Lyman Wight, George Miller, Pierce Hawley, Phineas R. Bird and John Young, to correspond with your reverend council, giving you our views concerning matters and things, and requesting your counsel on the same.

This committee views it inexpedient to purchase standing timber on so rapid and unnavigable a stream for the purpose of making lumber to gain wealth.

The Lamanites owning this land, notwithstanding their great anxiety to receive the Gospel and the Book of Mormon, have a strong desire, if counseled by us so to do, to go south-west, where game is more plentiful as their only resource here for a living is the pitiful annuities and proceeds from their pine timber, which timber is the only inducement to the Government to purchase their lands.

This committe is therefore led to take a brief view of the south and western part of North America, together with the Floridas, Texas, West India Islands, and the adjacent islands to the Gulf of Mexico, together with the Lamanites bordering on the United Territories from Green Bay to the Mexican Gulf, all crying with one voice, through the medium of their chiefs, Give us an understanding of your doctrine and principles, for we perceive that your ways are equal, and your righteousness far exceeds the righteousness of all the missionaries that we have yet become acquainted with,—that your conduct with one another is like that of ours, and that all your feasts and attendant ceremonies are precisely like ours.

Your servants, the committee, have viewed the Colorado river, with all its beautiful hills and valleys and fertile soil, with deep regret, when viewing the countless thousands of inhabitants on either side thereof, without the knowledge of God or the doctrine of the Church of Jesus

Christ of Latter-day Saints, and say in their hearts. Would it be expedient to form a mission of those true and full-blooded Ephraimites, who, from principle, and the love of the truth, have borne the most extreme burdens, fatigue, and hunger, to prosecute the mission, to procure lumber sufficient to build the two houses, to open the door to all the regions which we have named, which regions have never yet had an opportunity to hear the Gospel and to be made acquainted with the plan of salvation? or shall they continue to suffer the fatigues of hunger, wet and cold, in a rigid, inclement climate, for the pitiful sum that it shall avail them, after undergoing those hazardous perils? or shall they, like Timothy and Titus, with Paul, hazard the perils of the sea and land through the Southern States and West India Islands, and all the Lamanite world, go forth and proclaim to them the Gospel of our Lord and Savior Jesus Christ, and teach them to build up Zion?

Are there not thousands of the rich planters who would embrace the Gospel, and, if they had a place to plant their slaves, give all the proceeds of their yearly labor, if rightly taught, for building up the kingdom, being directed by the President of the whole Church to make the right application? We answer, Yes, we believe they would.

Your servants, the committee, are of the opinion that a concerted and reciprocity of action between the North and the South would greatly advance the building up of the kingdom.

The committee is well informed of the Cherokee and the Chocktaw nations who live between the state of Arkansas and the Colorado river of the Texans, owning large plantations and thousands of slaves, and that they are also very desirous to have an interview with the Elders of this Church, upon the principles of the Book of Mormon.

This committee is of the opinion that they can choose soldiers for this expedition who are as undeviating in the principles of the doctrine of Christ and the Book of Mormon as the sun in his daily course, and as indefatigable in their exertions in this cause as the earth is in its daily revolution.

This committee views it as a matter of investigation, whether would the Southerner, with his slaves and abundance of wealth, do better to take them to some slave-holding point, keep them in lively exercise according to his former customs and habits turning over his yearly proceeds into the hands of the Trustee-in-Trust for the whole Church, or to abolish slavery and settle himself in a climate uncongenial to his nature and entirely derogatory to his former occupations in life?

After having procured the lumber for those two houses, the committee is of the opinion that the preaching of the Gospel and raising funds in the south would be a far more speedy way of accomplishing the work than any other that could be introduced at the present time.

We, your servants, therefore, will wait patiently the result of your council, and submit ourselves to the same with all cheerfulness, our only object being to advance the cause and kingdom of God, stand ready to take hold wherever your wise council may consider it to be of the most advantage.

This committee view with deep regret the many different teachings this Church has received concerning the distribution of their property, such as raising funds for the printing of tracts, evidences of the Book of Mormon, and pamphlets of various descriptions, which we consider has not advanced the cause in the least degree, but has tended directly to sap the foundation of building the houses.

We therefore believe that no person embracing the doctrine of the Church of Jesus Christ of Latter-day Saints should give any part or parcel of the property without a direct counsel, written or oral, from the First Presidency of the Church.

Whereas the committee having appointed George Miller and Lyman Wight to write the views of the committee, each wrote separate and apart, having laid the same before the committee, the committee resolved that both productions be sent without alterations.

We, the committee, conclude by subscribing ourselves your friends and well-wishers in the Lord, praying a speedy answer from your worthy council, or the word of the Lord.

LYMAN WIGHT,
GEORGE MILLER,
PHINEAS R. BIRD,
PIERCE HAWLEY,
JOHN YOUNG,

Select Committee to write expressing the views of the branch of the Church at Black River Falls.

JOSEPH SMITH, SEN., P. C.
BRIGHAM YOUNG, P. T.
WILLARD RICHARDS, Clerk.

The brethren went into council on the subject matter of the letters during the evening.

Monday 11.—At home till nine; then spent the day in council in the lodge room over Henry Miller's house.

Special Council Meeting on Wight and Miller Letters.

Present—Joseph Smith, Hyrum Smith, Brigham Young, Heber C. Kimball, Willard Richards, Parley P. Pratt, Orson Pratt, John Taylor,

George A. Smith, William W. Phelps, John M. Bernhisel, Lucien Woodworth, George Miller, Alexander Badlam, Peter Haws, Erastus Snow, Reynolds Cahoon, Amos Fielding, Alpheus Cutler, Levi Richards, Newel K. Whitney, Lorenzo D. Wasson, and William Clayton, whom I organized into a special council, to take into consideration the subject matter contained in the above letters, and also the best policy for this people to adopt to obtain their rights from the nation and insure protection for themselves and children; and to secure a resting place in the mountains, or some uninhabited region, where we can enjoy the liberty of conscience guaranteed to us by the Constitution of our country, rendered doubly sacred by the precious blood of our fathers, and denied to us by the present authorities, who have smuggled themselves into power in the States and Nation.

CHAPTER XI.

ORSON PRATT SENT TO WASHINGTON AS AGENT OF NAUVOO—
AMOS FIELDING TO ENGLAND, DITTO—COMMENT ON THE
CANDIDACY OF JOSEPH SMITH FOR PRESIDENT OF THE U.
S.—CONSPIRACIES OF THE LAWS, HIGBEES, FOSTERS, ET
AL. AGAINST JOSEPH SMITH—THE PROPHET'S MEMORIAL
TO CONGRESS—OCCUPATION OF THE WEST CONTEM-
PLATED.

Tuesday, March 12, 1844.—At home in the morning.
At eleven a. m., I told Brother Cole I wanted the room
over the store for more important purposes, and wished
him to remove the school to Henry Miller's house immediately; which he did.

The brethren who were in council with me yesterday
assembled there in the afternoon and evening.

Gave the following recommend to Elder Orson Pratt.

Credentials of Orson Pratt as Agent for the City of Nauvoo.

CITY OF NAUVOO, ILLINOIS, March 12, 1844.

TO WHOM IT MAY CONCERN:—

We, the mayor and recorder of said city, do hereby certify that
Orson Pratt, Esq., the bearer, a councilor in city council of said city,
is sent as an agent by the authorities of said city or corporation to
transact such business as he may deem expedient and beneficial for the
community which he represents; and as such agent and gentleman of
principle and character, he by us is recommended to the due consideration of all the executive officers of the government, both houses of
Congress, and gentlemen generally of the United States.

In witness whereof we have hereunto set our hands and affixed the
seal of said corporation at the time and place aforesaid.

[CORPORATION SEAL.]

JOSEPH SMITH, Mayor.

WILLARD RICHARDS, Recorder.

A dull cloudy day.

A meeting of the inhabitants of the Tenth ward was held this evening at the schoolhouse on the hill, in Parley street, to take into consideration the propriety of establishing a store on the principle of co-operation or reciprocity. The subject was fully investigated, and the benefits of such an institution clearly pointed out.

Co--operative Store Planned.

The plan proposed for carrying out the object of the meeting was by shares of five dollars each.

The leading feature of the institution was to give employment to our own mechanics, by supplying the raw material, and manufacturing all sorts of domestic goods, and furnishing the necessaries and comforts of life on the lowest possible terms.

A committee was appointed to draft a plan for the government of said institute, to be submitted for adoption or amendment at their next meeting; after which an adjournment took place till next Tuesday evening, at half-past six o'clock, at the same place.

Wednesday, 13.—In special council from nine to twelve a. m. Orson Hyde, Wilford Woodruff and James Emmett were present, in addition to those of the preceding day. Willard Richards was appointed historian, and William Clayton clerk of the council.

It was decided that Amos Fielding should return to England, when I and my brother Hyrum gave him the following letter of attorney:—

Credentials of Elder Amos Fielding on Departing for England.

"This is to certify that the bearer thereof, our worthy brother Elder Amos Fielding, hath been appointed by the First Presidency of _the Church of Jesus Christ of Latter-day Saints, our agent, to transact such business as may be deemed necessary for the benefit of said Church, and such as he shall see proper throughout the island of Great Britain.

He is hereby authorized to receive moneys for the Temple in Nauvoo,

the poor, or for the Church; and the brethren will be safe should they
deposit money in his hands for any purpose pertaining to the Church
business in this place.

In witness whereof we have hereunto set our hands and placed the
corporation seal of City of Nauvoo this 13th day of March, A. D. 1844.

[CORPORATION SEAL.]   JOSEPH SMITH,
                                       HYRUM SMITH,

Presiding Elders of the whole Church of Jesus Christ of Latter-day
Saints.

Thursday, 14.—In special council over the store from
nine till one.

At two, went to see Brother John Wilkie. He had sent
to me to come and see him. He wanted to know what he
should do. I told him of the order of tithing, &c., and he
wanted I should come again.

At four, went to assembly room again. Lucien Woodworth sent on a mission to Texas. At seven, adjourned
to next Tuesday, at nine, a. m.

Friday 15.—Dull, cloudy day, north wind. Frosty
night. Spent the day in council.

Being in a strait to raise money to assist the hands in
the Pine country, I sent Elders Brigham and Willard
Richards to borrow some money from Mr. Orme, who, it
is believed, had a large sum of money lying idle, but they
did not get any.

I copy from the Law of the Lord:—

John Wilkie. The Blessing of the Prophet upon Him.

"This day President Joseph Smith rode over to Brother John Wilkie's at his special request, to give him some instructions relative to his
duty in regard to tithing and consecration.

Brother Wilkie has for a long time back been struggling with his
feelings, designing to do right. but laboring under many fears and prejudices, in consequence of having in some degree given way to believe
the base reports circulated by individuals for the purpose of injuring
the authorities of the Church, and also from various other causes. His
faithful companion has persevered diligently. and with fervent prayer
has called upon God in his behalf, until she has realized her utmost
wishes.

Brother Wilkie now feels anxious to do right in all things, and especially to pay his tithing to the full. President Joseph showed him the principles of consecration and the means whereby he might realize the fullness of the blessings of the celestial kingdom; and as an evidence that he desired to do right, he paid over to the Trustee-in-Trust the sum of three hundred dollars in gold and silver for the benefit of the Temple, and which is now recorded on consecration.

He also signified his intention of paying more as soon as he could get matters properly arranged. The president then pronounced a blessing upon him and his companion, that they should have the blessing of God to attend them in their basket and in their store—that they should have the blessing of health and salvation and long life, inasmuch as they would continue to walk in obedience to the commandments of God.

May the Lord grant his Spirit and peace to abide upon Brother Wilkie and his companion through the remainder of their days; may their hearts expand and become enlarged to receive the fullness of the blessings of the kingdom of heaven; may they have the light of eternal truth continually springing up in them like a well of living water; may they be shielded from the powers of Satan and the influence of designing men, and their faith increase from day to day until they shall have power to lay hold on the blessings of God and the gifts of the Spirit until they are satisfied; and, finally, may they live to a good old age; and when they have lived while they desire life, may they die in peace and be received into the mansions of eternal life, and enjoy a celestial glory forever and ever! Even so, amen.

The editors of the *Times and Seasons* published a short account of "Our City and the Present Aspect of Affairs," which we insert.

STATUS OF NAUVOO IN THE SPRING OF 1844.

Believing that our patrons and friends are pleased to hear of our prosperity, we feel happy in apprising them of the same, through the columns of our paper.

Owing to the scarcity of provision and the pressure in the money market during the past winter, commercial business has been somewhat dull; consequently, those who were not previously prepared have been obliged to employ the principal portion of their time in obtaining the necessary means for the sustenance of their families: therefore little improvement has been made. But old Boreas is now on his receding march, and spring has commenced its return with all its pleasantness.

Navigation is open, and steamboats are almost continually plying up and down our majestic river. They have already brought several families of emigrants to this place, who have cordially joined with their friends and brethren in the great work of the upbuilding of Zion and the rolling forth of the kingdom of God.

The work of improvement is now actively begun, and in every direction may be heard the sound of the mason's trowel, the carpenters's hammer, the teamster's voice, or, in other words, the hum of industry and the voice of merriment. Indeed, to judge from the present appearance, a greater amount of improvement will be done the ensuing summer than in the preceding one.

Almost every stranger that enters our city is excited with astonishment that so much has been done in so short a time; but we flatter ourselves, from the known industry, perseverance, and diligence of the Saints, that by the return of another winter so much more will be accomplished, that his astonishment will be increased to wonder and admiration.

Quite extensive preparations are being made by the farmers in this vicinity for the cultivation of land; and should the season prove favorable, we doubt not that nearly, if not a sufficient amount of produce will be raised to supply the wants of the city and adjacent country.

We are also pleased that we can inform our friends abroad that the Saints here of late have taken hold of the work on the Temple with the zeal and energy that in no small degree excites our admiration. Their united efforts certainly speak to us that it is their determination that this spacious edifice shall be enclosed, if not finished, this season.

And a word we would say to the Saints abroad, which is, that the Temple is being built in compliance with a special commandment of God not to a few individuals, but to all. Therefore we sincerely hope you will contribute of your means as liberally as your circumstances will allow, that the burden of the work may not rest upon a few, but pro. portionately upon all.

Where is the true-hearted Saint that does not with joy and delight contemplate the endowment of the servants of God and the blessings He has promised to His people on condition that they speedily build the Temple? Certainly you cannot reasonably expect to enjoy these blessings if you refuse to contribute your share towards its erection.

It is a thing of importance, and much depends upon its accomplishment: therefore we wish to forcibly impress the matter upon your minds, hoping you will become aroused to a sense of your duty—that every company of Saints, every Elder that comes here, and every mail may bring money and other property for this important work,—which, when completed, will stand, in one sense of the word, as a firm pillar in Zion, and which will greatly facilitate the prosperity of the great cause of truth which we all are actively engaged in.

Saturday, 16.—At home. At one p. m., I sat in council with Willard Richards, Orrin P. Rockwell, and Bishop George Miller.

The Female Relief Society had two meetings in the assembly room, as it would not hold all at once, and sanctioned the "Voice of Innocence from Nauvoo."

Sunday, 17.—Last night, Nauvoo was visited by a very strong wind from the west. It blew down a portion of the west wall of the new hall (28 by 40 feet on the ground,) which the Seventies had commenced on Bain street, and they had raised for the roof.

Wind Storm at Nauvoo.

The wind continued very strong all day. In the evening, had a smart snowstorm, which covered the ground, was succeeded by a frosty night.

Attended prayer meeting.

Monday, 18.—The frost of last night was so severe as to form ice inside the houses.

I stayed at home to recite German with Brother Neibaur.

Tuesday, 19.—Met in council in the assembly room. Elder Samuel Bent, Uriah Brown, Samuel James, John D. Parker, Orrin P. Rockwell, Sidney Rigdon, William Marks, and Orson Spencer met in council, in addition to the former names.

In the afternoon, heavy, driving rain. Northwest wind. Dull, cold day.

Wednesday, 20.—Severely cold northwest wind, with a snow and hail storm until ten a. m. Afternoon dull. West wind.

Spent the morning and afternoon in the assembly room, studying the languages.

Elder Woodruff read me a letter which he had written
to Colonel Solomon Copeland concerning his
nomination to be a candidate for the Vice-
President of the United States.

Col. Copeland
and the Vice-
Presidency.

The *Illinois Springfield Register* has the following:—

GENERAL JOSEPH SMITH A CANDIDATE FOR PRESIDENT.

It appears by the Nauvoo papers that the Mormon Prophet is actually
a candidate for the presidency. He has sent us his pamphlet, containing an extract of his principles, from which it appears that he is up to
the hub for a United States bank and a protective tariff. On these
points he is much more explicit than Mr. Clay, who will not say that he
is for a bank, but talks all the time of restoring a national currency.
Nor will Mr. Clay say what kind of a tariff he is for. He says to the
south that he has not sufficiently examined the present tariff, but
thinks very likely it could be amended.

General Smith posesses no such fastidious delicacy. He comes right
out in favor of a bank and a tariff, taking the true Whig ground, and
ought to be regarded as the real Whig candidate for President, until
Mr. Clay can so far recover from his shuffling and dodging as to declare
his sentiments like a man.

At present we can form no opinion of Clay's principles, except as
they are professed by his friends in these parts.

Clay himself has adopted the notion which was once entertained by
an eminent grammarian, who denied that language was intended as a
means to express one's ideas, but insisted that it was invented on purpose to aid us in concealing them.

The *Iowa Democrat* publishes the following:—

A New Candidate in the Field.

We see from the *Nauvoo Neighbor* that General Joseph Smith, the
great Mormon Prophet, has become a candidate for the next presidency.
We do not know whether he intends to submit his claims to the National
Convention, or not; but, judging from the language of his own organ,
we conclude that he considers himself a full team for all of them.

All that we have to say on this point is, that if superior talent, genius, and intelligence, combined with virtue, integrity, and enlarged
views, are any guarantee to General Smith's being elected, we think
that he will be a "full team of himself."

The *Missouri Republican* believes that it will be death to Van Buren, and all agree that it must be injurious to the Democratic ranks, inasmuch as it will throw the Mormon vote out of the field.

A traveler, having visited Nauvoo for a few days, wrote to the *Times and Seasons*—

"Mr. Editor,—Before I take my departure, permit me to express my views relative to the leading men of your city, where I have been these few days.

I have been conversant with the great men of the age; and, last of all I feel that I have met with the greatest, in the presence of your esteemed Prophet, General Joseph Smith. From many reports, I had reason to believe him a bigoted religionist, as ignorant of politics as the savages; but, to my utter astonishment, on the short acquaintance, I have found him as familiar in the cabinet of nations as with his Bible and in the knowledge of that book I have not met with his equal in Europe or America. Although I should beg leave to differ with him in some items of faith, his nobleness of soul will not permit him to take offense at me. No, sir; I find him open, frank, and generous,—as willing others should enjoy their opinions as to enjoy his own.

The General appears perfectly at home on every subject, and his familiarity with many languages affords him ample means to become informed concerning all nations and principles, which with his familiar and dignified deportment towards all must secure to his interest the affections of every intelligent and virtuous man that may chance to fall in his way, and I am astonished that so little is known abroad concerning him.

Van Buren was my favorite, and I was astonished to see General Smith's name as a competitor; but, since my late acquaintance, Mr. Van Buren can never re-seat himself in the Presidential chair on my vote while General Smith is in the field. Forming my opinions alone on the talents of the two, and from what I have seen, I have no reason to doubt but General Smith's integrity is equal to any other individual; and I am satisfied he cannot easily be made the pliant tool of any political party. I take him to be a man who stands far aloof from little caucus quibblings and squabblings, while nations, governments, and realms are wielded in his hand as familiarly as the top and hoop in the hands of their little masters.

Free from all bigotry and superstition, he dives into every subject, and it seems as though the world was not large enough to satisfy his capacious soul, and from his conversation one might suppose him as well acquinted with other worlds as this.

So far as I can discover, General Smith is the nation's man, and the man who will exalt the nation, if the people will give him the opportunity; and all parties will find a friend in him so far as right is concerned.

General Smith's movements are perfectly anomalous in the estimation of the public. All other great men have been considered wise in drawing around them wise men; but I have frequently heard the General called a fool because he has gathered the wisest of men to his cabinet, who direct his movements; but this subject is too ridiculous to dwell upon. Suffice it to say, so far as I have seen, he has wise men at his side—superlatively wise, and more capable of managing the affairs of a State than most men now engaged therein, which I consider much to his credit, though I would by no means speak diminutively of my old friend.

From my brief acquaintance, I consider General Smith (independent of his peculiar religious views, in which by-the-by, I have discovered neither vanity nor folly,) the *sine qua non* of the age to our nation's prosperity. He has learned the all-important lesson "to profit by the experience of those who have gone before;" so that, in short, General Smith begins where other men leave off. I am aware this will appear a bold assertion to some; but I would say to such, call, and form your acquaintance, as I have done; then judge.

Thus, sir, you have a few leading items of my views of General Smith, formed from personal acquaintance, which you are at liberty to dispose of as you think proper. I anticipate the pleasure of renewing my acquaintance with your citizens at a future day.

Yours respectfully,
A TRAVELER.

A writer in the *Quincy Herald* reflects very strongly upon the conduct of the *Quincy Whig*, *New York Tribune*, and other newspapers, for publishing slanderous falsehoods against the Saints.

Ten, p. m., commenced snowing again.

Thursday, 21.—A cold snow-storm through the night. In council in the assembly room, discussing the propriety of petitioning Congress for the privilege of raising troops to protect the making of setments in the uncivilized portions of our continent.

Origin of Memorial to Congress.

Willard Richards was appointed a committee to draw up a memorial to Congress.

Friday, 22.—Snow on the ground; cold, bleak north wind; cloudy.

At ten a. m., held Mayor's court, and afterwards read German in the reading room.

In the afternoon, met with the Twelve in prayer at President Brigham Young's house.

I advised the Seventies to pull down the remainder of the walls and rebuild the Seventies' hall on a permanent basis from the foundation, and not erect for themselves a trap, but build one two stories high. and strong enough to stand for a generation.

The Seventies' Hall, Instructions on Rebuilding.

Saturday, 23.—Day warmer. Rode out with Clayton to endeavor to raise money to furnish the hands in the Pinery with supplies. Visited the Temple and public works

Also called with William Clayton and Alexander Neibaur at Dr. Foster's. He was gone to Appanoose, and Mrs. Foster was at Mr. Gilman's.

I here extract from William Clayton's journal:—

President Smith's Interview With Mrs. Foster.

We went down there and saw her, [Mrs. Foster]. President Joseph asked Sister Foster if she ever in her life knew him guilty of an immoral or indecent act, She answered, "No." He then explained his reasons for asking; which were, he had been informed that Dr. Foster had stated that Joseph made propositions to his wife calculated to lead her astray from the path of virtue; and then asked if ever he had used any indecent or insulting language to her. She answered, "Never." He further asked if he ever preached anything like the "plurality of wife" doctrine to her other than what he had preached in public? She said, "No." He asked her if he ever proposed to have illicit intercourse with her, and especially when he took dinner during the doctor's absence. She said, "No." After some further conversation on the subject, we left. Mrs. Gillman was present all the time. President Joseph and Neibaur then went on foot to the farm.

Sunday, 24.—At ten, a. m., met at the stand near the

Temple. [The following very brief outline of the speeches is from the journal of Wilford Woodruff]:—

Discourse of President Smith—Conspiracies in Nauvoo.

"President Joseph Smith addressed the people. The following is the substance of what I heard him say:—

I have been informed by two gentlemen that a conspiracy is got up in this place for the purpose of taking the life of President Joseph Smith, his family, and all the Smith family, and the heads of the Church. One of the gentlemen will give his name to the public, and the other wishes it to be hid for the present: they will both testify to it on oath, and make an affidavit upon it. The names of the persons revealed at the head of the conspiracy are as follows:—Chancey L. Higbee, Dr. Robert D. Foster, Mr. Joseph H. Jackson, William and Wilson Law. And the lies that C. L. Higbee has hatched up as a foundation to work upon are—he says that I had men's heads cut off in Missouri, and that I had a sword run through the hearts of the people that I wanted to kill and put out of the way. I won't swear out a warrant against them, for I don't fear any of them: they would not scare off an old setting hen. I intend to publish all the iniquity that I know of them. If I am guilty, I am ready to bear it. There is sometimes honor among enemies. I am willing to do anything for the good of the people. I will give the name of one of the gentlemen who have divulged the plot: his name is M. G. Eaton. He will swear to it: he is a bold fellow. Joseph H. Jackson said a Smith should not be alive in two weeks,—not over two months anyhow. Concerning the character of these men, I will say nothing about it now; but if I hear anything more from them on this subject, I will tell what I know about them.

Elder Orson Spencer addressed the people as follows:—

While listening to President Smith's remarks, I thought of a figure, i.e., if a physician was going to dissect a body, he would not be likely to begin at the limbs but cut the head off first. So the adversary of the Saints has laid a plan to cut off the head of the Church with the intention of scattering and destroying the whole body. It was so in the days of Jesus Christ; the enemies of the truth sought to kill Him, that the body might be destroyed; which was also the case in the days of Elijah, Daniel, and many of the ancients.

I once heard a man say, who was opposed to this work, "That it might be true, but it gave Joseph Smith power." True, said I; but if his power be subordinate to the power of God, it is right. If a man set up a kingdom by the power of God, then let others seek power from the same source. God sets up kingdoms and pulls down kingdoms:

this makes men mad who will not submit to the kingdom of God. We all know the result of the power of Moses, who was the representative of God.

Judging from what is past, how will it be when God sets up His kingdom in the last days? Whether there is a conspiracy now, or not, I don't know; but no doubt there will be, if not now, for it has always been so. In the days of the Nephites, they had their Gadianton robbers. I have not any doubt but that the apostates will join with the other wicked powers to try to put down the power of God, and I am glad to have the power of the kingdom of God tested; I care not what sacrifice I am called to make for such a kingdom. If it is friends, wealth, or even life, at the purchase of such a kingdom, it is cheap. Did the ancient Apostles, Prophets, or Saints who died pay too much for that kingdom? ˉThey did not. It is necessary that men be put in possession of the knowledge and mysteries of the kingdom of God, in order to sin as far as they wish, that they may go to the highest pitch. How often men lay down their lives for their country and other purposes. How much better, then, to die for the cause of Zion! Good and righteous men will administer justice and rebuke evil. The Church should be cleansed from bad men, and the Lord will take His own way to cleanse the Church.

We should lift up our voice against wickedness of all kinds. But will the rulers of our land do it? No, they will not; they will be cowards until there is no man to fight, and then be brave. When Government will not do it, some man should take the helm of government that will do it. Will it be called treason, if the God of heaven should set up a kingdom? May the Lord give you more and more of His Spirit, light and intelligence, until you are cemented together in union and love. Amen.

Elder Sidney Rigdon addressed the meeting.

President Joseph Smith again arose and said—In relation to the power over the minds of mankind which I hold, I would say, It is in consequence of the power of truth in the doctrines which I have been an instrument in the hands of God of presenting unto them, and not because of any compulsion on my part. I wish to ask if ever I got any of it unfairly? if I have not reproved you in the gate? I ask, Did I ever exercise any compulsion over any man? Did I not give him the liberty of disbelieving any doctrine I have preached, if he saw fit? Why do not my enemies strike a blow at the doctrine? They cannot do it: it is truth, and I defy all men to upset it. I am the voice of one crying in the wilderness, "Repent ye of your sins and prepare the way for the coming of the Son of Man; for the kingdom of God has come unto you, and henceforth the ax is laid unto the root of the tree; and every tree that bringeth not forth good fruit, God Almighty (and not Joe Smith) shall hew it down and cast it into the fire."

After meeting, I rode out with Emma. The trees begin to bud forth.

In the evening, held a conversation with a large company of friends at my door.

Elder R. H. Kinnamon writes that during the last 22 months he has baptized over 100 persons while on a mission in Virginia and North Carolina, organized two branches in Virginia, and calls are continually made for preaching in every direction.

Monday, 25.—At home in the morning. After dinner rode up to the upper landing to see the *St. Louis Oak* steamer. Learned that a company of emigrants from England were expected soon. Called at my office on returning, and heard read the draft of a memorial to Congress which my clerk had been writing, as a committee appointed by the council on Thursday last, and was pleased with the instrument.

Progress on Memorial to Congress.

Millions of wild pigeons flying north, and millions of gnats dancing in the air. Dull day. At night thunder, lightning and rain.

Tuesday, 26.—Dull day. From nine to twelve, noon, in council; also from two to five p. m.

The memorial drawn up by Dr. Richards was read, discussed, and approved by the general council.

Started this morning to go to Ramus with Brother Amasa Lyman. Rode as far as the Temple, and found it so muddy that we turned back.

Issued a warrant on the complaint of Vernon H. Bruce, against Ianthus Rolfe, for stealing two stone-cutter's tools.

I wrote the following:—

The Prophet's Memorial to Congress.

To the Honorable the Senate and House of Representatives of the United States of America, in Congress Assembled:

Your memorialist, a free-born citizen of these United States, respectfully showeth that from his infancy his soul has been filled with the most intense and philanthropic interest for the welfare of his native country; and being fired with an ardor which floods cannot quench, crowns cannot conquer, nor diplomatic intrigue corrupt, to see those principles which emanated from the bosoms of the fathers of seventy-six, and which cost the noblest talents and richest blood of the nation, maintained inviolate and perpetuated to future generations; and the proud eagle of American freedom soar triumphant over every party prejudice and local sinistry, and spread her golden pinions over every member of the human family, who shall stretch forth their hands for succor from the lion's paw or the oppressor's grasp; and firmly trusting in the God of liberty, that He has designed universal peace and goodwill, union, and brotherly love to all the great family of man, your memorialist asks your honorable body to pass the following:—

ORDINANCE.

An Ordinance for the Protection of the Citizens of the United States Emigrating to the Territories, and for the Extension of the Principles of Universal Liberty.

PREAMBLE.

Whereas, many of the citizens of these United States have migrated and are migrating to Texas, Oregon, and other lands contiguous to this nation; and whereas, Texas has declared herself free and independent, without the necessary power to protect her rights and liberties; *and whereas* Oregon is without any organized government, and those who emigrate thither are exposed to foreign invasion and domestic feuds; *and whereas* the Oregon, by geographical location and discovery more rightfully belongs to these United States than any other general government; *and whereas* it is necessary that the emigrants of that newly settling territory should receive protection; *and whereas* the Texan Government has petitioned the United States to be received into our Union, but yet retains her national existence; *and whereas* the United States remember with gratitude the seasonable support they received in a like situation from a LaFayette; *and whereas* the United States desire to see the principles of her free institutions extended to all men, especially where it can be done without the loss of blood and treasure to the nation; *and whereas* there is an almost boundless extent of territory on the west and south of these United States, where exists little or no organization of protective Government; *and whereas* the lands thus unknown; unowned, or unoccupied, are among some of the richest and most fertile of the continent; *and whereas* many of the inhabitants of the Union would gladly embrace the opportunity of extending their researches and acquirements so soon as they can receive protection in their enterprise, thereby adding strength, durability, and wealth to the nation; *and whereas* the red man, the robber, and the desperado have frequenty interrupted such research and acquisition without justifiable cause; *and whereas* Joseph Smith has offered and does hereby offer these United States, to show his loyalty to our Confederate Union and the Constitution of our Republic; to prevent quarrel and bloodshed our frontiers; to extend the arm of deliverance to Texas; to on protect the inhabitants of Oregon from foreign aggressions and domestic broils; to prevent the crowned nations from encircling us as a nation on our western and southern borders, and save the eagle's talon from the lion's paw; to still the tongue of slander, and show the world that a Republic can be, and not be ungrateful; to open the vast regions of the unpeopled west and south to our enlightened and enterprising yeomanry; to protect them in their researches; to secure them in their locations, and thus strengthen the Government and enlarge her borders; to extend her influence; to inspire the nations with the spirit of freedom and win them to her standard; to promote intelligence; to cultivate and establish peace among all with whom we may have intercourse as neighbors; to settle all existing difficulties among those not organized into an acknowledged government bordering upon the United States and Territories; to save the national revenue in the nation's coffers; to supercede the necessity of a standing army on our western and southern frontiers; to create and maintain the principles of peace and suppress mobs, insurrections, and oppression in Oregon and all the lands bordering upon the United States and not incorporated into any acknowledged national government; to explore the unexplored regions of our continent; to open new fields for enterprise to our citizens, and protect them therein; to search out the antiquities of the land, and thereby promote the arts and sciences, and general information; to amalgamate the feelings of all with whom he may have intercourse on the principles of equity, liberty, justice, humanity and benevolence; to break down tyranny and oppression and exalt the standard of universal peace, provided he shall be protected in those rights and privileges which constitutionally belong to every citizen of this Republic; therefore, that the said memorialist may have the privilege, and that no citizen of the United States shall obstruct, or attempt to obstruct or hinder, so good, so great, so noble an enterprise to carry out those plans and principles as set forth in this preamble, and be shielded from every opposition by evil and designing men.

Section 1. *Be it ordained by the Senate and House of Representatives of the United States of America, in Congress Assembled,* that Joseph Smith, of the city of Nauvoo, in the State of Illinois, is hereby authorized and empowered to raise a company of one hundred thousand armed volunteers in the United States and Territories, at such times, and places and in such numbers, as he shall find necessary and convenient for the purposes specified in the foregoing preamble, and to execute the same.

Sec. 2. *And be it further ordained* that if any person or persons shall hinder or attempt to hinder or molest the said Joseph Smith from executing his designs in raising said volunteers, and marching and transporting the same to the borders of the United States and Territories, he, or they so hindering, molesting, or offending, shall be punished by a fine not exceeding one thousand dollars each for every offense, or by hard labor on some public work not exceeding two years, or both, at the discretion of the nearest District Court of the United States, where the hindrance or offense shall be committed, having jurisdiction.

See. 3. *And be it further ordained,* the more fully to remove all obstructions and hindrances to the raising, enlisting, and marching the volunteers as aforesaid, the said Joseph Smith is hereby constituted a member of the army of these United States, and is authorized to act as such in the United States and Territories, and on all lands bordering upon the United States and Territories, for the purposes specified in the foregoing preamble, provided said land shall not be within the acknowledged jurisdiction of any acknowledged national government.

Sec. 4. *And be it further ordained* that nothing in this ordinance shall be so construed by any individual or nation to consider the volunteers aforesaid as constituting any part of the army of the United States; neither shall the said Joseph Smith, as a member of the United States army, disturb the peace of any nation or government acknowledged as such, break the faith of treaties between the United States and any other nation, or violate any known law of nations, thereby endangering the peace of the United States.

Sec. 5. *And be it further ordained,* that the said Joseph Smith shall confine his operations to those principles of action specified in the preamble to this ordinance, the perpetuity of which shall be commensurate with the circumstances and specifications which have originated it.

And your memorialist will ever pray, &c.

JOSEPH SMITH.

CITY OF NAUVOO, ILLINOIS, March 26, 1844.

Dr. Willard Richards wrote to the Saints at Augusta, Lee County, Iowa, requesting a brief history of the settling of that branch, and also asking a donation of lumber for his house.

In the afternoon, Abiathar B. Williams made the following affidavit before Daniel H. Wells, Esq:—

Affidavit of Abiathar B. Williams, Concerning a Conspiracy against the Prophet.

STATE OF ILLINOIS, } ss.
HANCOCK COUNTY,

Personally appeared before me, Daniel H. Wells, Acting Justice of the Peace in and for the said county, Abiathar B. Williams, who, being duly sworn according to law, deposeth and saith that on or about the 15th day of March, A. D., 1844, Joseph H. Jackson came to my house and requested me to walk with him; which I did. During the time we were walking, said Joseph H. Jackson said that he was then coming direct from Mr. Law's; that there was going to be a secret meeting in the city of Nauvoo, probably tomorrow evening: but, as it was not decided, he could not say positively as to the time; but he would inform me in season. The said Joseph H. Jackson said that Doctor Foster, Chauncey L. Higbee, and the Laws were red hot for a conspiracy, and he should not be surprised if in two weeks there should not be one of the Smith family left alive in Nauvoo. After we arrived at Mr. Loomis', near the Masonic hall, in the city of Nauvoo, he related some things which he stated that Dr. Foster had said relative to his family. This he did in the presence of Mr. Eaton and myself, and strongly solicited myself and Mr. Eaton to attend the secret meeting and join them in their intentions. The said Joseph H. Jackson further said that Chauncey Higbee had said that he, the said Chauncey Higbee, had seen men tied hand and foot, and run through the heart with a sword, and their heads taken off, and then buried; and he durst not say a word. This the said Jackson said in Mr. Loomis' room. And further this deponent saith not.

A. B. WILLIAMS.

Sworn to and subscribed before me this 27th day of March, A. D. 1844.

[L. S.]   DANIEL H. WELLS, J. P.

Also M. G. Eaton made affidavit as follows:—

Affidavit of M. G. Eaton—A conspiracy Against Joseph Smith.

STATE OF ILLINOIS, }
HANCOCK COUNTY,   } SS.

Personally appeared before me, Daniel H. Wells, an acting Justice of the Peace, in and for the said county, M. G. Eaton, who being duly sworn according to law, deposeth and saith that on or about the fifteenth day of March, A. D. 1844, Joseph H. Jackson came to me several times and requested me to go on the hill with him. I finally consented went with him to the Keystone Store, in the city of Nauvoo. Dr. Foster and one of the Higbees (I think Chauncey L. Higbee) were in the store. The said Joseph H. Jackson, together with the said R. D. Foster and said Higbee, went into the back room of the store. They appeared to enter into private council. Soon after they went into the said room, the said Joseph H. Jackson invited me into the room where they were sitting. I immediately complied.

Soon after I went in, the said Higbee commenced talking about the spiritual wife system. He said he had no doubt but some of the Elders had ten or twelve apiece. He said they married them, whether the females were living or not; and they did it by recording the marriage in a large book, which book was sealed up after the record was made, and was not to be opened for a long time,—probably not till many of the husbands of those who were thus married were dead. They would then open the book and break the seals in the presence of those females, and when they saw their names recorded in that book they would believe that the doctrine was true and they must submit. He said this book was kept at Mr. Hyrum Smith's. I asked the Chauncey L Higbee.

*   *   *   *   *

[Here follows some expressions too indecent for insertion.]

The aforesaid R. D. Foster then asked me what I would think, if, during my absence from home, a carriage should drive up to my house, a person alight, and the carriage then drive off again; this person should then go into my house and begin to tell my wife a great many things against me to prejudice her mind against me, and use every possible means to do this, and finally would introduce and preach the spiritual wife doctrine to her, and make an attempt to seduce her; and further, this person should sit down to dine with my wife, bless the victuals, &c.; and while they were thus engaged, I should come home and find them thus associated, this person should rise up and say, "How do you do?" and bless me in a very polite manner, &c.; and also if, upon these appearances, I should feel jealous that something was wrong, and when the person was gone I would ask my wife what had been the conversation between her and this person, but she would refuse to tell me; I then draw a pistol and present it to her head and threaten to shoot her if she did not tell me all, but she would still refuse: I then would give her a double-barrelled pistol, and say to her, "Defend yourself; for if you don't tell me, either you or I would shoot:" she would then faint away through fear and excitement, and when she came to again, she would begin and tell how this person had been trying to poison your wife's mind against you, and, by preaching the spiritual wife system to her, had endeavored to seduce her. I replied, I should think he was a rascal: but who has had such a trial as that? The said R. D. Foster answered that he was the man who had had that trial, and who had been thus abused.

The said Dr. Foster, Higbee, and Joseph H. Jackson then remarked that they were about to hold a secret meeting to oppose and try to put a stop to such things. The said Joseph H. Jackson also said that if any person undertook to arrest him, he should begin to cut them.

The said R. D. Foster further said he was afraid of his life, and dared not be out at nights.

The said Higbee said he had not a doubt but there had been men killed in Missouri who had secrets that they were afraid they would divulge. He said he was afraid of his life.

The said Jackson further said he should not be surprised if there should be a real muss and an insurrection in the city in less than two months; and that if a disturbance should take place, the Carthagenians and others would come and help them.

He mentioned some names of persons who would come from Carthage, which names I do not remember. The same day, when in Mr. Loomis' room, I heard the said Jackson say that the Laws were ready to enter into a secret conspiracy, tooth and nails.

The said Higbee also said, while at the Keystone Store, that if ever he was brought before the Mayor's court again, and the Mayor told him to hold his tongue, he should get up and tell him he had a right to speak, and should do so; and then if any man attempted to put him out of court, he would shoot him through. And further this deponent saith not.

M. G. EATON.

Sworn to and subscribed before me, this 27th day of March, A. D., 1844.

[L. S.]   DANIEL H. WELLS, J. P.*

*In addition to these affidavits the Prophet was apprised by two young men, Dennison L. Harris and Robert Scott, the latter living in the family of William Law, of a secret movement then on foot to take his life, and the lives of several other leading men in the Church, among them the Prophet's brother, Hyrum. These

This evening, Dr. Reynolds, of Iowa City, lectured on astronomy in the assembly room.

Thursday, 28.—Dull day, drizzling rain, cold north-east wind.

Transferred the trial of Ianthus Rolfe to Aaron Johnson, J. P.

This afternoon, had the assembly room and office plastered where the same had been knocked off, &c.

Friday, 29.—Night boisterous: about eight, a. m., hail-storm, northeast wind, nipping frost; frost, hail, and strong wind all day.

Spent the day at home.

Saturday, 30.—This morning I heard there was some disturbance on the hill; I rode up and found it reported that a robbery had been committed at the Keystone Store, kept by Mr. Rollasson, of some $400 or $500, and some goods, and they were suspicious of a certain black man. I *The Robbery at Rollasson's Store in Nauvoo.* issued a search-warrant and returned to my office, where I found the black man, —— Chism, with his back lacerated from his shoulders to his hips, with twenty or more lashes. My clerk, Dr. Richards, kept him secreted, and called Aaron Johnson, a justice of the peace, who issued a warrant for —— ——, a Missourian, who had boarded at my house a few days, and on testimony fined him $5 and costs for whipping —— Chism. One Easton, a witness, said he could not testify without implicating himself, and he was apprehended and held in custody. W. H. J. Marr, Esq., refused to testify, because he was counsel.

I got prepared a memorial to his Excellency John Tyler,

young men were invited to the secret meetings by the conspirators, but before going conferred with the Prophet, who told them to go, but to take no part in the proceedings of these wicked men against himself. They carried out his instructions, and at the risk of their lives attended the secret meetings three times, and brought to President Smith a report of what they had witnessed. A full account of this conspiracy written by Horace Cummings—the narrative being detailed to him by Dennison L. Harris—was published in the *Contributor*, for April, 1884.

the President of the United States, embodying in it the same sentiments as are in my Petition to the

Memorial to the President of the United States. Senate and House of Representatives of the United States, dated 26th March, 1844, asking the privilege of raising 100,000 men to extend protection to persons wishing to settle Oregon and other portions of the territory of the United States, and extend protection to the people in Texas.

Sunday, 31.—Cold, fine day.

At home this morning until nine, when I went over to my reading-room, again heard read and signed m y memorial to Congress for the privilege of raising 100,000 volunteers to protect Texas, Oregon, &c., dated 26th instant; and also a memorial to the President for the same purpose, if the other fail.

Also signed an introductory letter to Elder Orson Hyde, who is going to carry the memorials* to Washington as follows:—

* President Smith's memorial to Congress, of the 26th of March, asking to be appointed "a member of the army of these United States," to be authorized "to raise 100,000 armed volunteers" to police the inter-mountain and Pacific slope west, was presented to the House of Representatives by Mr. John Wentworth, of Chicago, where the following occurred with reference to it:

MORMONS:

"Mr. Wentworth asked permission to present a memorial from Gen. Joseph Smith, the head of the Mormons, and required that it might be read by the clerk for the information of the House.

"The Clerk commenced the reading of the memorial.

"Before the reading was concluded.

"Mr. J. R. Ingersoll interposed, and objected to the reception at first, and still objected.

"Mr. Weber observed that if memorials of this kind were to be read, he was entrusted with the presentation of one of a peculiar character, from certain citizens of Frederick county, Md.

"Mr. Wentworth said he would move a suspension of the rules to enable him to have the paper read; and he wished to inquire of the chair whether it would be in order for him to assign his reasons for making such a motion.

"Mr. Duncan observed, if the gentleman would yield him the floor, he would move to suspend the rules, to go into committee of the whole on the Oregon bill.

"Mr. Wentworth said that, as he had the floor, he would make the motion. Mr. Wentworth then moved that the rules be suspended, for the purpose of going into committee of the whole on the Oregon Bill.

Credentials of Orson Hyde, Agent to Present the Prophet's Memorial to Congress.

CITY OF NAUVOO, ILLINOIS, March 30, 1844.

To whom it may concern: We, the Mayor and Recorder of said city, do certify that Orson Hyde, Esq., the bearer, a Councilor in the City Council of said city, is sent as our agent, by the authorities of said city, to transact such business as he may deem expedient and beneficial for the party whom he represents; and such agent and gentleman of principle and character, he by us is recommended to the due consideration of all the executive officers of the Government, both houses of Congress, and gentlemen generally of the United States.

In witness whereof, we have hereunto set our hands and affixed the seal of said corporation at the time and place aforesaid.

[CORPORATION SEAL.]

JOSEPH SMITH, Mayor.

WILLARD RICHARDS, Recorder.

About this time, Brother Alexander Mills, one of the police, informed me that Chauncey L. Higbee drew a pistol on him the night before, and threatened to shoot him. I instructed him to make complaint to Esquire Wells, and have him apprehended.

"The Speaker said that the question would be put on suspending the rules to go into committee of the whole. If that motion prevailed, the gentleman could move to take up any bill he pleased.

"Mr. Vance called for the yeas and nays on the question; which were ordered.

"Mr. McKay inquired if the House should refuse to go into committee of the whole, if it could by postponement of the previous orders, take up the naval appropriation bill which had been reported from the committee of the whole.

"The Speaker said a motion to that effect would require a vote of two-thirds.

"The question was put on suspending the rules and rejected—yeas 79, nays 86." ("Congressional Globe" for May 25th, 1844. Vol. 13, No. 39, p 624.)

CHAPTER XII.

THE AUTHORITIES OF NAUVOO VS. THE HIGBEES, ET. AL—DED-
ICATION OF THE MASONIC HALL—THE CHURCH CONFER-
ENCE OF APRIL, 1844—ADDRESS OF PRESIDENT SIDNEY
RIGDON; DITTO PATRIARCH HYRUM SMITH—HISTORICAL
RESUME, AND BUILDING THE TEMPLE.

Monday, April 1, 1844.—In the the court-room in the
Mansion, Mr. J. Easton was brought up as being accessory to whipping Chism, [a negro]. Referred the case to
Alderman Wells. On investigation, it appeared to the
satisfaction of the court that he had been on trial for the
same offense before Robert D. Foster, and acquitted.

I extract from the *Neighbor*:—

Comment on the Negro Chism's Case.

After the court dismissed the case, General Smith fearlessly stated
that he believed that it was a plot on the part of those who were instrumental in getting up the previous trial to thwart the ends of justice and
screen the prisoner from the condemnation he justly deserves. Mr.
Foster then stated, by way of an apology, that at the time he issued the
warrant he did not know that the prisoner was under an arrest, or
that there was any process out against him.

We hope, for the honor of such a man as Mr. Foster, that his
statement is true. Mr. Foster, however, called upon one of his jurors,
Mr. Carn, to corroborate what he had said; but, to our astonishment, he
replied that when Mr. Foster summoned him to appear and act as a
juryman, he was not informed what case he was to act upon, nor did
he learn until he entered the office, where he acted according to the
evidence given; but believed then, as well as now, that it was a sham
trial, and a mere mockery of justice. We state facts as they are,
and let the public judge for themselves.

The statement of the negro was that Messrs. Easton, Townsend, and Lawyer W. H. J. Marr were the persons engaged in this diabolical affair. Mr. Gibbs, one of the witnesses against Townsend, believed the above persons were engaged in it; but as a negro knows nothing in this state, and Mr. Gibbs could not positively swear to it, of course we don't know; but we have our opinion, and so have the public. We don't remember ever having seen more indignation manifest than was manifested on this occasion, and the public mind is not satisfied at the turn affairs have taken. Lynch law will not do in Nauvoo, and those who engage in it must expect to be visited by the wrath of an indignant people, not according to the rule of Judge Lynch, but according to law and equity.

It was thought best to acquit Easton and leave the case to the Circuit Court.

Francis M. Higbee and Chauncey L. Higbee were brought up before Esquire Wells for assaulting the police, and acquitted. Chauncey L. Higbee a lawyer, was brought before Daniel H. Wells Esq., on the charge of using abusive language to and insulting the city marshal while in the discharge of his official duty. He was fined ten dollars. *The Higbee Brothers in Trouble.*

Also Robert D. Foster, Esq., was taken before Isaac Higbee, J. P., and fined ten dollars, for a breach of the ordinance pertaining to gambling, &c.

We are sorry to find that our lawyers and magistrates should be taking the lead among gamblers and disorderly persons, and be numbered among the law-breakers, rather than supporting virtue, law, and the dignity of the city.

Tuesday, 2.—At home, somewhat unwell, and kept my house this fine day. John P. Greene, marshal; Andrew Lytle, and John Lytle, policemen, were arrested by a warrant issued by *Counter move of the Higbees.* Robert D. Foster, on complaint of Francis M. Higbee, for false imprisonment. As the case was going to trial, the prisoners were taken by John D. Parker, with a writ of *habeas corpus* before the Municipal Court; and tomorrow, at one, p. m., was fixed for trial.

Wednesdey, 3.—At one, p. m., presided in a special session of the Municipal Court, with Aldermen William Marks, Newel K. Whitney, Orson Spencer, George W. Harris, Gustavus Hills, George A. Smith, and Samuel Bennett as Associate-Justices. John P. Greene, Andrew Lytle, and John Lyttle were brought up on *habeas corpus* having been taken from the officer who held them on a writ issued by Robert D. Foster, before whom they had been arraigned on the complaint of Chauncey L. Higbee, charged with false imprisonment.

Joel S. Miles, Andrew Lytle, John Lytle, John P. Greene, and Robert D. Foster were sworn, gave testimony in the case, and the court decided that Greene and the two Lytles be discharged, and that Chauncey L. Higbee is a very disorderly person; that this case on *habeas corpus* originated in a malicious and vexatious suit, instituted by Chauncey L. Higbee against the petitioners now discharged; and that said Higbee pay the costs.

Warm and cloudy.

A conference was held in the city of New York; Elder William Smith presiding, and Elder William H. Miles, clerk. Fifteen branches were represented, containing 566 members, including 3 High Priests, 26 Elders, 15 Priests, 16 Teachers, and 9 Deacons.

Conference in New York.

Thursday. 14.—In a general council in the assembly room from nine to twelve, a. m., and from one to four, p. m.

I was visited by eleven Indians, who wanted counsel, and had an impressive interview.

Elder Orson Hyde was in the council, and left immediately for Washington.*

---

*The object of his mission was to assist Elders Orson Pratt and John E. Page in getting President Smith's Memorial, asking to be appointed "a member of the U. S. Army" and to be authorized to raise one hundred thousand armed volunteers to police the inter-mountain and Pacific coast west from Oregon to Texas.

A company of Saints arrived on the steamer *St. Croix.* Showery day.

Friday, 5.—Attended the dedication of the Masonic Temple, which was attended by about 550 members of the Masonic fraternity from various parts of the world. A procession was formed at Henry Miller's house, and was accompanied by the Nauvoo Brass Band to the hall. The dedicatory ceremonies were performed by the Worshipful Master Hyrum Smith. Elder Erastus Snow delivered an able Masonic address. Dr. Goforth and I also addressed the assembly. All the visiting Masons were furnished a dinner at the Masonic Hall at the expense of the Nauvoo Lodge. The building is admitted to be the most substantial and best finished Masonic Temple in the Western States. It has been erected under the direction of Mr. Lucius N. Scovil.

In consequence of ill health, I deferred preaching the funeral sermon of King Follett until Sunday. Elder Amasa Lyman addressed a very large assembly at the stand.

General Conference Minutes of the Church, April, 1844.

Conference met pursuant to adjournment. Present—President Joseph Smith, Hyrum Smith, Sidney Rigdon, and William Marks. Of the Twelve—Brigham Young, Heber C. Kimball, Willard Richards, Wilford Woodruff, John Taylor, and George A. Smith.

The members of the High Council, an immense number of Elders, and a very large concourse of people.

Presidents Joseph and Hyrum Smith came to the stand at a quarter-past ten o'clock, when the meeting was called to order by Elder Brigham Young. The choir sang a hymn, after which

Opening Address of President Joseph Smith.

President Joseph Smith rose to state to the congregation the nature of the business which would have to come before them. He stated that it had been expected by some that the little petty difficulties which have existed would be brought up and investigated before this conference, but it will not be the case: these things are of too trivial a nature to occupy the attention of so large a body. I intend to give you some instruction on the principles of eternal truth, but will defer it until others have spoken, in consequence of the weakness of my lungs. The Elders will give you instruction; and then, if necessary, I will offer such corrections as may be proper to fill up the interstices. Those who feel desirous of sowing the seeds of discord will be disappointed on this occasion. It is our purpose to build up and establish the principles of righteousness, and not to break down and destroy. The Great Jehovah has ever been with me, and the wisdom of God will direct me in the seventh hour. I feel in closer communion and better standing with God than ever I felt before in my life, and I am glad of this opportunity to appear in your midst. I thank God for the glorious day that He has given us. In so large a congregation it is necessary that the greatest order and decorum be observed. I request this at your hands, and believe that you will all keep good order.

Prayer was offered by W. W. Phelps, after which the choir sang a hymn.

Elder Sidney Rigdon.

Elder Sidney Rigdon then rose and said: It is with no ordinary degree of satisfaction I enjoy this privilege this morning. Want of health and other circumstances have kept me in silence for nearly the last five years. It can hardly be expected that when the violence of sickness has used its influence, and the seeds of disease have so long preyed upon me, that I can rise before this congregation, only in weakness. I am now come forth from a bed of sickness, and have enough of strength left to appear here for the first time in my true character. I have not come before a conference for the last five years in my true character. I shall consider this important privilege sacred in my family history during life. I hardly promise myself lungs to make this congregation hear me. I shall do the best I can, and the greatest can do no more.

The circumstance by which we are now surrounded point out the principles of my discourse—the history of this Church, which I have known from its infancy. My text is—"Behold the Church of God of the last days." I do not know that I can find it in the Bible. I do not think it necessary to have Paul to make a text for me; I can make a text for myself. I recollect in the year 1830 I met the whole Church of Christ in a little old log-house about 20 feet square, near Waterloo, N. Y., and we began to talk about the kingdom of God as if we had the world at our command. We talked with great confidence, and talked big things. Although we were not many people, we had big feelings.

We knew fourteen years ago that the Church would become as large as it is today. We were as big then as we ever shall be. We began to talk like men in authority and power. We looked upon the men of the earth as grasshoppers. If we did not see this people, we saw by vision the Church of God, a thousand times larger. And when men would say we wanted to upset the Government, although we were not enough to well man a farm, or meet a woman with a milk-pail, all the Elders, all the members met in conference in a room twenty feet square.

I recollect Elder Phelps being put in jail for reading the Book of Mormon. He came to see us, and expressed great astonishment, and left us, apparently pondering in his heart. He afterwards came to Kirtland, Ohio, and said he was a convert. Many things were taught, believed, and preached then, which have since come to pass. We knew the whole world would laugh at us; so we concealed ourselves, and there was much excitement about our secret meetings, charging us with designs against the Government, and with laying plans to get money, &c., which never existed in the hearts of any one else [i. e., but in the hearts of their accusers]. And if we had talked in public, we should have been ridiculed more than we were. The world, being entirely ignorant of the testimony of the Prophets, and without knowledge of what God was about to do, treated all we said with pretended contempt and much ridicule, and had they heard all we said, it would have made worse for us.

We talked about the people coming as doves to the windows; and that nations should flock unto it; that they should come bending to the standard of Jesus, saying, "Our fathers have taught falsehoods and things in which there is no profit," and of whole nations being born in one day. We talked such big things that men could not bear them, and they not only ridiculed us for what we did say in public, but threatened and inflicted much personal abuse; and if they had heard all we said, their violence would have been insupportable. God had great things to say for the salvation of the world, which, if they had been told the public, would have brought persecution upon us unto death: so we were obliged to retire to our secret chamber and commune ourselves with God. If we had told the people what our eyes behold this day, we should not have been believed; but the rascals would have shed our blood if we had only told them what we believed. There we sat in secret and beheld the glorious visions and powers of the kingdom of heaven pass and repass. We had not a mighty congregation to shelter us. If a mob came upon us, we had to run and hide ourselves to save our lives.

The time has now come to tell why we held secret meetings. We were maturing plans fourteen years ago which we can now tell. Were we maturing plans to corrupt the world, to destroy the peace of society? No. Let fourteen years' experience of the Church tell the story. The Church never would have been here if we had not done as we did in secret. The cry of "False prophet and imposter!" rolled upon us. I do not know that anything has taken place in the history of this Church which we did not then believe. It was written upon our hearts and never could be taken away. It was indelibly engraved; no power beneath yonder heavens could obliterate it. This was the period when God laid the foundation of the Church, and He laid it firmly, truly, and upon eternal truth.

If any man says it is not the work of God, I know he lies. Some of you who know you have a house, how long would it take to make you reason yourselves into a belief that you have no house where you now reside with your family? Neither have we any power whereby we can ever persuade ourselves that this is not the Church of God. We do not care who sinks or swims, or opposes, but we know here is the Church of God, and I have authority before God for saying so. I have the testimony of Jesus, which is the spirit of prophecy. I have slept with it,— I have walked with it. The idea has never been out of my heart for a moment, and I will reap the glory of it when I leave this world. I defy men and hell and devils to put it out of my heart. I defy all, and will triumph in spite of them.

I know God. I have gazed upon the glory of God, the throne, visions and glories of God, and the visions of eternity in days gone by. What is a man of God to do, when he sees all the madness, wrath and follies of our persecutors? He will do as God does—he will sit and laugh. * * * These were the beginning of good days—shut up in a room eating nothing but dry johnny-cake and buttermilk. Every man who had a little farm or clothes, sold them and distributed what he had among the rest, and did the best he could. I had a little to eat—little to wear, and yet it was the beginning of good days.

Some say "I want plenty to eat, plenty to drink, plenty to wear, and a good house to live in; and, say they then I will believe. But God will not give it until you have proved yourselves unto Him.

No wonder, then, that we should be joyful today. If the people will do as they are told, I will tell you what to do. Get the visions of heaven, and seek not what you shall eat or what you shall drink, but seek the will of God. Get into the presence of God, and then you will have johnny-cake and milk-and-water no more. Would you not be astonished if even now we should tell the glories and privileges of the Saints of God to you and to the world? We should be ridiculed; and no wonder we shut it up in secret. If we were to tell you when Jehovah is looked upon, lo it is beauty, it is heaven, it is felicity to look upon Jehovah. I should marvel if it were otherwise. If a man tells you one glory or one message, he is learning another at the same time. Do not be astonished, then, if we even yet have secret meetings, asking God for things for your benefit.

Do not be afraid. Go back to the commencement of this Church, and see what was concocted then. There was no evil concocted when we first held secret meetings, and it is the same now. Has God forgotten to be gracious, to be merciful to mankind? Did He ever concoct anything that was devilish for mankind? He could not do it. I never am afraid of God or man concocting anything to hurt me. I have faith to detect men, even if they did. I would ask God to detect them, and hold them fast before they should do it. I am not afraid of men or devils. I have none of those fears, jealousies, dreads, forebodings, surmisings, &c. I put my trust in God, and whatever God does for me is only for my salvation.

A man is a bad teamster who runs his team in the worst road. What I have already said is only to prepare the way. [Here five of the Pottawattomie tribe appeared with their interpreter, and were assisted to the stand by the President.] I am going to tell of something that surprised me at the beginning of the Church. I have handled, heard, seen and known things which I have not yet told.

After the Church began to grow, it was favored with marvelously wise men. They had so much wisdom that they could dispute what God said, and what His servant said. They were opposed to virtue. They would say they had revelations and visions, and were as certain that the Lord had given it as I was that the devil had.

He referred to the children of Israel who were snivelling and murmuring about their leeks and onions, &c., &c.; and so it is in these last days; some men are always yelling about what the Church believes and opposing every good thing.

I want devils to gratify themselves; and if howling, yelling and yelping will do you any good, do it till you are all damned.

If calling us devils, &c., will do you any good, let us have the whole of it, and you can then go on your way to hell without a grunt.

We hear these things ever since the Church existed. They have come up with us; they have had so much more wisdom, they knew all about the kingdom before God revealed it, and they know all things before they were heard; they understand more than God knows. We gather of all kinds. If we get all nations, we get all wisdom, cunning, and everything else.

The sectarians cannot be as wise as we are, for they have only got man's plans, the devil's plans, and, the best of all, we have God's plan.

I do not know whether there are any of these wise men here this morning or not; I have merely given this as a part of the history of this Church. I am disposed to give some reasons why salvation only belongs to the kingdom of God, and to that alone.

I will endeavor to show why salvation belongs to us more peculiarly, in contradistinction to all other bodies. Will this be clear enough?

I discover one thing: Mankind have labored under one universal mistake about this—viz., salvation was distinct from government; *i. e.*, that I can build a Church without government, and that thing have power to save me!

When God sets up a system of salvation, He sets up a system of government. When I speak of a government, I mean what I say. I mean a government that shall rule over temporal and spiritual affairs.

Every man is a government of himself, and infringes upon no government. A man is not an honorable man, if he is not above all law and above government.

I see in our town we have need of government. Some study law only for the purpose of seeing how many feuds, how many broils they can kick up, how much they can disturb the peace of the public without breaking the law, and then say—"I know my rights, and will have them;" "I did not know it was the marshal, or I would not have done it."

He is no gentleman. Gentlemen would not insult a poor man in the street, but would bow to him, as much as those who appear mor respectable. No marshal or any one else, should pull me up. We ought to live a great way within the circle of the laws of the land. I would live far above all law.

The law of God is far more righteous than the laws of the land. The kingdom of God does not interfere with the laws of the land, but keeps itself by its own laws. (Reported by Elder Thomas Bullock.)

Elder Rigdon stopped to refresh himself. The choir sang hymn 104.

Elder John Taylor, being called upon to address the congregation, said—It gives me pleasure to meet and associate with so large an assemblage of the Saints. I always feel at home among the brethren. I consider them the honorable of the earth; and if I can do anything to conduce to their happiness, or that will in anywise tend to their edification, I am satisfied.

I therefore address this congregation with cheerfulness and pleasure, and if by unfolding any of the principles of truth that I am in possession of, or laying before you anything pertaining to the kingdom—if my ideas will enlarge your minds, or produce beneficial results to any, I shall consider myself on this, as on all other occasions, amply repaid.

Many things have been spoken by Elder Rigdon concerning the early history of this Church. There is no person who has searched the oracles of eternal truth, but his mind will be touched with the remarks made by our venerable friend, which unfold the dispensation of Jehovah, and have a tendency to produce the most thrilling feelings in the bosoms of many who are this day present, and to promote our general edification. He traces with pleasure on the historic page—the rise of nations, kingdoms and empires. Historians dwell with great minuteness on the heroic deeds, the chivalrous acts, the dangers and deliverances, the tact, bravery, and heroism of their chieftains, generals and governments.

We, as Republicans, look back to the time when this nation was under the iron rule of Great Britain, and groaned under the power, tyranny and oppression of that powerful nation. We trace with delight the name of a Washington, a Jefferson, a LaFayette, and an Adams, in whose bosoms burned the spark of liberty. These themes are dwelt upon with delight by our legislators, our governors and presidents; they are subjects which fire our souls with patriotic ardor.

But if these things animate them so much, how much more great, noble and exalted are the things laid before us! They were engaged in founding kingdoms and empires that were destined to dissolution and decay; and although many of them were great, formidable and powerful, they now exist only in name. Their cloud-capped towers, their solemn temples, are dissolved, and nothing now remains of their former magnificence or ancient grandeur but a few dilapidated buildings and broken columns. A few shattered fragments remain to tell to this and to other generations the perishable nature of earthly pomp and worldly glory.

They were engaged in founding empires and establishing kingdoms and powers that had in themselves the seeds of destruction, and were destined to decay. We are laying the foundation of a kingdom that shall last forever—that shall bloom in time and blossom in eternity. We are engaged in a greater work than ever occupied the attention of mortals. We live in a day that prophets and kings desired to see, but died without the sight.

When we hear the history of the rise of this kingdom from one who has been with it from its infancy—from the lips of our venerable friend who has taken an active part in all the history of the Church, can we be surprised if he should feel animated, and that his soul should burn with heavenly zeal? We see in him a man of God who can contemplate the glories of heaven, the visions of eternity, and yet who looks forward to the opening glories which the great Elohim has manifested to him pertaining to righteousness and peace—a man who now beholds the things roll on which he has long since beheld in prophetic vision.

Most men have established themselves in authority by laying desolate other kingdoms and the destruction of other powers. Their kingdoms have been founded in blood, and supported in tyranny and oppression. The greatest chieftains of the earth have obtained their glory—if glory it can be called—by blood, carnage and ruin. One nation has been built up at the expense and ruin of another, and one man has been made at the expense of another; and yet these great men were called honorable for their inglorious deeds of rapine. They have slain their thousands, and caused the orphans to weep and the widows to mourn.

Men did these things because they could do it—because they had power to desolate nations, and spread terror and desolation. They have made themselves immortal as great men. The patriots of this country had indeed a laudable object in view—a plausible excuse for the course they took. They stood in defense of their rights, liberty and freedom. But where are now those principles of freedom? Where are the laws that protect all men in their religious opinions? Where the laws that say, "A man shall worship God according to the dictates of his own conscience? What say ye, ye Saints—ye who are exiles in the land of liberty? How came you here? Can you in this land of equal rights return in safety to your possessions in Missouri? No. You are exiles from thence, and there is no power, no voice, no arm to redress your grievance. Is this the gracious boon for which your fathers fought and struggled and died? Shades of the venerable dead, could you but gaze upon this scene, and witness tens of thousands of Americans in exile on Columbia's soil—if pity could touch your bosoms, how you would mourn for the oppressed! If indignation, how would you curse the heartless wretches that have so desecrated and polluted the temple of liberty? "How has the gold become dim, and the fine gold, how has it changed." Let it not be told among the monarchs of Europe, lest they laugh and say, "Ha; so would we have it."

Ye Saints, never let it go abroad that ye are exiles in the land of liberty, lest ye disgrace your republic in the eyes of the nations of the earth; but tell it to those who robbed and plundered and refused to give you your rights. Tell your rulers that all their deeds of fame are tarnished, and their glory is departed.

Are we now, indeed, in a land of liberty, of freedom, of equal rights? Would to God I could answer, Yes. But no, no, I cannot! They have robbed us, we are stripped of our possessions, many of our friends are slain, and our government says, "Your cause is just, but we can do nothing for you."

Hear it, ye great men, we are here in exile! Here are thousands of men in bondage in a land of liberty—of freedom! If ye have any patriotism, shake off your fetters and come and proclaim us free, and give us our rights. I speak of this government as being one of the best of governments—as one of the greatest and purest; and yet, what a melancholy picture! O ye venerable fathers who fought for your liberty, blush for your children, and mourn, mourn over your country's shame! We are now talking about a government which sets herself up as a pattern for the nations of the earth, and yet, oh, what a picture! If this is the best, the most patriotic, the most free, what is the situation of the rest?

Here we speak with national pride of a Washington, a LaFayette, a Monroe and a Jefferson, who fought for their liberties, achieved one of the greatest victories ever won; and scarcely has one generation passed away before fifteen thousand citizens petition government for redress of their wrongs, and they turn a deaf ear to their cry.

Let us compare this with the Church of Christ. Fourteen years ago a few men assembled in a log cabin; they saw the visions of heaven, and gazed upon the eternal world; they looked through the rent vista of futurity, and beheld the glories of eternity; they were planting those principles which were concocted in the bosom of Jehovah; they were laying a foundation for the salvation of the world, and those principles which they then planted have not yet begun to dwindle; but the fire still burns in their bones; the principles are planted in different nations and are wafted on every breeze.

When I gaze upon this company of men, I see those who are actuated by patriotic and noble principles, who will stand up in defense of the oppressed, of whatever country, nation, color or clime. I see it in their countenances. It is planted by the Spirit of God. They have received it from the great Elohim, and all the power or influence of mobs, priestcraft or corrupt men cannot quench it. It will burn. It is comprehensive as the designs of God, and as expansive as the universe and reaches to all the world. No matter whether it was an Indian, a negro, or any other man or set of men that are oppressed, you would stand forth in their defense.

I say unto you, continue to cherish those principles. Let them expand. And if the tree of liberty has been blasted in this nation—if it has been gnawed by worms, and already blight has overspread it, we will stand up in defense of our liberties, and proclaim ourselves free in time and in eternity.

The choir, by request, sang, "O stop and tell me, Red Man." After prayer by Elder John P. Greene, the meeting was adjourned for one hour.

CHAPTER XIII.

CONFERENCE OF THE CHURCH, APRIL, 1844, CONTINUED—
ADDRESS OF PATRIARCH HYRUM SMITH—THE BUILDING OF
THE TEMPLE.

Saturday, April 6, 1844, [*Conference Report Continued.*]

The President arrived at the stand at half-past two o'clock, p. m.
The choir sang a hymn; after which prayer by Elder John P. Greene,
when the choir sang another hymn.

Elder Rigdon resumed his history of the Church.

A little before five o'clock the assembly was dismissed without ceremony, until next morning, on the appearance of a shower. The people
had scarcely time to retire before a heavy shower of rain, wind, thunder and lightning followed. A splendid double rainbow seen in the
heavens.

Sunday, 7.

Very pleasant morning. The President arrived at ten o'clock, the
largest congregation ever seen in Nauvoo having assembled. The choir
sang the hymn, "Ye slumbering nations that have slept."

President Rigdon offered an affectionate appeal for the prayers of the
Saints on behalf of the sick, and then prayer by Elder George J.
Adams.

Choir sang the hymn, "The Spirit of God like a fire is burning," &c.

President Joseph Smith.

The Mayor requested the people to keep good order, and observed to
the police, who were round the outskirts of the congregation to keep
order, "Policemen, I want you to exercise your authority; and don't
say you can't do anything for us, for the constitutional power calls you
to keep good order, and God Almighty calls you, and we command you
to do it."

Elder Sidney Rigdon arose and continued his subject of yesterday.
Choir sang. Benediction. Intermission.

During the intermission, thirty-five were baptized in the Mississippi river for the remission of their sins.

Address of Elder Hyrum Smith, Patriarch to the Church.

At 2 o'clock p. m.

Patriarch Hyrum Smith arrived at the stand, and said he wanted to say something about the temple.

"We want 200,000 shingles, as we shall resume the work on the Temple immediately. All who have not paid their tithing, come on and do it. We want provisions, money, boards, planks, and anything that is good; we don't want any more old guns or watches. I thought some time ago I would get up a small subscription, so that the sisters might do something. In consequence of some misunderstanding, it has not gone on as at first. It is a matter of my own; I do not ask it as a tithing. I give a privilege to any one to pay a cent a week, or fifty cents a year. I want it by next fall to buy nails and glass. It is difficult to get money. I know that a small subscription will bring more than a large one. The poor can help in this way. I take the responsibility upon myself, and call again upon the sisters. I call again until I get about $1,000. It only requires two thousand subscribers.

I have sent this subscription plan to England and the branches. I am not to be dictated to by any one except the Prophet and God. I want you to pay in your subscriptions to me, and it shall always be said boldly by me, the sisters bought the glass in that house, and their names shall be written in the Book of the Law of the Lord. It is not a tax, but a free will offering to procure something which shall ever be a monument of your works. No member of the Relief Society got it up. I am the man that did it. They ought not to infringe upon it. I am not a member of the Female Relief Society! I am one of the committee of the Lord's House.

I wish to accomplish something, I wish all the Saints to have an opportunity to do something. I want the poor with the purse of five dollars to have a chance. The widow's two mites were more in the eyes of the Lord than the purse of the rich; and the poor woman shall have a seat in the house of God—she who pays her two mites as well as the rich, because it is all she has. I wish to have a place in that house. I intend to stimulate the brethren. I want to get the roof on this season. I want to get the windows in, in the winter, so that we may be able to dedicate the House of the Lord by this time next year, if nothing more than one room. I will call upon the brethren to do something.

I cannot make a comparison between the House of God and anything now in existence. Great things are to grow out of that house. There is a great and mighty power to grow out of it. There is an endowment. Knowledge is power. We want knowledge. We have frequently diffi-culties with persons who profess to be Latter-day Saints. When the sacrament will be administered in the Lord's House it will do away with a great deal of difficulty that is now in existence. If we can have a privilege and confess our faults unto God and one another every Sab-bath day,it will do away with these. * * * You sisters shall have a seat in that house. I will stand on the top of that pulpit and proclaim to all what the sisters have done. When you offer up your sacraments every Sabbath, you will feel well a whole week; you will get a great portion of the Spirit of God, enough to last you a week—and you will increase. We are now deprived of the privilege of giving the neces-sary instruction; hence we want a house.

All the money shall be laid out for what you design it. It shall not be paid for anything else. I am one of the committee. The committee tells me the quarry is blockaded; it is filled with rock. The stone cut-ters are wanting work. Come on with your teams as soon as conference is over. It is not necessary for me to tell who will come and do it. I will prophesy that you will do it. There is not one in the city but what will do right if he knows it, with only one or two exceptions, and they are not worth notice. God will take care of them, and if He doesn't, the devil will. I described them once, and you will always know them while you see them. They will keep hopping till they hop out of town. Some of them are tree toads, who climb the trees and are continually croaking.

We are now the most noble people on the face of the globe, and we have no occasion to fear tadpoles. We are designated by the All-seeing Eye to do good, not to stoop to anything low. We are apt to suffer prejudice to get into our hearts on hearing reports. We never should allow it—never should pass our judgment until we hear both sides.

I will tell a Dutch anecdote: A certain Dutchman had a case brought before him, and heard one side, and he gave in his decision—"Sure you have got the case;" and when the other party brought their witnesses, he said again, "Sure, you have got the case, too." If you hear of any one in high authority, that he is rather inclined to apostasy, don't let prejudice arise, but pray for him. God may feel after him, and he may return. Never speak reproachfully nor disrespectfully; he is in the hands of God. I am one of those peacemakers who take a stand above these little things. It has been intimated we should have investigations this conference. Do you think I would trouble this conference with it? If I have a difficulty with a man, I will go and settle it. Let them settle their difficulties. There is not a man who has had a difficulty

who would trouble this congregation about it.   We ask no favors; we
can settle it ourselves.   Don't think anything about persons who are on
the eve of apostasy; God is able to take care of them.   Let God judge.
do your duty and let men alone.

Never undertake to destroy men because they do some evil thing.   It
is natural for a man to be led, and not driven.   Put down iniquity by
good works.   Many men speak without any contemplation; if they had
given the matter a little contemplation it would not have been spoken
We ought to be careful what we say, and take the example of Jesus,
cast over men the mantle of charity, and try to cover their faults.
We are made to enlighten, and not to darken one another; save men,
not destroy them.   Do unto others what you would have them do unto
you.   It is well enough to root out conspiracy.   Do not fear, but if
you are in the right track, having God to guide you, He will save
you; for God will save you, if He has to destroy the wicked so as
by fire.

I want to put down all false influence.   If I thought I should be saved
and any in the congregation be lost, I should not be happy.   For this
purpose Jesus effected a resurrection.   Our Savior is competent to save
all from death and hell.   I can prove it out of the revelation.   I would
not serve a God that had not all wisdom and all power.

The reason why I feel so good is because I have a big soul.   There
are men with small bodies who have got souls like Enoch.   We have.
We have gathered our big souls from the ends of the earth.   The
Gospel picks the big souls out of all creation, and we will get the big
souls out of all the nations, and we shall have the largest city in the
world.

We will gather all the big souls out of every nation.   As soon as the
Gospel catches hold of noble souls, it brings them all right up to Zion.
There is a thing called guiding star.   The Gospel is similar.   We will
have a people great enough to be saved.

Popery could not write what Enoch preached.   He told the people
that the Spirit of God took him up into a high mountain, showed him
the distress of the people—the destruction of the world, and he said his
heart swelled wide as eternity.   But adherents of Popery could not
receive anything as large as that, and every man-made society is just
like them.   Men's souls conform to the society in which they live, with
very few exceptions, and when men come to live with the Mormons,
their souls swell as if they were going to stride the planets as I stride
the Republic of America.   I can believe that man can go from planet
to planet—a man gets so high in the mansions above.

A certain good sister came to my house, and she was troubled because
she heard so many big things.   She thought it weakened her faith.   I

told her she had too much faith. She believed too much. I will tell you how you may know whether the thing is true or not. When any one comes to you with a lie, you feel troubled. God will trouble you, and will not approbate you in such belief. You had better get some antidote to get rid of it. Humble yourself before God, and ask Him for His Spirit and pray to Him to judge it for you. It is better not to have so much faith, than to have so much as to believe all the lies.

Before this conference closes, I want to get all the Elders together.

I shall make a proclamation. I want to take the line and ax and hew you, and make you as straight as possible. I will make you straight as a stretched line. Every Elder that goes from Nauvoo to preach the Gospel, if he preaches anything else, we will silence him through the public print. I want all the Elders to meet and to understand; and if they preach anything but the pure truth, we will call them home.

At a quarter-past three p. m., President Smith having arrived, the choir sang a hymn. Elder Amasa Lyman offered prayer.

President Joseph Smith delivered a discourse before twenty thousand Saints, being the funeral sermon of Elder King Follett.

CHAPTER XIV.

CONFERENCE OF THE CHURCH, APRIL, 1844 (CONTINUED)—
THE KING FOLLETT SERMON—THE CHARACTER OF GOD—
RELIGIOUS FREEDOM—GOD AN EXALTED MAN—ETERNAL LIFE
TO KNOW GOD AND JESUS CHRIST—EVERLASTING BURNINGS
—MEANING OF THE HEBREW SCRIPTURES—A COUNCIL OF
THE GODS—MEANING OF THE WORD CREATE—THE IMMORTAL
INTELLIGENCE — THE RELATION OF MAN TO GOD — OUR
GREATEST RESPONSIBILITY—THE UNPARDONABLE SIN—THE
FORGIVENESS OF SIN—THE SECOND DEATH.

Sunday, April 7, 1844.—[Conference Report Continued.]

At quarter past three, p.m., the President having arrived, the
choir sang a hymn, Elder Amasa Lyman offered prayer.

President Joseph Smith delivered the following discourse before
about twenty thousand Saints, being the funeral sermon of Elder
King Follett. Reported by Willard Richards, Wilford Woodruff,
Thomas Bullock and William Clayton.*

Beloved Saints: I will call [for] the attention of this congregation
while I address you on the subject of the dead. The decease of our
beloved brother, Elder King Follett, who was crushed in a well by the
falling of a tub of rock, has more immediately led me to this
subject. I have been requested to speak by his friends and relatives,
but inasmuch as there are a great many in this congregation who
live in this city as well as elsewhere, who have lost friends, I feel
disposed to speak on the subject in general, and offer you my ideas,
so far as I have ability, and so far as I shall be inspired by the Holy
Spirit to dwell on this subject.

I want your prayers and faith that I may have the instruction of
Almighty God and the gift of the Holy Ghost, so that I may set forth
things that are true and which can be easily comprehended by you,

* This was not a stenographic report, but a carefully and skillfully prepared one
made by these men who were trained in reporting and taking notes. Evidently,
there are some imperfections in the report and some thoughts expressed by the
Prophet which were not fully rounded out and made complete; nevertheless it contains many wonderful truths pertaining to the subjects discussed and therefore is
valuable in giving us a better understanding than we would have without it.

and that the testimony may carry conviction to your hearts and minds of the truth of what I shall say. Pray that the Lord may strengthen my lungs, stay the winds, and let the prayers of the Saints to heaven appear, that they may enter into the ears of the Lord of Sabaoth, for the effectual prayers of the righteous avail much. There is strength here, and I verily believe that your prayers will be heard.

Before I enter fully into the investigation of the subject which is lying before me, I wish to pave the way and bring up the subject from the beginning, that you may understand it. I will make a few preliminaries, in order that you may understand the subject when I come to it. I do not calculate or intend to please your ears with superfluity of words or oratory, or with much learning; but I calculate [intend] to edify you with the simple truths from heaven.

The Character of God

In the first place, I wish to go back to the beginning—to the morn of creation. There is the starting point for us to look to, in order to understand and be fully acquainted with the mind, purposes and decrees of the Great Eloheim, who sits in yonder heavens as he did at the creation of the world. It is necessary for us to have an understanding of God himself in the beginning. If we start right, it is easy to go right all the time; but if we start wrong we may go wrong, and it will be a hard matter to get right.

There are but a very few beings in the world who understand rightly the character of God. The great majority of mankind do not comprehend anything, either that which is past, or that which is to come, as it respects their relationship to God. They do not know, neither do they understand the nature of that relationship; and consequently they know but little above the brute beast, or more than to eat, drink and sleep. This is all man knows about God or His existence, unless it is given by the inspiration of the Almighty.

If a man learns nothing more than to eat, drink and sleep, and does not comprehend any of the designs of God, the beast comprehends the same things. It eats, drinks, sleeps, and knows nothing more about God; yet it knows as much as we, unless we are able to comprehend by the inspiration of Almighty God. If men do not comprehend the character of God, they do not comprehend themselves. I want to go back to the beginning, and so lift your minds into more lofty spheres and a more exalted understanding than what the human mind generally aspires to.

I want to ask this congregation, every man, woman and child, to answer the question in their own hearts, what kind of a being God is? Ask yourselves; turn your thoughts into your hearts, and say if any of you have seen, heard, or communed with Him? This is a question that may occupy your attention for a long time. I again repeat the question—What kind of a being is God? Does any man or woman know? Have any of you seen Him, heard Him, or communed with Him? Here is the question that will, peradventure, from this time henceforth occupy your attention. The scriptures inform us that "This is life eternal that they might know thee, the only true God, and Jesus Christ whom thou hast sent."

If any man does not know God, and inquires what kind of a being He is,—if he will search diligently his own heart—if the declaration of Jesus and the apostles be true, he will realize that he has not eternal life; for there can be eternal life on no other principle.

My first object is to find out the character of the only wise and true, God, and what kind of a being He is; and if I am so fortunate as to be the man to comprehend God, and explain or convey the principles to your hearts, so that the Spirit seals them upon you, then let every man and woman henceforth sit in silence, put their hands on their mouths, and never lift their hands or voices, or say anything against the man of God or the servants of God again. But if I fail to do it, it becomes my duty to renounce all further pretensions to revelations and inspirations, or to be a prophet; and I should be like the rest of the world—a false teacher, be hailed as a friend, and no man would seek my life. But if all religious teachers were honest enough to renounce their pretensions to godliness when their ignorance of the knowledge of God is made manifest, they will all be as badly off as I am, at any rate; and you might just as well take the lives of other false teachers as that of mine. If any man is authorized to take away my life because he thinks and says I am a false teacher, then, upon the same principle, we should be justified in taking away the life of every false teacher, and where would be the end of blood? And who would not be the sufferer?*

The Privilege of Religious Freedom

But meddle not with any man for his religion: all governments ought to permit every man to enjoy his religion unmolested. No man is authorized to take away life in consequence of difference of religion, which all laws and governments ought to tolerate and protect, right or wrong. Every man has a natural, and, in our country, a constitutional right to be a false prophet, as well as a true prophet. If I show, verily, that I have the truth of God, and show that ninety-nine out of every hundred professing religious ministers are false teachers, having no authority, while they pretend to hold the keys of God's kingdom on earth, and was to kill them because they are false teachers, it would deluge the whole world with blood.

* It should be remembered that at the time of this discourse apostates and other enemies of the Prophet were seeking his life, and open threats were being made even in his presence. The forces of evil were determined that the Prophet should be destroyed. It was less than three months following the date of this discourse when he and his brother Hyrum were martyred.

I will prove that the world is wrong, by showing what God is. I am going to inquire after God; for I want you all to know Him, and to be familiar with Him; and if I am bringing you to a knowledge of Him, all persecutions against me ought to cease. You will then know that I am His servant; for I speak as one having authority.

God An Exalted Man

I will go back to the beginning before the world was, to show what kind of a being God is. What sort of a being was God in the beginning? Open your ears and hear, all ye ends of the earth, for I am going to prove it to you by the Bible, and to tell you the designs of God in relation to the human race, and why He interferes with the affairs of man.

God himself was once as we are now, and is an exalted man, and sits enthroned in yonder heavens! That is the great secret. If the veil were rent today, and the great God who holds this world in its orbit, and who upholds all worlds and all things by His power, was to make himself visible,—I say, if you were to see him today, you would see him like a man in form—like yourselves in all the person, image, and very form as a man; for Adam was created in the very fashion, image and likeness of God, and received instruction from, and walked, talked and conversed with Him, as one man talks and communes with another.

In order to understand the subject of the dead, for consolation of those who mourn for the loss of their friends, it is necessary we should understand the character and being of God and how He came to be so; for I am going to tell you how God came to be God. We have imagined and supposed that God was God from all eternity. I will refute that idea, and take away the veil, so that you may see.

These are incomprehensible ideas to some, but they are simple. It is the first principle of the gospel to know for a certainty the character of God, and to know that we may converse with Him as one man converses with another, and that He was once a man like us; yea, that God himself, the Father of us all, dwelt on an earth, the same as Jesus Christ Himself did; and I will show it from the Bible.

Eternal Life to Know God and Jesus Christ

I wish I was in a suitable place to tell it, and that I had the trump of an archangel, so that I could tell the story in such a manner that persecution would cease forever. What did Jesus say? (Mark it, Elder Rigdon!) The scriptures inform us that Jesus said, as the Father hath power in himself, even so hath the Son power— to do what? Why, what the Father did. The answer is obvious—in a manner to lay down his body and take it up again. Jesus, what are you going to do? To lay down my life as my Father did, and take it up again. Do you believe it? If you do not believe it you do not believe the Bible. The scriptures say it, and I defy all the learning and wisdom and all the combined powers of earth and hell together to refute it. Here, then, is eternal life—to know the only wise and true God; and you have got to learn how to be gods yourselves, and to be kings and priests to God, the same as all gods have done before you, namely, by going from one small degree to another, and from a small capacity to a great one; from grace to grace, from exaltation to exaltation, until you attain to the resurrection of the dead, and are able to dwell in everlasting burnings, and to sit in glory, as do those who sit enthroned in everlasting power. And I want you to know that God, in the last days, while certain individuals are proclaiming His name, is not trifling with you or me.*

The Righteous to Dwell in Everlasting Burnings

These are the first principles of consolation. How consoling to the mourners when they are called to part with a husband, wife, father, mother, child, or dear relative, to know that, although the earthly tabernacle is laid down and dissolved, they shall rise again to dwell in everlasting burnings in immortal glory, not to sorrow, suffer, or die any more, but they shall be heirs of God and joint heirs with Jesus Christ. What is it? To inherit the same power, the same glory and the same exaltation, until you arrive at the station of a god, and ascend the throne of eternal power, the same as those who have gone before. What did Jesus do? Why, I do the things I saw my Father do when worlds came rolling into existence. My Father worked out His kingdom with fear and trembling, and I must do the same; and when I get my kingdom, I shall present it to My Father, so that He may obtain kingdom upon kingdom, and it will exalt Him in glory. He will then take a higher exaltation, and I will take His place, and thereby become exalted myself. So that Jesus treads in the tracks of His Father, and inherits what God did before; and God is thus glorified and exalted in the salvation and exaltation of all His children. It is plain beyond disputation, and you thus learn some of the first principles of the gospel, about which so much hath been said.

When you climb up a ladder, you must begin at the bottom, and ascend step by step, until you arrive at the top; and so it is with

---

* The argument here made by the Prophet is very much strengthened by the following passage: "The Son can do nothing of himself, but what he seeth the Father do; for what things soever he [the Father] doeth, these also doeth the Son likewise. (John 5:19.)

Henry Drummond, for instance (following the Prophet by half a century), in his work, Natural Law in the Spiritual World, in his chapter on growth, has said: "The end of salvation is perfection, the Christ-like mind, character and life. * * * Therefore the man who has within himself this great formative agent, Life [spiritual life] is nearer the end than the man who has morality alone. The latter can never reach perfection, the former must. For the life must develop out according to its type; and being a germ of the Christ-life, it must unfold into a Christ."

the principles of the gospel—you must begin with the first, and go on until you learn all the principles of exaltation. But it will be a great while after you have passed through the veil before you will have learned them. It is not all to be comprehended in this world; it will be a great work to learn our salvation and exaltation even beyond the grave. I suppose I am not allowed to go into an investigation of anything that is not contained in the Bible. If I do, I think there are so many over-wise men here that they would cry "treason" and put me to death. So I will go to the old Bible and turn commentator today.

I shall comment on the very first Hebrew word in the Bible; I will make a comment on the very first sentence of the history of creation in the Bible—*Berosheit*. I want to analyze the word. *Baith*—in, by, through, and everything else. *Roch*—the head, *Sheit*—grammatical termination. When the inspired man wrote it, he did not put the baith there. An old Jew without any authority added the word; he thought it too bad to begin to talk about the head! It read first, "The head one of the Gods brought forth the Gods." That is the true meaning of the words. *Baurau* signifies to bring forth. If you do not believe it, you do not believe the learned man of God. Learned men can teach you no more than what I have told you. Thus the head God brought forth the Gods in the grand council.

I will transpose and simplify it in the English language. Oh, ye lawyers, ye doctors, and ye priests, who have persecuted me, I want to let you know that the Holy Ghost knows something as well as you do. The head God called together the Gods and sat in grand council to bring forth the world. The grand councilors sat at the head in yonder heavens and contemplated the creation of the worlds which were created at the time. When I say doctors and lawyers, I mean the doctors and lawyers of the scriptures. I have done so hitherto without explanation, to let the lawyers flutter and everybody laugh at them. Some learned doctors might take a notion to say the scriptures say thus and so; and we must believe the scriptures; they are not to be altered. But I am going to show you an error in them.

I have an old edition of the New Testament in the Latin, Hebrew, German and Greek languages. I have been reading the German, and find it to be the most [nearly] correct translation, and to correspond nearest to the revelations which God has given to me for the last fourteen years. It tells about Jacobus, the son of Zebedee. It means Jacob. In the English New Testament it is translated James. Now, if Jacob had the keys, you might talk about James through all eternity and never get the keys. In the 21st. of the fourth chapter of Matthew, my old German edition gives the word Jacob instead of James.

The doctors (I mean doctors of law, not physic) say, "If you preach anything not according to the Bible, we will cry treason." How can we escape the damnation of hell, except God be with us and reveal to us? Men bind us with chains. The Latin says Jacobus, which means Jacob; the Hebrew says Jacob, the Greek says Jacob and the German says Jacob, here we have the testimony of four against one. I thank God that I have got this old book; but I thank him more for the gift of the Holy Ghost. I have got the oldest book in the world; but I have got the oldest book in my heart, even the gift of the Holy Ghost. I have all the four Testaments. Come here, ye learned men, and read, if you can. I should not have introduced this testimony, were it not to back up the word *rosh*—the head, the Father of the Gods. I should not have brought it up, only to show that I am right.

A Council of the Gods

In the beginning, the head of the Gods called a council of the Gods; and they came together and concocted [prepared] a plan to create the world and people it. When we begin to learn this way, we begin to learn the only true God, and what kind of a being we have got to worship. Having a knowledge of God, we begin to know how to approach Him, and how to ask so as to receive an answer.

When we understand the character of God, and know how to come to Him, he begins to unfold the heavens to us, and to tell us all about it. When we are ready to come to him, he is ready to come to us.

Now, I ask all who hear me, why the learned men who are preaching salvation, say that God created the heavens and the earth out of nothing? The reason is, that they are unlearned in the things of God, and have not the gift of the Holy Ghost; they account it blasphemy in any one to contradict their idea. If you tell them that God made the world out of something, they will call you a fool. But I am learned, and know more than all the world put together. The Holy Ghost does, anyhow, and he is within me, and comprehends more than all the world; and I will associate myself with him.

Meaning of the Word Create

You ask the learned doctors why they say the world was made out of nothing, and they will answer, "Doesn't the Bible say He *created* the world?" And they infer, from the word create, that it must have been made out of nothing. Now, the word create came from the word *baurau*, which does not mean to create out of nothing; it means to organize; the same as a man would organize materials and build a ship. Hence we infer that God had materials to organize the world out of chaos—chaotic matter, which is element, and in which dwells all the glory. Element had an existence from the time He had. The pure principles of element are principles which can never be destroyed; they may be organized and re-organized, but not destroyed. They had no beginning and can have no end.*

* The view of the Prophet on this subject of creation is abundantly sustained by men of learning subsequent to his time. The Rev. Baden Powell of Oxford University, for instance, writing for Kitto's **Cyclopedia of Biblical Literature**, says: "The meaning of this word (create) has been commonly associated with the idea of 'making out of nothing.' But when we come to inquire more precisely into the subject, we can of course satisfy ourselves as to the meaning only from an examination of the original phrase." The learned professor then proceeds to say that three distinct Hebrew verbs are in different places employed with reference to the same divine act, and may be translated, respectively, "create," "make," "form or fashion." "Now," continues the professor, "though each of these has its shade of distinction, yet the best critics understand them as so nearly synonymous that, at least in regard to the idea of making out of nothing, little or no foundation for that doctrine can be obtained from the first of these words." And of course, if no foundation for the doctrine can be obtained from the first of these words—viz., the verb translated "create," then the chances are still less for there being any foundation for the doctrine of creation from nothing in the verb translated "made," "formed," or "fashioned."

Professor Powell further says: "The idea of 'creation,' as meaning absolutely 'making out of nothing,' or calling into existence that which did not exist before, in the strictest sense of the term, is not a doctrine of scripture; but it has been held by many on the grounds of natural theology, as enhancing the ideas we form of the divine power, and more especially since the contrary must imply the belief in the eternity and self existence of matter."

Dr. William Smith's great dictionary of the Bible, (Hackett edition, 1894) has no article on the term "create" or "creation," but in the article "earth," we have reference to the subject, and really an implied explanation as to why this work contains no treatise on "create" or "creation." The act of creation itself, as recorded in the first chapter of Genesis, is a subject beyond and above the experience of man, human language, derived, as it originally was, from the sensible and material world, fails to find an adequate term to describe the act; for our word 'create' and the Hebrew bara, though most appropriate to express the idea of an original creation, are yet applicable and must necessarily be applicable to other modes of creation; nor does the addition of such expressions as 'out of things that were not,' or 'not from things which appear,' contribute much to the force of the declaration. The absence of a term which shall describe exclusively an original creation is a necessary infirmity of language; as the events occured but once, the corresponding term must, in order to be adequate, have been coined for the occasion and reserved for it alone, which would have been impossible."

The philosophers with equal emphasis sustain the contention of the Prophet. Herbert Spencer, in his **First Principles** (1860), said:

"There was once universally current, a notion that things could vanish into absolute nothing, or arise out of absolute nothing. * * * The current theology, in its teachings respecting the beginning and end of the world, is clearly pervaded by it. * * * The gradual accumulation of experiences, has tended slowly to reverse this conviction; until now, the doctrine that matter is indestructible has become a commonplace. All the apparent proofs that something can come of nothing, a wider knowledge has one by one cancelled. The comet that is suddenly discovered in the heavens and nightly waxes larger, is proved not to be a newly-created body, but a body that was until lately beyond the range of vision. The cloud which in the course of a few minutes forms in the sky, consists not of substance that has begun to be, but of substance that previously existed in a more diffused and transparent form. And similarly with a crystal or precipitate in relation to the fluid depositing it. Conversely, the seeming annihilations of matter turn out, on closer observation, to be only changes of state. It is found that the evaporated water, though it has become invisible, may be brought by condensation to its original shape. The discharged

The Immortal Intelligence

I have another subject to dwell upon, which is calculated to exalt man; but it is impossible for me to say much on this subject. I shall therefore just touch upon it, for time will not permit me to say all. It is associated with the subject of the resurrection of the dead,—namely, the soul—the mind of man—the immortal spirit. Where did it come from? All learned men and doctors of divinity say that God created it in the beginning; but it is not so: the very idea lessens man in my estimation. I do not believe the doctrine; I know better. Hear it, all ye ends of the world; for God has told me so; and if you don't believe me, it will not make the truth without effect. I will make a man appear a fool before I get through; if he does not believe it. I am going to tell of things more noble.

We say that God Himself is a self-existing being. Who told you so? It is correct enough; but how did it get into your heads? Who told you that man did not exist in like manner upon the same principles? Man does exist upon the same principles. God made a tabernacle and put a spirit into it, and it became a living soul. (Refers to the Bible.) How does it read in the Hebrew? It does not say in the Hebrew that God created the spirit of man. It says, "God made man out of the earth and put into him Adam's spirit, and so became a living body."

The mind or the intelligence which man possesses is co-equal [co-eternal] with God himself.* I know that my testimony is true; hence,

fowling-piece gives evidence that though the gunpowder has disappeared, there have appeared in place of it certain gases, which, in assuming a larger volume, have caused the explosion."

Fiske follows Spencer, of course, and in his Cosmic Philosophy sums up the matter in these words: "It is now unconceivable that a particle of matter should either come into existence, or lapse into non-existence."

Robert Kennedy Duncan (1905), in his New Knowledge says: "Governing matter in all its varied forms, there is one great fundamental law which up to this time has been ironclad in its character. This law, known as the law of the conservation of mass, states that no particle of matter, however small, may be created or destroyed. All the king's horses and all the king's men cannot destroy a pin's head. We may smash that pin's head, dissolve it in acid, burn it in the electric furnace, employ, in a word, every annihilating agency, and yet that pin's head perists in being. Again, it is as uncreatable as it is indestructible. In other words, we cannot create something out of nothing. The material must be furnished for every existent article. The sum of matter in the universe is x pounds,—and, while it may be carried through a myriad of forms, when all is said and done, it is just— x pounds."

"The elements are eternal, and spirit and element inseparably connected receive a fulness of joy. * * * The elements are the tabernacle of God; yea, man is the tabernacle of God, even temples." (D. & C. Sec. 93:35.) Notes by Elder B. H. Roberts.

*It is obvious that the word "co-equal" should have been written "co-eternal," for we know the doctrines of the Church as revealed to, and taught by, the Prophet, teach us definitely that God "comprehendeth all things, and all things are before him, and all things are round about him, and he is above all things, and in all things, and is through all things, and is round about all things; and all things are by him, and of him, even God, for ever and ever." (D. & C. Sec. 88:41.) Moreover when I talk to these mourners, what have they lost? Their relatives and friends are only separated from their bodies for a short season: their spirits which existed with God have left the tabernacle of clay only for a little moment, as it were; and they now exist in a place where they converse together the same as we do on the earth,

I am dwelling on the immortality of the spirit of man. Is it logical to say that the intelligence of spirits is immortal, and yet that it has a beginning? The intelligence of spirits had no beginning, neither will it have an end. That is good logic. That which has a beginning may have an end. There never was a time when there were not spirits;** for they are co-equal [co-eternal] with our Father in heaven.

I want to reason more on the spirit of man; for I am dwelling on the body and spirit of man—on the subject of the dead. I take my ring from my finger and liken it unto the mind of man—the immortal part, because it had no beginning. Suppose you cut it in two; then it has a beginning and an end; but join it again, and it continues one eternal round. So with the spirit of man. As the Lord liveth, if it had a beginning, it will have an end. All the fools and learned and wise men from the beginning of creation, who say that the spirit of man had a beginning, prove that it must have an end; and if that doctrine is true, then the doctrine of annihilation would be true. But if I am right, I might with boldness proclaim from the house-tops that God never had the power to create the spirit of man at all. God himself could not create himself.

Intelligence is eternal and exists upon a self-existent principle. It is a spirit from age to age and there is no creation about it.* All the minds and spirits that God ever sent into the world are susceptible of enlargement.

in the Book of Abraham we read that the Lord said to Abraham: "These two facts do exist, that there are two spirits, one being more intelligent than the other; there shall be another more intelligent than they: I am the Lord thy God, I am more intelligent than they all." (Abraham 3:19.)

**It appears to be very clear that the Prophet had in mind the intelligence, when he said "the soul—the mind of man—the immortal spirit," was not created or made, and that there never was a time when there were not spirits for they are co-eternal with God. It is the doctrine of the scriptures, both in the Bible and in the Doctrine and Covenants, that we are the offspring of God. He is our Father; we are begotten sons and daughters unto Him. So Paul taught the Greeks on Mars' Hill. (Acts 17: 26-29.) It was taught by the resurrected Lord to Mary at the tomb, (John 20:17.) and by the Lord to the Prophet and Sidney Rigdon in the great vision (Sec. 76:22-24.) The reader is referred further to the official statement of the First Presidency and the Council of the Twelve Apostles, under the caption, The Father and The Son, in the Improvement Era, August, 1916.

"Man was also in the beginning with God. Intelligence, or the light of truth, was not created or made, neither indeed can be." (D. & C. Sec. 93.)

*It is clear in this statement that the terms "intelligence" and "spirit" are used synonymously and that the intelligent uncreated entity, spoken of as intelligence, is meant.

The first principles of man are self-existent with God. God himself, finding he was in the midst of spirits and glory, because he was more intelligent, saw proper to institute laws whereby the rest could have a privilege to advance like himself. The relationship we have with God places us in a situation to advance in knowledge. He has power to institute laws to instruct the weaker intelligences, that they may be exalted with Himself, so that they might have one glory upon another, and all that knowledge, power, glory, and intelligence, which is requisite in order to save them in the world of spirits.**

This is good doctrine. It tastes good. I can taste the principles of eternal life, and so can you. They are given to me by the revelations of Jesus Christ; and I know that when I tell you these words of eternal life as they are given to me, you taste them, and I know that you believe them. You say honey is sweet, and so do I. I can also taste the spirit of eternal life. I know that it is good; and when I tell you of these things which were given me by inspiration of the Holy Spirit, you are bound to receive them as sweet, and rejoice more and more.

The Relation of Man to God

I want to talk more of the relation of man to God. I will open your eyes in relation to the dead. All things whatsoever God in his infinite wisdom has seen fit and proper to reveal to us, while we are dwelling in mortality, in regard to our mortal bodies, are revealed to us in the abstract, and independent of affinity of this mortal tabernacle, but are revealed to our spirits precisely as though we had no bodies at all; and those revelations which will save our spirits will save our bodies. God reveals them to us in view of no eternal dissolution of the body, or tabernacle. Hence the responsibility, the awful responsibility, that rests upon us in relation to our dead; for all the spirits who have not obeyed the Gospel in the flesh must either

---

**"Behold this is my work and my glory—to bring to pass the immortality and eternal life of man."—(The Lord to Moses, Book of Moses, Chapt. 1:39: Pearl of Great Price)—that is "to bring to pass the immortality and eternal life of man," as man. This passage has reference doubtless to man as composed of spirit and body—a proper soul (see D. & C. Sec. 88:15-16)—"For the spirit and the body is the soul of man; and the resurrection of the dead is the redemption of the soul." In other words, the "work" and the "glory" of God are achieved in bringing to pass the "immortality and eternal life of man," as man, in the eternal union of the spirit and body of man through the resurrection—through the redemption of the soul. This brings into eternal union "spirit and element" declared by the word of God to be essential to a fulness of joy—"The elements are eternal, and spirit and element, inseparably connected, receive a fulness of joy; and when separated man cannot receive a fulness of joy." (D. & C. Sec. 93). Also "Adam fell that man might be: and men are that they might have joy." (2 Nephi 2:25). Indeed, the whole purpose of God in bringing to pass the earth-life of man is to inure to the welfare and enlargement of man as urged in the teaching of the Prophet in the paragraph above. God affects man only to his advantage. Note by Elder B. H. Roberts.

obey it in the spirit or be damned. Solemn thought!—dreadful thought! Is there nothing to be done?—no preparation—no salvation for our fathers and friends who have died without having had the opportunity to obey the decrees of the Son of Man? Would to God that I had forty days and nights in which to tell you all! I would let you know that I am not a "fallen prophet."

Our Greatest Responsibility

What promises are made in relation to the subject of the salvation of the dead? and what kind of characters are those who can be saved, although their bodies are mouldering and decaying in the grave? When His commandments teach us, it is in view of eternity; for we are looked upon by God as though we were in eternity; God dwells in eternity, and does not view things as we do.

The greatest responsibility in this world that God has laid upon us is to seek after our dead. The apostle says, "They without us cannot be made perfect"; for it is necessary that the sealing power should be in our hands to seal our children and our dead for the fulness of the dispensation of times—a dispensation to meet the promises made by Jesus Christ before the foundation of the world for the salvation of man.

Now, I will speak of them. I will meet Paul half way. I say to you, Paul, you cannot be perfect without us. It is necessary that those who are going before and those who come after us should have salvation in common with us; and thus hath God made it obligatory upon man. Hence, God said, "I will send you Elijah the prophet before the coming of the great and dreadful day of the Lord: he shall turn the heart of the fathers to the children, and the heart of the children to their fathers, lest I come and smite the earth with a curse."

The Unpardonable Sin

I have a declaration to make as to the provisions which God hath made to suit the conditions of man—made from before the foundation of the world. What has Jesus said? All sins, and all blasphemies, and every transgression, except one, that man can be guilty of, may be forgiven; and there is a salvation for all men, either in this world or the world to come, who have not committed the unpardonable sin, there being a provision either in this world or the world of spirits. Hence God hath made a provision that every spirit in the eternal world can be ferreted out and saved unless he has committed that unpardonable sin which cannot be remitted to him either in this world or the world of spirits. God has wrought out a salvation for all men, unless they have committed a certain sin; and every man who has a friend in the eternal world can save him, unless he has committed the unpardonable sin. And so you can see how far you can be a savior.

A man cannot commit the unpardonable sin after the dissolution of the body, and there is a way possible for escape. Knowledge saves a man; and in the world of spirits no man can be exalted but by knowledge. So long as a man will not give heed to the commandments, he must abide without salvation. If a man has knowledge, he can be saved; although, if he has been guilty of great sins, he will be punished for them. But when he consents to obey the gospel, whether here or in the world of spirits, he is saved.

A man is his own tormentor and his own condemner. Hence the saying, They shall go into the lake that burns with fire and brimstone. The torment of disappointment in the mind of man is as exquisite as a lake burning with fire and brimstone. I say, so is the torment of man.

I know the scriptures and understand them. I said, no man can commit the unpardonable sin after the dissolution of the body, nor in this life, until he receives the Holy Ghost; but they must do it in this world. Hence the salvation of Jesus Christ was wrought out for all men, in order to triumph over the devil; for if it did not catch him in one place, it would in another; for he stood up as a Savior. All will suffer until they obey Christ himself.

The contention in heaven was—Jesus said there would be certain souls that would not be saved; and the devil said he would save them all, and laid his plans before the grand council, who gave their vote in favor of Jesus Christ. So the devil rose up in rebellion against God, and was cast down, with all who put up their heads for him. (Book of Moses—Pearl of Great Price, Ch. 4:1-4; Book of Abraham, Ch. 3:23-28.)

The Forgiveness of Sins

All sins shall be forgiven, except the sin against the Holy Ghost; for Jesus will save all except the sons of perdition. What must a man do to commit the unpardonable sin? He must receive the Holy Ghost, have the heavens opened unto him, and know God, and then sin against him. After a man has sinned against the Holy Ghost, there is no repentance for him. He has got to say that the sun does not shine while he sees it; he has got to deny Jesus Christ when the heavens have been opened unto him, and to deny the plan of salvation with his eyes open to the truth of it; and from that time he begins to be an enemy. This is the case with many apostates of the Church of Jesus Christ of Latter-day Saints.

When a man begins to be an enemy to this work, he hunts me, he seeks to kill me, and never ceases to thirst for my blood. He gets the spirit of the devil—the same spirit that they had who crucified the Lord of Life—the same spirit that sins against the Holy Ghost.

You cannot save such persons; you cannot bring them to repentance; they make open war, like the devil, and awful is the consequence.

I advise all of you to be careful what you do, or you may by-and-by find out that you have been deceived. Stay yourselves; do not give way; don't make any hasty moves, you may be saved. If a spirit of bitterness is in you, don't be in haste. You may say, that man is a sinner. Well, if he repents, he shall be forgiven. Be cautious: await. When you find a spirit that wants bloodshed,—murder, the same is not of God, but is of the devil. Out of the abundance of the heart of man the mouth speaketh.

The best men bring forth the best works. The man who tells you words of life is the man who can save you. I warn you against all evil characters who sin against the Holy Ghost; for there is no redemption for them in this world nor in the world to come.

I could go back and trace every object of interest concerning the relationship of man to God, if I had time. I can enter into the mysteries; I can enter largely into the eternal worlds; for Jesus said, "In my Father's house are many mansions; if it were not so, I would have told you. I go to prepare a place for you." (John 14:2). Paul says, "There is one glory of the sun, and another glory of the moon, and another glory of the stars; for one star differeth from another star in glory. So also is the resurrection of the dead." (I Cor. 15:41). What have we to console us in relation to the dead? We have reason to have the greatest hope and consolation for our dead of any people on the earth; for we have seen them walk worthily in our midst, and seen them sink asleep in the arms of Jesus; and those who have died in the faith are now in the celestial kingdom of God. And hence is the glory of the sun.

You mourners have occasion to rejoice, speaking of the death of Elder King Follett; for your husband and father is gone to wait until the resurrection of the dead—until the perfection of the remainder; for at the resurrection your friend will rise in perfect felicity and go to celestial glory, while many must wait myriads of years before they can receive the like blessings; and your expectations and hopes are far above what man can conceive; for why has God revealed it to us?

I am authorized to say, by the authority of the Holy Ghost, that you have no occasion to fear; for he is gone to the home of the just. Don't mourn, don't weep. I know it by the testimony of the Holy Ghost that is within me; and you may wait for your friends to come forth to meet you in the morn of the celestial world.

Rejoice, O Israel! Your friends who have been murdered for the truth's sake in the persecutions shall triumph gloriously in the celestial world, while their murderers shall welter for ages in torment, even until they shall have paid the uttermost farthing. I say this for the benefit of strangers.

I have a father, brothers, children, and friends who have gone to a world of spirits. They are only absent for a moment. They are in the spirit, and we shall soon meet again. The time will soon arrive when the trumpet shall sound. When we depart, we shall hail our mothers, fathers, friends, and all whom we love, who have fallen asleep in Jesus. There will be no fear of mobs, persecutions, or malicious lawsuits and arrests; but it will be an eternity of felicity.

A question may be asked—"Will mothers have their children in eternity?" Yes! Yes! Mothers, you shall have your children; for they shall have eternal life, for their debt is paid. There is no damnation awaiting them for they are in the spirit. But as the child dies, so shall it rise from the dead, and be for ever living in the learning of God. It will never grow [in the grave]; it will still be the child, in the same precise form [when it rises] as it appeared before it died out of its mother's arms, but possessing all the intelligence of a God. Children dwell in the mansions of glory and exercise power, but appear in the same form as when on earth. Eternity is full of thrones, upon which dwell thousands of children, reigning on thrones of glory, with not one cubit added to their stature.*

I will leave this subject here, and make a few remarks on the subject of baptism. The baptism of water, without the baptism of fire and the Holy Ghost attending it, is of no use; they are necessarily and inseparably connected. An individual must be born of water and the spirit in order to get into the kingdom of God. In the German, the text bears me out the same as the revelations which I have given and taught for the past fourteen years on that subject. I have the testimony to put in their teeth. My testimony has been true all the time. You will find it in the declaration of John the Baptist. (Reads from the German.) John says, "I baptize you with water, but when Jesus comes, who has the power (or keys) He shall administer the baptism of fire and the Holy Ghost." Great God! Where is now all the sectarian world? And if this testimony is true, they are all damned as clearly as anathema can do it. I know the text is true. I call upon all you Germans who know that it is true to say, Eye. (Loud shouts of "Aye.")

Alexander Campbell, how are you going to save people with water alone? For John said his baptism was good for nothing without the baptism of Jesus Christ. "Therefore, *not* leaving the principles of

---

*It is clearly evident that in this passage concerning little children and their salvation and glorification after the resurrection, we do not have from the brethren, who made the notes, a perfect report on the status of little children after the resurrection. There was some lack of interpretation in the report of the Prophet's remarks, for he taught that little children would come forth from the dead in the same form and size in which their bodies were laid down but that they would grow after the resurrection to the full stature of the spirit. For an account of this teaching those who desire to investigate the matter more fully may consult the Documentary History of the Church, Vol. 4:556-7 and the footnote.

the doctrine of Christ, let us go on unto perfection; not laying again the foundation of repentance from dead works, and of faith towards God, of the doctrine of baptism, and of laying on of hands, and of resurrection of the dead, and of eternal judgment. And this will we do, if God permit." (Heb. 6:1-3).

There is one God, one Father, one Jesus, one hope of our calling, one baptism. All these three baptisms only make one. Many talk of baptism not being essential to salvation; but this kind of teaching would lay the foundation of their damnation. I have the truth, and am at the defiance of the world to contradict me, if they can.

I have now preached a little Latin, a little Hebrew, Greek, and German; and I have fulfilled all. I am not so big a fool as many have taken me to be. The Germans know that I read the German correctly.

The Second Death

Hear it, all ye ends of the earth—all ye priests, all ye sinners, and all men. Repent! Repent! Obey the gospel. Turn to God; for your religion won't save you, and you will be damned. I do not say how long. There have been remarks made concerning all men being redeemed from hell; but I say that those who sin against the Holy Ghost cannot be forgiven in this world or in the world to come; they shall die the second death. Those who commit the unpardonable sin are doomed to *Gnolom*—to dwell in hell, worlds without end. As they concocted scenes of bloodshed in this world, so they shall rise to that resurrection which is as the lake of fire and brimstone. Some shall rise to the everlasting burnings of God; for God dwells in everlasting burnings and some shall rise to the damnation of their own filthiness, which is as exquisite a torment as the lake of fire and brimstone.

I have intended my remarks for all, both rich and poor, bond and free, great and small. I have no enmity against any man. I love you all; but I hate some of your deeds. I am your best friend, and if persons miss their mark it is their own fault. If I reprove a man, and he hates me, he is a fool; for I love all men, especially these my brethren and sisters.

I rejoice in hearing the testimony of my aged friends. You don't know me; you never knew my heart. No man knows my history. I cannot tell it: I shall never undertake it. I don't blame any one for not believing my history. If I had not experienced what I have, I would not have believed it myself. I never did harm any man since I was born in the world. My voice is always for peace.

I cannot lie down until all my work is finished. I never think any evil, nor do anything to the harm of my fellow-man. When I am called by the trump of the archangel and weighed in the balance, you will all know me then. I add no more. God bless you all. Amen.

CHAPTER XV.

GENERAL CONFERENCE FOR APRIL, 1844, CONCLUDED—THE ANNOUNCEMENT THAT THE WHOLE LAND OF AMERICA IS ZION—INSTRUCTIONS TO ELDERS SET APART FOR MISSIONS —A GENERAL CONFERENCE IN ENGLAND.

Monday, April 8, 1844.—[*Conference Report Continued.*]

At three-quarters past 9 a. m., President Joseph Smith took his seat on the stand and requested the choir to sing a hymn. He called upon Elder Brigham Young to read 1st Corinthians, 15th chapter, as his own lungs were injured.

Elder Brigham Young said—to continue the subject of President Smith's discourse yesterday, I shall commence by reading the 15th chapter of 1st Corinthians, from an old Bible; and requested W. W. Phelps to read it.

Prayer by Elder Brigham Young, after which the choir sang a hymn.

President Joseph Smith's Remarks—The Whole of America Zion.

President Joseph Smith said:—It is just as impossible, for me to continue the subject of yesterday as to raise the dead. My lungs are worn out. There is a time to all things, and I must wait. I will give it up, and leave the time to those who can make you hear, and I will continue the subject of my discourse some other time. I want to make a proclamation to the Elders. I wanted you to stay, in order that I might make this proclamation. You know very well that the Lord has led this Church by revelation. I have another revelation in relation to economy in the Church—a great, grand, and glorious revelation. I shall not be able to dwell as largely upon it now as at some other time; but I will give you the first principles. You know there has been great discussion in relation to Zion—where it is, and where the gathering of the dispensation is, and which I am now going to tell you. The prophets have spoken and written upon it; but I will make a proclamation that will cover a broader ground. *The whole of America is Zion itself from north to south, and is described by the Prophets, who declare that it is the Zion where the mountain of the Lord should be, and that it should be in the center of the land.* When Elders shall take up and examine the old prophecies in the Bible, they will see it.

The declaration this morning is, that as soon as the Temple and baptismal font are prepared, we calculate to give the Elders of Israel their washings and anointings, and attend to those last and more impressive ordinances, without which we cannot obtain celestial thrones. But there must be a holy place prepared for that purpose. There was a proclamation made during the time that the foundation of the Temple was laid to that effect, and there are provisions made until the work is completed, so that men may receive their endowments and be made kings and priests unto the Most High God, having nothing to do with temporal things, but their whole time will be taken up with things pertaining to the house of God. There must, however, be a place built expressly for that purpose, and for men to be baptized for their dead. It must be built in this the central place; for every man who wishes to save his father, mother, brothers, sisters and friends, must go through all the ordinances for each one of them separately, the same as for himself, from baptism to ordination, washings and anointings, and receive all the keys and powers of the Priesthood, the same as for himself.

I have received instructions from the Lord that from henceforth wherever the Elders of Israel shall build up churches and branches unto the Lord throughout the States, there shall be a stake of Zion. In the great cities, as Boston, New York, &c., there shall be stakes. It is a glorious proclamation, and I reserved it to the last, and designed it to be understood that this work shall commence after the washings, anointings and endowments have been performed here.

The Lord has an established law in relation to the matter: there must be a particular spot for the salvation of our dead. I verily believe there will be a place, and hence men who want to save their dead can come and bring their families, do their work by being baptized and attending to the other ordinances for their dead, and then may go back again to live and wait till they go to receive their reward. I shall leave my brethren to enlarge on this subject: it is my duty to teach the doctrine. I would teach it more fully—the spirit is willing but the flesh is weak. God is not willing to let me gratify you; but I must teach the Elders, and they should teach you. God made Aaron to be the mouth piece for the children of Israel,* and He will make me be god to you in

---

* The scripture alluded to in the text is as follows:—Moses pleaded to be excused from the appointment to deliver Israel on the plea that he was not eloquent; whereupon the Lord said: "Is not Aaron the Levite thy brother? I know that he can speak well. And also, behold, he cometh forth to meet thee; and when he

His stead, and the Elders to be mouth for me; and if you don't like it, you must lump it. I have been giving Elder Adams instruction in some principles to speak to you, and if he makes a mistake, I will get up and correct him.

Elder G. J. Adams preached a discourse which occupied three hours, and which could be heard a great distance.

President Joseph Smith turned over the conference into the hands of the Twelve.

Choir sang a hymn. Prayer.

President Hyrum Smith called the conference to order at twenty-five minutes to four p. m., and spoke to the assembly one hour and a half.

He treated upon the subject of Elders preaching abroad. He said it was a matter of consequence that the Elders of Israel should know what they were about when they go to preach the Gospel. They should, like Paul, be ready to give a reason for the hope of their calling. When they are sent to preach the Gospel, they should preach the Gospel and nothing else, if they wish to stand approved themselves. The Elders are sent into the world to preach faith, repentance, baptism for the remission of sins, and the laying on of hands for the reception of the Holy Ghost and they should let the mysteries alone.

God has commanded you to preach repentance to this generation; and if this generation will not receive the first principles of the Gospel and the Book of Mormon, they will receive nothing greater. Just go and do as you are told and God will bless you.

It is the power of God that is going to convert the world, and nothing but the power of God. Every man who knows me knows that I have taught these principles from the beginning. It is the honest and pure in heart that will harken to the everlasting covenant. They are those who are noble and good; they will feed and clothe you and receive your testimony; and we want the Elders to gather out the good seed to Nauvoo. The day will come when you will see the wicked flee when no man pursueth. I want you to be wise as serpents and harmless as doves. Preach principles that will stand the test of ages; teach them good precepts and save souls, go forth as men of God, and you will find friends wherever you go. Drink deep of the Spirit of Truth and a great and mighty work shall be wrought in the world; hundreds

---

seeth thee, he will be glad in his heart. And thou shalt speak unto him, and put words in his mouth;   *   *   *   And he shall be thy spokesman unto the people: *   *   *   *   he shall be to thee instead of a mouth, and thou shalt be to him instead of God" (Exodus iv: 14-16.)

Somewhat later this passage occurs: "And the Lord said unto Moses, See, I have made thee a god to Pharaoh; and Aaron thy brother shall be thy prophet" (Exodus vii: 1.)

and tens of thousands shall flock to the standard and go up to Zion.

Many other remarks were made by the speaker.

After which Sidney Rigdon made a few remarks, and concurred in what Brother Hyrum had said.

Twelve minutes to six, adjourned to April 9th, at eight o'clock, a. m.

Special Meeting of Elders.

Tuesday, 9.—[*Conference Report Continued*]. At 8 a. m., the Elders assembled at the stand, (President Brigham Young presiding,) and were addressed by Elder Amasa Lyman; after which: President Brigham Young said—

Address of Brigham Young.

What has been given is correct; the speech and conduct of Elders one towards another is frequently wrong; one Elder will speak evil of another; and while you trample others you will sink yourself. A man has sinking principles; but if his feelings are elevated, he will build up others and build up himself. Just as sure as one Elder tries to build himself upon the destruction of another, he will surely sink himself.

I would like to sit and hear the brethren teach for a week; but as business is pressing, we must hurry through. Preach repentance to this generation. Faith must go before repentance, and of course all men must follow the course and obey the laws and ordinances for the remission of sins, so as to receive the gift of the Holy Ghost, and then your mission is done. Let a man who goes into the vineyard build up all he can. If a man preaches anything in error, pray to God that no man may remember it any more. No Elder will correct another in public before unbelievers unless he has the sinking principle. I call all the Elders together to witness that I always use charity, for it covers a multitude of sins.

North and South America Zion.

Let us obey the proclamation of Joseph Smith concerning the Elders going forth into the vineyard to build up the Temple, get their endowments, and be prepared to go forth and preach the Gospel. You may build up Zion, and learn to be men, and not children. It was a perfect sweepstakes when the Prophet called North and South America Zion. Let us go to and build the Temple with all our might, that we may build up the kingdom when established and her cords lengthened. It is a perfect knock-down to the devil's kingdom. There is not a faithful Elder who cannot, if he is humble and diligent, build up the Church. There are many men who will give you large sums to build a

Stake of Zion where they live. It proves the words of the Prophet of the last days.

The Priesthood is fitted to every capacity in the world. There are blessings and conditions in that Priesthood that suit every man. This will suit the condition of thousands, because it is as broad as the heavens, deep as hell, and wide as eternity.

I am asked all sorts of questions about making gods and devils, and organizing the eternal worlds; but we could not get it precisely into our understandings so as to make them. The God we serve is the God of Abraham, Isaac, and Jacob. There is no need of breaking the law of the land if you keep the law of the Lord. I want a wife that can take care of my children when I am away, who can pray, lay on hands, anoint with oil, and baffle the enemy; and this is a spiritual wife.

The sweepstakes is a perfect knock-down to the devil. We will build up churches and establish Zion and her stakes. This is a fire which, cannot be put out: it has spread far faster than ever it did before. If you kick us and cuff us, we will turn the world upside down, and make the cart draw the horse. We want to build the Temple and have the roof on this fall, in the name of Israel's God. There are hundreds of Elders who will sell their property to build up the Temple. Let us pay up our tithing. If there are any men who have not paid their tithing, they will not get in there. Let the branches send teams with provisions to work all the year.

We are aquainted with the views of Gen. Smith, the Democrats and Whigs and all factions. It is now time to have a President of the United States. Elders will be sent to preach the Gospel and electioneer. The government belongs to God. No man can draw the dividing line between the government of God and the government of the children of men. You can't touch the Gospel without infringing upon the common avocations of men. They may have helps and governments in the Church, but it is all one at last.

Address of Hyrum Smith the Patriarch.

Patriarch Hyrum Smith said: I never knew a proclamation to be understood at once. President Brigham Young wished to draw the attention of the brethren, first to build the Temple and get your washings, anointings, and endowments; after that to build up branches throughout the nations. We must do all we can to build up the Temple, and after that to build churches. The gathering will continue here until the Temple is so far finished that the Elders can get their endowments; and after that the gathering will be from the nations to North and South America, which is the land of Zion. North and South America, are the symbols of the wings. The gathering from the old countries will always be to headquarters, and I have no doubt this conference will do a great deal of good.

We have every power and principle to teach the people. Say what God says, and say no more. Never deviate one fraction from what God tells you. Elder Rigdon's remarks were very correct. Give out the simple principles. A man never fails who only says what he knows; and if any man says more,and can't give reasons, he falls short. Preach the first principles of the Gospel—preach them over again: you will find that day after day new ideas and additional light concerning them will be revealed to you. You can enlarge upon them so as to comprehend them clearly. You will then be able to make them more plainly understood by those who teach, so that you will meet with scarcely any honest man but will obey them, and none who can oppose. Adduce sufficient reason to prove all things, and you can convert every honest man in the world.The knowledge of the Gospel of Jesus Christ is not prevalent in the world, although it is written in the Holy Book. You can prove it by the Holy Book they profess to believe in, and your arguments will be so strong and convincing,that people will hear and obey it by thousands. The Savior says that to you it is given to know the mysteries of God, but to the world it is not given. You have power; you are authorized to put down every foolish thing you hear. A wise man will put it out of existence as he goes along; for light cleaveth unto light, knowledge to knowledge, and intelligence to intelligence.

We engage in the election the same as in any other principle: you are to vote for good men, and if you do not do this it is a sin: to vote for wicked men, it would be sin. Choose the good and refuse the evil. Men of false principles have preyed upon us like wolves upon helpless lambs. Damn the rod of tyranny; curse it. Let every man use his liberties according to the Constitution. Don't fear man or devil; electioneer with all people, male and female, and exhort them to do the thing that is right. We want a President of the U. S , not a party President, but a President of the whole people; for a party President disfranchises the opposite party. Have a President who will maintain every man in his rights.

I wish all of you to do all the good you can. We will try and convert the nations into one solid union. I despise the principle that divides the nation into party and faction. I want it to grow up like a green bay tree. Damn the system of splitting up the nation into opposite belligerent parties. Whatever are the rights of men guaranteed by the Constitution of these United States, let them have them. Then, if we were all in union, no one dare attempt to put a warlike foot on our soil. I don't like to see the rights of Americans trampled down. I am opposed to the policy of all such persons as would allow Great Britain

or any other power to take from us Oregon or any portion of our
national territory; and damn all who attempt it. Lift up your voices
like thunder: there is power and influence enough among us to put in a
President. I don't wonder at the old Carthagenian lawyer being
afraid of Joseph Smith being elected.

[A unanimous vote was passed by the immense assembly for Joseph
Smith to be the candidate for the next President.]

Address of Heber C. Kimball.

Elder Heber C. Kimball arose and said—What Brother Hyrum has
told you is God's truth, and will eventually come to pass. As he was
making his observations to the Elders, it made me think of the first
time that I went out into the vineyard to preach. I dwelt on one subject till it branched like unto a tree that was cultivated, until the
branches shot forth in all directions. Suppose you had only one seed
to plant, and that seed was an acorn, and you spend your time in cultivating it till it comes forth a great and mighty tree, branching forth
with many branches, and bearing fruit abundantly after its own kind.
So it is with the first principles of the Gospel, they branch out in all
directions, unfolding new light continually. They are eternal principles. I never preached anything else but the first principles. When
first we went to England, we preached nothing else, and never even
touched on the gathering, as there was no place of gathering, the
Church having been driven from Jackson County and also from Kirtland, and the Prophets, Patriarchs, Apostles and Saints were wandering in the wilderness seeking for a home; but as soon as the people
were baptized and received the Holy Ghost, the most of them had the
spirit of prophecy, and prophesied of coming to this land, as being the
land of Zion; and the time would come that they should come here.
Yet we never taught the doctrine of the gathering or Book of Doctrine
and Covenants.

If you tell the people to stay, they will gather here stronger than
ever. If you want to cut anything off, you should know how to restore.
You should never cut off the ears of the people until you are able to make
them others. It is no matter what way you convert them so you do convert
them to believe the doctrines of the very Bible they have always professed
to believe. It is no use attempting to teach them other things until you
can make them believe the principles contained in the Bible which they
have been taught to reverence and believe from their infancy. It
teaches the gathering and all the principles of the Gospel necessary to
be taught to the unbelieving world. This is the thrashingfloor, where
the wheat is gathered to be thrashed. There are a great many green
heads, and they of course have to be pelted a little harder. After the

wheat is thrashed, it has to go through the fanning-mill, and then the screen, and then the smut-mill; then it has to be ground and to be bolted: but many bolt away and leave. If you get a cudgeling, don't be mad, for your heads are green. We are going to arrange a plan for Conferences, and we design to send Elders to all the different States to get up meetings and protracted meetings, and electioneer for Joseph to be the next President.

A great many of the Elders will necessarily have to leave their families, and the mothers will have to assume the responsibility of governing and taking care of the children to a much greater extent than when their husbands were at home. I therefore exhort them to be humble, faithful, and diligent, seeking to the Lord for wisdom to rear up their children in righteousness and prepare them to roll on the work of the Lord when their fathers shall have been worn out in the ministry. The mothers, therefore, are the persons who will more or less have to train the children.

Twenty minutes to 11: A call was made for the volunteers to go preaching to pass out to the green. A great company moved out and returned to the right of the stand, and were numbered 244.

Twenty minutes to 1: Adjourned for one hour.

Met according to adjournment. The names of the volunteers were called, and places assigned to each.

Brigham Young's Instruction to the Elders.

President Brigham Young said: Take care of yourselves, be wise, be humble, and you will prosper. I curse all who degrade themselves with corruption and licentiousness, as many have done. Magnify your calling, keep yourselves pure and innocent, and your path shall be clear as the horizon. We have all manner of prejudices to contend with. We thank God for the Gospel, the Book of Mormon, and the Temple, and sing glory to God; and yet there are characters among us who from mere covetousness will squeeze a sixpence two inches long, and we have all their iniquity to bear.

We have the honor to be the first fruits of this dispensation, and have to contend with floods of oppression. Go humbly and prayerfully, trusting and believing in God, and what you desire to do you will accomplish. Cease not to ask the Father what you shall do, and He will give you the Spirit. You know not the day of your visitation. What is asked for in the name of Jesus Christ will be granted. J. C. Bennett's power fell like the lightning. God was asked not to let Joe Duncan be governor, and it was so. We asked the Lord to deliver us from Governor Reynolds, of Missouri; and he shot himself, and has gone to hell. As for Squire Warren, of Quincy, it takes two of him to make a shadow.

The Lord is cutting off the bitterest branches. Look at the explosion of the big gun on board of the *Princeton* war-steamer at Washington. God will deliver His faithful Saints. You will be innocent, and do a good work: you will come back, and bring your sheaves with you, rejoicing. Every man has the privilege of practicing godliness and virtue, and of manifesting himself as a servant of the Most High God. Doctor Foster lost his money by gambling, and joined blacklegs. Those men who say there is evil in the Church are evil themselves. This doctrine is the best for any man to practice, and will do him good. Ask of God that you may have wisdom to do all things. If you hear anything of an Elder preaching false doctrine, ask of God in full faith that it may be taken off the minds of the people.

A contribution was taken up for President Joseph Smith, $100 was raised, and another $100 loaned.

Tuesday, April 9th, [Continued]:—The weather has been beautiful for the conference; and they have been the greatest, best, and most glorious five consecutive days ever enjoyed by this generation. Much good was done. Many spectators were present from Quincy, Alton, Warsaw, Fort Madison, and other towns. When we consider the immense number present, and the good order that was preserved, it speaks much in favor of the morality of the city.

Comment of President Smith on the Conference.

In the afternoon I rode out with Emma, Dr. Goforth, and others to the mound. The peach trees look beautiful.

The Mayor and Marshal received a notification to produce docket and other papers in case of O. F. Bostwick, before the circuit court at Carthage; also a similar notification to produce papers in case of Amos Davis, appealed before Circuit Court.

A General Conference in England Beginning April 6th, and Continuing Until April 9th, 1844.

According to previous announcement, the general conference of the various branches of the Church of Jesus Christ of Latter-day Saints, commenced its sittings in the Music Hall, Liverpool, on the 6th of April,

1844, Elder Reuben Hedlock, president of the mission, presiding, and Elder J. S. Cantwell, acting as clerk.

Morning Session.

After opening meeting by singing and prayer, it was voted unanimously that Elder Reuben Hedlock preside over the conference and that Elder J. S. Cantwell, act as clerk.

The number of officers present at the opening are as follows:—High Priests, 10; Elders, 23; Priests, 5; Teachers, 3; Deacons, 2. The representation of the various conferences was then called for:—

Manchester Conference represented by Elder Charles Miller, including the branches of Manchester, Stockport, Ashton, Duckenfield, Newton Moor, Mottram, Bolton, Edgeworth Moor, Edgerton, Leith, Chewmoor, Breightmet Fold, Bradshaw, Tottington, Summerseat, Bury, Haslingden, Royton, Oldham, Rochdale, Eccles, Pendlebury, Heatons, Ratcliffe, Halfare, Crossmoor, Didsbury, Middleton, Crompton Fold, Marble Bridge, Ashworth Tops, Vale House. Comprises 1583 members, 2 High Priests, 41 Elders, 100 Priests, 56 Teachers, 19 Deacons. Baptized since last general conference, 194.

Liverpool Conference represented by Elder Mitchelson, including Liverpool, the Isle of Man, Chester, part of Wales, Warrington, St. Helens, and Graseby. Comprises 596 members, 3 High Priests, 29 Elders, 39 Priests, 19 Teachers, 11 Deacons. Baptized since last general conference, 107.

Preston Conference represented by Elder John Banks, including Preston, Lancaster, Kendal, Brigsteer Holme, Heskin, Hunter's Hill, Euxton, Leyland, Southport, and Longton. Comprises 594 members, 1 High Priest, 16 Elders, 23 Priests, 17 Teachers, 4 Deacons. Baptized since last general conference, 21.

London Conference represented by Elder John Cairns, including London, Newbury, Woolwich, Dover, and Luton. Comprises 324 members, 1 High Priest, 11 Elders, 21 Priests, 5 Teachers, 5 Deacons. Baptized since last general conference, 47.

Macclesfield Conference represented by Elder Galley, including Macclesfield, Bollington, Middlewich, Northwich, Plumbley, and Crewe. Comprises 219 members, 1 High Priest, 10 Elders, 22 Priests, 14 Teachers, 7 Deacons. Baptized since last general conference, 15.

Birmingham Conference represented by Elder Crook, including Birmingham, Gritsgreen, Oldbury, Wolverhampton, Dudley, Brittlelane, Bilston, Kidderminster, Leamington, Bloxwich, Stratford-upon-Avon, Catthorpe, Westbromwich, Penydarren, Abersychan, Beaufort, Rumny, Tredegar, Merthyr Tydvil, Aberdare. Comprises 707 members,

38 Elders, 49 Priests, 27 Teachers, 12 Deacons. Baptized since last general conference, 200.

Wooden Box represented by Elder Robert Crook, including Wooden Box, Dunstall, Branstone, Barton, and Colebille. Comprises 96 members, 9 Elders, 10 Priests, 6 Teachers, 5 Deacons. Baptized since last general conference, 60.

Staffordshire Conference represented by Elder George Simpson, including Burslem, Hanley, Stoke-upon-Trent, Newcastle, Baddely Edge, Bradley Green, Knutton Heath, Longton, Coxbank, Prees, Tunstall, Leek, Longport, Hassell Green, Allsager's Bank. Comprises 370 members, 1 High Priest, 29 Elders, 48 Priests, 20 Teachers, 11 Deacons.

Edinburgh Conference represented by Elder George P. Waugh, including Edinburgh, Wemyss, Sterling, and Pathead. Comprises 330 members, 11 Elders, 16 Priests, 7 Teachers, 3 Deacons. Baptized since November, 1843, 37.

Garaway Conference represented by Elder Blakey, including Garaway, Llanfoist, Buckle, Ewaisharold, Llanthony, and Llanvano. Comprises 172 members, 4 Elders, 9 Priests, 8 Teachers, 1 Deacon.

Glasgow Conferennce represented by Elder James Houston, including Glasgow, Paisley, Kilbirnie, Bridge of Weir, Thorny Bank and Shaws, Campsie, Renfrew, Greenock, Ayr, Bonhill, Balfrone, Johnstone, Airdrie, Irvine, and Calry. Comprises 833 members, 1 High Priest, 26 Elders, 39 Priests, 30 Teachers, 19 Deacons.

Sheffield Conference represented by letter, including Sheffield, Woodhouse, Dennington, and Brampton. Comprises 201 members, 5 Elders, 9 Priests, 5 Teachers, 3 Deacons.

Bradford Conference represented by Elder William Speakman, including Bradford, Idle, Leeds, Doncaster. Comprises 206 members, 9 Elders, 15 Priests, 8 Teachers, 6 Deacons. Baptized since last general conference, 44.

Ireland represented by Elder Sloan, including Hillsborough, Crawfordsburn, and Melusk, Comprises 52 members, 5 Elders, 1 Priest, 1 Teacher.

Lincolnshire Conference represented by letter. Comprises 27 members, 2 Elders, 2 Priests, 1 Teacher, 1 Deacon. Baptized since last general conference, 17.

Worcestershire Conference represented by Elder Thomas Smith, including Earls Common, Pinyin, Flyford Flavel, Worcester, Bromsgrove, Randan Woods, Barford, St. John's, and Milton. Comprises 140 members, 6 Elders, 10 Priests, 3 Teachers, 3 Deacons. Baptized since last general conference, 28.

Clitheroe Conference represented by Elder William Snalam, including

Clitheroe, Chatburn, Downham. Waddington, Ribchester, Chaigley, and Settle. Comprises 299 members, 16 Elders, 22 Priests, 18 Teachers, 4 Deacons. Baptized since last general conference, 14.

Leicester Conference represented by Elder Thomas Margetts, including Leicester and Nottingham. Comprises 127 members, 5 Elders, 10 Priests, 1 Teacher, 2 Deacons.

Cheltenham Conference represented by letter, consisting of 18 branches. Comprises 532 members, 17 Elders, 30 Priests, 13 Teachers, 5 Deacons. Baptized since last General Conference, 90.

Bath represented by letter, comprising 31 members, 1 Elder, 2 Priests.

Wolverton represented by letter. Comprises 8 members, 1 Elder, 2 Priests.

Carlisle represented by letter. Comprises 160 members, 8 Elders, 19 Priests, 8 Teachers, 3 Deacons; and contains four branches.

Littlemoor represented by letter. Comprises 6 members, 1 Priest.

Bedfordshire Conference represented by letter, including 12 branches Comprises 184 members, 14 Elders, 20 Priests, 9 Teachers, 2 Deacons.

The number of members and authorities of each conference being ascertained as nearly as possible, it was determined that the delegates should represent the condition of each conference, and what alterations or measures were necessary to be adopted for the wellbeing of each other.

Elder Charles Miller having remarked that he had been challenged to discussion, and had accepted it, it led to some remarks from Elder Ward as to the very little good effected in general by discussions; and that it was beneath the servants of God to turn aside from the path of duty to wrangle and dispute like the people of the world; and that while the professors of modern religion were in a manner devouring each other, the path of the Saints ought to be onward in the proclamation of the principles of truth.

Elder Hedlock agreed with the remarks of Elder Ward, and stated that they were in perfect accordance with the advice of the First Presidency, and that the evil ought to be guarded against as much as possible.

[The remaining sessions of the conference were devoted to hearing reports from the several conferences comprising the mission, giving instruction relative to ordaining men to the ministry, and the manner of conducting the ministry of the Church to make it effective. Among other items of interest was a communication from the Twelve in Nauvoo making the nomination of Elders Reuben Hedlock and Thomas Ward to preside over the British Mission, which nomination was accepted by the conference, and these brethren were unanimously sustained as the presidency of the mission. The publication of the *Millennial Star* had been ordered suspended by the Twelve, but the conference voted by unanimous acclamation that this conference request the quorum of the Twelve to permit the continued publication of that periodical. The minutes of the conference state that—

"Elder Hedlock addressed the assembly on the subject of the publications, and was desirous of taking the sense of that meeting on the same. It was true that the quorum of the Twelve had advised that the publication of the *Millennial Star* be stopped, and had given him authority to publish a circular as occasion might require; but he believed most sincerely that the stoppage of the *Star* would have a most injurious tendency.

"Several having spoken to the same effect, Elder Ward remarked that, if a publication was to be issued at all, it appeared trifling with the interest of the cause to change the name, inasmuch as the office had received the name of the *Millennial Star* Office, and many letters came to them with that address."

[Then followed the action of the conference upon the subject noted above. Permission must have been given soon afterwards to renew the publication of the *Star*, since it missed but one issue, that of May, 1844 —it was then published monthly. See vols. v and vi.]

CHAPTER XVI.

DIFFICULTIES WITH THE HIGBEES AND FOSTERS—CONFER-
ENCES APPOINTED BY THE TWELVE THROUGHOUT THE
UNITED STATES—INSTRUCTIONS TO REUBEN HEDLOCK,
PRESIDENT OF THE BRITISH MISSION—PREPARATIONS FOR
ENLARGEMENT OF THE WORK—FRANCIS M. HIGBEE'S
SUIT AGAINST PRESIDENT SMITH—THE PROPHET RELEASED.

Wednesday, April 10, 1844.—The Twelve were in council arranging a plan for appointing conferences.

Thursday, 11.—In general council in Masonic Hall,
morning and afternoon. Had a very interesting time.
The Spirit of the Lord was with us, and we closed the
council with loud shouts of Hosanna!

Friday, 12.—The Twelve met in council. Rode out
with Brothers Parker and Clayton to look at some land.

A conference was held at Cypry, Tuscaloosa County,
Alabama. Elder Benjamin L. Clapp, president, and
John Brown, clerk. Seven branches were represented,
consisting of 192 members, 12 Elders, 5 Priests, 4 Teachers, and 2 Deacons, all in good standing.

Saturday, 13.—At 10 a. m. met in City Council. George
P. Styles was appointed City Attorney. I advise that the
council take such a course as would protect the innocent:
that in many cases the attorney would get his pay off the
individual employing him; that the appointment would be
a valuable consideration, and for one year a salary of $100
would be sufficient; perhaps $160 the next year, &c.,
increasing as the city increases; and if $100 would not
satisfy, we had better have no attorney. "I would

rather give my services as counselor, &c., than levy a tax the people are not able to pay; and that every man ought to be willing to help prop the city by bearing a share of the burden till the city is able to pay a higher salary. My opinion is that the officers of the city should be satisfied with a very small compensation for their services. I have never received twenty-five dollars for my services; [as counselor] but the peace I have enjoyed in the rights and liberties of the city has been ample compensation."

I suggested the propriety of inserting a clause in the ordinance to be made relating to the City Attorney, authorizing him to claim fees of parties in certain cases, and the small salary satisfy the attorney in cases where he can get no fees from his client. "I would rather be docked $100 in my salary than have the $200 given to the City Attorney by the city."

I also proposed that the Council take into consideration the payment of the police; also proposed that a public meeting be called in each ward to see if they will not, then the council will take the case into consideration.

At 1 p. m., the Municipal Court sat in the assembly room, where I asked Dr. R. D. Foster if he bore my expenses to Washington, or any part thereof.

Foster replied he did not.

I stated that Dr. Goforth had said that he was taken in a secret council when Foster told him he had paid my expenses.

Dr. Foster replied he never had a secret interview with Dr. Goforth, and gave his version of the meeting.

I then asked him—"Have I ever misused you any way?"

Foster said—"I do not feel at liberty to answer this question, under existing circumstances?"

I again asked him—"Did I ever misuse you?"

He again replied—"I do not feel at liberty to answer under existing circumstances"

I then asked—"Did I ever wrong you in deal, or personally misuse you in any shape?"

Foster said,"I do not feel at liberty to answer. I have treated you Christianly and friendly too, so far as I have had the ability."

I then asked him to tell me where I had done wrong, and I will ask his forgiveness; for I want you to prove to this company by your testimony that I have treated you honorably.

Foster then said—"I shall testify no further at present."

I then asked Justice Aaron Johnson—"Did I ever make oath before you against Simpson?"

He replied—"Not before the prosecution."

I then told the whole story.

Andrew Colton then came up before the Municipal Court on *habeas corpus,* and was discharged on the insufficiency of the papers.

After which, I preferred the following charge before the High Council against Dr. Robert D. Foster "for unchristianlike conduct in general, for abusing my character privily, for throwing out slanderous insinuations against me, for conspiring against my peace and safety, for conspiring against my life, for conspiring against the peace of my family, and for lying."

A charge was preferred against Harrison Sagers for teaching spiritual wife doctrine and neglecting his family, which was handed over to the High Council to act upon.

At 2 p. m., Elder John Taylor delivered a political discourse.

About 5 p. m., the *"Maid of Iowa"* arrived at the Nauvoo House wharf, filled with passengers from England, led by William Kay. 210 souls started from Liverpool, and nearly all arrived in good health and spirits, one smaller company having previously arrived.

Sunday, 14.—Rainy day. No meeting at the stand. I preached on board the *"Maid of Iowa."*

Committee of the Council met in the afternoon at my office.

Monday, 15.—At home settling with Dan Jones for steamboat *"Maid of Iowa."* She has returned in debt about $1,700. After much conversation and deliberation, I agreed to buy out Jones, by giving him property in the city worth $1,231, and assuming the debts.

I rode out in the afternoon.

The Twelve Apostles arranged the appointments for the general conferences in the United States as follows:

Quincy, Ill.,	Sat. and Sun. May	4	5
Princess Grove, Ill.,	" " "	11	12
Ottowa, Ill.,	" " "	18	19
Chicago, Ill.,	" " "	25	26
Comstock, Kallamazoo county, Mich.,	" " June	1	2
Pleasant Valley, Mich.,	" " "	8	9
Frankland, Oakland county, Mich ,	" " "	15	16
Kirtland, Ohio,	" " "	22	23
G. A. Neal's six miles west of Lockport,N.Y.	" " "	29	30
Batavia, N. Y,,	" " July	6	7
Portage, Alleghany county, N. Y.,	" " "	13	14
Hamilton, Madison county, N. Y.,	" " "	20	21
Oswego, N. Y.,	" " June	29	30
Adams, Jefferson county, N. Y,,	" " July	6	7
London, Caledonia county, N. Y.	" " June	15	16
Northfield, Washington county, ten miles of Montpelier, at Lyman Houghton's, N.Y.	" " "	29	30
Fairfield, Essex Co., at Elder Tracy's, N. Y.	" " July	13	14
Boston, Mass.,	" " June	29	30
Salem, "	" " July	6	7
New Bedford, Mass.,	" " "	13	14
Peterboro, N. H.,	" " "	13	14
Lowell, Mass.,	" " "	27	28
Scarboro, Maine,	" " "	6	7
Vinal Haven "	" " "	13	14
Westfield, Mass.,	" " "	27	28
Farmington, Mass.,	" " Aug.	3	4
New Haven, Conn.,	" " "	10	11
Canaan, Conn.,	" " "	17	18
Norwalk, "	" " "	24	25
New York City, N. Y.,	" " "	17	18
Philadelphia, Pa.,	" " Aug.31	Sep. 1	
Dresden, Weekly county, Tenn.,	" " May 25	26	

Eagle Creek, Benton county, Tenn., ... Sat and Sun June 8	9
Dyer county, C. H., ... " " " 22	23
Rutherford county, C. H., Tenn., ... " " July 20	21
Lexington, Henderson county, Tenn., ... " " Aug. 3	4
New Albany, Clinton county, Ky., ... " " June 29	30
Alquina, Fayette county, Ia., ... " " ." 1	2
Pleasant Garden, Ia., ... " " " 15	16
Fort Wayne, Ia., ... " " " 29	30
Northfield, Boon county, Ia., ... " " July 13	14
Cincinnati, Ohio, ... " " May 18	19
Pittsburgh, Pa., ... " " June 1	2
Leechburg, " .... " " " 15	16
Running Water Branch, Noxuble Co., Miss., ·· " " " 1	2
Tuscaloosa, Ala., ... " " " 22	23
Washington City, D. C., ...Sept. 7, 8, 9, 10, 11, 12, 13, 14, 15.	

We also publish the names of the Elders who are appointed to the several states, together with their appointments. Those who are numbered with the figures 1 and 2 will take the presidency of the several states to which they are appointed.

MAINE.

J. Butterfield, 1st
Elbridge Tufts, 2nd
S. B. Stoddard

Jonathan H. Hale
Henry Herriman,
John Moon

NEW HAMPSHIRE.

W. Snow, 1st
Howard Egan, 2nd
Alvin Cooley
John S. Twiss,
Charles A. Adams,
Bethuel Miller
A. D. Boynton.

Harley Morley
Israel Barlow
David Clough, Sen.
Calvin Reed
Chilion Mack
Isaac Burton

MASSACHUSETTS.

Daniel Spencer, 1st
Milton F. Bartlett
Daniel Loveland
Joseph J. Woodbury
W. H. Woodbury
John R. Blanchard

George Lloyd
Orlando D. Hovey
Nathaniel Ashby
Samuel P. Hoyt
Daniel W. Gardner

RHODE ISLAND.

William Seabury, 1st   Melvin Wilbur
Thomas McTaggart

CONNECTICUT.

E. H. Davis, 1st   Quartus S. Sparks

VERMONT.

Erastus Snow, 1st   Warren Snow
William Hyde   Dominicus Carter
Denman Cornish,   Levi W. Hancock
Jeremiah Hatch   Alfred Cordon
Martin Titus   Charles Snow
William Haight   James C. Snow
John D. Chase   A. M. Harding
Josiah H. Perry   Isaac Houston
Amos Hodges.

NEW YORK.

C. W. Wandell, 1st   William Newland
Marcellus Bates, 2nd   Allen Wait
Truman Gillett   William H. Parshall,
A. A. Farnham   C. H. Wheelock
Edmund Ellsworth,   Timothy B. Foote
Gregory Bentley   George W. Fowler
Homer C. Hoyt   Henry L. Cook
Isaac Chase,   William W. Dryer
Simeon A. Dunn   Elijah Reed
Daniel Shearer   Solon Foster
James W. Phippin   Hiram Bennett
J. H. Van Natta   Chandler Holbrook
Samuel P. Bacon   Lyman Hall
Bradford W, Elliott   William Felshaw
J. R. G. Phelps   Daniel Fisher,
Joseph P. Noble   D. H. Redfield
John Tanner   Martin H. Tanner
Thomas Fuller   G. D, Goldsmith
O. M. Duel   Charles Thompson
Samuel White   B. C. Elsworth
W. R. R. Stowell   Archibald Bates
William D. Pratt   David Pettigrew
Marcellus McKeown   Ellis Eames
Horace S. Eldredge

NEW JERSEY.

Ezra T. Benson, 1st	John Pack

PENNSYLVANIA.

D. D. Yearsley, 1st	Wm. P. McIntyre
Edson Whipple, 2nd	Jacob Zundall
John Duncan	Orrin D. Farlin
Stephen Post	Henry Mouer
G. W. Crouse	G. Chamberlain
Jacob Shoemaker	Thomas Hess
Stephen Winchester	A. J. Glæfke
Hyrum Nyman	Henry Dean
J. M. Cole	James Downing
Charles Warner.	

DELAWARE.

John Jones	Jonathan O. Duke
Warren Snow	Justus Morse

MARYLAND.

Jacob Hamblin	Patrick Norris
Lyman Stoddard.	

VIRGINIA.

B. Winchester, 1st	James Park
S. C. Shelton, 2nd	A. W. Whitney
Geo. D. Watt. 3rd	Pleasant Ewell
Chapman Duncan	W. E. Higginbottom
Joseph King	John F. Betts
Peter Fife	Alfred B. Lambson
Robert Hamilton	David Evans

NORTH CAROLINA.

A. McRae, 1st	John Holt
Aaron Razer, 2nd	John Houston
Thomas Guymon	James Sanderson
George Watt.	

SOUTH CAROLINA.

Alonzo LeBaron, 1st	Ekells Truly
John M. Emell	William Smith
William D. Lyman.	

GEORGIA.

Morgan L. Gardner	Miles Anderson
Isaac Beebe	S. E. Carpenter

KENTUCKY.

John D. Lee, 1st
D. H. Rogers
Samuel B. Frost
John O. Angus
Charles Spry
John H. Reid
William Watkins.

D. D. Hunt
M. B. Welton
Horace B. Owens
Joseph Holbrook
Hiram W. Mikesell
Garret W. Mikesell

TENNESSEE.

A. O. Smoot, 1st
Alphonzo Young, 2nd
W. W. Riley
Amos Davis
L. T. Coon
Jackson Smith
W. P. Vance
H. D. Buys
A. D. Young
Joseph Younger
G. W. Langley
G. Penn

J. J. Castell
J. A. Kelting
J. Hampton
Alfred Bell
Armstead Moffitt
D. P. Rainey
James Holt,
Warren Smith
J. J. Sasnett
H. B. Jacobs
John L. Fullmer
Joseph Mount

ALABAMA.

B. L. Clapp, 1st
G. W. Brandon

L. D. Butler
T. J. Brandon

MISSISSIPPI.

J. B. Walker
Ethan Barrus.

Daniel Tyler

LOUISIANA.

J. B. Bosworth, 1st
H. H. Wilson
Wm. Nelson

John Kelly
George Pew
Lorenzo Moore

ARKANSAS.

A. A. Simmons
Darwin Chase

J. A. McIntosh
Nathaniel Leavitt

OHIO.

Lorenzo Snow, 1st
L. Brooks, 2nd
Alfred Brown
J. J. Riser

William Batson
G. C. Riser
Clark Lewis
B. W. Wilson

J. Carroll
L. O. Littlefield
J. M. Powers
Milo Andrus
John Lovelace
W. H. Folsom
John Cooper
S. Carter
John Nichols
David Jones
Nathaniel Childs
Jesse Johnson
J. A. Casper
Joseph Rose
W. Brothers
Jared Porter
John W. Roberts

A. W. Condit
Loren Babbitt
Elijah Newman
Milton Stow
Edson Barney
Hiram Dayton
Jacob Morris
Ezra Strong
J. M. Emmett
Allen Tulley
P. H. Young
S. P. Hutchins
J. H. Foster
Nathan T. Porter
Ezra Vincent
Lysander Dayton

INDIANA.

Amasa Lyman, 1st
G. P. Dykes, 2nd
A. L. Lamoreaux
Charles Hopkins
F. M. Edwards
Salmon Warner
F. D. Richards
S. W. Richards
John Mackey
James Newberry
Abraham Palmer
John G. Smith

U. V. Stewart
Washington Lemon
Edward Carlin
L. D. Young
Wm. Snow
Nathan Tanner
Wm. Martindale
Henry Elliott
A. F. Farr
John Jones
Frederick Ott

MICHIGAN.

Charles C. Rich, 1st
Harvey Green, 2nd
Thomas Dunn
R. C. Sprague
Joseph Curtis
Zebedee Coltrin
Reuben W. Strong
L. N. Kendall

Wm. Savage
David Savage
Graham Coltrin
Samuel Parker
Jeremiah Curtis
C. W. Hubbard
S. D. Willard
Wm. Gribble

ILLINOIS.

E. H. Groves, 1st

Morris Phelps, 2nd

John Vance
H. Olmstead, Galena
H. W. Barnes, do.
Hiram Mott,
David Candland
W. A. Duncan
Wm. O. Clark
Almon Bathrick
P. H. Buzzard
Zachariah Hardy
John Hammond
G. W. Hickerson
Daniel Allen
David Judah
Thomas Dobson
James Nelson
David Lewis

S. Mulliner
John Gould
Zenus H. Gurley
Jefferson Hunt
Jacob L. Burnham
D. J. Kershner
N. Leavitt
John Laurence
Nathan A. West
Levi Jackman
Abel Lamb
Howard Coray
Stephen Markham
Levi Stewart
James Graham
Timothy S. Hoit
Duncan McArthur

MISSOURI.

A. H. Perkins, 1st
John Lowry 2nd
Wm. G. Rule

Wm. Coray
O. M. Allen
Wm. H. Jordan

WISCONSIN TERRITORY.

S. H. Briggs

FREE.

F. Nickerson, 1st   A. C. Nickerson   L. S. Nickerson

Those Elders who are numbered in the foregoing list to preside over the different states will appoint conferences in all places in their several states where opportunities present, and will attend all the conferences, or send experienced and able Elders, who will preach the truth in righteousness, and present before the people "General Smith's Views of the Powers and Policy of the General Government," and seek diligently to get up electors who will go for him for the Presidency. All the Elders will be faithful in preaching the Gospel in its simplicity and beauty, in all meekness, humility, long-suffering and prayerfulness; and the Twelve will devote the season to traveling, and will attend as many conferences as possible.

Elder B. Winchester is instructed to pass through Mississippi, Alabama, Georgia, North and South Carolina and Virginia, to visit the churches, hold conferences, and preside over them.

BRIGHAM YOUNG, President

W. RICHARDS, Clerk of the Quorum of the Twelve.

Tuesday, 16.—Rode out to Brother Greenwood's, but he had not returned.   Five p. m. had a long talk with Chauncey L. Higbee and Esq. Marr, in front of my house, and read to them Dr. A. B. Williams' and M. G. Eaton's affidavit before Esq. Wells.

The Twelve Apostles met in council.

Wednesday 17.—Rode out with Brother Heber C. Kimball and William Clayton to the steamboat landing. Remainder of the day at home.

Thursday, 18.—Nine a. m. went into general council until noon and introduced J. W. Coolidge, D. S. Hollister, and added Lyman Wight's name.

While at dinner I made mention of the report that Foster, Higbee, *et al.* were paying someone's board at my table so as to catch something against me; so that, if the report is true, they may have something to carry back.

Two to five thirty p. m. in council.

At 6 p. m. Brigham Young, Willard Richards, John Taylor, George A. Smith, Heber C. Kimball, Wilford Woodruff, of the Twelve Apostles; Alpheus Cutler, Samuel Bent, George W. Harris, A. Johnson, William Marks, of the City Council; Charles C. Rich, Amasa M. Lyman, of the High Council; William W. Phelps, Newel K. Whitney, John Smith, John M. Bernhisel, Joseph Fielding, George J. Adams, Erastus Snow, Reynolds Cahoon, J. W. Coolidge, John Scott, John D. Lee, Levi W. Hancock, S. Williams, Jos. Young, John P. Greene, John D. Parker, Alexander McRae, George D. Watt, and William Clayton held a council and unanimously cut off Robert D. Foster, Wilson Law, William Law and Jane Law, of Nauvoo, and Howard Smith of Scott county, Illinois, from the Church of Jesus Christ of Latter-day Saints, for unchristianlike conduct; and their names were published in the *Times and Seasons*.

Excommunication of the Laws, Fosters, *et al.*

Friday, 19.—A company of about eighty Saints arrived. In the evening rode to the upper steamboat landing.

Saturday, 20.—Emma started for St. Louis to purchase goods.

I rode out with Dr. Bernhisel and my boys Frederick and Alexander to the prairie, which is now very green.

Elders Brigham Young and Wilford Woodruff rode to Lima and spent the night with Father Morley.

Sunday, 21.—At home; rainy day. A meeting at the Stand. Elder Erastus Snow preached on "The Law of Nature."

Elders Young and Woodruff attended a conference and preached to the Saints in Lima, where twenty-six Elders volunteered to go out preaching.

Elder Kimball attended a conference at Ramus.

Monday, 22.—All night lightning, thundering, raining, with strong east wind which continued through the day.

The river very high; all the mills in the city stopped on account of the high water.

This morning a man, who had put up at my house told me he wanted to see me alone. I went into my room with him, when he told me he was a prophet of God, that he came from Vermont, and he prophecied that this Government, was about to be overthrown, and the kingdom which Daniel speaks of was about to be established somewhere in the West, and he thought in Illinois.

My brother William arrived from New Jersey with some forty or fifty Saints. I spent some time with him in the evening.

Elders Young and Woodruff started for Nauvoo; but on account of a tremendous storm of hail and rain, they were glad to take shelter at Brother William Draper's, where they spent the night.

Tuesday, 9.—From 9 to 12 a general meeting of citizens friendly to my election, was held in the hall, to elect a delegate to go to the Baltimore Convention, to be held on the first Monday in May. D. S. Hollister was elected.

From 3 to 5 p. m. again assembled, and many speeches were made, &c.; and appointed the second Monday in May to hold a State Convention at Nauvoo.

In the evening, visited Agnes, my brother Carlos' widow, and Dr. Richards, with Hyrum.

Wednesday, 24.—Rode up to the steamboat landing, where we found Elder J. M. Grant, who introduced me to Judge William Richards, of New Jersey, took him to Brother Winchester's.

In the evening Brother Ezra Thayer, Dr. Richards, and Dr. Williams were in my room, and a man who boarded at the Masonic Hall. At their request, I gave them a history of the Laws' proceedings, in part, in trying to make a difficulty in my family, &c.

Gave recommendations to Elders Amasa M. Lyman and D. S. Hollister.

Thursday, 25.—Emma returned from St. Louis.

A brother who works in the *St. Louis Gazette* office came up at the same time, and wanted to know by what principle I got so much power, how many inhabitants and armed men we had, &c. I told him I obtained power on the principles of truth and virtue, which would last when I was dead and gone, &c.

In general council from 10 till 12, and from 2 to 5, when they adjourned *sine die*, after appointing a State Convention to meet in Nauvoo on 17th May. The council then dispersed to go abroad in the nations.

Instructed Dr. Richards to make out a writ of *habeas corpus* for Mr. Jeremiah Smith, of Iowa, who was expecting to be arrested by the U. S. Marshal for getting money which was due him, as he says, at Washington.

A play on rational amusement was to commence this evening, but a most tremendous shower of rain and large hail from the southwest commenced about six p. m. which prevented it. The small creeks rose over four feet high, overflowed their banks, sweeping away fences, and doing considerable damage.

The Mississippi river is higher at this place than ever known by the oldest inhabitant.

Friday 26.—At home. At 10 a. m. the Marshal went up on the hill to arrest Augustine Spencer for an assault on his brother, Orson Spencer, in his own house. Robert D. Foster, Charles Foster and Chauncey L. Higbee came down. Charles Foster drew a pistol pointed towards me, and threatened to shoot while standing on the steps of my office. I ordered him to be arrested and the pistol taken from him, when a struggle ensued, in which Charles Foster, Robert D. Foster and Chauncey L. Highbee resisted, and I ordered them to be arrested also, and I as the Mayor ordered the policemen to be called; then went on to try Augustine Spencer. He was fined $100, and required to give bonds in $100 to keep the peace for six months. He appealed the case at once to the Municipal Court.

Violence of the Fosters and Higbees.

Robert D. Foster, Chauncey L. Higbee, and Charles Foster were also tried for resisting the authorities of the city.

O. P. Rockwell sworn. Marshal John P. Greene sworn:— Said Dr. Foster swore by God that he would not assist the Marshal, and swore by God they would see the Mayor in hell before they would go; and that Charles Foster drew a pistol and presented at the Mayor, which was being wrested from him when Dr. Robert D. Foster interfered. Charles Foster and Chauncey L. Higbee said they would be G— d——d if they would not shoot the Mayor. They breathed out many hard threatenings and menacing sayings. They said they would consider themselves the favored of God for the privilege of shooting or ridding the world of such a tyrant (referring to the Mayor).

Joseph W. Coolidge sworn, and confirmed the Marshal's testimony.

Elbridge Tufts sworn, and confirmed the foregoing statements.

Robert D. Foster, Charles Foster and Chauncey L. Higbee were each fined $100.   They immediately took an appeal to the Municipal Court.

I issued a warrant for Robert D. Foster, on complaint of Willard Richards, for a breach of ordinance, in that Foster said to Richards: "You," shaking his fist in the doctor's face, "are another d—ned black-hearted villain! You tried to seduce my wife on the boat, when she was going to New York and I can prove it; and the oath is out against you."

Saturday, 27.—A large company of gentlemen from St. Louis and other places on the river, called at the Mansion.   After spending some time, they returned to the boat, but it was gone, when they again returned to the Mansion.

At 9 a. m. the case of Dr. Robert D. Foster came up for trial before the Municipal Court.   I had a conversation with Foster in which he charged me with many crimes, and said that Daniteism was in Nauvoo; and he used a great variety of vile and false epithets and charges.

The court adjourned to Monday, the 29th at 9 a. m.

Foster agreed to meet me on the second Monday in May, at the Stand, and have a settlement, and he would publish the result of it in the Warsaw papers.   I told him if he did not agree to be quiet, and not attempt to raise a mob, I would not meet him; if he would agree to be quiet, I would be willing to publish the settlement in the *Neighbor*.   But Foster would not agree to be quiet.   I then told him I had done my duty; the skirts of my garments were free from his (Foster's) blood; I had made the last overtures of peace to him; and then delivered him into the hands of God, and shook my garments against him as a testimony thereof.

I continued in the office some time afterwards in conversation, and then went into the big room and read in the *Warsaw Signal* a vile article against the Saints.

Elder Hiram Smith arrived from Liverpool accompanied by one hundred and fifty immigrating Saints.

There was a meeting at the Stand at one o'clock, to give instructions to the Elders going out electioneering. They were addressed by President Rigdon and William Smith.

Dr. Richards prosecuted Robert D. Foster for slander, &c.

Sunday, 28.—At home. A beautiful clear day.

My brother Hyrum preached at the Stand in the morning, and among other things, said the time will shortly come that when one man makes another an offender for a word, he shall be cut off from the Church of Jesus Christ. There were prophets before, but Joseph has the spirit and power of all the prophets.

President Brigham Young also spoke very pointedly and very truly about Dr. Foster and others. Dr. Foster was cursed, and the people cried "Amen."

Several persons were baptized in the river at the foot of Main street.

There was a meeting of the Twelve Apostles, Seventies and others, in the Seventies' Hall, in the afternoon.

Prayer meeting in the evening: the brethren prayed for the sick, a deliverance from our enemies, a favorable termination to lawsuits, &c., &c. I had been suddenly taken sick, and was therefore unable to attend.

A conference of Elders assembled at Yelrome, or Morley Settlement, Lima, Isaac Morley presiding, when a quorum of High Priests was organized, consisting of thirty-one members. Horace Rawson president, Philip Gardner and Joseph S. Allen, his counselors, and James C. Snow, clerk.

There was a meeting at Wilson Law's, near the sawmill, of those who had been cut off from the Church, and their dupes. Several affidavits which they had taken against me and others were read. William Law, Wilson

Law, Austin A. Cowles, John Scott, Sen., Francis M. Higbee, Robert D. Foster, and Robert Pierce were appointed a committee to visit the different families in the city, and see who would join the new church; *i. e.*, as they had decided that I was a fallen prophet, &c.; and they appointed William Law in my place, who chose Austin Cowles and Wilson Law as his counselors. Robert D. Foster and Francis M. Higbee to be two of the Twelve Apostles, &c., &c., as report says.

Elder James Blackeslee preached in the forenoon, bearing a faithful testimony of the truth of the work and my being a true prophet, and in the afternoon joined the "Anties." They chose Charles Ivins Bishop.

A conference was held in Sheffield, England, representing 215 members, 7 Elders, 19 Priests, 5 Teachers, and 3 Deacons.

Monday, 29.—At home; received a visit from L. R. Foster of New York, who gave me a good pencil case, sent me by Brother Theodore Curtis, who is now in New York; and the first words I wrote with it were, "God bless the man!"

At 11 a. m., Robert D. Foster came up for trial. I transferred the case to Alderman William Marks. Foster objected to the jurisdiction of the court, also to an informality in the writ, &c.

The court decided he had not jurisdiction. Esquire Noble, from Rock river, assisted the City Attorney. Esquire Patrick was present.

I called a special session of the City Council at 3:30 p. m., when it was voted that W. W. Phelps take the place of John Taylor during his absence this season; also Aaron Johnson in place of Orson Hyde; Phineas Richards in place of Heber C. Kimball; Edward Hunter in place of Daniel Spencer; Levi Richards in place of Brigham Young as councilors in the City Council; and Elias Smith as alderman in place of George A. Smith.

Lieutenant Williams filed his affidavit *versus* Major-

General Wilson Law, and he was suspended from office to
await his trial before a court-martial of the Nauvoo Legion for ungentlemanly conduct, &c.; and he was notified
of his command in the Legion being suspended, and Charles
C. Rich was notified to take command, and also notified
seven officers to sit as a court-martial.

William Law was supended for trial about the same
time.

Steamer *Mermaid* touched at Nauvoo House, landing at
5 p. m. for a short time when going down.

John P. Greene published the following in the
Neighbor: (Impression of May 1st.)

The Foster-Higbee Embroilment.

All is peace at Nauvoo, among the Saints:

But, Mr. Taylor, I wish you to give the following outrage an insertion in the *Neighbor*, that the public mind may be disabused, and the
disgrace and shame fall on those who have justly deserved it and merited
the people's rebuke!

On Friday morning, the 26th inst., I was informed by Mr. Orrin P. Rockwell that one Mr. Augustine Spencer had committed an assault on the
person of Alderman Orson Spencer, and the Mayor of the city had sent
for Augustine Spencer, and found him in Mr. Marr's law office, made
him a prisoner, and informed him he must go with me to the Mayor's
office, when he said he would not go.

I then called upon Robert D. Foster, Chauncey L. Higbee, and Charles
A. Foster to assist me in taking said Spencer to the Mayor's office; but
they swore they would not, and used many threatening oaths and asper-
sions, saying they would see the Mayor and the city damned, and then
they would not; but soon followed me and Mr. Augustine Spencer
to the office door, when the Mayor ordered me to arrest these three
men for refusing to assist me in the discharge of my duty; and when
attempting to arrest them, they all resisted, and with horrid imprecations threatened to shoot.

I called for help, and there not being sufficient, the Mayor laid hold on
the two Fosters at the same time. At that instant Charles A. Foster drew
a double-barrel pistol on Mr. Smith, but it was instantly wrenched from
his hand; and afterwards he declared he would have shot the Mayor, if
we had let his pistol alone, and also he would thank God for the privil-
edge of ridding the world of a tyrant! Chauncey L. Higbee responded
to Foster's threats, and swore that he would do it.

However, the three were arrested and brought before the Mayor, whereupon Orrin P. Rockwell, Joseph Coolidge, John P. Greene and E. Tufts testified to the amount of the above statements; upon which evidence the court assessed a fine of one hundred dollars to each of the above-named aggressors, who appealed to the Municipal Court.

I wish the public to know who it is that makes insurrections and disturbs the peace and quiet of the people of the city of Nauvoo; and in order to do this I need only to tell the world that this Robert D. Foster is a county magistrate, and the same Robert D. Foster that was fined for gambling a few weeks since; and that this Chauncey L. Higbee is a lawyer and notary public of Hancock county, and the same Chauncey L. Higbee that was fined for insulting the city officers (the marshal and constable) when in the discharge of their official duties, a few weeks since.

"When the wicked rule the people mourn, but righteousness exalteth any nation"—SOLOMON.

J. P. GREENE, City Marshal.

N. B.—We wish it to be distinctly understood that neither of the three above-named individuals are members of the Church of Latter-day Saints, but we believe Charles A. Foster is a Methodist.—J. P. G.

Tuesday, 30.—At home counseling the brethren about many things; received much company, &c.

In the afternoon in council with Hiram Clark and Brigham Young, at Brigham Young's house, on the affairs of the Church in England.

A complaint was commenced against William and Wilson Law in the Masonic Lodge, &c.

Sent notification to two more officers to sit in the court-martial on the trial of William and Wilson Law.

The *Osprey* steamer touched at the Nauvoo House landing in the evening.

Wednesday, May 1.—Heavy rain and wind last night.

At home counseling the brethren, and rode out a short time in the afternoon with a gentleman from Quincy.

Elder Lyman Wight and Bishop George Miller arrived from the Pine country.

Mr. Thomas A. Lyne, a tragedian from New York, assisted by George J. Adams and others, got up a theatrical exhibition in the lower room of the Masonic Hall, which was fitted up with very tasteful scenery. They performed "Pizarro," "The Orphan of Geneva," "Douglas," "The Idiot Witness," "Damon and Pythias," and other plays with marked success. The Hall was well attended each evening, and the audience expressed their entire satisfaction and approbation.

Thursday, 2.—Very windy all night, breaking down large trees; a thunder storm also.

At home and counseling the brethren.

Sent William Clayton to Wilson Law to find out why he refused paying his note, when he brought in some claims as a set-off which Clayton knew were paid, leaving me no remedy but the glorious uncertainty of the law.

At 10 a. m. the *Maid of Iowa* steamer started for Rock River for a load of wheat and corn to feed the laborers on the Temple.

William Clayton and Colonel Stephen Markham started to attend court at Dixon, on the case of "Joseph Smith vs. Harmon T. Wilson and Joseph H. Reynolds."

In the afternoon I rode to the prairie to sell some land, and during my absence Lucien Woodworth returned from Texas.

Lieut. Aaron Johnson made the following affidavit:

Nauvoo, May 2nd, 1844.

State of Illinois, Hancock Co., } ss
City of Nauvoo.

Personally appeared before me, John Taylor, Judge-Advocate of the Nauvoo Legion, Aaron Johnson; and being duly sworn deposes and says that on or about the 28th day of April, 1844, at the dwelling house of Wilson Law in Nauvoo aforesaid, Colonel R. D. Foster, Surgeon-in-Chief, and Brevet Brigadier-General of said Nauvoo Legion, while talking about General Joseph Smith, said that General Smith kept a gang of robbers and plunderers about his house for the purpose of robbing and plundering, and he (Smith) received half the spoils; also that said General Joseph Smith tried to get him (Foster) to go and kill Boggs, with many other ungentlemanly and unofficer-like observations concerning said General Smith and others.   Aaron Johnson,
2nd Lieut., 1st Comp,, 1st Regiment, 2nd Cohort, Nauvoo Legion.

Personally appeared, Aaron Johnson, the signer of the above complaint, and made oath the same was true according to the best of his knowledge and belief, the day and year above written before me.

JOHN TAYLOR,
Judge-Advocate of the Nauvoo Legion.

Friday, *3.*—At home giving advice to brethren who were constantly calling to ask for counsel. Several thunder showers during the day.

In general council from 2 to 6, and from 8 to 10 p. m. Lucien Woodworth gave an account of his mission.

Wrote a letter to Uncle John Smith, and requested him to attend general council next Monday.

The following letter was written:

Letter: Brigham Young and Willard Richards to Reuben Hedlock—Instructions on Immigration Matters.

NAUVOO, May 3rd, 1844.

Elder Reuben Hedlock:

DEAR BROTHER—Your long communication by Elder Kay was received two weeks last Saturday, also the one by Elder Clark last Saturday, and we feel to thank you for the care you have taken to write us so particularly. We are glad to receive such communications, and wish you to continue the same course as opportunities present. The brethren have all had good passages (four ships). Elder Clark was only five weeks and three days to New Orleans. All things safe.

All things are going on gloriously at Nauvoo. We shall make a great wake in the nation. Joseph for President. Your family is well, and friends generally. We have already received several hundred volunteers to go out electioneering and preaching and more offering. We go for storming the nation. But we must proceed to realities.

The whisperings of the Spirit to us are that you do well to content yourself awhile longer in old England, and let your wife remain where she is. We hope the Temple may be completed, say one year from this spring, when in many respects changes will take place. Until then, who can do better in England than yourself! But we will not leave you comfortless; we will send Elders to your assistance. For three or four months we want all the help we can get in the United States; after which you may expect help.

In the meantime you are at liberty to print as many *Stars*, pamphlets hymn books, tracts, cards, &c., as you can sell; and make all the money you can in righteousness. Don't reprint everything you get from Nauvoo. Many things are printed here not best to circulate in England. Select and write doctrine, and matter, (new) such as will be useful to the Saints in England and new to us; so that when we exchange papers all will be edified. God shall give you wisdom, if you will seek to Him, and you shall prosper in your printing.

We also wish you to unfurl your flag on your shipping office, and send all the Saints you can to New York, or Boston, or Philadelphia or any other port of the United States, but not at our expense any longer. We have need of something to sustain us in our labors, and we want you to go ahead with printing and shipping, and make enough to support yourself and help us a bit. You will doubtless find it necessary to employ Brother Ward. Keep all your books straight, so that we in the end can know every particular.

Ship everybody to America you can get the money for—Saint and sinner—a general shipping-office. And we would like to have our shipping-agent in Liverpool sleep on as good a bed, eat at as respectable a house, keep as genteel an office, and have his boots shine as bright, and blacked as often as any other office-keeper. Yes sir; make you money enough to wear a good broadcloth, and show the world that you represent gentlemen of worth, character and respectability.

We will by-and-by have offices from the rivers to the ends of the earth, and we will begin at Liverpool from this time and increase and increase and *increase* the business of the office as fast as it can be done in safety, and circumstances will permit. Employ a runner, if necessary, and show the world you can do a better and more honorable business than anybody else, and more of it. Don't be afraid to blow your trumpet.

We need not say, deal with everybody so that they will want to deal with you again, and make all the money you honestly can. Send no more emigrants on emigration books or *Star* money. Temple orders for emigrants may be filled on Temple funds. Keep account of all moneys in their separate departments and favor us with a report occasionally.

Sell the Books of Mormon the first opportunity, if it be at a reduced price, and forward the money by the first safe conveyance to Brigham Young.

We will pay your wife as you requested in your letter, as soon as possible. We wish you to take care of yourself and family, and withal help us besides; and we have now put you in possession of means to do it.

Let nobody know your business but the underwriters. Our wives know not all our business, neither does any wise man's wife know all things, for the secret of the Lord is with those that fear Him and do His business. A hint to the wise is sufficient. But we will add, if you want us to do anything for your wife, write us, and we will do it; but keep our business from your wife and from everybody else

We are glad to hear a door is open in France, and sure we have no objections to your going over and preaching, &c.; but we think perhaps you will now find as much to do in England as you can find time to do it in; if not, go by all means. We are in hopes of sending a special messenger to France in a few days; if so, very likely he may call on you, and you pass over and give him an introduction: this would be pleasant for you all.

Brother Hedlock, a word with you privately. Joseph said, last conference, that Zion included all North and South America; and after the Temple was done, and the Elders endowed, they would spread and build up cities all over the United States; but at present we are not to teach this doctrine. Nay, hold your tongue. But by this you can see why it is wsidom for the Saints to get into the United States—anywhere rather than stay in England to starve.

The prophet has a charter for a dam from the lower line of the city to the island opposite Montrose, and from thence to the sand-bar above in the Mississippi. Could five, six or seven thousand dollars be raised to commence the dam at the lower extremity, and erect a building, any machinery might be propelled by water. The value of a steam-engine would nearly build the dam sufficient for a cotton-factory, which we much need. Start some capitalists, if you can: 'tis the greatest speculation in the world: a world of cotton and woollen goods are wanted here.

We have proposed to Brother Clark to return to your assistance in the shipping business soon; also to enter into exchanges of goods and produce. Which he will do, he has not decided. What will hinder your doing a good business in shipping this season? Good? Yes, in competing with the first offices in the city, and by next season taking the lead, if not this! When the Saints get to New York, Boston, &c., let them go to work, spread abroad in the land, or come to Nauvoo, as they find convenient and have means, and when the season arrives, start again for New Orleans. Write soon after the receipt of this, and let us know the prospect.

Tell the Saints, when they arrive in America, to make themselves as comfortable as they can, and be diligent in business, and not be over-anxious if they cannot come to Nauvoo. They will find Elders in all the states who will be ready to give them instruction; and if they can gather something by the way by their industry to assist themselves with when they arrive here, it will be well for them.

We have dropped the Nauvoo House until the Temple can be completed, and the Temple is going on finely. We have had an open winter and a forward spring. The Twelve are holding general conferences all over the United States. They will go East soon, and Brother Young will write to you as soon as he gets the information to tell what house you can remit the book money to in New York.

We shall have a State Convention at Nauvoo on the 17th inst.,—an election. A great many are believing the doctrine. If any of the brethren wish to go to Texas, we have no particular objection. You may send a hundred thousand there if you can, in eighteen months, though we expect before that you will return to receive your endow-ments; and then we will consult your interest, with others who may be going abroad, about taking their families with them.

The kingdom is organized; and, although as yet no bigger than a grain of mustard seed, the little plant is in a flourishing condition, and our prospects brighter than ever. Cousin Lemuel is very friendly, and cultivating the spirit of peace and union in his family very extensively.

William and Wilson Law, Robert D. Foster, Chauncey L. and Francis Higbee, Father Cowles, &c., have organized a new church. (Laws and Fosters were first cut off). William Law is Prophet; James Blakesley and Cowles, Counselors; Higbee and Foster of the Twelve. Cannot learn all particulars. Charles Ivins, Bishop; old Dr. Green and old John Scott, his counselors. They are talking of sending a mission to England. but it will probably be after this when they come among you. 'Tis the same old story over again—"The doctrine is right, but Joseph is a fallen prophet."

Your brethren in the new covenant,

BRIGHAM YOUNG,
WILLARD RICHARDS.

Elder Parley P. Pratt wrote from Richmond, Mass., as follows:

Letter: Parley P. Pratt to Joseph Smith et al., Denouncing Augustine Spencer.

Dear Brother Joseph and Brother Orson Spencer, or whom it may concern:
This is to forewarn you that you have a snake in the grass—a base traitor and hypocrite in your midst, of whom perhaps you may not be fully aware. You may think these harsh terms, but I speak from good evidence and speak the truth.

Mr. Augustine Spencer, brother to Elder Orson Spencer, has written a letter from Nauvoo, which is now going the rounds in this neighbor-hood, and is fraught with the most infamous slander and lies concern-ing Joseph Smith and others, and which is calculated to embitter the minds of the people who read or hear it. It affirms that Joseph Smith is in the habit of drinking, swearing, carousing, dancing all night, &c.,

and that he keeps six or seven young females as wives, &c., and many other such like insinuations.

At the same time he cautions the people to whom he writes to keep the letter in such a way that a knowledge of its contents may not reach Nauvoo, as he says he is on intimate terms and confidential friendship with the "Prophet Joe" and the Mormons, and that he hopes to get into office by their means. This is his own acknowledgment of his own baseness, imposition and hypocrisy. I have not seen the letter myself, but have carefully examined the testimony of those who have, and I have also seen and witnessed its baneful effect upon the people here.

Now, I say to the Saints, Let such a man alone severely; shun him as they would the pestilence; be not deceived by a smooth tongue nor flattering words; neither accept of any excuse or apology until he boldly contradicts and counteracts his lying words abroad; but rather expose and unmask him in your midst, that he may be known and consequently become powerless, if he is not already so. I am well and expect to be in Boston tomorrow.

I remain, as ever, your friend and brother, in the love of truth,

P. P. PRATT.

RICHMOND, MASS., May 3rd, 1844.

Saturday, 4.—Rode out on the prairie to sell some land. The stone work for four circular windows finished cutting for the middle story of the Temple. Elder Wilford Woodruff moved into his new brick house.

A court-martial was detailed as follows:

HEADQUARTERS NAUVOO LEGION May 4, 1844.

To Alanson Ripley, Sergeant-Major, 2nd Cohort, Nauvoo Legion:

You are hereby forthwith commanded to notify the following named officers of the Nauvoo Legion to assemble at the office of Lieut.-General Joseph Smith, on Friday, the 10th inst., at 9 o'clock a. m., as members of a court-martial detailed for the trial of Robert D. Foster, Surgeon-in-Chief and Brevet Brigadier-General of the Nauvoo Legion, on the complaint of Lieut. Aaron Johnson for unofficer-like and unbecoming conduct, and hereof fail not, and make returns of your proceedings to the President of the Court on the first day of its sitting—*viz.*

Brig.,-Gen. George Miller as President; Brevet Brig.-Gen. Hugh McFall, Brevet Brig.-General Daniel H. Wells, Brevet Brig.-Gen. John S. Fullmer, Colonel Jonathan Dunham, Colonel Stephen Markham, Colonel Hosea Stout, Colonel John Scott, Lieut.-Colonel John D. Parker, Lieut.-Colonel Jonathan H. Hale, Lieut.-Colonel Theodore Turley, as members of said court, and Colonel John Taylor as Judge-Advocate

Also to summons Willard Richards and Aaron Johnson to appear at the same time and place as witnessses.

Given under my hand the day and year above written.

CHARLES C. RICH,

Major-General N. L., Commanding.

Dr. Richards wrote a letter, at President Brigham Young's request, to Reuben Hedlock.

Sunday, 5.—At home. Rainy day. Elder Jedediah M. Grant preached at the Mansion at 2 p. m. A large company of friends at my house afternoon and evening, whom I addressed on the true policy of this people in our intercourse with the national government.

A conference was held at Marsh Hill, (formerly Froom's Hill) England, comprising 681 members, 22 Elders, 43 Priests, 15 Teachers, 7 Deacons.

Monday, 6.—Attended general council all day. Elder J. M. Grant was added to the council. Voted to send Almon W. Babbitt on a mission to France and Lucien Woodworth to Texas. Sidney Rigdon was nominated as a candidate for the Vice-Presidency of the United States.

I had a warrant served on me by John D. Parker, issued by the clerk of the Circuit Court at Carthage, on the complaint of Francis M. Higbee, who had laid his damages at $5,000, but for what the writ does not state. I petitioned the Municipal Court for a writ of *habeas corpus*, which I obtained.

At 6 p. m. I was in conversation with Jeremiah Smith and a number of gentlemen, in my office on the subject of Emma's correspondence with Governor Carlin.

Beautiful day. West wind.

Tuesday 7.—Rode out on the prairie at nine a. m., with some gentlemen, to sell them some land. A tremendous thunder shower in the afternoon, with a strong wind and rain, which abated about sunset, and I stayed at my farm all night.

Esquire Daniel H. Wells issued a writ of ejectment against all persons who had bought land of Robert D.

Foster on the block east of the Temple, Foster having given them warranty deeds, but not having paid for the land himself.

An opposition printing press arrives at Dr. Foster's.

The following notice was issued by the Recorder:

STATE OF ILLINOIS, }
CITY OF NAUVOO. }

To the Marshal of the said City, greeting:

You are hereby required to notify Phineas Richards, Edward Hunter and Levi Richards, that they have been elected members of the City Council of said city; and Elias Smith, that he has been elected Alderman of said city by said City Council; and the said Councilors and Alderman and Gustavus Hills are required to appear, receive their oath of office, and take seats in said Council on Saturday, the 8th of June, 1844. at 10 o'clock a. m., at the Council Chamber. By order of the Council.

Witness my hand and corporation seal this 7th May, 1844.

[L. S.]   W. RICHARDS. Recorder.

Thursday, 8.—Returned home. At 10 a. m. went before the Municipal Court on the case, "Francis M. Higbee *versus* Joseph Smith."

The Prophet's Petition for Writ of Habeas Corpus.

MUNICIPAL COURT, CITY OF NAUVOO, ILLINOIS.

Third day, regular term, May 8, 1844.

Before Alderman N. K. Whitney, acting Chief Justice, and Aldermen Daniel H. Wells, William Marks, Orson Spencer, George W. Harris, Gustavus Hills, George A. Smith and Samuel Bennett, Associate Justices presiding.

Ex-parte   } Messrs. Styles and
Joseph Smith, Sen., } Rigdon, Counsel for
on *habeas corpus.* } Smith.

This case came before the court upon a return to a writ of *habeas corpus*, which was issued by this court on the 6th of May instant, upon the petition of Joseph Smith, Sen., as follows:

STATE OF ILLINOIS, } Sct.
CITY OF NAUVOO, }

To the Honorable Municipal Court and for the City of Nauvoo:

The undersigned, your petitioner, most respectfully represents that he is an inhabitant of said city. Your petitioner further represents that he is under arrest in said city, and is now in the custody of one John D. Parker, deputy sheriff of the county of Hancock, and state of

Illinois; and that the said Parker holds your petitioner by a writ of *Capias ad respondendum*, issued by the clerk of the Circuit Court of the county of Hancock and state of Illinois, at the instance of one Francis M. Higbee of said county, requiring your petitioner to answer the said Francis M. Higbee, "of a plea of the case;" damage, five thousand dollars. Your petitioner further represents that the proceedings against him are illegal; that the said warrant of arrest is informal, and not of that character which the law recognizes as valid; that the said writ is wanting and deficient in the plea therein contained; that the charge or complaint which your petitioner is therein required to answer is not known to the law.

Your petitioner further avers that the said writ does not disclose in any way or manner whatever any cause of action; which matter your petitioner most respectfully submits for your consideration, together with a copy of the said warrant of arrest which is hereunto attached.

Your petitioner further states that this proceeding has been instituted against him without any just or legal cause; and further that the said Francis M. Higbee is actuated by no other motive than a desire to persecute and harass your petitioner for the base purpose of gratifying feelings of revenge, which, without any cause, the said Francis M. Higbee has for a long time been fostering and cherishing.

Your petitioner further states that he is not guilty of the charge preferred against him, or of any act against him, by which the said Francis M. Higbee could have any charge, claim or demand whatever against your petitioner.

Your petitioner further states that he verily believes that another object the said F. M. Higbee had in instituting the proceeding was and is to throw your petitioner into the hands of his enemies, that he might the better carry out a conspiracy which has for some time been brewing against the life of your petitioner.

Your petitioner further states that the suit which has been instituted against him has been instituted through malice, private pique and corruption.

Your petitioner would therefore most respectfully ask your honorable body to grant him the benefit of the writ of *habeas corpus*, that the whole matter may be thoroughly investigated, and such order made as the law and justice demand in the premises: and your petitioner will ever pray.   JOSEPH SMITH, SEN.

Order of the Municipal Court.

STATE OF ILLINOIS, } Sct.   NAUVOO, May 6th, 1844.
CITY OF NAUVOO, }

The people of the State of Illinois, to the Marshal of said city, greeting:

Whereas application has been made before the Municipal Court of said city, that the body of one Joseph Smith, Senior, of the said city of Nauvoo, is in the custody of John D. Parker, deputy sheriff of Hancock county and state aforesaid.

These are therefore to command the said John D. Parker, of the county aforesaid, to safely have the body of said Joseph Smith, Senior, of the city aforesaid, in his custody detained, as it is said, together with the day and cause of his caption and detention, by whatsoever name the said Joseph Smith, Senior, may be known or called, before the Municipal Court of said city forthwith, to abide such order as the said court shall make in this behalf; and further, if the said John D. Parker, or other person or persons, having said Joseph Smith, Senior, of said city of Nauvoo, in custody, shall refuse or neglect to comply with the provisions of this writ, you, the marshal of said city, or other person authorized to serve the same, are hereby required to arrest the person or persons so refusing or neglecting to comply as aforesaid, and bring him or them, together with the person or persons in his or their custody, forthwith before the Municipal Court aforesaid, to be dealt with according to law; and herein fail not and bring this writ with you.

Witness, Willard Richards, clerk of the Municipal Court at Nauvoo, this 6th day of May, in the year of our Lord one thousand eight hundred and forty-four.

WILLARD RICHARDS,
Clerk M. C. C. N.

I hold the within-named Joseph Smith, Senior, under arrest, by virtue of a *capias ad respondendum.*

HANCOCK COUNTY COURT.
To May Term, A. D. 1844.

Francis M. Higbee ⎫
　　vs.　　⎬ In case.
Joseph Smith 　 ⎭

The day of his caption, May 6th, 1844.
To damage five thousand dollars.

WM. BACKENSTOS, S. H. C.
By J. D. PARKER, D. S.

STATE OF ILLINOIS, ⎫ ss
　HANCOCK COUNTY. ⎭

The people of the state of Illinois to the Sheriff of said county, greeting:

We command you that you take Joseph Smith, if to be found within your county, and him safely keep, so that you have his body before the Circuit Court of said county of Hancock on the first day of the next term thereof, to be holden at the Courthouse in Carthage on the third

Monday in the month of May instant, to answer Francis M. Higbee, of a plea of the case; damage, the sum of five thousand dollars, as he says; and you have then there this writ, and make due return thereon in what manner you execute the same.

Witness, J. B. Backenstos, clerk of said Circuit Court

[Seal]　　　at Carthage, this first day of May, in the year of our Lord, one thousand eight hundred and forty-four.

J. C. BACKENSTOS, Clerk.

By D. E. HEAD, Deputy.

This is a true copy of the original now in the possession of William B. Backenstos, Sheriff of Hancock county.

By J. D. PARKER, Deputy.

STATE OF ILLINOIS, ⎫
HANCOCK COUNTY, ⎬ Sct.
CITY OF NAUVOO. ⎭

To Mr. Francis M. Higbee:

SIR.—You will please to take notice that Joseph Smith, Senior, has petioned for a writ of *habeas corpus* from the Municipal Court of said city, praying that he may be liberated from the custody of John D. Parker, deputy sheriff of Hancock county, by whom he is held in custody on a *capias ad respondendum*, issued by the Circuit Court of Hancock county, on the first day of May instant, to answer Francis M. Higbee on a plea of the case, etc.; which writ is granted; and you will have the opportunity to appear before the Municipal Court at 10 o'clock a. m. on the 7th of May instant, at the Council Chamber in said city, and show cause why said Joseph Smith, Senior, should not be liberated on said *habeas corpus.*

[Seal]　　　Witness my hand and seal of court this 5th day of May, 1844.

WILLARD RICHARDS, CLERK M. C. C. N.

The case was argued at length by Messrs. George P. Styles and Sidney Rigdon. After which the court allowed the petitioner and his counsel to proceed with the case. Whereupon President Joseph Smith, Brigham Young, Sidney Rigdon, Hyrum Smith, Orrin Porter Rockwell, Cyrus H. Wheelock, Joel S. Miles, Henry G. Sherwood, Heber C. Kimball, were permitted to testify proving (1) the very bad and immoral character of Francis M. Higbee; and (2) the maliciousness of his prosecution of Joseph Smith. In the course of his testimony the Prophet said: "The only sin I ever committed was in exercising sympathy and covering up their [the Higbees', Fosters', Laws' and Dr. Bennett's] iniquities, on their solemn promise to reform, and of this I am ashamed, and will never do so again." After hearing these witnesses the Judge said: "It is considered and ordained by the court—

"1st. That the said Joseph Smith, Senior, be discharged from the said arrest and imprisonment complained of in said petition, on the illegality of the writ upon which he was arrested, as well as upon the writ of the case, and that he go hence without day.

"2nd. Francis M. Higbee's character having been so fully shown as infamous, the court is convinced that this suit was instituted through malice, private pique, and corruption, and ought not to be countenanced; and it is ordained by the court that the said Francis M. Higbee pay the costs."

　　　　　　　In testimony whereof I hereunto set my hand and affix
[Seal]　　the seal of said court at the city of Nauvoo, this 8th
　　　　　　　day of May, 1844.

WILLARD RICHARDS, Clerk.

1 copy the following from the *Neighbor* of this date:

Hurrah for the General! The following which we extract from the *St. Louis Organ*, shows how the public mind is turning, and what their feelings are in regard to the Prophet, his views and theirs also in regard to the Presidency.

Forebear awhile—we'll hear a little more. The matter is now settled with Messrs. Clay, Tyler and Van Buren. Let Mr. Clay return at once from his political perambulations in the South, Mr. Tyler abandon his hopes of re-election by aid of the "immediate annexation" of Texas, and let Mr. Van Buren be quiet at Kinderhook, that he may watch the operations of the "sober second thought" of the people!

General Joseph Smith, the acknowledged modern Prophet, has got them all in the rear; and from the common mode of testing the success of candidates for the Presidency, to wit., by steamboat elections, he (Smith) will beat all the other aspirants to that office two to one. We learn from the polls of the steamboat *Osprey*, on her last trip to this city, that the vote stood for General Joseph Smith, 20 gents and 5 ladies; Henry Clay, 16 gents and 4 ladies; Van Buren, 7 gents and 0 ladies.

Attended theatre in the evening.

CHAPTER XVII.

ADDRESS OF THE PROPHET—HIS PROPHETIC CALLING AND THE
RESURRECTION—STATUS OF AFFAIRS AT NAUVOO—HYDE'S
REPORTS FROM WASHINGTON ON THE WESTERN MOVEMENT
—OREGON.

Thursday, May 9, 1844.—A court-martial was held in my
office for the trial of Major-General Wilson Law, on a
charge of ungentlemanly and unofficer-like conduct. Present
—Generals Hyrum Smith, Charles C. Rich, Lyman Wight,
George Miller and Albert P. Rockwood; Cols. John Scott
and Hosea Stout; Judge-Advocate John Taylor; and Secretary Thomas Bullock.   The charge was sustained and
Wilson Law cashiered.

Theatricals in   Evening, attended theatre, and saw "Damon
Nauvoo.   and Pythias," and "The Idiot Witness" performed.

Elders Wilford Woodruff and George A. Smith called
upon me this morning, and said they were ready to start
on their mission to attend the conferences appointed
throughout the north of Illinois, Indiana and Michigan. I
blessed them in the name of the Lord, and told them to
go, and they should prosper and always prosper.   They
left in company with Elders Jedediah M. Grant and Ezra
Thayer.

Friday, 10—Rode out after breakfast to the prairie to
sell some land to some brethren.

The court-martial was held in the Mayor's office on the
charge against Robert D. Foster, Surgeon-General, for
unbecoming and unofficer-like conduct, &c.; Brigadier-
General George Miller presiding.   The charges were sustained.

A prospectus of the *Nauvoo Expositor* was distributed among the people by the apostates.

The jury of Lee county, Illinois, awarded $40 damages and the costs against Joseph H. Reynolds and Harmon T. Wilson for illegal imprisonment and abuse, which I suffered from them last June in that county.

Saturday, 11.—At 10 a. m. I attended City Council, and stayed till half-past eleven; but there not being a quorum, adjourned until next regular session. At 1 p. m. at my office, and had a conversation with Mr. Lyne on the theatre; and at 6 p. m. attended prayer meeting: John P. Greene and Sidney Rigdon present. Several showers of rain during the day. The Nauvoo Legion had a company muster.

Sunday, 12.—At 10 a. m. I preached at the Stand. The following brief synopsis of my discourse was reported by my clerk, Thomas Bullock:

President Joseph Smith's Address—Defense of his Prophetic Calling—
Resurrection of the Dead—Fullness of Ordinances
Necessary Both for the Living and Dead.

The Savior has the words of eternal life. Nothing else can profit us. There is no salvation in believing an evil report against our neighbor. I advise all to go on to perfection, and search deeper and deeper into the mysteries of Godliness. A man can do nothing for himself unless God direct him in the right way; and the priesthood is for that purpose.

The last time I spoke on this stand it was on the resurrection of the dead, when I promised to continue my remarks upon that subject. I still feel a desire to say something on this subject. Let us this very day begin anew, and now say, with all our hearts, we will forsake our sins and be righteous. I shall read the 24th chapter of Matthew, and give it a literal rendering and reading; and when it is rightly understood, it will be edifying. [He then read and translated it from the German].

I thought the very oddity of its rendering would be edifying anyhow —"*And it will preached be, the Gospel of the kingdom, in the whole world, to a witness over all people: and then will the end come.*" I will now read it in German [which he did, and many Germans who were present said he translated it correctly].

The Savior said when these tribulations should take place, it should be committed to a man who should be a witness over the whole world:

the keys of knowledge, power and revelations should be revealed to a witness who should hold the testimony to the world. It has always been my province to dig up hidden mysteries—new things—for my hearers. Just at the time when some men think that I have no right to the keys of the Priesthood—just at that time I have the greatest right. The Germans are an exalted people. The old German translators are the most correct—most honest of any of the translators; and therefore I get testimony to bear me out in the revelations that I have preached for the last fourteen years. The old German, Latin, Greek and Hebrew translations all say it is true: they cannot be impeached, and therefore I am in good company.

All the testimony is that the Lord in the last days would commit the keys of the priesthood to a witness over all people. Has the Gospel of the kingdom commenced in the last days? And will God take it from the man until He takes him Himself? I have read it precisely as the words flowed from the lips of Jesus Christ. John the Revelator saw an angel flying through the midst of heaven, having the everlasting Gospel to preach unto them that dwell on the earth.

The scripture is ready to be fulfilled when great wars, famines, pestilence, great distress, judgments, &c., are ready to be poured out on the inhabitants of the earth. John saw the angel having the holy priesthood, who should preach the everlasting Gospel to all nations. God had an angel—a special messenger—ordained and prepared for that purpose in the last days. Woe, woe be to that man or set of men who lift up their hands against God and His witness in these last days: for they shall deceive almost the very chosen ones!

My enemies say that I *have* been a true prophet. Why, I had rather be a fallen true prophet than a false prophet. When a man goes about prophesying, and commands men to obey his teachings, he must either be a true or false prophet. False prophets always arise to oppose the true prophets and they will prophesy so very near the truth that they will deceive almost the very chosen ones.

The doctrine of eternal judgments belongs to the first principles of the Gospel, in the last days. In relation to the kingdom of God, the devil always sets up his kingdom at the very same time in opposition to God. Every man who has a calling to minister to the inhabitants of the world was ordained to that very purpose in the Grand Council of heaven before this world was. I suppose that I was ordained to this very office in that Grand Council. It is the testimony that I want that I am God's servant, and this people His people. The ancient prophets declared that in the last days the God of heaven should set up a kingdom which should never be destroyed, nor left to other people; and the very time that was calculated on, this people were struggling to bring it out. He that arms himself with gun, sword, or pistol, except in the defense of truth, will sometime be sorry for it. I never carry any weapon with me bigger than my penknife. When I was dragged before the cannon and muskets in Missouri, I was unarmed. God will always protect me until my mission is fulfilled.

I calculate to be one of the instruments of setting up the kingdom of Daniel by the word of the Lord, and I intend to lay a foundation that will revolutionize the whole world. I once offered my life to the Missouri mob as a sacrifice for my people, and here I am. It will not be by sword or gun that this kingdom will roll on: the power of truth is such that all nations will be under the necessity of obeying the Gospel. The prediction is that army will be against army: it may be that the Saints will have to beat their ploughs into swords, for it will not do for men to sit down patiently and see their children destroyed.

My text is on the resurrection of the dead, which you will find in the 14th chapter of John—"In my Father's house are many mansions." It should be—"In my Father's kingdom are many kingdoms," in order that ye may be heirs of God and joint-heirs with me. I do not believe the Methodist doctrine of sending honest men and noble-minded men to hell, along with the murderer and the adulterer. They may hurl all their hell and fiery billows upon me, for they will roll off me as fast as they come on. But I have an order of things to save the poor fellows at any rate, and get them saved; for I will send men to preach to them in prison and save them if I can.

There are mansions for those who obey a celestial law, and there are other mansions for those who come short of the law, every man in his own order. There is baptism, &c., for those to exercise who are alive, and baptism for the dead who die without the knowledge of the Gospel.

I am going on in my progress for eternal life. It is not only necessary that you should be baptized for your dead, but you will have to go through all the ordinances for them, the same as you have gone through to save yourselves. There will be 144,000 saviors on Mount Zion, and with them an innumerable host that no man can number. Oh! I beseech you to go forward, go forward and make your calling and your election sure; and if any man preach any other Gospel than that which I have preached, he shall be cursed; and some of you who now hear me shall see it, and know that I testify the truth concerning them.

In regard to the law of the priesthood, there should be a place where all nations shall come up from time to time to receive their endowments; and the Lord has said this shall be the place for the baptisms for the dead. Every man that has been baptized and belongs to the kingdom has a right to be baptized for those who have gone before; and as soon as the law of the Gospel is obeyed here by their friends who act as proxy for them, the Lord has administrators there to set them free.

A man may act as proxy for his own relatives; the ordinances of the Gospel which were laid out before the foundations of the world have thus been fulfilled by them, and we may be baptized for those whom we have much friendship for; but it must first be revealed to the man of God, lest we should run too far. "As in Adam all die, even so in Christ shall all be made alive;" all shall be raised from the dead. The Lamb of God hath brought to pass the resurrection, so that all shall rise from the dead.

God Almighty Himself dwells in eternal fire; flesh and blood cannot go there, for all corruption is devoured by the fire. "Our God is a consuming fire." When our flesh is quickened by the Spirit, there will be no blood in this tabernacle. Some dwell in higher glory than others.

Those who have done wrong always have that wrong gnawing them. Immortality dwells in everlasting burnings. I will from time to time reveal to you the subjects that are revealed by the Holy Ghost to me. All the lies that are now hatched up against me are of the devil, and the influence of the devil and his servants will be used against the kingdom of God. The servants of God teach nothing but principles of eternal life, by their works ye shall know them. A good man will speak good things and holy principles, and an evil man evil things. I feel, in the name of the Lord, to rebuke all such bad principles, liars, &c., and I warn all of you to look out whom you are going after. I exhort you to give heed to all the virtue and the teachings which I have given you. All men who are immortal dwell in everlasting burnings. You cannot go anywhere but where God can find you out. All men are born to die, and all men must rise; all must enter eternity.

In order for you to receive your children to yourselves you must have a promise—some ordinance; some blessing, in order to ascend above principalities, or else it may be an angel. They must rise just as they died; we can there hail our lovely infants with the same glory—the same loveliness in the celestial glory, where they all enjoy alike. They differ in stature, in size, the same glorious spirit gives them the likeness of glory and bloom; the old man with his silvery hairs will glory in bloom and beauty. No man can describe it to you—no man can write it.

When did I ever teach anything wrong from this stand? When was I ever confounded? I want to triumph in Israel before I depart hence and am no more seen. I never told you I was perfect; but there is no error in the revelations which I have taught. Must I, then, be thrown away as a thing of naught?

I enjoin for your consideration—add to your faith virtue, love, &c. I say, in the name of the Lord, if these things are in you, you shall be fruitful. I testify that no man has power to reveal it but myself—things in heaven, in earth and hell; and all shut your mouths for the future. I commend you all to God, that you may inherit all things; and may God add His blessing. Amen.

My brother Hyrum and Elder Lyman Wight also addressed the Saints.

My brother Hyrum received an anonymous letter, supposed to have been written by Joseph H. Jackson, threatening his life, and calling upon him to make his peace with God for he would soon have to die.

At 3 p. m. I attended prayer meeting in the council room. William Smith and Almon W. Babbitt were present. The room was full and we all prayed for deliverance from our enemies and exaltation to such offices as will enable the servants of God to execute righteousness in the earth.

I copy the following from the *Times and Seasons:*

FOR THE NEIGHBOR.

Nauvoo and President Smith.

Before taking my farewell of your beautiful and growing city, I avail myself of a few leisure moments in expressing some of my views and conclusions of the "Prophet Joe" and the Mormons. In the first place, allow me to say that the Mormons, as a people, have been most woefully misrepresented and abused, and, in ninety-nine instances out of a hundred, by persons who know nothing of their principles and doctrines.

Before visiting the place, my mind was very much prejudiced against the Mormons, from reports which I had listened to in traveling through the different states; and I presume, if I had never taken occasion to inform myself of their religion and views, my mind would have remained in the same condition. There is not a city within my knowledge that can boast of a more enterprising and industrious people than Nauvoo. Her citizens are enlightened, and possess many advantages in the arts and sciences of the day, which other cities of longer standing cannot boast: in a word, Nauvoo bids fair to soon outrival any city in the West.

General Smith is a man who understands the political history of his country as well as the religious history of the world, as perfectly as any politician or religionist I have ever met with. He advances ideas which if carried into effect would greatly benefit the nation in point of commerce and finance; and while he maintains and philosophically shows that our country is approaching a fearful crisis, which, if not arrested, will end in disgrace to the country, and cause our national banner to hug its mast in disgust and shame, clearly points out the remedy.

Shall the liberty which our fathers purchased at so dear a price be wrenched from the hand of their children? Shall our national banner, which floated so proudly in the breeze at the Declaration of Independence, be disgraced and refuse to show its motto? Shall we, as American citizens, fold our arms and look quietly on, while the shackles of slavery are being fastened upon our hands, and while men only seek office for the purpose of exalting themselves into power? I say, shall we still rush blindly on and hasten on our own destruction by placing men in power who neither regard the interests of the people nor the prayers of the oppressed? Every American citizen will shout at the top of his voice—no!

Mr. Smith's "Views of the Powers and Policy of the Government" manifest a Republican spirit, and if carried out, would soon place the nation in a prosperous condition and brighten the prospects of those who now toil so incessantly to suppport the profligate expenditures and luxurious equipage of the present rulers and representatives of our nation.

Joseph Smith is a man who is in every way calculated to make a free people happy. He is liberal in his sentiments and allows every man the free expression of his feelings on all subjects; he is sociable and easy in his manners, is conversant and familiar on all exciting topics, expresses himself freely and plainly on the different methods of administering the Government, while he is not ashamed to let the world know his views and criticise upon his opinions.

I am, sir, in no way connected with the Mormon Church, but am disposed to listen to reason in all cases. I have heretofore been a warm advocate of the measures of the Whig party; but, considering General Smith's views and sentiments to be worthy the applause of every citizen of the United States, and especially the yeomanry of the country, I shall in every instance advocate his principles and use my utmost influence in his favor. I am, sir, yours in haste,

AN AMERICAN.

NAUVOO MANSION, May 12, 1844.

Monday 13.—Heavy thunder showers during the night. At 10 a. m. went to my office and conversed with several of the brethren. Sold Ellis M. Sanders one hundred acres of land, received $300 in cash, and his note for $1,000, and $20 for the Temple. Paid Sisson Chase $298 and took up a note of Young, Kimball & Taylor, given for money they had borrowed for me; and gave $10 to Heber C. Kimball.

At 2 p. m. attended meeting of the general council, at which the following letter from Orson Hyde was read:

Letter: Elder Orson Hyde's Report of Labors in Washington: President Smith's Memorial for Western Movement Before Congressmen.

WASHINGTON, April 25, 1844.

HONORED SIR:—I take the liberty to transmit through you to the council of our Church the result of my labors thus far. I arrived in this place on the 23rd instant, by way of Pittsburg, Philadelphia, and New Jersey.

I found Elder Orson Pratt here, Elder Page having been called home to Pittsburg on account of his wife's ill health. Elder Orson Pratt has been indefatigable in his exertions in prosecuting the business entrusted to his charge. His business has been before the Senate, and referred to the Committee on the Judiciary; and the report of said committee is not yet rendered, which is the cause of his delay in writing to you.

Yesterday we conversed with Messrs. Hoge, Hardin, Douglas and Wentworth; and last evening we spent several hours with the Hon. Mr. [James] Semple.* They all appear deeply interested in the Oregon question, and received us with every demonstration of respect that we could desire. Mr. Hoge thought the bill would not pass, from the fact that there already exists between England and America a treaty for the joint occupancy of Oregon, and that any act of our government authorizing an armed force to be raised, and destined for that country, would be regarded by England as an infraction of that treaty, and a cause of her commencing hostilities against us.

But my reply was, These volunteers are not to be considered any part or portion of the army of the United States, neither acting under the direction or authority of the United States; and, said I, for men to go there and settle in the character of emigrants cannot be regarded by our government as deviating in the least degree from her plighted faith, unless she intends to tamely submit to British monopoly in that country.

Mr. Hoge said he would present the memorial, if we desired it. I thanked him for his kind offer, but observed that I was not yet prepared for the bill to be submitted, but wished to elicit all the facts relative to the condition of Oregon, and also advise with many other members relative to the matter; and we could better determine then how the bill

* This was Illinois' senior Senator at the time.

should be introduced.   We do not want it presented and referred to a standing committee, and stuck away with five or ten cords of petitions, and that be the last of it; but we want the memorial read, a move made to suspend the rules of the House, and the bill printed, &c.

Mr. Wentworth said, "I am for Oregon, any how. You may set me down on your list, and I will go for you if you will go for Oregon."

Judge Douglas has been quite ill, but is just recovered; he will help all he can; Mr. Hardin likewise.   But Major Semple says that he does not believe anything will be done about Texas or Oregon this session, for it might have a very important effect upon the presidential election; and politicians are slow to move when such doubtful and important matters are likely to be effected by it.   He says that there are already two bills before the House for establishing a territorial government in Oregon, and to protect the emigrants there; and now, he says, "Were your bill to be introduced, it might be looked upon that you claimed the sole right of emigrating to and settling the new country to the exclusion of others.   He was in favor of the Oregon being settled, and he thought the bills already before the House would extend equal protection to us; and equal protection to every class of citizens was what the Government could rightly do, but particular privileges to any one class they could not rightly do."

I observed that the bill asks for no exclusive rights.   It asks not for exclusive rights in Oregon, neither do we wish it.   Other people might make a move to Oregon, and no prejudices bar their way, and their motives would not be misinterpreted.

But, said I, Missouri, knows her guilt; and should we attempt to march to Oregon without the government throwing a protective shield over us, Missouri's crimes would lead her first to misinterpret our intentions, to fan the flame of popular excitement against us, and scatter the firebrands of a misguided zeal among the combustible materials of other places, creating a flame too hot for us to encounter—too desolating for us to indulge the hope of successfully prosecuting the grand and benevolent enterprise we have conceived.*   We have been compelled to

---

*The reason for this reference to Missouri and of possible difficulty arising from the Saints going to Oregon without a guarantee of protection from the general government grew out of the fact that nearly all the early settlers of the Oregon territory were from Missouri.   Even in this month of May, 1844, Cornelius Gilliam, the inveterate enemy of the Saints, and who took so prominent a part in the troubles about Far West, was collecting a large company at Independence, Missouri, numbering over three hundred persons, to start for Oregon that season; and all along the Oregon route on the south side of the Platte river, the road was thronged during the next several years by emigrants, very many of whom, and for some time the most of whom, were from Missouri.   (*See Western Missouri Expositor*, May 18 1844.   Also Bancroft's *Oregon* Vol. I, page 449, *Passim*).

relinquish our rights in Missouri. We have been forcibly driven from our homes, leaving our property and inheritances as spoil to the oppressor; and more or less in Illinois we have been subject to the whims and chimeras of illiberal men, and to threats, to vexatious prosecutions and lawsuits.

Our government professes to have no power to help us, or to redress the wrongs which we have suffered; and we now ask the government to protect us while raising our volunteers. And when we get into Oregon we will protect ourselves and all others who wish our protection. And after subduing a new country, encountering all its difficulties and hardships, and sustaining the just claims of our nation to its soil, we believe that the generosity of our government towards us will be equal to our enterprise and patriotism; and that they will allow us a grant or territory of land, which will be both honorable to them and satisfactory to us.

This, he says, is all very just and reasonable. But still he thinks that Congress will take no step in relation to Oregon, from the fact that his resolution requesting the President of the United States to give notice to the British Government for the abolition of the treaty of joint occupation was voted down; and while that treaty is in force, our government dare do nothing in relation to that country. This resolution was introduced by Mr. Semple to pave the way for the passage of those bills in relation to a territorial government in Oregon.

All our members [Illinois delegation] join in the acknowledgment that you now have an undoubted right to go to Oregon with all the emigrants you can raise. They say the existing laws protect you as much as law can protect you; and should Congress pass an additional law, it would not prevent wicked men from shooting you down as they did in Missouri. All the Oregon men in Congress would be glad we would go to that country and settle it.

I will now give you my opinion in relation to this matter. It is made up from the spirit of the times in a hasty manner, nevertheless I think time will prove it to be correct:—That Congress will pass no act in relation to Texas or Oregon at present. She is afraid of England, afraid of Mexico, afraid the Presidential election will be twisted by it. The members all appear like unskillful players at checkers—afraid to move, for they see not which way to move advantageously. All are figuring and play round the grand and important questions. In the days of our Lord the people neglected the weightier matters of the law, but tithed mint, rue, anise and cummin; but I think here in Washington they do little else than tithe the *mint*.

A member of Congress is in no enviable situation; if he will boldly advocate true principles, he loses his influence and becomes unpopular;

and whoever is committed and has lost his influence has no power to benefit his constituents, so that all go to figuring and playing around the great points.

Mr. Semple said that Mr. Smith could not constitutionally be constituted a member of the army by law; and this, if nothing else, would prevent its passage. I observed that I would in that case strike out that clause. Perhaps I took an unwarrantable responsibility upon myself; but where I get into a straight place I can do no better than act according to what appears most correct.

I do not intend the opinion that I have hastily given shall abate my zeal to drive the matter through, but I have given the opinion for your benefit that your indulgence of the hope that Congress will do something for us may not cause you to delay any important action.

There is already a government established in Oregon to some extent; magistrates have been chosen by the people, &c. This is on the south of the Columbia. North of that river the Hudson Bay Company occupy. There is some good country in Oregon, but a great deal of sandy, barren desert. I have seen a gentleman who has been there, and also in California.

The most of the settlers in Oregon and Texas are our old enemies, the mobocrats of Missouri. If, however, the settlement of Oregon and Texas be determined upon, the sooner the move is made the better; and I would not advise any delay for the action of our government, for there is such jealousy of our rising power already, that government will do nothing to favor us. If the Saints possess the kingdom I think they will have to take it; and the sooner it is done the more easily it is accomplished.

Your superior wisdom must determine whether to go to Oregon, to Texas, or to remain within these United States, and send forth the most efficient men to build up churches, and let them remain the time being; and in the meantime send some wise men among the Indians, and teach them civilization and religion, to cultivate the soil, to live in peace with one another and with all men. But whatever you do, don't be deluded with the hope that government will foster us and thus delay an action for which the present perhaps is the most proper time that ever will be.

Oregon is becoming a popular question: the fever of emigration begins to rage. If the Mormons become the early majority, others will not come; if the Mormons do not become the early majority, the others will not allow us to come.

Elder Pratt is faithful, useful and true; he has got the run of matters here very well, and is with me in all my deliberations, visitings, &c.

Major Semple goes with us this evening to introduce us to the President and to view the White House.

My heart and hand are with you.　May heaven bless you and me. As ever, I am

ORSON HYDE.

To the Council of the Church of Jesus Christ of Latter-day Saints.

Also the following letter:

Letter: Orson Hyde's Second Letter from Washington Anent the Western Movement of the Church—the Probable Route.

WASHINGTON, April 26, 1844.

DEAR SIR:—Today I trouble you with another communication, which you will please have the goodness to lay before our council.

We were last evening introduced to the President at the White House by the politeness of Major Semple, where we spent an hour very agreeably. The President is a very plain, homespun, familiar, farmer-like man. He spoke of our troubles in Missouri, and regretted that we had met with such treatment. He asked us how we were getting along in Illinois. I told him that we were contending with the difficulties of a new country, and laboring under disadvantageous consequences of being driven from our property and homes in Missouri.

We have this day had a long conversation with Judge Douglas. He is ripe for Oregon and the California. He said he would resign his seat in Congress if he could command the force that Mr. Smith could, and would be on the march to the country in a month.

I learn that the eyes of many aspiring politicians in this place are upon that country, and that there is so much jealousy between them that they will probably pass no bill in relation to it. Now all these politicians rely upon the arm of the government to protect them there; and if government were to pass an act establishing a Territorial Government west of the Rocky Mountains there would be at once a tremendous rush of emigration; but if government pass no act in relation to it, these men have not stamina or sufficient confidence in themselves and their own resources to hazard the enterprise.

The Northern Whig members are almost to a man against Texas and Oregon; but should the present administration succeed in annexing Texas, then all the Whigs would turn around in favor of Oregon; for if Texas be admitted slavery is extended to the South; then free states must be added to the West to keep up a balance of power between the slave and the free states.

Should Texas be admitted, war with Mexico is looked upon as inevitable. The Senate have been in secret session on the ratification of the treaty of annexation; but what they did we cannot say. General Gaines who was boarding at the same house with Judge Douglas, was secretly

ordered to repair to the Texan frontier four days ago, and left immediately. I asked Judge Douglas if that did not speak loud for annexation. He says no. Santa Anna, being a jealous, hot-headed pate,
might be suspicious the treaty would be ratified by the Senate, and upon
mere suspicion might attempt some hostilities, and Gaines has been
ordered there to be on the alert and ready for action, if necessary.
Probably our navy will in a few days be mostly in the Guif of Mexico.

There are many powerful checks upon our government, preventing
her from moving in any of these important matters; and for aught I
know these checks are permitted to prevent our government from
extending her jurisdiction over the territory which God designs to give
to His Saints. Judge Douglas says he would equally as soon go to
that country without an act of Congress as with; "and that in five years
a noble state might be formed; and then if they would not receive us
into the Union, we would have a government of our own." He is decidedly of the opinion that Congress will pass no act in favor of any particular man going there; but he says if any man will go and desires that
privilege, and has confidence in his own ability to perform it, he already
has the right, and the sooner he is off the better for his scheme.

It is the opinion here among politicians that it will be extremely difficult to have any bill pass in relation to the encouragement of emigration
to Oregon; but much more difficult to get a bill passed designating any
particular man to go. But all concur in the opinion that we are authorized already.

In case of a removal to that country, Nauvoo is the place of general
rendezvous. Our course from thence would be westward through Iowa
bearing a little north until we came to the Missouri River, leaving the
state of Missouri on the left, thence onward, until we came
to the Platte, thence up the north fork of the Platte to the
mouth of the Sweetwater river in longitude 107 degree, 45 W.;
and thence up said Sweetwater river to the South Pass of the
Rocky Mountains, about eleven hundred miles from Nauvoo; and
from said South Pass, in latitude 42°28 north, to the Umpqua and Klamet
valleys in Oregon, bordering on California, is about six hundred miles,
making the distance from Nauvoo to the best portions of Oregon one
thousand seven hundred miles.

There is no government established there; and it is so near California
that when a government shall be estalished there, it may readily
embrace that country likewise. There is much barren country, rocks
and mountains in Oregon; but the valleys are very fertile. I am persuaded that Congress will pass no act in relation to that country, from
the fact that the resolution requesting the President to give notice to
the British Government for the discontinuance of the treaty of joint

occupation of Oregon was voted down with a rush; and this notice must be given before any action can be had unless Congress violates the treaty; at least so say the politicians here.

Judge Douglas has given me a map of Oregon, and also a report on an exploration of the country lying between the Missouri river and the Rocky Mountains on the line of the Kansas and great Platte rivers, by Lieut. J. C. Fremont, of the corps of Topographical Engineers. On receiving it I expressed a wish that Mr. Smith could see it. Judge Douglas says "It is a public document, and I will frank it to him." I accepted his offer, and the book will be forthcoming to you. The people are so eager for it here that they have even stolen it out of the library. The author is Mr. Benton's son-in-law.* Judge Douglas borrowed it of Mr. Benton. I was not to tell any one in this city where I got it. The book is a most valuable document to any one contemplating a journey to Oregon. The directions which I have given may not be exactly correct, but the book will tell correctly. Judge Douglas says he can direct Mr. Smith to several gentlemen in California who will be able to give him any information on the state of affairs in that country: and when he returns to Illinois, he will visit Mr. Smith.

Brother Pratt and myself drafted a bill this morning, and handed it into the committee on the judiciary from the Senate, asking an appropriation of two million dollars for the relief of the sufferers among our people in Missouri in 1836-9, to be deposited in the hands of the City Council of Nauvoo, and by them dealt out to the sufferers in proportion to their loss. We intend to tease them until we either provoke them or get them to do something for us. I have learned this much—that if we want Congress to do anything for us in drawing up our memorial, we must not ask what is right in the matter, but we must ask what kind of a thing will Congress pass? Will it suit the politics of the majority? Will it be popular or unpopular? For you might as well drive a musket ball through a cotton bag, or the Gospel of Christ through the heart of a priest, case-hardened by sectarianism, bigotry and superstition, or a camel through the eye of a needle, as to drive anything through Congress that will operate against the popularity of politicians.

I shall probably leave here in a few days, and Brother Pratt will remain. I go to get money to sustain ourselves with.

I shall write again soon, and let you know what restrictions, if any, are laid upon our citizens in relation to passing through the Indian Territories. I shall communicate everything I think will benefit. In the meantime, if the council have any instructions to give us, we shall be happy to receive them here or at Philadelphia.

John Ross is here; we intend to see him. It is uncertain when Con-

---

* This was John C. Fremont.

gress rises. It will be a long pull, in my opinion. As ever, I am, yours sincerely,

ORSON HYDE.

P. S.—Elder Pratt's best respects to the brethren.

Willard Richards was instructed to answer the above letters, and Elders Lyman Wight and Heber C. Kimball were instructed to carry the answers.

Council adjourned at 6 p. m.

The steamer *Maid of Iowa* returned from Rock River with four hundred bushels of corn, and two hundred bushels of wheat, which had been purchased for the Temple. At 8 p. m. I went on board with Dr. Willard Richards, and visited Captain Dan Jones.

I insert a lettter which I received from Henry Clay:

Letter: Henry Clay to the Prophet.

ASHLAND, November 15, 1843.

DEAR SIR.—I have received your letter in behalf of the Church of Jesus Christ of Latter-day Saints, stating that you understand that I am a candidate for the presidency, and inquiring what will be my rule of action relative to you as a people should I be elected.

I am profoundly grateful for the numerous and strong expressions of the people in my behalf as a candidate for president of the United States; but I do not so consider myself. That must depend upon future events and upon my sense of duty.

Should I be a candidate, I can enter into no engagements, make no promises, give no pledge to any particular portion of the people of the United States. If I ever enter into that high office I must go into it free and unfettered, with no guarantees but such as are to be drawn from my whole life, character and conduct.

It is not inconsistent with this declaration to say that I have viewed with lively interest the progress of the Latter-day Saints; that I have sympathized in their sufferings under injustice, as it appeared to me, which have been inflicted upon them; and I think, in common with other religious communities, they ought to enjoy the security and protection of the Constitution and the laws.

I am, with great respect, your friend and obedient servant,

H. CLAY.

To Joseph Smith, Esq.

The Prophet's Answer to Clay's Letter.

[Under the date of the Journal's entry here being followed, May 13,

1844, President Smith sent a reply to the above eminent statesman's letter, taking him severely to task for his evident desire to be non-committal with reference to the problem presented by the wrongs which had been inflicted upon the Latter-day Saints by Missouri. Vexed by remembrance of the cruelty and injustice endured by the Saints in Missouri and the general indifference to their suffering among public men, the letter was written in a caustic and, at times, vehement vein.]

I instructed Thomas Bullock to take charge of the books of the *Maid of Iowa* and go on board as clerk.

Tuesday, 14.—Rode out about 7 a. m. The *Maid of Iowa* started for St. Louis at 8:30 a. m.

This afternoon, Mr. Reid, my old lawyer* gave a lecture on the stand, relating the history of some of my first persecutions. I spoke after he closed, and continued my history to the present time, relating some of the doings of the apostates in Nauvoo.

At 4 p. m. prayer meeting; few present. Prayed for Elder Woodworth's daughter, who was sick. Elder Lyman Wight was present.

Wednesday, 15.—At home; much rain through the day; river rising rapidly. Mr. Adams, son of John Quincy Adams, with Dr. Goforth, called to see me at the Mansion.

At 5 p. m. went to my office, and heard my letter to Mr. Clay read. At 7 p. m. rode to the upper landing with Mr. Adams.

I insert the following from the *Times and Seasons:*

STATUS OF AFFAIRS AT NAUVOO.

We take pleasure in announcing to the Saints abroad that Nauvoo continues to flourish, and the little one has become a thousand. Quite a number of splendid houses are being erected, and the Temple is rapidly progressing, insomuch that there is one universal expectation that before next winter closes in upon us the cap-stone will have been raised and the building enclosed.

The Saints continue to flock together from all parts of the widespread continent and from the islands of the sea. Three ship's com-

* For the part taken by Mr. Reid in defending the Prophet in those early experiences, see this HISTORY Vol. I, pp. 89-96 and *note* p. 94 *et seq.*

panies have arrived this spring from England, and are now rejoicing in the truths of the everlasting Gospel.

The Prophet is in good health and spirits, and unwearied in his anxiety and labors to instruct the Saints in the things of God and the mysteries of the Kingdom of Jesus Christ. Indeed we may truly say that those who come to scoff remain to pray.

Many have come here filled with prejudice and strange anticipations, but have been convinced that report with her thousand tongues is false, and have almost invariably left a testimony behind them. Instead of finding Mr. Smith the cunning, crafty, and illiterate character that he had been represented to be, they have found in him the gentleman and scholar—open, generous, and brave.

But it is his immediate connections and associates alone that can appreciate his virtues and his talents. While his face is set as a flint against iniquity from every quarter, the cries of the oppressed ever reach his heart, and his hand is ever ready to alleviate the sufferings of the needy.

A few heartless villains can always be found who are watching for his downfall or death; but the Lord has generally caused them to fall into their own pit, and no weapon formed against him has prospered. One or two disaffected individuals have made an attempt to spread dissension; but it is like a tale that is nearly told, and will soon be forgotten.

It was first represented as a monster calculated to spread desolation around; but we are credibly informed by a person who attended their first meeting, that there was much difficulty in raising a committee of seven, for there was some objection to Father——; but as none could be found to fill the vacuum, he constituted one of the seven *stars!*

It will be unneccessary for us to say much about those luminaries of the last days, as they shine forth in their true colors in our columns this week in the trial of President Smith. But to say anything by way of warning to the brethren abroad would resemble the "ocean into tempest tossed, to waft a feather or drown a fly." "By their fruits ye shall know them. Do men gather grapes of thorns or figs of thistles?"

The glad tidings of salvation and the fullness of the Gospel are fast spreading from city to city and from nation to nation. The little stone will still increase till the knowledge of God covers the earth and righteousness and truth extend from pole to pole.

I copy from the *Neighbor*:

WITHDRAWAL OF WILLIAM SMITH AS CANDIDATE FOR THE LEGISLATURE.

To the Friends and Voters of Hancock County: Elder William Smith (late representative) wishes to say to the friends and voters of Hancock county, that in consequence of the sickness of his family, now in the hands of a doctor in the city of Philadelphia, he relinquishes the idea of offering himself as a candidate for a seat in the next Legislature of Illinois; but, as a matter of the highest consideration, would recommend his brother Hyrum Smith as a suitable and capable person to fill that office and worthy of the people's confidence and votes.

We know of no person that would be more qualified to fill his station than General Hyrum Smith (his, William's, brother). We are not informed whether the General will accept of the office or not. If he will, we don't know of any gentleman in Hancock county who would be more competent. General Smith is a man of sterling integrity, deep penetration and brilliant talents. He is well versed in politics and as unchangeable as the everlasting hills. He is a man of probity and virtue, and an unwavering patriot.

If General Hyrum Smith will allow his name to be brought forth, we go it for him; and we know from the confidence and respect that are entertained for him as a gentleman and a patriot, he will be elected. What say you, General?

Thursday, 16.—Went to my office at 8 a. m., and heard a letter written by Elder Willard Richards, in behalf of the council to Elders Orson Hyde and Orson Pratt at Washington.

I ordered the Municipal Court to meet at one p. m. and spent the morning in reading.

Session of Municipal Court—Case of Jeremiah Smith.

At one p, m. I presided in Municipal Court. The case of Jeremiah Smith, Sen., who had been arrested by Jones on the charge of procuring money under false pretenses, came up on *habeas corpus*. The complainant, T. B. Johnson, by his counsel, Chauncey L. Higbee, asked for and obtained an adjournment for one week in order to procure witnesses. The petitioner by his counsel, George P. Stiles, objected to the plea, supposing the prosecuting party always ready for a trial. The court decided that it was an important case, and it was not best to be in haste; and if the prisoner is discharged on the merits of the case after a full investigation, he goes free forever. The majority of the court decided to adjourn until Thursday next.

I was about home the rest of the day and read in the

Neighbor the report of the trial in the Municipal Court on the 8th inst.

The following appears in the *Times and Seasons:*

LETTER: WILLIAM CLAYTON DESCRIBING THE FARCICAL PROCEEDINGS OF THE COURT AT DIXON IN THE CASE OF JOSEPH SMITH VS. JOSEPH H. REYNOLDS OF MISSOURI AND HARMON T. WILSON.

DEAR SIR.—I have just returned from the north part of this state, where I have been on business for our beloved President Joseph Smith; and it feels so good to breathe the pure air of liberty and friendship after spending some three or four days in a swamp, or rather a slough of religious prejudice and political hypocrisy, which are equally nauseous and offensive, that I cannot let this opportunity pass without giving vent to some of my feelings in regard to what passed while I remained at Dixon, on Rock River.

My principle business was to appear in the Lee county Circuit Court as a witness in the case of Joseph Smith, *vs.* Joseph H. Reynolds and Harmon T. Wilson, for false imprisonment and using unnecessary force and violence in arresting the plaintiff.

A plea had been entered in this suit by this counsel for the defendants, to which the counsel for the plaintiff demurred. The demurrer was argued on Wednesday morning, the 8th inst., and the parties finally joined issue on the charge of using unnecssary force and violence; and the court gave permission, by consent of the bar, to proceed with the trial, but the counsel not being fully prepared, it was laid over until the following morning, the 9th inst.

On Thursday morning, after the usual preliminaries of opening court, the above case was called up for trial, and the clerk ordered to impanel a jury; and here, sir, a scene took place which ought to make every honest American citizen blush and weep for the credit and honor of his country and laws. A number of men were called up, and when questioned as to whether they had previously expressed opinions in relation to the suit now pending, nearly the whole answered in the affirmative. The further question was then put as to whether they had any prejudice against either of the parties; to which a great majority replied they had against Smith. They were then questioned as to what their prejudice had reference—his religious sentiments, or general course of conduct. The greater part replied, to his religious sentiments; and the remainder said they were opposed to his general course of conduct.

About twenty men had to be called upon, one after another, out of the number the court finally selected twelve as competent jurors though the majority of these decidedly expressed their feelings of prejudice against the plaintiff. They were, however, accepted on the ground that they said they thought they could do justice to both parties, although some of them expressed a doubt whether they could do justice or not.

The jury being sworn, the court, or rather the counsel, proceeded to examine the witnesses on the part of the plaintiff, which occupied nearly the whole day. But little of the real matter of fact could be set before the court on account of their being confined to the charge of unnecesary force and violence; but this was proven in the clearest point of light.

I must refer to the testimony of old Mr. Dixon, whose silvery locks seem to tell an age of many years. His evidence related to the circumstance of the Missouri sheriff refusing for a length of time to give the plaintiff the privilege of *habeas corpus*, and threatening to drag him to Missouri in fifteen minutes from the time they arrived at Dixon. The old gentleman seemed to tremble with indignation while relating the simple facts as they transpired at the time; and, like a true lover of his country, appeared proud of the privilege of telling those men that the citizens of Dixon would not suffer themselves to be disgraced by permitting them to drag away a citizen of this state to a foreign state for trial, without the privilege of a trial by *habeas corpus*—a privilege which is guaranteed to every individual under like circumstances, and especially when it was understood that he was to be dragged to Missouri, amongst a people whose hands are yet dripping with the blood of murdered innocence, and who thirst for the blood of General Joseph Smith as the howling wolf thirsts for his prey. Surely such a picture would melt the heart of anything but an adamantine. There are those, and men too who profess to be the followers of the Lord Jesus Christ, who can bear such things and still wish the Missourians had got General Smith to Missouri to murder him without judge or jury, and surely they are no better than murderers themselves, and only lack the opportunity to make them shedders of innocent blood.

After the evidence was through on the part of the plaintiff, the witness for the defense was examined, which only occupied a few minutes. The arguments were then advanced on both sides, during which time I could not help noticing how apt the respectable gentleman of the opposite counsel was to sing the song of "old Joe Smith," &c., which might appear very gentlemanly in his mind, but to me it seemed as contemptible as the voice of a stupid ass, or the tongue of slander.

Finally the case was submitted to the jury, who were charged by the court, and then ordered to retire and bring in a sealed verdict the following morning at nine o'clock. Friday morning came and with it the verdict, and it proved to be in favor of the plaintiff and against the detendants for forty dollars and costs of suit. I confess I was astonished when I heard it, and could not help thinking that prejudice sometimes overrules justice even in the jury box. I could not help comparing the results of this trial with one which came off the day previous, wherein a certain person complained of another for destroying his cow by setting his dogs on the animal until they worried her. It appeared the cow of the plaintiff had seen fit to break into the defendant's lot without asking leave, and the defendant, or rather his men, not liking such treatment, set the dogs on her and destroyed her. Well, the result of this trial was a verdict of damages for the plaintiff of thirty dollars and costs!

Now, sir, compare the two cases. On the one hand here is a citizen of the United States near two hundred miles from his home and his friends; he is on a visit with his family, not dreaming of danger or difficulty. Two men—or rather wolves in sheep's clothing—for it is a fact that when Wilson and Reynolds made inquiry for General Smith at Dixon at the time of the arrest, they said they were "Mormon Elders," and wanted to see President Smith, &c.—two men, I say, while he is thus enjoying himself with his family, came upon him with each a loaded pistol in his hand, and threatened to shoot him dead if he offered the least resistance, although no resistance had been offered. They then began to haul him about; and when he asked them what they wanted with him, and what was their authority, they replied they were going to take him to Missouri; and jamming their pistols at his side, swore that was their authority. He requested them to let him go into the house to bid his family good-by; but this they positively refused, not even giving him the privilege to get his hat. They then forced him into the wagon and placing themselves one on each side, with a loaded pistol pressed close against his side, and repeatedly striking him with them, so as to make him lame and sore for two weeks afterwards, they drove him to Dixon, and ordered horses ready in fifteen minutes to drag him among his murderers, and otherwise abused, insulted, threatened, and treated him in the cruelest manner possible, filling his family with the most excruciating pangs, and rending the heart of his beloved companion with grief to witness their ferocious cruelty, not knowing but his life would be sacrificed before morning; and finally pursued their persecutions until it cost him from $3,500 to $5,000 expenses; and all this without a cause; and when he sues for justice against these men, he obtains damages to the amount of forty dollars!

On the other hand, a man loses a cow which had broke into his neighbor's lot, and he obtained damages to the amount of thirty dollars.

Now, sir, if this is not the effects of prejudice amounting to oppression, then I am no judge of right and wrong. I am very much inclined to think that if General Joseph Smith or any of his friends had treated any citizen of this state or any other state in the manner he was treated by these men, and they had sued for damages as he did, the case would have terminated very differently. However, so it is.

The idea of a man yielding to such a degree of prejudice as to render him incapable of executing justice between man and man, merely from rumor and report, is to me perfectly ridiculous and contemptible, as well as wicked and unjust. And when a man is all the day long boasting of the rights and privileges guaranteed to every citizen of the United States under the Constitution and laws, and at the same time is so prejudiced against one of the most peaceable citizens that he does not know whether he can render him justice in a court of equity, but would rather strengthen the hands of mobocrats and law-breakers, the inference that one must naturally draw is that such a man is a consummate scoundrel and hypocrite, or that he is guilty of the most flagrant violation of the most sacred constitutional principles embraced in the fundamental doctrines of this republic. I am happy, sir, to have evidence daily that no such corrupt prejudice exists in the heart of General Joseph Smith, nor in the community, so far as I have been able to discover.

Now, as to the exceptions these men have taken in regard to General Smith's religious views or general course of conduct, it matters not much. His religious views are his inalienable right, and are nobody's business; and the man who cannot render him justice on that account is a wilful violator of the laws he professes to admire; and, sir, I have for more than two years last past been a close observer of General Smith's general course of conduct, as well as his private life; and justice to him, to myself, and the community at large, compels me to say that, in all my intercourse with men, I never associated with a more honorable, upright, charitable, benevolent, and law-abiding man than is the much persecuted General Smith; and, sir, when I hear men speak reproachfully of him, I never ask for a second evidence of their corruptness and baseness. General Smith, sir, is a man of God, a man of truth, and a lover of his country; and never did I hear him breathe out curses or raillery at any man because he saw fit to differ in religious matters. Shame on the principle—shame on the man or set of men who show themselves so degraded and miserably corrupt.

The last night of our stay at Dixon, I had the privilege of speaking on the principles of my religion to a number of individuals in a kind of argument with two men; and, sir, although it is near some four years since I have made a practice of preaching, it felt as sweet as ever. Truth to an honest heart is sweet, but to a wicked man is like a piercing sword, as was manifest on that occasion; for although the principles of the Gospel were laid down so plain and clear that it was impossible to misunderstand, yet the opposing party repeatedly misconstrued my language, and even his own admission.

I cannot persuade myself that the prejudice referred to above is a general thing. There are many honorable exceptions, and I presume if the Mormons had signified their intentions of supporting the Democratic candidate for the presidency at the ensuing election, instead of nominating an independent candidate of their own choice, their prejudice would not have been so great at the trial of Reynolds and Wilson, and perhaps General Smith would have obtained a judgment somewhat equivalent to the injuries he sustained from that unholy prosecution. But the Mormon people are too noble-minded to be bought or biased by fear or favor, and have been too often deceived by the plausible pretensions of demagogues to put trust in any but tried friends. General Smith has ever been an undeviating friend, not only to this community, but to the oppressed of every name or society, and we consider him as competent and qualified for the highest office of the United States as any other man, and a little more so; and a great deal more worthy of it.

In conclusion, let me say that whatever others may say, I consider it an honor to be associated with such a man as General Joseph Smith, and all true followers of the Lord Jesus Christ; and the more wicked men despise and misrepresent the principles and conduct of President Smith, the more I love him and delight in his society; and this I can do without prejudice or animosity against any man or set of men. I believe in the broad principle of equal rights and privileges, so far as religion or politics are concerned; and while I seek to enjoy my religion according to the knowledge in me, I will interfere with the rights of no man, nor persecute because my neighbor does not think as I do.

A multitude of business compels me to close, and I must forbear. I have the honor to be your brother in the everlasting covenant.

WILLIAM CLAYTON.

Nauvoo, May 16, 1844.

From the *Neighbor:*—

STEAMBOAT ELECTION.

On the last upward voyage of the *Osprey* from St. Louis to this place as usual, the merits of the several candidates for the next Presidential election were discussed. A vote was taken, and the following was the state of the polls as handed to us by a gentleman who came as passenger:—

General Joseph Smith, 26 gentlemen, 3 ladies.

Henry Clay, 6 gentlemen, 2 ladies.

Van Buren, 2 gentlemen, 0 ladies.

The ladies are altogether forsaking Van Buren, and the gentlemen as a matter of course are following after. There is a wonderful shrinkage in Henry Clay, but the General is going it with a rush. *Hurrah for the General!*

CHAPTER XVIII.

Friday, May 17, 1844.—The State Convention met in the assembly room. I copy the minutes.

State Convention at Nauvoo.

Convention met according to appointment, and was organized by appointing General Uriah Brown to the chair, and Dr. F. Merryweather secretary.

Dr. G. W. Goforth presented the following letter, and took his seat in the convention. Several letters of the same character were presented by other gentlemen, but we have not room to insert them.

MUSCOUTAH, ST. CLAIR COUNTY, ILL., May 4th, 1844.

Mr. G. W. Goforth:

Sir,—At various meetings held in this county, where I had the honor of attending, and the interesting topic of the selection of a suitable person for the high station of President of the United States being at this time the most important to Americans, and with the names that are now before the people, Joseph Smith of Nauvoo is recognized respectfully as a candidate, declarative in the principles of Jeffersonianism, or Jefferson democracy, free trade, and sailor's rights, and the protection of person and property.

A convention being about to be held in the City of Nauvoo on the 17th of this month (May), your name has been on every occasion given as a delegate to said convention, and through me the message to be imparted you, asking you to represent our expressions in the case.

Please say for us, as Americans, that we will support General Joseph Smith in preference to any other man that has given, or suffered his name to come before us as a candidate. And at the great Baltimore Convention, to be held on the 13th of July, our delegation to said convention be authorized to proclaim for us submission to the nominee as may be by them brought before the people, in case of a failure to nominate Joseph Smith (our choice), and unite approbatively for his support.

Respectfully, sir, this communication and authority usward is forwarded you as your voucher at said convention, with our hearty prayers for the success of him whose special name is given in the important affairs.   HENRY B. JACOBS,

Agent for the friends of General Joseph Smith.

Mr. Clay's letter to General Joseph Smith was then read by Mr. Phelps, and also General Joseph Smith's rejoinder, which was applauded by three cheers.

It was moved and seconded that the following gentlemen be appointed a committee to draft resolutions for the adoption of this convention:—

Dr. G. W. Goforth, John Taylor, Wm. W. Phelps, William Smith, and Lucian R. Foster.

It was moved and seconded that he correspondence of the Central Committee for Government Reform of New York be read by W. W. Phelps, also General Joseph Smith's answer to the same.

NEW YORK, April 20, 1844.

Joseph Smith, Esq.,

SIR,—The subscribers, the Central Committee of the National Reform Association, in accordance with a duty prescribed by their constitution, respectively solicit an expression of your views as a candidate for public office, on a subject that, as they think, vitally affects the rights and interests of their constituents.

We see this singular condition of affairs, and while wealth in our country is rapidly accumulating, while internal improvements of every description are fast increasing, and while machinery has multiplied the power of production to an immense extent, yet with all these national advantages, the compensation for useful labor is getting less and less.

We seek the cause of this anomaly, and we trace it to the monopoly of the land, which places labor at the mercy of capital. We therefore desire to abolish the monopoly, not by interfering with the conventional rights of persons now in possession of the land, but by arresting the further sale of all lands not yet appropriated as private property, and by allowing these lands hereafter to be freely occupied by those who may choose to settle on them.

We propose that the public lands hereafter shall not be owned, but occupied only, the occupant having the right to sell or otherwise dispose of improvements to any one not in possession of other land; so that, by preventing any individual from becoming possessed of more than a limited quantity, every one may enjoy the right.

This measure, we think, would gradually establish an equilibrium between the agricultural and other useful occupations, that would ensure to all full employment and fair compensation for their labor, on the lands now held as private property, and to each individual on the public lands the right to work for himself on his own premises, or for another, at his option.

An answer, as soon as convenient, will much oblige your fellow-citizens.

JOHN WINDT,
EGBERT S. MANNING,
JAMES MAXWELL,
LEWIS MASQUERIER,
DANIEL WITTER,
GEORE H. EVANS.
ELLIS SMALLEY.

NAUVOO, ILL., May 16th, 1844.

To John Windt, Egbert S. Manning, James Maxwell, Lewis Masquerier, Daniel Witter, George H. Evans, and Ellis Smalley, Esqrs.

GENTLEMEN:—

Your communication of April 20th, soliciting my views relative to the public lands, is before me; and I answer, that as soon as the greater national evils could be remedied by the consolidated efforts of a virtuous people and the judicious legislation of wise men, so that slavery could not occupy one-half of the United States for speculation, competition, prodigality, and fleshy capital, and so that enormous salaries, stipends, fees, perquisites, patronage, and the wages of spiritual wickedness in ermine and lace could not swallow up forty or fifty millions of public revenue, I would use all honorable means to bring the wages of mechanics and farmers up, and salaries of public servants down, increase labor and money by a judicious tariff, and advise the people—who are only the sovereigns of the soil—to petition Congress to pass a uniform land law! that the air, the water, and the land, of the asylum of the oppressed, might be free to free men!

With consideration of the highest regard for unadulterated freedom I have the honor to be your obedient servant.

JOSEPH SMITH.

After which, the meeting adjourned for one hour.

It was moved and seconded that the following gentlemen be constituted a committee to appoint electors for this State:—

Dr. G. W. Goforth, L. Robinson, L. N. Scoville, Peter Hawes, and John S. Reid.

It was moved and seconded that the following gentlemen be constituted a central committee of correspondence, having power to increase their number:—

Dr. Willard Richards, Dr. J. M. Bernhisel, W. W. Phelps, and Luciar R. Foster.

The following delegates from the different states of the Union were then received by vote:—

NAMES.	COUNTIES.	STATES.
Dr. G. W. Goforth	St. Clair	Illinois
Meyers, Esq.,	Adams	"
J. Sene,	Quincy	"
A. Badlock,	Joe Davis,	"
J. C. Wright,	Scott,	"
L. Wight,	Crawford,	"
S. Brown,	Brown,	"
W. B. Idle,	Sangamon,	"
J. Browning,	Adams,	"
W. W Phelps,	Hancock,	"
W. Green,	"	"
Ebenezer Robinson,	"	"
Johh Taylor,	'	"
Henry G. Sherwood,	"	"
F. Merryweather,	"	"
John S. Reid, Esq.,	Chemung	New York.
E. Reece, Esq.,	Buffalo,	"
L. R. Foster,	New York City,	"
Dr. J. M. Bernhisel,	"	"
Hugh Herinshaw,	West Chester,	"
E. Thompson,	"	"
S. A. Perry,	Essex,	"
Wm. Miller,	Livingston,	"
Mr. Dorlan,	Kings,	"
E. Swakhammer,	New York City,	"
P. Bowen,	Chester,	Pennsylvania·
W. Smith,	Philadelphia,	"
J. H. Newton,	"	"
Edward Hunter,	West Chester,	"
E. Woolley,	Columbiana.	Ohio
W. G. Ware,	Cincinnati,	"
Thos. Martin,	Hamilton,	"
C. Brooks,	Lake,	"
Dusten Arne,	"	"
W. W. Dryer,	Lorain,	"
M. J. Coltrin,	Cuyahoga,	"
W. Vanausdell,	Green Briar,	Virginia.
L. B. Lewis,		Massachusetts

Dr. Willard Richards,	Berkshire,	Massachusetts.
E. Dougherty,	Essex,	New Jersey.
W. Richardson,	Burlington,	"
J. Horner,	Monmouth,	"
Thomas Atkins,	Burlington,	"
Capt. R. Jones,	New Orleans,	Louisiana.
E. Ludington,	"	"
J. Harman	Monroe,	Mississippi.
Mr. Palman,	"	"
S. Gully,	Lawrence,	"
E. M. Sanders,	"	Delaware·
E. F. Sheets,	"	"
J. Hatch,	Alice,	Vermont.
J. Houston,	Madison,	"
J. A. Mikesell,	"	Missouri.
Col. Cowan,	Oxford,	Maine.
M. Anderson,	Rutherford,	Tennessee.
H. Stout,	Mercer,	Kentucky.
Gen. G. Miller,	Madison,	"
Mr. Hunt,	Switzerland,	Indiana.
A. Johnson,	Middletown,	Connecticut.
L. N. Scovil,		Maryland.
Dr. L. Richards,	Providence,	Rhode Island.
M. Wilber,		"
J. S. Swiss,		New Hampshire.
Dr. Shenask,		Michigan.
Abraham Williams,		Georgia.
J. Haws,		Alabama.
R. Alexander,	Union District,	South Carolina.
Y. Maccauslin,	Randolph,	North Carolina.
D. J. Putton,		Iowa.
Capt. Hathaway,*		Arkansas.

It was moved, seconded, and carried by acclamation. that General Joseph Smith, of Illinois, be the choice of this convention for President of the United States.

It was moved, seconded, and carried by acclamation, that Sidney Rigdon, Esq., of Pennsylvania, be the choice of the Convention for Vice-President of the United States.

The nine following resolutions were then adopted, the fifth of which was carried by acclamation.

Resolutions.

1. *Resolved*, that from all the facts and appearances that are now

* It is to be observed that these delegates named from the various States were now, and for some time past had been, residents of Nauvoo, Ill.

visible in the United States, we believe that much imbecility and fraud is practiced by the officers of Government; and that to remedy these evils it is highly necessary that a virtuous people should arise in the panoply of their might, and with one heart and one mind correct these abuses by electing wise and honorable men to fill the various offices of Government.

2. *Resolved*, that as union is power, the permanency and continuance of our political institutions depend upon the correction of the abuses.

3. *Resolved*, that as all political parties of the present day have degraded themselves by adhering more or less to corrupt principles and practices, by fomenting discord and division among the people, being swallowed in the vortex of party spirit and sectional prejudices, until they have become insensible to the welfare of the people and the general good of the country; and knowing that there are good men among all parties, in whose bosoms burn the fire of pure patriotism, we invite them, by the love of liberty, by the sacred honor of freemen, by the patriotism of the illustrious fathers of our freedom, by the glorious love of country, and by the holy principles of '76, to come over and help us to reform the Government.

4. *Resolved*, that to redress all wrongs, the government of the United States, with the President at its head, is as powerful in its sphere as Jehovah is in His.

5. *Resolved*, that the better to carry out the principles of liberty and equal rights, Jeffersonian democracy, free trade, and sailor's rights, and the protection of person and property, we will support General Joseph Smith, of Illinois, for the President of the United States at the ensuing election.

6. *Resolved*, that we will support Sidney Rigdon, Esq., of Pennsylvania, for the Vice-Presidency.

7. *Resolved*, that we will hold a National Convention at Baltimore on Saturday, the 13th day of July.

8. *Resolved*, that we call upon the honest men of all parties in each state to send their delegates to said convention.

9. *Resolved*, that all honest editors throughout the United States are requested to publish the above resolutions.

10. *Resolved*, that those gentlemen who stand at the head of the list, who have gone to the several states to take charge of our political interests, be requested to use every exertion to appoint electors in the several electoral districts of the States which they represent, and also to send delegates to the Baltimore Convention.

11. *Resolved*, that Dr. Goforth and John S. Reid, Esq., be requested to furnish a copy of their speeches for publication.

12. *Resolved*, that the electors be instructed to make stump speeches in their different districts.

13. *Resolved*, that the thanks of this meeting be given to Mr. Hancock for his patriotic song.

It was moved and seconded that Orson Hyde, Heber C. Kimball, David S. Hollister, Orson Pratt, and Lyman Wight represent this convention at the convention to be held in Baltimore on the 13th of July next.

Sidney Rigdon, Esq., then addressed the meeting, and was succeeded by the following gentlemen:—Gen. Joseph Smith, Dr. G. W. Goforth, Lyman Wight, W. W. Phelps, John Taylor, Hyrum Smith, and John S. Reid, Esq.

It was moved, seconded, and carried, that the thanks of this meeting be given to the chairman and secretary.

The Convention was addressed in an eloquent speech by Sidney Rigdon, Esq., showing the political dishonesty of both Henry Clay and Martin VanBuren, and stating his views, and the present condition of the country.

Dr. Goforth rose and addressed the convention. [Dr. Goforth dealt chiefly with the past glories of the republic, and the wrongs suffered by the Latter-day Saints in Missouri].

*Synopsis of the Remarks of Hon. John S. Reid.**

Mr. Chairman:

I cannot leave this subject and do justice to my own feelings and the character of Gen. Smith, without giving a short history of the first persecution that came upon him in the counties of Chenango and Broome, in the State of New York, commenced by that class of people calling themselves Christians.

The first acquaintance I had with Gen. Smith was about the year 1823. He came into my neighborhood, being then about eighteen years of age, and resided there two years; during which time I became intimately acquainted with him. I do know that his character was irreproachable; that he was well known for truth and uprightness; that he moved in the first circles of the community, and he was often spoken of as a young man of intelligence and good morals, and possessing a mind susceptible of the highest intellectual attainments.

I early discovered that his mind was constantly in search of truth, expressing an anxious desire to know the will of God concerning His children here below, often speaking of those things which professed Christians believe in. I have often observed to my best informed friends

---

* This was the "former lawyer" who defended the Prophet in his first prosecution in the State of New York, before local justices of the peace in Chenango and Broome counties, 1830; see this HISTORY, vol. I, ch. XX.

(those that were free from superstition and bigotry) that I thought Joseph was predestinated by his God from all eternity to be an instrument in the hands of the great Dispenser of all good to do a great work. What it was I knew not. After living in that neighborhood about three years, enjoying the good feelings of his acquaintance as a worthy youth, he told his particular friends that he had had a revelation from God to go to the west about eighty miles to his father's, in which neighborhood he should find hid in the earth an old history written on golden plates, which would give great light and knowledge concerning the will of God towards His people in this generation, unfolding the destiny of all nations, kindreds and tongues. He said that he distinctly heard the voice of him that spake. Joseph Knight, one of the fathers of your Church, a worthy man, and my intimate friend, went with him. When I reflect upon our former friendship, Mr. Chairman, and upon the scenes that he had passed through in consequence of mal-administration, mobocracy and cruelty, I feel to lift up my voice to high heaven, and pray God to bless the aged veteran, and that his silver locks may go down to the grave in peace, like a shock of corn fully ripe. In a few days his friends [Joseph Smith's] returned with the glad news that Joseph had found the plates and had gone down to his father-in-law's for the purpose of translating them. I believe he remained there until he finished the translation. After the book was published, he came to live in the neighborhood of Father Knight's, about four miles from me, and began to preach the Gospel; and many were pricked in their hearts, believed, and were baptized in the name of the Lord Jesus. He soon formed a Church at Colesville; his meetings were numerously attended, and the eyes of all people were upon him with astonishment. Oh, Mr. Chairman, the world was turned upside down at once, and the devil,—always ready to assist and help along in all difficulties that arise among men—personified in some of the religionists, began to prick up his ears and jump, and kick and run about, like Jim Crow, calling for rotten eggs to help in the wake. You would have thought, sir, that Gog and Magog were let loose on the young man. He called upon the world's people (as they are called) but got no help; he then flew about in the sectarian churches, like lightning, and they immediately came to his aid, and uniting their efforts, roared against him like the thunders of Mount Sinai. When those fiery bigots were let loose, they united in pouring the red hot vials of their wrath upon his head. Their cry of "False Prophet! False Prophet!" was sounded from village to village, and every foul epithet that malice and wicked ingenuity could invent were heaped upon him. Yes, sir; the same spirit that influenced the Presbyterians of Massachusetts about one hundred and fifty years ago, in their persecution of the Quakers, when they first began to preach their doctrines in that state, was fully manifested by those religious bigots, who were afraid if they let them alone, their own doctrines would come to naught.   What was the result of the persecution in Massachusetts? Why, sir, warrants were made out by those churches having authority, and the Quakers were tried for heresy.   But what was the result of those trials.   The sentence of death was passed upon the Quakers for heresy by those religious fanatics, and three of them were hanged by the neck on Bloody Hill, in Boston. to make expiation for that unpardonable crime.   "Tell it not in Gath," nor publish it not on the tops of the mountains in this boasted land of freedom, that the Puritans of New England, who had fled from the Old World in consequence of religious intolerance, that they might enjoy the sweets of liberty, so soon became persecutors themselves, and shed innocent blood, which still cries aloud from the dust for vengeance upon their heads.   Let shame cover our faces when we mention the name of freedom in our grand republic.

O my God! when in one portion of our country blood is flowing from the crime of worshiping our Creator according to the dictates of conscience, or as the Spirit directs, and in the other are great rejoicings in consequence thereof, where, I ask, is the boasted freedom for which our fathers fought and bled?

O Thou who holdest the destinies of all things in Thine hands here below, return these blessings unto us. that we may keep them as precious jewels till time is no more.   But, Mr. Chairman, I am wandering too far from the subject.   I will return to the persecutions which followed General Smith, when his cheeks blossomed with the beauty of youth, and his eyes sparkled with innocence.

These bigots soon made up a false accusation against him, and had him arraigned before Joseph Chamberlain, a justice of the peace, a man who was always ready to deal out justice to all, and a man of great discernment of mind.

The case came up about 10 o'clock a. m.   I was called upon to defend the prisoner, the prosecutors employed the best counsel they could get, and ransacked the town of Bainbridge and county of Chenango for witnesses that would swear hard enough to convict the prisoner; but they entirely failed.   Yes, sir; let me say to you that not one blemish nor spot was found against his character.   He came from that trial, notwithstanding the mighty efforts that were made to convict him of crime by his vigilant persecutors, with his character unstained by even the appearance of guilt.

The trial closed about twelve o'clock at night.   After a few moments' deliberation, the court pronounced the words, "Not guilty," and the prisoner was discharged.   But, alas! the devil, not satisfied with his defeat, stirred up a man not unlike himself, who was more fit to dwell among the fiends of hell than to belong to the human family, to go to Colesville and get another writ and take him to Broome county for another trial.   They were sure they could send that boy to hell or to Texas, they did not care which; and in half an hour after he was discharged by the court, he was arrested again, and on the way to Colesville for another trial.

I was again called upon by his friends to defend him against his malignant persecutors, and clear him from the false charges they had preferred against him. I made every reasonable excuse I could, as I was nearly worn down through fatigue and want of sleep, as I had been engaged in lawsuits for two days and nearly the whole of two nights. But I saw the persecution was great against him; and here let me say, Mr. Chairman, singular as it may seem, while Mr. Knight was pleading with me to go, a peculiar impression or thought struck my mind that I must go and defend him, for he was the Lord's anointed. I did not know what it meant, but thought I must go and clear the Lord's anointed.   I said I would go, and started with as much faith as the Apostles had when they could remove mountains, accompanied by Father Knight, who was like the old patriarch that followed the ark of God to the city of David.

We rode on till we came to the house of Hezekiah Peck, where a number of Mormon women were assembled, as I was informed, for the purpose of praying for the deliverance of the Prophet of the Lord. The women came out to our wagon, and Mrs. Smith among the rest.

O my God, sir, what were my feeling when I saw that woman who had but a few days before given herself, heart and hand, to be a consort for life, and that so soon her crimson cheeks must be wet with tears that came streaming from her eyes! Yes, sir; it seemed that her very heart strings would be broken with grief. My feelings, sir, were moved with pity and sorrow for the afflicted, and on the other hand they were wrough up to the highest pitch of indignation against those fiends of hell who had thus caused the innocent to suffer.

The next morning about ten o'clock, the court was organized. The prisoner was to be tried by three justices of the peace, that his departure out of the county might be made sure.   Neither talents nor money were wanting to ensure them success. They employed the ablest lawyer in that county, and introduced twenty witnesses before dark, but proved nothing.

They sent out runners and ransaked the hills and vales, grog-shops and ditches, gathered together a company that looked as if they had come from hell, and had been whipped by the soot-boy thereof, which they brought forward to testify one after another, but with no better success.   Although they wrung and twisted into every shape, in trying to tell something that would criminate the prisoner, nothing was proven against him whatever.

Having got through with the examination of their witnesses about two o'clock in the morning, the case was argued about two hours. There was not one particle of testimony against the prisoner. No, sir; he came out like the three children from the fiery furnace, without the smell of fire upon his garments.

The court deliberated upon the case for half an hour with closed doors, and then we were called in. The court arraigned the prisoner and said—"Mr. Smith, we have had your case under consideration, examined the testimony, and find nothing to condemn you; and therefore you are discharged."

They then proceeded to reprimand him severely—not because anything derogatory to his character in any shape had been proven against him by the host of witnesses that had testified during the trial, but merely to please those fiends in human shape who were engaged in the unhallowed persecution of an innocent man, sheerly on account of his religious opinions.

After they had got through, I arose and said—"This court puts me in mind of a certain trial held before Felix of old, when the enemies of Paul arraigned him before that venerable judge for some alleged crime, and nothing was found in him worthy of death or bonds. Yet, to please the Jews who were his accusers, he was left bound, contrary to law, and the court had served Mr. Smith in the same way, by their unlawful and uncalled for reprimand after his discharge to please his accusers."

We got him away that night from the midst of three hundred people without his receiving any injury; but I am well aware that we were assisted by some higher power than man; for to look back on the scene, I cannot tell how we succeeded in getting him away. I take no glory to myself: it was the Lord's work, and marvelous in our eyes.

This, Mr. Chairman, is a true history of the first persecution that came upon General Smith in his youth among professed Christians, and in a country heralded to the ends of the earth as a land of freedom, where all men have the constitutional right to worship as they please and believe what they please, without molestation, so long as they do not interfere with the rights and privileges of others—yes, sir; a persecution got up through the influence of religious bigotry by as vile a set of men as ever disgraced the family of man. But their devices against him were brought to naught by the Overruling Power that controls all things and brings to naught the counsels of the wicked.

Mr. Chairman, little did I think that I was defending a boy that would rise to eminence like this man—a man whom God delights to honor as a

Prophet and leader of His people—one to whom He has given the keys of heaven and earth, and the power of David, and said to him, Whatever you bind on earth shall be bound in heaven, and the gates of hell shall not prevail against you. And may he live to put his foot upon the neck of his enemies in love and meekness! I know, sir, that God has made him a leader of many thousands of people; and may he teach them in meekness and with that wisdom and judgment that God shall direct.

I add no more.

The Convention adjourned *sine die*

URIAH BROWN, President,

F. MERRRYWEATHER, Secretary.

I rode out in the afternoon.

About 6 p. m., a caucus was held; but, Emma being sick, I could not attend. At night a large assemblage burned a barrel of tar in the street. I went out to see what was the matter, and found they were giving toasts; and as soon as they became aware of my presence, they carried me on their shoulders twice round the fire, and escorted me to the Mansion by a band of music.

Elders Eranklin D. Richards and Joseph A. Stratton were ordained High Priests and set apart to go on a mission to England by Elders Brigham Young and Heber C. Kimball and Willard Richards.

CHAPTER XIX.

CHARGES AGAINST PRESIDENT SMITH BEFORE THE CIRCUIT
COURT—HIS VOLUNTARY APPEARANCES AT COURT—
TREATMENT—RETURN TO NAUVOO.

Saturday, May 18, 1844.—At 9 a. m., I went with Heber
C. Kimball to visit President Brigham Young, and afterwards went out to the regimental training, and also in the
afternoon riding on my horse, "Joe Duncan."

At 5 p. m., two cannons were fired opposite my old
house, and the regiments were dismissed.

The high Council cut off from the Church James Blakesley, Francis M. Higbee, Charles Ivins, and Austin Cowles,
for apostasy.

Sunday, 19.—Cloudy morning; rain about noon. I remained at home. Elder Lyman Wight preached at the
stand in the morning. The usual prayer meeting at 2 p
m. was dispensed with on account of the mud and rain.

In the evening I talked to the brethren at my house,
Esquire Reid, my old lawyer, being present. W. W.
Phelps read my last letter to Henry Clay to the company.

Monday, 20.—Emma continued very sick, and I was with
her most of the time.

At 10 a. m., there was a meeting at the stand for the
purpose of collecting means to enable Elder Lyman Wight
to go to Washington.

The Circuit Court commenced its sitting at Carthage,
Court Session   Judge Thomas presiding. Brother Phelps and
at Carthage.   many of the brethren went to Carthage.
Phelps returned in the evening with the intelligence that

a summons was supposed to be issued for me to appear on the same case on which I was set free by *habeas corpus* on the 8th inst.* The lawyers agreed to move an abatement. A good influence in favor of the Saints appears to have prevailed.

A general court-martial of the Legion was held, Brevet Major General Hyrum Smith presiding. It was adjourned to the 10th of June next.

Tuesday, 21.—A very pleasant morning. I rode out on horseback to the prairie, with Porter Rockwell and Mr. Reid. At 7. a. m., Elders Brigham Young, Heber C. Kimball, Lyman Wight, and about a hundred Elders, left this city on the steamer *Osprey* (Captain Anderson) for St. Louis.

The *Maid of Iowa* arrived at 8 a. m., with sixty-two Saints from the Eastern States on board, all in good health and spirits. The clerk, Thomas Bullock, reported the fields on each side of the river covered with water to the depth of upwards of sixteen feet, and all the farms on the flats of the Mississippi river were submerged, and the river was still rising eight inches per day. The *Maid of Iowa* started up the river for Wapello on the Iowa river at 3 p. m.

I was at home towards night with Emma, who is somewhat better. I shoveled dirt out of the ditch, while Wasson stood on the corner of the fence to watch. An officer arrived having a summons and an attachment to take me to Carthage, but he could not find me. I rode out in the evening to see David Yearsley's child, who was sick, and returned home at 9 p. m.

I copy from the *Times and Seasons*:—

LETTER: GEORGE A. SMITH TO "TIMES AND SEASONS"—CONFERENCE AT NEWARK, ILLINOIS.

"NEWARK, KENDALL COUNTY, ILL., May 21, 1844.

Editor of the Times and Seasons:—

DEAR SIR,—We arrived at Ottawa on the 17th inst., after driving

* Case of Chauncey L. Higbee vs. Joseph Smith, see Ch. XVI.

four days through the constant rains, and over roads almost impassable for man or beast.   We were soon informed that the conference was removed twenty miles up Fox River, at the Newark Branch.

Notice had been given for a political address to be delivered in the Court House in the evening by one of the Twelve; several hundred citizens assembled, and were addressed by Elder G. A. Smith.   The speaker considered General Smith the smartest man in the United States, and best calculated to fill the presidential chair, which was applauded by the assembly.   His political views as presented on that occasion seemed to please most of the people.   At the close of the speech the congregation quietly dispersed.   Elder Woodruff continued his journey ten miles, and held a meeting with the LaSalle Branch of 46 members, mostly emigrants from Norway.   On the 18th we arrived at Newark, and attended the Conference according to appointment.

The following is a copy of the minutes, which we forward for publication:—

NEWARK, KENDALL COUNTY, ILL., May 18, 1844.

Conference convened pursuant to notice.

There were present two of the quorum of the Twelve, one High Priest, two Seventies, nine Elders, one Priest, and one Teacher.

Conference called to order by Elder Woodruff.

Elder George A. Smith called to the chair.

Conference opened by singing, and prayer by the president.

Representation of the several branches was called for, when the following branches were represented as follows:

Newark Branch, 35 members, 1 Elder. 1 Teacher; La Salle Branch, 46 members, 2 Elders: Ottawa Branch, 16 members. 2 Elders; Bureau Branch, 15 members. 3 Elders; Pleasant Grove, McHenry County, 19 members, 2 Elders; Indian Creek Branch, 5 members; Big Vermillion Branch, 4 members; French Creek Grove Branch, 2 members.   Total 133 members, 10 Elders, and 1 Teacher,

Canute Petersen, Severt Olson. Zimri H. Baxter, Levi Lightfoot, S. D. Huffaker, Mades Madison, Vance Jacobs, and Oder Jacobson, were ordained Priests; Ole Johnson and Peter Maclin ordained Teachers, under the hands of Elders Wilford Woodruff, Geo. A. Smith, and Ezra Thayer.

Appropriate remarks were then made by Elders Woodruff and Smith by way of counsel and instruction to those who had been ordained; followed by Elder David Savage.

Adjourned until Sunday morning, 10 o'clock.

Sunday, 19th.

Met according to adjournment.

Opened by singing and prayer by Elder A. M. Wilsey.

A discourse was then delivered by Elder Wilford Woodruff, in which he instructed the Elders to be careful to preach the first principles of the Gospel and doctrines of Christ, and not to spend their time in warring with the opinions of other men; showed the importance of revelation, and the necessity of a Prophet of God, as the head of the Church on earth, being as necessary in order to exist and advance in knowledge as for a natural body to possess a head in order to live. He considered we were enjoying the society of as good a Prophet in this day as any people ever enjoyed in any age of the world, and believed all good men would think so, if they were fully acquainted with him and his principles.

He was followed by Elder Geo. A. Smith, who bore testimony to the truth of the fullness of the Gospel, counseled the Elders to be humble, and not get head and shoulders above their brethren, lest they fall, like the tallest trees of the forest, that are first swept down by the raging storm.

Two o'clock, met according to adjournment, when the sacrament was administered, and many testimonies given from the Elders and members present concerning the truth of the work they had received.

Conference was dismissed amid the best of feelings, which were manifested not only by all the Saints, but by the whole congregation of citizens that attended. Good order prevailed through the whole conference. Attention, kindness, and civility, were manifested by all.

GEO. A. SMITH, President.

ASA MANCHESTER, Clerk.

At the close of the Conference, Elders C. C. Rich, David Fullmer, Norton Jacobs, and Moses Smith arrived direct from Nauvoo, on their way to Michigan.

20th—We have appointed a political meeting in Newark, this evening, and one at Joliet tomorrow evening, where we expect to present to the citizens General Smith's Views of the Powers and Policy of the Government, and discuss the subject of politics.

WILFORD WOODRUFF.

GEO. A. SMITH.

Wednesday, 22.—At home, watching, as the officers from Carthage were after me.

At 10 a. m., about 40 Indians of the Sacs and Foxes came up in front of the Mansion, four or five of them being mounted ,among whom was Black Hawk's brother, Kis-kish-kee, &c. I was obliged to send word I could not see them at present. They encamped in the Council Chamber afternoon

Visit of Sac and Fox Indians to Nauvoo.

and night. I was with the police on duty, and saw several individuals lurking around.

Very pleasant day.

President Brigham Young preached to the brethren in St. Louis this evening.

Thursday, 23.—Emma rather better. Read Hebrew with Neibaur, and counseled with various friends.

At 10 a. m., the Municipal Court met, Newel K. Whitney presiding; but there not being a quorum present, adjourned for one week.

At one p. m., had a talk with the Sac and Fox Indians in my back kitchen. They said—"When our fathers first came here, this land was inhabited by the Spanish; when the Spaniards were driven off, the French came, and then the English and Americans; and our fathers talked a great deal with the Big Spirit." They complained that they had been robbed of their lands by the whites, and cruelly treated.

Address of the Prophet to the Indians

I told them I knew they had been wronged, but that we had bought this land and paid our money for it. I advised them not to sell any more land, but to cultivate peace with the different tribes and with all men, as the Great Spirit wanted them to be united and to live in peace. "The Great Spirit has enabled me to find a book [showing them the Book of Mormon], which told me about your fathers, and Great Spirit told me, 'You must send to all the tribes that you can, and tell them to live in peace;' and when any of our people come to see you, I want you to treat them as we treat you."

At 3 p. m., the Indians commenced a war dance in front of my old house. Our people commenced with music and firing cannon. After the dance, which lasted about two hours, the firing of cannon closed the exercise, and with our music marched back to the office. Before they commenced dancing, the Saints took up a collection to get the Indians food.

A. A. Lathrop came to my clerk, Dr. Richards, and told him an officer was on his way with an attachment for him, and that the grand jury had found a bill against me for adultery, on the testimony of William Law; he had come from Carthage in two hours and thirty minutes to bring the news. Dr. Richards came to my house and stayed all night.

Aaron Johnson came from Carthage, and said that Foster had been swearing that I swore to the complaint on which Simpson was arrested. I instructed Johnson and Rockwell to go to Carthage in the morning, and have him indicted for perjury, as I never did swear to the complaint. The officer was after John D. Parker also, and report says Brigham Young, Heber C. Kimball and W. Clayton.

Past nine p. m., I walked a little way with Dr. Richards for exercise.

My brother Hyrum called in the evening, and cautioned me against speaking so freely about my enemies, &c., in such a manner as to make it actionable. I told him that six months would not roll over his head before they would swear twelve as palpable lies about him as they had about me.

Hyrum's Caution to the Prophet on the Freedom of Speaking.

President Brigham Young left St. Louis at noon in the steamboat *Louis Philippe*.

Friday, 24.—With my family all day.

Aaron Johnson and Orrin P. Rockwell went to Carthage to get Robert D. Foster indicted; but they returned again as the grand jury had risen. Joseph H. Jackson was at Carthage, and had sworn falsely against me.

At 6 p. m., went to Dr. Bernhise's room, and had counsel with Brothers Richards and Phelps. I ordered a meeting of the City Council for tomorrow, and returned to my family after being absent about one hour.

The Central Committee wrote a letter to Hugh Clark Esq.:—

Letter: Central Campaign Committee to Hugh Clark, Esq.,—Presidential Election Matters.

NAUVOO, ILLINOIS, May 24, 1844.

SIR.—Having received your address through our mutual friend, Mr. Edward Doughty, we forward with this per next mail the Nauvoo *Neighbor* of the 22nd inst., through which you will learn the doings of a State Convention held in this place on the 17th; and this communication has been drawn forth, in a great degree, through our sympathies for a people who are now being mobbed in the city of brotherly love (Philadelphia) as we have been for many years in Missouri; and for what? For our religion, although called by another name.

The Mormons and the Catholics are the most obnoxious to the sectarian world of any people, and are the only two who have not persecuted each other and others in these the United States, and the only two who have suffered from the cruel hand of mobocracy for their religion under the name of foreigners; and to stay this growing evil, and establish Jeffersonian democracy, free trade and sailor's rights, and protection of person and property," we have nominated General Joseph Smith for the next president of the nation—a man with whom we are thoroughly acquainted, and have no fear in pledging our lives, our fortunes and our sacred honor, that, if elected, he will give and secure these inestimable blessings to every individual and society of men, no matter what their religious faith. Help us to elect this man, and we will help you to secure these privileges which belong to you, and break every yoke.

You will please to consider yourself a member of the corresponding committee with us, agreeable to the resolution of the State Convention, and lay this subject before your people, giving us your views on receipt hereof, and open such correspondence as wisdom shall dictate.

General Smith's prospects are brightening every day. With sentiments of the highest consideration, we are your obedient servants,

WILLARD RICHARDS,
JOHN M. BERNHISEL,
W. W. PHELPS,
LUCIAN R. FOSTER,

Central Committee of Correspondence for the Election of General Joseph Smith to the Presidency.

HUGH CLARK, ESQ. Alderman.

Corner of Fourth and Masters Street, Northern Liberties, Philadelphia.

Rainy evening.

A conference was held at Chicago, Alfred Cordon, president, and James Burgess, clerk. Eleven Elders were present, and a very favorable impression was made upon the minds of the people.

Saturday, 25.—At home, keeping out of the way of the expected writs from Carthage. Towards evening, Edward Hunter and William Marks, of the grand jury returned from Carthage; also Marshal John P. Greene and Almon W. Babbitt, who informed me there were two indictments found against me, one charging me with false swearing on the testimony of Joseph H. Jackson and Robert D. Foster, and one charging me with polygamy, or something else, on the testimony of William Law, that I had told him so! The particulars of which I shall learn hereafter. There was much false swearing before the grand jury. Francis M. Higbee swore so hard that I had received stolen property, &c., that his testimony was rejected. I heard that Joseph H. Jackson had come into the city. I therefore instructed the officers to arrest him for threatening to take life, &c.

Reported Indictments of the Prophet.

I had a long talk with Edward Hunter, my brother Hyrum, Dr. Richards, William Marks, Almon W. Babbitt, Shadrach Roundy, Edward Romney and others, and concluded not to keep out of the way of the officers any longer.

At 2 p. m. I was in council in my north room, and heard the letters from Elder O. Hyde read, and instructed Dr. Richards to write an answer, which he did as follows:

Letter: Willard Richards to Orson Hyde—Answering Hyde's Letter on Western Movement.

NAUVOO, May 26, 1844.

Orson Hyde, Esq.:

SIR.—Yours of April 30th is received. The council convened this afternoon, and, after investigation, directed an answer, which must be brief to correspond with the press of business.

All the items you refer to had previously received the deliberation of the council.

Messrs. Lyman Wight and Heber C. Kimball will doubtless be in Washington before you receive this, from whom you will learn all things relative to Texas, &c.   Our great success at present depends upon our faith in the doctrine of election; and our faith must be made manifest by our works and every honorable exertion made to elect Gen. Smith.

Agricultural pursuits will take care of themselves, regulating their own operations and the rich also; but the poor we must gather and take care of, for they are to inherit the kingdom.

Nauvoo will be a "corner stake of Zion" forever, we most assuredly expect.   Here are the house and the ordinance, extend where else we may.

Press the bills through the two houses, if possible.   If Congress will not pass them, let them do as they have a mind with them.   If they will not pass our bills, but will give us "something," they will give what they please, and it will be at our option to accept or reject.

Men who are afraid of "hazarding their influence" in the council or political arena are good for nothing.   'Tis the fearless, undaunted and persevering who will gain the conquest of the forum.

Sidney Rigdon, Esq., is about to resign the postoffice at Nauvoo, in favor of Gen. Joseph Smith, the founder of the city.   He has the oldest petitions now on file in the general postoffice for that station, and has an undoubted claim over every other petitioner, by being the founder and supporter of the city, and by the voice of nineteen-twentieths of the people, and every sacred consideration; and it is the wish of the council that you engage the Illinois delegation to use their influence to secure the office to General Smith without fail, and have them ready to act on the arrival of Mr. Rigdon's resignation, and before too, if expedient.

We are also writing to Justin Butterfield, Esq., U. S. Attorney for the district of Illinois, who has kindly offered his services to secure the post office to the General, he having been here and seen for himself the situation; and probably his letter to the department will arrive nearly as soon as this.

The election on the principle of Jeffersonian democracy, free trade, and protection of person and property, is gaining ground in every quarter.   All is well in Nauvoo, although some of the Anties are trying to do us injury; but their efforts are palsied, and they make very little headway.   You remember the Preston motto, "Truth will prevail!* Therefore we go ahead.

---

* Referring to the motto that was displayed in the streets of Preston, England, on the arrival of Elders Kimball and Hyde as missionaries to that city in 1837.   See this HISTORY, vol. II, pp. 498-9.

You have the best wishes of the council and friends here.
I am, sir, most respectfully yours,

W. RICHARDS, Recorder.
By order of the council.

N. B.   Your families and friends were well last information.

Sidney Rigdon resigned the office of postmaster of Nauvoo, and recommended me as his successor.

The *Maid of Iowa* arrived at five p. m.

The High Council have directed the following testimony to be published in the *Neighbor*, I copy it with the editor's remarks, to show the character of the men who are now seeking to destroy my life and usefulness, and overthrow the work of the Lord which He has commenced through my instrumentality:

[Here follow the affidavits of Margaret J. Nyman, Matilda J. Nyman, Sarah Miller, and an extract from the testimony of Catherine Warren before the High Council of the Church to the effect that Chauncey L. Higbee had brought about their ruin by deceit in representing that Joseph Smith taught that promiscuous sexual relations were not sinful when kept secret, and by this misrepresentation he, the said Chauncey L. Higbee, accomplished his wicked purposes].

Editorial Comment.

We have abundance of like testimony on hand which may be forthcoming if we are compelled; at present the foregoing may suffice.

"Why have you not published this before?" We answer—on account of the humility and entreaties of Higbee at the time; and on account of the feelings of his parents, who are highly respectable, we have forborne until now.   The character of Chauncey L. Higbee is so infamous, and his exertions such as to destroy every principle of righteousness, that forbearance is no longer a virtue.

After all that this Chauncey L. Higbee has done in wickedly and maliciously using the name of Joseph Smith to persuade innocent females to submit to gratify his hellish lusts, and then blast the character of the most chaste, pure, virtuous and philanthropic man on earth, he, to screen himself from the law of the land and the just indignation of an insulted people, and save himself from the penitentiary, or whatever punishment his unparalleled crimes merit, has entered into a conspiracy with the Laws and others against the lives of those who are knowing to his abandoned conduct, thus hoping to save himself from the disgrace which must follow an exposure, and wreak his vengeance and gratify his revenge for his awful disappointment.

A two days' conference was held in Jefferson county, New York, at 10 a. m.   Present 300 Saints, 150 of whom had embraced the Gospel since last autumn. Nine branches were represented, containing 289 members, 16 Elders, 8 Priests and 1 Teacher.   An immense concourse of people assembled to hear the Elders preach.   Elder Benjamin Brown was President, and J. W. Crosby, Clerk.

Conference in Jefferson Co., N. Y.

A three days' conference was held at Dresden, Weakly county, Tennessee.   Elder A. O. Smoot was chosen president, and D. P. Raney, secretary.   A large congregation assembled, but the proceedings were interrupted by a mob headed by some of the leading men of the county; yet a candidate for elector was appointed by my friends.

Conference, Dresden, Tenn.

Sunday, 26.—At 10 a. m. I preached at the Stand. The following synopsis was reported by Mr. Thos. Bullock, clerk of the steamer, *Maid of Iowa.*

Address of the Prophet—His Testimony Against the Dissenters at Nauvoo.

President Joseph Smith read the 11th Chap. II Corinthians. My object is to let you know that I am right here on the spot where I intend to stay.   I, like Paul, have been in perils, and oftener than anyone in this generation.   As Paul boasted, I have suffered more than Paul did. I should be like a fish out of water, if I were out of persecutions.   Perhaps my brethren think it requires all this to keep me humble.   The Lord has constituted me so curiously that I glory in persecution.   I am not nearly so humble as if I were not persecuted.   If oppression will make a wise man mad, much more a fool.   If they want a beardless boy to whip all the world, I will get on the top of a mountain and crow like a rooster: I shall always beat them.   When facts are proved, truth and innocence will prevail at last.   My enemies are no philosophers: they think that when they have my spoke under, they will keep me down; but for the fools, I will hold on and fly over them.

God is in the still small voice.   In all these affidavits, indictments, it is all of the devil—all corruption.   Come on! ye prosecutors! ye false swearers!   All hell, boil over!   Ye burning mountains, roll down your lava!   for I will come out on the top at last.   I have more to boast of than ever any man had.   I am the only man that has ever been able to keep a whole church together since the days of Adam. A large majority of the whole have stood by me. Neither Paul, John, Peter, nor Jesus ever did it. I boast that no man ever did such a work as I. The followers of Jesus ran away from Him; but the Latter-day Saints never ran away from me yet. You know my daily walk and conversation. I am in the bosom of a virtuous and good people. How I do love to hear the wolves howl! When they can get rid of me, the devil will also go. For the last three years I have a record of all my acts and proceedings, for I have kept several good, faithful, and efficient clerks in constant employ: they have accompanied me everywhere, and carefully kept my history, and they have written down what I have done, where I have been, and what I have said; therefore my enemies cannot charge me with any day, time, or place, but what I have written testimony to prove my actions; and my enemies cannot prove anything against me. They have got wonderful things in the land of Ham. I think the grand jury have strained at a gnat and swallowed the camel.

A man named Simpson says I made an affidavit against him, &c. Mr. Simpson says I arrested him. I never arrested Mr. Simpson in my life. He says I made an affidavit against him. I never made an affidavit against him in my life. I will prove it in court. I will tell you how it was: Last winter I got ready with my children to go to the farm to kill hogs. Orrin P. Rockwell was going to drive. An Englishman came in and wanted a private conversation with me. I told him I did not want any private conversations. "I demand one of you!" Such a one I am bound to obey anyhow. Said he—"I want a warrant against the man who stabbed Brother Badham. He said it was a man who boarded at Davis'. He said it was Mr. Simpson—it answered his description. I said I had no jurisdiction out of the city. He said—"The man must be arrested, or else he will go away." I told him—"You must go to Squire Wells, Johnson, or Foster." Mr. Lytle stepped up and said—"I am a policeman." I jumped into my carriage, and away I went.

When I came back I met Mr. Jackson. He said—"You did wrong in arresting Mr. Simpson." I told him I did not do it. I went over and sat down, and related the circumstances. He turned round and said—"Mr. Smith, I have nothing against you; I am satisfied." He went and supped with me. He declared in the presence of witnesses, that he had nothing against me. I then said—"I will go over to Esquire Johnson, and testify what the Englishman told me." I told him not to make out that I believe he is the man, but that I believe he is innocent. I don't want to swear that he is the man. Messrs. Coolidge, Rockwell, Hatfield, and Hawes were present.

Mr. Johnson made one [a complaint] out in due form: and as I sat down in a bustle the same as I do when one of the clerks brings a deed for me to sign. Johnson read it. I said—"I can't swear to that affidavit; I don't believe it: tear up that paper." Mr. Simpson agreed to come before Badham and make it up. I did not swear to it [*i. e.* to the complaint.]

After a while, Dr. Foster and others came in. They called me up to testify. I told it all the same as I do here. Mr. Simpson rose up, and asked—"Do you believe now that I am the man who stabbed Mr. Badham?" I replied—"No sir, I do not now, nor ever did: the magistrate says I did not swear to it." He considered, and made a public declaration that he was satisfied with me.

Aaron Johnson went before the grand jury and swore I did not swear to it. when Dr. Foster goes and swears that I swore to it, and that he was in the room when he was not in. Chauncey wanted me to stay and have a conversation. Dr. Foster asked Aaron Johnson for the writ and affidavit. He handed them to Dr. Foster, who read them, and then threw them into the fire. I said—"Doctor, you ought not to have burned it; it was my paper." Dr. Foster goes to the grand jury and swears he did not burn only one; but I say he burnt both. This is a fair sample of the swearing that is going on against me.

The last discharge was the 40th; now the 41st, 42nd, 43rd; all through falsehood. Matters of fact are as profitable as the Gospel, and which I can prove. You will then know who are liars, and who speak the truth I want to retain your friendship on holy grounds.

Another indictment has been got up against me. It appears a holy prophet has arisen up, and he has testified against me: the reason is, he is so holy. The Lord knows I do not care how many churches are in the world. As many as believe me, may. If the doctrine that I preach is true, the tree must be good. I have prophesied things that have come to pass, and can still.

Inasmuch as there is a new church, this must be old, and of course we ought to be set down as orthodox. From henceforth let all the churches now no longer persecute orthodoxy. I never built upon any other man's ground. I never told the old Catholic that he was a fallen true prophet God knows, then, that the charges against me are false.

I had not been married scarcely five minutes, and made one proclamation of the Gospel, before it was reported that I had seven wives. I mean to live and proclaim the truth as long as I can.

This new holy prophet [William Law] has gone to Carthage and swore that I had told him that I was guilty of adultery. This spiritual wifeism! Why, a man dares not speak or wink, for fear of being accused of this.

William Law testified before forty policemen, and the assembly room full of witnesses, that he testified under oath that he never had heard or seen or knew anything immoral or criminal against me. He testified under oath that he was my friend, and not the "Brutus." There was a cogitation who was the "Brutus." I had not prophesied against William Law. He swore under oath that he was satisfied that he was ready to lay down his life for me, and he swears that I have committed adultery.

I wish the grand jury would tell me who they are—whether it will be a curse or blessing to me. I am quite tired of the fools asking me.

A man asked me whether the commandment was given that a man may have seven wives; and now the new prophet has charged me with adultery. I never had any fuss with these men until that Female Relief Society brought out the paper against adulterers and adulteresses.

Dr. Goforth was invited into the Laws' clique, and Dr. Foster and the clique were dissatisfied with that document, and they rush away and leave the Church, and conspire to take away my life; and because I will not countenance such wickedness, they proclaim that I have been a true prophet, but that I am now a fallen prophet.

Jackson has committed murder, robbery, and perjury; and I can prove it by half-a-dozen witnesses. Jackson got up and said—"By God, he is innocent," and now swears that I am guilty. He threatened my life.

There is another Law, not the prophet, who was cashiered for dishonesty and robbing the government. Wilson Law also swears that I told him I was guilty of adultery. Brother Jonathan Dunham can swear to the contrary. I have been chained. I have rattled chains before in a dungeon for the truth's sake. I am innocent of all these charges, and you can bear witness of my innocence, for you know me yourselves.

When I love the poor, I ask no favors of the rich. I can go to the cross—I can lay down my life; but don't forsake me. I want the friendship of my brethren.—Let us teach the things of Jesus Christ. Pride goes before destruction, and a haughty spirit before a downfall.

Be meek and lowly, upright and pure; render good for evil. If you bring on yourselves your own destruction, I will complain. It is not right for a man to bear down his neck to the oppressor always. Be humble and patient in all circumstances of life; we shall then triumph more gloriously. What a thing it is for a man to be accused of committing adultery, and having seven wives, when I can only find one.

I am the same man, and as innocent as I was fourteen years ago; and I can prove them all perjurers. I labored with these apostates myself until I was out of all manner of patience; and then I sent my brother Hyrum, whom they virtually kicked out of doors.

I then sent Mr. Backenstos, when they declared that they were my enemies. I told Mr. Backenstos that he might tell the Laws, if they had any cause against me I would go before the Church, and confess it

to the world. He [Wm. Law] was summoned time and again,but refused
to come. Dr. Bernhisel and Elder Rigdon know that I speak the truth. I
cite you to Captain Dunham, Esquires Johnson and Wells, Brother
Hatfield and others, for the truth of what I have said.   I have said this
to let my friends know that I am right.

As I grow older, my heart grows tenderer for you. I am at all times
willing to give up everything that is wrong, for I wish this people to
have a virtuous leader,   I have set your minds at liberty by letting you
know the things of Christ Jesus.   When I shrink not from your defense
will you throw me away for a new man who slanders you?   I love you
for your reception of me.   Have I asked you for your money? No; you
know better. I appeal to the poor. I say, Cursed be that man or woman
who says that I have taken of your money unjustly.   Brother Babbitt
will address you. I have nothing in my heart but good feelings.

I rode out in the afternoon. On my return, my lawyers,
Col. Richardson and Almon W. Babbitt, called upon me
on the subject of the writs which were out against me.

A man called and informed me that John Eagle
and several others intended to kidnap Jere-
Threat to
Kidnap Jere-
miah Smith. miah Smith during the night.   I therefore stationed an extra police in order to protect him.

President Brigham Young arrived at Cincinnati at 5 p.m.

Monday, *27.*—About 8 a. m., I started on horsback
President
Smith Vol-
untarily goes
to Carthage
to Meet In-
dictments. with a few friends, went by the Temple, and
pursued my course towards Carthage, think-
ing it best for me to meet my enemies before
the Circuit Court, and have the indictments
against me investigated.   After I had passed my farm on
the prairie, most of the following brethren joined my
company, and the remainder soon after my arrival in
Carthage—viz: Aaron Johnson, Dr. Bernhisel, Joseph
W. Coolidge, John Hatfield, Orrin P. Rockwell, Lorenzo
Rockwell, William Walker, Harrison Sagers, Hyrum
Smith, John P. Greene, Judge William Richards, Shadrach Roundy, Theodore Turley, Jedediah M. Grant, John
Lytle, Joseph B. Noble, Edward Bonney, Lucien Woodworth, Cornelius P. Lott, Johathan Dunham, and other
friends.

We arrived at Hamilton's hotel about noon. Charles A. Foster overtook us three or four miles from the city, and accompanied us to Carthage. I had considerable conversation with him, and he appeared to be more mild than previously, and as though he was almost persuaded that he had been influenced to some extent by false reports.

Joseph H. Jackson, Francis M. Higbee, and Chauncey L. Higbee were in Hamilton's hotel when we arrived. Soon after our arrival there, Charles A. Foster took me into a private room and told me in a friendly manner that there was a conspiracy against my life. Robert D. Foster told some of the brethren (with tears in his eyes) that there was evil determined against me; and that there were some persons who were determined I should not go out of Carthage alive. Jackson was seen to reload his pistols, and was heard to swear he would have satisfaction of me and Hyrum.

I had a short interview with Judge Thomas, who treated me with the utmost courtesy. He is a great man and a gentleman. After dinner (at the second or third table) we retired to our room, when Jackson, who had been to the Court House, came towards the hotel. Some person told him Hyrum had arrived, when he immediately turned towards the Court House again.

My lawyers, Messrs. Richardson, Babbitt, and Skinner, used all reasonable exertions to bring forward my trial on the charge of perjury; but the prosecuting party were not ready,—one Withers, a material witness (as they asserted in court), being absent.

My attorneys frequently called on me to report the state of things in court, and I was ready to go in at a moment's warning, being anxious for my trial; but the case was deferred till next term. I was left to give bail to the sheriff at his option. He told me I might go home, where he would call and take bail at his own convenience.

We immediately called for our horses; and while they

were being harnessed, Chauncey L. Higbee came to me and wanted me to stay as a witness in a certain case in which he was employed as attorney. He urged me considerably, but I told him I did not recollect the occurrence he referred to particularly enough to testify in the case, and got him to excuse me.

At half-past four p. m., we started on our return; but when we had got as far as Brother George D. Grant's, a heavy shower of rain commenced, and I went

The Return to Nauvoo.

into the house, while most of the brethren went into the barn until the shower abated. After the storm had subsided, we went forward, and I, Hyrum, and some others arrived at home about 9 p. m., and found Emma sick. My carriage, with Joseph B. Noble, arrived a little after. It was upset on the Temple Hill, but no one was hurt. I rode on horseback all the way on "Joe Duncan."

As we left the tavern in Carthage, and passed the Court House, there were many people about in small groups. Jackson stood on the green with one or two men some distance off.

While at Hamilton's, Chauncey L. Higbee offered some insulting language concerning me to Orrin P. Rockwell, who resented it nobly as a friend ought to do. Hamilton, seeing it, turned Rockwell out of doors.

It was afterwards reported to me by James Flack that Robert D. Foster, Charles A. Foster, Wm. H. Rollinson, and the Higbees were on the hill when I passed in the morning. They immediately gathered their pistols, mounted their horses, and were in Carthage before me, excepting Charles A. Foster.

Also Mr. Powers was talking with Mr. Davies, a tailor, about my going to Carthage, and said they would attempt to kill Joseph Smith. Mr. Davies replied, "O no, I think not." Mr. Powers rejoined, "They will, by G—; and you know it, by G—."

Samuel Smith, of Montebello, heard at five this morning, that 1 had been taken prisoner to Carthage by a mob. He immediately gathered a company of twenty-five men for the purpose of assisting me, and arrived at Carthage about the time I did.

CHAPTER XX.

CASE OF JEREMIAH SMITH BEFORE MUNICIPAL COURT AT NAUVOO—AFFIDAVITS OF CRIMES OF CHAUNCEY L. HIGBEE —APPEARANCE OF THE "EXPOSITOR."

Tuesday, 28.—At home all day. Rain in the afternoon. The *Maid of Iowa* started for the Iowa river at 11 a. m.

I received a letter from Mr. J. Bronder, dated Philadelphia, May 20th, expressing his strong desires that I should allow my name to stand as candidate for the Presidency of the United States, urging many reasons for his request.

Wednesday, 29.—At home. Rain in the morning.

Arrest of Jeremiah Smith, by U. S. Authority. Luther W. Hicock, of Burlington, Iowa, came in and arrested Jeremiah Smith on a warrant issued by Nathanial Pope, Judge of the U. S. Circuit Court. During our conversation in the afternoon we learned to our mutual joy that Jeremiah Smith and I were of one origin.

Received the following letter:

Letter: D. S. Hollister to Joseph Smith—Presidential Election Matters.

BALTIMORE, May 9th, 1844.

DEAR BROTHER JOSEPH.—From the time of my departue to that of my arrival here on Saturday last, I was blessed with prosperity. The feelings manifested by the passengers on the boat to St. Louis were quite favorable.

At St. Louis I embarked on board the steamer *Valley Forge*, with about 125 cabin passengers. I gradually introduced myself to those whose faces gave indications of honest hearts and intelligent minds.

On Sunday I was invited to give, in a public discourse, the points of difference between faith of the Latter-day Saints and other professors of the Christian religion. There was a Methodist preacher on board, with whom arrangements were made, to follow me and blow Mormonism to the four winds. Well, I led off in a discourse of an hour and a half. After dinner the Methodists tried to rally their preacher; but he could not be induced to undertake the fulfillment of his engagements.

I spent the time in conversing with groups of inquirers, and giving further information to those who sought it. After tea, the Methodist priest was, by much persuasion, induced to preach; but, to the astonishment of all, never once mentioned "Mormonism."

By-the-by, we had a beautiful specimen of Missouri treatment of the Saints on board. While I was speaking, I referred to the many false statements which found their way to the public through the papers. A case in point was that of Joseph Smith having just discarded his wife.

After I had finished speaking, and was standing on the guard of the boat, a Missourian stepped up to me, asking me if I wished to be understood that all who said Jo Smith had discarded his wife were liars. On my answering him in the affirmative, he drew his bowie knife on me; but some passengers, who had heard him threaten my life, were watching, and caught him as he was in the act of striking and I in the act of pitching him overboard; but they saved him, and I am glad of it. The whole affair turned much to my advantage. It was an occular demonstration to the crowd of Missourians' feeling toward the Church of Christ.

By this time the way was pretty well paved for introducing national matters; and from this on to our arrival at Wheeling, the time was principally occupied on that subject—reading your views on political economy, &c.

On arriving at Wheeling, a stranger might have imagined me to be a man of some consequence, for it was, "Will you take a seat in our coach?" "Go with us in this stage." "Hold on, and take a seat with us," says the third. In fact, the Mormon was quite a lion among the passengers.

But passing the minutiæ, I arrived in the city two days after the great Whig convention. All is joy and enthusiasm among the Whigs, while doubt and consternation are manifested among the Democrats. The convention has been got up at an immense expense; hundreds of thousands of dollars have been expended.

The Democratic convention comes off on the 27th inst. In the meantime I shall do what is in my power for the promotion of the good cause, and endeavor to be well accoutred for that occasion. I expect to co-operate with Hyde, Pratt and Page, though as yet I have not heard from them.

I shall expect to receive from you the proceedings of the convention held at Nauvoo on Monday last, together with such instructions as you deem proper to give.

D. S. HOLLISTER.

Thursday, 30.—Municipal Court met at 10 a. m., over which I presided as mayor and chief justice. Present, William Marks, Orson Spencer, George W. Harris, Gustavus Hills and Samuel Bennett, alderman, associate justices. Jeremiah Smith, Sen., was brought up on *habeas corpus* from the custody of T. B. Johnson, the complainant.

Municipal Court—Case of Jeremiah Smith.

T. B. Johnson being called by the court answered that he did not acknowledge the jurisdiction of this court; that his writ was only to keep Smith until he could get another writ for him; that Mr. Hickock had a writ from Judge Pope, and he considered Mr. Smith his prisoner, and he attended this court as a matter of courtesy; and if any one offered resistance, he was instructed by Government to give their names, &c., and wrote the names of the court, &c.

Smith's counsel replied to such a subterfuge writ.

The court thought it due the court to hear the reasons why the jurisdiction of the court was not regarded.

T. B. Johnson said he did not come to make a speech; but was instructed to arrest the man. He intended to make no defense. He was an agent of the United States. "Your writ of *habeas corpus* had nothing more to do with this case than with a man in the moon. I have not been able to get authority, and did not come to make defense." Read from Charles B. Penrose's handwriting (so purporting) 33 sec. of Act Sept. 24th, 1789, Act of Congress. Had agreed to wait the decision of this court, but had not agreed to abide the decision.

James A. McCanse was called by the court and asked, "Do you subscribe to the decision of Mr. Johnson in the matter?"

McCanse would not decide. Would like counsel.

T. B. Johnson said he did not ask any favors of the court. He was a United States agent.

Councilor Hugins said—"If McCanse surrenders his claim we will not go into the merits of the case; but if McCanse claims the prisoner, we will go into the merits."

Councilor Hugins read a petition of Jeremiah Smith for another writ of *habeas corpus.* G. P. Stiles, counsel for prisoner, said that Johnson had given up the prisoner on the first claim.

T. B. Johnson said he did not surrender his claim; had nothing to say about it. "Take your own course, gentlemen."

Stiles said he has given him up on the first writ, and now says he says nothing about it; and upon this ground we claim a discharge.

T. B. Johnson said—"We would be defending the writ before Judge Pope. I come here as an agent of the United States. The prisoner has been taken out of my hand, I consider illegally. I do not come here to prosecute or to defend a writ of *habeas corpus.* There is no law for these proceedings. I know my rights. If this court thinks it right to discharge the prisoner, let them do it—let them do it. I do not ask any favors of the court—I ask justice. The laws of Illinois have no power over the United States laws. Let this court discharge him, and I shall take another course—I do not say against you as a court. I came here to arrest Jeremiah Smith."

Justice Harris asked if he meant to intimidate the court by threats.

The chief justice remarked that it was the duty of the United States and Federal Government to treat their subjects and constituents with all that complacency and good feeling which they wished in return, and to avoid every threatening aspect, every intimidating and harsh treatment. He respected the United States laws, but would not yield up any right ceded to the court. The United States have no right to trample our laws under their feet.

The court is bound by oath to support the Constitution of
the United States, and State of Illinois and writ of *habeas
corpus*. The Constitution of the United States and *habeas
corpus* shall not be denied. If the court deny the writ of
habeas corpus, they perjure themselves. The United
States have no right to usurp power to intimidate, and the
court would see them all destroyed before he would perjure himself. We have asked no power. Mr. Smith
asked us to investigate. We were bound to do so. Let
the Federal Government hurl on us their forces, dragoons,
&c.; we are not to be intimidated. The court is clothed
with *habeas corpus*, [power] and will execute it according
to the law. "I understand some law and more justice, and
know as much about the rights of American citizens as
any man."

T. B. Johnson said—"If I did say anything indecorus
to the court, I take it back."

Court responded—"All is right."

Court ordered that the prisoner be discharged, the complainant having refused to prosecute his claim; and that
judgment be entered up *v.* T. B. Johnson, as agent, for
costs of suit.

Afterwards another petition for another writ of *habeas
corpus* was presented and the writ issued and tried. I
copy the minutes from the municipal docket:

Municipal Court Minutes in the case of Jeremiah Smith.

STATE OF ILLINOIS, } Municipal Court.
    CITY OF NAUVOO,

United States, vs. Jeremiah Smith, on Habeas Corpus.

May 30th, 1844, came Jeremiah Smith, and upon the reading and fil-
ing the petition for a writ of *habeas corpus* to be directed to one Luther
W. Hickock to have forthwith before the Municipal Court the body of
the said Jeremiah Smith upon said writ. Said writ was granted by the
court in accordance with the prayer of the petitioner.

The writ of *habeas corpus* was served instanter by the Marshal in cour-
and petitioner present; which writ with Marshal's return thereon, is on
file in the clerk's office.

The foregoing petition of said Jeremiah Smith, together with a certified copy of the warrant, by virtue of which the said Hickock held the said Jeremiah Smith in custody, are on file in the clerk's office.

Present, Joseph Smith, mayor and chief justice; and William Marks, Orson Spencer, George W. Harris, Gustavus Hills, and Samuel Bennett, aldermen, associate justices.

Luther W. Hickock was called by the court to answer in the case, who said he had a writ from Judge Pope, and should consider Smith his prisoner until he was compelled to give him up. Wanted an adjournment.

The court informed Hickock that Smith was their prisoner.

H. T. Hugins and George P. Stiles, counsel for Smith, objected to an adjournment, as there had been two weeks' adjournment for the Government to procure witnesses in another suit which had closed, arising out of the same case, and which had been abandoned by the prosecuting party.

T. B. Johnson appeared before the court and said—"I stand here as an agent for the Government to act in the case of Smith in any state where he may be found; and if we are to go into an investigation on the merits of the case, and go behind the writ, I must have time to send to Washington for witnesses; and I am instructed to consult with Justin Butterfield, Esq., Governor Chambers of Iowa, and Mr. McPherson of St. Louis.

The marshal, J. P. Greene, presented the prisoner for trial.

The court ordered the marshal to take charge of the prisoner, and have him forthcoming from time to time for trial.

Hickock asked for an adjournment until afternoon.

Hugins said—"If they want to go into the merits of the case, we will give them any time; but we propose to dispense with the merits, and move a discharge on the insufficiency of the papers. Dr. Hickock has no legal authority to arrest the prisoner," and read from page 51, Revised Statutes of Illinois, sec. 399.

T. B. Johnson said he could show the law different, and asked for one week's adjournment.

One o'clock p. m., court adjourned until after dinner to hear the pleas.

Three o'clock, p. m., court sat, the same as in the morning.

H. T. Hugins and George P. Stiles, counsel for Smith, read and filed their plea, moving the court that said Smith be discharged, and suffered to go at large.

1st. Because the person issuing the warrant on which he has been arrested is unauthorized to issue the same.

2nd. Because the process has been issued in a case and under circumstances where the law does not allow process.

3rd. Because the person having custody of said Smith is unauthorized to execute the warrant under which he is acting, and is not the person empowered by law to detain him.

4th. Because said Smith has been, by and before a competent court, legally examined and discharged in relation to the subject matter set forth in said warrant.

5th. Because said writ is defective in a substantial form required by law.

L. W. Hickock was called, and persisted in considering the authority under which he acted good and sufficient.

Counselor Hugins urged the first and second count in his plea, and read from the Constitution of the United States, Art. 4, 2nd sec, 2nd part. 3rd count, read Revised Statutes of Illinois, page 51, sec. 399, and page 324; 4th count, read the certificate of John S. Dunlap, clerk of the District Court for the county of DesMoines, Iowa Territory, dated May 21st, 1844, a copy of which is on file in the clerk's office.

L. W. Hickock said he had nothing to say; and the case was submitted.

DECISION—The court are of opinion, when they take into consideration their oath to support the Constitution of the United States, that the certificate of John S. Dunlap, clerk of the District Court for the county of DesMoines, Territory of Iowa, is sufficient to authorize the discharge or the prisoner, because the Constitution says no person shall twice be put in jeopardy of life for the same offense. The decision of the court is that the prisoner be discharged on all the points for which plea has been made in his behalf, and that judgment be entered against the prosecutor for cost.

Evening, T. B. Johnson was going to Burlington. Jeremiah Smith swore out an execution for $77.75. Mr. Johnson acknowledged the fee bill, and afterwards threatened to bring the dragoons in order to get Jeremiah Smith.

Mr. Hickock called for a copy of the proceedings of the Municipal Court.

I wrote the following letter to Judge Pope:—

Letter: *Joseph Smith to Judge Pope Introducing Jeremiah Smith.*

NAUVOO, May 30, 1844.

SIR,—Permit me to introduce to your particular notice and confidence as "brethren of the mystic tie," Mr. Jeremiah Smith of Iowa Territory, and Mr. H. T. Hugins. of Burlington, in said Territory Mr. Smith is a gentleman whose statements can be relied on, and Mr. Hugins a lawyer, of sound principles, as well as promising talents; and I always take pleasure in extending the reputations of honorable men among honorable men, especially when it appears to me that the benevolence and clemency extended by me is needed and merited by worthy men. Conscious, too, that your Honor is liberal and just in your sphere, and will appreciate "the golden rule," I have only to greet you with my best wishes for your welfare and happiness.

Respectfully, I have the honor to be,

Your humble servant,
JOSEPH SMITH.

JUDGE POPE.

A Presidential election was recently held on board the *Osprey* and the result was as follows:—

Joseph Smith, 65 gentlemen and 6 ladies.
Henry Clay, 27   "   " 3 "
Van Buren, 12   "   " 0 "

Friday, 31st.—

Affidavit H. T. Hugins, Anent Threat to Bring Dragoons Against Nauvoo.

STATE OF ILLINOIS, } ss.
CITY OF NAUVOO,

May 31, 1844.

Then and there personally appeared before me, Joseph Smith, Mayor of the City of Nauvoo, the undersigned H. T. Hugins, of Burlington, Iowa Territory, and made solemn oath that Thomas B. Johnson did, on the 30th day of May, 1844, declare in his presence that he intended to bring dragoons and troops of the United States from Iowa Territory into this city, for the purpose of resisting the authority and power of the Municipal Court of said city, and that he should disregard entirely the authority of said court, and that he deemed the authority of said court of no effect. Deponent further states that said Johnson, in his said conversation, had reference to the case of Jeremiah Smith, which had been decided by said court.

H. T. HUGINS.

Subscribed and sworn to before me, this 31st day of May, 1844.

WM. W. PHELPS, Clerk M. C.

Upon the foregoing affidavit, I issued a *capias* to arrest Thomas B. Johnson for threatening the peace of the city with United States dragoons. At 10 a. m., called at my office.   At 1 p. m., called to see Sister Richards, who was sick. I administered to her the laying on of hands, when she felt better.   Afternoon I attended general council, when Brother Emmett made his report.   Rode out in the evening to Van Orden's, and paid him $100.   Two or three Indians staid in the hall at night.

Saturday, June 1.—At home.   Some gentle showers.

At one, p. m., I rode out with Dr. Richards and Orrin P. Rockwell. Called on Davis at the boat.   Paid Manhard $90.   Met George J. Adams, and paid him $50. Then went to John P. Greene's, and paid him and another brother $200.   Called at William Clayton's, while Dr. Richards and Orrin P. Rockwell called at the doctor's new house.   Returned home at 4:30 p. m.

At 8 p. m., Peter Maughan, John Saunders, and Jacob Peart called at Dr. Richards' to consult about a coal-bed on Rock River. I suggested it would be profitable to employ the *Maid of Iowa* in the business of carrying the coal, &c; and all approved of this plan.

President Brigham Young and Elder John E. Page held a conference in Pittsburg.

I received the following letter:—

*Joel H. Walker to Joseph Smith—Proposes to Join Prophet in Western
Volunteer Movement.*

BOSTON, May 9th, 1844.

MY DEAR SIR.—Being so closely confined in the postoffice in this city, where I have been but a short time, I have not, before this morning been aware that you had petitioned Congress in relation to raising a military force to protect our Southern Frontier.

My purpose in addressing you is to offer my services, either in military or civil duty, as 1 am so much confined that my health must suffer if I remain a great length of time.

If I can make myself known to you by reputation which I think possible, I have every confidence, if in your power, you will favor my wishes.

At any rate, I hope you will write me at your earliest convenience upon receipt of this.

I was born in Peacham, Vermont, October 14th, 1813.　My father is Col. Joel Walker, now of Belvidere, Illinois.　Hon. E. Peck, of Springfield, Illinois, is my brother-in-law.　I was in the mercantile business in Chicago from 1836 to '39, (one of the firm of King, Walker & Co.,) since which time I have been here, with the exception of a year; have been in the military since the age of sixteen, and am considered somewhat proficient, having devoted much attention to the study of its principles, and an ardent love for the art.　I have received a good academical and mercantile education; and if there is in your place anything which would be for our mutual advantage,

I am yours respectfully,

JOEL HAMILTON WALKER.

GENERAL JOSEPH SMITH, Nauvoo.

I replied as follows:

Letter: Joseph Smith to Joel H. Walker.

NAUVOO, ILLINOIS, June 1st, 1844.

SIR.—Yours of May 9th is before me, and according to my custom I answer off hand.　I have not yet ascertained whether Congress will, by special act, authorize me to protect our beloved country.　If it should, I have not a doubt but your services could be agreeably used.

As to what you could do in Nauvoo, I am unable to say.　Gentlemen with a small capital, or a large one, can easily employ it to good advantage, our city is so rapidly improving.

Truth, virtue, and honor, combined with energy and industry, pave the way to exaltation, glory and bliss.

Respectfully, I have the honor to be your obedient servant,

JOSEPH SMITH.

JOEL HAMILTON WALKER, Boston, Mass.

A conference was held at Kalamazoo, Michigan.　Present, Wilford Woodruff, George A. Smith, of the Twelve; S. Bent, C C Rich and B. Fullmer, of the High Council; also 5 High Priests, 8 Seventies, 14 Elders, 2 Priests, and 1 Deacon. Elder Wilford Woodruff presided.　Seven branches were represented, containing 126 members, 15 Elders, 4 Priests, 1 Teacher and 2 Deacons.　Two Elders were ordained; also 1 Priest and 1 Teacher.

Conference at Kalamazoo, Michigan.

A conference was held at Alquina, Fayette Co.,

Indiana. Elder Amasa Lyman presided. 5 High Priests, 2 Seventies and 4 Elders present.

Sunday, 2.—At home. Pleasant day.

A conference was held in Glasgow, Scotland, representing 1,018 members, including 1 High
Priest, 30 Elders, 46 Priests, 36 Teachers and
20 Deacons.

Conference at
Glasgow,
Scotland.

Monday, 3.—At home. Received the following letter:

Letter: "Horace" to President Joseph Smith—Threatened Invasion of Nauvoo.

BURLINGTON, IOWA, June 2nd, 1844.

FRIEND SMITH.—I have just received intimation that there is a project on foot here to visit Nauvoo with a body of from five to six hundred armed men, for the purpose of liberating Dr. Hickock, who, it is stated, is confined in your prison. I, as a friend to your society, consider it my duty to make you aware of the danger you may be in, that you may be prepared to meet them. I think it best to keep my name from you, for were it known here that I had given notice of their proceedings, it would not be safe for me to remain. Do not think it a humbug, and treat it lightly; but prepare yourselves for the coming storm. From what I can learn, they intend going on the the next boat. I hope this may reach you in time.

I am, with respect, your friend,

HORACE.

Rode out on the hill about 9 a. m.

Municipal Court sat. I was not present. The appealed cases of Augustine Spencer, Chauncey L. Higbee, Charles A. Foster, and Robert D. Foster, came up; but as they failed to appear, the cases were referred back to the court below.

At 5 p. m. I read German with Alexander Neibaur.

President Brigham Young left Pittsburg, and preached in the evening to an attentive congregation in Old Britain.

Tuesday, 4.—At home.

Arthur Morrison and Pulaski Cahoon proposed to give $100 per month for the use of the *Maid of Iowa.* Made out their own bonds with their own security; but I would not receive them.

In the afternoon I went out to my farm, and accidentally broke the whippletree of my buggy.

Wrote the following letter to Mr. Tewkesbury, Boston.

Letter: Joseph and Hyrum Smith to Mr. Tewkesbury—Seeking to Restore Latter to Fellowship.

NAUVOO, ILLINOIS, June 4th, 1844.

SIR.—We understand that you have been cut off from the Church of Jesus Christ of Latter-day Saints; and feeling an ardent desire for the salvation of the souls of men, we take pleasure in feeling after you; and therefore would, in the sincerity of men of God, advise you to be rebaptized by Elder Nickerson, one of the servants of God, that you may again receive the sweet influences of the Holy Ghost, and enjoy the fellowship of the Saints.

The law of God requires it, and you cannot be too good. Patience is heavenly, obedience is noble, forgiveness is merciful, and exaltation is godly; and he that holds out faithful to the end shall in no wise lose his reward. A good man will endure all things to honor Christ, and even dispose of the whole world, and all in it, to save his soul. Grace for grace is a heavenly decree, and union is power where wisdom guides.

Respectfully,

JOSEPH SMITH,
HYRUM SMITH.

The Municipal Court issued an execution against Francis M. Higbee for $36.26½ for costs incurred on 8th May last.

At 6 p. m. I was in council with Elders John Taylor, Hyrum Smith, Willard Richards, Almon W. Babbitt, Lucien Woodworth, and William W. Phelps on the propriety of prosecuting the Laws and Fosters for perjury, slander, &c. Counseled Taylor to go on with the prosecution in behalf of Maria Lawrence. I concluded to go to Quincy with Taylor, and give up my bonds of guardianship as administrator of the Lawrence estate.

Prosecution of the Laws and Fosters Discussed.

Alpheus Cutler and Reynolds Cahoon are so anxious to get property, they will all flat out as soon as the Temple is completed and the faith of the Saints ceases from them, &c.

At 7 p. m. I walked out with Lucien Woodworth.

Wednesday, 5.—I went to the prairie to show some land, and returned home towards night.

At 8 p. m. I walked out with Dr. Richards. The lightning in the north was most beautiful. About 10 a shower of rain passed over, with continued distant thunder. There has not been any rain for some days back. Thermometer stood at 94½ degrees in the shade. Very warm.

I received a book entitled *"An Original History of the Religious Denominations at Present Existing in the United States,"** and wrote the following acknowledgment:

Letter: Joseph Smith to L. Daniel Rupp—Book on Religious Sects.

NAUVOO, ILLINOIS, June 5th, 1844.

DEAR SIR.—He pasa Ek-klesia, &c., together with your note, has safely reached me, and I feel very thankful for so valuable a treasure. The design, the propriety, the wisdom of letting every sect tell its own story, and the elegant manner in which the work appears, have filled my breast with encomiums upon it, wishing you God speed.

Although all is not gold that shines, any more than every religious creed is sanctioned with the so eternally sure word of prophecy, satisfying all doubt with "Thus saith the Lord;" yet, "by proving contraries," truth is made manifest," and a wise man can search out "old paths, wherein righteous men held communion with Jehovah, and were exalted through obedience.

I shall be pleased to furnish further information at a proper time, and render you such further service as the work and vast extension of our Church may demand for the benefit of truth, virtue and holiness.

Your work will be suitably noticed in our papers for your benefit.

With great respect, I have the honor to be,

Your obedient servant,

JOSEPH SMITH.

L. D. RUPP, ESQ., Lancaster City, Pa.

Thursday, 6.—About 9 a. m. I ordered my carriage for a ride; but it stood at the door till nearly noon, while I read my lettter to Henry Clay to many strangers, in the

* An article prepared by President Smith, under the title "The Latter-day Saints," is published in this work.

bar-room,* among whom was one who advocated the claims of Henry Clay for the presidency. I argued with him for a long time to show the subject in its true light, and that no man could honestly vote for a man like Clay, who had violated his oath, and not acted on constitutional principles.

About half-past twelve Dimick B. Huntington came and said that Robert D. Foster felt very bad, and he thought there was a chance for his return, if he could be reinstated in his office in the Legion, &c., &c.; and that Foster had all the affidavits of the anti-Mormons under his control. I told Huntington that if Foster would return, withdraw all the suits he had commenced, and do right, he should be restored.

I rode out in the carriage with several persons for an hour or two. At 7 p. m. a heavy shower of rain, accompanied by thunder and lightning, and another shower at 9. p. m.

I issued the following caution to the public:

Having once notified the public against receiving a certain currency called "Kirtland Safety Society;" I again caution all persons against receiving or trading in said paper money, as all that was issued as genuine was redeemed. After the first officers who signed said bills retired, a new set of officers were appointed, and the vault of the institution was broken open and robbed of several hundred thousand dollars, the signatures forged upon the said stolen bills, and those bills are being slyly bartered or had in trade, for the purpose of wilful and malicious prosecution and collection.

In the first place the bills are not collectable by law in an unchartered institution. In the second place, they are spurious, the signature being a forgery, and every person passing or trading a bill is guilty of passing counterfeit money, besides the bare-faced act of swindling. And lastly, he that uses said bills in any way, as a medium of trade is guilty of fraud, and shows a wicked and corrupt determination to wilfully, maliciously and feloniously rob the Latter-day Saints; and if the executors of the laws are as ready to mete out even handed justice to such

*This was the public sitting room of the Mansion, which, it will be remembered was used at this time as a hotel.

men as the Mormons, more indictments will indicate more honesty. Time will show.

JOSEPH SMITH.

Nauvoo, June 6, 1844.

Friday, 7.—Robert D. Foster called professedly to make some concessions in order to return to the Church. He wanted a private interview, which I declined. I had some conversation with him in the hall, in the presence of several gentlemen. I told him I would meet with him in the presence of friends. I would choose three or four, and he might choose an equal number, and that I was willing to settle everything on righteous principles. In the evening a report was circulated that Foster had said that I would receive him back on any terms, and give him a hatful of dollars into the bargain.

Prophet's Conversation with Dr. Foster.

I went to the printing office about 2 p. m., and instructed Elder John Taylor to answer a certain bill or receipt of George W. Harris.

First number of the Expositor.

The first and only number of the *Nauvoo Expositor* was published, edited by Sylvester Emmons.

In the evening I received an extremely saucy and insulting letter from Robert D. Foster. Pleasant evening.

Saturday, 8.—From 10 a. m. to 1 p. m. in City Council; also from 3 to 6:30 p. m. The subject the *Nauvoo Expositor* was taken under consideration. An ordinance was passed concerning the City Attorney and his duties.

Elder Jedediah M. Grant preached in the Mansion this evening. Thunder and rain this evening and during the night.

A ferry-boat came down from Burlington with a pleasure party, and landed at the Nauvoo House at 2 p. m.

I sent William Clayton to Carthage to give in some lots for assessments; and while there Backenstos told him that Walter Bagby had been gone eight days to Missouri to try to get another writ for me. Brother Clayton also got

news that the Democrats had dropped Van Buren, and sub-
stituted James K. Polk, of Tennessee for president, and
Silas Wright of New York, for vice-president.

I walked out in the evening with Brother Clayton.

A conference was held at Pleasant Valley, Michigan.
Present of the Twelve, Wilford Woodruff,
and George A. Smith. Elder Wilford Woodruff presided. Six branches were represented,
comprising 89 members, 5 Elders, 2 Priests, 4 Teachers,
and 3 Deacons. Five Elders were ordained.

Sunday, 9.—At home. My health not very good, in
consequence of my lungs being impaired by so much public speaking. My brother Hyrum preached at the Stand.

At 2 p. m. several passengers of the steamer *Osprey*
from St. Louis and Quincy arrived, and put up at the
Mansion. I helped to carry in their trunks, and chatted
with them in the bar-room.

There was a meeting at the Mansion at 6 p. m.

CHAPTER XXI.

THE DESTRUCTION OF THE "NAUVOO EXPOSITOR"—PROCEED-
INGS OF THE NAUVOO CITY COUNCIL AND MAYOR.

Monday, June 10, 1844.—I was in the City Council from
Nauvoo Ex- 10 a. m., to 1:20 p. m., and from 2:20 p. m.
positor before to 6:30 p. m. investigating the merits of the
Nauvoo City
Council. *Nauvoo Expositor,* and also the conduct of
the Laws, Higbees, Fosters, and others, who have formed
a conspiracy for the purpose of destroying my life, and
scattering the Saints or driving them from the state.

An ordinance was passed concerning libels.   The Council passed an ordinance declaring the *Nauvoo Expositor* a
nuisance, and also issued an order to me to abate
Ordinance on the said nuisance.   I immediately ordered the
Libels.
Marshal to destroy it without delay, and at the
same time issued an order to Jonathan Dunham, acting
Major-General of the Nauvoo Legion, to assist the Marshal with the Legion, if called upon so to do.

About 8 p. m., the Marshal returned and reported that
he had removed the press, type, printed paper, and fixtures into the street, and destroyed them.   This was done
because of the libelous and slanderous character of the
paper, its avowed intention being to destroy the municipality and drive the Saints from the city.   The *posse*
accompanied by some hundreds of the citizens, returned
with the Marshal to the front of the Mansion, when I gave
them a short address, and told them they had done right
and that not a hair of their heads should be hurt for it;
that they had executed the orders which were given me by

the City Council; that I would never submit to have
another libelous publication established in the city; that I
did not care how many papers were printed in the city, if
they would print the truth: but would submit to no libels
or slanders from them.   I then blessed them in the name
of the Lord.   This speech was loudly greeted by the
assembly with three-times-three cheers.   The *posse* and
assembly then dispersed all in good order.   Francis M.
Higbee and others made some threats.

East wind.   Very cold and cloudy.

I here insert the

Ordinance Concerning Libels and for Other Purposes.

Whereas the Saints in all ages of the world have suffered persecution
and death by wicked and corrupt men under the garb of a more holy
appearance of religion; and whereas the Church of Jesus Christ of
Latter day Saints, from the moment that its first truth sprang out of
the earth till now, has been persecuted with death, destruction, and
extermination; and, whereas men to fulfill the Scriptures that a man's
enemies are they of his own household, have turned traitors in the
Church, and combined and leagued with the most corrupt scoundrels
and villains that disgrace the earth unhung, for the Heaven-daring and
damnable purpose of revenge on account of disappointed lust, disappointed projects of speculation, fraud, and unlawful designs to rob and
plunder mankind with impunity; and, whereas such wicked and corrupt men have greatly facilitated their unlawful designs, horrid intentions, and murderous plans by polluting, degrading and converting the
blessings and utility of the press to the sin-smoking and blood-stained
ruin of innocent communities—by publishing lies, false statements,
coloring the truth, slandering men, women, children, societies, and
countries—by polishing the characters of blacklegs, highwaymen, and
murderers as virtuous; and whereas a horrid, bloody, secret plan,
upheld, sanctioned and largely patronized by men in Nauvoo and out of
it, who boast that all they want for the word *go*, to exterminate or ruin
the Latter day Saints, is for them to do one unlawful act, and the
work shall be done, is now fostered, cherished, and maturing in Nauvoo,—by men, too, who helped to obtain the very charter they would
break, and some of them drew up and voted for the very ordinances
they are striving to use as a scarecrow to frighten the surrounding
country in rebellion, mobbing, and war; and whereas, while the blood of

our brethren from wells, holes and naked prairies, and the ravishment of female virtue from Missouri, and the smoke from the altars of infamy, prostituted by John C. Bennett, and continued in the full tide of experiment and disgraceful damnation by the very self-called fragments of a body of degraded men that have got up a press in Nauvoo to destroy the charter of the city—to destroy Mormonism, men, women, and children as Missouri did; by force of arms—by fostering laws that emanate from corruption and betray with a kiss; wherefore to honor the State of Illinois, and those patriots who gave the charter, and for the benefit, convenience, health, and happiness of said city:—

Sec. 1.   Be it ordained by the City Council of Nauvoo that if any person or persons shall write or publish in said city any false statement or libel any of the citizens, for the purpose of exciting the public mind against the chartered privileges, peace, and good order of said city, or shall slander (according to the definition of slander or libel by Blackstone or Kent, or the act in the statute of Illinois,) any portion of the inhabitants of said city, or bribe any portion of the citizens of said city for malicious purposes, or in any manner or form excite the prejudice of the community against any portion of the citizens of said city, for evil purposes, he, she, or they shall be deemed disturbers of the peace; and, upon conviction before the Mayor or Municipal Court, shall be fined in any sum not exceeding five hundred dollars, or imprisoned six months, or both, at the discretion of said Mayor or court.

Sec. 2.   Be it further ordained that nothing in the foregoing section shall be so construed as to interfere with the right of any person to be tried by a jury of his vicinage, with the freedom of speech or the liberty of the press, according to the most liberal meaning of the Constitution, the dignity of freemen, the voice of truth, and the rules of virtue.

Sec. 3.   And be it further ordained that this ordinance shall be in force from and after its passage.

Passed June 10th, 1844.

GEO. W. HARRIS, President, pro tem.

W. RICHARDS, Recorder.

I also insert a brief synopsis of the proceedings of the City Council of the city of Nauvoo, relative to the destruction of the press and fixtures of the *Nauvoo Expositor*.

Synopsis of Proceedings in the City Council against the Nauvoo Expositor.

CITY COUNCIL, REGULAR SESSION,
June 8th, 1844.

In connection with other business as stated in last week's paper, the

Mayor remarked that he believed it generally the case, that when a man goes to law, he has an unjust cause, and wants to go before some one who wants business, and that he had very few cases on his docket; and referring to Councilor Emmons, editor of the *Nauvoo Expositor*, suggested the propriety of first purging the City Council; and, referring to the character of the paper and proprietors, called up Theodore Turley, a mechanic, who being sworn, said that the Laws (William and Wilson,) had brought bogus dies to him to fix.

Councilor Hyrum Smith inquired what good Foster and his brother and the Higbees and Laws had ever done. While his brother Joseph was under arrest from the Missouri persecution, the Laws and Robert D. Foster would have been ridden on a rail, if he had not stepped forward to prevent it, on account of their oppressing the poor.

Mayor said, while he was under arrest by writ from Governor Carlin William Law sued him for $40 he was owing Law, and it took the last expense money he had to pay it.

Councilor Hyrum Smith referred to J. H. Jackson's coming to this city, &c. Mayor said that William Law had offered Jackson $500 to kill him.

Councilor Hyrum Smith continued—Jackson told him he (Jackson) meant to have his daughter, and threatened him if he made any resistance. Jackson related to him a dream, that Joseph and Hyrum were opposed to him, but that he would execute his purposes; that Jackson had laid a plan with four or five persons to kidnap his daughter, and threatened to shoot any one that should come near after he had got her in the skiff; that Jackson was engaged in trying to make bogus, which was his principal business. Referred to the revelation read to the High Council of the Church, which has caused so much talk, about multiplicity of wives; that said revelation was in answer to a question concerning things which transpired in former days. That when sick, William Law confessed to him that he had been guilty of adultery, and was not fit to live, and had sinned against his own soul, &c., and inquired who was Judge Emmons? When he came here he had scarce two shirts to his back; but he had been dandled by the authorities of the city, &c., and was now editor of the *Nauvoo Expositor*, and his right hand man, was Francis M. Higbee, who had confessed to him that he had had the——!

Washington Peck sworn, said—"Soon after Joseph H. Jackson came here, he came to witness to borrow money, which witness loaned him and took some jewelry as security.

Soon after a man from across the river came after the jewelry. Jackson had stolen the jewelry from him.

At another time wanted to get money of witness. Asked witness if he would do anything dishonorable to get a living. Witness said he would not. Jackson said witness was a damn fool, for he could get a living, a deal easier than he was then doing, by making bogus; and some men high in the Church, are engaged in the business.

Witness asked if it was Joseph. "No," said Jackson; "I dare not tell it to Joseph." Witness understood him the Laws are engaged in it. Jackson said he would be the death of witness, if he ever went to Joseph, or anyone else, to tell what he had said.

AFTERNOON.—Ordered by the Council that Sylvester Emmons be suspended until his case could be investigated, for slandering the City Council. That the Recorder notify him of his suspension, and that his case would come up for investigation at the next regular session of the Council. (The order is in the hands of the Marshal).

Councilor John Taylor said that Counci or Emmons helped to make the ordinances of the city, and had never lifted his voice against them in the Council, and was now trying to destroy the ordinances and the charter.

Lorenzo Wasson sworn, said Josoph H. Jackson had told witness that bogus-making was going on in the city; but it was too damned small business. Wanted witness to help him to procure money, for the General (Smith) was afraid to go into it; and with $500 he could get an engraving for bills on the Bank of Missouri, and one on the State of New York, and could make money. Said many times witness did not know him. Believed the General had been telling witness something. "G—d d—n him; if he has, I will kill him. Swore he would kill any man that should prove a traitor to him," Jackson said, if he could get a company of men to suit him, he would go into the frontiers and live by highway robbery; had got sick of the world.

Mayor suggested that the Council pass an ordinance to prevent misrepresentations and libelous publications and conspiracies against the peace of the city; and, referring to the reports that Dr. Foster had set afloat, said he had never made any proposals to Foster to come back to the Church. Foster proposed to come back; came to Mayor's house, and wanted a private interview. Had some conversation with Foster in the hall, in presence of several gentlemen, on the 7th inst. Offered to meet him and have an interview in presence of friends, three or four, to be selected by each party; which Foster agreed to, and went to bring his friends for the interview; and the next notice he had of him was the following letter:—

To General Joseph Smith:

June 7th, 1844.

Sir,—I have consulted my friends in relation to your proposals of settlement, and they as well as myself, are of opinion that your conduct, and that of your unworthy, unprincipled clan, is so base, that it would be morally wrong, and detract from the dignity of gentlemen, to hold any conference with you. The repeated insults and abuses I, as well as my friends, have suffered from your unlawful course towards us, demands honorable resentment. We are resolved to make this our motto.

Nothing on our part has been done to provoke your anger, but have done all things as become men. You have trampled upon everything we hold dear and sacred. You have set all law at defiance, and profaned the name of the Most High to carry out your damnable purposes; and I have nothing more to fear from you than you have already threatened; and I, as well as my friends, will stay here and maintain and magnify the law as long as we stay; and we are resolved never to leave until we sell or exchange our property that we have here.

The proposals made by your agent, Dimick Huntington, as well as the threats you sent to intimidate me, I disdain and despise as I do their unhallowed author. The right of my family and my friends demands at my hand a refusal of all your offers. We are united in virtue and truth, and we set hell at defiance, and all her agents. Adieu.

R. D. Foster.

Mayor continued—And when Foster left his house, he went to a shoe shop on the hill, and reported that Joseph said to him, if he would come back he would give him Law's place in the Church, and a hat-full of specie.

Lucien Woodworth sworn. Said that the conversation as stated by the Mayor was correct. Was at the Mansion June 7th, when Dr. Foster rode up and inquired if General Smith was at home. Dr. Foster went into the house; witness followed. Dr. Foster was there, the General, and others, looking at some specimens of penmanship. Something was said respecting a conversation at that time between the General and the Doctor, Gen. Smith observed to Foster, if he had a conversation, he would want others present. The Doctor said he would have a word with him by himself, and went into the hall. Witness went to the door that he might see and hear what was passing. They still continued to talk on the subject of a conversation that they might have afterwards with others present, whom Mr. Smith and Foster might choose. Foster left, and went for those that he said he wanted pres-

ent, and would return soon with them.   He heard all the conversation.
Heard nothing about Gen. Smith's making any offers to Foster to settle.

Mayor said he wished it distinctly understood that he knew nothing
about Dimick Huntington going to see Foster.

Woodworth said he sent Dimick Huntington to Foster, and Joseph
knew nothing about it.

Councilor Hyrum Smith said Dimick Huntington came to him on the
7th inst. and said he had had an interview with Dr. Foster, and thought
he was about ready to come back, and a word from him or Joseph
would bring it about.

Mayor said—"The conduct of such men and such papers are calculated to destroy the peace of the city, and it is not safe that such things
should exist, on account of the mob spirit which they tend to produce."
He had made the statements he had, and called the witnesses to prepare the council to act in the case.

Emmons was blackguarded out of Philadelphia, and dubbed with the
title of Judge (as he had understood from citizens of Philadelphia);
was poor, and Mayor helped him to cloth for a coat before he went
away last fall, and he (Emmons) labored all winter to get the postoffice
from Mr. Rigdon (as informed).

Mayor referred to a writing from Dr. Goforth, showing that the
Laws presented the communication from the Female Relief Society in
the *Nauvoo Neighbor* to Dr. Goforth, as the bone of contention, and said
if God ever spake by any man, it will not be five years before this city
is in ashes and we in our graves, unless we go to Oregon, California or
some other place, if the city does not put down everything which tends
to mobocracy, and put down murderers, bogus-makers, and scoundrels.
All the sorrow he ever had in his family in this city has arisen through
the influence of William Law.

Councilor H. Smith spoke in relation to the Laws, Fosters, Higbees,
editor of the *Signal*, &c., and of the importance of suppressing that
spirit which has driven us from Missouri, &c.; that he would go in for
an effective ordinance.

Mayor said, at the time Governor Carlin was pursuing him with his
writs, William Law came to his house with a band of Missourians for
the purpose of betraying him.   Came to his gate, and was prevented by
Daniel Carn, who was set to watch.   Law came within his gate and
called, "Mayor," and the Mayor reproved Law for coming at that time
of night with a company of strangers.

Daniel Carn sworn.   Said that about ten o'clock at night a boat came
up the river with about a dozen men.   William Law came to the gate
with them.   Witness on guard, stopped them.   Law called Joseph to

the door, and wanted an interview. Joseph said—"Brother Law, you know better than to come here at this hour of the night," and Law retired. Next morning Law wrote a letter to apologize, which witness heard read, which was written apparently to screen himself from the censure of a conspiracy; and the letter betrayed a conspiracy on the face of it.

Adjourned at half-past 6 p. m., till Monday, 10th, 10 o'clock a. m.

Ajourned session, June 10th, 10 o'clock a, m. Alderman Harris presiding.

Mayor referred to Dr. Foster, and again read his letter of the 7th instant (as before quoted).

Cyrus Hills (a stranger) sworn. Said one day last week, believed it Wednesday, a gentleman whom witness did not know, came into the sitting room of the Nauvoo Mansion, and requested the Hon. Mayor to step aside; he wanted to speak with him. Mayor stepped through the door into the entry by the foot of the stairs, and the General (Mayor) asked him what he wished? Foster (as witness learned since was his name) said he wanted some conversation on some business witness did not understand at the time. The General refused to go any farther, and said he would have no conversation in private, and what should be said should be in public, and told Foster, if he would choose three or four men, he would meet him with the same number of men (among whom was his brother Hyrum), and they would have a cool and calm investigation of the subject; and by his making a proper satisfaction, things should be honorably adjusted. Witness judged, from the manner in which Foster expressed himself, that he agreed to the Mayor's proposals, and would meet him the same day in the presence of friends. Heard no proposals made by Mayor to Foster for settlement. Heard nothing about any offers of dollars, or money, or any other offer except those mentioned before. Nothing said about William Law. Was within hearing of the parties at the time conversation was going on.

Orrin P. Rockwell sworn. Some day last week saw Dr. Foster ride up to the Nauvoo Mansion and go in. Witness went in and found the Mayor and Dr. Foster in conversation. General Smith was naming the men he would have present, among whom were Hyrum Smith, William Marks, Lucien Woodworth, and Peter Haws; and Dr. Foster had leave to call an equal number of his friends, as witness understood, for the purpose of having an interview on some matters in contention.

The Doctor's brother was proposed. General said he had no objection; wanted him present. Dr. Foster started, saying he would be back shortly. Before Dr. Foster left, the men whom General Smith had named to be present at the conversation were sent for.

Cross-examined. Witness went into the house as Mayor and Dr. Foster were coming out of the bar-room into the hall   Nothing said by the Mayor to Dr. Foster about his coming back.   Made no offer to Foster about a settlement.

Mayor said the first thing that occurred to his mind, when he stepped into the hall with Foster, was that he wanted to assassinate him.   He saw something shining below his vest.   Mayor put his finger on it and said—"What is that?"   Foster replied—"It's my pistol," and immediately took out the pistol, and showed it openly, and wanted the Mayor to go with him alone.   Mayor said he would not go alone.   Mayor never saw the pistol before.   Had a hook on its side to hang on his waist-band.

Andrew L. Lamoreaux sworn. Said that in 1839 or '40, while President Joseph Smith, Elder Rigdon, Judge Higbee, Orrin P. Rockwell, and Dr. Robert D. Foster were on their way to Washington, called at witness' house in Dayton, Ohio; that the evening was spent very agreeably, except some dissatisfaction on the part of certain females with regard to the conduct of Dr. Foster.   On their return from Washington, witness informed President Smith of Foster's conduct.   President Smith said he had frequently reproved Foster for such conduct, and he had promised to do better, and told witness to reprove Foster, if he saw anything out of the way.   That evening Foster refused to join the company, and walked through the town till about 8 o'clock, when he came in and interrupted President Smith, who was expounding some passages of the Scripture, and changed the conversation.   Soon after the company were invited to Mr. Brown's at the next door, whither they all repaired. While at Mr. Brown's, conversation was going on, and the room much crowded.   Dr. Foster and one of the ladies he had paid so much attention to before took their seats in one corner of the room.   [Here follows statement of such lewdness in speech and conduct on the part of Foster that it would violate propriety to print it.]   Next morning witness went in while Foster and others were at breakfast, and related what he had seen.   Foster denied it.   President Smith told him not to deny it, for he saw it himself, and was ashamed of it.   Foster confessed it was true, and promised to reform.

Peter Haws sworn. Said that he came to Nauvoo before the Laws and brought considerable property.   It was a short time after the Church had been driven out of Missouri, and had arrived in this place. The families having been robbed of all in Missouri, were in a starving condition.   By the counsel of the Presidency, witness converted his funds to feeding the poor, bringing in meat and flour, &c.; and while thus engaged, drew upon the Laws, who were at that time engaged in merchandise, to the amount of some six hundred dollars, which, on account of expenditure for the poor, he was not able to pay within seventy or eighty dollars, which they pressed him for as soon as they wanted it, although he offered them good property at considerable less than the market value, as witness was obliged to leave the city on Church business for a little season. William Law threatened and intimidated witness' family during his absense for the pay.

Dr. Foster made a public dinner on the 4th of July. Witness was obliged to be absent, and deposited meat, flour, &c., with William Law to give to the poor at that dinner, and Law handed it out as his own private property. Witness carried a load of wheat to Law's mill to be ground. Law would not grind it only to give a certain quantity of flour in return by weight. Law used up the flour, promising from time to time he would refund it. As witness was about to start on a mission to the south with his valise in his hand saw Law before his door talking with Hyrum Smith. Called on Law. and told him he was going away, and his family wanted the flour. Law promised on the honor of a gentleman and a Saint, that his family should have the flour when they wanted.

Councilor Hyrum Smith said he recollected the time and circumstance.

Hawes said when he returned he found his family must have starved, if they had not borrowed money to get food somewhere else; could not get it of Law; and Law was preaching punctuality, *punctuality, punctuality*, as the whole drift of his discourses to the Saints, and abusing them himself and grinding the poor.

Mayor said, if he had a City Council who felt as he did, the establishment (referring to the *Nauvoo Expositor*) would be declared a nuisance before night; and then he read an editorial from the *Nauvoo Expositor*. He then asked who ever said a word against Judge Emmons until he attacked this Council? or even against Joseph H. Jackson or the Laws. until they came out against the city? Here is a paper (*Nauvoo Expositor*) that is exciting our enemies abroad. Joseph H. Jackson has been proved a murderer before the Council, and he declared the paper a nuisance—a greater nuisance than a dead carcass. They make it a criminality for a man to have a wife on the earth while he has one in heaven, according to the keys of the Holy Priesthood; and he then read a statement of William Law's from the *Expositor*, where the truth of God was transformed into a lie concerning this thing. He then read several statements of Austin Cowles in the *Expositor* concerning a private interview, and said he never had any private conversations with Austin Cowles on these subjects; that he preached on the stand from the Bible, showing the order in ancient days. What the opposition party want is to raise a mob on us and take the spoil from us, as they did in Missouri. He said it was as much as he could do to keep his clerk, Thompson, from publishing the proceeding of the Laws and causing the people to rise up against them. Said he would rather die tomorrow and have the thing smashed, than live and have it go on, for it was exciting the spirit of mobocracy among the people, and bringing death and destruction upon us.

Peter Hawes recalled a circumstance which he had forgotten to mention concerning a Mr. Smith who came from England and soon after died. The children had no one to protect them. There was one girl sixteen or seventeen years old, and a younger sister. Witness took these girls into his family out of pity. Wilson Law, then Major-General of the Nauvoo Legion, was familiar with the oldest daughter. Witness cautioned the girl. Wilson was soon there again, and went out in the evening with the girl, who, when charged by the witness' wife, confessed that Wilson Law had seduced her. Witness told her he could not keep her. The girl wept, made much ado, and many promises. Witness told her if she would do right she might stay; but she did not keep her promise. Wilson came again and she went out with him. Witness then required her to leave the house.

Mayor said certain women came to complain to his wife that they had caught Wilson Law with the girl [in compromising relations] at Mr. Hawes' in the night.

Councilor Hyrum Smith proceeded to show the falsehood of Austin Cowles in the *Expositor*, in relation to the revelation referred to.

Mayor said he had never preached the revelation in private; but he had public. Had not taught to the anointed in the Church in private, which statement many present confirmed; that on inquiring concerning the passage on the resurrection concerning "they neither marry nor are given in marriage," &c., he received for answer, "Man in this life must marry in view of eternity, otherwise they must remain as angels, or be single in heaven," which was the doctrine of the revelation referred to; and the Mayor spoke at considerable length in explanation of this principle, and was willing, for one, to subscribe his name to declare the *Expositor* and whole establishment a nuisance.

Two o'clock p. m. Willard Richards, the clerk of the Council, bore testimony of the good character and high standing of Mr. Smith and his family, whose daughter was seduced by Wilson Law, as stated by the last witness before the morning council; that Mrs. Smith died near the mouth of the Mississippi, and the father and eldest daughter died soon after their arrival in this place; and that the seduction of such a youthful, fatherless and innocent creature, by such a man in high standing as the Major-General of the Nauvoo Legion, was one of the darkest, damnedest, and foulest deeds on record.

Councilor Hyrum Smith concurred in the remarks made by the clerk concerning the excellent character of Mr. Smith and his family.

Mayor said the Constitution did not authorize the press to publish libels, and proposed that the Council make some provision for putting down the *Nauvoo Expositor.*

Councilor Hyrum Smith called for a prospectus of the *Expositor.*

Councilor Phelps read article 8, sec. 1, Constitution of Illinois.

Mayor called for the charter.

The clerk read the prospectus of the *Nauvoo Expositor* as follows:

PROSPECTUS OF THE "NAUVOO EXPOSITOR."

The *Nauvoo Expositor* will be issued on Friday of each week, on an imperial sheet, with a new press and materials of the best quality, and rendered worthy of the patronage of a discerning and enlightened public.

The *Expositor* will be devoted to a general diffusion of useful knowledge, and its columns open for the admission of all courteous communications of a religious, moral, social, literary, or political character without taking a decided stand in favor of either of the great political parties in the country. A part of its columns will be devoted to a few primary objects, which the publishers deem of vital importance to the public welfare. Their particular locality gives them a knowledge of the many *gross abuses exercised under the "pretended" authorities of the Charter of the City of Nauvoo,* by the legislative authorities of said city and the *insupportable oppression* of the *Ministerial powers in carrying out the unjust, illegal and unconstitutional ordinances of the same.* The publishers therefore deem it a sacred duty they owe to their country and their fellow-citizens to advocate through the columns of the *Expositor* THE UNCONDITIONAL REPEAL OF THE NAUVOO CITY CHARTER, to restrain and correct the abuses of the UNIT POWER, to ward off the iron rod which is held over the devoted heads of the citizens of Nauvoo and the surrounding country, to advocate unmitigated DISOBEDIENCE TO POLITICAL REVELATIONS, and to censure and decry gross moral imperfections wherever found, either in the plebeian, patrician or SELF-CONSTITUTED MONARCH—to advocate the pure principles of morality, the pure principles of truth, designed not to destroy, but to strengthen the mainspring of God's moral government—to advocate and exercise the freedom of speech in Nauvoo, independent of the ordinances abridging the same—*to give free toleration to every man's religious sentiment,* and sustain ALL in worshiping their God according to the monitions of their consciences, as guaranteed by the Constitution of our country, and to oppose with uncompromising hostility any UNION OF CHURCH AND STATE, or any preliminary step tending to the same—to sustain ALL *however humble,* in their equal and constitutional rights, and oppose the sacrifice of the liberty, the property and the happiness of the MANY, to the *pride* and *ambition* of the FEW; in a word, to give a full, candid and succinct statement of FACTS AS THEY REALLY EXIST IN THE CITY OF NAUVOO *fearless of whose particular case the facts may apply*—being governed by the laws of editorial courtesy, and the inherent dignity which is inseparable from honorable minds, at the same time exercising their own judgment in cases of flagrant abuses of moral delinquencies,—to use such terms and names as they deem proper, when the object is of such high importance that the end will justify the means. In this great and indispensable work, we confidently look to an enlightened public to aid us in our laudable effort.

The columns of the *Expositor* will be open to the discussion of all matters of public interest, the production of all correspondents, sub- ject to the decision of the editor alone, who shall receive or reject at his option.   National questions will be in place, but no preference given to either of the political parties.   The editorial department will contain the political news of the day, proceedings of Congress, election returns &c.   Room will be given for articles on agriculture, the mechanic arts, commercial transactions, &c.

The first number of the *Expositor* will be issued on Friday, the 7th day of June, 1844.   The publishers bind themselves to issue the paper weekly for one year, and forward 52 copies to each subscriber during the year.   Orders should be forwarded as soon as possible, that the publishers may know what number of copies to issue.

The publishers take pleasure in announcing to the public that they have engaged the service of Sylvester Emmons, Esq., who will have entire charge and supervision of the editorial department.   From an acquaintance with the dignity of character and literary qualifications of this gentleman, they feel assured that the *Nauvoo Expositor* must and will sustain a high and honorable reputation.

All letters and communications must be addressed to Charles A. Foster, Nauvoo, Ill., postpaid, in order to insure attention.

WILLIAM LAW,
WILSON LAW,
CHARLES IVINS,
FRANCIS M. HIGBEE,
CHAUNCEY L. HIGBEE,
ROBERT D. FOSTER,
CHARLES A. FOSTER,
                Publishers.

Nauvoo, Ill., May 10th, 1844.

Mayor read the statements of Francis M. Higbee from the *Expositor*, and asked—"Is it not treasonable against all chartered rights and privileges, and against the peace and happiness of the city?"

Councilor Hyrum Smith was in favor of declaring the *Expositor* a nuisance.

Councilor Taylor said no city on earth would bear such slander, and he would not bear it, and was decidedly in favor of active measures.

Mayor made a statement of what William Law said before the City Council under oath, that he was a friend to the Mayor, &c., and asked if there were any present who recollected his statement, when scores responded, Yes.

Councilor Taylor continued—Wilson Law was President of this Council during the passage of many ordinances, and referred to the records. "William Law and Emmons were members of the Council, and Emmons has never objected to any ordinance while in the Council, but has been more like a cipher, and is now become editor of a libelous paper, and is trying to destroy our charter and ordinances." He then read from the Constitution of the United States on the freedom of the press, and said—"We are willing they should publish the truth; but it is unlawful to publish libels. The *Expositor* is a nuisance, and stinks in the nose of every honest man."

Mayor read from Illinois Constitution, article 8, section 12, touching the responsibility of the press for its constitutional liberty.

Councilor Stiles said a nuisance was anything that disturbs the peace of a community, and read Blackstone on private wrongs, vol. 2, page 4; and the whole community has to rest under the stigma of these false-hoods (referring to the *Expositor*); and if we can prevent the issuing of any more slanderous communications, he would go in for it. It is right for this community to show a proper resentment; and he would go in for suppressing all further publications of the kind.

Councilor Hyrum Smith believed the best way was to smash the press and pi the type.

Councilor Johnson concurred with the Councilors who had spoken.

Alderman Bennett referred to the statement of the *Expositor* concerning the Municipal Court in the case of Jeremiah Smith as a libel, and considered the paper a public nuisance.

Councilor Warrington considered his a peculiar situation, as he did not belong to any church or any party. Thought it might be considered rather harsh for the Council to declare the paper a nuisance, and pro-posed giving a few days limitation, and assessing a fine of $3,000 for every libel; and if they would not cease publishing libels, to declare it a nuisance; and said the statutes made provisions for a fine of $500.

Mayor replied that they threatened to shoot him when at Carthage, and the women and others dare not go to Carthage to prosecute; and read a libel from the *Expositor* concerning the imprisonment of Jeremiah Smith.

Councilor Hyrum Smith spoke of the *Warsaw Signal*, and disapprobated its libelous course.

Mayor remarked he was sorry to have one dissenting voice in declaring the *Expositor* a nuisance.

Councilor Warrington did not mean to be understood to go against the proposition; but would not be in haste in declaring a nuisance.

Councilor Hyrum Smith referred to the mortgages and property of the proprietors of the *Expositor*, and thought there would be little chance of collecting damages for libels.

Alderman Elias Smith considered there was but one course to pursue that the proprietors were out of the reach of the law; that our course was to put an end to the things at once. Believed by what he had heard that if the City Council did not do it, others would.

Councilor Hunter believed it to be a nuisance. Referred to the opinion of Judge Pope on *habeas corpus*, and spoke in favor of the charter, &c. Asked Francis M. Higbee, before the jury, if he was not the man he saw at Joseph's house making professions of friendship· Higbee said he was not. (Hundreds know this statement to be false.) He also asked R. D. Foster if he did not state before hundreds of people that he believed Joseph to be a Prophet. "No," said Foster. They were under oath when they said it. (Many hundreds of people are witness to this perjury).

Alderman Orson Spencer accorded with the views expressed, that the *Nauvoo Expositor* is a nuisance. Did not consider it wise to give them time to trumpet a thousand lies. Their property could not pay for it. If we pass only a fine or imprisonment, have we any confidence that they will desist? None at all. We have found these men covenantbreakers with God, with their wives, &c. Have we any hope of their doing better? Their characters have gone before them. Shall they be suffered to go on, and bring a mob upon us, and murder our women and children, and burn our beautiful city! No! I had rather my blood would be spilled at once, and would like to have the press removed as soon as the ordinance would allow; and wish the matter might be put into the hands of the Mayor, and everybody stand by him in the execution of his duties, and hush every murmur.

Councilor Levi Richards said he had felt deeply on this subject, and concurred fully in the view General Smith had expressed of it this day; thought it unnecessary to repeat what the Council perfectly understood; considered private interest as nothing in comparison with the public good. Every time a line was formed in Far West, he was there—for what? To defend it against just such scoundrels and influence as the *Nauvoo Expositor* and its supporters were directly calculated to bring against us again. Considered the doings of the Council this day of immense moment, not to this city alone, but to the whole world; would go in to put a stop to the thing at once. Let it be thrown out of this city, and the responsibility of countenancing such a press be taken off our shoulders and fall on the State, if corrupt enough to sustain it.

Councilor Phineas Richards said that he had not forgotten the transaction at Haun's Mill, and that he recollected that his son George Spencer then lay in the well referred to on the day previous, without a winding-sheet, shroud or coffin. He said he could not sit still when he saw the same spirit raging in this place. He considered the publication of the *Expositor* as much murderous at heart as David was before the death of Uriah; was prepared to take stand; by the Mayor, and whatever he proposes; would stand by him to the last. The quicker it is stopped the better

Councilor Phelps had investigated the Constitution, Charter, and laws. The power to declare that office a nuisance is granted to us in the Springfield Charter, and a resolution declaring it a nuisance is all that is required.

John Birney sworn. Said Francis M. Higbee and Wm. Law declared they had commenced their operations, and would carry them out, law or no law.

Stephen Markham sworn. Said that Francis M. Higbee said the interest of this city is done the moment a hand is laid on their press.

Councilor Phelps continued, and referred to Wilson Law in destroying the character of a child—an orphan child, who had the charge of another child.

Warren Smith sworn. Said F. M. Higbee came to him, and proposed to have him go in as a partner in making bogus money. Higbee said he would not work for a living; that witness might go in with him if he would advance fifty dollars; and showed him (witness) a half-dollar which he said was made in his dies.

Councilor Phelps continued and he felt deeper this day than ever he felt before, and wanted to know, by "Yes,"if there was any person who wanted to avenge the blood of that innocent female who had been seduced by the then Major-General of the Nauvoo Legion, Wilson Law; when "Yes!" resounded from every quarter of the house. He then referred to the tea plot at Boston, and asked if anybody's rights were taken away with that transaction; and are we offering, or have we offered to take away the rights of anyone these two days? ("No!" resounded from every quarter.) He then referred also to Law's grinding the poor during the scarcity of grain, while the poor had nothing but themselves to grind; and spoke at great length in support of active measures to put down iniquity, and suppress the spirit of mobocracy.

Alderman Harris spoke from the chair, and expressed his feelings that the press ought to be demolished.

The following resolution was then read and passed unanimously, with the exception of Councilor Warrington:—

"Resolved, by the City Council of the city of Nauvoo, that the printing-office from whence issues the *Nauvoo Expositor* is a public nuisance and also all of said *Nauvoo Expositors* which may be or exist in said establishment; and the Mayor is instructed to cause said printing establishment and papers to be removed without delay, in such manner as he shall direct.

GEORGE W. HARRIS,
President, *pro tem.*

W. RICHARDS, Recorder.

The following order was immediately issued by the Mayor:—

STATE OF ILLINOIS,   } ss.
  CITY OF NAUVOO,   }

To the Marshal of said City, greeting.

You are here commanded to destroy the printing press from whence issues the *Nauvoo Expositor*, and pi the type of said printing establishment in the street. and burn all the *Expositors* and libelous handbills found in said establishment; and if resistance be offered to your execution of this order by the owners or others, demolish the house; and if anyone threatens you or the Mayor or the officers of the city, arrest those who threaten you, and fail not to execute this order without delay, and make due return hereon.

By order of the City Council,
JOSEPH SMITH. Mayor.

Marshal's return—"The within-named press and type is destroyed and pied according to order, on this 10th day of June, 1844, at about 8 o'clock p. m.

J. P. GREENE, C. M.
HEADQUARTERS. NAUVOO LEGION,
June 10th, 1844.

To Jonathan Dunham, acting Major-General of the Nauvoo Legion.

You are hereby commanded to hold the Nauvoo Legion in readiness fortwith to execute the city ordinances. and especially to remove the printing establishment of the *Nauvoo Expositor;* and this is what you are required to do at sight, under the penalty of the laws, provided the Marshal shall require it and need your services.

JOSEPH SMITH,
Lieut-General, Nauvoo Legion.

Tuesday 11.—Spent the forenoon in council with the brethren at my house. Went to the office and conversed with my brother Hyrum, Dr. Richards, George G. Adams, and others.

I issued the following.

PROCLAMATION.

By virtue of my office as Mayor of the city of Nauvoo, I do hereby strictly enjoin it upon the municipal officers and citizens of said city to use all honorable and lawful means in their power to assist me in maintaining the public peace and common quiet of said city. As attempts have already been made to excite the jealousy and prejudice of the people of the surrounding country, by libels and slanderous articles upon the citizens and City Council, for the purpose of destroying the charter of said city, and for the purpose of raising suspicion, wrath, and indignation among a certain class of the less honorable portion of mankind, to commit acts of violence upon the innocent and unsuspecting, in a certain newspaper called the *Nauvoo Expositor*, recently established for such purposes in said city, and which has been destroyed as a nuisance, according to the provision of the charter. I further call upon every officer, authority, and citizen to be vigilant in preventing, by wisdom the promulgation of false statements, libels, slanders, or any other malicious or evil-designed concern that may be put in operation to excite and ferment the passions of men to rebel against the rights and privileges of the city, citizens, or laws of the land; to be ready to suppress the gathering of mobs; to repel, by gentle means and noble exertion, every foul scheme of unprincipled men to disgrace and dishonor the city, or state, or any of their legally-constituted authorities; and, finally to keep the peace by being cool, considerate, virtuous, unoffending, manly, and patriotic, as the true sons of liberty ever have been, and honorably maintain the precious boon our illustrious fathers won.

In witness whereof I have hereunto set my hand and affixed the seal of said corporation at the city of Nauvoo, this 11th day of June, 1844.

JOSEPH SMITH, Mayor.

I had an interview with Elder G. J. Adams out of doors and then returned home to dinner.

At 2 p. m. I went into court. Many people were present. I talked an hour or two on passing events, the mob

party, &c., and told the people I was ready to fight, if
the mob compelled me to, for I would not be in bondage.
I asked the assembly if they would stand by me, and they
cried "Yes" from all quarters. I returned home.

The Recorder issued a summons for Sylvester Emmons
to attend the City Council on the second Saturday in July,
at 10 a. m. to answer charges then and there to be preferred against him for slandering the City Council.

Dr. Richards came to me at my room as I was talking
to my brother Hyrum, Eaton Bonney and others, and
read the following letter:

*Letter: L. W. Hickok to Joseph Smith—Probability of Indictment of the
Prophet et al, at Springfield.*

SPRINGFIELD, ILL., June 6th, 1844.

General Joseph Smith or Dr. Richards:

GENTLEMEN.—I arrived at this place on yesterday, safe and sound, in
company with Major Smith, who is in good health, and wishes to be
remembered to you and all his friends.

I have just learned that T. B. Johnson, the individual who figured so
large at Nauvoo is about to present the case, or his case, before the
grand jury at this place. This is to inform you of the fact, that you
may take the necessary precaution, or do what you think advisable in
the case. From what I can gather, you are all to be indicted who were
present in the case according to the law of the city of Nauvoo.

I remain a friend to humanity, "equal rights," and justice to all
mankind.

L. W. HICKOK.

P. S.—I have just learned that Elder Wight is in this place, and shall
put this in his hands, thinking that he may act with more efficiency than
the mail.

I am, &c.,
L. W. H.

Our communications by mail appear to be cut off, as no
part of our extensive correspondence has come to hand by
the U. S. mail for the last three weeks, and Dr. Hickok
seems to be aware of it. Instructed Dr. Richards to

answer Dr. Hickok's letter, and then rode out with O. P. Rockwell.

I received the following letter:

Letter: H. T. Hugins to Joseph Smith—Warning the Prophet of Probable Indictment.

SPRINGFIELD, ILL., June 6, 1844.

DEAR SIR.—I have just received information that T. B. Johnson is making an effort to procure from the grand jury for the United States, now in session at this place, an indictment against the members of your Municipal Court for exercising their legal and constitutional rights, and discharging their sworn duty in acting in the matter of Jeremiah Smith's petition for *habeas corpus.* I could hardly have supposed that he would succeed, had I not been informed that there is no doubt that he will accomplish his object. I give you this information that you may be able to act as circumstances may require. Mr. Smith has not had a hearing, and will not till tomorrow morning.

Yours truly,

H. T. HUGINS.

GENERAL JOSEPH SMITH, Nauvoo.

Elders Jedediah M. Grant and George J. Adams preached at my house in the evening. Cloudy and cool day.

The captain of the steamer *Osprey* called this forenoon at the printing office to see me. I rode with him to his boat, which was at the upper landing. When I came up, Charles A. Foster called the passengers to see the meanest man in the world. Mr. Eaton stopped him, and told the passengers that it was Foster who was the meanest man in the world. Rollison attempted to draw a pistol, but Eaton silenced him, and kept them all down.

David Harvey Redfield reported that last evening, while on the hill, just before the police arrived, Francis M. Higbee said while speaking of the printing press of the *Nauvoo Expositor*, if they lay their hands upon it or break it, they may date their downfall from that very hour, and in ten days there will not be a Mormon left in Nauvoo. What they do, they may expect the same in return. Addison Everett also heard him.

Jason R. Luse reported that Ianthus Rolf said, while the press was burning that before three weeks the Mansion House would be strung to the ground, and he would help to do it; and Tallman Rolf said the city would be strung to the ground within ten day.   Moses Leonard also heard him, Joshua Miller being also present.

Bryant, (merchant of Nauvoo) said before he would see such things, he would wade to his knees in blood.

It is reported that runners have gone out in all directions to try to get up a mob; and the mobbers are selling their houses in Nauvoo and disposing of their property.

CHAPTER XXII.

PRESIDENT SMITH ARRESTED FOR RIOT IN RELATION TO
"EXPOSITOR" AFFAIR—HABEAS CORPUS PROCEEDINGS BE-
FORE MUNICIPAL COURT—A CALL FROM ARKANSAS—THE
PROPHETS'S DREAMS—MASS MEETING AT WARSAW—LET-
TERS TO GOVERNOR FORD ON "EXPOSITOR" AFFAIR.

Wednesay, June 12, 1844.—At 10 a. m. in my office.
At half-past one I was arrested by David Bettisworth
on the following writ:

STATE OF ILLINOIS, } ss.
  HANCOCK COUNTY,

*The People of the State of Illinois to all Constables, Sheriffs and Coroners
of State, Greeting:* ·

Whereas complaint hath been made before me, one of the justices of
the peace within and for the county of Hancock aforesaid, upon the
oath of Francis M. Higbee of said county, that Joseph Smith, Samuel
Bennett, John Taylor and William W. Phelps, Hyrum Smith, John P.
Greene, Stephen Perry, Dimick B. Huntington, Jonathan Dunham,
Stephen Markham, William Edwards, Jonathan Holmes, Jesse P.
Harmon, John Lytle, Joseph W. Coolidge, Harvey D. Redfield, Porter
Rockwell and Levi Richards, of said county did on the 10th day of June
instant commit a riot at and within the county aforesaid, wherein they,
with force and violence broke into the office of the *Nauvoo Expositor*,
and unlawfully and with force burned and destroyed the printing press,
type and fixtures of the same, being the property of William Law. Wilson Law, Charles Ivins, Francis M. Higbee, Chauncey L. Higbee, Robert
D. Foster, and Charles A. Foster.

These are therefore to command you forthwith to apprehend the said
Joseph Smith, Samuel Bennett, John Taylor, William W. Phelps,
Hyrum Smith, John P. Greene, Stephen Perry, Dimick B. Huntington,
Jonathan Dunham, Stephen Markham, William Edwards, Jonathan
Holmes, Jesse P. Harmon, John Lytle, Joseph W. Coolidge, Harvey
D. Redfield. Porter Rockwell and Levi Richards, and bring them
before me or some other justice of the peace, to answer the premises,
and further to be dealt with according to Law.

Given under my hand and seal at Carthage, in the county aforesaid, this 11th day of June, A. D. 1844.

    [Seal]   THOMAS MORRISON, J. P.

After the officer got through reading the writ, I referred him to the clause in the writ—"Before me or some other justice of the peace of said county," saying, "We are ready to go to trial before Esquire Johnson or any justice in Nauvoo, according to the requirements of the writ;" but Bettisworth swore he would be damned but he would carry them to Carthage before Morrison, who issued the writ and seemed very wrathy. I asked him if he intended to break the law, for he knew the privilege of the prisoners, and they should have it. I called upon all present to witness that I then offered myself (Hyrum did the same) to go forthwith before the nearest justice of the peace, and also called upon them to witness whether the officer broke the law or not.

The Prophet Asserts his Rights Under the Law.

I felt so indignant at his abuse in depriving me of the privilege of the statute of Illinois in going before "some other justice," that I determined to take out a writ of *habeas corpus*, and signed the following petition:

The Prophet's Petition for Writ of Habeas Corpus.

STATE OF ILLINOIS, CITY OF NAUVOO.

To the Honorable Municipal Court in and for the said City of Nauvoo:

Your petitioner, Joseph Smith, respectfully represents that he is now under arrest in the said city of Nauvoo.

That he is in the custody of one David Bettisworth, a constable in and for said county of Hancock, who holds your petitioner, as he says by virtue of a warrant issued by one Thomas Morrison, an acting justice of the peace in and for the said county of Hancock, and State of Illinois, which warrant was issued upon the affidavits of one Francis M. Higbee, charging your petitioner with being guilty of a riot, or of having committed a riot within the county aforesaid.

Your petitioner further represents that the warrant of arrest, by virture of which the said David Bettisworth has made this arrest, does not disclose sufficiently clear and explicit the charge they have preferred.

Your petitioner further avers that this proceeding against him has been instituted through malice, private pique and corruption.

Your petitioner further avers that the design and intention of the said F. M. Higbee in commencing this prosecution is to commit and carry out more easily a conspiracy against the life of your petitioner; and that the said Higbee has publicly declared that it was his determination to do everything in his power to throw your petitioner into the hands of his enemies: and that there is a determination upon the part of said Higbee and his unhallowed coadjutors to commit an unlawful act, and to set the rights and privileges of your petitioner at defiance, and bring down upon his head this corrupt and unhallowed prosecution.

Your petitioner further avers that he is not guilty of the charge preferred against him; that he seeks an investigation before an impartial tribunal, and fears not the result.

Your petitioner would therefore ask your honorable body to grant him the benefit of the writ of *habeas corpus*, that this matter may be investigated upon legal principles, and that the legal and constitutional rights of your petitioner may be determined by your honorable body. And your petitioner, as in duty bound, will ever pray.

JOSEPH SMITH.

Subscribed and sworn to this 12th day of June, 1844, before me.

WILLARD RICHARDS, M. C. C. N.

Whereupon the clerk issued the following:

Petition of the Prophet Granted.

STATE OF ILLINOIS, CITY OF NAUVOO.

The People af the State of Illinois to the Marshal of Said City Greeting:

Whereas, application has been made before the Municipal Court of said city, that the body of one Joseph Smith, of the city aforesaid, is in the custody of one David Bettisworth, constable of the county of Hancock, and State aforesaid.

These are therefore to command the said David Bettisworth, constable as aforesaid, to safely have the body of said Joseph Smith, of the city aforesaid, in his custody detained, as it is said, together with the day and cause of his caption and detention, by whatsoever name the said Joseph Smith may be known or called, before the Municipal Court of the said city forthwith, to abide such order as the said court shall make in his behalf. And further, if the said David Bettisworth, or other person or persons having said Joseph Smith of said city of Nauvoo in custody shall refuse or neglect to comply with the provisions of this writ, you, the marshal of said city, or other person authorized to serve the same, are hereby required to arrest the person or persons so refusing or neglecting to comply, as aforesaid, and bring him or them together with the person or persons in his or their custody, forthwith before the Municipal Court aforesaid, to be dealt with according to law. And herein fail not, and bring this writ with you.

Witness, Willard Richards, clerk of the Municipal Court at Nauvoo, this 12th day of June, in the year of our Lord one thousand eight hundred and forty-four.

[Seal]   WILLARD RICHARDS,
Clerk of the Municipal Court of the City of Nauvoo.

At 5 p. m. I appeared before the Municipal Court on the above *habeas corpus*. The following is a copy of their docket.

Hearing on the Expositor affairs Before the Municipal Court of Nauvoo—
Habeas Corpus Proceedings.

Special session, June 12th, 1844, 5 o'clock p. m.

Present—Alderman N. K. Whitney, Orson Spencer, George W. Harris, Gustavus Hills, Elias Smith, and Samuel Bennett, associate justices. The Mayor being on trial, George W. Harris was elected president *pro tem*.

John P. Greene, Marshal, made his return on the writ of *habeas corpus;* "the body of Joseph Smith in court."

David Bettisworth made his return on the copy of the warrant which was attached to the petition as follows:—"I hold the body of Joseph Smith by virtue of a writ, of which the within is a copy. David Bettisworth, constable."

7th section of Addenda of City Ordinance read by Councilor George P. Styles. Resolution of City Council June 10th, 1844, declaring printing establishment of the *Nauvoo Expositor* a nuisance read. Mayor's order to the Marshal to execute the same was also read, and Lieut.-General's order of June 10th, 1844, to Major-General Dunham to assist the Marshal to destroy said printing establishment.

Theodore Turley sworn, said that the order of the Marshal was executed quietly and peaceably. There was no riot or disturbance, no noise, no exultation; the Marshal endeavored to keep peace and silence, and the officers did also. The two companies under command of Dunham and Markham retired in perfect order; no exultation or shouting. Marched in front of the Mansion, and were dismissed.

J. R. Wakefield confirmed the statements of Theodore Turley: said the Marshal stated his authority, and demanded the keys of the building, which Higbee denied; and Marshal ordered the door to be forced, and the press was broken, and type pied in the street.

James Jackson, sworn, confirmed the statements of previous witnesses; heard no noise on opening the door. Most of the confusion he heard was Higbee and his company throwing blackguard language to the posse, which they did not regard: saw the whole proceedings till they were dismissed; all was done in order. Higbee's blackguard language was not answered to at all by the ranks. Heard nothing said about shooting. Heard some one damn the city authorities. Understood it was Charles Foster. I am a stranger in this place.

John Kay, Robert Clift, Augustus A. Farnham, Joseph A. Kelting, Henry G. Sherwood, Augustus Stafford, Cyrus Canfield, John Gleason sworn.

Henry G. Sherwood confirmed the statements of previous witnesses. Pullin called for Dr. Foster and the officer commanded silence. Francis M. Higbee's threats have been lavish towards General Smith and Hyrum for a long time; has threatened injury upon them and the property of the Smiths. His conspiracies and threats have not been a little.

Orrin P. Rockwell sworn. Some three or four weeks ago said Francis M. Higbee said he would go his death against Joseph and Hyrum Smith. Francis said, "I know my course is wrong; but if I stop I shall get hell, and if I go on I shall only get hell;" and would do what he intended at the risk of his life, and would destroy the General if possible. Said the Council had ordered the press destroyed and "who lays his hands on the press it is death to them." Witness has frequently heard Higbee tell lies about the General to injure his character.

John Hughes, Joseph Dalton, William Clayton and James Goff sworn. John Hughes said, Higbee said, "By God, all I want to live for is to see this city sunk down to the lowest hell, and by God it shall!" This was just previous to the Marshal's arriving on the 10th. William Clayton said two years ago this June Francis M. Higbee confessed he was concerned with John C. Bennett in his iniquity, and had a bad disorder: said he knew his character was ruined. From time to time since that, witness knew Higbee had been threatening General Smith's character and property.

Leonard Soby heard Higbee threaten to shoot General Smith at Rollinson's store, and Higbee said the destinies of this people are this day sealed in the archives of heaven, and there shall not be left one stone upon another on that temple.

Jonn P. McEwan: Higbee said, in reference to Joseph Smith, "G—d—— him, I will shoot him and all that pertains to him; and before ten suns shall go over our heads, the Temple, Nauvoo House and Mansion shall all be destroyed, and it will be the total downfall of this community."

Cyrus Canfield: Higbee said he would never let things go till he had accomplished the downfall of General Smith; that he did not value his life to produce the downfall of General Smith.

Joseph Dalton: Higbee said, if they laid their hands on the press, from that hour they might date their downfall; that ten suns should not roll over their heads till the city was destroyed.

Court decided that Joseph Smith had acted under proper authority in destroying the establishment of the *Nauvoo Expositor* on the 10th inst.; that his orders were executed in an orderly and judicious manner, without noise or tumult; that this was a malicious prosecution on the part of Francis M. Higbee; and that said Higbee pay the costs of suit, and that Joseph Smith be honorably discharged from the accusations and of the writ, and go hence without delay.

I received the following letter:

Letter: Washington Tucker to President Smith—Asking that Elders be Sent to Arkansas.

ELDORADO, UNION COUNTY, ARKANSAS, May 4th, 1844.

To General Joseph Smith of Nauvoo, Illinois:

REVEREND SIR.—Last winter, while in the State of Mississippi, I became acquainted with one of your missionaries who was laboring at the time in that state. Also at the same time, I had an opportunity of perusing some of your sacred books; and from what I have been able to learn, as well from reading as from observation, I am constrained to be very favorably impressed towards the new doctrine. Although to me it certainly appears quite novel, yet I cannot do otherwise than believe there is great reality in it; so much so, indeed, that I am extremely anxious to become better informed on this all important and truly vital matter.

And, moreover, I am not the only one in this part who is an ardent seeker after truth. Indeed, the subject is beginning to produce a great deal of inquiry and some excitement in this country. Hundreds who never before heard of the new revelation are opening their eyes and staring and gaping to know more about it.

Some few days ago, several emigrants arrived here from Mississippi, who speak in the highest terms of the Latter-day Saints. Their report has greatly increased the inquiry and excitement previously going the rounds in this quarter. I hear a number speak of visiting Nauvoo, some of taking their families with them, and so remain there. But it is the general wish of a great many here in Union county for you to send a minister here immediately to instruct us and lead us more fully into the light of this wonderful and new revealed religion, and direct us into the true road to salvation.

This is the only subject on which my thoughts dwell both day and night; for, indeed, during my waking hours nothing diverts my meditation from this absorbing topic, and while asleep I dream of nothing else.

If you please, be so good as to send a laborer among us immediately; for indeed the harvest is great, and the laborers but few, or none at all, I have not the least doubt but that a Latter-day Saint would succeed here as well as the most sanguine could promise himself. His labors, I am sure, would be crowned with success, and the salvation of many a precious yet perishing soul might be rescued from death and prove the rich fruits of the missionary's toil.

The principal denominations here are the Methodists, the Baptists and Campbellites. A great many of the people, however, are none-professors, the greater majority of whom are quite moral, and many of them religiously inclined.

I shall look for a minister from you within two or three months. When he does come, I will see that he is hospitably received and entertained.

Your obedient and humble servant,
WASHINGTON TUCKER.

To which 1 wrote the following reply:

Letter: Joseph Smith to Washington Tucker, Promising that an Elder Should be Sent.

NAUVOO, ILLINOIS, June 12th, 1844.

SIR.—Your letter, dated May 4th, has reached me, and its contents duly considered. A multiplicity of business keeps me from writing as freely to correspondents as I could wish; still my heart is large enough for all men, and my sensibilities keen enough to have compassion for every case when justice, mercy, virtue, or humanity require it. Be pleased to accept my thanks for your very kind letter; study the Bible, and as many of our books as you can get; pray to the Father in the name of Jesus Christ, have faith in the promises made to the fathers, and your mind will be guided to the truth. An Elder shall be sent as soon as the Twelve can make the necessary arrangements.

In the Gospel of our Lord Jesus Christ,
I am your obedient servant,
JOSEPH SMITH.

WASHINGTON TUCKER, Eldorado, Arkansas.

The editor of the *Neighbor* writes:

RETRIBUTIVE JUSTICE.

A knot of base men, to further their wicked and malicious designs towards the Church of Jesus Christ of Latter-day Saints and to bolster up the intents of blacklegs and bogus-makers,and advocate the characters of murderers, established a press in this city last week, and issued a paper entitled the *Nauvoo Expositor*. The prospectus showed an intention to destroy the charter, and the paper was filled with libels and slanderous articles upon the citizens and City Council from one end to the other.

"A burnt child dreads the fire." The Church as a body and individually has suffered till "forebearance has ceased to be a virtue." The cries and pleadings of men, women and children, with the authorities were, "Will you suffer that servile, murderous paper to go on and vilify and slander the innocent inhabitants of this city, and raise another mob to drive and plunder us again as they did in Missouri?" Under these pressing cries and supplications of afflicted innocence, and in the character, dignity, and honor of the corporate powers of the charter, as granted to the city of Springfield, and made and provided as a part of our charter for legislative purposes—viz., "to declare what shall be a nuisance and to prevent and remove the same." The City Council of Nauvoo on Monday, the 10th instant, declared the establishment and *Expositor* a nuisance; and the city marshal, at the head of the police, in the evening, took the press, materials and paper into the street and burned them.

And in the name of freemen, and in the name of God, we beseech all men who have the spirit of honor in them to cease from persecuting us, collectively or individually. Let us enjoy our religion, rights and peace like the rest of mankind. Why start presses to destroy rights and privileges, and bring upon us mobs to plunder and murder? We ask no more than what belongs to us—the rights of Americans.

Thursday, 13.—At nine a. m. presided in Municipal Court, which sat in the Seventies' Hall. Present, William Marks, Newel K. Whitney, George W. Harris, Gustavus Hills, and Elias Smith, associate justices. Hyrum Smith, John P. Greene, William W. Phelps, Stephen Markham, Harvey D. Redfield, John Lytle, Dimick B. Huntington, John Taylor, Levi Richards, Stephen Perry, Jonathan H. Holmes, Jonathan Dunham, Samuel Bennett and William W. Edwards were arrested on the complaint of Francis M. Higbee, before Thomas Morrison, J. P., of

Further Action of Municipal Court on Expositor Case.

Carthage, by David Bettisworth, constable of Hancock county. They petitioned for and obtained a writ of *habeas corpus*. I sat as chief-justice; William Marks, Newel K. Whitney, George W. Harris, Gustavus Hills, and Elias Smith as associate justices.

Addison Everett and James Jackson gave their testimony under oath, when they were all honorably discharged from the accusations and arrest, the court deciding that said Higbee pay the costs; whereupon execution was issued for the amount.

In the evening I attended meeting in the Seventies' Hall. George J. Adams preached and I made some observations afterwards, and related a dream which I had a short time since. I thought I was riding out in my carriage, and my guardian angel was along with me. We went past the Temple, and had not gone much further before we espied two large snakes so fast locked together that neither of them had any power. I inquired of my guide what I was to understand by that. He answered, "Those snakes represent Dr. Foster and Chauncey L. Higbee. They are your enemies and desire to destroy you; but you see they are so fast locked together that they have no power of themselves to hurt you. I then thought I was riding up Mulholland street, but my guardian angel was not along with me. On arriving at the prairie, I was overtaken and siezed by William and Wilson Law and others, saying, "Ah! ah! we have got you at last! We will secure you and put you in a safe place!" and, without any ceremony dragged me out of my carriage, tied my hands behind me, and threw me into a deep, dry pit, where I remained in a perfectly helpless condition, and they went away. While struggling to get out, I heard Wilson Law screaming for help hard by. I managed to unloose myself so as to make a spring, when I caught hold of some grass which grew at the edge of the pit.

The Prophet's Dreams on Condition of Apostates at Nauvoo.

I looked out of the pit and saw Wilson Law at a little distances attacked by ferocious wild beasts, and heard him cry out, "Oh! Brother Joseph, come and save me!" I replied, "I cannot, for you have put me into this deep pit." On looking out another way, I saw William Law with outstretched tongue, blue in the face, and the green poison forced out of his mouth, caused by the coiling of a large snake around his body. It had also grabbed him by the arm, a little above the elbow, ready to devour him. He cried out in the intensity of his agony, "Oh, Brother Joseph, Brother Joseph, come and save me, or I die!" I also replied to him, "I cannot, William; I would willingly, but you have tied me and put me in this pit, and I am powerless to help you or liberate myself." In a short time after my guide came and said aloud, "Joseph, Joseph, what are you doing there?" I replied, "My enemies fell upon me, bound me and threw me in." He then took me by the hand, drew me out of the pit, set me free, and we went away rejoicing.

Two of the brethren arrived this evening from Carthage, and said that about three hundred mobbers were assembled there, with the avowed intention of coming against Nauvoo; also that Hamilton was paying a dollar per bushel for corn to feed their animals.

Threats of Carthage Mob against Nauvoo.

The following was published in the *Warsaw Signal* office. I insert it as a specimen of the unparalleled corruption and diabolical falsehood of which the human race has become capable in this generation:

MASS MEETING AT WARSAW.

At a mass meeting of the citizens of Hancock county, convened at Carthage on the 13th day of June, 1844 Mr. Knox was appointed president, John Doty and Lewis F. Evans, vice-presidents; and William Y. Head, secretary.

Henry Stephens, Esq., presented the following resolutions, passed at a meeting of the citizens of Warsaw, and urged the adoption of them as the sense of this meeting.

Preamble and Resolutions.

Whereas information has reached us, about which there can be no question, that the authorities of Nauvoo did recently pass an ordinance declaring a printing press and newspaper published by the opponents of the Prophet a nuisance, and in pursuance thereof did direct the Marshal of the city and his adherents to enter by force the building from whence the paper was issued, and violently (if necessary) to take possession of the press and printing materials, and thereafter to burn and destroy the same; and whereas, in pursuance of said ordinance, the Marshal and his adherents, together with a mob of Mormons, did, after sunset on the evening of the 10th instant, violently enter said building in a tumultuous manner, burn and destroy the press and other materials found on the premises.

And whereas Hyrum Smith did, in the presence of the City Council and the citizens of Nauvoo, offer a reward for the destruction of the printing press and materials of the *Warsaw Signal,* a newspaper also opposed to his interests;

And whereas the liberty of the press is one of the cardinal principles of our government, firmly guaranteed by the several constitutions of the states, as well as the United States;

And whereas, Hyrum Smith has within the last week publicly threatened the life of one of our valued citizens, Thomas C. Sharp, the editor of the *Signal;*

Therefore, be it solemnly

Resolved by the citizens of Warsaw in public meeting assembled, that we view the recent ordinance of the city of Nauvoo, and the proceedings thereunder as an outrage of an alarming character, revolutionary and tyrannical in tendency, and being under color of law as calculated to subvert and destroy in the minds of the community all reliance on the law.

Resolved, that as a community we feel anxious, when possible, to redress our grievances by legal remedies; but the time has now arrived when the law has ceased to be a protection to our lives and property. A mob at Nauvoo, under a city ordinance, has violated the highest privilege in government; and to seek redress in the ordinary mode would be utterly ineffectual.

Resolved, that the public threat made in the Council of the city, not only to destroy our printing-press, but to take the life of its editor, is sufficient, in connection with the recent outrage, to command the efforts and the services of every good citizen to put an immediate stop to the career of the mad prophet and his demoniac coadjutors. We must not only defend ourselves from danger, but we must resolutely carry the war into the enemy's camp. We do therefore declare that we will sustain our press and the editor at all hazards; that we will take full vengeance, terrible vengeance, should the lives of any of our citizens be lost in the effort; that we hold ourselves at all times in readiness to co-operate with our fellow-citizens in this state, Missouri and Iowa, to exterminate, utterly exterminate the wicked and abominable Mormon leaders, the authors of our troubles.

Resolved, that a committee of five be appointed forthwith to notify all persons in our township suspected of being the tools of the prophet to leave immediately on pain of instant vengeance. And we do recommend the inhabitants of the adjacent townships to do the same, hereby pledging ourselves to render all the assistance they may require.

Resolved, that the time, in our opinion, has arrived, when the adherents of Smith, as a body, should be driven from the surrounding settlements into Nauvoo. That the prophet and his miscreant adherents should then he demanded at their hands; and, if not surrendered, a war of extermination should be waged to the entire destruction, if necessary for our protection, of his adherents. And we hereby recommend this resolution to the consideration of the several townships, to the Mass Convention to be held at Carthage, hereby pledging ourselves to aid to the utmost the complete consummation of the object in view, that we may thereby be utterly relieved of the alarm, anxiety and trouble to which we are now subjected.

Resolved that every citizen arm himself to be prepared to sustain the resolutions herein contained.

Mr. Roosevelt rose and made a brief but eloquent speech, and called upon the citizens throughout the country to render efficient aid in carrying out the spirit of the resolutions. Mr. Roosevelt then moved a committee of seven be appointed by the chair to draft resolutions expressive of our action in future.

Mr. Catlin moved to amend the motion of Mr. Roosevelt, so that the committee should consist of one from each precinct; which motion, as amended, was adopted.

The chair then appointed the following: Col. Levi. Williams, Rocky Run precinct; Joel Catlin, Augusta; Samuel Williams, Carthage; Elisha Worrell, Chili; Captain Maddison, St. Mary's; John M. Ferris, Fountain Green; James Rice, Pilot Grove; John Carns, Bear Creek; C. L. Higbee, Nauvoo; George Robinson, La Harpe; and George Rockwell, Warsaw, were appointed said committee.

On motion of Mr. Sympson, Walter Bagby, Esq., was requested to address the meeting during the absence of the committee. He spoke long and eloquently upon the couse of our grievances, and expressed his belief that the time was now at hand when we were individually and collectively called upon to repel the innovations upon our liberties, and suggested that points be designated as places of encampment at which to rendezvous our forces, that we may be ready when called upon for efficient action.

Dr Barnes, one of the persons who went with the officers to Nauvoo for the purpose of arresting the rioters, having just arrived, came into the meeting and reported the result of their proceedings, which was, that the persons charged in the writs were duly arrested, but taken from the officers' hands on a writ of *habeas corpus* from the Municipal Court, and discharged, and the following potent words entered upon the records—*honorably released.*

On motion of O. C. Skinner, Esq., a vote of thanks was tendered to Dr. Barnes for volunteering his services in executing said writs.

Francis M. Higbee was now loudly called for. He stated his personal knowledge of the Mormons from their earliest history—throughout their hellish career in Missouri and this state—which has been characterized by the darkest and most diabolical deeds which have ever disgraced humanity.

The committee appointed to draft resolutions brought in the following report, which, after some considerable discussion, was unanimously adopted:

Whereas, the officer charged with the execution of a writ against Joseph Smith and others, for riot in the county of Hancock, which said writ said officer has served upon said Smith and others; and whereas said Smith and others refuse to obey the mandate of said writ; and whereas in the opinion of this meeting, it is impossible for said officer so raise a posse of sufficient strength to execute said writ; and whereas it is the opinion of this meeting that the riot is still progressing and that violence is meditated and determined on, it is the opinion of this meeting that the circumstances of the case require the interposition of executive power. Therefore,

Resolved, that a deputation of two discreet men be sent to Springfield to solicit such interposition.

2nd, Resolved, that said deputation be furnished with a certified copy of the resolution, and be authorized to obtain evidence, by affidavits and otherwise, in regard to the violence which has already been committed, and is still further meditated.

Dr. Evans here arose and expressed his wish that the above resolutions would not retard our operations, but that we would each one arm and equip ourselves forthwith.

The resolutions passed at Warsaw were again read by Dr. Barnes, and passed by acclamation.

On motion of A. Sympson, Esq., the suggestion of Mr. Bagby,

appointing places of encampment, was adopted—to-wit., Warsaw, Carthage, Green Plains, Spilman's landing, Chili and La Harpe.

On motion, O. C. Skinner and Walter Bagby, Esqs.,were appointed a committee to bear the resolutions adopted by this meeting to his Excellency the Governor, requiring his executive interposition.

On motion of J. H. Sherman, a central corresponding committee was appointed.

Order that J. H. Sherman, H. T. Wilson, Chauncey Robinson, William S. Freeman, Thomas Morrison, F. M. Higbee, Lyman Prentiss, and Stephen H. Tyler be said committee,

On motion of George Rockwell,

Resolved that constables in the different precincts hold themselves in readiness to obey the officer in possession of the writs, whenever called upon, in summoning the posse.

On motion, the meeting adjourned.

> JOHN KNOX, President.
> JOHN DOTY,
> LEWIS F. EVANS,Vice-Presidents.
> W. Y. HEAD, Secretary.

Friday, 14.—Wrote to Governor Ford as follows:

Letter: Joseph Smith to Governor Ford—Explaining Action of City Council in Proceedings in "Expositor" Affairs.

NAUVOO, June 14, 1844.

His Excellency Thomas Ford:

SIR.—I write you this morning, briefly, to inform you of the facts relative to the removal of the press and fixtures of the *Nauvoo Expositor* as a nuisance.

The 8th and 10th instant were spent by the City Council of Nauvoo in receiving testimony concerning the character of the *Expositor*, and the character and designs of the proprietors.

In the investigation it appeared evident to the council that the proprietors were a set of unprincipled, lawless debauchers, counterfeiters, bogus-makers, gamblers, peace-disturbers, and that the grand object of said proprietors was to destroy our constitutional rights and chartered privileges. To overthrow all good and wholesome regulations in society, to strengthen themselves against the municipality, to fortify themselves against the Church of which I am a member, and destroy all our religious rights and privileges by libels, slanders, falsehoods, perjury, &c., and sticking at no corruption to accomplish their hellish purposes; and that said paper of itself was libelous of the deepest dye, and very injurious as a vehicle of defamation, tending to corrupt the morals and disturb the peace, tranquility and happiness of the whole community, and especially that of Nauvoo.

After a long and patient investigation, of the *Expositor* and the character and design of its proprietors, the constitution, the charter, (see Addenda to Nauvoo Charter from the Springfield Charter, sec. 7) and all the best authorities on the subject; (See Chitty's Blackstone Bk. iii: v, and n., &c., &c.) the City Council decided that it was necessary for the "peace, benefit, good order and regulations" of said city, "and for the protection of property," and for "the happiness and prosperity of the citizens of Nauvoo," that said *Expositor* should be removed, and declaring said *Expositor* a nuisance ordered the Mayor to cause them to be removed without delay; which order was committed to the Marshal by due process, and by him executed the same day, by removing the paper, press and fixtures into the streets and burning the same; all which was done without riot, noise, tumult or confusion, as has already been proved before the municipality of the city; and the particulars of the whole transaction may be expected in our next *Nauvoo Neighbor.*

I send you this hasty sketch that your Excellency may be aware of the lying reports that are now being circulated by our enemies that there has been a "mob at Nauvoo," and "blood and thunder," and "swearing that two men were killed," &c., &c., as we hear from abroad, are false—false as Satan himself could invent, and that nothing has been transacted here but what has been in perfect accordance with the strictest principles of law and good order on the part of the authorities of this city; and if your Excellency is not satisfied, and shall not be satisfied after reading the whole proceedings which will be forthcoming soon, and shall demand an investigation of our municipality before Judge Pope, or any legal tribunal at the Capitol, you have only to write your wishes, and we will be forthcoming. We will not trouble you to fill a writ or send an officer for us.

I remain, as ever, a friend of truth, good order, and your Excellency's humble servant,

JOSEPH SMITH.

The following letters were also written:

Letter: John M. Bernhisel to Governor Ford—Confirming Correctness of the Prophet's Report of "Expositor" Affair.

NAUVOO, June 14th, 1844.

To His Excellency Governor Ford:

SIR.—Though I have not the honor of a personal acquaintance with you, I take the liberty of stating to you that I arrived here from the city of New York about a year since, where I was engaged in the practice of medicine for many years; that General Smith's letter to you of this date has been read in my hearing; that the statement contained therein in relation to the proceedings of the municipal authorities for the removal of the press whence issued a scandalous sheet entitled the *Nauvoo Expositor* are correct, having been an eye- and ear-witness of them.

The whole affair was conducted by the City Marshal and his posse in the most quiet and orderly manner, without the least noise, riot or tumult; and when the nuisance was abated, they immediately retired and were dismissed.

Having been a boarder in General Smith's family for more than nine months, and having therefore had abundant opportunities of contemplating his character and observing his conduct, I have concluded to give you a few of my "impressions" of him.

General Joseph Smith is naturally a man of strong mental powers, and is possessed of much energy and decision of character, great penetration, and a profound knowlege of human nature. He is a man of calm judgment, enlarged views, and is eminently distinguished by his love of justice. He is kind and obliging, generous and benevolent, sociable and cheerful, and is possessed of a mind of a contemplative and reflective character. He is honest, frank, fearless and independent, and as free from dissimulation as any man to be found.

But it is in the gentle charities of domestic life, as the tender and affectionate husband and parent, the warm and sympathizing friend, that the prominent traits of his character are revealed, and his heart is felt to be keenly alive to the kindest and softest emotions of which human nature is susceptible; and I feel assured that his family and friends formed one of the greatest consolations to him while the vials of wrath were poured upon his head, while his footsteps were pursued by malice and envy, and reproach and slander were strewn in his path, as well as during numerous and cruel persecutions, and severe and protracted sufferings in chains and loathsome prisons, for worshiping God according to the dictates of his own conscience.

He is a true lover of his country, and a bright and shining example of integrity and moral excellence in all the relations of life. As a relig-ious teacher, as well as a man, he is greatly beloved by this people. It is almost superfluous to add that the numerous ridiculous and scandalous reports in circulation respecting him have not the least foundation in truth.

In haste, I have the honor to be your Excellency's most obedient and humble servant,

JOHN M. BERNHISEL.

Letter: Wakefield to Governor Ford—Anent the "Expositor" Affair.

CITY OF NAUVOO, June 14th, 1844.

Hon. *Governor Ford:*

Being a stranger in the city of Nauvoo, but fully acquainted with the facts as stated in Gen. Smith's letter of June 14th, I assert that they are true in every particular, and that the press. in the minds of all unprejudiced people, was a nuisance of the worst character, and that the authorities acted perfectly proper in destroying it; and in accomplishing the act there was no noise, tumult or riot.   Furthermore, having remained for a few weeks at General Smith's house, I think it my duty to state that I have seen nothing in his deportment but what is correct in all his domestic relations, being a kind husband and an affectionate father; and all his affairs, both domestic and official, have not only been free from censure, but praiseworthy, and ought to be imitated by every one desirous of order and peace.

Yours, sir, most obediently,

J. R. WAKEFIELD, M. D.

Letter: Sidney Rigdon to Governor Ford—"Expositor" Affair.

POST OFFICE, NAUVOO, ILL., June 14 1844.

His Ecellency, Thomas Ford:

DEAR SIR.—I address this letter to your Excellency by the hand of Mr. Samuel James, in consequence of the difficulties now existing in this county, difficulties in which I have had no concern; and fearing as I do, that in the midst of an excitement so great as I have understood now exists in this county, (I say understood, for it is by report only that I speak) there may be attempts made to prejudice your mind to take some measures of a violent character that may seriously affect the citizens of this place, and injure innocent and unoffending persons, which I am satisfied would grieve your Excellency, as well as every other thinking and humane man.

There have for a length of time difficulties existed between a number of the citizens of this place, which kept increasing. One of the parties had recourse to the *Warsaw Signal* as a medium through which they communicate their difficulties to the world.   These productions were inflammatory to a high degree, and the party thus assailed charged the matter as libelous and highly abusive.   To these exposures responses appeared in the papers of this place, charging the matter as being false and the authors as defamers and slanderers.

Things continued thus until a paper was established in this place called the *Nauvoo Expositor*. The first number of this paper made its appearance, and it was inflammatory and abusive to an extreme. This raised the excitement to a degree beyond control, and threatened serious consequence.

At this particular juncture all the authorities of the city feeling a common interest in the peace and quiet of the place, and fearing the worst consequences must follow if something were not done, the City Council met and took the matter into consideration, and, after deliberating on the subject and examining the charter, came to the conclusion to hazard all the consequences of declaring the press a nuisance, and accordingly ordered its removal.   The city marshal, in obedience to this order, went and removed the press and destroyed it.   This was done without tumult or disorder.   When the press was destroyed, all returned home, and everything has been perfectly quiet ever since.

Within the last three days warrants have been issued from a justice of the peace in Carthage, calling for the bodies of the persons who destroyed the press.   The officer having the matter in charge, refuses the persons a hearing before any other justices of the peace than the one issuing the warrants.   With this demand they refused to comply, as there is a large assembly of persons assembled at Carthage making threats of violence; and they say, and I have no doubt they verily believe that by going there their lives will be in danger; and from the intelligence which I received last evening from a person in no way connected with the affair, and one of undoubted veracity, I must think so myself. This gentleman informs me that he has been in Carthage since Monday last at the land sales, and he heard threatenings by the persons assembled there that if they could get into Nauvoo they would murder indiscriminately, and those who wanted to escape must leave.   This your Excellency would abhor as I do.

The citizens of this county who do not reside in Nauvoo, and those of other counties, have indeed no interest of a personal kind at stake in this matter. There are no persons disturbing them, nor going to do so; and this great excitement does savor of something else to me than a regard for the laws.   Why not let the parties, as in all other cases of the kind settle their difficulties as the laws of the country in such cases have provided.

Have the citizens of Nauvoo ever interfered with cases of difficulty existing in other parts of the county, held public meetings to inflame the public mind in favor of one party, and prejudice it against the other party?   Most assuredly they have not.   Why, then, must the citizens of this place be scourged with such attempts?

If the citizens of Hancock want the supremacy of the laws maintained let these tumultuous assemblies disperse, and let the civil officers, if resisted, do as in other cases—call for aid instead of assembling in advance, and then call for persons to be brought into their midst as prisoners amidst threats and insults.

From the confidence I have in your Excellency's superior intelligence, and sound discretion, I doubt not that your Excellency will arrive at just conclusions when the matter is submitted to your consideration, as I understand it is about being.

I can see no need for executive interference in this case, but disperse all uncalled for assemblies, and let the laws have their regular course, which they can have if these assemblies will disperse. If not, I fear the consequences.

I send this to your Excellency as confidential, as I wish not to take any part in the affair, or be known in it.

With consideration of high regard, I am, dear sir, your Excellency's most obedient servant,

SIDNEY RIGDON.

I read the doings of the City Council to Dr. Wakefield, and gave him a volume of the *Times and Seasons.* About 4 p. m., I rode out with Dr. Bernhisel. Pleasant and warm day. Towards night some clouds.

A Mr. Norton was tried before Esq. Aaron Johnson, J. P., on a charge of firing Foster's printing office, and acquitted.

Saturday, 15.—At home. Two brethren came from Lima, and said that Colonel Levi Williams had demanded the arms belonging to the Mormons in that neighborhood. They wished my advice on the subject. I told them that when they gave up their arms, to give up their lives with them as dearly as possible.

It is reported that a company of men were constantly training at Carthage. Mr. John M. Crane, from Warsaw, said that several boxes of arms had arrived at Warsaw from Quincy. There was some considerable excitement, but expected they were going to wait the meeting at Carthage, which was fixed for the middle of next week.

The Prophet's Advice on giving up Arms.

The *Maid of Iowa* arrived at half-past two p. m., while I was examining the painting, "Death on the Pale Horse," by Benjamin West, which has been exhibiting in my reading room for the last three days. The *Maid* had lost her lighter, which was loaded at the time with corn and lumber, it having broken in two on a snag in the Iowa river.

This morning Samuel James started for Springfield to carry letters and papers to Governor Ford concerning the destruction of the *Expositor* press.

About 7 p. m. I rode out with Orrin P. Rockwell.

I received the following letter:

Letter: A. Ladd to Joseph Smith—Wharfage Matter.

FORT MADISON, June 15th, 1844.

Gen. Joseph Smith:

DEAR SIR.—1 have been informed that a writ was issued against the steam ferry, *New Purchase*, for wharfage, on Tuesday last, but no such writ has been served or shown to me, and I am anxious to learn the facts of the case. If it is required, I will pay wharfage with the greatest of pleasure; but I would dislike to have cost to pay in addition. I expect to visit this place with my boat at least once a week during the season. You will confer a favor on me by informing me in relation to the ordinance, &c.

It has been rumored that the *New Purchase* was employed to convey to Nauvoo an armed force to attack the citizens in connection with other companies, on account of the late difficulties at your place; but it is not true. I assure you that the boat will not be employed in any unlawful enterprise, and I further assure you that there is no unkind feeling existing in our place against the people of your place.

I remain yours with respect,

A. LADD.

Captain of the *New Purchase*.

GEN. JOSEPH SMITH, Nauvoo, Ill.

CHAPTER XXIII.

DISCOURSE OF THE PROPHET—THE GODHEAD—THE MOB UP-
RISING—ARREST OF PRESIDENT SMITH, ET AL. OVER THE
"EXPOSITOR" AFFAIR—TRIAL BEFORE ESQUIRE WELLS.

A conference was held at Franklin, Michigan. Present
of the Twelve, Wilford Woodruff and George A. Smith;
Elder George A. Smith presided. Nine   Conference in
branches were represented, comprising 170   Michigan.
members, 8 Elders, 5 Priests, 5 Teachers and 3 Deacons.
There were ordained 1 High Priest, 9 Elders, 2 Priests,
and 1 Deacon, under the hands of Elders Wilford Woodruff, George A. Smith and Charles C. Rich.

Sunday, June 16, 1844.—I preached at the stand at
10 a. m. Before I closed my remarks it rained severely.
The following synopsis was reported by Elder Thomas
Bullock, whom I had transferred from the duties of
clerk of the *Maid of Iowa* to my office.

SERMON BY THE PROPHET—THE CHRISTIAN GODHEAD—PLURALITY
OF GODS.

Meeting in the Grove, east of the Temple, June 16, 1844.

Prayer by Bishop Newel K. Whitney.

Choir sang, "Mortals Awake."

President Joseph Smith read the 3rd chapter of Revelation, and took
for his text 1st chapter, 6th verse—"And hath made us kings and
priests unto God and His Father: to Him be glory and dominion forever
and ever. Amen.

It is altogether correct in the translation. Now, you know that of
late some malicious and corrupt men have sprung up and apostatized
from the Church of Jesus Christ of Latter-day Saints, and they declare
that the Prophet believes in a plurality of Gods, and, lo and behold!
we have discovered a very great secret, they cry—"The Prophet says
there are many Gods, and this proves that he has fallen."

It has been my intention for a long time to take up this subject and lay it clearly before the people, and show what my faith is in relation to this interesting matter. I have contemplated the saying of Jesus (Luke 17th chapter, 26th verse)—"And as it was in the days of Noah, so shall it be also in the days of the Son of Man." And if it does rain, I'll preach this doctrine, for the truth shall be preached.

I will preach on the plurality of Gods. I have selected this text for that express purpose. I wish to declare I have always and in all congregations when I have preached on the subject of the Deity, it has been the plurality of Gods. It has been preached by the Elders for fifteen years.

I have always declared God to be a distinct personage, Jesus Christ a separate and distinct personage from God the Father, and that the Holy Ghost was a distinct personage and a Spirit: and these three constitute three distinct personages and three Gods. If this is in accordance with the New Testament, lo and behold! we have three Gods anyhow, and they are plural; and who can contradict it?

Our text says "And hath made us kings and priests unto God and His Father." The Apostles have discovered that there were Gods above, for Paul says God was the Father of our Lord Jesus Christ. My object was to preach the scriptures, and preach the doctrine they contain, there being a God above, the Father of our Lord Jesus Christ. I am bold to declare I have taught all the strong doctrines publicly, and always teach stronger doctrines in public than in private.

John was one of the men, and apostles declare they were made kings and priests unto God, the Father of our Lord Jesus Christ. It reads just so in the Revelation. Hence, the doctrine of a plurity of Gods is as prominent in the Bible as any other doctrine. It is all over the face of the Bible. It stands beyond the power of controversy. A wayfaring man, though a fool, need not err therein.

Paul says there are Gods many and Lords many. I want to set it forth in a plain and simple manner; but to us there is but one God— that is *pertaining to us;* and he is in all and through all. But if Joseph Smith says there are Gods many and Lords many, they cry, "Away with him! Crucify him! crucify him!"

Mankind verily say that the scriptures are with them. Search the scriptures, for they testify of things that these apostates would gravely pronounce blasphemy. Paul, if Joseph Smith is a blasphemer, you are. I say there are Gods many and Lords many, but to us only one, and we are to be in subjection to that one, and no man can limit the bounds or the eternal existence of eternal time. Hath he beheld the eternal world, and is he authorized to say that there is only one God? He makes himself a fool if he thinks or says so, and there is an end of his career or progress in knowledge. He cannot obtain all knowledge, for he has sealed up the gate to it.

Some say I do not interpret the scripture the same as they do. They say it means the heathen's gods. Paul says there are Gods many and Lords many; and that makes a plurality of Gods, in spite of the whims of all men. Without a revelation, I am not going to give them the knowledge of the God of heaven. You know and I testify that Paul had no allusion to the heathen gods. I have it from God, and get over it if you can. I have a witness of the Holy Ghost, and a testimony that Paul had no allusion to the heathen gods in the text. I will show from the Hebrew Bible that I am correct, and the first word shows a plurality of Gods; and I want the apostates and learned men to come here and prove to the contrary, if they can. An unlearned boy must give you a little Hebrew. *Berosheit baurau Eloheim ait aushamayeen vehau auraits*, rendered by King James' translators, "In the beginning God created the heaven and the earth." I want to analyze the word *Berosheit*. *Rosh*, the head; *Sheit*, a grammatical termination, The *Baith* was not originally put there when the inspired man wrote it, but it has been since added by an old Jew. *Baurau* signifies to bring forth; *Eloheim* is from the word *Eloi*, God, in the singular number; and by adding the word *heim*, it renders it Gods. It read first, "In the beginning the head of the Gods brought forth the Gods," or, as others have translated it, "The head of the Gods called the Gods together." I want to show a little learning as well as other fools—

> A little learning is a dangerous thing.
> Drink deep, or taste not the Pierian spring.
> There shallow draughts intoxicate the brain,
> And drinking largely sobers us up again.

All this confusion among professed translators is for want of drinking another draught.

The head God organized the heavens and the earth. I defy all the world to refute me. In the beginning the heads of the Gods organized the heavens and the earth. Now the learned priests and the people rage, and the heathen imagine a vain thing. If we pursue the Hebrew text further, it reads, "*Berosheit baurau Eloheim ait aashamayeen vehau auraits*"—"The head one of the Gods said, Let us make a man in our own image." I once asked a learned Jew, "If the Hebrew language compels us to render all words ending in *heim* in the plural, why not render the first *Eloheim* plural?" He replied, "That is the rule with few exceptions; but in this case it would ruin the Bible." He acknowledged I was right. I came here to investigate these things precisely as I believe them. Hear and judge for yourselves; and if you go away satisfied, well and good.

In the very beginning the Bible shows there is a plurality of Gods beyond the power of refutation. It is a great subject I am dwelling on. The word *Eloheim* ought to be in the plural all the way through— Gods. The heads of the Gods appointed one God for us; and when you take [that] view of the subject, it sets one free to see all the beauty, holiness and perfection of the Gods. All I want is to get the simple, naked truth, and the whole truth.

Many men say there is one God; the Father, the Son and the Holy Ghost are only one God! I say that is a strange God anyhow—three in one, and one in three! It is a curious organization. "Father, I pray not for the world, but I pray for them which thou hast given me." "Holy Father, keep through Thine own name those whom thou hast given me, that they may be one as we are." All are to be crammed into one God, according to sectarianism. It would make the biggest God in all the world. He would be a wonderfully big God—he would be a giant or a monster. I want to read the text to you myself—"I am agreed with the Father and the Father is agreed with me, and we are agreed as one." The Greek shows that it should be agreed. "Father, I pray for them which Thou hast given me out of the world, and not for those alone, but for them also which shall believe on me through their word, that they all may be agreed, as Thou, Father, art with me, and I with Thee, that they also may be agreed with us," and all come to dwell in unity, and in all the glory and everlasting burnings of the Gods; and then we shall see as we are seen, and be as our God and He as His Father. I want to reason a little on this subject. I learned it by trans-lating the papyrus which is now in my house. I learned a testimony concerning Abraham, and he reasoned concerning the God of heaven. "In order to do that," said he, "suppose we have two facts: that sup-poses another fact may exist—two men on the earth, one wiser than the other, would logically show that another who is wiser than the wisest may exist. Intelligences exist one above another, so that there is no end to them."

If Abraham reasoned thus—If Jesus Christ was the Son of God, and John discovered that God the Father of Jesus Christ had a Father, you may suppose that He had a Father also. Where was there ever a son without a father? And where was there ever a father without first being a son? Whenever did a tree or anything spring into existence without a progenitor? And everything comes in this way. Paul says that which is earthly is in the likeness of that which is heavenly, Hence if Jesus had a Father, can we not believe that *He* had a Father also? I despise the idea of being scared to death at such a doctrine, for the Bible is full of it.

I want you to pay particular attention to what I am saying. Jesus said that the Father wrought precisely in the same way as His Father had done before Him. As the Father had done before. He laid down His life, and took it up the same as His Father had done before. He did as He was sent, to lay down His life and take it up again; and then was committed unto Him the keys, &c. I know it is good reasoning.

I have reason to think that the Church is being purged. I saw Satan fall from heaven, and the way they ran was a caution. All these are wonders and marvels in our eyes in these last days. So long as men are under the law of God, they have no fears—they do not scare themselves.

I want to stick to my text, to show that when men open their lips against these truths they do not injure me, but injure themselves. To the law and to the testimony, for these principles are poured out all over the scriptures. When things that are of the greatest importance are passed over by weak-minded men without even a thought, I want to see truth in all its bearings and hug it to my bosom. I believe all that God ever revealed, and I never hear of a man being damned for believing too much; but they are damned for unbelief.

They found fault with Jesus Christ because He said He was the Son of God, and made Himself equal with God. They say of me, like they did of the apostles of old, that I must be put down. What did Jesus say? "Is it not written in your law, I said, Ye are Gods? If He called them Gods unto whom the word of God came, and the scriptures cannot be broken, say ye of Him whom the Father had sanctified and sent into the world, Thou blasphemest, because I said I am the Son of God?" It was through Him that they drank of the spiritual rock. Of course He would take the honor to Himself. Jesus, if they were called Gods unto whom the word of God came, why should it be thought blasphemy that I should say I am the son of God?

Oh, poor, blind apostates! did you never think of this before? These are the quotations that the apostates take from the scriptures. They swear that they believe the Bible, the Book of Mormon and the Doctrine and Covenants and then you will get from them filth, slander, and bogus-makers plenty. One of the apostate Church official members prophesied that Joseph would never preach any more, and yet I am now preaching.

Go and read the vision in the Book of Covenants. There is clearly illustrated glory upon glory—one glory of the sun, another glory of the moon, and a glory of the stars; and as one star differeth from another star in glory, even so do they of the telestial world differ in glory, and every man who reigns in celestial glory is a God to his dominions. By the apostates admitting the testimony of the Doctrine and Covenants, they damn themselves. Paul, what do you say? They impeached Paul and all went and left him.   Paul had seven churches, and they drove him off from among them; and yet they cannot do it by me.   I rejoice in that.   My testimony is good.

Paul says, "There is one glory of the sun, and another glory of the moon, and another glory of the stars; for one star differeth from another star in glory.   So is also the resurrection of the dead."   They who obtain a glorious resurrection from the dead, are exalted far above principalities, powers, thrones, dominions and angels, and are expressly declared to be heirs of God and joint heirs with Jesus Christ, all having eternal power.

The scriptures are a mixture of very strange doctrines to the Christian world, who are blindly led by the blind.   I will refer to another scripture.   "Now," says God, when He visited Moses in the bush, (Moses was a stammering sort of a boy like me) God said, "Thou shalt be a God unto the children of Israel."   God said, "Thou shalt be a God unto Aaron, and he shall be thy spokeman."   I believe those Gods that God reveals as Gods to be sons of God, and all can cry, "Abba, Father!"   Sons of God who exalt themselves to be Gods, even from before the foundation of the world, and are the only Gods I have a reverence for.

John said he was a king.   "And from Jesus Christ, who is the faithful witness, and the first begotten of the dead, and the Prince of the kings of the earth.   Unto Him that loved us, and washed us from our sins in His own blood, and hath made us kings and priests unto God, and His Father; to him be glory and dominion forever and ever Amen."   Oh, Thou God who art King of kings and Lord of lords, the sectarian world, by their actions, declare, "We cannot believe Thee."

The old Catholic church traditions are worth more than all you have said.   Here is a principle of logic that most men have no more sense than to adopt.   I will illustrate it by an old apple tree.   Here jumps off a branch and says, I am the true tree, and you are corrupt.   If the whole tree is corrupt, are not its branches corrupt?   If the Catholic religion is a false religion, how can any true religion come out of it?   If the Catholic church is bad, how can any good thing come out of it?   The character of the old churches have always been slandered by all apostates since the world began.

I testify again, as the Lord lives, God never will acknowledge any traitors or apostates.   Any man who will betray the Catholics will betray you; and if he will betray me, he will betray you.   All men are liars who say they are of the true Church without the revelations of Jesus Christ and the Priesthood of Melchisedek, which is after the order of the Son of God.

It is in the order of heavenly things that God should always send a new dispensation into the world when men have apostatized from the truth and lost the priesthood; but when men come out and build upon other men's foundations, they do it on their own responsibility, without authority from God; and when the floods come and the winds blow, their foundations will be found to be sand, and their whole fabric will crumble to dust.

Did I build on any other man's foundation? I have got all the truth which the Christian world possessed, and an independent revelation in the bargain, and God will bear me off triumphant. I will drop this subject. I wish I could speak for three or four hours; but it is not expedient on account of the rain: I would still go on, and show you proof upon proofs; all the Bible is equal in support of this doctrine, one part as another.

[On account of the rain it was impossible for Thomas Bullock to report any more].

Judge Jesse B. Thomas came to Nauvoo, and advised me to go before some justice of the peace of the county, and have an examination of the charges specified in the writ from Justice Morrison of Carthage; and if acquitted or bound over, it would allay all excitement, answer the law and cut off all legal pretext for a mob, and he would be bound to order them to keep the peace.

Advice of Judge Thomas on Expositor Affair.

Some forty gentlemen from Madison came down on a steamer to inquire into our difficulties. I met them at the Masonic Hall at 2 p. m., and gave them the desired information. Dr. Richards, the city recorder, read the minutes of the council declaring the *Nauvoo Expositor* a nuisance. They expressed themselves satisfied. I then went to the Temple stand and met some thousands of the brethren. I instructed them to keep cool, and prepare their arms for defense of the city, as it was reported that a mob was collecting in Carthage and other places. I exhorted them to be quiet and make no disturbance, and instructed the brethren to organize into the capacity of a public meeting and send delegates to all the surrounding towns and villages, to explain the cause of the disturbance, and show

Inquiry of Delegation from Madison.

them that all was peace at Nauvoo, and that there was no cause for any mobs.

A messenger arrived stating that the clerk of the county court expected to be driven out of Carthage tomorrow, and the only way to prevent the shedding of blood was to get the Governor in person to come down with his staff.

I wrote to Governor Ford stating the facts as follows:

Letter: Joseph Smith to Governor Ford—Inviting the Governor to Nauvoo.

NAUVOO, ILLINOIS, June 16th, 1844.

His Excellency Thomas Ford:

SIR.—I am informed from credible sources, as well as from the proceedings of a public meeting at Carthage, &c., as published in the *Warsaw Signal* extra, that an energetic attempt is being made by some of the citizens of this and the surrounding counties to drive and exterminate "the Saints" by force of arms; and I send this information to your Excellency by a special messenger, Hugh McFall, Adjutant-General, Nauvoo Legion, who will give all particulars; and I ask at your hands immediate counsel and protection.

Judge Thomas has been here and given his advice in the case, which I shall strictly follow until I hear from your Excellency, and in all cases shall adhere to the Constitution and laws.

The Nauvoo Legion is at your service to quell all insurrection and support the dignity of the common weal.

I wish, urgently wish your Excellency to come down in person with your staff and investigate the whole matter without delay, and cause peace to be restored to the country; and I know not but this will be the only means of stopping an effusion of blood.

The information referred to above is before me by affidavit.

I remain, sir, the friend of peace, and your Excellency's humble servant,

JOSEPH SMITH.

I enclosed a copy of the following affidavit:

Affidavit: Mob Movements.

STATE OF ILLINOIS, HANCOCK CO., } ss.
CITY OF NAUVOO.

June 16th, 1844. Personally appeared before me Willard Richards, clerk of the Municipal Court of the City of Nauvoo, Thomas G. Wilson; and after being duly sworn according to law, deposeth and saith that during the last evening Robert Johnson, of the county aforesaid, told deponent that fifteen hundred Missourians would assemble at Warsaw, in said county, on the morning of the 17th instant; that the arms of the Quincy Greys had been sent up to Warsaw; that they had five cannon at Warsaw; that said Missourians, and others who would join them, would proceed to Carthage, and the Quincy Greys and other companies from Adams county were to meet the Missourians in Carthage at the time before stated; that from Carthage they were going round to the branches of the Church of Latter-day Saints in said county, and inform them that they must deny Joseph's being a Prophet, and if they did not deny Joseph, they must leave immediately: and on Thursday next the whole mob were to proceed to Nauvoo and demand Joseph and Hyrum Smith, and the City Council of said city, and if Joseph and Hyrum and the City Council were not given up they would blow up the city, and kill and exterminate all the inhabitants of said city.

THOMAS G. WILSON.

[Seal of Municipal Court.]

Subscribed and sworn to before me, Willard Richards, clerk. In testimony whereof I have hereunto set my hand and seal of the Municipal Court of said city, at the time and place above written.

WILLARD RICHARDS,
Clerk of the Municipal Court, City of Nauvoo.

I have compared the within affidavit with the original, and find it a true copy.

In witness whereof I have hereunto set my hand and seal of court at the city of Nauvoo, this 16th day of June, 1844.

WILLARD RICHARDS.
Clerk of the Municipal Court, City of Nauvoo.

Brother Butler, from Bear Creek, came in and made affidavit before the Recorder that fifteen hundred Missourians were to cross the Mississippi to Warsaw the next morning, on their way to Carthage.

I received a letter from Father Morley:

Letter: Isaac Morley to Joseph Smith—Mob Threats.

President Joseph Smith:

SIR.—Believing it to be my duty to inform you of the proceedings of a wicked clan against the Saints in this place, I improve this opportunity. On yesterday, George Baker, in company with Joseph Barber, a Mr. John Banks, Luther Perry and one more, (his name I have not got) came to my house. Mr. Baker came to my door and said he had some business, and wished to speak with me.   I went out into my door-yard with him, and he came in company with a Mr. Banks and others. They informed me they were a committee appointed to inform me and our people that they had three propositions to make to us.   In the first place, yourself and about seventeen others had broken the law and good order of society; that we, the Mormon people, must take up arms and proceed with them for your arrest, or take our effects and proceed immediately to Nauvoo, otherwise give up our arms, and remain quiet until the fuss is over.   We have until Monday morning next to make up our minds.   We have made up our minds that we shall not comply with any of these proposals, but stand in our own defense.   We have no signature from the Governor, or any official officer, to accept of such wicked proposals.

We are informed that the company must be at Col. Williams' tomorrow morning at eight o'clock to proceed to Nauvoo.

I have thought it my duty to inform you of the proceedings here.

This from your humble servant,

ISAAC MORLEY.

June 16th, 1844,

We certify the above is true.

GARDNER SNOW,
EDMUND DURFEE,
IRA WILLSEY.

I sent the following answer by Joseph S. Allen:

Letter: Joseph Smith to Isaac Morley—Instructions on Resisting Mob.

HEADQUARTERS NAUVOO LEGION, NAUVOO.
LIEUT-GENERAL'S OFFICE,
June 16th, 1844.

Col. Isaac Morley:

SIR.—In reply to yours of this date, you will take special notice of the movements of the mob party that is stirring up strife and endeavoring to excite rebellion to the government and destroy the Saints, and cause all the troops of said Legion in your vicinity to be in readiness to act at a moment's warning; and if the mob shall fall upon the Saints by force of arms, defend them at every hazard unless prudence dictate the retreat of the troops to Nauvoo, in which case the mob will not disturb your women and children; and if the mob move towards Nauvoo, either come before them or in their rear and be ready to co-operate with the main body of the Legion. Instruct the companies to keep cool, and let all things be done decently and in order.

Give information by affidavit before a magistrate and special messengers to the Governor of what has occurred, and every illegal proceed-ing that shall be had on the subject, without delay.   Also notify me of the same, and demand instruction and protection from the Governor.

JOSEPH SMITH.
Lieut.-Gen. Nauvoo Legion.

I insert the minutes of a public meeting:

Minutes of a Public Meeting at Nauvoo.

A public meeting was held in the city of Nauvoo on Sunday evening, the 16th inst.

Mr. John Taylor was unanimously called to the chair, and William Clayton appointed clerk.

The chairman stated briefly the object of the meeting, whereupon it was unanimously

Resolved, that inasmuch as many false reports are being circulated through this county by designing characters for the purpose of bring-ing persecution upon the peaceable citizens of this city we will use our endeavors to disabuse the public mind, and present a true statement of facts before them as speedily as possible.

Resolved that for the more speedy accomplishment of this object, this meeting appoint delegates to go to the different precincts throughout the county to lay a true statement of facts before the public.

The following delegates were then appointed;

To Warsaw precinct, Messrs. Joseph A. Kelting, Hugh McFall and John T. Barnett.

Rocky Run precinct, Messrs. Anson Call, E. Horner, Nicholas Bos-cow and David Evans.

Carthage precinct, Messrs. Lewis Robinson, Jeremiah Hatch, Jun., and Dr. Robinson.

Lima precinct, Messrs. William Allen, Elam Luddington, and Charles Warner.

La Harpe and Pilot Grove, Messrs. Benjamin Warrington and Hiram Kimball.

Spilman's Landing and Appanoose, Messrs. Elijah R. Swackhammer, and Truman Gillett, Jun.

St. Mary's and Chili, Messrs. Philander Colton and Averett.

Fountain Green and Macedonia, Messrs. Moses Claire and Andrew H. Perkins.

Augusta and Plymouth, Messrs. Peter Slater, Darwin Chase and John McIllwrick.

On motion, meeting adjourned *sine die.*

JOHN TAYLOR, President.
WILLIAM CLAYTON, Secretary.

And I issued the following:

PROCLAMATION.

MAYOR'S OFFICE, NAUVOO, June 16th, 1844.

As there are a number of statements in circulation which have for their object the injury of the Latter-day Saints, all of which are false and prompted by black-hearted villains, I therefore deem it my duty to disabuse the public mind in regard to them, and to give a plain statement of facts which have taken place in the city within a few days past, and which have brought upon us the displeasure of the unprincipled and the uninformed, and seems to afford an opportunity to our enemies to unite and arouse themselves to mob. And already they have commenced their hellish operations by driving a few defenseless "Mormons" from their houses and homes in the vicinity of Warsaw and Carthage.

A short time since a press was started in this city which had for its object the destruction of the institutions of the city, both civil and religious. Its proprietors are a set of unprincipled scoundrels, who attempted in every possible way to defame the character of the most virtuous of our community, and change our peaceful and prosperous city into a place as evil and polluted as their own black hearts. To rid the city of a paper so filthy and pestilential as this became the duty of every good citizen who loves good order and morality. A complaint was made before the City Council, and after a full and impartial investigation it was voted (without one dissenting voice) a public nuisance, and to be immediately destroyed. The peace and happiness of the place demanded it, the virtue of our wives and daughters demanded it, and our consciences demanded it at our hands as conservators of the public peace.

That we acted right in this matter we have the assurance of one of the ablest expounders of the laws of England, namely, Blackstone, the Constitution of the state of Illinois, and our own chartered rights,

If, then, our charter gives us the power to decide what shall be a nuisance, and cause it to be removed, where is the offense? What law is violated? If, then, no law has been violated, why this ridiculous excitement and bandying with lawless ruffians to destroy the happiness of a people whose religious motto is "Peace and good will toward all men?"

Our city is infested with a set of blacklegs, counterfeiters and debauchers, and that the proprietors of this press were of that class the minutes of the Municipal Court fully testify, and in ridding our young and flourishing city of such characters we are abused by not only villainous demagogues, but by some who from their station and influence in society, ought rather to raise than repress the standard of human excellence.

We have no disturbance nor excitement among us, save what is made by the thousand-and-one idle rumors afloat in the country. Everyone is protected in his person and property, and but few cities of a population of twenty thousand people, in the United States, have less of dissipation or vice of any kind than the city of Nauvoo.

Of the correctness of our conduct in this affair, we appeal to every high court in the state, and to its ordeal we are willing to appear at any time that his Excellency, Governor Ford, shall please call us before it. I therefore, in behalf of the Municipal Court of Nauvoo, warn the lawless not to be precipitate in any interference in our affairs; for, as sure as there is a God in Israel, we shall ride triumphant over all oppression.

JOSEPH SMITH, Mayor.

I received a letter from my uncle, John Smith:

Letter: John Smith to Joseph Smith—Accompanying Delegation to the Prophet.

MACEDONIA, ILLINOIS, Sunday, June 16th, 1844.

President Smith:

DEAR SIR.—We send you Brothers Perkins, two faithful brethren, who will give you all the information which is within our knowledge of the proceedings of our enemies; and as we have not heard or received communication from Nauvoo as regards the course we should pursue, we now ask your counsel, and you will please forward per Brother Perkins. We should have sought your counsel sooner, only on account of high water. Please communicate in writing the course we in this part of the country should pursue. The brethren in these parts are in good faith, spirits, and health generally, and may be relied on.

Respectfully,
JOHN SMITH.

GENERAL JOSEPH SMITH.

Monday, 17.—I wrote the following to my uncle, John Smith:

Letter: Joseph Smith to John Smith—Instructions in Case of Mob Violence.

NAUVOO, June 17th, 1844.

Uncle John:

DEAR SIR.—The brethren from Ramus arrived here this morning. We were glad to see them, and to hear that you were all alive in the midst of the ragings of an infatuated and blood thirsty mob. I write these few lines to inform you that we feel determined in this place not to be dismayed if hell boils over all at once. We feel to hope for the best, and determined to prepare for the worst; and we want this to be your motto in common with us, "That we will never ground our arms until we give them up by death." Free trade and sailor's rights, protection of persons and property, wives and families.

If a mob annoy you, defend yourselves to the very last; and if they fall upon you with a superior force, and you think you are not able to compete with them, retreat to Nauvoo. But we hope for better things. But remember, if your enemies do fall upon you, be sure and take the best and most efficient measures the emergency of the case may require.

Remember the front and the rear of your enemies, because if they should come to Nanvoo to attack it unlawfully and by mob force, a little annoyance upon the rear with some bold fellows would be a very good thing to weaken the ranks of an enemy.

It is impossible to give you correct information what to do before-hand; but act according to the emergency of the case, but never give up your arms, but die first.

The brethren will give you information of the conversation between us. We have sent to the Governor, and are about to send again, and we want you to send affidavits and demand the attention of the Governor, and request protection at his hand, in common with the rest of us that by our continual wearying we may get him to come and investigate the whole matter.

I now conclude with my best wishes, and must refer you to the brethren for further information.

JOSEPH SMITH.
Mayor of the City of Nauvoo, and Lieut.-General of the Nauvoo Legion.

My brother Hyrum wrote the following letter to President Brigham Young.

Letter: Hyrum Smith to Brigham Young—Calling Home the Twelve.

CITY OF NAUVOO, June 17th, 1844.

Dear Brother Brigham Young:

There has been for several days a great excitement among the inhabitants in the adjoining counties. Mass meetings are held upon mass meetings drawing up resolutions to utterly exterminate the Saints. The excitement has been gotten up by the Laws, Fosters and the Higbees, and they themselves have left the city and are engaged in the mob. They have sent their runners into the State of Missouri to excite them to murder and bloodshed, and the report is that a great many hundreds of them will come over to take an active part in murdering the Saints. The excitement is very great indeed.

It is thought best by myself and others for you to return without delay, and the rest of the Twelve, and all the Elders that have gone out from this place, and as many more good, faithful men as feel disposed to come up with them. Let wisdom be exercised; and whatever they do, do it without a noise. You know we are not frightened, but think it best to be well prepared and be ready for the onset; and if it is extermination, extermination it is, of course.

Communicate to the others of the Twelve with as much speed as possible, with perfect stillness and calmness. A word to the wise is sufficient; and a little powder, lead and a good rifle can be packed in your luggage very easy without creating any suspicion.

There must be no excuses made, for wisdom says that a strict compliance with our request will be for our safety and welfare.

In haste, I remain yours in the firm bonds of the new and everlasting covenant,

HYRUM SMITH.

P. S.—Large bodies of armed men, cannon and munitions of war are coming on from Missouri in steamboats. These facts are communicated to the Governor and President of the United States, and you will readily see that we have to prepare for the onset.

In the bonds of the new and everlasting covenant, I remain yours,

JOSEPH SMITH.

This morning [17th of June] I was arrested, together with Samuel Bennett, John Taylor, William W. Phelps, Hyrum Smith, John P. Greene, Dimick B. Huntington, Jonathan Dunham, Stephen Markham, Jonathan H. Holmes, Jesse P. Harmon, John Lytle, Joseph W. Coolidge, H. David Redfield, O. P. Rockwell, and Levi Richards, by Constable Joel S. Miles, on a writ issued by Daniel H. Wells, on complaint of W. G. Ware, for a riot on the 10th inst. in destroying the *Nauvoo Expositor* press. At 2 p. m. we went before Justice Wells at his house; and after a long and close examination we were discharged. The following is a copy of the minutes of this trial.

Arrest of the Prophet et al. for Destroying the Expositor.

Minutes of the Trial of Joseph Smith et al. Before Esquire Wells—
"Expositor" Affair.

FOR THE "NEIGHBOR."

STATE OF ILLINOIS   } ss.
COUNTY OF HANCOCK. }

Justice's Court, June 17th, 1844, Daniel H. Wells, Justice of the Peace, presiding.

State of Illinois *v.* Joseph Smith, Samuel Bennett, John Taylor, William W. Phelps, Hyrum Smith, John P. Greene, Stephen Perry, Dimick B. Huntington, Jonathan Dunham, Stephen Markham, Jonathan H. Holmes, Jesse P. Harmon, John Lytle, Joseph W. Coolidge, H. David Redfield, Orrin Porter Rockwell and Levi Richards.

Defendants were brought before the court by Joel S. Miles, constable of the county aforesaid, by virtue of a warrant issued by the court on complaint of W. G. Ware, for a "riot committed in the city of Nauvoo, county aforesaid, on or before the 10th day of June, 1844, by forcibly entering a brick building in said city, occupied as a printing office and taking therefrom by force, and with force of arms, a printing-press, types and paper, together with other property, belonging to William Law, Wilson Law, Robert D. Foster, Charles A. Foster, Francis M. Higbee, Chauncey L. Higbee and Charles Ivins, and breaking in pieces and burning the same in the streets.

George P. Stiles, Esq., appeared as counsel for the defense, and Edward Bonny, Esq., for the prosecution.

W. G. Ware sworn. Said he was present when the City Council passed an order for the destruction of the press. Went up to the Temple and heard the Marshal read the order of the Mayor. Did not know how they got into the building. The press was taken out and destroyed.

Defendants' counsel objected to witness' stating who voted for the passage of the bill in the council and read Burns' definition of a riot, and said there could be no accessory.

Councilor Bonny read from the statute, page 173, and pleaded there might be an accessory to a riot. Court decided there might be an accessory to any crime either before or after the fact.

Witness knew some who voted for the order in the City Council. Heard Gen. Dunham give orders for the destruction of the press. Dunham, Redfield and Richards took an active part in the destruction of the press. Did not know all the persons.

Cross-examined: City Council considered the press a nuisance, and ordered it to be abated. Was present at the execution of the Mayor's orders. No unnecessary noise. All was done peaceably. Saw no disorder. Heard no language by the prisoners calculated to disturb the peace.

Henry O. Norton sworn. Was at the printing office, Heard Marshal Greene give orders to open the door. Markham carried out the press and type. Recollected Dunham. Could not identify any others. No contention between the marshal and Higbee. Marshal asked Charles A. Foster for the key, which he refused to give. Heard no threats concerning the destruction of the press any time.

O. F. Moesseur sworn. Saw many of the people gather around the printing office. Went over, back, and over again. Could not identify any person. Heard no loud talking or noise.

P. T. Rolfe sworn. Was at work in the printing office last Monday night. Chauncey Higbee came in and said the Council was about to destroy the press, and took some papers from the desk. Marshal Greene came with a company and demanded the key. Foster and Higbee forbade him. Door was opened by Lytle, as witness thought. The press and fixtures were destroyed, and some paper and a desk belonging to Dr. Foster, containing several thousand dollars of property, four thousand dollars auditor's warrants, and other valuable papers.

Cross-examined, Did not know the amount of warrants and papers. Presumed they were destroyed, Did not know whether they were destroyed. Was from the office long enough to have them taken out. Said Greene, Dunham, Markham, Holmes, Perry, Edwards and Harmon helped to move the press. Never knew anything against Joseph Smith personally.

B. Warrington sworn. Was present at the Council when the bill passed to destroy the press.

Joseph Smith objected to calling in question the doings of the City Council, and referred to the proceedings of Congress to show that all legislative bodies have a right to speak freely on any subject before them, and that Congress is not responsible for a riot which might arise on the execution of their order by the Marshal; that the execution of such order could not be a riot, but a legal transaction; that the doings of the City Council could only be called in question by the powers above them, and that a magistrate had not that power; that the City Council was not arraigned here for trial, but individuals were arraigned for a riot. If the City Council had transcended their powers, they were amenable to the Supreme Court; and that Judge Thomas had decided that an action could not lie if no riot had been committed.

Councilor Bonny said, if the act was committed under an ordinance of the city, they might show it in justification.

Court decided that the gentlemen arraigned were arraigned in their individual capacity, and could not be recognized by the court in their official capacity.

Witness said that all he heard the prisoners say was said as councilors.

Testimony on the prosecution closed.

Councilor Stiles moved that the prisoners be dismissed for want of a case being made out.

Councilor Bonny read the riot act, and pleaded a case had been made out.

Motion overruled by the Court.

Dr. Wakefield, Willard Richards and Edward Wingott sworn.

Dr. J. R. Wakefield, of New York, said he went on the hill after the order passed the Council. Saw some portion of the Legion collected, walking quietly along as though they were walking to the "Dead March in Saul." There was no noise or tumult. Higbee asked the Marshal his authority, Marshal stated his authority from the Mayor for abating the nuisance. Higbee set them all at defiance. Some twelve men were called out, who went up stairs and opened the door. Did not know how the door was opened. There was not more than one thump. Marshal Greene asked one of the officers if anything was destroyed except what belonged to the press? and the officer replied, "No." All was done in perfect order—as peaceably as people move on a Sunday. Was present all the time. All that was done was done in their official capacity as officers of the city.

Councilor Bonny objected to the testimony, as it was not before the Court that there was any city.

Court decided that any knowledge in possession of the Court was testimony in the Court.

E. Wingott, of Boston, concurred in Dr. Wakefield's statements. Was by the door when it was opened, and knew that nothing more than a knee was put against it. All was done quietly. Was present in the City Council when the order passed. Nothing said in Council except what was said in capacity of councilors and aldermen. Was by the door all the time when the press and type and things used in connection with the press were destroyed. There was no other property taken from the building.

Cross-examined: Did not know the name of the man who opened the door. Knew Orrin P. Rockwell.

Willard Richards read the resolutions of the City Council of the 10th instant, declaring the press a nuisance, &c., and the Mayor's order to the Marshal to destroy the press, and the Lieut.-General's order to Major-General Dunham to assist the Marshal with the Legion, if needed, to abate the nuisance, and the Marshal's return that the press and type were destroyed (as published in the *Neighbor*, June 19).

Court queried about the destruction of the desk.

Dr. Wakefield was again called up.   Heard Marshal tell the officers and men to hurt no property, except the press, type and fixtures; and after the abatement, Marshal inquired if his order had been obeyed, and the officers said it had.

E. Wingott called again.   Heard Mr. Foster ask Higbee for the key of the office, and afterward saw him deliver the key to Mr. Higbee. There was nothing destroyed but what pertained to the press.

Addison Everett of New York, sworn.   Saw the press and type taken out and burned.   Saw no other property burned.   Desk might have been taken away before.   Should not have seen it, if it had been. Saw no desk burned.   Does not believe any desk was burned.

Joel S. Miles sworn. Foster said his docket was not burned. Witness was sure that Dr. Foster said he had taken other papers out of the desk.

W. G. Ware called again.   Saw Charles Foster coming from the office and go into Foster's house with books under his arm.   Looked like account books.   Saw nothing but the press and fixtures brought out, except a chair, and the Marshal ordered it to be carried back.

E. Wingott recalled.   Stood close by the door.   Could see all that was done.   Did not believe a desk could be brought out and he not see it.

Dr. Wakefield recalled. Joseph Smith and Hyrum were not on the hill at all that evening.

Joseph W. Coolidge was discharged by the Court and sworn.   Charles Foster asked Francis Higbee for the key to the office.   Higbee hesitated.   Foster said he wanted to get a desk that had some valuable papers in it.   Foster got the key and went in.   Did not see him remove the desk. Might have removed it, and witness not see it.   There was no desk burned.

The councilors submitted the case without plea, and the court discharged the prisoners.

CHAPTER XXIV.

RUMORS OF INVASION FROM MISSOURI—THE LEGION ORDERED
TO ASSIST THE CITY MARSHAL—NAUVOO PLACED UNDER
MARTIAL LAW—THE MAYOR'S ADDRESS TO THE LEGION.

Monday, June, 17, 1844, (continued).—Edward Hunter, Philip B. Lewis and Major John Bills started with the affidavit of Thomas G. Wilson and my letter, &c., to take to Governor Ford. I charged Edward Hunter, under oath, to tell Governor Ford all he knew concerning me, good or bad, as he has known me for several years; and I said to him, "Brother Hunter, you have always wished you had been with us from the commencement. If you will go to Springfield and do this business for me now in this time of danger, it shall be as though you had been in Missouri and had always been with us."

Stephen Markham made the following affidavit:

Affidavit of Stephen Markham—Nauvoo to be Attacked.

STATE OF ILLINOIS } ss.
CITY OF NAUVOO. }

On the 17th day of June, 1844, came Stephen Markham before me, Willard Richards, recorder of said city; and after being duly sworn, deposeth and saith that, from the public papers, especially the Warsaw papers, and from reports from the various precincts, a mob may be expected to make an immediate attack upon the citizens and city of Nauvoo, on account of the gatherings at the various precincts, and threats to exterminate the Latter-day Saints.

STEPHEN MARKHAM.

Sworn and subscribed to before me this 17th day of June, 1844.

WILLARD RICHARDS.
Recorder of the city of Nauvoo.

As soon as the affidavit came to my knowledge, I issued the following:

PROCLAMATION.

NAUVOO, June 17th, 1844.

To John P. Greene, Marshal of the City of Nauvoo, &c.:

SIR.—Complaint having been made to me on oath that a mob is collecting at sundry points to make an attack on this city, you will therefore take such measures as shall be necessary to preserve the peace of said city according to the provisions of the charter and the laws of the state; and with the police and the Legion, see that no violent act is committed. General Dunham is hereby instructed to act with the Marshal in keeping the peace, according to law.

JOSEPH SMITH, Mayor.

And also:

ORDER TO THE LEGION.

HEADQUARTERS NAUVOO LEGION,
NAUVOO, June 17th, 1844.

To Major General in Command, Jonathan Dunham:

Complaint having been made on oath that a mob is preparing to make an attack upon this city and citizens of Nauvoo, and having directed the Marshal to keep the peace, you are hereby commanded to order the Nauvoo Legion to be in readiness to assist said Marshal in keeping the peace, and doing whatever may be necessary to preserve the dignity of the state and city.

JOSEPH SMITH, Lieut.-General N. L.

Also:

LEGION PLACED AT COMMAND OF CITY MARSHAL.

HEADQUARTERS NAUVOO LEGION, June 17th, 1844.

To Major-General in Command, Jonathan Dunham:

You are hereby instructed to execute all orders of the Marshal, and perform all services with as little noise and confusion as possible, and take every precaution to prevent groups of citizens, &c., from gathering on the bank of the river, on the landing of boats or otherwise, and allay every cause and pretext of excitement as well as suspicion, and let your operations be efficient and decided.

JOSEPH SMITH, Lieut.-Gen. N. L.

I also issued an order to Col. A. P. Rockwood to call out

my guard and staff immediately to my headquarters; and
I also ordered the Legion to parade tomorrow at 10 a. m.

HEADQUARTERS NAUVOO LEGION,
LIEUT.-GENERAL'S OFFICE
June 17th, 1844.

To Col. A. P. Rockwood:

You are hereby commanded to notify my guard and staff to appear at
headquarters without delay, armed and equipped according to law for
military duty and inspection, with powder and ball.

JOSEPH SMITH, Lieut.-Gen. N. L.

I advised my brother Hyrum not to mail his letter to
President Young at present.

I directed my clerk, Thomas Bullock, to remain in the
Masonic Hall and take affidavits of the men who are constantly coming in with news of the movements of the mob
and preserve copies to forward to the Governor.

I received the following letter:

*Letter: H. T. Hugins to Joseph Smith—Probable Indictment of the Prophet
at Springfield.*

BURLINGTON, IOWA TERRITORY,
June 17th, 1844.

DEAR SIR.—I write to inform you that Jeremiah Smith arrived here
yesterday in safety and free from arrest.   He desires, through me, to
thank you for your kindness and attention to him while at
Nauvoo.

I wrote from Springfield to apprise you that an effort was making to
procure an indictment against the members of your Municipal Court for
the part they acted in trying the *habeas corpus* petitions.   Through the
efforts of myself and Dr. Hickock, that result was prevented, and T. B.
Johnson exposed.   The boat is casting off, and I must close.   Dr. Dunlop will write to apprise you of the William and Wilson Law's proceedings here.   You will hear from me again soon.

Yours truly,
H. T. HUGINS.

GENERAL JOSEPH SMITH, Nauvoo, Ill.

The mob is still increasing in numbers at Carthage and
other places.

It is reported that William and Wilson Law have laid a plan to burn the printing office of the *Nauvoo Neighbor* this night. I therefore stationed a strong police round the premises and throughout the city.

The captain of the steamer *Osprey* called upon me.

About 11 p. m. a negro came into my office with an open letter, without any date or name, and said that Dr. Foster gave it to him at Madison to give Henry O. Norton. In that letter Foster said that Dunham and Richards swore in my presence that they would kill him (Foster) in two days, and that there was a man in Madison would swear he had heard them say so at my house.

Charge of Threats Against Foster's Life.

I closed the issuing of orders about 12 at night, ready to retire to rest. Pleasant weather.

To refute the lying slanders of the *Warsaw Signal*, as published in the proceedings of a meeting held at Carthage an the 13th instant, I insert the following certificate.*

TO THE PUBLIC.

We, whose names are undersigned, having seen in the *Warsaw Signal*, containing the proceedings of a meeting held at Carthage on the 13th instant, many statements calculated to arouse the indignation and wrath of the people against the citizens of Nauvoo, do certify that Hyrum Smith did not make any threats, nor offer any reward against the *Signal* or its editor in the City Council.

JOHN TAYLOR,	GEORGE W. HARRIS,
AARON JOHNSON,	PHINEHAS RICHARDS,
WILLIAM BOLES,	THOMAS SMITH,
GEORGE P. STILES,	EDWARD HUNTER,
W. W. PHELPS,	MOSES F. CLARK,
ALANSON RIPLEY,	LEVI RICHARDS,
ORSON SPENCER,	ADDISON EVERETT,
JOHN P. GREENE,	PHILIP B. LEWIS.

NAUVOO, June 17, 1844.

* This was published in the *Nauvoo Neighbor* impressions of June 19 1844.

A *Nauvoo Neighbor* extra was issued with the following editorial:

TO THE PUBLIC.

As a soft breeze on a hot day mellows the air, so does the simple truth calm the feelings of the irritated; and so we proceed to give the proceedings of the City Council relating to the removal of the *Nauvoo Expositor* as a nuisance. We have been robbed, mobbed and plundered with impunity some two or three times; and as every heart is more apt to know its own sorrows, the people of Nauvoo had ample reason, when such characters as the proprietors and abettors of the *Nauvoo Expositor* proved to be before the City Council, to be alarmed for their safety.

The men who got up the press were constantly engaged in resisting the authority or threatening something. If they were fined, an appeal was taken, but the slander went on; and when the paper came, the course and the plan to destroy the city was marked out. The destruction of the city charter and the ruin of the Saints was the all-commanding topic.

Our lives, our city, our charter and our characters are just as sacred, just as dear, and just as good as other people's; and while no friendly arm has been extended from the demolition of our press in Jackson county, Missouri, without law, to this present day, the City Council with all the law of nuisance, from Blackstone down to the Springfield charter, knowing that if they exceeded the law of the land a higher court could regulate the proceedings, abated the *Nauvoo Expositor*.

The proceedings of the Council show, as sketched out, that there was cause for alarm. The people, when they reflect, will at once say that the feelings and rights of men ought to be respected. All persons otherwise, who, without recourse to justice, mercy or humanity, come out with inflammatory publications, destructive resolutions, or more especially extermination, show a want of feeling a want of respect and a want of religious toleration that honorable men will deprecate among Americans as they would the pestilence, famine, or horrors of war. It cannot be that the people are so lost to virtue as to coolly go to murdering men, women and children. No; candor and common sense forbid it!

Dr. Richards and Thomas Bullock sat up all last night writing the proceedings of the City Council for the press.

Tuesday, 18.—At 8 a. m. the Legion assembled according to orders, and organized at 9 a. m., under Acting Major-General Jonathan Dunham. The first cohort under the command of Colonel Stephen Markham, acting

Brigadier-General, and the second cohort under Colonel Hosea Stout, acting Brigadier-General.

Just before, I was informed that there were several boxes of arms landed at the upper stone house, which were secured by the Marshal. Soon after it was discovered that the arms (40 stand) had been sent by Henry G. Sherwood, and the Marshal bought them for the city.

About 1:45 p. m. I proclaimed the city under martial law, and caused the following orders to be issued from the Mayor's office:

DECLARATION OF MARTIAL LAW.

PROCLAMATION.

MAYOR'S OFFICE, CITY OF NAUVOO,
June 18th, 1844.

To the Marshal of the City of Nauvoo:

From the newspapers around us, and the current reports as brought in from the surrounding country, I have good reason to fear that a mob is organizing to come upon this city, and plunder and destroy said city, as well as murder the citizens; and by virtue of the authority vested in me as Mayor, and to preserve the city and the lives of the citizens, I do hereby declare the said city, within the limits of its incorporation, under martial law. The officers, therefore, of the Nauvoo Legion, the police as well as all others, will strictly see that no persons or property pass in or out of the city without due orders.

JOSEPH SMITH, Mayor.

About 2 p. m. the Legion was drawn up in the street close by the Mansion. I stood in full uniform on the top of the frame of a building.

Judge Phelps read the *Warsaw Signal* extra of the 17th, wherein all the "old citizens" were called upon to assist the mob in exterminating the leaders of the Saints and driving away the people.

I addressed the Legion for about an hour and a half.

[The following synopsis of this address was compiled by George A. Smith, from the verbal reports of Joseph G. Hovey, William G. Sterrett, Robert Campbell and many others who heard the Prophet on the occasion]:

The Last Speech of President Smith to the Legion.

It is thought by some that our enemies would be satisfied with my destruction; but I tell you that as soon as they have shed my blood they will thirst for the blood of every man in whose heart dwells a single spark of the spirit of the fullness of the Gospel. The opposition of these men is moved by the spirit of the adversary of all righteousness. It is not only to destroy me, but every man and woman who dares believe the doctrines that God hath inspired me to teach to this generation.

We have never violated the laws of our country. We have every right to live under their protection, and are entitled to all the privileges guaranteed by our state and national constitutions. We have turned the barren, bleak prairies and swamps of this state into beautiful towns, farms and cities by our industry; and the men who seek our destruction and cry thief, treason, riot, &c., are those who themselves violate the laws, steal and plunder from their neighbors, and seek to destroy the innocent, heralding forth lies to screen themselves from the just punishment of their crimes by bringing destruction upon this innocent people. I call God, angels and all men to witness that we are innocent of the charges which are heralded forth through the public prints against us by our enemies; and while they assemble together in unlawful mobs to take away our rights and destroy our lives, they think to shield themselves under the refuge of lies which they have thus wickedly fabricated.

We have forwarded a particular account of all our doings to the Governor. We are ready to obey his commands, and we expect that protection at his hands which we know to be our just due.

We have taken the counsel of Judge Thomas, and have been tried before a civil magistrate on the charge of riot—not that the law required it, but because the Judge advised it as a precautionary measure, to allay all possible pretext for excitement. We were legally acquitted by Esq. Wells, who is a good judge of law. Had we been before the Circuit, the Supreme, or any other court of law in the state or nation, we would have been acquitted, for we have broken no law.

Constable Bettisworth came here with a writ requiring us to go before Mr. Morrison, "or some other justice of the peace of the county," to answer to the charge of riot. We acknowledged ourselves his prisoners, and were ready to go before any magistrate in any precinct in this part of the county, or anywhere else where our lives could be protected from the mob who have published the resolutions for our extermination which you have just heard read. This is a privilege the law guarantees to us, and which the writ itself allows. He broke the law and refused us this privilege, declaring that we should go before Morrison in Carthage, and no one else, when he knew that a numerous mob was collected there who are publicly pledged to destroy our lives.

It was under these circumstances that we availed ourselves of the legal right of the ancient, high, and constitutional privilege of the writ of *habeas corpus*, and were brought before the Municipal Court of this city and discharged from the illegal detention under which we were held by Constable Bettisworth.   All mob-men, priests, thieves, and bogus makers, apostates and adulterers, who combine to destroy this people, now raise the hue and cry throughout the state that we resist the law, in order to raise a pretext for calling together thousands more of infuriated mob-men to murder, destroy, plunder and ravish the innocent.

We are American citizens.   We live upon a soil for the liberties of which our fathers periled their lives and spilt their blood upon the battlefield.   Those rights so dearly purchased, shall not be disgracefully trodden under foot by lawless marauders without at least a noble effort on our part to sustain our liberties.

Will you all stand by me to the death, and sustain at the peril of your lives, the laws of our country, and the liberties and privileges which our fathers have transmitted unto us, sealed with their sacred blood? ("Aye!" shouted thousands.) He then said, "It is well. If you had not done it, I would have gone out there (pointing to the west) and would have raised up a mightier people."

I call upon all men, from Maine to the Rocky Mountains, and from Mexico to British America, whose hearts thrill with horror to behold the rights of freemen trampled under foot, to come to the deliverance of this people from the hand of oppression, cruelty, anarchy and misrule to which they have long been made subject. Come, all ye lovers of liberty, break the oppressor's rod, loose the iron grasp of mobocracy, and bring to condign punishment all those who trample under foot the glorious Constitution and the people's rights. [Drawing his sword, and presenting it to heaven, he said] I call God and angels to witness that I have unsheathed my sword with a firm and unalterable determination that this people shall have their legal rights, and be protected from mob violence, or my blood shall be spilt upon the ground like water, and my body consigned to the silent tomb.   While I live, I will never tamely submit to the dominion of cursed mobocracy.   I would welcome death rather than submit to this oppression; and it would be sweet, oh, sweet, to rest in the grave rather than submit to this oppression, agitation, annoyance, confusion, and alarm upon alarm, any longer.

I call upon all friends of truth and liberty to come to our assistance; and may the thunders of the Almighty and the forked lightnings of heaven and pestilence, and war and bloodshed come down on those ungodly men who seek to destroy my life and the lives of this innocent people.

I do not regard my own life. I am ready to be offered a sacrifice for this people; for what can our enemies do? Only kill the body, and their power is then at an end. Stand firm, my friends; never flinch. Do not seek to save your lives, for he that is afraid to die for the truth, will lose eternal life. Hold out to the end, and we shall be resurrected and become like Gods, and reign in celestial kingdoms, pricipalities, and eternal dominions, while this cursed mob will sink to hell, the portion of all those who shed innocent blood.

God has tried you. You are a good people; therefore I love you with all my heart. Greater love hath no man than that he should lay down his life for his friends. You have stood by me in the hour of trouble, and I am willing to sacrifice my life for your preservation.

May the Lord God of Israel bless you for ever and ever. I say it in the name of Jesus of Nazareth, and in the authority of the Holy Priesthood, which He hath conferred upon me.

(The people said "Amen.")

Hyrum said that the statement of Sharp in the *Warsaw Signal*, that he (Hyrum) had threatened to take his life, was false as hell—there was not a syllable of truth in it.

About 3:15 p. m., I took the command, and with my staff rode in front of the Legion, marched up Main Street, and returned to our former parade ground. The number on parade was very large, considering the number of Elders who had been sent on missions. After dismissing the Legion to their several commands, I returned home and gave orders to the several commanders only to receive official communications through my aides-de-camp, the proper official channel. I appointed Edward Bonney one of my aids-de-camp.

Truman Gillett, Jr., made the following affidavit:

Affidavit: Truman Gillett—the Treachery of William Law.

STATE OF ILLINOIS,   } ss.
CITY OF NAUVOO,   }

June 18th, 1844.—Personally appeared Truman Gillett, Jr., before me, Willard Richards, recorder of the city of Nauvoo; and after being duly sworn, deposeth and saith that on or about the first day of June, 1842, while passing up the Ohio river on the steamboat *Massachusetts,* deponent overheard two men, one a resident of Missouri and the other of Ohio, as reported, conversing together concerning incidents on the Upper Mississippi, when one said to the other. "If Law could have succeeded in getting an introduction for us to Joe Smith, damn him, we would have gagged him and nabbed him; and, damn him, all hell could not have rescued him from our hands."

The next morning deponent got in conversation with the man before mentioned from Missouri, who stated that he had been on the Upper Mississippi on business; that he stopped at Nauvoo on his way down with some twelve or fourteen other men, who laid a plan to kidnap Joe Smith; that some of the company queried about getting access to him, but one of them said he knew they could if he could find William Law. They called on William Law in the evening to get an introduction to their great Prophet, and Law went with them to the gate, where they were stopped by the police; "and it was well for him that we did not succeed in getting an introduction to him."

Deponent said, "Did William Law know your business?" And he said "Yes." Deponent asked, "What have you against Joseph Smith? Did he ever injure you?" The man replied, "No; but he has others." "Did you ever see him?" "Yes. I was one who helped to run the Mormons from Missouri," and related many circumstances concerning the Missouri mob.

Deponent said to the man, he was acquainted with William Law; considered he was an honorable man, and was led to doubt his being engaged with them in a conspiracy against Joseph Smith. He replied, "G—d d—n you, it is true, whether you believe it or not," and repeatedly affirmed it. Deponent did not believe the statements of the man from Missouri as mentioned above until after hearing the recent developments before the City Council.　　　TRUMAN GILLETT, JR.

[Seal]　　　Sworn and subscribed at the time and place above written, before me.

WILLARD RICHARDS, Recorder C. N.

At 8 p. m. I wrote the following:

Letter: Joseph Smith to H. T. Hugins—Congratulating Jeremiah Smith on his release.

NAUVOO, ILL., June 18th, 1844.

H. T. Hugins, Esq.

SIR.—I received your communication from Burlington per Captain Anderson; also Dr. Hickock's from Springfield; and I feel grateful for your favors, and congratulate you and Mr. Smith also.

The enemy, or mob, is prowling in the southern and eastern part of the county, and threatening us with extermination; and we ask the friends of peace and good government everywhere to use their influence in suppressing the spirit of mobocracy, and sustain us in our righteous course.

So far as you can conscientiously speak in our behalf, and lend your influence in our favor for the public good your favors will be highly appreciated.

Please show this to Dr. Hickock and such confidential friends as you think proper. Also request Mr. Dunlop to direct his letter to me.

The bearer, Dr. Wakefield, will give you all particulars.

In haste, I remain your friend, respectfully,

                                          JOSEPH SMITH.

I sent the letter by Dr. Wakefield to Burlington.

Nine messengers arrived from Carthage, and report that the mob had received intelligence from the Governor, who would take no notice of them; and they damned the Governor as being as bad as Joe Smith. They did not care for him, and they were just as willing he would not help them as if he would.

Governor Ford's Treatment of the Mob.

There was a body of armed men in Carthage, and a mob meeting at Fountain Green, which attracted considerable attention.

Shadrach Roundy, a policeman, reported at 10 p. m., after I had retired, that a man by the name of Norton had threatened to shoot me. An examination was immediately had, but no proof was found.

Threat Against the Prophet's Life

This evening I appointed Theodore Turley Armorer-General of the Legion.

I insert the following affidavit:

Affidavit, Canfield and Belknap—Concerning Threats of Invasion from Missouri.

STATE OF ILLINOIS, } ss.
CITY OF NAUVOO,   }

                    HANCOCK COUNTY, June 18, 1844.

Personally appeared before me, Aaron Johnson, a justice of the peace, Cyrus Canfield and Gilbert Belknap, of Hancock county; and being duly sworn depose and say that on yesterday, June 17th, 1844, certain persons—to-wit, Dr. Barnes and Joseph H. Jackson, having entered into conversation with your deponents, among other things declared that the Governor of Illinois was as big a scoundrel as Joseph Smith, and that he is the d—dest scoundrel that was ever suffered to live; that they did not care for the Governor, and had rather that the Governor would side with Smith; that they (the mob) were coming to Nauvoo with a sufficient force to take Smith; and if the people endeavored to prevent them, they should kill the people; and that if Smith had left Nauvoo, they had determined to destroy the Mansion and other buildings. And your deponents further say that one John Eller declared that he had lived in Missouri and was at the massacre of the Mormons at Haun's Mill, that he had killed one Mormon, and that he had left Missouri on purpose to fight the Mormons, and would hunt a Mormon as he would a deer. And your deponents further say that they heard that about one hundred persons had already arrived from Missouri, and were expecting as many more from that State. And your deponents further say, that they heard in Carthage that they had already received a number of guns and ammunition and provisions from St. Louis, in order to prosecute their attack upon Nauvoo. And, further your deponents say not.

CYRUS CANFIELD,
GILBERT BELKNAP.

Sworn and subscribed to before me, this eighteenth day of June, 1844.

AARON JOHNSON,
A Justice of the Peace.

CHAPTER XXV.

ATTEMPTS TO DRAFT SAINTS INTO MOB SERVICE AGAINST
NAUVOO—THREATENED INVASION FROM MISSOURI—JAMES A.
BENNETT URGED TO COME TO NAUVOO.

Wednesday, June 19, 1844.—The Legion assembled on
the parade-ground.   A company of the Legion came in
from Green Plains about 11 a. m.   I met them at the
front of the Mansion, and an escort came down from the
parade-ground below the Temple and escorted them to
the ground.

At 1 p. m. a company of volunteers arrived from Iowa
and were also escorted to the parade-ground.

On Sunday, the 16th, a committee of the mob, headed
by James Charles, a constable of Hancock county, went
to the house of Captain Chester Loveland,
who lives four miles southeast of Warsaw, and
required him to call out his company to join
the *posse* of David Bettisworth to go to Nauvoo and arrest me and the City Council.   He peremptorily refused to comply with their request.   The same *posse*
returned on the 17th with an order, as they stated, from
the Governor, which Loveland believed (and no doubt correctly) to be a forgery, and therefore still refused to go on
any terms.   The *posse* then reported his refusal to Colonel
Williams, who appointed a committee of twelve to lynch,
tar and feather Captain Loveland on the 18th; which
committee went that evening and arrived about midnight.

Loveland, who had been informed of Williams' order,
prepared himself for defense and kept watch.   As soon as
they came and he saw their number, and that they were

Effort to Draft Chester Loveland into Mob Service.

provided with tar bucket, bag of feathers and a bundle of withes, in addition to their fire-arms, he blew out his light and placed himself in a suitable position to defend the door (which he had fastened) and the window. They went around his house several times, tried his door, rapped, called him by name, and consulted together. Some were for breaking the door; others thought it too dangerous. They knew he must be in there, for they were near his door when the light was blown out. Finally their courage failed; and notifying him to leave the country immediately, they took their departure. During this trying time Loveland did not speak.

In the afternoon I gave orders to General Dunham to have a picket-guard under Col. Markham, posted on all the roads leading out of the city; also an inner guard, under Major Jesse P. Harmon, posted in all the streets and alleys in the city, and also on the river bank. I also gave orders to have all the powder and lead in the city secured, and to see that all the arms were in use, and that all unclaimed arms be put in the hands of those who could use them. *Roads Leading into Nauvoo Picketed.*

I insert the affidavit of Anson Call, David Evans and William E. Horner:

Affidavit: Call, Evans and Horner—Treatment of Nauvoo Committee by Levi Williams, et al.

STATE OF ILLINOIS. }
CITY OF NAUVOO, } ss.

HANCOCK COUNTY, June 19, 1844.

Personally appeared before me, Aaron Johnson, justice of the peace of said county, Anson Call, David Evans and William E. Horner. of Hancock county and state aforesaid; and being duly sworn,depose and say that on Monday, the 17th instant, we started for Rocky Run precinct, and arived yesterday. We then went to Col. Williams' of that place, and there soon assembled twenty or thirty men. We were informed that Col. Williams had gone to Lima to get the colonel there to bring on his regiment. We then informed them that we were delegated on behalf of the people of Nauvoo to transact business with them

They informed us they had a committee set apart to do their business, and that one was absent, and the other two would shortly be here. That while a person was seeking the two men, we observed to the people that General Smith was willing to be tried in any state, for any crime or supposed crime that he had ever committed, except in the state of Missouri.

One of the persons objected to General Smith being tried by the Municipal Court in Nauvoo, and declared that nothing else would do but for him to be taken upon the old writ, and by the same person who took him in custody before, and tried at the place where the writ was issued.

It was then observed that Judge Thomas had advised General Smith to enter into bonds to be tried before the Circuit Court, and this would allay all the excited feelings of the people.

It was then moved by one of their company, and sanctioned by the people, that a committee should wait on the Judge who gave General Smith this advice, and give him a coat of tar and feathers; when one John Elliott, of notoriety, agreed to find the tar and feathers for that purpose.

After some further conversation, a man whom they called Lawyer Stephens came in from Warsaw, and asked where Col. Williams was. He was told that he had gone to Lima. They then observed to the lawyer that we were delegates from Nauvoo, when he replied, "We are expecting delegates, too, at Warsaw;" and he said the people were talking of introducing them to the Mississippi river; and says he, "Gentlemen, you can do with your delegates what you think proper."

A Mr. Crawford, one of the committee, observed that he went against such proceedings, and advised them as a body to keep cool. They then told the lawyer the advice that the Judge of the Circuit Court had given to General Smith, when he said it was unlawful advice, and it was a second time moved and assented to that a committee should wait on Judge Thomas and give him a coat of tar and feathers. The remainder of the committee having come in, they stated to us that they had written to the Governor to obtain aid from other counties; and if the Governor did not send them aid, they were too weak to go themselves now, but were summoning all the people that would come into the county until they got force enough to come up and take Joseph Smith with the first warrant, and take him to the place where the writ was first issued; and nothing less than that would satisfy the people.

ANSON CALL,
DAVID EVANS,
WM. E. HORNER.

Sworn and subscribed to this 19th day of June, 1844.

AARON JOHNSON, J. P.

From the best information they could learn, there were two hundred armed men at Rocky Run precinct, two hundred at Warsaw, two hundred in Missouri, and the whole receiving constant additions.

At 9 p. m. I was at home. The city all quiet.

Thursday, 20.—At daybreak I went with my staff and Major-General Dunham to the prairie, to view the situation of the ground, and to devise plans for the defense of the city, and select the proper locations to meet the mob, and made arrangements for provisions for the city, instructing my agent to pledge my farms for the purpose.

Preparations for an Attack.

At 10 a. m. Dr. Southwick from Louisiana arrived, and reported that there was not much excitement in St. Louis; that a cannon had arrived at Warsaw from Quincy, and that it had been reported to him that there was great excitement in Upper Missouri.

Report of Dr. Southwick.

At 11, I reviewed the Legion facing the Mansion, and went to parade on the banks of the river.

I insert the affidavit of Carlos W. Lyon.

Affidavit: Carlos W. Lyon.

STATE OF ILLINOIS, } ss
CITY OF NAUVOO. }

On the 20th day of June, 1844, came before me, Willard Richards, recorder of the city aforesaid, Carlos W. Lyon; and after being duly sworn, deposeth and saith that while at St. Louis, Mo., on Monday, the 17th instant, it was a common topic that they were furnishing arms and ammunition to be sent by steamboat to Warsaw, Illinois; and said if the people of Warsaw need five hundred men, to give notice by the steamer *Boreas*, and the men should be sent from St. Louis to Warsaw; and that your said affiant also saw a cannon landed from the steamer *Mermaid* at Warsaw; and further he saith not.

CARLOS W. LYON.

Subscribed and sworn to before me this 20th day of June, 1844.
WILLARD RICHARDS,
Recorder of the City of Nauvoo.

Wrote to John Tyler, President of the United States, as follows:

An Appeal to President Tyler.

CITY OF NAUVOO, ILLINOIS, June 20th, 1844.

SIR.— I have just enclosed to the Governor of the State of Illinois copies of the enclosed affidavits and extra. I am sorry to say that the State of Missouri, not contented with robbing, driving and murdering many of the Latter-day Saints, are now joining the mob of this state for the purpose of the "utter extermination" of the Mormons, as they have resolved. And now, sir, as President of the United States, will you render that protection which the Constitution guarantees in case of "insurrection and rebellion," and save the innocent and oppressed from such horrid persecution?

With great respect, I have the honor to be your obedient servant,

JOSEPH SMITH, Mayor.

JOHN TYLER, President of the U. S., Washington, D. C.

I here insert affidavits of Hiram B. Mount and John Cunningham:

Affidavit: Mount and Cunningham—Attempt to Draft them into the Mob Service.

STATE OF ILLINOIS, } ss.
HANCOCK COUNTY, }

CITY OF NAUVOO, June 20th, 1844.

Personally appeared before me, Aaron Johnson, an acting justice of the peace in and for the county of Hancock, Hiram B. Mount and John Cunningham, who being duly sworn, depose and say that George Baker, John Banks, Joseph Barber, and two others came to your deponents on Saturday the 15th inst., at Morley Settlement, in said county, and demanded our arms. We replied that we had none, when they required of us to go with them to Nauvoo to take Joseph Smith and other prisoners, and they promised to supply us with arms. Second, if we would not do so, that we were required to leave our homes and go to Nauvoo. We must either go against Smith, or take part with him.

They then told us they intended to go to Nauvoo to take Smith; and if they could not take him, they would take some of the head men of Smith's clan, and hold them under bonds of death until Smith was delivered up to them. And your deponents further say that John Banks

told them if they could not get volunteers enough, they would get a
force that would take him.

HIRAM B. MOUNT,
JOHN CUNNINGHAM, (x—his mark).

[Seal]   Subscribed and sworn to this 20th day of June, 1844,
before me,

AARON JOHNSON, J. P.

Affidavit: Allen T. Wait—Attempt to Draft him into Mob Service.

STATE OF ILLINOIS, } ss
HANCOCK COUNTY. }

CITY OF NAUVOO, June 20th, 1844.

Personally appeared before me, Aaron Johnson, an acting justice of
the peace in and for said county, Allen T. Wait, of Morley Settlement
in said county; and being first duly sworn, deposeth and saith that on
Saturday morning he was at the house of Colonel Levi Williams, when
he told me that I must take up arms and go and fight against Joseph
Smith, or I must leave the place immediately, or else I must give up
my arms and stay at home.

He also said they would take Smith by law if they could; or if the
Governor would not grant a writ to take him they would take him anyhow. He also said, if the people would not give Smith up, they would
lay the whole city of Nauvoo in ashes.

I inquired what they would do with those people of Nauvoo who
would not fight? He said they must make some signal, or else they
must share the same fate—they must all perish, men, women, and children.

I then left in order to go home, when Captain Harrison P. Crawford
overtook me, and told me if the Governor would not help them they did
not care for the Governor anyhow. He said Governor Ford was an
unconstitutional man; he had issued two illegal writs, and they were
done so on purpose: and any such man ought not to hold any office
whatever; and they intended to proceed against the Mormons whether
they got any authority from the Governor or not.

ALLAN T. WAIT.

[Seal]   Subscribed and sworn to this 20th day of June, 1844,
before me,

AARON JOHNSON, J. P.

Likewise the affidavit of Isaac Morley, Gardner Snow
John Edmiston and Edmund Durfee.

Affidavit: Isaac Morley et al.—Attempt to Draft them into Mob Service,

STATE OF ILLINOIS,   }
HANCOCK COUNTY,   } ss

CITY OF NAUVOO, June 20th, 1844.

Personally appeared before me, Aaron Johnson, an acting justice of the peace in and for said county, Isaac Morley, Gardner Snow, John Edmiston and Edmund Durfee, all of Hancock county aforesaid; and being first duly sworn, depose and say that on Saturday, the 15th day of June, 1844, at Morley Settlement in said county, certain persons—to wit.,George Baker, farmer, John Banks, Esq., Luther Perry, constable, Joseph Barber, farmer; and another person whose name we do not know, called upon your deponent, Isaac Morley, when John Banks said they waited on him to make three propositions—namely: first, that we were to take up arms, join with, and go along with them to Nauvoo, to arrest one Joseph Smith and others, about seventeen in number, living in Nauvoo; second, to remove our effects to Nauvoo; or third, to give up our arms to them and remain neutral. And said Isaac Morley was required to notify all the brethren in the neighborhood, and report to the said committee, which of these propositions we accepted, by 8 o'clock on Monday morning following; and that one of the above resolutions was to be complied with within that time.

On the same day said Joseph Barber and Luther Perry went to where your deponent, Edmund Durfee, was at work in a field in the same neighborhood, and said they had come to notify him that said Durfee must comply with one of the above propositions; if not that said Durfee would smell thunder.

And all your deponents further depose and say that they have been compelled to leave their homes and flee to Nauvoo for protection. "For we were afraid to stay there on account of the mobs threatening to utterly exterminate us," according to a *Warsaw Signal* extra of June, 14th, 1844, if we stayed at home; and further your deponents say not.

ISAAC MORLEY,
GARDNER SNOW,
JOHN EDMISTON,
EDMUND DURFEE.

[Seal]   Subscribed and sworn to this 20th day of June, 1844, before me,

AARON JOHNSON, J. P.

Also the affidavit of Solomon Hancock, William Garner, and John G. Lofton:

Affidavit: Hancock, Garner, Lofton—Attempt to Draft them into Mob Service.

STATE OF ILLINOIS, ⎫ ss
HANCOCK COUNTY. ⎭

CITY OF NAUVOO, June 20th, 1844.

Personally appeared before me, Aaron Johnson, an acting justice of the peace, Solomon Hancock, William Garner and John G. Lofton, who being first duly sworn, depose and say that on Saturday, the 15th day of June, 1844, at Morley Settlement in said county, certain persons, —to wit., John Clark, John Crawford, Jeremiah Bently, and three others, all farmers, came to your deponents and made three several propositions to them, to wit: first, that we were to take up our arms and join with them in going to Nauvoo, to take Joseph Smith and others prisoners; second, to remove with our effects to Nauvoo immediately; or, third, to give up our arms to Col. Levi Williams and remain neutral.

We were ordered to give in our decision on Monday then next by 8 o'clock in the morning; and if we would not agree to their decision, we must abide the consequences. And in consequence of mobs gathering in the neighborhood, we have been obliged to leave our homes in order to save our lives, and are come to Nauvoo for protection.

Solomon Hancock further deposeth and saith that said John Clark did on Tuesday, 18th instant, inform your deponent that one of their party had gone to St. Louis and had obtained three cannon, and were expecting three companies of volunteers from St. Louis to join them in going to Nauvoo to exterminate the Mormons; and further your deponents say not.

SOLOMON HANCOCK,
WILLIAM GARNER,
JOHN G. LOFTON.

[Seal]   Subscribed and sworn to this 20th day of June, 1844, before me,

AARON JOHNSON.

Also the affidavit of James Guyman:

Affidavit: James Guyman—Threats of Invasion from Missouri.

STATE OF ILLINOIS, ⎫ ss
HANCOCK COUNTY. ⎭

CITY OF NAUVOO, June 20th, 1844.

Personally appeared before me, Aaron Johnson, an acting justice of the peace in and for said county, James Guyman, of Green Plains precinct in said county; and being first duly sworn deposeth and saith that on Saturday morning, the 15th instant, he was at Rocky Run precinct, when one Captain Wyers, captain of an "Independent Anti-Mormon Minute Men Company," came to a house where your deponent was staying. He inquired for a drum. He wanted either to borrow it or buy it until the affray with the Mormons was over.

I asked him how he was going to proceed to take Smith. He then said Missouri had offered to send over two thousand men, to come over to assist and take him.

I asked whether it was legal for them to come over here. He replied when they came over the constables were going to summons them, and also to summons every man who was in or would come into the county.

I asked if it was according to law to proceed that way, and he replied it was, and he went in for the law and democracy. He said they had sent two men to the Governor to order the militia out in their favor to help to take those criminals: and if he would not do just right, they would execute him by taking his head from his shoulders.

I replied, "You said you were a democracy man, and went for the law." I said, "Do you call that democracy or mobocracy?"

He said if they went that far, and if the Governor ordered the militia against them instead of in favor of them, he would turn mob, and the militia would join him, and they would take the Governor's head from his shoulders. He repeated it two or three times.

I enquired if it was law to go and drive those innocent Mormons who were living in the neighborhood, or tyrannically compel them to do things not agreeable to their will? He allowed that in this case it was.

I asked what he was going to do with these old settlers who would neither take up arms and fight against Smith nor in favor of him; when he replied they must fight either for one side or the other, or they must share the same fate as the Mormons.

Your deponent further saith that he is not a Mormon, and does not belong to the Church of Jesus Christ of Latter-day Saints; and further saith not.

JAMES GUYMAN.

[Seal]   Subscribed and sworn to this 20th day of June, 1844, before me,

AARON JOHNSON, J. P.

Also the affidavit of Obadiah Bowen:

Affidavit: Obadiah Bowen—Attempt to Draft him into Service of Mob.

STATE OF ILLINOIS, }
HANCOCK COUNTY. } ss

CITY OF NAUVOO, June 20th, 1844.

Personally appeared before me, Aaron Johnson, an acting justice of the peace, in and for said county, Obadiah Bowen, of Morley Settlement, in said county; and being first duly sworn, deposeth and saith that on Saturday the 15th instant, John Clark rode up to where I was at work in Morley Settlement, and said he was afraid the Mormons would come and destroy their property; "and," said he, "if I have any destroyed by any person, I shall make my resort upon the nearest Mormons, and take their property in place of that which shall be taken away;" wherever he could find it, so long as it was a Mormon's; and that on Tuesday, the 18th instant, as I was coming from my house to the road leading to Lima, a mob was at the forks of the road standing still and consulting together; I came on the road about twenty rods ahead of them. In a few moments Colonel Levi Williams, John Clark and five others rode along the same road after me.

I heard them talking about shooting the Mormons, when Clark said, "It is no disgrace to shoot a Mormon, anyhow," when they all laughed. They overtook me, and Col. Williams asked me where I lived. I replied in Morley Settlement. He asked me if I was a Mormon, when Clark said it was no odds—he is on their part.

Col. Williams then threatened me, and said I must be sure and be at his house by nine o'clock in the morning; if not I must either get out of Morley Settlement, or be served the same sauce as the Mormons. He gave me to understand that they were going to make a total destruction of Morley Settlement tomorrow, and I had better get out of it.

He then talked about Joseph Smith, when I replied I understood Joseph Smith had a fair trial and was bound over to the Supreme Court. He said, "If he is not, we do not care, it is illegally done;" and he should go ahead. He should gather the troops, and there would be two thousand men landed tomorrow from Missouri. He said they were volunteers. They should meet next day at Carthage, and then go against Joseph Smith and demolish the city of Nauvoo, for have him at any rate they would. He was in a very great passion, and let out a great many oaths and [said] other things that I have not mentioned.

In consequence of their threats, and to save our lives, we were obliged to leave our homes in a very stormy night, and had to cross a dangerous stream that was swollen by the rain, and was unable to protect myself from great sufferings and hardships, and came to the city of Nauvoo for protection.

OBADIAH BOWEN.

[Seal]   Subscribed and sworn to this 20th day of June, 1844, before me,

AARON JOHNSON, J. P.

Also the affidavit of Alvah Tippitts:

Affidavit: Alvah Tippetts—Violence of John Williams Upon.

STATE OF ILLINOIS, ⎱ ss
HANCOCK COUNTY. ⎰

CITY OF NAUVOO. June 20th, 1844.

Personally appeared before me, Aaron Johnson, a justice of the peace in and for the said county, Alvah Tippetts, of Warsaw, in Hancock county and state aforesaid; and being first duly sworn, deposeth and saith that on Wednesday, June 12th, at Green Plains, one Col. Levi Williams came to your deponent about sunrise, and ordered me out of the house that very day.

I replied he was very hasty. He again ordered me out of the house, and said, if I spoke a word, he would put me out of the house immediately.

I then took away part of my goods and left the house accordingly, because I was afraid to stay there another night.

The next day I went back after the remainder of my property, and called at the house of Col. Levi Williams for some things belonging to me.

When I arrived there John Williams, the son of said Levi Williams, aged about twenty-eight years, abused me for placing confidence in Joseph Smith and the people of Nauvoo. He then took me by the back of my neck and pushed me away, and said he would not have such stuff in his house. The second time he pushed me by the neck, and his foot to my back. He pushed me several times and kicked me. Again, when in the street, he kept kicking and pushing me, and abusing me with his tongue. I am sixty-one years old. I did not say anything to him to cause this abuse; but it was all on account of my believing that Joseph Smith and the people of Nauvoo would do nothing but what was according to law.

                                        ALVAH TIPPETTS.

[Seal]   Subscribed and sworn to this 20th day of June, 1844, before me,

                                        AARON JOHNSON, J. P.

I had sent orders to Captain Almon W. Babbitt, commander of the company at Ramus, to come immediately with his company to Nauvoo, and help to defend the place; and this morning my brother-in-law, William McLeary, informs me that when the letter was read to the company, Babbitt refused to come, and said it was a foolish move, and

Reinforcement for Nauvoo from Ramus.

objected to any of the company coming. The company was marshaled into line, when Babbitt said, "If any of you go, not one will ever get to Nauvoo alive," when immediately my Uncle John Smith stepped in front of the line and said, "Every man that goes at the call of the Prophet shall go and return safe, and not a hair of his head shall be lost; and I bless you in the name of the Lord."

The company immediately threw the command upon Uriah H. Yager, who accepted of it, and started for Nauvoo, although many of them were destitute of boots or shoes. The company had not traveled five miles before they suddenly came upon double their number of the mob, who had two red flags flying, and who had paraded their company and taken a position in a wood that commanded the road. The company from Macedonia opened file about ten feet apart and marched past them within rifle shot, while the mob fired several guns at them, the balls whizzing past their heads. They came here at daybreak this morning, and I directed the quartermaster to furnish those who needed with shoes.

I wrote the following letter:

Letter: Joseph Smith to Ballantyne and Slater—Advice on moving into Nauvoo.

NAUVOO, June 20th, 1844.

BROTHERS BALLANTYNE AND SLATER:—On information from you by J. McIllrick, I would advise that your families remain where they are and be quiet, as the mob will not be likely to disturb them; but any amount of wheat or provisions you may have you had better remove without delay to Nauvoo, as it will be better for you to bring it here and have your pay than to leave it for the mob to consume and destroy.

I remain your brother in Christ Jesus,

JOSEPH SMITH.

BALLANTYNE AND SLATER, Doyles Mills, near Plymouth, Ill.

I here insert the affidavit of John P. Greene and John M. Bernhisel:

Affidavit: Greene and Bernhisel—Threatened Invasion from Missouri.

STATE OF ILLINOIS,   }
  COUNTY OF HANCOCK. } ss

CITY OF NAUVOO.

On the 20th day of June,1844, personally appeared before me, Aaron Johnson, a justice of the peace within and for said county, John P. Greene, marshal of said city, and John M. Bernhisel; and after being duly sworn, depose and say that a body of citizens, in a mass meeting convened on the 13th instant at Carthage, resolved to exterminate the Latter-day Saints of the said city of Nauvoo, and for that purpose, according to the purport of the *Warsaw Signal* extra, dated June 14, 1844, bodies of armed men are coming from the State of Missouri, and also from the territory of Iowa, and the cannon and ammunition are being transported from the state of Missouri to Illinois for the purpose of utterly exterminating the Latter-day Saints. And your affiants would further state that these bodies of armed men, cannon, arms, and munitions of war are transported in steamboats navigating the waters of the United States, and that the name of one of these boats is the *Die Vernon*.

JOHN P. GREENE,
JOHN M. BERNHISEL.

[Seal]   Subscribed and sworn to before me, this 20th day of June, 1844.

AARON JOHNSON, J. P.

Dr. Richards wrote the following:

Letter: Willard Richards to Jas Arlington Bennett—Affairs in Nauvoo—Western Movement.

MAYOR'S OFFICE, NAUVOO, June 20th, 1844.

DEAR GENERAL.—Yours of the 14th of April was received at a late date. A multiplicity of business on account of the peculiar state of affairs, has prevented a reply till now. Your views about the nomination of General Smith for the Presidency are correct. We will gain popularity and external influence. But this is not all: we mean to elect him, and nothing shall be wanting on our part to accomplish it; and why? Because we are satisfied, fully satisfied, that this is the best or only method of saving our free institutions from a total overthrow.

You will discover by this day's extra *Nauvoo Neighbor*, and previous papers which I shall forward with this, that we are already being surrounded by an armed mob; and, if we can believe a hundredth part of their statements we have no alternative but to fight or die. All the horrors of Missouri's murders are crowding thick upon us, and the citizens of this county declare in mass-meetings, "No peace till the Mormons are utterly exterminated from the earth." And for what?

A band of thieves, counterfeiters, bogus-makers, gamblers, debauchers, murderers, and all that is vile, established a printing-press in this city for the purpose of carrying on all their hellish plans and overthrowing every principle of righteousness; and after publishing one number, called the *Nauvoo Expositor*, filled on every column with lies and libel the most dark and damnable it were possible for men or demons on the earth or in the shades of Gehenna, calculated to destroy every chartered right to our peaceful city, and constitutional principles to our nation, being destitute of every vestige of truth, and without one redeeming quality, either in the paper or the characters of its publishers.

The City Council, on the 10th instant, ordered the press and fixtures to be abated as a nuisance which order was executed by the proper authorities without delay, without noise, tumult or confusion.

The proprietors immediately evacuated their houses and the city, and the night following fired one or more of their buildings, just as they did in Missouri, thinking to raise a hue-and-cry that the Mormons had done it, and by that means bring a mob on us without a moment's delay; but our vigilant police discovered the fire and abated that also.

Chagrined at their disappointment, and drunk with madness, they next went to Carthage, the county seat and headquarters of mobocracy, and swore that Joseph and about seventeen others had committed a riot, and sent a warrant for their apprehension. They offered to go before any magistrate in the vicinity and answer to the charge. The officer would not consent, but would take them to Carthage. They had threatened their lives at Carthage and did not consider it safe to go thither, and prayed out a writ of *habeas corpus* from the Municipal Court, and were set free.

This only enraged the mob the more, and another writ was issued by a county magistrate in the vicinity, not a Mormon, before whom they were brought, and every exertion made to convict them, but the magistrate discharged them.

This does not satisfy them. They are determined to have "Joe Smith," brought before themselves for trial at the headquarters of mobocracy swearing that all they want is to get him out of the city; and they will shoot the "damned rascal."

Cannon, ammunition and men are passing over the Mississippi from Missouri to Illinois, and the mob is collected by hundreds at different points in the county swearing everlasting vengeance; and when their oaths and writs will end, God knows.

We have sent messengers to the Governor, but had no returns, and shall dispatch messages to the President of the United States next boat.

If the virtuous part of the community, the state, the nation, will come to the rescue of innocence and the rights our fathers bled to purchase, that our peace and happiness may be secured to us in common with others, it is all we ask; but if they will not, and the mob goes on, we say a dishonorable life is worse than an honorable death, and we are ready for the onset; and we call upon all patriots, far and near, to lend a helping hand to put down the mob and restore peace.

If this is not done immediately, and the mob attempt to execute their threats, you may soon have the opportunity of beholding that glorious "vision in the west" you have sublimely contemplated in your letter.

I write you at this time at the request of the Prophet, and I invite you to come to our assistance with as many volunteers as you can bring.   And if the mob cannot be dispersed, and the Government will not espouse our righteous cause, you may soon, very soon, behold the second birth of our nation's freedom; for live without the free exercise of thought, and the privilege of worshiping God according to the dictates of our consciences, we will not!   We will die rather, and go where the wicked cease to trouble.   But we firmly believe there are virtuous men and patriots enough yet left to sustain those principles which alone are worth living for.   Will you come?

Here is Oregon.   Here is California.   Where is your ambition? Patriotism?   Your "separate and independent empire," if you sit calmly still and see the most virtuous and noble people that ever trod upon the footstool of Jehovah ground to powder by a miscreant mob and not stretch forth your potent arm for their defense in all the majesty of a God?   If you do not, your turn may come next; and where will it cease?

Let the first blow be struck upon us from this hour, and this field is open for every honest patriot from the east to the west sea, and from the river Mississippi to the ends of the earth.

General, will you stand neutral?   Come, and you will know for yourself.

I close in haste, with good wishes to yourself and family.

W. RICHARDS.

GENERAL J. A. BENNETT,
    Arlington House, N. Y.

CHAPTER XXVI.

THE TWELVE CALLED FROM EASTERN MISSION—GOVERNOR
FORD AT CARTHAGE —NAUVOO DELEGATION TO GOVERNOR—
THREATS AND CONSPIRACY AGAINST THE PROPHET'S LIFE—
GOVERNOR FORD INVITED TO NAUVOO TO INVESTIGATE CON-
DITIONS.

Thursday, June 20, 1844 [*continued*].—I wrote to those
of the Twelve Apostles who are absent on missions to
come home immediately, namely, Brigham
Young, Boston; Heber C. Kimball, Washing-   The Apostles
ton; Orson Hyde, Philadelphia; Parley P.   Called Home.
Pratt, New York; Orson Pratt, Washington; Wilford
Woodruff, Portage, New York; William Smith, Philadelphia; George A. Smith, Peterboro; John E. Page, Pittsburg; and Lyman Wight, Baltimore. Also to Amasa
Lyman, Cincinnati, Ohio, and George Miller, Richmond,
Madison county, Kentucky. I sent the letters by express
by Aaron M. York to the Illinois river, on account of the
stoppage of the mails.

At 8 p. m. Thomas Bullock came and read to me the
affidavits of Isaac Morley, Gardner Snow, John Edmiston,
Edmund Durfee, Solomon Hancock, Allen T. Waite,
James Guyman, Obadiah Bowen, Alvah Tippetts, Hiram
B. Mount, and John Cunningham, with the affiants; and
afterward the affidavits were all sworn to before Aaron
Johnson, Esquire.

Ten p. m. John Pike and Henry Gates went to the
quarters of the Major-General, and informed him they had
seen a number of men driving about three hundred head
of cattle in the direction of the mob camp. The drovers
reported themselves as having come from Missouri, and
were about nine miles from Nauvoo.

I gave directions to Theodore Turley to commence the manufacture of artillery. He asked me if he should not rent a building, and set some men to repairing the small arms which were out of order. I told him in confidence that there would not be a gun fired on our part during this fuss.

A Prophecy —No Gun Fired on Part of Saints.

I extract the following from a letter from Robert D. Foster dated "Carthage, June 20th, 1844, to John Proctor, Sen., Nauvoo."

Letter: Robert D. Foster to John Proctor—Fragment—Instruction as to Property.

We have a hundred barrels of flour here for the folks, and Nauvoo has no means to live, only from the country, and that is cut off sure There are thousands of armed men ready now and thousands more coming from Missouri and the country around. Tell John to sleep in the barn, and take care of fire and robbery, and all my things there, as I shall be home soon. Tell Amos Davis to keep his eyes open, as we learn that consecration law will soon commence on him. This we know, and he had better look out sharp. Let him read this sheet. Tell Norton Gibbs and all my boys that I should be glad to see them a minute, but I cannot come. They must be patient and faithful, and I will be there and reward every man according to his desert; and I won't forget the perjured villains there either.

I advised my brother Hyrum to take his family on the next steamboat and go to Cincinnati. Hyrum replied, "Joseph, I can't leave you." Whereupon I said to the company present, "I wish I could get Hyrum out of the way, so that he may live to avenge my blood, and I will stay with you and see it out."

Hyrum Smith's Fidelity to the Prophet.

Friday, 21.—About 10 a. m. I rode out with my guard up Main Street past the Major-General's quarters, and reviewed the Legion. I returned to headquarters about 2:30 p. m., having met Col. Elam L. Freeman and Mr. Bartlett, who came as express from the Governor who had arrived at Carthage this morning, and they delivered me the following letter:

Letter: Governor Ford to Mayor and Council of Nauvoo Asking Representatives to Meet him at Carthage.

HEADQUARTERS CARTHAGE, June 21st, 1844.

To the Honorable the Mayor and Common Council of the City of Nauvoo:

GENTLEMEN.—Having heard of the excitement in this part of the country, and judging that my presence here might be necessary to preserve the peace and enforce the laws, I arrived at this place this morning. Both before and since my arrival, complaints of a grave character have been made to me of certain proceedings of your honorable body. As chief magistrate, it is my duty to see that impartial justice shall be done, uninfluenced either by the excitement here or in your city.

I think before any decisive measure shall be adopted, that I ought to hear the allegations and defenses of all parties. By adopting this course I have some hope that the evils of war may be averted, and, at any rate, I will be enabled by it to understand the true merits of the present difficulties, and shape my course with reference to law and justice.

For these reasons I have to request that you will send out to me at this place, one or more well-informed and discreet persons, who will be capable of laying before me your version of the matter, and of receiving from me such explanations and resolutions as may be determined on.

Col. Elam L. Freeman will present you this note in the character of a herald from the Governor. You will respect his character as such and permit him to pass and repass free from molestation.

Your messengers are assured of protection in person and property, and will be returned to you in safety.

I am, gentlemen, with high consideration most respectfully,

Your obedient servant,

THOMAS FORD.

Governor and Commander in Chief.

I immediately notified the City Council to meet in session at 4 p. m. About 11 a. m. a rumor was circulated at General Dunham's headquarters that Joseph H. Jackson was seen at Davidson Hibberd's. He [Dunham] ordered out a *posse* to arrest him, which went accordingly, but returned without success.

Joseph H. Jackson at Nauvoo.

At 4 p. m. I met with the City Council, when the affidavits of the following persons were read—namely

Isaac Morley, Gardner Snow, John Edmiston, Edward
Durfee, Solomon Hancock, William Gardner, John G.
Lofton, Allen T. Waite, James Guyman, Obadiah Bowen,
Alvah Tippetts, Hiram B. Mount, John Cunningham,
Cyrus Canfield, Gilbert Belknap, Anson Call, David Evans,
William E. Horner, Stephen Markham, Thomas G. Wil-
son, John P. Greene, John M. Bernhisel, Truman Gillett,
Jr., Carlos W. Lyon, and H. T. Hugins; when Dr. J.
M. Bernhisel, Councilor John Taylor, and Dr. Willard
Richards were appointed by the council to return with the
express to the Governor at Carthage, and carry said
affidavits with the following letter:

Letter: Joseph Smith to Governor Ford—Submitting Documents.

NAUVOO, June 21, 1844.

SIR —The affidavits and handbills herewith connected, are submitted
for your Excellency's consideration.

Respectfully, I have the honor to be your Excellency's obedient
servant,

JOSEPH SMITH.

THOMAS FORD, Governor of Illinois, Carthage.

Messrs. Taylor and Bernhisel went accordingly, but Dr.
Richards tarried to prepare additional documents.

The following affidavit was taken:

Affidavit: John P. Greene—Joseph H. Jackson,—Threatens Prophet's Life.

STATE OF ILLINOIS, HANCOCK CO., } ss.
CITY OF NAUVOO.

June 21st, 1844.—Personally appeared John P. Greene before me,
Willard Richards, recorder of said city; and after being duly sworn,
deposeth and saith that on or about the 27th day of May, 1844, while at
Hamilton's tavern, in Carthage, county aforesaid, in company with
Joseph Smith and others, Robert D. Foster called deponent into a private room, and there and then said, "For God's sake, don't suffer that
man, Joseph Smith, to go out of doors; for if he steps outside of the
door his blood will be spilt;" to which statement deponent replied he
had no such fears; when said Foster confirmed said statements with considerable emotion, and said he knew that Smith could not go out of
doors, but his blood would be spilt.

Deponent asked Foster who would do it. Foster said he would not tell; but he knew the proud spirit of Jackson, that he would not be insulted, and that he would kill Joseph Smith if he had to die on the spot; and there were many others in Carthage who would assist to do the same thing. Joseph H. Jackson was in the house below at the time.

A day or two previous to the above conversation, while at Carthage aforesaid, deponent heard Joseph H. Jackson say that Joseph Smith was the damnedest rascal in the world, and he would be damned if he did not take vengeance on him, if he had to follow him to the Rocky Mountains; and said Jackson made many more such like threats against Joseph Smith and Hyrum Smith.

JOHN P. GREENE.

Sworn and subscribed this 21st day of June, 1844, before me,
[Seal]   WILLARD RICHARDS,
Recorder of the city of Nauvoo.

And as this affidavit confirms what was told me in Carthage, I made the following affidavit:

Affidavit: Joseph Smith—Conspiracy Against Affiant's Life.

STATE OF ILLINOIS,   } ss
COUNTY OF HANCOCK. }

CITY OF NAUVOO, June 21st, 1844.

Personally appeared Joseph Smith before me, Willard Richards, recorder of the City of Nauvoo; and after being duly sworn deposeth and saith that while at Hamilton's tavern at Carthage, in the county aforesaid, on or about the 27th day of May, 1844, whither deponent had gone to transact business in the Circuit Court of the county aforesaid, Charles A. Foster took deponent into a private room, and told deponent there was a conspiracy against the life of deponent, and that deponent had not better go out of doors. If he did, his blood would be shed. Foster said he was deponent's friend, and did not want to see bloodshed.

JOSEPH SMITH.

[Seal]   Sworn and subscribed this 21st day of June, 1844, before me,
WILLARD RICHARDS,
Recorder of the City of Nauvoo.

I instructed my clerks, Willard Richards, William Clayton, Thomas Bullock and John McEwan, to prepare all necessary papers and affidavits ready to be sent to the Governor tomorrow morning.

Joseph Jackson made the two following affidavits:

Affidavit: Joseph Jackson—Francis M. Higbee's Threat to Kill the Prophet.

STATE OF ILLINOIS, } ss
CITY OF NAUVOO. }

On the 21st day of June, 1844, came before me, W. W. Phelps, clerk of the Mayor's Court, Joseph Jackson; and after being duly sworn, deposeth and saith that on Tuesday, the 11th instant, he was in Nauvoo, when Francis M. Higbee, while speaking of the destruction of the printing press, said he was very sorry, for the proprietors had set up that press for the destruction of the city, and that he meant to kill Joseph Smith and Hyrum Smith; and he saith no further.

JOSEPH JACKSON.

Subscribed and sworn to before me, this 21st day of June, 1844.

WILLIAM W. PHELPS, Clerk M. C.

Affidavit: Joseph Jackson—Reporting Mob at Pilot Grove.

STATE OF ILLINOIS, } ss
CITY OF NAUVOO. }

On the 21st day of June, 1844, came before me, W. W. Phelps, clerk of the Mayor's Court for said city, Joseph Jackson; and after being duly sworn, deposeth and saith, that on the 19th day of June instant, at his residence near Pilot Grove, in the afternoon, about twenty-four persons fired about twenty-six guns at him, and that the balls whistled close by his head. Thus this mob, of which John McKay was one, fired about one hundred guns, but not all at your affiant; and that this mob was very noisy, cursing and swearing that they would kill every damned Mormon; and he says no further.

JOSEPH JACKSON.

Subscribed and sworn to before me, this 21st day of June, 1844.

WILLIAM W. PHELPS, Clerk M. C.

At 7 p. m. James Emmett went by order of the Sergeant of the Guard at the Stone House to the Major-General and reported the crew of the *Maid of Iowa* for firing five guns contrary to orders, which were, that any firing of guns was an alarm.

After the news had reached the city of the Governor's

arrival at Carthage, an express was sent to Keokuk to stop an express which I had sent to the Governor at Springfield before I had learned of his arrival at Carthage.

An officer of the United States army, having arrested a deserter, came to Nauvoo, and stayed at my house all night.

Col. Brewer and lady arrived at the Mansion about 9 p. m. Also James W. Woods, Esq., my attorney from Burlington.

At 10 p. m., Private —— Minor gave information that as he was passing, an hour since, about two miles out of the city to his home, he was fired upon by some unknown person. General Stephen Markham ordered out a detachment to proceed to the designated place, scour that part of the country, and see that all was right.

[*Saturday, June 22.—*]

Letter: Joseph Smith to Governor Ford—Inviting the Governor to Come to Nauvoo and Investigate Conditions.

NAUVOO, Saturday Morning, June 22, 1844.

To His Excellency Thomas Ford, Governor:

DEAR SIR.—I this morning forward you the remainder of the affidavits which are ready to present to you, by the hands of a gentleman who is fully competent to give you information on the whole subject which has been the cause of the origin of our present difficulties. I would respectfully recommend the bearer, Col. Woodworth, as one of my aides, and a man whose testimony can be relied upon.

I presume you are already convinced that it would be altogether unsafe for me or any of the City Council to come to Carthage on account of the vast excitement which has been got up by false report and libelous publications. Nothing could afford me a greater pleasure than a privilege of investigating the whole subject before your Excellency in person; for I have ever held myself in readiness to comply with your orders and answer for my proceedings before any legal tribunal in the state.

I would hereby respectfully pray your Excellency to come to Nauvoo, if congenial with your feelings, and give us a privilege of laying the whole matter before you in its true colors, and where abundance of testimony can be forthcoming, to prove every point by disinterested persons—men of character and of worth and notoriety, strangers—who were here all the time.   But I am satisfied your Excellency does not wish men to expose the lives of the citizens of this place by requiring them to put themselves into the power of an infuriated, blood-thirsty mob, a part of whom have already several times fired upon our people without the least shadow of cause or provocation.

I am informed this morning that some gentleman has made affidavit that he had a private conversation with me, in which I stated that I had secret correspondence with you, &c. If any person has been wicked enough to do this, he is a perjured villain; for in the first place, I do not suffer myself to hold private conversation with any stranger; and, in the second place, I have never even intimated anything of the kind as having secret correspondence with your Excellency.

Our troubles are invariably brought upon us by falsehoods and misrepresentations by designing men. We have ever held ourselves amenable to the law; and, for myself, sir, I am ever ready to conform to and support the laws and Constitution, even at the expense of my life. I have never in the least offered any resistence to law or lawful process, which is a well-known fact to the general public; all of which circumstances make us the more anxious to have you come to Nauvoo and investigate the whole matter.

Now, sir, is it not an easy matter to distinguish between those who have pledged themselves to exterminate innocent men, women and children, and those who have only stood in their own defense, and in defense of their innocent families, and that, too, in accordance with the Constitution and laws of the country, as required by the oaths, and as good and law-abiding citizens?

In regard to the destruction of the press, the truth only needs to be presented before your Excellency to satisfy you of the justice of the proceedings. The press was established by a set of men who had already set themselves at defiance of the law and authorities of the city, and had threatened the lives of some of its principal officers, and who also made it no private matter that the press was established for the express purpose of destroying the city, as will be shown by the affidavit of Joseph Jackson, and as they stated to me in their threats.

Mr. Babbitt informs me that reports are in circulation that we have taken property which belongs to the Messrs. Law and others. There has been no property meddled with, to my knowledge, belonging to any person, except property we have purchased of the rightful owners.

Mr. Law turned over some property to a Mr. Hicks, to pay a debt. This I purchased of Mr. Hicks, and I am responsible to him for the amount. We have been especially careful to preserve the property of those who are exciting the public against us, inasmuch as we know that every means would be used which could be invented to raise excitement; and we have appointed the police to watch this property and see that no harm was done to it by any person, as they had tried to fire their own building and were detected in the act. The fire was extinguished by the policemen, and no property damaged.

There have been no prisoners taken in this city, neither any person held as hostage, only some who are residents of this place, who had broken the laws. No stranger has been interfered with or detained in the city under any circumstances.

In haste, I have the honor to remain, dear sir, your most obedient servant,

JOSEPH SMITH.

Lieut.-Gen. N. L.

This letter was accompanied by other affidavits, and was sent by Lucien Woodworth, who was delegated to go in place of Dr. Richards. He started at noon in company with Squire Woods of Burlington.

CHAPTER XXVII.

PREPARATIONS TO DEFEND NAUVOO—MOB MOVEMENTS ON
CARTHAGE ROAD—GOVERNOR FORD'S REVIEW OF HANCOCK
COUNTY DIFFICULTIES—JOSEPH SMITH'S ACCOUNT OF THE
SAME DIFFICULTIES, DEFENSE OF HIS OWN AND ASSOCIATES'
COURSE.

Saturday, June 22 [*continued*].—Legion met as usual; and
after receiving instructions, were dismissed until 6 p. m.,
when they met again.

At 7 p. m. I instructed General Dunham to cause the
regiment of the 2nd cohort to turn out tomorrow, and work by turns three or four hours
each, with entrenching tools, and to take the
best measures in case of attack. I also gave orders that
a standard be prepared for the nations.

Orders for
Nauvoo's En-
trenchment.

Almon W. Babbitt arrived from Carthage this morning,
having come at the request of the Governor, who thought
it not wisdom to have Richards and Phelps and others of
the City Council go to Carthage.

Edward Robinson made the following affidavit:

Affidavit: Edward Robinson—Threats Against Nauvoo.

STATE OF ILLINOIS, }
    CITY OF NAUVOO, } ss

On the 22nd day or June, 1844, came before me, W. W. Phelps,
clerk of the Mayor's Court, in said city, Dr. Edward Robinson, who,
after being duly sworn, deposeth and saith that while at Carthage, on
the 18th and 19th instant, I heard several persons who had assembled
together for warlike purposes, (having their arms and one cannon with
them) say that they were gathering together for the purpose of destroying the property of General Joseph Smith, or, as they said, "Joe
Smith," and his followers, and the City Council, with the exception of

one; and finally said they would destroy the town and exterminate the Latter-day Saints.

EDWARD ROBINSON.

Subscribed and sworn to before me this 22nd day of June, 1844.

WILLIAM W. PHELPS, Clerk M. C.

James Olive made the following affidavit:

Affidavit: James Olive—Mob Movements on the Carthage Road.

STATE OF ILLINOIS, }
HANCOCK COUNTY. } ss

CITY OF NAUVOO, June 22nd, 1844.

Personally appeared before me, Aaron Johnson, a justice of the peace in and for said county, James Olive; who being first duly sworn, deposeth and saith that on Friday afternoon, the 21st instant, about 3 o'clock, he was at his own house, about two miles from Appanoose. In a southeasterly direction, he saw a four-horse wagon with some men before it, all traveling towards Appanoose. They went about a quarter of a mile beyond my house; there met a two horse wagon and a company of men, about fifteen in number. Both parties then took the road towards the Big Mound. A part of the men were mounted and a part were on foot. The mounted men were forward; and after passing my house, they wheeled and rode back to the footmen who were some little distance behind, and said to them, "There are some fellows on the Mound; you had better hurry on, and we will take those fellows and carry them to Carthage." They used profane language. I watched them until they got near the Mound, and saw the guard on the Mound turn and run towards Nauvoo. After that the company went on to the Mound, and halted near the spot where the guard had run from.

On the same evening, about sundown, there was a man by the name of Milton Hamilton came into my house and told me to arm and equip myself according to the law and stand in readiness; that the Governor had demanded Joseph Smith according to law, and that he would not come it (meaning that Joseph Smith would not surrender); that the General had issued orders for the militia to be in readiness to take said Smith. I asked him what general, and he observed that he believed it was Col. Williams. I asked him if it was done by orders of the Governor, and he said that was the understanding. He told me he acted under the orders of Captain McAuley; and further saith not.

JAMES OLIVE.

[Seal]   Subscribed and sworn to this 22nd day of June, 1844, before me,

AARON JOHNSON, J. P.

Phebe Levett states that she saw Finch, Rollison, Foster, and Squire McAuley in the company who fired on the guard on the La Harpe road.

George G. Johnstone made the following affidavit:

Affidavit: George G. Johnstone—Militia Under Governor to Move on Nauvoo.

STATE OF ILLINOIS, } ss
COUNTY OF HANCOCK. }

CITY OF NAUVOO, June 22nd, 1844.

Personally appeared before me, Aaron Johnson, a justice of the peace in and for the county of Hancock, George G. Johnstone, living on Spring Creek in McDonough county; who, being first duly sworn, deposeth and saith that yesterday, Napoleon Hardin came to your deponent and said that the Governor had sent orders for the militia to be called out for today at 4 o'clock p. m., and to start on the 22nd to Carthage, there to wait until all were ready from the different counties in the state, and then they should march out to the prairie. They should stop on the prairie and send a flag of truce to Nauvoo, and demand the body of General Joseph Smith. If the people of Nauvoo refused to give him up, then they should exterminate the whole of them.

GEORGE G. JOHNSTONE.

[Seal]   Subscribed and sworn to this 22nd day of June, 1844, before me,

AARON JOHNSON, J. P.

Gideon Gibbs made the following affidavit:

Affidavit: Gideon Gibbs—Mob on La Harpe Road.

STATE OF ILLINOIS, } ss
CITY OF NAUVOO. }

On the 22nd day of June, 1844, came before me, William W. Phelps, clerk of the Mayor's Court for said city, Gideon Gibbs, and after being duly sworn deposeth and saith that on the afternoon of the 21st instant, about a half-mile southeast of the Big Mound on the La Harpe road, a party of about eight or ten men, in a warlike attitude, in company with two teams, passed your said affiant, and one of them said he fired at two men near the Big Mound. Thought he killed them both; and your deponent saith no further.

GIDEON GIBBS.

Subscribed and sworn to before me, this 22nd day of June, 1844.

WILLIAM W. PHELPS, Clerk M. C.

Luman H. Calkins made the following affidavit:

*Affidavit: Luman H. Calkins—Nauvoo Conspiracy Against the Prophet's
Life.*

STATE OF ILLINOIS, }
CITY OF NAUVOO, } ss

June 22nd, 1844.

Personally appeared before me, George W. Harris, an alderman acting in and for the city of Nauvoo, Luman H. Calkins; and being first
duly sworn, deposeth and saith that about seven weeks ago I came on
the steamboat *Ohio* from St. Louis to Nauvoo, when William Nesbit,
who was on board, entered into conversation with your deponent.

I asked him if he knew anything about the conspiracy in Nauvoo to
kill Joseph and Hyrum, and all that believed on them. He said he did.
It was intended that they should be killed between then and the 1st of
July.

I asked him who was at the head of the conspiracy. He replied he
was sworn not to tell who the head one was. I asked him if there were
any in Nauvoo concerned. He replied there was, and named the two
Laws, two Fosters, two Higbees, Charles Ivins, and several others. I
asked if it was to be made a public thing. He replied the first blow
was to be struck in Nauvoo by those who were opposed to Joseph. I
asked how many they could rely on in Nauvoo. He said they could
rely on five hundred, if they could only get arms for them.

He said as soon as the first blow was struck in Nauvoo, there were
about seven thousand men ready in Missouri to join them to exterminate all who believed on Joseph Smith. He also told me that the *Die
Vernon*, when she came on her pleasure-trip to Nauvoo, that there were
none but spies, and who came on purpose to see the places in order to
know how to strike when the time comes to strike; and he also said
"the Reformers" had got spies continually passing Nauvoo in order to
spy out all that took place; that there was not a thing took place in
Nauvoo but what was made known to them in St. Louis as soon as a
steamboat landed.

I told him I should think he would be afraid to stop here. He said
he should stay in Nauvoo and carry on his butchering as usual, as if
there was nothing taking place; that he had as good a gun as any man
ever put to his face, and that the first shot he should fire would be to
kill Joseph and Hyrum. Said I, "The people will surely kill you then."
He replied he would rush through a thousand people to wash his hands
in Joseph's blood, and especially in Hyrum's, if he was to be immediately cut into a thousand pieces. He said he should be willing to die as
soon as he had killed them.

About five weeks since I had another conversation with William Nesbit, when he confirmed the whole of the foregoing conversation; and he also said he had made arrangements with Mr. Bostwick of St. Louis to send him a brace of the best pistols, for the purpose of being ready when he wanted them. He also said that he would kill Hyrum any time he could get an opportunity without being detected. I then asked him if Hyrum could be put in his way so that no man would mistrust him, would you kill him? He said, "By God, I would." I asked if he would not be afraid to kill him in cold blood. He replied, "No, I would not; I would do it in a moment if I could get an opportunity."

The day following I left for Galena, and returned on Tuesday, the 18th instant, and on the 19th I saw William Nesbit in the ranks, and I cautioned Richard Brazier to keep an eye on Nesbit, for he had sworn to wash his hands in Joseph's and Hyrum's blood.

LUMAN H. CALKINS.

Subscribed and sworn to this 22nd day of June, 1844, before me,
GEORGE W. HARRIS,
Alderman of the City of Nauvoo.

At 12, noon, orders were sent to the different guards and pickets to let persons pass and repass without hailing until further orders.

I issued the following:

GENERAL ORDERS.

MAYOR'S OFFICE AND HEADQUARTERS, OF THE NAUVOO LEGION,
NAUVOO, June 22nd, 1844.

To Col. Jonathan Dunham, Acting Major-General Nauvoo Legion:

SIR.—You will proceed without delay, with the assistance of the Nauvoo Legion, to prepare the background [Eastern part] of said city for defense against an invasion by mobs, cause the Legion to be furnished with tents, and make your encampment in the vicinity of your labor.

JOSEPH SMITH,
Mayor of the City of Nauvoo, and Lieut.-Gen. Nauvoo Legion.

TO COL. JONATHAN DUNHAM, Major-General in command Nauvoo Legion.

At 6 p. m. I prophesied that in the sickly seasons sickness would enter into the houses of the mob and vex
A Prophecy.   them until they would fain repent in dust and ashes. They will be smitten with the scab, &c.

At 7 p. m. I received the following:

A Petition to Hear the Prophet Speak.

We, the undersigned citizens of Hancock county, respectfully request General Joseph Smith to preach on tomorrow, and that we have liberty of seats near enough to the stand to hear, inasmuch as we have an opportunity to hear him but seldom, and some of us have not heard him at all.

Yours respectfully,

JAMES HAMILTON AND CO., Capt. at the Liberty Branch.

NATHANIEL CASE, Capt. 7th Co., 4th Reg., 2nd Cohort, N. L. from La Harpe.

URIAH H. YAGER AND CO., Captain at the Branch of Macedonia, 2nd Cohort.

HIRAM CLARK 1st Lieut. at the Midland Branch Company.

Z. D. WILSON'S COMPANY.

ALNA L. TIPPETT'S COMPANY.

S. HANCOCK, Major of the First Battalion of the 3rd Regiment.

WARREN SNOW, Captain and Co., 4th Reg. 2nd Cohort of N. Legion.

At 10 p. m. I received the following letter by the hands of Captain Yates, who accompanied Elder John Taylor and Dr. John M. Bernhisel on their return from Carthage:

Letter: Governor Ford to Mayor and Council of the City of Nauvoo:

HEADQUARTERS CARTHAGE, June 22nd, 1844.

To the Mayor and Council of the City of Nauvoo:

GENTLEMEN.—After examining carefully all the allegations on the part of the citizens of the country in Hancock county, and the defensive matters submitted to me by the committee of your citizens concerning the existing disturbances, I find that there appears to be but little contradiction as to important facts, so that it may be safely assumed that the immediate cause of the existing excitement is the destruction of the press and *Nauvoo Expositor,* and the subsequent refusal of the individuals accused to be accountable therefor according to the general laws of this state, and the insisting on your parts to be accountable only before your own municipal court, and according to the ordinances of your city.

Many other facts have been asserted on both sides as tending to increase the excitement; but as they mostly relate merely to private persons, and committed by individuals, and tend simply to show the present state of affairs, I will not further notice them in this communication.

The material facts to be noticed are that a newspaper called the *Nauvoo Expositor* was established in Nauvoo; that this newspaper was deemed offensive to the people of that city; that the Common Council, without notice or process to the owners, entered into a trial and heard statements not under oath, and evidence which was under oath, in relation to the character, conduct and designs of the owners and editors of the press; that, upon hearing such statements and evidence, the Common Council passed an ordinance or resolution declaring said press and paper to be a public nuisance, and ordered the same to be abated as such; that a writ was issued by the Mayor to the Marshal of the city for that purpose; that a military order was issued at the same time by the Mayor, who is also Lieutenant-General of the Nauvoo Legion, to the Major-General in command of that Legion, for a force sufficient to ensure the execution of the writ aforesaid.

It appears also the press was destroyed in obedience to the foregoing ordinance and writ, according to a return on the same by the Marshal in the following words: "The within press and type is destroyed and pied according to order on this 10th day of June, 1844, at about six o'clock p. m.—J. P. GREENE, C. M."

It appears also that the owners of the press obtained from a justice of the peace at Carthage a warrant against the authors of this destruction for a riot; that the constable charged with the execution of this process, arrested some of the persons accused, who immediately obtained writs of *habeas corpus* from the Municipal Court of your city, by virtue of which they were tried in Nauvoo and discharged from arrest, and that they have ever since refused to be arrested or to submit to a trial at any other place or before any other court, except in the city and before the Municipal Court aforesaid.

It has also been reported to me that martial law has been declared in Nauvoo; that persons and property have been and are now forcibly imprisoned and detained there, and that the Legion has been ordered under arms to resist any attempt to arrest the persons accused. I have not particularly inquired into the truth of these latter reports; for although they may become matters of great importance in the sequel, they are not necessary to be ascertained and acted upon at present.

I now express to you my opinion that your conduct in the destruction of the press was a very gross outrage upon the laws and the liberties of the people. It may have been full of libels, but this did not authorize you to destroy it.

There are many newspapers in this state which have been wrongfully abusing me for more than a year, and yet such is my regard for the liberty of the press and the rights of a free people in a republican government that I would shed the last drop of my blood to protect those presses from any illegal violence. You have violated the Constitution in at least four particulars. You have violated that part of it which declares that the printing presses shall be free, being responsible for the abuse thereof, and that the truth may be given in evidence.

This article of the Constitution contemplates that the proprietors of a libelous press may be sued for private damages, or may be indicted criminally, and that upon trial they should have the right to give the truth in evidence. In this case the proprietors had no notice of the proceeding.

The Constitution also provides that the people shall be protected against unreasonable searches and seizures of their property and "That no man shall be deprived of life, liberty or property, except by the judgment of his peers (which means a jury trial) and the law of the land," which means due process of law and notice to the accused.

You have also violated the Constitution and your own charter in this: Your Council, which has no judicial powers, and can only pass ordinances of a general nature, have undertaken to pass judgment as a court and convict without a jury a press of being libelous and a nuisance to the city.

The Council at most could only define a nuisance by general ordinance, and leave it to the courts to determine whether individuals or particulars accused came within such definition.

The Constitution abhors and will not tolerate the union of legislative and judicial power in the same body of magistracy, because, as in this case, they will first make a tyrannical law, and then execute it in a tyrannical manner.

You have also assumed to yourselves more power than you are entitled to in relation to writs of *habeas* under your charter. I know that you have been told by lawyers, for the purpose of gaining your favor that you have this power to any extent. In this they have deceived you for their own base purposes. Your charter supposes that you may pass ordinances, a breach of which will result in the imprisonment of the offender.

For the purpose of insuring more speedy relief to such persons, authority was given to the Municipal Court to issue writs of *habeas corpus* in all cases arising under the ordinances of the city.

It was never supposed by the Legislature, nor can the language of your charter be tortured to mean that a jurisdiction was intended to be conferred which would apply to all cases of imprisonment under the general laws of the state or of the United States, as well as the city ordinances.

It has also been reserved to you to make the discovery that a news-paper charged to be scurrilous and libellous may be legally abated or removed as a nuisance. In no other state, county, city, town or territory in the United States has ever such a thing been thought of before. Such an act at this day would not be tolerated even in England. Just such another act in 1830 hurled the king of France from his throne, and caused the imprisonment of four of his principal ministers for life. No civilized country can tolerate such conduct, much less can it be tolerated in this free country of the United States.

The result of my deliberations on this subject is, that I will have to require you and all persons in Nauvoo accused or sued to submit in all cases implicitly to the process of the court, and to interpose no obstacles to an arrest, either by writ of *habeas corpus* or otherwise; and that all of the people of the city of Nauvoo shall make and continue the most complete submission to the laws of the state, and the process of the courts and justices of the peace.

In the particular case now under consideration, I require any and all of you who are or shall be accused to submit yourselves to be arrested by the same constable, by virtue of the same warrant and be tried before the same magistrate whose authority has heretofore been resisted. Nothing short of this can vindicate the dignity of violated law and allay the just excitement of the people.

I am anxious to preserve the peace. A small indiscretion may bring on a war. The whole country is now up in arms, and a vast number of people are ready to take the matter into their own hands. Such a state of things might force me to call out the militia to prevent a civil war. And such is the excitement of the country that I fear the militia, when assembled, would be beyond legal control.

You are wrong in the first instance, and I can call out no portion of the militia for your defense until you submit to the law. You have made it necessary that a *posse* should be assembled to execute legal process; and that *posse*, as fast as it assembles is in danger of being imbued with the mobocratic spirit, If you, by refusing to submit, shall make it necessary to call out the militia, I have great fears that your city will be destroyed, and your people many of them exterminated.

You know the excitement of the public mind. Do not tempt it too far. A very little matter may do a very great injury; and if you are disposed to continue the causes of excitement and render a force necessary to coerce submission, I would say that your city was built, as it were, upon a keg of powder which a very little spark may explode.

It is my intention to do all I can to preserve the peace, and even, if obliged, to call the militia to prosecute the war so as not to involve the innocent and comprehend all in the same punishment. But excitement is a mattter which grows very fast upon men when assembled. The affair, I much fear, may assume a revolutionary character, and the men may disregard the authority of their officers.

I tell you plainly that if no such submission is made as I have indicated, I will be obliged to call out the militia; and if a few thousand will not be sufficient, many thousands will be.

I sincerely hope that your people may do nothing which will make such a proceeding necessary. I hope also that they will be well-disposed to co-operate with me in allaying the excitement of the public mind. Immediately discharge such persons as you have under martial law. Let them go without molestation. Abstain from all injury to private property. Let people go where they please without swearing them first to take no part against you. All such proceedings tend only to inflame the public mind, and raise up ten men disposed to fight you for every one thus foolishly disabled.

Your committee assures me that you are sincerely desirous of preserving the peace; and if so, I hope you will co-operate with me in everything necessary to allay the excitement in the minds of the people.

The following-named persons are reported to me as being detained against their will by martial law: John A. Hicks, H. O. Norton, A. J. Higbee, John Eagle, P. J. Rolf, Peter Lemon, and T. J. Rolf. It will tend greatly to allay excitement if they shall be immediately discharged and suffered to go without molestation.

It is also reported here, and generally believed, (but whether true or not I have not yet learned) that there are many foraging parties abroad from Nauvoo committing depredations upon the cattle and property in the vicinity These acts, if correctly reported, must absolutely cease immediately, if you expect any person here to have the power to preserve the peace.

In case the persons accused should make no resistance to arrest, it will be against orders to be accompanied by others. If it should become necessary to have witnesses on the trials, I will see that such persons shall be duly summoned, *and I will also guarantee the safety of all such persons as may thus be brought to this place from Nauvoo either for trial or as witnesses for the accused.*

If the individuals accused cannot be found when required by the constable it will be considered by me as an equivalent to a refusal to be arrested, and the militia will be ordered accordingly.

I am, gentlemen, with great respect, your obedient servant,

THOMAS FORD,
Governor and Commander-in-Chief.

To which I wrote the following answer:

Letter: Joseph Smith to Governor Ford—Defending the action of the City
Council in the "Expositor" Affair.

NAUVOO, June 22nd, 1844, 12 o'clock p. m.

To His Excellency, Thomas Ford:

SIR.—Yours of this date is received by Messrs. Taylor and Bernhisel.
A part of the same delegation, Mr. Woodworth, who was detained
yesterday, started for Carthage at 12 noon, this date, who, we perceive,
had not arrived at your last date.   Some documents conveyed by him
would tend to counteract some of the views expressed in your Excellency's communication, and we feel confident, if all the facts could be
before your Excellency, you would have come to different conclusions.

Our "insisting to be accountable only before our own Municipal
Court," is totally incorrect.   We plead a *habeas corpus* as a last resort
to save us from being thrown into the power of the mobocrats, who
were then threatening us with death, and it was with great reluctance
we went before the Municipal Court, on account of the prejudice which
might arise in the minds of the unbiased; and we did not petition for
a *habeas corpus* until we had told the constable that on our lives we dare
not go to Carthage for trial, and plead with him to go before any county
magistrate he pleased in our vicinity, (which occurrence is common in legal proceedings) and not a member of our society, so that our
lives might be saved from the threats thus already issued against us.

The press was declared a nuisance under the authority of the charter
as written in 7th section of Addenda, the same as in the Springfield
charter, so that if the act declaring the press a nuisance was unconstitutional, we cannot see how it is that the charter itself is not unconstitutional: and if we have erred in judgment, it is an official act, and
belongs to the Supreme Court to correct it, and assess damages *versus*
the city to restore property abated as a nuisance.   If we have erred in
this thing, we have done it in good company, for Blackstone on
"Wrongs," asserts the doctrine that scurrilous prints may be abated as
nuisances.

As to martial law, we truly say that we were obliged to call out the
forces to protect our lives; and the Constitution guarantees to every
man that privilege; and our measures were active and efficient, as the
necessity of the case required; but the city is and has been continually
under the special direction of the marshal all the time.   No person, to
our knowledge, has been arrested only for violation of the peace, and
those some of our own citizens, all of whom we believe are now dis-

charged. And if any property has been taken for public benefit without a compensation, or against the will of the owner, it has been done without our knowledge or consent, and when shown shall be corrected, if the people will permit us to resume our usual labors.

If we "have committed a gross outrage upon the laws and liberties of the people," as your Excellency represents, we are ready to correct that outrage when the testimony is forthcoming. All men are bound to act in their sphere on their own judgment, and it would be quite impossible for us to know what your Excellency's judgment would have been in the case referred to; consequently acted on our own and according to our best judgment, after having taken able counsel in the case. If we have erred, we again say we will make all right if we can have the privilege.

"The Constitution also provides that the people shall be protected against all unreasonable search and seizure." True. The doctrine we believe most fully, and have acted upon it; but we do not believe it unreasonable to search so far as it is necessary to protect life and property from destruction.

We do not believe in the "union of legislative and judicial power," and we have not so understood the action of the case in question.

Whatever power we have exercised in the *habeas corpus* has been done in accordance with the letter of the charter and Constitution as we confidently understood them, and that, too, with the ablest counsel; but if it be so that we have erred in this thing, let the Supreme Court correct the evil. We have never gone contrary to constitutional law, so far as we have been able to learn it. If lawyers have belied their profession to abuse us, the evil be on their heads.

You have intimated that no press has been abated as a nuisance in the United States. We refer your Excellency to Humphrey *versus* Press in Ohio, who abated the press by his own arm for libel, and the courts decided on prosecution no cause of action. And we do know that it is common for police in Boston, New York, &c., to destroy scurrilous prints: and we think the loss of character by libel and the loss of life by mobocratic prints to be a greater loss than a little property, all of which, life alone excepted, we have sustained, brought upon us by the most unprincipled outlaws, gamblers, counterfeiters, and such characters as have been standing by me, and probably are now standing around your Excellency—namely, those men who have brought these evils upon us.

We have no knowledge of men's being sworn to pass our city. And upon receipt of your last message the Legion was disbanded and the city left to your Excellency's disposal.

How it could be possible for us now to be tried constitutionally by the same magistrate who first issued the writ at Carthage we cannot see, for the Constitution expressly says no man shall twice be put in jeopardy of life and limb for the same offense; and all you refer to, have been, since the issuance of the *habeas corpus*, complied with for the same offense, and trial before Daniel H. Wells, justice of the peace for Hancock county, and, after a full investigation, were discharged. But, notwithstanding this, we would not hesitate to stand another trial according to your Excellency's wish, were it not that we are confident our lives would be in danger. We dare not come. Writs, we are assured, are issued against us in various parts of the country. For what? To drag us from place to place, from court to court, across the creeks and prairies, till some bloodthirsty villain could find his opportunity to shoot us. We dare not come, though your Excellency promises protection. Yet, at the same time, you have expressed fears that you could not control the mob, in which case we are left to the mercy of the merciless. Sir, we dare not come, for our lives would be in danger, and we are guilty of no crime.

You say, "It will be against orders to be accompanied by others, if we come to trial." This we have been obliged to act upon in Missouri; and when our witnesses were sent for by the court, (as your honor promises to do) they were thrust into prison, and we left without witnesses. Sir, you must not blame us, for "a burnt child dreads the fire." And although your Excellency might be well-disposed in the matter, the appearance of the mob forbids our coming. We dare not do it.

We have been advised by legal and high-minded gentlemen from abroad, who came on the boat this evening to lay our grievances before the Federal Government, as the appearance of things is not only treasonable against us, but against the state on the part of Missouri, unless the same has been requested of Governor Ford by the Federal Government. And we suppose your Excellency is well aware by this time that the mass-meetings of the county declared utter extermination of the Mormons, and that the Legion was not called out until complaints were made to the Mayor, and the citizens were afraid of their lives, and losing their confidence in the authorities of the city, and that nothing on the part of the city authorities had been wanting, legally and judiciously, to allay excitement and restore peace. We shall leave the city forthwith to lay the facts before the General Government, and, as before stated, the city is left open and unprotected; and by everything that is sacred, we implore your Excellency to cause our helpless women and children to be protected from mob violence, and let not the blood of innocence cry to heaven against you. We again say, if anything wrong has been done on our part, and we know of nothing, we will make all things right if the Government will give us the opportunity. Disperse the mob, and secure to us our constitutional privileges, that our lives may not be endangered when on trial.

I remain most respectfully, your Excellency's humble servant,

JOSEPH SMITH,
Mayor, and Lieut.-Gen. N. L.

CHAPTER XXVIII.

GOVERNOR FORD'S WRONG VIEWPOINT — ELDER TAYLOR'S ACCOUNT OF THE INTERVIEW WITH THE GOVERNOR AT CARTHAGE—CLOSE OF THE PROPHET'S JOURNAL NARRATIVE OF HIS LIFE.

[*Saturday, June 22nd, 1844, continued*].—It appears that the Governor, on arriving at Carthage, ordered the entire mob into service, adopted the lies and mis-representations circulated against us by our enemies as truth, turned Supreme Court, and decided on the legality of our municipal ordinances and proceedings, which is the business of the judiciary alone. He charges us in his letter, based upon most cursed false-hoods, with violations of law and order, which have never been thought of by us. He treated our delegates very rudely. My communications that were read to him were read in the presence of a large number of our worst ene-mies, who interrupted the reader at almost every line with, "That's a damned lie!" and "That's a G— d——d lie!" He never accorded to them the privilege of saying one word to him only in the midst of such interruptions as, "You lie like hell!" from a crowd of persons pres-ent. These facts show conclusively that he is under the influence of the mob spirit, and is designedly intending to place us in the hands of murderous assassins, and is conniving at our destruction, or else that he is so ignorant and stupid that he does not understand the corrupt and diabolical spirits that are around him.

Gov. Ford's Biased Judgment.

Elder John Taylor gave the following account of his interview with the Governor:

Elder John Taylor's Account of Interview With Governor Ford at Carthage.

After waiting the Governor's pleasure for some time, we had an audience—but such an audience! He was surrounded by some of the vilest and most unprincipled men in creation. Some of them had an appearance of respectability, but many of them lacked even that. Wilson, and, I believe, William Law were there, Foster, Frank and Chauncey Higbee, Mr. Marr, a lawyer from Nauvoo, a mobocratic merchant from Warsaw, Joseph H. Jackson, a number of his associates, and the Governor's secretary—in all fifteen or twenty persons, most of whom were recreant to virtue, honor, integrity and everything that is considered honorable among men. I can well remember the feelings of disgust that I had in seeing the Governor surrounded by such an infamous group, and on being introduced to men of so questionable a character; and had I been on private business, I should have turned to depart, and told the Governor that if he thought proper to associate with such questionable characters, I should beg leave to be excused; but coming. as we did, on public business, we could not of course consult our private feelings.

We then stated to the Governor that, in accordance with his request, General Joseph Smith had, in response to his call, sent us to him as a committee of conference; that we were acquainted with most of the circumstances that had transpired in and about Nauvoo lately, and were prepared to give him the information; that, moreover, we had in our possession testimony and affidavits confirmatory of what we should say, which had been forwarded to him by General Joseph Smith; that communications had been forwarded to his Excellency by Messrs. Hunter, James and others, some of which had not reached their destination, but of which we had duplicates with us. We then in brief related an outline of the difficulties, and the course we had pursued from the commencement of the troubles up to the present, and, handing him the documents, respectfully submitted the whole. During our conversation and explanations with the Governor, we were frequently rudely and impudently contradicted by the fellows he had around him, and of whom he seemed to take no notice.

He opened and read a number of the documents himself, and as he proceeded he was frequently interrupted by, "That's a lie!" "That's a G— d——d lie!" "That's an infernal falsehood!" "That's a blasted lie!" &c.

These men evidently winced on an exposure of their acts, and thus vulgarly, impudently and falsely repudiated them. One of their number, Mr. Marr, addressed himself several times to me while in conversation with the Governor. I did not notice him until after a frequent repetition of his insolence, when I informed him that my business at that time was with Governor Ford, whereupon I continued my conversation with his Excellency.

During the conversation the Governor expressed a desire that Joseph Smith and all parties concerned in passing or executing the city law in relation to the press had better come to Carthage; that however repugnant it might be to our feelings, he thought it would have a tendency to allay public excitement and prove to the people what we professed— that we wished to be governed by law.

We represented to him the course we had taken in relation to this matter, our willingness to go before another magistrate other than the Muncipal Court, the illegal refusal by the constable, of our request, our dismissal by the Municipal Court, a legally constituted tribunal, our subsequent trial before Esq. Wells at the instance of Judge Thomas (the circuit judge), and our dismissal by him; that we had fulfilled the law in every particular; that it was our enemies who were breaking the law, and, having murderous designs, were only making use of this as a pretext to get us into their power.

The Governor stated that the people viewed it differently, and that, notwithstanding our opinions, he would recommend that the people should be satisfied.

We then remarked to him that, should Joseph Smith comply with his request, it would be extremely unsafe, in the present excited state of the country, to come without an armed force; that we had a sufficiency of men, and were competent to defend ourselves, but that there might be danger of collision should our forces and those of our enemies be brought in such close proximity.

He strenuously advised us not to bring any arms, and pledged his faith as Governor, and the faith of the state, that we should be protected, and that he would guarantee our perfect safety.

At the termination of our interview, and previous to our withdrawal, after a long conversation and the perusal of the documents which we had brought, the Governor informed us that he would prepare a written communication for General Joseph Smith, which he desired us to wait for. We were kept waiting for this instrument some five or six hours.

About five o'clock in the afternoon we took our departure with not the most pleasant feelings. The associations of the Governor, the spirit that he manifested to compromise with these scoundrels, the length of time that he had kept us waiting, and his general deportment, together with the infernal spirit that we saw exhibited by those whom he admitted to his counsels, made the prospect anything but promising.

I had a consultation for a little while with my brother Hyrum, Dr. Richards, John Taylor and John M. Bernhisel, and determined to go to Washington and lay the matter before President Tyler.*

About 7 p. m, I requested Reynolds Cahoon and Alpheus Cutler to stand guard at the Mansion, and not to admit any stranger inside the house.

At sundown I asked O. P. Rockwell if he would go with me a short journey, and he replied he would.

[Abraham C. Hodge says that soon after dusk, Joseph called Hyrum, Willard Richards, John Taylor, William W. Phelps, A. C. Hodge, John L. Butler, Alpheus Cutler, William Marks and some others, into his upper room and said, "Brethren, here is a letter from the Governor which I wish to have read.   After it was read through Joseph remarked, "There is no mercy—no mercy here." Hyrum said, "No; just as sure as we fall into their hands we are dead men." Joseph replied, "Yes; what shall we do, Brother Hyrum?" He replied, "I don't know." All at once Joseph's countenance brightened up and he said, "The way is open. It is clear to my mind what to do. All they want is Hyrum and myself; then tell everybody to go about their business, and not to collect in groups, but to scatter about. There is no doubt they will come here and search for us. Let them search; they will not harm you in person or property, and not even a hair of your head. We will cross the river tonight, and

* "At this juncture the council was interrupted by the withdrawal of President Smith to give an interview to two gentlemen—one of whom was a son of John C. Calhoun—who had arrived at the Mansion and were anxious to meet with the Prophet" (Life of John Taylor, page 125). Elder Taylor withdrew at a late hour from the council because of great weariness. "Shortly after he [Elder Taylor] retired, however, the Prophet returned, and the informal council meeting was resumed. The project of laying the case before President Tyler was abandoned. Joseph had received an inspiration to go west and all would be well" (Ibid).

go away to the West.'' He made a move to go out of the house to cross the river. When out of doors he told Butler and Hodge to take the *Maid of Iowa*, (in charge of Repsher) get it to the upper landing, and put his and Hyrum's families and effects upon her; then go down the Mississippi and up the Ohio river to Portsmouth, where they should hear from them. He then took Hodge by the hand and said, ''Now, Brother Hodge, let what will come, don't deny the faith, and all will be well.'']

*I told Stephen Markham that if I and Hyrum were ever taken again we should be massacred, or I was not a prophet of God. I want Hyrum to live to avenge my blood, but he is determined not to leave me.**

* Here the direct narrative of the Prophet ends; what happened in the next few days of his life occurred under such circumstances as not to permit of his dictating an account of it to his secretary or clerks, as was his custom.

Concerning the statement in the text about the Prophet's desire to have Hyrum live, and the purpose of it, Mr. Edward Tullidge, in his *Life of Joseph the Prophet,* gives a different version of it. He states it: *"I want Hyrum to live to lead the Church, but he is determined not to leave me"* (Tullidge, p. 491). On what authority Mr. Tullidge makes the change is not known; but there is evidence in addition to his statement that the Prophet did desire Hyrum Smith to succeed him in the presidency of the Church, and even "ordained" him to take that place. At the October conference following the martyrdom of the two brothers, President Brigham Young said: *"Did Joseph ordain any man to take his place? He did. Who was it? It was Hyrum. But Hyrum fell a martyr before Joseph did"* (*Times and Seasons* Vol. V, page 683).

CHAPTER XXIX.

THE PROPHET STARTS FOR THE ROCKY MOUNTAINS—THE
COUNSEL OF FALSE BRETHREN—THE RETURN TO NAUVOO
—THE SURRENDER AND ARRIVAL AT CARTHAGE.

*An account of the arrest, imprisonment and martyrdom of President Joseph
Smith and Patriarch Hyrum Smith in Carthage jail, Hancock county,
Illinois, as collected from the journal kept at the time by Willard Richards
and the statements published by John Taylor, Messrs. Reid and Woods and
John S. Fullmer, and the writings and statements of Dan Jones, Cyrus
H. Wheelock, Stephen Markham and many other persons, who   were
personally acquainted with the transactions.*—By the Historian.†*

Saturday, June 22, 1844.—About 9 p. m. Hyrum came
out of the Mansion and gave his hand to Reynolds Cahoon,
at the same time saying, "A company of men
are seeking to kill my brother Joseph, and the
Lord has warned him to flee to the Rocky
Mountains to save his life. Good-by, Brother
Cahoon, we shall see you again." In a few minutes
afterwards Joseph came from his family. His tears were
flowing fast. He held a handkerchief to his face, and
followed after Brother Hyrum without uttering a word.

The Warning
to Flee to the
Rocky
Mountains.

Between 9 and 10 p. m. Joseph, Hyrum and Willard,
while waiting on the banks of the river for the skiff, sent

* This is the title of the first *Compilation of Data* as it appears in the *Millennial Star*, Vol. XXIV, p. 332. A *Second Compilation* was made by the Church
Historian, extending from the 22nd of June to the 8th of August, 1844, at which
time the Twelve were accepted for the time as the Presiding Council of the Church;
and the claims of Sidney Rigdon rejected.

† George A. Smith was the Historian from 1854 to 1875. Consequently this
pilation was made under his supervision.

for William W. Phelps, and instructed him to take their
families to Cincinnati by the second steamboat, arriving
at Nauvoo; and when he arrived there to commence petitioning the President of the United States and Congress
for redress of grievances, and see if they would grant the
Church liberty and equal rights.   Joseph then said: "Go
to our wives, and tell them what we have concluded to do,
and learn their feelings on the subject; and tell Emma
you will be ready to start by the second steamboat, and
she has sufficient money wherewith to pay the expenses.
If you ascertain by tomorrow morning that there is anything wrong, come over the river to Montrose, to the
house of Captain John Killien, and there you will learn
where we are."

About midnight, Joseph, Hyrum and Dr. Richards
called for Orrin P. Rockwell at his lodgings, and all went
up the river bank until they found Aaron Johnson's boat,
which they got into, and started about 2 a. m to cross
the Mississippi river.   Orrin P. Rockwell rowed the skiff,
which was very leaky, so that it kept Joseph, Hyrum
and the doctor busy baling out the water with their boots
and shoes to prevent it from sinking.

Sunday, 23.—At daybreak arrived on the Iowa side of
the river.   Sent Orrin P. Rockwell back to Nauvoo with
instructions to return the next night with
horses for Joseph and Hyrum, pass them over
the river in the night secretly, and be ready
to start for the Great Basin in the Rocky Mountains.

Preparations
for the West-
ern Journey.

Joseph, Hyrum and Dr. Richards walked up to Captain
John Killien's house, where they arrived at sunrise; but
he not being at home, they went from thence to Brother
William Jordan's.   About 9 a. m. Dr. Bernhisel came
over the river to visit Joseph; also Reynolds Cahoon,
who made some explanations respecting Governor Ford's
letter.

Early in the morning a *posse* arrived in Nauvoo to

arrest Joseph, but as they did not find him, they started back to Carthage immediately, leaving one man of the name of Yates behind them, who said to one of the brethren that Governor

Arrival of the Constable's Posse.

Ford designed that if Joseph and Hyrum were not given up, he would send his troops and guard the city until they were found, if it took three years to do it.

At 1 p. m. Emma sent over Orrin P. Rockwell, requesting him to entreat of Joseph to come back. Reynolds Cahoon accompanied him with a letter which Emma had written to the same

Emma's Message to the Prophet.

effect, and she insisted that Cahoon should persuade Joseph to come back and give himself up. When they went over they found Joseph, Hyrum and Willard in a room by themselves, having flour and other provisions on the floor ready for packing.

Reynolds Cahoon informed Joseph what the troops intended to do, and urged upon him to give himself up, inasmuch as the Governor had pledged his faith and the faith of the state to protect him while he underwent a legal and fair trial. Reynolds Cahoon, Lorenzo D. Wasson and Hiram Kimball accused Joseph of cowardice for wishing to leave the people, adding that their property would be destroyed, and they left without house or home. Like the fable, when the wolves came the shepherd ran from the flock, and left the sheep to be devoured. To which Joseph replied, "If my life is of no value to my friends it is of none to myself."

Joseph said to Rockwell, "What shall I do?" Rockwell replied, "You are the oldest and ought to know best; and as you make your bed, I will lie with you." Joseph then turned to Hyrum,

Consultation with Rockwell.

who was talking with Cahoon, and said, "Brother Hyrum, you are the oldest, what shall we do?" Hyrum said, "Let us go back and give ourselves up, and see the thing out." After studying a few moments, Joseph said, "If

you go back I will go with you, but we shall be butchered." Hyrum said, "No, no; let us go back and put
our trust in God, and we shall not be harmed. The Lord
is in it. If we live or have to die, we will be reconciled to
our fate."

After a short pause, Joseph told Cahoon to request Captain Daniel C. Davis to have his boat ready at half-past
five to cross them over the river.

Joseph and Hyrum then wrote the following letter:

*Letter: Joseph and Hyrum Smith to Governor Ford—Consenting to go to
Carthage.*

BANK OF THE RIVER MISSISSIPPI,
Sunday, June 23rd, 1844, 2 p. m.

His Excellency Governor Ford:

SIR.—I wrote you a long communication at 12 last night, expressive
of my views of your Excellency's communication of yesterday. I
thought your letter rather severe, but one of my friends has just come
to me with an explanation from the captain of your *posse* which softened
the subject matter of your communication, and gives us greater assurance of protection, and that your Excellency has succeeded in bringing
in subjection the spirits which surround your Excellency to some extent.
And I declare again the only objection I ever had or ever made on trial
by my country at any time, was what I have made in my last letter—
on account of assassins, and the reason I have to fear deathly consequences from their hands.

But from the explanation, I now offer to come to you at Carthage on
the morrow, as early as shall be convenient for your *posse* to escort us
into headquarters, provided we can have a fair trial, not be abused nor
have my witnesses abused, and have all things done in due form of
law, without partiality, and you may depend on my honor without the
show of a great armed force to produce excitement in the minds of the
timid.

We will meet your *posse*, if this letter is satisfactory, (if not, inform
me) at or near the Mound, at or about two o'clock tomorrow afternoon.
which will be as soon as we can get our witnesses and prepare for trial.
We shall expect to take our witnesses with us, and not have to wait a
subpœna or part at least, so as not to detain the proceedings, although
we may want time for counsel.

We remain most respectfully, your Excellency's humble servants,

JOSEPH SMITH.
HYRUM SMITH.

Also wrote to Horace T. Hugins, Esquire:

Letter: Joseph Smith to H. T. Hugins—Engaging Counsel.

NAUVOO, Sunday, June 23, 1844.

H. T. Hugins, Esq:

SIR.—I have agreed to meet Governor Ford at Carthage tomorrow to attend an examination before Justice Morrison, and request your attendance professionally with the best attorney you can bring.

I meet the Governor's *posse* on the Mound at 10 a. m.; in Carthage at 12 noon. Do not fail me, and oblige,

Yours respectfully,

JOSEPH SMITH.

per W. RICHARDS, Clerk.

P. S.—Dr. J. R. Wakefield I wish as witness, &c.

And also to Dr. J. Wakefield as follows:

Letter: Joseph Smith to J. R. Wakefield Soliciting Latter's Attendance as Witness.

NAUVOO, June 23, 1844.

Dr. J R. Wakefield:

SIR.—I would respectfully solicit your attendance at court in Carthage tomorrow at 12 noon, as witness in case "State of Illinois on complaint of Francis M. Higbee, *versus* Joseph Smith and others." Dear sir, do not fail me, and oblige your old friend,

JOSEPH SMITH,

per WILLARD RICHARDS, Clerk.

P. S.—Esq. Hugins and co-partner are expected. We meet the Governor's *posse* on the Mound at 10 a. m.: at Carthage at 12 noon. Bearer will give particulars.

About 4 p. m. Joseph, Hyrum, the Doctor and others started back. While walking towards the river, Joseph fell behind with Orrin P. Rockwell. The others shouted to come on. Joseph replied, "It is of no use to hurry, for we are going back to be slaughtered," and continually expressed himself that he would like to get the people once more together, and talk to them tonight. Rockwell said if that was his wish he would get the people together, and he could talk to them by starlight.

The Prophet Returns to Nauvoo.

It was the strong persuasions of Reynolds Cahoon, Lorenzo D. Wasson and Hiram Kimball, who were carrying out Emma's instructions, that induced Joseph and Hyrum to start back to Nauvoo. They re-crossed the river at half-past five. When they arrived at the Mansion in Nauvoo, Joseph's family surrounded him, and he tarried there all night, giving up the idea of preaching to the Saints by starlight.

He sent the letter of this date to Governor Ford by Col. Theodore Turley and Elder Jedediah M. Grant, who carried it to Carthage, where they arrived about 9 p.m. They gave the letter to Governor Ford, who first agreed to send a *posse* to escort General Smith in safety to Carthage. Immediately afterwards Mr. Skinner came in and made a very bitter speech to the Governor, in which Wilson Law and Joseph H. Jackson joined, telling him naught but lies, which caused Elder Grant to ask if messengers to him were to be insulted in that manner. The Governor treated them coldly, and rescinded his previous promise, and refused to send or allow an escort to go with Joseph, as he said it was an honor not given to any other citizen. He would not allow the messengers to stay in Carthage through the night, but ordered them to start at 10 o'clock, and return to Nauvoo with orders for General Smith to be in Carthage at 10 o'clock tomorrow morning without an escort; and he threatened that if General Smith did not give himself up at that time, that Nauvoo would be destroyed and all the men, women and children that were in it. Messrs. Grant and Turley immediately started; but on account of their horses being wearied, they did not arrive in Nauvoo until about four a. m. of the 24th, when they went to General Smith to report to him the state of excitement in Carthage. He would not hear one word of the warning, as he was determined to go to Carthage and give himself up to the Governor.

Vacillation of Governor Ford.

At night Joseph conversed with Captain Anderson, who reported that the mob at Warsaw had stopped his boat, and threatened to fire into her with his cannon. He gave the following certificate:

Certificate: Captain Anderson—on Retention of People in Nauvoo.

NAUVOO, June 23rd, 1844.

This is to certify that on Tuesday morning last, I stated to General Joseph Smith that the number of passengers leaving that day might produce the effect on the public mind that they were afraid of being attacked, and prove injurious; and I further observed, in order to preserve peace and good order, that it would be better to use his endeavors to retain those in the city until the excitement should abate.

GEORGE C. ANDERSON,
Captain steamer *Osprey*.

Joseph received the following letter:

Letter: Ed. Johnston to Joseph Smith—About Counsel.

Sunday Evening, June 23rd, 1844.

General Joseph Smith:

SIR.—I have this moment received your favor of this day per the hands of Mr. Adams. I regret to say, in reply, that I am now awaiting every moment a boat for St. Louis, whither my business requires me to go, and which, of course will deter me from acceding to your request. I have introduced Mr. Adams to a friend who is entirely competent to do full justice to your cause.

In great haste, yours respectfully,

ED. JOHNSTON.

PORT MADISON, IOWA.

Preparations are making for an early start tomorrow morning for Carthage. Joseph gave directions to gather some horses for the purpose of carrying him and his friends to Carthage tomorrow.

Preparations for Going to Carthage.

Although the Governor has threatened to send his troops into the city, none have appeared as yet.

Monday, 24.—Francis M. Higbee having sworn out a writ before Thomas Morrison, a justice of the peace at

Carthage on the 11th instant, against Joseph Smith, Hy-

Defendants in the *Expositor* Case. rum Smith, Samuel Bennet, John Taylor, William W. Phelps, John P. Greene, Stephen C. Perry, Dimick B. Huntington, Jonathan Dunham, Stephen Markham, William W. Edwards, Jonathan Holmes, Jesse P. Harmon, John Lytle, Joseph W. Coolidge, David Harvey Redfield, Orrin P. Rockwell and Levi Richards for riot, in destroying the *Nauvoo Expositor* press, the property of William and Wilson Law and others, on the 10th instant, and Governor Ford having sent word by the *posse* that those eighteen persons should be protected by the militia of the state, they, upon the assurance of that pledge at half-past six a. m. started for Carthage, Willard Richards, Dan Jones, Henry G. Sherwood, Alfred Randall, James Davis, Cyrus H. Wheelock, A. C. Hodge and several other brethren, together with James W. Woods as counsel, accompanying them.

When they arrived at the top of the hill, Joseph sent Rockwell with a horse for Dr. Southwick, a Southern

Incidents *en route* for Carthage. gentleman who had been staying some days at the Mansion, and who wished General Joseph Smith to buy considerable property in Texas; but Ed. Bonny took possession of the horse, so that Dr. Southwick could not then go.

Joseph paused when they got to the Temple, and looked with admiration first on that, and then on the city, and remarked, "This is the loveliest place and the best people under the heavens; little do they know the trials that await them." As he passed out of the city, he called on Daniel H. Wells, Esq., who was unwell, and on parting he said, "Squire Wells, I wish you to cherish my memory, and not think me the worst man in the world either."

At ten minutes to 10 a. m. they arrived at Albert G. Fellows' farm, four miles west of Carthage, where they

Meeting with Captain Dunn. met Captain Dunn with a company of about sixty mounted militia, on seeing which Joseph said, "Do not be alarmed, brethren, for they

cannot do more to you than the enemies of truth did to the
ancient Saints—they can only kill the body." The
company made a halt, when Joseph, Hyrum and several
others went into Fellows' house with Captain Dunn, who
presented an order from Governor Ford for all the state
arms in possession of the Nauvoo Legion, which Joseph
immediately countersigned.

Henry G. Sherwood went up to Joseph and said,
"Brother Joseph, shall I return to Nauvoo and regulate
about getting the arms and get the receipts
for them?" Joseph inquired if he was under   A Pathetic
                                              Prophecy.
arrest, or expected to be arrested. Sherwood answered "No," when Joseph directed him to
return ahead of the company, gather the arms and do as
well as he could in all things. Joseph then said to the
company who were with him, "*I am going like a lamb to
the slaughter, but I am calm as a summer's morning. I
have a conscience void of offense toward God and toward
all men. If they take my life I shall die an innocent man,
and my blood shall cry from the ground for vengeance, and
it shall be said of me 'He was murdered in cold blood!'*"
He then said to Father Sherwood, "Go, and God bless
you." Sherwood then rode as swiftly as he could to
Nauvoo.

Esquire Woods left the company there, and continued
his journey to Carthage.

This order for the delivery of the state arms was evidently designed to drive the citizens of Nauvoo to desper-
ation, so that in the heat of their indignation they might
commit some overt act which the Governor could con-
strue into treason, and thus have a shadow of excuse for
his mob militia to destroy the Mormons.

Captain Dunn requested the company to return to
Nauvoo to assist in collecting the arms, and   Dunn's Re-
pledged his word as a military man, that   quest that the
                                              Prophet Re-
Joseph and his friends should be protected   turn to Nau-
even if it were at the expense of his own life,   voo:

and his men responded to the pledge by three cheers. Captain Dunn, no doubt feared that the order of the Governor would excite the inhabitants of Nauvoo beyond endurance, and therefore chose to depend on the well-known integrity of General Smith than to risk the chances of exciting the feelings of a much-abused people. At the same time Joseph sent a messenger to the Governor with the following letter:

Letter: Joseph Smith to Governor Ford—Explaining his Return to Nauvoo.

FOUR MILES WEST OF CARTHAGE MOUND,
HANCOCK COUNTY, ILLINOIS,
Monday, 10 o'clock.

His Excellency Governor Ford:

DEAR SIR.—On my way to Carthage to answer your request this morning, I here met Captain Dunn, who has here made known to me your orders to surrender the state arms in possession of the Nauvoo Legion, which command I shall comply with; and that the same may be done properly and without trouble to the state, I shall return with Captain Dunn to Nauvoo, see that the arms are put into his possession, and shall then return to headquarters in his company, when I shall most cheerfully submit to any requisition of the Governor of our state.

With all due respect to your Excellency, I remain your obedient servant.

JOSEPH SMITH.

He also issued the following order:

Order: Joseph Smith to General Dunham—Complying with Governor Ford's Demand for State Arms.

HEADQUARTERS NAUVOO LEGION,
Prairie Four Miles West of Carthage,
June 24th, 1844, 10 o'clock and 10 minutes.

To Major-General Jonathan Dunham and all commissioned and non-commissioned officers and privates of the Nauvoo Legion:

You are hereby ordered to comply strictly with the within order of the Commander-in-Chief, Governor Ford.

JOSEPH SMITH.
Lieut.-Gen. Nauvoo Legion.

And requested that the state arms should be taken to the Masonic Hall without delay.

Hyrum then said to Abram C. Hodge, "You go on into Carthage and see what is going on, and hear what is said on this matter." *Messenger Sent to Carthage.*

Joseph and his company then returned with Captain Dunn, and arrived in Nauvoo at half-past two p. m.

When Hodge arrived at Carthage, he met with Rev. Mr. Dodge, who had some time previously been very kindly treated by Hyrum. He warned Hodge that as sure as Joseph and Hyrum came to Carthage, they would be killed. Hodge also saw Hamilton, the innkeeper, who, pointing to the Carthage Greys, said, "Hodge, there are the boys that will settle you Mormons." Hodge replied, "We can take as many men as there are there out of the Nauvoo Legion, and they would not be missed."

When the fact of the order for the state arms was known in Nauvoo, many of the brethren looked upon it as another preparation for a Missouri massacre; nevertheless, as Joseph requested that it should be complied with, they very unwillingly gave up the arms. *Surrender of State Arms.*

About 6 p. m., when all the states' arms were collected, and the company were ready to start, Captain Dunn and Quartermaster-General Buckmaster made a short speech, expressing their gratitude at the peaceable conduct of the citizens of Nauvoo, and that while they thus conducted themselves they would protect them.

It appears that Governor Ford feared that the Nauvoo Legion, although disbanded, might avenge any outrage that might hereafter be committed on the persons of their leaders, and so thought he had better disarm them as he had previously disbanded them; yet the mob was suffered to retain their portion of the state's arms, even when within a half-day's march of Nauvoo, and they in a threatening and hostile attitude, while the Nauvoo Legion had not evinced the least disposition whatever, except to defend their city in case it should be attacked; and they had not set a foot outside the limits of the corporation.

Joseph rode down home twice to bid his family farewell.
The Prophet's Farewell to his Family.
He appeared solemn and thoughtful, and expressed himself to several individuals that he expected to be murdered. There appeared no alternative but that he must either give himself up, or the inhabitants of the city would be massacred by a lawless mob under sanction of the Governor.

The company (about fifteen) then started again for Carthage, and when opposite to the Masonic Hall, Joseph
Looking Back-Sadness.
said, "Boys, if I don't come back, take care of yourselves; I am going like a lamb to the slaughter." When they passed his farm he took a good look at it, and after they had passed it, he turned round several times to look again, at which some of the company made remarks, when Joseph said: "If some of you had got such a farm and knew you would not see it any more, you would want to take a good look at it for the last time." When they got to the edge of the woods near Nauvoo, they met A. C. Hodge returning from Carthage. He reported to Hyrum what he had heard in Carthage, told him what his feelings were and said, "Brother Hyrum, you are now clear, and if it was my duty to counsel you, I would say, do not go another foot, for they say they will kill you, if you go to Carthage," but as other persons gathered around, nothing further was said. About this time Joseph received the following letter:

Letter: Messrs. Reid and Woods to Joseph Smith—Documents for Defense.

CARTHAGE, 5 o'clock p. m.

General Joseph Smith:

DEAR SIR.—In accordance with previous arrangements with Elder Adams, I am here at your service; and it will be necessary for us to have, on the examination here before the justice, a certified copy of the city ordinance for the destruction of the *Expositor* press, or a copy which has been published by authority. We also wish the original order issued by you to the marshal for the destruction of said press, and such witnesses as may be necessary to show by whom the press was destroyed, and that the act was not done in a riotous or tumultuous manner.

Yours respectfully,

H. T. REID.

DEAR SIR.—I concur fully as to the above, and will add, from an interview with Governor Ford, you can, with the utmost safety, rely on his protection, and that you will have as impartial an investigation as could be expected from those opposed to you. The excitement is much allayed, and your opponents (those who wish to make capital out of you) do not want you to come to Carthage. Mr. Johnson has gone east, and that will account for Mr. Reed being here.

Respectfully, your obedient servant,

JAMES W. WOOD.

CARTHAGE, 24th June, 1844.

The company arrived at Fellows' house, four miles west of Carthage, about 9 p. m., where they stopped about half an hour, and partook of such refreshments as they had brought with them. Captain Dunn and his company of mounted militia, returning with the state arms from Nauvoo, joined them here, and escorted them into Carthage, where they arrived at five minutes before 12 at night, and went to Hamilton's tavern. While passing the public square many of the troops, especially the Carthage Greys, made use of the following expressions, which were re-echoed in the ears of the Governor and hundreds of others, "Where is the damned prophet?" "Stand away, you McDonough boys, and let us shoot the damned Mormons." "G—d— you, old Joe, we've got you now." "Clear the way and let us have a view of Joe Smith, the prophet of God. He has seen the last of Nauvoo. We'll use him up now, and kill all the damned Mormons." The rear platoon of the Carthage Greys repeatedly threw their guns over their heads in a curve, so that the bayonets struck the ground with the breech of their guns upward, when

The Prophet's Arrival at Carthage.

they would run back and pick them up, at the same time whooping, yelling, hooting and cursing like a pack of savages.

On hearing the above expressions, the Governor put his head out of the window and very fawningly said, "I know your great anxiety to see Mr.

The Governor Pacifies the Mob.

Smith, which is natural enough, but it is quite too late tonight for you to have the opportunity; but I assure you, gentlemen, you shall have that privilege tomorrow morning, as I will cause him to pass before the troops upon the square, and I now wish you, with this assurance, quietly and peaceably to return to your quarters." When this declaration was made, there was a faint "Hurrah for Tom Ford," and they instantly obeyed his wish.

There was a company of apostates also quartered at Hamilton's hotel—namely William and Wilson Law, the Higbees and Fosters, Augustine Spencer, Henry O. Norton, John A. Hicks, (formerly president of the Elder's quorum) and others.

The Apostates at Carthage.

Hicks stated to C. H. Wheelock that it was determined to shed the blood of Joseph Smith by not only himself, but by the Laws, Higbees, Fosters, Joseph H. Jackson, and many others, whether he was cleared by the law or not. Jackson talked freely and unreservedly on that subject, as though he were discoursing upon the most common occurrence of his life. Said he, you will find me a true prophet in this respect. Wheelock told Ford what Hicks had said, but he treated it with perfect indifference, and suffered Hicks and his associates to run at liberty and mature their murderous plans.

A writ was also issued by Robert F. Smith against Joseph W. Coolidge on complaint of Chauncey L. Higbee, charging him with the illegal detention of Charles A. Foster.

CHAPTER XXX.

ARREST OF JOSEPH AND HYRUM SMITH ON A CHARGE OF TREASON—FALSE IMPRISONMENT—ELDER TAYLOR'S PROTEST—FALSE IMPRISONMENT.

Tuesday, June 25, 1844.—This morning the prisoners voluntarily surrendered themselves to the constable, Mr. Bettisworth, who held the writ against them. The Governor was at headquarters in person, and had pledged his own faith and the faith of the state of Illinois, that the Smiths and other persons should be protected from personal violence, and should have a fair and impartial trial, if they would surrender themselves to be dealt with according to law. During the Governor's stay in Carthage, he repeatedly expressed to the legal counselors of the Smiths his determination to protect the prisoners, and to see that they should have a fair and impartial examination.

The Governor's Pledge of Protection.

At 8 a. m. President Smith had an interview with William G. Flood of Quincy, U. S. Receiver of Public Moneys. While in conversation with him, Constable David Bettisworth arrested Joseph for treason against the state of Illinois, with the following writ, which had been granted on the oath of Augustine Spencer:

The Arrest for Treason.

Writ of Arrest on the Charge of Treason—Joseph Smith.

STATE OF ILLINOIS, ⎫ ss
CITY OF NAUVOO. ⎭

The people of the State of Illinois, to all sheriffs, coroners and constables of said state greeting:

Whereas complaint has been made before me, one of the justices of

36 Vol. VI

the peace in and for said county aforefaid, upon the oath of Augustine Spencer, that Joseph Smith, late of the county aforesaid, did, on or about the nineteenth day of June. A. D. 1844, at the county and state aforesaid, commit the crime of treason against the government and people of the State of Illinois aforesaid.

These are therefore to command you to take the said Joseph Smith if he be found in your county, or if he shall have fled, that you pursue after the said Smith into another county within this state, and take and safely keep the said Joseph Smith, so that you have his body forthwith before me to answer the said complaint, and be further dealt with according to law.

[Seal]   Given under my hand and seal this 24th day of June, A. D. 1844.

R. F. SMITH, J. P.

Hyrum Smith was also arrested at the same time for treason on the same writ, granted on the affidavit of Henry O. Norton:

Writ of Arrest for Treason—Hyrum Smith.

STATE OF ILLINOIS, }
HANCOCK COUNTY.   } ss

The people of the State of Illinois, to all sheriffs, coroners and constables, greeting:

Whereas complaint has been made before me, one of the justices of the peace, in and for the county of Hancock, upon the oath of one Henry O. Norton, that one Hyrum Smith, late of the county of Hancock and state of Illinois, did, on the 19th day of June, 1844, commit the crime of treason against the government and people of the state of Illinois aforesaid.

These are therefore to command you to take the body of the said Hyrum Smith, if he be found in your county, or if he shall have fled that you pursue after the said Hyrum Smith into any county within this state, and take and safely keep the said Hyrum Smith, so that you have his body forthwith before me, to answer unto the said complaint, and be further dealt with according to law.

[Seal]   Given under my hand and seal, this 24th day of June. 1844.

R. F. SMITH, J. P.

8:30 a. m.—Governor Ford called all the troops and ordered them to form a hollow square on the public ground near the Court House; and when formed, he

mounted an old table, and addressed them in a most
inflammatory manner, exciting the feelings of indignation
against Generals Joseph and Hyrum Smith
which were already burning in their breasts,
occasioned by the falsehoods and misrepresentations that were in circulation, giving his assent and
sanction to the rumors that had gathered them together,
and stating that although they were dangerous men in
the community, and guilty of all that they might have
alleged against them, still they were in the hands of the
law, which must have its course. He continued speaking
twenty or thirty minutes.

Governor
Ford's Speech
to the Troops.

9:15 a. m.—The Governor came in and invited Joseph
to walk with him through the troops. Joseph
solicited a few moments' private conversation
with him, which the Governor refused. While
refusing, the Governor looked down at his
shoes, as though he was ashamed. They then walked
through the crowd with Brigadier-General Miner R. Deming and Dr. Richards, to General Deming's quarters. The
people appeared quiet until a company of Carthage Greys
flocked around the doors of General Deming in an uproar-
ious manner, of which notice was sent to the Governor. In
the meantime the Governor had ordered the McDonough
troops to be drawn up in line for Joseph and Hyrum to
pass in front of them, they having requested that they
might have a clear view of the Generals Smith. Joseph
had a conversation with the Governor for about ten minutes, when he again pledged the faith of the state that he
and his friends should be protected from violence.

The Prophet's
Request for
an Interview
with Gov.
Ford.

Robinson, the postmaster, said, on report of martial
law being proclaimed in Nauvoo, he had stopped the mail
and notified the Postmaster-General of the state of things
in Hancock county.

From the General's quarters Joseph and Hyrum went
in front of the lines, in a hollow square of a company of

Carthage Greys.   At seven minutes before ten they
arrived in front of the lines, and passed before
the whole, Joseph being on the right of General
Deming, and Hyrum on his left, Elders Richards, Taylor and Phelps following. Joseph and Hyrum were
introduced by the Governor about twenty times along the
line, as General Joseph Smith and General Hyrum Smith,
the Governor walking in front on the left. The Carthage
Greys refused to receive them by that introduction, and
some of the officers threw up their hats drew their swords
and said they would introduce themselves to the damned
Mormons in a different style. The Governor mildly
entreated them not to act so rudely, but their excitement
increased. The Governor, however, succeeded in paci-
fying them by making a speech, and promising them that
they should have "full satisfaction." General Smith and
party returned to their lodgings at five minutes past ten.

10:30.—News reached Joseph at the hotel that the Carthage Greys had revolted, and were put under guard by
General Deming.   Joseph told all his friends
to stay in the two rooms occupied by them in
the hotel.

10:50.—Quietness was apparently restored among the
Carthage Greys.

11:15.—News arrived that the Warsaw troops were
near Carthage, and had come of their own accord.

Mr. Prentice, U. S. Marshal for Illinois, called to see
Joseph.

12 minutes before 1.—Intelligence was given to Joseph
that the Laws, Higbees, Fosters and others,
were going to Nauvoo to plunder.   The Governor called at the door with some gentlemen,
when Joseph informed him of what he had
heard, and requested him to send a guard to protect the
city of Nauvoo.

Willard Richards wrote a letter to his wife.

1:30 p. m.—After dinner, Mark Aldrich of Warsaw called to see Joseph.

2:30.—The Governor communicated that he had ordered Captain Singleton with a company of men from McDonough county, to march to Nauvoo to co-operate with the police in keeping the peace; and he would call out the Legion, if necessary.

Joseph wrote to Emma as follows:

Letter: The Prophet to Emma Smith—Governor Ford Going to Nauvoo.

CARTHAGE, June 25th, 1844.

2:30 o'clock p. m.

DEAR EMMA.—I have had an interivew with Governor Ford, and he treats us honorably. Myself and Hyrum have been again arrested for treason because we called out the Nauvoo Legion; but when the truth comes out we have nothing to fear. We all feel calm and composed.

This morning Governor Ford introduced myself and Hyrum to the militia in a very appropriate manner, as General Joseph Smith and General Hyrum Smith. There was a little mutiny among the Carthage Greys, but I think the Governor has and will succeed in enforcing the laws. I do hope the people of Nauvoo will continue pacific and prayerful.

Governor Ford has just concluded to send some of his militia to Nauvoo to protect the citizens, and I wish that they may be kindly treated. They will co-operate with the police to keep the peace. The Governor's orders will be read in the hearing of the police and officers of the Legion, as I suppose.

3 o'clock.—The Governor has just agreed to march his army to Nauvoo, and I shall come along with him. The prisoners, all that can, will be admitted to bail. I am as ever,

JOSEPH SMITH.

EMMA SMITH.

Joseph also sent a message to Orrin P. Rockwell not to come to Carthage, but to stay in Nauvoo, and not to suffer himself to be delivered into the hands of his enemies, or to be taken a prisoner by any one. *The Prophet's Warning to Rockwell.*

It was reported by Israel Barlow that he had heard resolutions of the Warsaw troops read, to the effect that they would return to Warsaw at 3 p. m., then go to Golden's Point on Thursday, and thence to Nauvoo.

Several of the officers of the troops in Carthage, and
other gentlemen, curious to see the Prophet, visited Joseph
in his room. General Smith asked them if
there was anything in his appearance that
indicated he was the desperate character his
enemies represented him to be; and he asked
them to give him their honest opinion on the subject.
The reply was, "No, sir, your appearance would indicate
the very contrary, General Smith; but we cannot see what
is in your heart, neither can we tell what are your intentions." To which Joseph replied, "Very true, gentlemen,
you cannot see what is in my heart, and you are therefore
unable to judge me or my intentions; but I can see what
is in your hearts, and will tell you what I see. I can see
that you thirst for blood, and nothing but my blood will
satisfy you. It is not for crime of any description that I
and my brethren are thus continually persecuted and harassed by our enemies, but there are other motives, and
some of them I have expressed, so far as relates to myself;
and inasmuch as you and the people thirst for blood, I
prophesy, in the name of the Lord, that you shall witness
scenes of blood and sorrow to your entire satisfaction.
Your souls shall be perfectly satiated with blood, and
many of you who are now present shall have an opportunity to face the cannon's mouth from sources you think not
of; and those people that desire this great evil upon me
and my brethren, shall be filled with regret and sorrow
because of the scenes of desolation and distress that await
them. They shall seek for peace, and shall not be able to find
it. Gentlemen, you will find what I have told you to be true."

12 minutes to 4.—Report came to Joseph that William
and Wilson Law, Robert D. Foster, Chauncey
L. Higbee and Francis M. Higbee had said *that
there was nothing against these men; the law
could not reach them but powder and ball would,*
and they should not go out of Carthage alive.

The Prophet's Interview with Militia Officers.

Law Cannot Reach Them —Powder and Ball Must.

Joseph, Hyrum and thirteen others, were Arraigned on the *Expositor* Affair. taken before Robert F. Smith, a justice of the peace residing in Carthage (he being also captain of the Carthage Greys) on the charge of riot destroying the printing press of the *Nauvoo Expositor*.

It is worthy of notice here, that when the defendants went before Esquire Wells, the prosecution objected, and insisted that they should be taken before the justice who issued the writ—viz., Thomas Morrison, and that Governor Ford had also stated in his letter to General Joseph Smith that he must go before the justice in Carthage who issued the writ. But when the prosecution had the defendants in their own power in Carthage, they could then ride over their own objections by taking them before another justice, who was known to be a greater enemy to the defendants than Justice Morrison, and moreover, before one who was not only a justice of the peace, but also the military commander of a company of Carthage Greys, who had already been arrested for mutiny.

Chauncey L. Higbee, one of the prosecutors, moved an adjournment.

H. T. Reid and James W. Woods on behalf of the defendants, objected to an adjournment, and said that the court was not authorized to take recognizance without their acknowledging their guilt, or having witnesses to prove it, and we admit the press was destroyed by order of the Mayor, it having been condemned by the City Council as a nuisance.

They read law to show that justices could not recognize without admission of guilt, and offered to give bail.

Mr. Reid stated that the law quoted by the prosecution belonged to civil, not criminal cases.

The prosecution insisted to have a commission of the crime acknowledged.

After a good deal of resistance on the part of the prosecution, court asked if the parties admitted that there was

Prophet *et al.*
Bound over to
Circuit Court.
sufficient cause to bind over, and the counsel for the defense admitted there was, and offered to enter into cognizance in the common form, in order to prevent, if possible, any increase of excitement.

5 p. m.—Court acknowledged the admission and ordered recognizances, whereupon Joseph Smith, Hyrum Smith, John Taylor, William W. Phelps, John P. Greene, Stephen C. Perry, Dimick B. Huntington, Jonathan Dunham, Stephen Markham, Jonathan H. Holmes, Jesse P. Harmon, John Lytle, Joseph W. Coolidge, David Harvey Redfield, and Levi Richards gave bonds, with John S. Fullmer, Edward Hunter, Dan Jones, John Benbow, and other unexceptionable sureties, in the sum of $500 for each of the defendants, total $7,500, for their appearance at the next term of the Circuit Court for Hancock county.

The Sureties
for the
Prophet.

It was evident that the magistrate intended to overreach the wealth of the defendants and their friends, so as to imprison them for want of bail; but it happened that there was strength to cover the demand, for some of the brethren went security to the full extent of their property; and Justice Smith adjourned his court over, and left the court house without calling on Joseph and Hyrum to answer to the charge of treason, or even intimating to those prisoners, or their counsel that they were expected to enter into an examination that night.

Captain Smith, the only magistrate who could grant subpoenas for witnesses, disappeared until a late hour, as if purposely to prevent the appearing of the defendant's witnesses, and in keeping with the conviction expressed by Joseph's enemies the previous day, that the law cannot touch them, but that powder and ball will.

About 6:30 p. m.—Dan Jones heard Wilson Law, whilst endeavoring to get another warrant against Joseph Smith for treason, declare that while he (Mr. Smith) was once preaching from Daniel 2nd chapter, 44th verse, said that the

kingdom referred to was already set up, and that he was the
king over it. He also heard Joseph H. Jackson, and
other leaders of the mob, declare that they
had eighteen accusations against Joseph, and
as one failed, they would try another to detain
him there, and that they had had so much
trouble and hazard, and worked so hard in getting him to
Carthage, that they would not let him get out of it alive.
Jackson pointed to his pistols and said, "The balls are in
there that will decide his case." Jones immediately went
up stairs to Joseph and informed him what he had heard
Jackson say.

Another Warrant Sought—Daniel's Kingdom and Treason.

About 7:30 p. m.—Dr. Levi Richards and most of the
brethren, after they had signed the bonds, left for Nauvoo
when Joseph and Hyrum went into the Governor's room
and spoke with him, as Governor Ford had promised them
an interview. After a few moments' conversation, the Governor left them to order the captain of the guard to give
the brethren some passes. They then went to supper.

8 p. m.—Constable Bettisworth appeared at the lodgings
of Joseph and Hyrum, and insisted that
they should go to jail. Joseph demanded a
copy of the mittimus, which was refused.
Messrs. Woods and Reid, as counsel, insisted
that the prisoners were entitled to be brought before a
justice of the peace for examination before they could be
sent to jail. The constable, to their surprise, then exhibited the following mittimus:

Illegal Imprisonment of the Smith Brothers.

The False Mittimus.

STATE OF ILLINOIS, ⎱ ss.
HANCOCK COUNTY, ⎰

*The people of the State of Illinois to the keeper of the jail of said County,
Greeting:*

Whereas Joseph Smith and Hyrum Smith, of the county aforesaid,
have been arrested upon oath of Augustine Spencer and Henry O.
Norton, for the crime of treason, and have been brought before me as

a justice of the peace in and for the said county, for trial at the seat of justice thereof, which trial has been necessarily postponed by reason of the absence of the material witnesses—to wit, Francis M. Higbee and others. Therefore, I command you, in the name of the people, to receive the said Joseph Smith and Hyrum Smith into your custody in the jail of the county aforesaid, there to remain until discharged by due course of law.

[Seal]   Given under my hand and seal this 25th day of June, A. D. 1844.

(Signed)   R. F. SMITH J. P.

Joseph remonstrated against such bare-faced, illegal, and tyrannical proceedings, but the constable still insisted that they should go to jail. Lawyer Woods requested the officer to wait until he could see Governor Ford, and was told by Bettisworth that he could only wait five minutes.

Joseph and Hyrum again remonstrated, and the constable waited until about nine o'clock, when they heard by Mr. Wood that the Governor did not think it within the sphere of his duty to interfere, as they were in the hands of the civil law, and therefore he had not the power to stay process, or the due course of law, and that he could not interrupt a civil officer in the discharge of his duty.

Governor Ford Refuses to Interfere with Illegal Proceedings.

Governor Ford knew this [proceeding] was illegal, (for he had formerly been an associate-justice of the Supreme Court of the state) and when he was appealed to by Captain Robert F. Smith to know what he must do, as he had found his mittimus as a magistrate was illegal, and therefore that it was a false committal, Governor Ford replied, "You have the Carthage Greys at your command." *Captain Smith* therefore commanded his "Greys" to execute and carry into effect his illegal mittimus as *a magistrate*, thus practically blending the civil and military in the same person at the same time; and the prisoners were violently and illegally dragged to jail without any examination whatever, while his Excellency was in the the adjoining room from that from which they were thus taken. So much for his professions that *the law must be executed.*

Thus a justice of the peace acting as a military officer also by virtue of his commission as such, orders his command to appear under arms and to incarcerate the prisoners whom he had just before ordered to commit to jail by *mittimus without having them brought before him for examination;* and the Governor, having been himself at one time a judge upon the bench, knew and well understood the illegality of the above proceedings.

He also well knew that military power and [civil] authority had been used by one and the same person, and yet he, acting at that time as Commander-in-Chief, which gave him the supervision over all his officers, and in fact made him responsible for all their acts and movements, refused to interfere when requested by the prisoners to interpose his authority in their behalf against an illegal civil process, and also refused to countermand the illegal, oppressive and unofficer-like order of one of his captains.

Moreover, having taken the oath of office, as Governor of the state of Illinois, he was by virtue of that oath bound to see the laws faithfully executed, and not, as in this instance, see them violated and trodden under foot, and even prompt one of his officers in his lawless course. Thus he violated his solemn pledges and oath of office.

Elder John Taylor says, "As I was informed of this illegal proceeding, I went immediately to the Governor and informed him of it; whether he was apprized of it before or not, I do not know, but my opinion is that he was. I represented to him the character of the parties who had made oath, the outrageous nature of the charge, the indignity offered to men in the position which they [the prisoners] occupied, and that he knew very well that it was a vexatious prosecution, and that they were not guilty of any such thing."

Elder Taylor's Remonstrance with Governor Ford.

The Governor replied that he was very sorry that the

thing had occurred; that he did not believe the charges, but that he thought that the best thing to be done in the premises was to let the law take its course.

"I then reminded him that we had come out there at his instance, not to satisfy the law, which we had done before, but the prejudices of the people in relation to the affair of the press; that we had given bonds, which we could not by law be required to do, to satisfy the people at his instance, and that it was asking too much to require gentlemen in their position in life to suffer the degradation of being immured in a jail at the instance of such worthless scoundrels as those who had made this affidavit.

"The Governor replied that it was an unpleasant affair, and looked hard, but that it was a matter over which he had no control, as it belonged to the judiciary; that he, as the executive could not interfere with their proceedings, and that he had no doubt but that they would be immediately dismissed.

"I told him that we had looked to him for protection from such insults, and that I thought we had a right to do so from the solemn promises he had made to me and Dr. Bernhisel in relation to our coming without a guard or arms; that we had relied upon his faith and had a right to expect him to fulfill his engagements, after we had placed ourselves implicitely under his care, and complied with all his requests, although extra-judicial.

"He replied that he would detail a guard, if we required it, and see us protected, but that he could not interfere with the judiciary.

"I expressed my dissatisfaction at the course taken, and told him that if we were to be subject to mob rule, and to be dragged contrary to law into prison, at the instance of every infernal scoundrel whose oath could be bought for a dram of whiskey, his protection availed very little, and we had miscalculated his promises.

"Seeing there was no prospect of redress from the Governor, I returned to the room and found the Constable,

Bettisworth, very urgent to hurry Brothers Joseph and Hyrum to prison, whilst the brethren were remonstrating with him.

"At the same time a great rabble was gathered in the streets and around the door, and from the rowdyism manifested, I was afraid there was a design to murder the prisoners on the way to the jail.

"Without conferring with any person, my next feeling was to procure a guard, and seeing a man habited as a soldier in the room, I went to him and said, "I am afraid there is a design against the lives of the Messrs. Smith, will you go immediately and bring your captain, and if not convenient, any other captain of a company, and I will pay you well for your trouble."

Elder Taylor Takes Independent Action.

"He said he would, and departed forthwith, and soon returned with his captain, whose name I have forgotten* and introduced him to me.

"I told him of my fears, and requested him immediately to fetch his company. He departed forthwith, and arrived at the door with them, just as the time that the constable was hurrying the brethren downstairs.

"A number of brethren went along, and one or two strangers, and all of us safely lodged in prison, remained there during the night."

As Esquire Woods went to the door he met Captain Dunn, with some twenty men, they having come to guard the prisoners in jail. Mr. Woods accompanied Governor Ford to (Captain) Justice Robert F. Smith, who gave as a cause for issuing the warrant of committal, that the prisoners were not personally safe at the hotel. Mr. Woods then requested the Governor to have a company of troops from some other county detailed to guard the jail.

Captain Dunn, with his company, escorted Joseph and

---

* This was Captain Dunn, of Augusta township, who had been sent to Nauvoo a few days before to collect the state arms at Nauvoo, and who afterwards escorted the Prophet and his friends into Carthage.

Hyrum Smith from their lodgings, together with Willard Richards, John Taylor, John P. Greene, Stephen Markham, Dan Jones, John S. Fullmer, Dr. Southwick, and

In Carthage Jail.

Lorenzo D. Wasson, to the jail. Markham had a very large hickory cane, which he called "the rascal-beater." Dan Jones had a smaller walking-stick, and they walked on either side of Joseph and Hyrum, keeping off the drunken rabble, who several times broke through the ranks.

They were received by the jailer, Mr. George W. Stigall, and put into the criminal's cell; but he afterwards gave them the debtors' apartment, where the prisoners and their friends had amusing conversations on various interesting subjects, which engaged them till late. Prayer was offered, which made Carthage prison into the gate of heaven for a while. They laid promiscuously on the floor, where they all slept from 11:30 until 6 a. m. of the 26th.

Counselor H. T. Reid, in his published statement, writes as follows: "The recitals of the mittimus, so far as they relate to the prisoners, having been brought before the justice for trial, and it there appearing that the necessary witnesses of the prosecution were absent, are wholly untrue, unless the prisoners could have appeared before the justice, without being present in person or by counsel; nor is there any law of Illinois which permits a justice to commit persons charged with crimes to jail, without examination as to the probability of their guilt."

CHAPTER XXXI.

Wednesday, June 26, 1844; 7 a. m.—Joseph Hyrum, and the rest of the brethren, took breakfast with Stigall, and were then removed to the room upstairs.

Dr. Southwick went to see the Governor

At 7:30 a. m., Markham, Wasson, and Jones were severally sent by Joseph with messages to the Governor, but at 8 a. m., got no return. He also sent word to his counsel that he wanted a change of venue to Quincy, Adams County. Messages to the Governor

At 8 a. m., Joseph and Hyrum had a conversation with the jailor, Mr. Stigall, who said a week last Wednesday the mob were calculating to have made an attack on Nauvoo, and they expected about 9000 persons, but only about 200 came. They had sent runners to Missouri, and all around the counties in Illinois

At ten minutes past 8 o'clock a. m. Joseph wrote to Governor Ford, as follows and sent it by Mr. Stigall:—

Letter—Joseph Smith to Governor Ford—Soliciting an Interview.

CARTHAGE JAIL, June 26, 1844.
Ten minutes past 8 a. m.

His Excellency Governor Ford:

SIR,—I would again solicit your excellency for an interview having been much disappointed the past evening. I hope you will not deny me this privilege any longer than your public duties shall absolutely require.

We have been committed under a false mittimus, and consequently the proceedings are illegal, and we desire the time may be hastened when all things shall be made right, and we relieved from this imprisonment.   Your servant,

                                    JOSEPH SMITH.

P. S.—Please send an answer per bearer.

At 8:30 a. m., Markham and Jones returned, stating that the Governor said he was taken by surprise last evening, and was very sorry. Was afraid we would think he had forfeited his word about having an interview, that the wrath of the people was about to turn on the head of Jackson, the mob,&c. That the Governor was doing as fast as he could.

Word from Governor Ford.

Twelve minutes before 9. Received the following reply on the same sheet:—

"The interview will take place at my earliest leisure to-day.
                                    "GOVERNOR FORD."

Ten minutes to 9. Mr. Reid and others arrived at the jail and investigated the merits of the case, and concluded to take a change of venue before Justice Greenleaf, of Augusta, Hancock county, and to send for Dr. James H. Lyon, Col. J. Brewer, Edward Bonney, M. G. Eaton, Dr. Abiathar Williams, Thomas A. Lyne, George J. Adams, Dr. J. M. Bernhisel, Daniel H. Wells, Daniel Spencer, Orson Spencer, Dr. J. R. Wakefield, George P. Stiles, Jonathan Dunham, Albert P. Rockwood, Captain G. C. Anderson, William Marks, Hiram Kimball, Lorenzo D. Wasson, and Samuel Searles, as witnesses.

Consultation With Counsel

9:27 a. m. The Governor, in company with Col. Thomas Geddes, arrived at the jail, when a lengthy conversation was entered into in relation to our difficulties; and after some preliminary remarks, at the Governor's request Brother Joseph gave him a general outline of the state of the coun-

Interview with Gov. Ford.

try, the tumultuous, mobocratic movements of our enemies, the precautionary measures used by himself, (Joseph Smith) the acts of the City Council, the destruction of
the press, and the moves of the mob and ourselves up to
that time.

*The Following Account of this Interview is from the Manuscript History of
the Church in the Historian's Office, and not Hitherto Published.*

Joseph Smith stated to them [Governor Ford and Col. Geddes] the
origin of the difficulty, the facts relating to the *Expositor* press, the
course pursued by the City Council; the legality, as they thought, of
their legislation; the pledges that he had made by letter and sent by
expresses to his Exellency, that he was willing to satisfy all legal claims
in case it should be shown that the City Council had transcended their
legal bounds, etc., and that the Legion had been called out for the protection of the city, while it was threatened with immediate hostilities by
an infuriated mob, until his Excellency could afford relief, and not for
the purpose of invasion. (The Governor seemed to be satisfied that
this was the truth, but still he did not interfere in their illegal imprisonment). Joseph adverted to all the leading causes which gave
rise to the difficulties under consideration in a brief, but lucid, energetic and impressive manner. The Governor said he was satisfied it
was the truth. General Smith then read copies of the orders and proceedings of the City Council of Nauvoo, concerning the destruction of
the *Expositor* press, and of the correspondence forwarded to his Excellency, in relation thereto; and also informed him concerning the calling out of the Legion, and the position they occupied of absolute necessity, not to make war upon, or invade the rights of any portion of
the citizens of the State; but it was the *last resort*, and *only* defense, *in
the absence of executive protection*, against a large, organized military
and mobocratic foe.

General Smith reminded his Excellency that the question in dispute [the
Expositor case] was a *civil* matter, and to settle which needed no resort to
arms, and that he was ready at any time, and had always been ready to
answer any charge that might be preferred against him, either as the Lieutenant General of the Legion, the Mayor of the City, or as a private
individual, in any court of justice, which was unintimidated by a mob
or military array, *and make all the satisfaction that the law required, if
any, etc.* The Governor said he had not called out this force; [i. e.,

the one then gathered at Carthage] but found it assembled in military
array, without his orders, on his arrival at Carthage, and that the laws
must be enforced, but that the prisoners must and should be protected,
and he again pledged his word, and the faith and honor of the State,
that they should be protected. He also stated that he intended to march
his forces (that is, those who had assembled for mobocratic purposes;
and whom he had mustered into his service) to Nauvoo to gratify *them*,
and that the prisoners should accompany them, and then return again
to attend the trial before the said magistrate, which he said had been
postponed for the purpose of making this visit. (John S. Fullmer)
Joseph alluded to the coming of Constable Bettisworth when he
gave himself up, also to his offer to go before *any other justice of the
peace,* and called upon some twenty bystanders to witness that he submitted to the writ, but for fear of his life if he went to Carthage he had
preferred to go before Esq. Daniel H. Wells, a gentleman of high legal
attainments, who is in no way connected with the Mormon Church.

Joseph also said that he had sent frequent expresses and letters to
the Governor; that Dr. J. R. Wakefield, Dr. J. M. Bernhisel and Mr.
Sidney Rigdon also had written letters to the Governor; that he had
written another letter to the Governor which was sent on the 15th of
June by Mr. James; that he had written again on the 16th of June,
enclosing affidavits, and sent them by Messrs. Edward Hunter, Phillip
B. Lewis and John Bills. He also read Captain Anderson's certificate
of the proceedings of the mob at Warsaw; also his Proclamation, his
orders as Lieutenant General to Major General Dunham, the proceedings of the City Council of Nauvoo, and copies of communications forwarded to Springfield; also his letter of the 21st of June which was
sent by Dr. Bernhisel, and Mr. John Taylor, and his letter of the 22nd,
which was sent by Lucien Woodworth and Squire Woods.

Marshal John P. Greene explained about giving passes to persons
going in and out of the city, and denied that any arrests had been
made.

The Governor referred to the trial before Esq. Wells, which did not
satisfy the feelings of the people in and about Carthage. The Governor admitted that sufficient time had not been allowed by the posse for
the defendants to get ready, or to gather their witnesses, said it can be
very safely admitted that your statements are true, and was satisfied
now that the people of Nauvoo had acted according to the best of their
judgment.

Mr. Reid said that it was very evident from the excitement created
by Mr. Smith's enemies it would have been unsafe for him to come to
Carthage, for under such circumstances he could not have had an
impartial trial.

The Governor said he came here to enforce the laws on all the people whether Mormons or not; and then expressed his feelings about the destruction of the *Expositor* press.

Joseph spoke of his imprisonment in Missouri, and of the shameful kidnapping of his witnesses, and their being thrust into prison to prevent them from giving their testimony in his favor.

Governor Ford spoke of the Constitution.

Joseph said we were willing to pay for the press, as he did not want the owners to suffer any loss by it, [i. e. its suppression] neither did he wish such a libelous paper to be published in Nauvoo. As for calling out the Nauvoo Legion, if it was intended to resist the government of the State, it would be treason; but, as they believed, they were endeavoring to defend themselves, and had no such intention as to resist the government—it was all right.

The following report is by Elder John Taylor.*

Elder John Taylor's Account of Governor Ford's and President Smith's Interview.

Governor—General Smith, I believe you have given me a general outline of the difficulties that have existed in the country, in the documents forwarded to me by Dr. Bernhisel and Mr. Taylor; but, unfortunately, there seems to be a discrepancy between your statements and those of your enemies. It is true that you are substantiated by evidence and affidavit, but for such an extraordinary excitement as that which is now in the country, there must be some cause, and I attribute the last outbreak to the destruction of the *Expositor,* and to your refusal to comply with the writ issued by Esq. Morrison. The press in the United States is looked upon as the great bulwark of American freedom, and its destruction in Nauvoo was represented and looked upon as a high-handed measure, and manifests to the people a disposi-

---

*This report of the Prophet's interview with Governor Ford, it is only proper to say, was not written until a number of years after the interview took place. (See ms. Statement, Feb. 22, 1847, on Atlantic Ocean; also in *Taylor's Journal*, kept at Nauvoo, c. f. with "The Martyrdom of Joseph and Hyrum Smith, opening paragraphs, published in Tyler's "Mormon Battalion.") The extract above quoted is taken from "Taylor's Martyrdom of Joseph and Hyrum Smith," written at the request of George A. Smith and Wilford Woodruff "Church Historian," hence no earlier than 1854-1856, since Geo. A. Smith did not become Historian until the year first given, and Wilford Woodruff, assistant Historian in the second. The interview therefore, though given in dialogue form, can only be Elder Taylor's recollection of it, and could not be a *verbatum* report.

tion on your part to suppress the liberty of speech and of the press; this, with your refusal to comply with the requisition of a writ, I conceive to be the principal cause of this difficulty, and you are, moreover, represented to me as turbulent and defiant of the laws and institutions of your country.

Gen. Smith.—Governor Ford, you, sir, as Governor of this State, are aware of the prosecutions and persecutions that I have endured. You know well that our course has been peaceable and law-abiding, for I have furnished this State, ever since our settlement here, with sufficient evidence of my pacific intentions, and those of the people with whom I am associated, by the endurance of every conceivable indignity and lawless outrage perpetrated upon me and upon this people since our settlement here, and you yourself know that I have kept you well posted in relation to all matters associated with the late difficulties. If you have not got some of my communications, it has not been my fault.

Agreeably to your orders, I assembled the Nauvoo Legion for the protection of Nauvoo and the surrounding country against an armed band of marauders, and ever since they have been mustered I have almost daily communicated with you in regard to all the leading events that have transpired; and whether in the capacity of mayor of the city, or lieutenant-general of the Nauvoo Legion, I have striven to preserve the peace and administer even-handed justice to all; but my motives are impugned, my acts are misconstrued, and I am grossly and wickedly misrepresented. I suppose I am indebted for my incarceration here to the oath of a worthless man that was arraigned before me and fined for abusing and maltreating his lame, helpless brother.

That I should be charged by you, sir. who know better, of acting contrary to law, is to me a matter of surprise. Was it the Mormons or our enemies who first commenced these difficulties? You know well it was not us; and when this turbulent, outrageous people commenced their insurrectionary movements, I made you acquainted with them, officially, and asked your advice, and have followed strictly your counsel in every particular:

Who ordered out the Nauvoo Legion? I did, under your direction. For what purpose? To suppress these insurrectionary movements. It was at your instance, sir, that I issued a proclamation calling upon the Nauvoo Legion to be in readiness, at a moment's warning, to guard against the incursions of mobs, and gave an order to Jonathan Dunham acting major-general, to that effect. Am I then to be charged for the acts of others; and because lawlessness and mobocracy abound, am I when carrying out your instructions, to be charged with not abiding the law? Why is it that I must be held accountable for other men's acts? If there is trouble in the country, neither I nor my people made it, and all that we have ever done, after much endurance on our part, is to maintain and uphold the Constitution and institutions of our country, and to protect an injured, innocent, and persecuted people against mis-rule and mob violence.

Concerning the destruction of the press to which you refer, men may differ somewhat in their opinions about it; but can it be supposed that after all the indignities to which we have been subjected outside, that this people could suffer a set of worthless vagabonds to come into our city, and right under our own eyes and protection, vilify and calumniate not only ourselves, but the character of our wives and daughters, as was impudently and unblushingly done in that infamous and filthy sheet? There is not a city in the United States that would have suffered such an indignity for twenty-four hours.

Our whole people were indignant, and loudly called upon our city authorities for redress of their grievances, which, if not attended to they themselves would have taken the matter into their own hands, and have summarily punished the audacious wretches, as they de-served.

The principles of equal rights that have been instilled into our bos-oms from our cradles, as American citizens, forbid us submitting to every foul indignity, and succumbing and pandering to wretches so infamous as these. But, independent of this, the course that we pur-sued we considered to be strictly legal; for, notwithstanding the insult we were anxious to be governed strictly by law, and therefore con-vened the City Council; and being desirous in our deliberations to abide law, summoned legal counsel to be present on the occasion.

Upon investigating the matter, we found that our City Charter gave us power to remove all nuisances; and, furthermore, upon consulting Blackstone upon what might be considered a nuisance, that distin-guished lawyer, who is considered authority, I believe, in all our courts, states, among other things, that a libelous and filthy press may be considered a nuisance, and abated as such.

Here, then one of the most eminent English barristers, whose works are considered standard with us, declares that a libelous press may be considered a nuisance: and our own charter, given us by the legisla-ture of this State, gives us the power to remove nuisances; and by ordering that press abated as a nuisance, we conceived that we were acting strictly in accordance with law. We made that order in our corporate capacity, and the City Marshal carried it out. It is possible there may have been some better way, but I must confess that I could not see it.

In relation to the writ served upon us, we were willing to abide the consequences of our own acts, but were unwilling, in answering a writ of that kind, to submit to illegal exactions sought to be imposed upon us under the pretense of law, when we knew they were in open violation of it.

When that document was presented to me by Mr. Bettisworth, I offered, in the presence of more than 20 persons, to go to any other magistrate, either in our city or Appanoose, or any other place where we should be safe, but we all refused to put ourselves into the power of a mob.

What right had that constable to refuse our request? He had none according to law; for you know, Governor Ford, that the statute law in Illinois is, that the parties served with the writ shall go before him who issued it, or some other justice of the peace. Why, then, should we be dragged to Carthage, where the law does not compel us to go? Does not this look like many others of our prosecutions with which you are acquainted? And had we not a right to expect foul play?

This very act was a breach of law on his part—an assumption of power that did not belong to him, and an attempt, at least, to deprive us of our legal and constitutional rights and privileges. What could we do under the circumstances different from what we did do? We sued for, and obtained a writ of *habeas corprus* from the Municipal Court, by which we were delivered from the hands of Constable Bettisworth, and brought before and acquitted by the Municipal Court.

After our acquittal, in a conversation with Judge Thomas, although he considered the acts of the party illegal, he advised, that to satisfy the people, we had better go before another magistrate who was not in our Church.

In accordance with his advice we went before Esq. Wells, with whom you are well acquainted; both parties were present, witnesses were called on both sides, the case was fully investigated, and we were again dismissed.

And what is this pretended desire to enforce law, and these lying, base rumors put into circulation for, but to seek, through mob influence, under pretense of law, to make us submit to requisitions that are contrary to law, and subversive of every principle of justice?

And when you, sir, reqired us to come out here, we came, not because it was legal, but because you required it of us, and we were desirous of showing to you and to all men that we shrunk not from the most rigid investigation of our acts.

We certainly did expect other treatment than to be immured in a jail at the instance of these men, and I think, from your plighted faith, we had a right to, after disbanding our own forces, and putting ourselves entirely in your hands; and now, after having fulfilled my part, sir, as a man and an American citizen, I call upon you, Governor Ford, and think I have a right to do so, to deliver us from this place, and rescue us from this outrage that is sought to be practiced upon us by a set of infamous scoundrels.

Gov. Ford—But you have placed men under arrest. detained men as prisoners, and given passes to others, some of which I have seen.

John P. Greene, City Marshal—Perhaps I can explain. Since these difficulties have commenced, you are aware that we have been placed under very peculiar circumstance, our city has been placed under a very rigid police guard; in addition to this, frequent guards have been placed outside the city to prevent any sudden surprise, and those guards have questioned suspected or suspicious persons as to their business.

To strangers, in some instances, passes have been given, to prevent difficulty in passing those guards. It is some of those passes that you have seen. No person, sir, has been imprisoned without a legal cause in our city.

Gov.—Why did you not give a more speedy answer to the *posse* that I sent out?

Gen. Smith.—We had matters of importance to consult upon. Your letter showed anything but an amicable spirit. We have suffered immensely in Missouri from mobs, in loss of property, imprisonment, and otherwise.

It took some time for us to weigh duly these matters. We could not decide upon the matters of such importance immediately, and your *posse* were too hasty in returning. We were consulting for a large people, and vast interests were at stake.

We had been outrageously imposed upon, and knew not how far we could trust anyone; besides, a question necessarily arose, how shall we come? Your request was that we should come unarmed. It became a matter of serious importance to decide how far promises could be trusted, and how far we were safe from mob violence.

Geddes—It certainly did look from all I have heard, from the general spirit of violence and mobocracy that here prevails, that it was not safe for you to come unprotected.

Gov.—I think that sufficient time was not allowed by the *posse* for you to consult and get ready. They were too hasty; but I suppose they found themselves bound by their orders. I think, too, there is a great deal of truth in what you say, and your reasoning is plausible; yet, I must beg leave to differ from you in relation to the acts of the City Council. That council in my opinion, had no right to act in a legislative capacity, and in that of the judiciary.

They should have passed a law in relation to the matter, and then the Municipal Court, upon complaint, could have removed it; but for the City Council to take upon themselves the law-making and the execution of the laws, in my opinion, was wrong; besides, these men ought to have had a hearing before their property was destroyed; to destroy it without was an infringement of their rights; besides, it is so contrary to the feelings of the American people to interfere with the press.

And furthermore, I cannot but think that it would have been more judicious for you to have gone with Mr. Bettisworth to Carthage, notwithstanding the law did not require it. Concerning your being in jail, I am sorry for that, I wish it had been otherwise. I hope you will soon be released, but I cannot interfere.

Joseph Smith—Governor Ford, allow me, sir, to bring one thing to your mind, that you seem to have overlooked. You state that you think it would have been better for us to have submitted to the requisition of Constable Bettisworth, and to have gone to Carthage.

Do you not know, sir, that that writ was served at the instance of an anti-Mormon mob, who had passed resolutions and published them to the effect that they would exterminate the Mormon leaders; and are you not informed that Captain Anderson was not only threatened when coming to Nauvoo, but had a gun fired at his boat by this said mob at Warsaw, when coming up to Nauvoo, and that this very thing was made use of as a means to get us into their hands, and we could not, without taking an armed force with us, go there without, according to their published declarations, going into the jaws of death?

To have taken a force would only have fanned the excitement, as they would have stated that we wanted to use intimidation, therefore we thought it the most judicious to avail ourselves of the protection of the law.

Gov.—I see, I see.

Joseph Smith—Furthermore, in relation to the press, you say that you differ with me in opinion; be it so, the thing after all is a legal difficulty, and the courts I should judge competent to decide on that matter.

If our act was illegal, we are willing to meet it; and although I cannot see the distinction that you draw about the acts of the City Council, and what difference it could have made in point of fact, law, or justice, between the City Council's acting together or separate, or how much more legal it would have been for the Municipal Court, who were a part of the City Council, to act separate, instead of with the councilors.

Yet, if it is deemed that we did a wrong in destroying that press, we refuse not to pay for it. We are desirous to fulfill the law in every particular, and are responsible for our acts.

You say that the parties ought to have had a hearing. Had it been a civil suit, this of course would have been proper; but there was a flagrant violation of every principle of right, a nuisance, and it was abated on the same principle that any nuisance, stench, or putrified carcase would have been removed.

Our first step, therefore, was to stop the foul, noisome, filthy sheet, and then the next, in our opinion, would have been to have prosecuted the men for a breech of public decency.

And furthermore, again, let me say, Governor Ford, I shall look to you for our protection. I believe you are talking of going to Nauvoo; if you go, sir, I wish to go along. I refuse not to answer any law, but I do not consider myself safe here.

Gov. I am in hopes that you will be acquitted; but if I go, I will certainly take you along. I do not, however, apprehend danger. I think you are perfectly safe, either here or anywhere else. I cannot, however, interfere with the law. I am placed in peculiar circumstances and seem to be blamed by all parties.

Joseph Smith—Governor Ford, I ask nothing but what is legal. I have a right to expect protection at least from you; for, independent of law, you have pledged your faith, and that of the State, for my protection, and I wish to go to Nauvoo.

Gov.—And you shall have protection, General Smith. I did not make this promise without consulting my officers, who all pledged their honor to its fullfillment. I do not know that I shall go tomorrow to Nauvoo, but if I do, I will take you along.*

*Thomas Gregg, author of the History of Hancock County, page 372, gives the following statement of Col. Thomas Geddes mentioned in the above interview as the companion of Governor Ford. If true, and it is quite in keeping with all the circumstances and with both the character and subsequent actions of the Governor, then it is a very important statement as showing the double dealing of which Governor Ford was always suspected in relation to his course with reference to the difficulties between the citizens of Nauvoo and their enemies. And now Col. Geddes as reported by Gregg:

"While the Smiths were in jail, I went to the jail in company with Governor Ford, and there we conversed with them for some time, the burden of Smith's

10:15 a. m.—The Governor left after saying that the prisoners were under his protection, and again pledging himself that they should be protected from violence, and telling them that if the troops marched the next morning to Nauvoo, as he then expected, they should probably be taken along, in order to insure their personal safety, with how much sincerity may be seen by the following affidavits:—

Affidavit—Alfred   Randall—Threats   Against   the   Prophet's   Life   in Carthage.

TERRITORY OF UTAH, } ss
GREAT SALT LAKE CITY. }

Personally appeared before me, Thomas Bullock, Recorder of Great Salt Lake County, Alfred Randall, who deposes and says, that about ten o'clock on the morning of the (26th) twenty sixth day of June, one thousand eight hundred and forty-four, he was in Carthage, Hancock county, Illinois, and as the troops, under Governor Thomas Ford, were in squads around the square, he went up to several of them, and heard one of the soldiers say: "When I left home I calculated to see old Joe dead before I returned," when several others said, "So did I," "So did I," and "I'll be damned if I don't," was the general reply.

One fellow then spoke up and said "I shouldn't wonder if there is some damned Mormon hearing all we have to say." Another who stood next to Randall, replied, "If I knew there was, I would run him through with my bayonet."

In a few minutes Randall went to another crowd of soldiers, and heard one say, "I guess this will be the last of old Joe." From there Randall went to Hamilton's Hotel, where Governor Thomas Ford was standing by the fence side, and heard another soldier tell Governor Thomas Ford, "The soldiers are determined to see Joe Smith dead before they leave here." Ford replied, "If you know of any such thing keep it to yourself."

In a short time Randall started for his own home, stayed all night, and arrived in Nauvoo on the twenty-seventh of June, when Governor

talk being that they were only acting in self-defense, and only wanted to be let alone. After leaving the jail, and while returning from it, the Governor and I had still further conversation about the subject matter. After some time the Governor exclaimed, "O, it's all nonsense; you will have to drive these Mormons out yet!" I then said: "If we undertake that, Governor, when the proper time comes, will you interfere?" "No, I will not," said he; then, after a pause, adding, "until you are through!"

Ford was making his notorious speech to the citizens. And further this deponent saith not.

ALFRED RANDALL.

Subscribed and sworn to before me this twelfth day of February, one thousand eight hundred and fifty-five.

THOMAS BULLOCK,
Recorder, Great Salt Lake County.

Affidavit—Jonathan C. Wright—Conspiracy against the Prophet's Life at Carthage.

On the 26th day of June, A. D. 1844, near the mansion in the city of Nauvoo, I fell in company with Col. Enoch C. March and Geo. T. M. Davis, Esq., from Alton, Illinois, editor of the *Telegraph*, who had just arrived from Carthage, where they said they had been for some days, in company with Governor Ford and others, in council upon the subject of the arrest and trial of Joseph and Hyrum Smith, who were then prisoners in the county jail in Carthage.

After considerable conversation between myself and them on the subject of the Mormon religion, and the reasons why I had embraced that faith, and renounced my former religious discipline—viz, that of the Methodists, Mr. March asked me what I thought of Joe Smith, and if I had any hopes of his return to Nauvoo in safety.

I answered that I knew Joseph Smith was a true Prophet of the living God, as good and virtuous a man as ever lived upon the earth; that the Book or Mormon was true as holy writ, and was brought forth precisely in the way and manner it purported to be, by the gift and power of the Lord Almighty, and from no other source; and that the revelations he had received and published were eternal truth, and heaven and earth would pass away before one jot or tittle of the same should fail, and all that he pretended and testified to concerning the ministration of holy angels from the heavens to him, the Urim and Thummim, the voice of God, his correspondence with the heavens, was the truth and nothing but the truth; and that in relation to his return I had no doubt but that he would be honorably discharged upon his trial by the court, and would be preserved in safety from the power of his enemies; that he was in the hands of his God, whom he loved and faithfully served; and He, who held the destinies of nations in His own hands, would deliver him from his enemies, as He had done hundreds of times before.

Col. March replied, "Mr. Wright, you are mistaken, and I know it; you do not know what I know; I tell you they will kill Joe Smith before he leaves Carthage, and I know it, and you never will see him alive again." Said I, "Enoch, I do not believe it, he is in the hands of God, and God will deliver him." Says he, "I know better; when you hear of him again, you will hear he is dead, and I know it. The people at Carthage wanted permission from the Governor to kill you all and burn up your city, and Ford (the Governor) asked me if I thought it was best to suffer it. I replied, "No, no, for God's sake, Ford, don't suffer it, that will never do, no never. Just see for a moment, Ford, what that would do; it would be the means of murdering thousands of innocent men, women and children, and destroying thousands of dollars' worth of property, and that would never do, it would not be sanctioned, it would disgrace the nation. You have now got the principle men here under your own control, they are all you want, what more do you want? When they are out of the way the thing is settled, and the people will be satisfied, and that is the easiest way you can dispose of it; and Governor Ford concluded upon the whole that was the best policy, and I know it will be done."

Mayor's Office, Great Salt Lake City, Utah Territory,
Jan. 13th, A. D. 1855.

Personally appeared before me, Jedediah M. Grant, Mayor of said City, Jonathan Calkins Wright, who being duly sworn, deposeth and saith that the foregoing statements contained in his report of the conversation between himself and Enoch C. March, in presence of Geo. T. M. Davis, Esq., on the 26th day of June, 1844, in the city of Nauvoo, is true to the best of his knowledge and belief; and further this deponent saith not.

JONATHAN CALKINS WRIGHT.

Sworn to and subscribed before me, this 13th day of January, 1855, in Great Salt Lake City, Utah Territory.

J. M. GRANT,
Mayor of Great Salt Lake City.

Affidavit:—Orrin P. Rockwell—Gov. Ford in Nauvoo.

Personally appeared before me, Thomas Bullock, County Recorder in and for Great Salt Lake County, in the Territory of Utah, Orrin P. Rockwell, who being first duly sworn, deposeth and saith that about the hour of 3 o'clock in the afternoon of the 27th day of June, one thousand eight hundred forty-four, a short time only before Governor Ford addressed the citizens of Nauvoo, he (Ford) and his suit occupied an upper room in the mansion of Joseph Smith, in the city of Nauvoo, when he, the said Rockwell, had of necessity to enter said upper room for his hat, and as he entered the door, all were sitting silent except one man, who was standing behind a chair making a speech, and while in the act of dropping his right hand from an uplifted position, said, "The deed is done before this time," which were the only words I heard while in the room, for on seeing me they all hushed in silence. At that time I could not comprehend the meaning of the words, but in a few hours after I understood them as referring to the murder of Joseph and Hyrum Smith in Carthage jail.

ORRIN P. ROCKWELL,

Subscribed and sworn to before me, the fourteenth day of April, 1856.

THOMAS BULLOCK.

Recorder of Great Salt Lake County.

Affidavit:—Wm. G. Sterrett—Conduct of Gov. Ford and Posse While in Nauvoo.

STATE OF DESERET, GREAT SALT LAKE COUNTY.

Personally appeared before me, Thomas Bullock, Recorder in and for Great Salt Lake County, this third day of October, one thousand eight hundred and fifty, William G. Sterrett, who being first duly sworn, deposeth and saith that on the twenty-seventh day of June, one thousand eight hundred and forty-four, in the city of Nauvoo, county of Hancock, and State of Illinois, I heard Thomas Ford, Governor of Illinois, address an assembly of several thousand citizens, gathered around the frame of a building situated at the corner of Water and Main streets. He reproached the people in severe terms for the course they had taken in resising the *posse comitatus,* and among other things, "The retribution thereof will be terrible, and you must make up your minds for it. I hope you will not make any more trouble, but be a law-abiding people, for if I have to come again it will be worse for you."

And your deponent further saith, that about half-past five in the afternoon the said Governor Thomas Ford and his guard visited the Temple and the workshops on the Temple block.

Mr. Alpheus Cutler, one of the building committee of the Temple, sent me to watch them in and about the Temple. I was close to the Governor when one of his men called him to look at one of the oxen of the font in the basement of the Temple, that had part of one horn broken off. The Governor stepped up to it, and laying his hand on it remarked, "This is the cow with the crumply horn, that we read of." One of the staff continued, "That tossed the maiden all forlorn," and they all had a laugh about it.

Several of the horns were broken off the oxen by the Governor's attendants. A man who stood behind me said, "I'll be damned but I should like to take one of those horns home with me, to show as a curiosity, but it is a pity to break them off."

After they had passed round the font, one of them remarked, "This temple is a curious piece of workmanship, and it was a damned shame that they did not let Joe Smith finish it, so that we could have seen what sort of a finish he would have put on it, for it is altogether a different style of architecture from any building I have ever seen or read about." Another said, "But he is dead by this time, and he will never see this temple again."

I replied, "They cannot kill him until he has finished his work." The Governor thereupon gave a very significant grin, when one of his suit who stood next to me said, "Whether he has finished his work or not by God he will not see this place again, for he's finished before this time."

Another of his suit pulled out his watch and said, "Governor, it's time we were off, we have been here too long already. Whether you go or not, I'm going to leave, and that damned quick." The Governor said, "Yes, it's time for us to be going." They then all left the stone shop, mounted their horses, which were hitched near the temple, and went out of the city towards Carthage by way of Mulholland Street, taking with them one of the horns that the company had knocked off. Further this deponent saith not.

WM. G. STERRETT.

Sworn to and subscribed before me, this day and year first above written.

THOMAS BULLOCK,
Great Salt Lake County Recorder.

While Joseph was writing at the jailor's desk, William Wall stepped up, wanting to deliver a verbal message to him from his uncle John Smith. He turned round to speak to Wall, but the guard refused to allow them any communication.

At noon Joseph wrote to Judge Thomas as follows:

Letter: Joseph Smith to Judge Thomas—Engaging Thomas as Legal Counsel.

CARTHAGE JAIL, June 26, 1844.

His Hon. Judge Thomas.

DEAR SIR,—You will perceive by my date that I am in prison. Myself and brother Hyrum were arrested yesterday on charge of treason without bringing us before the magistrate; last evening we were committed on a mittimus from Justice Robert F. Smith, stating that we had been before the magistrate, which is *utterly false*; but from the appearance of the case at present, we can have no reasonable prospect of anything but partial decisions of law, and all the prospect we have of justice being done is to get our case on *habeas corpus* before an impartial judge; the excitement and prejudice is such in this place, testimony is of little avail.

Therefore, sir, I earnestly request your honor to repair to Nauvoo without delay, and make yourself at home at my house until the papers can be in readiness for you to bring us on *habeas corpus*. Our witnesses are all at Nauvoo, and there you can easily investigate the whole matter, and I will be responsible to you for all the trouble and expense.

CHAPTER XXXII.

THE PROPHET IN CARTHAGE PRISON—THE UNION OF JUDICIAL,
EXECUTIVE, AND MILITARY AUTHORITY IN DEALING WITH
THE PRISONERS—THE LAST NIGHT IN PRISON.

Wednesday, June 26, 1844.—(*Noon*)—Willard Richards made copies of the orders of Joseph Smith as Mayor to Marshal John P. Greene, and as Lieut.-General to Major-General Jonathan Dunham.

Joseph remarked, "I have had a good deal of anxiety
The Prophet's Anxiety for His own Safety. about my safety since I left Nauvoo, which I never had before when I was under arrest. I could not help those feelings, and they have depressed me." Most of the forenoon was spent by Dan Jones and Col. Stephen Markham in hewing with a penknife a warped door to get it on the latch, thus preparing to fortify the place against any attack.

The Prophet, Patriarch, and their friends took turns preaching to the guards, several of whom were relieved before their time was out, because they admitted they were convinced of the innocence of the prisoners. They frequently admitted they had been imposed upon, and more than once it was heard, "Let us go home, boys, for I will not fight any longer against these men."

During the day Hyrum encouraged Joseph to think that the Lord, for his Church's sake, would release him
Hyrum as Comforter. from prison. Joseph replied, "Could my brother, Hyrum but be liberated, it would not matter so much about me. Poor Rigdon, I am glad he is gone to Pittsburg out of the way; were he to preside he

would lead the Church to destruction in less than five years."

Dr. Richards was busily engaged writing as dictated by the Prophet, and Elder Taylor amused him by singing. Joseph related his dream about William and Wilson Law, also his dream about trying to save a steamboat in a storm.

One of the counsel for the prosecution expressed a wish to Esq. Reid, that the prisoners should be brought out of jail for examination on the charge of treason. He was answered that the prisoners had already been committed "until discharged by due course of law," and therefore the justice *Status of Prisoners Under the Law.* and constable had no further control of the prisoners, and that if the prosecutors wished the prisoners brought out of jail, they might bring them out on a writ of *habeas corpus*, or some other "due course of law," when we would appear and defend.

12:30, noon—Dr. Bernhisel arrived at the jail.

Mr. Reid came with the following letter from General Deming.

Letter—Gen. Miner R. Deming to Joseph Smith—Protection and Admission to Presence of the Prophet.

Messrs. Smith,—I was requested by the governor to order you such protection as circumstances might require. The guard have been acting upon the supposition that your protection excluded all persons but those admitted by a pass. I have caused the officer of the guard to be correctly instructed of his duties, so that you need suffer no further inconvenience.

M. R. DEMING, Brig.-Gen'l.

Headquarters,
    Carthage, June 26, 1844.

Counselor Reid said that he had got the magistrate on a pin hook, for the magistrate had committed them without examination, and had no further jurisdiction in the case, *Effect of a False Commitment.*

and he would not agree to a trial unless (Captain)
Justice Smith would consent to go to Nauvoo for
examination, where witnesses could be had.

Reid said that a week ago, Harmon T. Wilson and
another, had concocted a scheme for a writ to take
Joseph, and when he was apprehended, to take him to
Missouri; and Harmon T. Wilson returned from Missouri
the night before the burning of the press.

1 p. m.—Willard Richards wrote to his wife, and sent
the letter by Cyrus C. Canfield.

It was common conversation on the camp ground and
in the dining-room of the hotel, in the presence of Governor Ford, "The law is too
short for these men, but they must not
be suffered to go at large;" and, "if the law will not reach
them, powder and ball must."

Threats in the Governor's Presence.

Half past 2—Constable Bettisworth came with Alexander Simpson, and wanted to come in, with an order to
the jailor demanding the prisoners; but as
Mr. Stigall, the jailor, could find no law authorizing a justice of the peace to demand prisoners committed to his charge, he refused to give them
up until discharged from his custody by due course of
the law.

Loyalty of Mr. Stigall to His prisoners.

Justice Robert F. Smith then inquired what he
must do. Governor Ford replied, "We have plenty
of troops; there are the Carthage Greys under
your command, bring them out." Joseph
sent Lorenzo D. Wasson to inform the Governor of what had just taken place, and also to
inform his counsel, Messrs. Reid and Woods.

Conference of Gov. Ford and Justice Smith.

Twenty minutes to 3—Dr. Bernhisel returned from the
Governor, and said apparently the Governor was doing
all he could.

3 p. m.—Wrote to Messrs. Woods and Reid as follows
which was carried by Elder John Taylor.

*Letter: Joseph Smith   to Messrs. Woods and Reid—Anent Excitement
in Carthage.*

CARTHAGE JAIL, June 26, 3 p. m.

Messrs. Woods and Reid.

SIRS,—Constable Bettisworth called a little while since, and wanted to come in, the guard would not [allow it]. We have since learned that he wanted to take us before the magistrate, and we have since learned that there is some excitement because we did not go, and we wish to see you without delay.

We are informed that Dr. Foster has said that they can do nothing with us, only by powder and ball, as we have done nothing against the law.

Yours,

JOSEPH SMITH,

Per W. RICHARDS.

Twenty minutes to 4—Upon the refusal of the jailor to give up the prisoners, the constable with the company of Carthage Greys, under the command of Frank Worrell, marched to the jail, and by intimidation and   threats, compelled the jailor, against his will and conviction of duty, to deliver Joseph and Hyrum to the Constable, who forthwith, and contrary to their wishes, compulsorily took them.

Joseph and Hyrum Smith Forced from Prison.

Joseph, seeing the mob gathering and assuming a threatening aspect, concluded it best to go with them then, and putting on his hat, walked boldly into the midst of a hollow square of the Carthage Greys; yet evidently expecting to be massacred in the streets before arriving at the Court House, politely locked arms with the worst mobocrat he could see, and Hyrum locked arms with Joseph, followed by Dr. Richards, and escorted by a guard. Elders Taylor, Jones, Markham, and Fullmer followed, outside the hollow square, and accompanied them to the court room.

4 o'clock.—Case called by Robert F. Smith, Captain of

the Carthage Greys. The counsel for the prisoners then
appeared, and called for subpoenas for witnesses on the part of the prisoners, and expressed their wish to go into the examination
as soon as the witnesses could be brought from Nauvoo to
Carthage. This was objected to most vehemently by the
opposite counsel.

Prisoners Before the Court.

4:25.—Took copy of order to bring prisoners from jail
for trial, as follows:—

Copy of Order to Bring Prisoners into Court.

STATE OF ILLINOIS, ⎱ ss
HANCOCK COUNTY. ⎰

To David Bettisworth, Constable of said county.

You are hereby commanded to bring the bodies of Joseph Smith and
Hyrum Smith from the jail of said county, forthwith before me at my
office, for an examination on the charge of treason, they having been
committed for safe keeping until trial could be had on such examination, and the state now being ready for such examination.

Given under my hand and seal this 26th day of June, 1844.

(Signed)   R. F. SMITH, J. P. [L. S.]

4:30—Made a copy of the list of witnesses.

4:35—C. L. Higbee, O. C. Skinner, Thos. Sharp,
Sylvester Emmons and Thos. Morrison, appeared as
counsel for the State.

The writ was returned, endorsed,

"Served on June 25th," which was false.

Mr. Wood said, they were committed to jail without any
examination whatever.

Mr. Reid urged a continuance of the case till the witnesses could be obtained from Nauvoo for the defense.

4:45 p. m.—Mr. Skinner suggested that the court
adjourn until 12 o'clock tomorrow.

Mr. Wood proposed that the court adjourn until witnesses could be got together, or until tomorrow at any
time, and again adjourn if they are not ready, without
bringing the prisoners into court.

Mr. Reid hoped no compulsory measures would be made

use of by the prosecution in this enlightened country.

Mr. Skinner: "If witnesses cannot be had after due diligence by the defense, a continuance will be granted.

Court said this writ was served yesterday, (which was not the case, unless it could be served without the prisoners or their counsel knowing it).

On motion of counsel for the prisoners, examination was postponed till tomorrow at 12 o'clock noon, and subpoenas were granted to get witnesses from Nauvoo, twenty miles distance, whereupon the prisoners were remanded to prison with the following mittimus:— **Examination Postponed.**

Second Mittimus Remanding Smith Brothers to Prison.

STATE OF ILLINOIS, } ss
HANCOCK COUNTY. }

To the keeper of the jail of Hancock County, Illinois, greeting:

Whereas Joseph Smith and Hyrum Smith have been arrested and brought before me, Robert F. Smith, a justice of the peace in and for said county, for examination on the charge of treason against the State of Illinois, and have applied for a continuance, which is granted until the 27th June, 1844, at 12 o'clock, m.

These are therefore to command you to receive the said Joseph Smith and Hyrum Smith into your custody in the jail of the county, there to remain until they are brought before me for said examination according to law.

Given under my hand and seal this 26th day of June, 1844.

R. F. SMITH, J. P. [L. S.]

5:30.—Returned to jail, and Joseph and Hyrum were thrust into close confinement.

Patriarch John Smith came from Macedonia to jail to see his nephews Joseph and Hyrum. The road was thronged with mobbers. Three of them snapped their guns at him, and he was threatened by many others who recognized him. The guard at the jail refused him admittance. **Brave Patriarch John Smith.**

Joseph saw him through the prison window, and said to

the guard, "Let the old gentleman come in, he is my uncle." The guard replied they did not care who the hell he was uncle to, he should not go in.

Joseph replied, "You will not hinder so old and infirm a man as he is from coming in," and then said, "Come in uncle;" on which, after searching him closely the guard let him pass into the jail, where he remained about an hour. He asked Joseph if he thought he should again get out of the hands of his enemies, when he replied, "My brother Hyrum thinks I shall. I wish you would tell the brethren in Macedonia that they can see by this, that it has not been safe for me to visit them; and tell Almon W. Babbitt I want him to come and assist me as an attorney at my expected trial tomorrow before Captain R. F. Smith."

Pathetic Interview Between the Prophet and "Uncle John."

Father Smith then left the jail to convey this message to A. W. Babbitt, who was at Macedonia.

6 p. m.—Copied witnesses' names and mittimus.

Dr. Bernhisel brought the following:—

The Governor's Suggestions to the Jailor.

I would advise the jailor to keep the Messrs. Smith in the room in which I found them this morning, unless a closer confinement should be clearly necessary to prevent an escape.

THOMAS FORD,
Governor and Commander-in-Chief.

June 26th, 1844.

6:15 p. m.—Received the following letter from William Clayton:—

Letter:—William Clayton to Joseph Smith—Conditions in Nauvoo.

NAUVOO, June 26, 1844.

DEAR PRESIDENT,—

I write this line to inform you that Mr. Marsh, who lives down the river, and of whom you have had corn, pork, etc., has sent word if you want any bail he is ready for one to any amount; and further, that he has got some corn left which he wants you to have, lest the mob get it. (We will endeavor to obtain it.)

They have already taken two loads, but he has charged them a dollar a bushel for it.

The *Amaranth* has just landed at the foot of Main Street, and unloaded 200 bbls. flour,—95 for Mr. Kimball, and the balance for Bryant.

Captain Singleton, who came at the head of the police this morning, is sending a request to the Governor to call them home. He says he finds no difficulties to settle here, but there is plenty to settle at home. He furthermore says that while the police were at Carthage they were treated as soldiers, but since they came to Nauvoo they have been treated as gentlemen.

The company all got home safe and well last night.

A messenger is about to start forthwith to Judge Thomas.

All is peace in Nauvoo. Many threats keep coming that the mob are determined to attack the city in your absence, but we have no fears.

With fervency and true friendship, I remain yours eternally,

WILLIAM CLAYTON.

This letter was sent from Nauvoo by Joel S. Miles. Joseph instructed Cahoon to return to Nauvoo with all haste, and fetch a number of documents for the promised trial.

Twenty-five minutes to 7.—Sent a message to Counselor Woods to get subpoenas for Samuel James, Edward Hunter, and Philip B. Lewis, with instructions to bring with them the papers that they carried to the Governor at Springfield, and which the Governor had not seen, as he had started for Carthage before they arrived at Springfield.

Fifteen minutes to 8.—Supper.

8 p. m.—Counselors Woods and Reid called with Elder John P. Greene, and said that the Governor and military officers had held a council which had been called by the Governor, and they decided that the Governor and all the troops should march to Nauvoo at eight o'clock to-morrow, except one company of about 50 men, in order to gratify the troops, and return next day, the company

Militia Council meeting at Carthage.

of fifty men to be selected by the Governor
from those of the troops whose fidelity he could most
rely on, to guard the prisoners, who should be left in
Carthage jail; and that their trial be deferred until Saturday, the 29th.

After the consultation, the justice, (Robert F. Smith),
who was one of the officers in command, altered the return
of the subpoenas until the 29th. This was done without
consulting either the prisoners or their counsel.

About 8:15, p. m.—Patriarch John Smith met Lawyer
Babbitt, and delivered the message, when Babbitt replied
"You are too late, I am already engaged on the other
side."

9 p. m.—Messrs. Woods, Reid, and Greene returned to
Hamilton's Hotel.

9:15.—Elder John Taylor prayed. Willard Richards,
John Taylor, John S. Fullmer, Stephen Markham, and
Dan Jones stayed with Joseph and Hyrum in the front
room.

During the evening the Patriarch Hyrum Smith read
and commented upon extracts from the Book of Mormon,
on the imprisonments and deliverance of the
servants of God for the Gospel's sake. Joseph
bore a powerful testimony to the guards of
the divine authenticity of the Book of Mormon, the restoration of the Gospel, the administration of angels, and
that the kingdom of God was again established upon the
earth, for the sake of which he was then incarcerated in
that prison, and not because he had violated any law of
God or man.

The Last
Night in
Carthage
Prison.

They retired to rest late. Joseph and Hyrum occupied
the only bedstead in the room, while their friends lay
side by side on the matresses on the floor. Dr. Richards
sat up writing until his last candle left him in the dark.
The report of a gun fired close by caused Joseph to arise,
leave the bed, and lay himself on the floor, having Dan
Jones on his left, and John S. Fullmer on his right.

Joseph laid out his right arm, and said to John S. Fullmer, "Lay your head on my arm for a pillow, Brother John;" and when all were quiet they conversed in a low tone about the prospects of their deliverance. Joseph gave expression to several presentiments that he had to die, and said "I would like to see my family again." and "I would to God that I could preach to the Saints in Nauvoo once more." Fullmer tried to rally his spirits, saying he thought he would often have that privilege, when Joseph thanked him for the remarks and good feelings expressed to him.

Conversation with John S. Fullmer.

Soon after Dr. Richards retired to the bed which Joseph had left, and when all were apparently fast asleep, Joseph whispered to Dan Jones, "are you afraid to die?" Dan said, "Has that time come, think you? Engaged in such a cause I do not think that death would have many terrors." Joseph replied, "You will yet see Wales, and fulfill the mission appointed you before you die."

Prophecy on the Head of Dan Jones.

CHAPTER XXXIII.

THE DAY OF MARTYRDOM—THREATS—REPEATED WARNINGS OF
THE PRISONERS' DANGER GIVEN TO GOVERNOR FORD—THE
CARTHAGE GREYS AS GUARDS.

Tuesday, 27, 5 a. m.—John P. Greene and William W.
Phelps called at the jail, on their way to Nauvoo.

5:30 a. m.—Arose. Joseph requested Dan Jones to
descend and inquire of the guard the cause
of the disturbance in the night. Frank Worrel, the officer of the guard, who was one of the
Carthage Greys, in a very bitter spirit said, "We have
had too much trouble to bring Old Joe here to let him ever
escape alive, and unless you want to die with him you had
better leave before sundown; and you are not a damned
bit better than him for taking his part, and you'll see
that I can prophesy better than Old Joe, for neither he
nor his brother, nor anyone who will remain with them will
see the sun set today."

Joseph directed Jones to go to Governor Ford and
inform him what he had been told by the
officer of the guard. While Jones was going
to Governor Ford's quarters, he saw an
assemblage of men, and heard one of them,
who was apparently a leader, making a speech, saying
that, "Our troops will be discharged this morning in obedience to orders, and for a sham we will leave the town; but
when the Governor and the McDonough troops have left

(marginal notes:) Threats of Frank Worrell.

Governor Ford Warned of Worrell's Threat.

for Nauvoo this afternoon, we will return and kill those men, if we have to tear the jail down." This sentiment was applauded by three cheers from the crowd.

Captain Jones went to the Governor, told him what had occurred in the night, what the officer of the guard had said, and what he had heard while coming to see him, and earnestly solicited him to avert the danger.

His Excellency replied, "You are unnecessarily alarmed for the safety of your friends, sir, the people are not that cruel."

Irritated by such a remark, Jones urged the necessity of placing better men to guard them than professed assassins, and said, "The Messrs. Smith are American citizens, and have surrendered them- Jones' Warn ing to Gov. Ford. selves to your Excellency upon your pledging your honor for their safety; they are also Master Masons, and as such I demand of you protection of their lives."

Governor Ford's face turned pale, and Jones remarked, "If you do not do this, I have but one more desire, and that is if you leave their lives in the hands of those men to be sacrificed——"

"What is that, sir?" he asked in a hurried tone.

"It is," said Jones, "that the Almighty will preserve my life to a proper time and place, that I may testify that you have been timely warned of their danger."

Jones then returned to the prison, but the guard would not let him enter. He again returned to the hotel, and found Governor Ford standing in front of the McDonough troops, who were in line ready to escort him to Nauvoo.

The disbanded mob retired to the rear, shouting loudly that they were only going a short distance out Boasts of the Mob. of town, when they would return and kill old Joe and Hyrum as soon as the Governor was far enough out of town.

Jones called the attention of the Governor to the threats

then made, but the Governor took no notice of them, although it was impossible for him to avoid hearing them.

Jones then requested the Governor to give him passports for himself and friends to pass in and out of the prison, according to his promise made to the prisoners. He refused to give them, but he told General Deming to give one to Dr. Willard Richards, Joseph Smith's private secretary.

Chauncey L. Higbee's Declared Intention to Kill the Prophet

While obtaining this, Jones' life was threatened, and Chauncey L. Higbee said to him in the street, "We are determined to kill Joe and Hyrum, and you had better go away to save yourself."

At 7 a. m., Joseph, Hyrum, Dr. Richards, Stephen Markham and John S. Fullmer ate breakfast together. Mr. Crane ate with them, and wanted to know if the report was true that Joseph fainted three times on Tuesday, while being exhibited to the troops. He was told it was a false report.

8 a. m.—Cyrus H. Wheelock, at Joseph's request, applied to the Governor, and obtained the following passes:

Cyrus H. Wheelock's Passes.

Suffer Mr. C. H. Wheelock to pass in to visit General Joseph Smith and friends in Carthage jail unmolested.

THOMAS FORD.

Governor and Commander-in-Chief.

June, 27th, 1844.

Protect Mr. C. H. Wheelock in passing to and from Carthage and Nauvoo.

THOMAS FORD,

Governor and Commander-in-Chief.

June 27th, 1844.

While receiving these passes he related to the Governor the numerous threats he had heard.

John S. Fullmer went to the Governor to get a pass.

8:20 a. m.—Joseph wrote to Emma as follows:

Letter: Joseph Smith to Emma Smith—Prophet's Instruction as to
Reception of the Governor.

CARTHAGE JAIL, June 27th, 1844.

20 minutes past eight a. m.

DEAR EMMA.—The Governor continues his courtesies, and permits us to see our friends. We hear this morning that the Governor will not go down with his troops today to Nauvoo, as we anticipated last evening; but if he does come down with his troops you will be protected; and I want you to tell Brother Dunham to instruct the people to stay at home and attend to their own business, and let there be no groups or gathering together, unless by permission of the Governor, they are called together to receive communications from the Governor, which would please our people, but let the Governor direct.

Brother Dunham of course will obey the orders of the government officers, and render them the assistance they require. There is no danger of any extermination order. Should there be a mutiny among the troops (which we do not anticipate, excitement is abating) a part will remain loyal and stand for the defense of the state and our rights.

There is one principle which is eternal; it is the duty of all men to protect their lives and the lives of the household, whenever necessity requires, and no power has a right to forbid it, should the last extreme arrive, but I anticipate no such extreme, but caution is the parent of safety.

JOSEPH SMITH.

P. S.—Dear Emma, I am very much resigned to my lot, knowing I am justified, and have done the best that could be done. Give my love to the children and all my friends, Mr. Brewer, and all who inquire after me; and as for treason, I know that I have not committed any, and they cannot prove anything of the kind, so you need not have any fears that anything can happen to us on that account. May God bless you all. Amen.

8:30.—John S. Fullmer returned to jail.

9:40 a. m.—Mr. Woods and Mr. Reid called. They said another consultation of the officers had taken place, and the former orders of the Governor for marching to Nauvoo with the whole army were countermanded.

Dr. Southwick was in the meeting, seeing what was going on. He afterward told Stephen Markham that the purport of the meeting was to take into consideration the best way to stop Joseph Smith's career, as his views on government were widely circulated and took like wildfire.

Dr. Southwick's Report of the Carthage Meeting. They said if he did not get into the Presidential chair this election, he would be sure to the next time; and if Illinois and Missouri would join together and kill him, they would not be brought to justice for it. There were delegates in said meeting from every state in the Union except three. Governor Ford and Captain Smith were also in the meeting.

Captain Dunn and his company were ordered to accompany the Governor to Nauvoo. The Carthage Appointment of the Carthage Greys to Guard the Prisoners. Greys, who had but two days before been under arrest for insulting the commanding general, and whose conduct had been more hostile to the prisoners than that of any other company, were selected by Governor Ford to guard the prisoners at the jail; and other troops composed of the mob whom the Governor had found at Carthage, and had mustered into the service of the State and who had been promised "full satisfaction" and that they should be marched to Nauvoo, were disbanded and discharged in Carthage; yet Governor Ford suffered two or three hundred armed men to remain encamped about eight miles off on the Warsaw road,* apparently under the control of Col. Levi Williams, a notoriously sworn enemy to Joseph, and who had on many occasions threatened the destruction of Nauvoo and the death of Joseph. Moreover it was the duty of

---

* It is the record of the case, however, that Governor Ford did send an order disbanding the regiment from Warsaw which he had ordered to rendezvous at Golden's Point for the purpose of marching with the rest of the Governor's troops into Nauvoo. "The Governor," remarks the late John Hay, who is the authority for the incident of disbanding the Warsaw troops—"the Governor, fearing he could not control the inflammable material he had gathered together, had determined to scatter it again" (*Atlantic Monthly,* December, 1869). The courier of the Governor to the Warsaw troops was Mr. David Matthews, a well-known citizen of Warsaw. But after receiving the order for disbandment, while most of the troops returned to their homes, about one hundred and fifty volunteered to follow several of the militia captains—leaders on their own responsibilty—to Nauvoo; of whom about seventy-five reached that place and participated in the murder of the Brothers Smith.

the Governor to dismiss the troops into the hands of their several officers in order to be marched home and there disbanded, and not to have disbanded them at a distance from home, and at a time and place when they were predisposed to acts of lawless violence, rapine and murder.

Cyrus H. Wheelock, states that previous to leaving Carthage he said to the Governor, "Sir, you must be aware by this time that the prisoners have no fears in relation to any lawful demands made against them, but you have heard sufficient to justify you in the belief that their enemies would destroy them if they had them in their power; and now, sir, I am about to leave for Nauvoo, and I fear for those men; they are safe as regards the law, but they are not safe from the hands of traitors, and midnight assassins who thirst for their blood and have determined to spill it; and under these circumstances I leave with a heavy heart." *Wheelock's Remonstrance to Gov. Ford.*

Ford replied: "I was never in such a dilemma in my life; but your friends shall be protected, and have a fair trial by the law; in this *pledge* I am not alone; I have obtained the *pledge* of the whole of the army to sustain me."

After receiving these assurances, Wheelock prepared to visit the prison. The morning being a little rainy, favored his wearing an overcoat, in the side pocket of which he was enabled to carry a six shooter, and he passed the guard unmolested. During his visit in the prison he slipped the revolver into Joseph's pocket. Joseph examined it, and asked Wheelock if he had not better retain it for his own protection. *Arms Given to the Prisoners.*

This was a providential circumstance, as most other persons had been very rigidly searched. Joseph then handed the single barrel pistol which had been given him by John S. Fullmer, to his brother Hyrum, and said,

"You may have use for this." Brother Hyrum observed, "I hate to use such things or to see them used." "So do I," said Joseph, "but we may have to, to defend ourselves;" upon this Hyrum took the pistol.

Wheelock was intrusted with a verbal request to the commanders of the Legion to avoid all military display, or any other movement calculated to produce excitement during the Governor's visit. He was especially charged to use all the influence he possessed to have the brethren and friends of Joseph remain perfectly calm and quiet, inasmuch as they respected the feelings and well-being of the Prophet and Patriarch.

Said Joseph, "Our lives have already become jeopardized by revealing the wicked and bloodthirsty purposes of our enemies; and for the future we must cease to do so. All we have said about them is truth, but it is not always wise to relate all the truth. Even Jesus, the Son of God had to refrain from doing so, and had to restrain His feelings many times for the safety of Himself and His followers, and had to conceal the righteous purposes of His heart in relation to many things pertaining to His Father's kingdom. When still a boy He had all the intelligence necessary to enable Him to rule and govern the kingdom of the Jews, and could reason with the wisest and most profound doctors of law and divinity, and make their theories and practice to appear like folly compared with the wisdom He possessed; but He was a boy only, and lacked physical strength even to defend His own person, and was subject to cold, to hunger and to death. So it is with the Church of Jesus Christ of Latter-day Saints; we have the revelation of Jesus, and the knowledge within us is sufficient to organize a righteous government upon the earth, and to give universal peace to all mankind, if they would receive it, but we lack the physical strength, as did our Savior when a child, to defend our principles, and we have of necessity to be afflicted, persecuted and smitten, and to

Reflections of the Prophet on Exposing Wickedness.

bear it patiently until Jacob is of age, then he will take care of himself."

Wheelock took a list of witnesses' names that were wanted for the expected trial on Saturday. When the list was read over, a number of names were stricken out, among whom were Alpheus Cutler and Reynolds Cahoon, it being deemed by Brother Hyrum unnecessary for them to attend. Brother Joseph asked why they should not come. Hyrum answered, "They may be very good men, but they don't know enough to answer a question properly." Brother Joseph remarked, "That is sufficient reason."

The prisoners also sent many verbal messages to their families. They were so numerous that Dr. Richards proposed writing them all down, fearing Wheelock might forget, but Brother Hyrum fastened his eyes upon him, and with a look of penetration said, "Brother Wheelock will remember all that we tell him, and he will never forget the occurrences of this day." *The Prisoners' Messages to Friends in Nauvoo.*

Joseph related the following dream which he had last night:

"I was back in Kirtland, Ohio, and thought I would take a walk out by myself, and view my old farm, which I found grown up with weeds and brambles, and altogether bearing evidence of neglect and want of culture. I went into the barn, which I found without floor or doors, with the weather-boarding off, and was altogether in keeping with the farm. *The Prophet's Dream of his Kirtland Farm*

"While I viewed the desolation around me, and was contemplating how it might be recovered from the curse upon it, there came rushing into the barn a company of furious men, who commenced to pick a quarrel with me.

"The leader of the party ordered me to leave the barn and farm, stating it was none of mine, and that I must give up all hope of ever possessing it.

"I told him the farm was given me by the Church, and

although I had not had any use of it for some time back, still I had not sold it, and according to righteous principles it belonged to me or the Church.

"He then grew furious and began to rail upon me, and threaten me, and said it never did belong to me nor to the Church.

"I then told him that I did not think it worth contending about, that I had no desire to live upon it in its present state, and if he thought he had a better right I would not quarrel with him about it but leave; but my assurance that I would not trouble him at present did not seem to satisfy him, as he seemed determined to quarrel with me, and threatened me with the destruction of my body.

"While he was thus engaged, pouring out his bitter words upon me, a rabble rushed in and nearly filled the barn, drew out their knives, and began to quarrel among themselves for the premises, and for a moment forgot me, at which time I took the opportunity to walk out of the barn about up to my ankles in mud.

"When I was a little distance from the barn, I heard them screeching and screaming in a very distressed manner, as it appeared they had engaged in a general fight with their knives. While they were thus engaged, the dream or vision ended."

Both Joseph and Hyrum bore a faithful testimony to the Latter-day work, and the coming forth of the Book of Mormon, and prophesied of the triump of the Gospel over all the earth, exhorting the brethren present to faithfulness and persevering diligence in proclaiming the Gospel, building up the Temple, and performing all the duties connected with our holy religion.

Testimony of Joseph and Hyrum to the Book of Mormon.

Joseph dictated the following postscript to Emma:

Letter: Postscript.

P. S.—*20 minutes to 10.*—I just learn that the Governor is about to disband his troops, all but a guard to protect us and the peace, anu come himself to Nauvoo and deliver a speech to the people. This is right as I suppose.

He afterwards wrote a few lines with his own hand, which were not copied.

The letter was sent by Joel S. Mills and Cyrus H. Wheelock.

John P. Greene, (Nauvoo city marshal) told Governor Ford that if he went to Nauvoo, leaving only the Carthage Greys to guard the jail, that there was a conspiracy on foot to take the lives of Joseph and Hyrum Smith during his absence, to which the Governor replied, "Marshal Greene, you are too enthusiastic."

Gov. Ford Warned of the Conspiracy Against Prisoners' Lives.

CHAPTER XXXIV.

DEPARTURE OF GOVERNOR FORD FOR NAUVOO—THE AFTER-
NOON IN CARTHAGE PRISON—THE ASSAULT ON THE
PRISON—THE MARTYRDOM OF JOSEPH AND HYRUM
SMITH.

Thursday, June 27, [*continued*] *10:30.,*—Governor Ford
went to Nauvoo some time this forenoon, escorted by a
portion of his troops, most friendly to the prisoners, and
leaving the known enemies of the Prophet, ostensibly to
guard the jail, having previously disbanded the remainder.

Joseph sent a request to the Governor by Dan Jones
for a pass for his private secretary, Dr. Willard Richards.

11 a. m.—John S. Fullmer left the jail for Nauvoo,
with a verbal charge to assist Wheelock in gathering and
forwarding witnesses for the promised trial.

James W. Woods, Esq., Joseph's principal lawyer,
left Carthage for Nauvoo.

11:20 a. m.—Dan Jones returned with the following pass
for Dr. Richards:—

Pass for Willard Richards.

Permit Dr. Richards, the private secretary of Joseph Smith, to be
with him, if he desires it, and to pass and repasss the guard.

THOMAS FORD,
Commander-in-Chief.

June 27th, 1844.

Jones said he could not get one for himself.

Dan Jones met Almon W. Babbitt in the street, and
informed him that Joseph wanted to see him.

11:30.—A.W.Babbitt arrived at the jail and read a letter from Oliver Cowdery.

Joseph, Hyrum, and Dr. Richards tried to get Jones past the guard, but they persisted in refusing to admit him.

12:20 noon.—Joseph wrote for Lawyer Browning of Quincy to come up on Saturday as his attorney, as follows:—

Letter: Joseph Smith to O. H. Browning—Engaging Browning as Legal Counsel.

CARTHAGE JAIL, June 27th, 1844.

Lawyer Browning:—

SIR,—Myself and brother Hyrum are in jail on charge of treason, to come up for examination on Saturday morning, 29th inst., and we request your professional services at that time, on our defense, without fail.

Most respectfully, your servant,

JOSEPH SMITH.

P. S.—There is no cause of action, for we have not been guilty of any crime, neither is there any just cause of suspicion against us; but certain circumstances make your attendance very necessary.

J. S.

Almon W. Babbitt took the letter and left the jail. He handed it to Jones, with directions to take it to Quincy forthwith. The guard being aware of the letter, told the mob that, "old Joe" had sent orders to raise the Nauvoo Legion to come and rescue him. The mob gathered around Jones, and demanded the letter; some of them wanted to take it from him by force, and said that Jones should not get out of Carthage alive, as a dozen men had started off with their rifles to waylay him in the woods. Having previously ordered his horse, Jones took advantage of their disagreement, and started off at full speed. He, by mistake, took the Warsaw road, and so avoided the men who were lying in wait for him. When he emerged on the prairie, he saw the Governor and his

The Guard's False Alarm Over the Nauvoo Legion.

posse, whereupon he left the Warsaw road for the Nauvoo road.

Dr. Southwick called at the jail. Joseph gave him a note to Governor Ford or General Deming, requesting them to furnish him with a pass.

1:15. p. m.—Joseph, Hyrum, and Willard dined in their room. Taylor and Markham dined below.

1:30 p. m.—Dr. Richards was taken sick, when Joseph said, "Brother Markham, as you have a pass from the Governor to go in and out of the jail, go and get the doctor something that he needs to settle his stomach," and Markham went out for medicine. When he had got the remedies desired, and was returning to jail, a man by the name of Stewart called out, "Old man, you have got to leave town in five minutes." Markham replied, "I shall not do it." A company of Carthage Greys gathered round him, put him on his horse, and forced him out of the town at the point of the bayonet.

Markham Forced. out of Carthage.

3:15. p. m.—The guard began to be more severe in their operations, threatening among themselves, and telling what they would do when the excitement was over.

Elder Taylor sang the following:—

The Poor Wayfaring Man of Grief.

A poor wayfaring man of grief
Had often crossed me on my way,
Who sued so humbly for relief
That I could never answer, Nay.

I had not power to ask his name;
Whither he went or whence he came;
Yet there was something in his eye
That won my love, I knew not why.

Once, when my scanty meal was spread,
He entered—not a word he spake!
Just perishing for want of bread;
I gave him all; he blessed it, brake,

And ate, but gave me part again;
Mine was an angel's portion then,
For while I fed with eager haste,
The crust was manna to my taste.

I spied him where a fountain burst,
Clear from the rock—his strength was gone,
The heedless water mock'd his thirst,
He heard it, saw it hurrying on.

I ran and raised the suff'rer up;
Thrice from the stream he drain'd my cup,
Dipp'd, and returned it running o'er;
I drank and never thirsted more.

'Twas night, the floods were out, it blew
A winter hurricane aloof;
I heard his voice, abroad, and flew
To bid him welcome to my roof.

I warmed, I clothed, I cheered my guest,
I laid him on my couch to rest;
Then made the earth my bed, and seem'd
In Eden's garden while I dream'd.

Stripp'd, wounded, beaten nigh to death,
I found him by the highway side;
I rous'd his pulse, brought back his breath,
Revived his spirit, and supplied

Wine, oil, refreshment—he was heal'd;
I had myself a wound conceal'd;
But from that hour forgot the smart,
And peace bound up my broken heart,

In pris'n I saw him next—condemned
To meet a traitor's doom at morn;
The tide of lying tongues I stemmed,
And honored him 'mid shame and scorn.

My friendship's utmost zeal to try,
He asked, if I for him would die;
The flesh was weak, my blood ran chill,
But the free spirit cried, "I will!"

Then in a moment to my view,
The stranger started from disguise:
The tokens in his hands I knew,
The Savior stood before mine eyes.

He spake—and my poor name he named—
"Of me thou hast not been asham'd;
These deeds shall thy memorial be;
Fear not thou didst them unto me."

When he got through, Joseph requested him to sing it again, which he did.

Hyrum read extracts from Josephus.

4 p. m.—The guard was again changed, only eight men being stationed at the jail, whilst the main body of the Carthage Greys were in camp about a quarter of a mile distant, on the public square.

4:15 p. m.—Joseph commenced conversing with the guard about Joseph H. Jackson, William and Wilson Law, and others of his persecutors.

Hyrum and Dr. Richards conversed together until quarter past five.

5 p. m.—Jailor Stigall returned to the jail, and said that Stephen Markham had been surrounded by a mob, who had driven him out of Carthage, and he had gone to Nauvoo.

Stigall suggested that they would be safer in the cell. Joseph said, "After supper we will go in." Mr. Stigall Anxiety went out, and Joseph said to Dr. Richards, of the "If we go into the cell, will you go in with Jailor. us?" The doctor answered, "Brother Joseph you did not ask me to cross the river with you—you did not ask me to come to Carthage—you did not ask me to come to jail with you—and do you think I would forsake you now? But I will tell you what I will do; if you are condemned to be hung for treason, I will be hung in your stead, and you shall go free." Joseph said, "You cannot." The doctor replied, "I will."

Before the jailor came in, his boy brought in some water, and said the guard wanted some wine. Joseph gave Dr. Richards two dollars to give the Wine for the guard; but the guard said one was enough, Guard. and would take no more.

The guard immediately sent for a bottle of wine, pipes, and two small papers of tobacco; and one of the guards brought them into the jail soon after the jailor went out. Dr. Richards uncorked the bottle, and presented a glass to Joseph, who tasted, as also Brother Taylor and the doctor, and the bottle was then given to the guard, who turned to go out. When at the top of the stairs some one below called him two or three times, and he went down.

Immediately there was a little rustling at the outer door of the jail, and a cry of surrender, and also a discharge of three or four firearms followed instantly. The doctor glanced an eye by the curtain of the window, and saw about a hundred armed men around the door.

It is said that the guard elevated their firelocks, and boisterously threatening the mob discharged their firearms over their heads. The mob encircled the building, and some of them rushed by the guard up the flight of stairs, burst open the door, and began the work of death, while others fired in through the open windows.

In the meantime Joseph, Hyrum, and Elder Taylor had their coats off. Joseph sprang to his coat for his six-shooter, Hyrum for his single barrel, Taylor for Markham's large hickory cane, and Dr. Richards for Taylor's cane. All sprang against the door, the balls whistled up the stairway, and in an instant one came through the door.

Joseph Smith, John Taylor and Dr. Richards sprang to the left of the door, and tried to knock aside the guns of the ruffians.

Hyrum was retreating back in front of the door and snapped his pistol, when a ball struck him in the left side of his nose, and he fell on his back on the floor saying, "I am a dead man!" As he fell on the floor another ball from the outside entered his left side, and passed through his body with such force that it completely broke to pieces the watch he wore in his vest pocket, and at the same instant another ball from the door grazed his breast, and entered his head by the throat; subsequently a fourth ball entered his left leg.

A shower of balls was pouring through all parts of the room, many of which lodged in the ceiling just above the head of Hyrum.

Joseph reached round the door casing, and discharged his six shooter into the passage, some barrels missing fire. Continual discharges of musketry came into the room. Elder Taylor continued parrying the guns until they had got them about half their length into the room, when he found that resistance was vain, and he attempted to jump out of the window, where a ball fired from within struck him on his left thigh, hitting the bone, and passing through to within half an inch of the other side. He fell on the window sill, when a ball fired from the outside struck his watch in his vest pocket, and threw him back into the room.

The "Handsome Fight" of Joseph Smith and John Taylor.

After he fell into the room he was hit by two more balls, one of them injuring his left wrist considerably, and the other entering at the side of the bone just below the left knee. He rolled under the bed, which was at the right of the window in the south-east corner of the room.

Taylor Wounded and Helpless.

While he lay under the bed he was fired at several times from the stairway; one ball struck him on the left hip, which tore the flesh in a shocking manner, and large quantities of blood were scattered upon the wall and floor.

When Hyrum fell, Joseph exclaimed, "Oh dear, brother Hyrum!" and opening the door a few inches he discharged his six shooter in the stairway (as stated before), two or three barrels of which missed fire.

Joseph, seeing there was no safety in the room, and no doubt thinking that it would save the lives of his brethren in the room if he could get out, turned calmly from the door, dropped his pistol on the floor, and sprang into the window when two balls pierced him from the door, and one entered his right breast from without, and he fell outward into the hands of his murderers, exclaiming. "O Lord, my God!"

The Death of the Prophet.

Dr. Richards' escape was miraculous; he being a very large man, and in the midst of a shower of balls, yet he stood unscathed, with the exception of a ball which grazed the tip end of the lower part of his left ear. His escape fulfilled literally a prophecy which Joseph made over a year previously, that the time would come that the balls would fly around him like hail, and he should see his friends fall on the right and on the left, but that there should not be a hole in his garment.

Willard Richards' Remarkable Escape.

The following is copied from the *Times and Seasons*:—

TWO MINUTES IN JAIL.

Possibly the following events occupied near three minutes, but I think only about two, and have penned them for the gratification of many friends.

CARTHAGE, June 27, 1844.

A shower of musket balls were thrown up the stairway against the door of the prison in the second story, followed by many rapid footsteps.

While Generals Joseph and Hyrum Smith, Mr. Taylor, and myself, who were in the front chamber, closed the door of our room against the entry at the head of the stairs, and placed ourselves against it, there being no lock on the door, and no catch that was usable.

The door is a common panel, and as soon as we heard the feet at the stairs head, a ball was sent through the door, which passed between us, and showed that our enemies were desperadoes, and we must change our position.

General Joseph Smith, Mr. Taylor and myself sprang back to the front part of the room, and General Hyrum Smith retreated two-thirds across the chamber directly in front of and facing the door.

A ball was sent through the door which hit Hyrum on the side of his nose, when he fell backwards, extended at length, without moving his feet.

From the holes in his vest (the day was warm, and no one had his coat on but myself), pantaloons, drawers, and shirt, it appears evident that a ball must have been thrown from without, through the window, which entered his back on the right side, and passing through, lodged against his watch, which was in his right vest pocket, completely pulverizing the crystal and face, tearing off the hands and mashing the whole body of the watch. At the same instant the ball from the door entered his nose.

As he struck the floor he exclaimed emphatically, "I am a dead man." Joseph looked towards him and responded, "Oh, dear brother Hyrum!" and opening the door two or three inches with his left hand, discharged one barrel of a six shooter (pistol) at random in the entry, from whence a ball grazed Hyrum's breast, and entering his throat passed into his head, while other muskets were aimed at him and some balls hit him.

Joseph continued snapping his revolver round the casing of the door into the space as before, three barrels of which missed fire, while Mr. Taylor with a walking stick stood by his side and knocked down the bayonets and muskets which were constantly discharging through the doorway, while I stood by him, ready to lend any assistance, with another stick, but could not come within striking distance without going directly before the muzzle of the guns.

When the revolver failed, we had no more firearms, and expected an immediate rush of the mob, and the doorway full of muskets, half way in the room, and no hope but instant death from within.

Mr. Taylor rushed into the window, which is some fifteen or twenty feet from the ground. When his body was nearly on a balance, a ball from the door within entered his leg, and a ball from without struck his watch, a patent lever, in his vest pocket near the left breast, and smashed it into "pie," leaving the hands standing at 5 o'clock, 16 minutes, and 26 seconds, the force of which ball threw him back on the floor, and he rolled under the bed which stood by his side, where he lay motionless, the mob from the door continuing to fire upon him, cutting away a piece of flesh from his left hip as large as a man's hand, and were hindered only by my knocking down their muzzles with a stick; while they continued to reach their guns into the room, probably left handed, and aimed their discharge so far round as almost to reach us in the corner of the room to where we retreated and dodged, and then I recommenced the attack with my stick.

Joseph attempted, as the last resort, to leap the same window from whence Mr. Taylor fell, when two balls pierced him from the door, and one entered his right breast from without, and he fell outward, exclaiming, "Oh Lord, my God!" As his feet went out of the window my head went in, the balls whistling all around. He fell on his left side a dead man.

At this instant the cry was raised, "He's leaped the window!" and the mob on the stairs and in the entry ran out.

I withdrew from the window, thinking it of no use to leap out on a hundred bayonets, then around General Joseph Smith's body.

Not satisfied with this I again reached my head out of the window, and watched some seconds to see if there were any signs of life, regardless of my own, determined to see the end of him I loved. Being fully satisfied that he was dead, with a hundred men near the body and more coming round the corner of the jail, and expecting a return to our room, I rushed towards the prison door, at the head of the stairs, and through the entry from whence the firing had proceeded, to learn if the doors into the prison were open.

When near the entry, Mr. Taylor called out, "Take me." I pressed my way until I found all doors unbarred, returning instantly, caught Mr. Taylor under my arm and rushed by the stairs into the dungeon, or inner prison, stretched him on the floor and covered him with a bed in such a manner as not likely to be perceived, expecting an immediate return of the mob.

I said to Mr. Taylor, "This is a hard case to lay you on the floor, but if your wounds are not fatal, I want you to live to tell the story." I expected to be shot the next moment, and stood before the door awaiting the onset.   WILLARD RICHARDS.

While Willard Richards and John Taylor were in the cell, a company of the mob again rushed up stairs, but finding only the dead body of Hyrum, they were again descending the stairs, when a loud cry was heard, "The Mormons are coming!" which caused the whole band of murderers to flee precipitately to the woods.

The following communication was written and sent to Nauvoo:—

First Message to Nauvoo.

CARTHAGE JAIL, 8:05 o'clock, p. m., June 27th, 1844.

Joseph and Hyrum are dead. Taylor wounded, not very badly.* I am well. Our guard was forced, as we believe, by a band of Mis-

---

* This statement was made at Elder Taylor's request, that he might not alarm his family; he was, however, severely wounded, as the narrative in the text bears witness. When the note above was being prepared, Elder Taylor said, "Brother Richards, say I am *slightly* wounded;" and when it was brought to him he signed his name as quickly as he could, lest the tremor of his hand should be noticed, and the fears of his family aroused (*The Life of John Taylor*, pp. 144-5).

sourians from 100 to 200. The job was done in an instant, and the party fled towards Nauvoo instantly. This is as I believe it. The citizens here are afraid of the Mormons attacking them. I promise them no!   W. RICHARDS.
                                                JOHN TAYLOR.

N. B.—The citizens promise us protection. Alarm guns have been fired.

The above note was addressed to Governor Ford, Gen. Dunham, Col. Markham, Emma Smith, Nauvoo.

This letter was given to William and John Barnes, two mobocrats, who were afraid to go to Nauvoo, fearing that the Mormons would kill them and lay everything waste about Carthage; they therefore carried it to Arza Adams, who was sick with the ague and fever, about two and a half miles north of Carthage. He was afraid to go on the main road; and after two hours persuasion Mr. Benjamin Leyland consented to pilot Adams by "a blind road," and about midnight they started, and arrived in Nauvoo a little after sunrise. They found the news had arrived before them, for about a dozen men were talking about it at the Mansion, but not knowing what to believe until Adams handed in the above official letter.

CHAPTER XXXV.

GOVERNOR FORD IN NAUVOO—NEWS OF THE MARTYRDOM—
MESSAGES TO NAUVOO —ARRIVAL OF THE BODIES—SORROW-
FUL SCENES—THE BURIAL.

Thursday, June 27th (continued).—In the meantime the
Governor was making to the Saints in Nauvoo one of the
most infamous and insulting speeches that ever   Governor
fell from the lips of an executive. Among   Ford in Nau-
                                                 voo.
other things he said, ''A great crime has been
done by destroying the *Expositor* press and placing the
city under martial law, and a severe atonement must be
made, so prepare your minds for the emergency. Another
cause of excitement is the fact of your having so many
firearms. The public are afraid that you are going to use
them against government. I know there is a great prejudice against you on account of your peculiar religion, but
you ought to be praying Saints, not military Saints.
Depend upon it, a little more misbehavior from the citizens, and the torch, which is already lighted, will be
applied, and the city may be reduced to ashes, and extermination would inevitably follow; and it gives me great
pain to think that there is danger of so many innocent
women and children being exterminated. If anything of
a serious character should befall the lives or property of
the persons who are prosecuting your leaders, you will be
held responsible.''

The Governor was solicited to stay until morning, but
he declined, and left Nauvoo at about 6:30 p. m.; and in
passing up Main Street his escort performed   Military Dis-
the sword exercise, giving all the passes,   play.
guards, cuts and thrusts, taking up the entire width of

the street, and making as imposing a show as they could, until they passed Lyon's store, near the Masonic Hall. This was apparently done to intimidate the people, as the Governor had remarked in his speech that they need not expect to set themselves up against such "well disciplined troops."

Soon after Captain Singleton and his company left for home.

When the Governor and his party had proceeded about three miles from Nauvoo, they met two messengers (George D, Grant and David Bettisworth) hastening with the sad news to Nauvoo. The Governor took them back to Grant's house, one and one-half miles east of Carthage, with him in order to prevent their carrying the news until he and the authorities had removed the county records and public documents, and until most of the inhabitants had left Carthage. The Governor then proceeded towards Carthage, when Grant took another horse and rode into Nauvoo with the news that night.

Gov. Ford's Interception of Grant and Bettisworth.

Second Message to Nauvoo.

12 o'clock at night, 27th June,
CARTHAGE, HAMILTON'S TAVERN,

To Mrs. Emma Smith and Major-General Dunham, &c.:

The Governor has just arrived; says all things shall be inquired into, and all right measures taken.

I say to all the citizens of Nauvoo, my brethren, be still, and know that *God reigns. Don't rush out of the city*—don't rush to Carthage—stay at home, and be prepared for an attack from Missouri mobbers. The Governor will render every assistance possible—has sent out orders for troops. Joseph and Hyrum are dead. We will prepare to move the bodies as soon as possible.

The people of the county are greatly excited, and fear the Mormons will come out and take vengeance. I have pledged my word the Mormons will stay at home as soon as they can be informed, and no violence will be on their part, and say to my brethren in Nauvoo, in the name of the Lord, be still, be patient, only let such friends as choose come here to see the bodies. Mr. Taylor's wounds are dressed and not serious. I am sound.

WILLARD RICHARDS,
JOHN TAYLOR,
SAMUEL H. SMITH.

Defend yourselves until protection can be furnished necessary. June 27th, 1844.

THOMAS FORD,
Governor and Commander-in-Chief.

Mr. Orson Spencer:

DEAR SIR:—Please deliberate on this matter—prudence may obviate material destruction. I was at my residence when this horrible crime was committed. It will be condemned by three-fourths of the citizens of the county. Be quiet, or you will be attacked from Missouri.

M. R. DEMING.

It was near midnight before Dr. Richards could obtain any help or refreshment for John Taylor, who was badly wounded, nearly all the inhabitants of Carthage having fled in terror.

Friday, 28.—1 a. m. The Governor said the matter should be investigated, and that there was a great responsibility resting upon him. He also said he would send a messenger with an express for Dr. Richards, and wrote an order for the citizens of Nauvoo to defend themselves.

Departure of the Governor from the Danger Zone.

He then went to the public square, and advised all who were present to disperse, as he expected the Mormons would be so exasperated that they would come and burn the town, whereupon the citizens of Carthage fled in all directions, and the Governor and his *posse* fled towards Quincy, and did not consider themselves safe until they had reached Augusta, eighteen miles distant from Carthage.

Captain Singleton, of Brown county arrived in Carthage from Nauvoo with his troops.

About 8 a. m. Dr. Richards started for Nauvoo with the bodies of Joseph and Hyrum on two wagons, accompanied by their brother Samuel H. Smith, Mr. Hamilton, and a guard of eight soldiers who had been detached for that purpose by General Deming. The bodies were covered with bushes to keep them from the hot sun. They were met by a great assemblage of citizens of Nauvoo, on Mulholland Street, about a mile east of the Temple, about three p. m. under direction of the city marshal.

The Start for Nauvoo with the Bodies of the Martyrs.

The City Council, the Lieut.-General's staff, Major. General Jonathan Dunham and staff, the acting Brigadier-General Hosea Stout and staff, commanders and officers of the Legion, and several thousands of the citizens were there amid the most solemn lamentations and wailings that ever ascended into the ears of the Lord of Hosts to be avenged of their enemies.

When the procession arrived, the bodies were both taken into the Nauvoo Mansion. The scene there cannot be described.

About eight or ten thousand persons were addressed by Dr. Willard Richards, William W. Phelps, Esquires Woods and Reid of Iowa, and Col. Stephen Markham. Dr. Richards admonished the people to keep the peace, stating that he had pledged his honor, and his life for their good conduct, when the people with one united voice resolved to trust to the law for a remedy of such a high-handed assassination, and when that failed, to call upon God to avenge them of their wrongs.

The Address of Dr- Richards *et al.*

O, Americans, weep, for the glory of freedom has departed!

When the bodies of Joseph and Hyrum arrived at the Mansion, the doors were closed immediately. The people were told to go quietly home, and the bodies would be viewed the next morning at eight o'clock.

Dimick B. Huntington, with the assistance of William Marks and William D. Huntington, washed the bodies from head to foot. Joseph was shot in the right breast, also under the heart, in the lower part of his bowels and the right side, and on the back part of the right hip. One ball had come out at the right shoulder-blade. Cotton soaked in camphor was put into each wound, and the bodies laid out with fine plain drawers and shirt, white neckerchiefs, white cotton stockings and white shrouds. (Gilbert Goldsmith was doorkeeper at the time).

Preparation of the Bodies for Burial.

After this was done, Emma (who at the time was pregnant) also Mary (Hyrum's wife) with the children of the martyred Prophet and Patriarch, were admitted to see the bodies. On first seeing the corpse of her husband, Emma screamed and fell back, but was caught and supported by Dimick B. Huntington. She then fell forward to the Prophet's face and kissed him, calling him by name, and begged him to speak to her once. Mary, (the Patriarch's wife) manifested calmness and composure throughout the trying scene, which was affecting in the extreme. Relatives and particular friends were also permitted to view the remains during the evening.

Saturday 29.—At 7 a. m. the bodies were put into the coffins which were covered with black velvet fastened with brass nails. Over the face of each corpse a lid was hung with brass hinges, under which was a square of glass to protect the face, and the coffin was lined with white cambric. The coffins were then each put into a rough pine box.

At 8 a. m. the room was thrown open for the Saints to view the bodies of their martyred Prophet and Patriarch, and it is estimated that over ten thousand persons visited the remains that day, as there was a perfect living stream of people entering in at the west door of the Mansion and out at the north door from 8 a. m. to 5 p. m., at which hour a request was made

Lying in State.

that the Mansion should be cleared, so that the family could take their farewell look at the remains.

The coffins were then taken out of the boxes into the little bedroom in the northeast corner of the Mansion, and there concealed and the doors locked.   Bags of sand were then placed in each end of the boxes, which were nailed up, and a mock funeral took place, the boxes being put into a hearse and driven to the graveyard by William D. Huntington, and there deposited in a grave with the usual ceremonies.

This was done to prevent enemies of the martyred Prophet and Patriarch getting possession of the bodies, as they threatened they would do.   As the hearse passed the meeting ground accompanied by a few men, William W. Phelps was preaching the funeral sermon.

About midnight the coffins containing the bodies were

The Real Burial.   taken from the Mansion by Dimick B. Huntington, Edward Hunter, William D. Huntington, William Marks, Jonathan H. Holmes, Gilbert Goldsmith, Alpheus Cutler, Lorenzo D. Wasson, and Philip B. Lewis, preceded by James Emmett as guard with his musket.

They went through the garden, round by the pump, and were conveyed to the Nauvoo house, which was then built to the first joists of the basement, and buried in the basement story.

After the bodies were interred, and the ground smoothed off as it was before, and chips of wood. and stone and other rubbish thrown over, so as to make it appear like the rest of the ground around the graves, a most terrific shower of rain, accompanied with thunder and lightning, occurred, and obliterated all traces of the fact that the earth had been newly dug.

The bodies remained in the cellar of the Nauvoo House where they were buried, until the fall, when they were removed by Dimick B. Huntington, William D. Huntington, Jonathan H. Holmes, and Gilbert Goldsmith, at Emma's request, to near the Mansion, and buried side by side, and the bee house then moved and placed over their graves.

The deceased children of Joseph were afterwards removed and interred in the same place. It was found at this time that two of Hyrum's teeth had fallen into the inside of his mouth, supposed to have been done by a ball at the time of the martyrdom, but which was not discovered at the time he was laid out, in consequence of his jaws being tied up.

*   *   *   *   *   *   *

[It is thought proper that this volume, which brings the HISTORY OF THE CHURCH to the close of its first Period— the administration of its First President, and, by way of pre-eminence *the* Prophet of the New Dispensation of the Gospel, should close with the official statement of the Martyrdom of the Prophet and the Patriarch. A statement so true, and conservative, and excellent that now for a long time it has been published in the "Doctrine and Covenants."]

MARTYRDOM OF JOSEPH SMITH, THE PROPHET, AND HIS BROTHER HYRUM.

(*From the Doctrine and Covenants*).

To seal the testimony of this book and the Book of Mormon, we announce the Martyrdom of Joseph Smith the Prophet, and Hyrum Smith the Patriarch. They were shot in Carthage jail, on the 27th of June, 1844, about 5 o'clock p. m., by an armed mob, painted black— of from 150 to 200 persons. Hyrum was shot first and fell calmly, exclaiming, "*I am a dead man!*" Joseph leaped from the window and was shot dead in the attempt, exclaiming, "*O Lord, my God!*" They were both shot after they were dead in a brutal manner, and both received four balls.

John Taylor and Willard Richards, two of the Twelve, were the only persons in the room at the time; the former was wounded in a savage manner with four balls, but has since recovered; the latter through the providence of God, escaped, "without even a hole in his robe."

Joseph Smith, the Prophet and Seer of the Lord, has done more (save Jesus only) for the salvation of men in this world, than any

other man that ever lived in it.   In the short space of twenty years he
has brought forth the Book of Mormon, which he translated by the gift
and power of God, and has been the means of publishing it on two con-
tinents; has sent the fullness of the everlasting Gospel which it contained to the four quarters of the earth; has brought forth the revela.
tions 'and commandments which compose this Book of Doctrine and
Covenants, and many other wise documents and instructions for the
benefit of the children of men; gathered many thousands of the Latter-
day Saints, founded a great city; and left a fame and name that cannot be slain.   He lived great, and he died great in the eyes of God and
his people, and like most of the Lord's anointed in ancient times, has
sealed his mission and his works with his own blood—and so has his
brother Hyrum.   In life they were not divided, and in death they were
not separated!

When Joseph went to Carthage to deliver himself up to the pretended
requirements of the law,two or three days previous to his assassination,
he said:

*"I am going like a lamb to the slaughter; but I am calm as a summer's
morning; I have a conscience void of offense towards God and towards all
men.   I shall die innocent, and it shall yet be said of me—he was murdered in cold blood."*

The same morning after Hyrum had made ready to go—shall it be
said to the slaughter?   Yes, for so it was,—he read the following paragraph near the close of the fifth chapter of Ether, in the Book of Mormon, and turned down the leaf upon it:

*"And it came to pass that I prayed unto the Lord that He would give unto
the Gentiles grace that they might have charity.   And it came to pass that
the Lord said unto me, if they have not charity, it mattereth not unto you,
thou hast been faithful; wherefore thy garments are clean.   And because
thou hast seen thy weakness thou shalt be made strong, even unto the sitting
down in the place which I have prepared in the mansions of my Father.
And now I   . . .   bid farewell unto the Gentiles; yea, and also unto my
brethren whom I love, until we shall meet before the judgment-seat of Christ
where all men shall know that my garments are not spotted with your blood."*

The testators are now dead, and their testament is in force.

Hyrum Smith was forty-four years old, February, 1844, and Joseph
Smith was thirty-eight in December, 1843: and henceforward their
names will be classed among the martyrs of religion; and the reader in
every nation will be reminded that the Book of Mormon and this Book
of Doctrine and Covenants of the Church, cost the best blood of
the nineteenth century to bring them forth for the salvation of a ruined
world; and that if the fire can scathe a *green tree* for the glory of God,
how easy it will burn up the "dry trees" to purify the vineyard of cor-

ruption. They lived for glory, they died for glory; and glory is their eternal reward. From age to age shall their names go down to posterity as gems for the sanctified.

They were innocent of any crime, as they had often been proved before, and were only confined in the jail by the conspiracy of traitors and wicked men; and their innocent blood on the floor of Carthage jail, is a broad seal affixed to "Mormonism" that cannot be rejected by any court on earth; and their *innocent blood* on the escutcheon of the State of Illinois with the broken faith of the State, as pledged by the Governor, is a witness to the truth of the everlasting gospel, that all the world cannot impeach; and their *innocent blood* on the banner of liberty, and on the *magna charta* of the United States is an ambassador for the religion of Jesus Christ that will touch the hearts of honest men among all nations; and their *innocent blood* with the *innocent blood* of all the martyrs under the altar that John saw, will cry unto the Lord of Hosts, till He avenges that blood on the earth. Amen.

(END OF PERIOD I.)

INDEX TO VOLUME VI.

Smith's answer, 425; "Horace" to Joseph Smith 426; Joseph and Hyrum Smith to Tewkesbury, 427; Joseph Smith to I. Daniel Rupp, 428; Hickok to Joseph Smith, 450; Hugins to Joseph Smith, 451; Washington Tucker to Joseph Smith, 458-459; Prophet's answer to Tucker, 459; Joseph Smith to Governor Ford—defense in *Expositor* case, 466; Bernhisel to Governor Ford, 467-468; Wakefield to Governor Ford, 469; Sidney Rigdon to Gov. Ford, 469; Ladd to Joseph Smith, 472; Joseph Smith to Gov. Ford —urges Governor to come to Nauvoo, 480; Morley to Joseph Smith—mob threats, 481-482; John Smith to the Prophet, 485; the Prophet's answer, 485-486; Hyrum Smith to Brigham Young—calling home the Twelve, 486-487; Hugins to Joseph Smith, 494; Joseph Smith to H. F. Hugins, 501; Joseph Smith to Ballantyne and Slater, 515; Richards to James A. Bennett, 516-518; Foster to John Procter, 520; Governor Ford to Mayor of Nauvoo, 521; Joseph Smith to Gov. Ford— urging latter to come to Nauvoo, 525-527; Gov. Ford to Mayor and City Council of Nauvoo —on *Expositor* affair, 533-537; Joseph Smith in answer to above, 538-541; Joseph and Hyrum Smith to Gov. Ford, 550; Joseph Smith to Hugins, 551; Joseph Smith to J. R. Wakefield, 551; Johnston to Joseph Smith, 553; Joseph Smith to Gov. Ford, 556; Reid and Woods to Joseph Smith, 558-559; the Prophet to Emma Smith, 565; Joseph Smith to Gov. Ford, 575; Joseph Smith to Judge Thomas, 590; Miner R. Deming to Joseph Smith, 593; Joseph Smith to Messrs. Woods and Reid, 595; William Clayton to Joseph Smith, 598-599; Joseph Smith to Emma

Smith, 605; P. S. 605; Richards, *et al.* to Saints at Nauvoo— second message announcing martyrdom, 624-625. Lytle, Andrew and John, trial of, before Municipal Court, 286.
Life, Eternal, to know God and Jesus Christ, 305.
Loveland, Chester, threats of violence against, 504-505.
Lyne, Thomas A., a tragedian, 349.

M

Maid of Iowa, arrives at Nauvoo with English passengers, 333; Mansion, Nauvoo, made a hotel, 33; party and dinner at, 42.
Markham, Col. Stephen, attends court at Dixon, 350; with the Prophet in Carthage prison, 592,614; forced out of Carthage, 614.
Marks, William, police difficulties of, 166-170.
Marriage, plural, 46.
Meetings, public, at Nauvoo, 101; at Nauvoo—appeal to government on local affairs, 107; at Nauvoo—aggressions of Missouri, 111-113; mass, at Warsaw, 462-466; public at Nauvoo —to correct false reports, 483.
Memorial to Congress, 84.
Memorial to Congress, 123.
Memorial to U. S. Congress, 84, *et seq;* action of meeting on, 88; officially signed by Mayor and city council, 116; of the city council to Congress, 125-132; origin of Joseph Smith's Western Memorial, 270; memorial to Congress, Joseph Smith's, 275; before House of Representatives, 282 (note); Joseph Smith's to President John Tyler, 281-282.
Metoka, sailing of, with Saints, 4.
Miller, Bishop George, returns from mission, 61.
Misrepresentations, corrected, 67.
Missouri, peace proposals to, 218-220; "Friendly Hint" to, 245-247.